INTRACTABLE CONFLICTS

This book provides a comprehensive, interdisciplinary, and holistic analysis of the socio-psychological dynamics of intractable conflicts. Daniel Bar-Tal's original conceptual framework is supported by evidence drawn from different disciplines, including empirical data and illustrative case studies. His analysis rests on the premise that intractable conflicts share certain socio-psychological foundations, despite differences in context and other characteristics. He describes the full cycle of intractable conflicts – outbreak, escalation, deescalation, and peace building through reconciliation. Bar-Tal's framework provides a broad theoretical view of the socio-psychological repertoire that develops in the course of long-term and violent conflicts, outlines the factors affecting its formation, demonstrates how it is maintained, points out its functions, and describes its consequences. The book also elaborates on the contents, processes, and other factors involved in the peace-building process.

Daniel Bar-Tal is the Branco Weiss Professor of Research in Child Development and Education at Tel-Aviv University. His primary research interests are political and social psychology, particularly the socio-psychological foundations of intractable conflicts and peace building. Professor Bar-Tal is the recipient of a number of major awards, including the Otto Klineberg Intercultural and International Relations Prize of the Society for the Psychological Study of Social Issues, the Golestan Fellowship at the Netherlands Institute for Advanced Study in the Humanities and Social Sciences, the Peace Scholar Award of the Peace and Justice Studies Association, and the 2011 Lasswell Award and 2012 Nevitt Sanford Award of the International Society of Political Psychology. He has published widely in the areas of conflict and peace studies. His 2005 book *Stereotypes and Prejudice in Conflict*, coauthored with Yona Teichman, received the Alexander George Award from the International Society of Political Psychology.

Intractable Conflicts

Socio-Psychological Foundations and Dynamics

DANIEL BAR-TAL

Tel-Aviv University

CAMBRIDGE UNIVERSITY PRESS
Cambridge, New York, Melbourne, Madrid, Cape Town,
Singapore, São Paulo, Delhi, Mexico City

Cambridge University Press
32 Avenue of the Americas, New York, NY 10013-2473, USA

www.cambridge.org
Information on this title: www.cambridge.org/9780521867085

© Daniel Bar-Tal 2013

This publication is in copyright. Subject to statutory exception
and to the provisions of relevant collective licensing agreements,
no reproduction of any part may take place without the written
permission of Cambridge University Press.

First published 2013

Printed in the United States of America

A catalog record for this publication is available from the British Library.

Library of Congress Cataloging in Publication data
Intractable conflicts : socio-psychological foundations and dynamics / Daniel Bar-Tal.
p.   cm.
Includes bibliographical references and index.
ISBN 978-0-521-86708-5 (hardback)
1. Conflict management.   2. Social psychology.   I. Title.
HM1126.B368   2013
303.6′9 – dc23   2012021365

ISBN 978-0-521-86708-5 Hardback

Cambridge University Press has no responsibility for the persistence or accuracy of URLs for
external or third-party Internet Web sites referred to in this publication and does not guarantee
that any content on such Web sites is, or will remain, accurate or appropriate.

Contents

Preface		*page* vii
	Introduction	1
	PART I EVOLUTION OF INTRACTABLE CONFLICTS	
1	Nature of Intractable Conflicts	33
2	Eruption of Intractable Conflicts	61
3	Escalation of Intractable Conflicts	101
	PART II SOCIETAL PSYCHOLOGICAL REPERTOIRE OF CONFLICTS	
4	Collective Memory of Intractable Conflicts	137
5	Ethos of Conflict	174
6	Collective Emotional Orientations in Intractable Conflicts	213
	PART III MAINTAINING CONFLICTS	
7	Institutionalization of the Culture of Conflict	247
8	Socio-Psychological Barriers to Peaceful Conflict Resolution	281
	PART IV DEESCALATION AND PEACE BUILDING	
9	Breaking the Cycles of Intractable Conflicts	323
10	Peace Building: Concepts and Their Nature	367
11	Peace Building: Processes and Methods	400
	Epilogue	434
References		459
Index		547

Preface

I have spent almost all my life in the natural laboratory of a conflict, living under the conditions of intractable conflict between Jews and Arabs, especially Palestinians. As an adolescent and then as a soldier, first in the regular service and then for almost 35 years in the reserves and as a civilian, I personally experienced the tremendous costs of living under the conditions of intractable conflict. This recognition was reinforced by my opportunities to live for years outside the environment of the conflict. In these periods I realized that many members of society living continuously in a confrontational context become so used to their way of life that they do not even think that there is a possibility to live differently. They experience the normality and the banality of violence, not being aware of the price they pay individually and collectively. But even more striking to me was the recognition that many of those living under the conditions of intractable conflict are often unaware of the particular worldview imparted by authorities to mobilize members of society to participate in the conflict. They think that it is an inseparable part of collective life to adhere to conflict goals, to delegitimize the rival, to view themselves as eternal victims and as moral soldiers – not realizing that this worldview is a result of their indoctrination. More importantly, I recognized the dramatic effects of living under threat. In my view, this is one of the most potent mechanisms leading to closed-mindedness. With time, many of the society members involved in violent conflicts are not only greatly affected by the perceptions of threats; they also cannot differentiate where real threats end and where threats manipulated by the authorities begin. Indeed, this distinction is difficult to make, as threat perception is in many cases a subjective evaluation.

These realizations led me to devote almost my entire career to the study of the socio-psychological foundations and dynamics of intractable conflicts. In the course of personal development, visiting places of bloody intergroup confrontations, and reading much about other conflicts, I became confident that the society of which I am part is not unlike other societies involved in intractable conflicts and that these other societies also develop similar processes and the same general socio-psychological repertoire.

In the early 1980s I began to elucidate these processes and the socio-psychological repertoire associated with intractable conflict. The first ideas were about the opposing narratives that rival societies construct in order to mobilize society members and rationalize the initiation and continuation of the conflict. Through the years I began to assemble pieces of the puzzle by elucidating various elements and processes of the socio-psychological dynamics of intractable conflicts. In finding and exposing each piece, I attempted to view it from a general perspective as well as from the particular perspective of the Israeli Jewish society. Over the years, the pieces of the puzzle have multiplied, and the picture they provided has expanded. This inductive process has allowed me to develop a comprehensive and holistic view. The book is the result of this ongoing process. It focuses mostly on ideas that I have developed and less on reviews of the literature. It illuminates the general view of intractable conflict, because a specific book about Israeli society's "living with the conflict" was written in Hebrew and published in Israel in 2007. The present book, while drawing upon the knowledge I have collected through the years and upon the many relevant publications, offers extended and elaborated observations organized in a comprehensive, systematic, and holistic conceptual framework with new illuminations.

Because this book is intended for a wide audience, it uses illustrations from different conflicts, though with special emphasis on the Israeli-Palestinian conflict from the Israeli Jewish perspective with which I am familiar. My hope is that a book shedding light on the socio-psychological aspects of intractable conflicts will be of interest not only to academics but also to a wider audience, including decision makers and practitioners.

Although I began collecting materials and writing this book in 2004, it was a sabbatical at Brandeis University in 2010–2011 that provided the perfect time to bring this long journey to an end. I am very thankful to the Maurice and Marilyn Cohen Center for Modern Jewish Studies and especially its director, Professor Leonard Saxe, who provided me with this golden opportunity.

But I must acknowledge that this project is inspired tremendously by work with those who were originally my students but who soon became my colleagues and friends. They were, and many are, still part of a group that has met regularly for the past 15 years to present their own work, discuss various issues related to conflict and peacemaking, and hear lectures. Coming from different departments and different universities, they became a cohesive and professional collective that turned into a supportive and friendly group as well as a social network. My friend and colleague Amiram Raviv helped me lead this wonderful group, and I am indebted to him for his long-term friendship and cooperation.

I cannot begin to imagine my professional life without such colleagues, as they are very dear to me. They offer not only inspiration but also the best critiques and evaluations of my work. In addition, each of them through his or her academic work has contributed greatly to expand the conceptual framework presented in this book. Many of them worked with me while pursuing their master's theses and doctoral dissertations, postdoctoral study, and many other projects that extended the knowledge about intractable conflicts. I list them in alphabetical order: Guy Abutbul, Dalia Aloni, Rinat Arviv-Abromovich, Hadas Baram, Shiry Dagan, Ohad David, Talie Fried, Shai Fuxman, Corinna Gayer, Amit Goldenberg, Uri Gopher, Betty Goren, Nimrod Goren, Dana Guy, Eran Halperin, Dennis Kahn, Neta-ley Kolonimus, Shiri Landman, Eyal Levin, Tamir Magal, Eman Nahhas, Meytal Nasie, Rafi Nets-Zehngut, Neta Oren, Ruthi Pliskin, Roni Porat, Michal Reifen, Yigal Rosen, Nimrod Rosler, Noa Schori-Eyal, Eldad Shahar, Ronni Shaked, Keren Sharvit, Ofer Shinar, Anat Trope, Doron Tzur, Soli Vered, and Anat Zafran. Some of them – Rinat Arviv-Abromovich, Shai Fuxman, Nimrod Goren, Eran Halperin, Shiri Landman, Tamir Magal, Rafi Nets-Zehngut, Neta Oren, Nimrod Rosler, Keren Sharvit, and Ofer Shinar – read at least one chapter of this book and some even three, providing helpful comments that allowed me to improve the final manuscript. My friends and colleagues Maria Jarymowicz and Eran Halperin had an important part in my revision of Chapter 6 about emotions. Dario Paez, Dario Spini, and Ervin Staub provided valuable feedback on the Epilogue. I am grateful to all of them.

Finally, but not the least, this work would be impossible to do without the help and encouragement of my immediate family, my wife, Svetlana, and my daughter, Galiya. They endured the many days I spent before the computer with only warm words of support. I love them and thank them for the privilege of spending my life with them.

Introduction

Although intergroup conflicts are an inseparable part of intergroup relations, intractable conflicts that are viciously violent and prolonged constitute a special threat to the societies involved and often to the international community. Among the populations of the participating countries, they cause tremendous suffering, which can sometimes spill beyond their borders. Such conflicts can affect other societies and often play a significant role in the policies and actions of the world's organizations and states. Some have been terminated through peaceful resolution (such as in South Africa or in Guatemala); others still endure with intermittent or regular violent confrontations. Intractable conflicts continue, for example, in Sri Lanka, Chechnya, Kashmir, and the Middle East. These conflicts, which may last decades and even centuries, involve disputes over real issues, including territory, natural resources, power, self-determination, statehood, and religious dogmas. Such basic issues have to be addressed in conflict resolution. Almost all conflicts, however, are accompanied by intense socio-psychological forces, which make them especially difficult to resolve. The present book focuses exactly on these difficult conflicts, elucidating their socio-psychological foundations and dynamics. The Guatemalan and the Israeli-Palestinian conflict can serve as examples in our discussion; the former was eventually resolved peacefully, while the latter still goes on.

For many years Guatemala was ruled by dictators, and only in 1945 was a president elected democratically. The new president and his successor carried out reforms, including an agrarian land reform plan. But the succeeding president was overthrown in a coup orchestrated by the United States in 1954, with the support of the Guatemalan armed forces and members of the political and economic elite, who viewed these reforms as negating their interest. A period of repression begun by the new leaders especially harmed leftist political parties, along with labor organizations and peasant groups.

The repression, together with socio-economic discrimination and racism, led to feelings of threat and deprivation, especially by Guatemala's indigenous peoples, such as the Maya. Although the dark-skinned native Guatemalans constituted more than half of the national populace, they were almost landless. At the same time, the upper classes, white-skinned descendants of European immigrants to Guatemala, controlled most of the land. The grave conditions led to formulation of goals for societal change. As these goals were rejected by the ruling establishment, the wish to achieve them led to a decision to use violent struggle.

Over the next three and a half decades, the U.S.-trained and U.S.-equipped Guatemalan Army battled the guerrillas in bloody counterinsurgency campaigns, often operating in cooperation with paramilitary groups organized into Civil Self-Defense Patrols or Patrullas de Autodefensa Civil (PACs). Some paramilitary groups acted as death squads in both rural and urban areas, terrorizing those associated with leftist or opposition activities. Despite the repression, guerrilla groups, organized loosely under the Guatemalan National Revolutionary Unity (URNG), continued to operate in parts of the country. The violence caused severe losses and suffering, especially among civilians, but neither side could win the conflict. Eventually, leaders of the rival groups understood that the conflict had to be resolved peacefully and began a process of democratization and negotiation to end the violence. Despite violent objection by spoiler groups, the democratic transition continued as succeeding elected governments pursued peace talks with guerrilla groups. Backed by the international community and under UN mediation, these talks culminated on 29 December 1996 with the signing of peace accords that officially put an end to 36 years of civil war, which claimed more than 200,000 killed and more than 40,000 disappeared citizens, mostly among the Maya indigenous people.

The Israeli-Palestinian conflict, which constitutes the core of the Israeli-Arab conflict, began at the beginning of the 20th century as a communal conflict between Jews and Palestinians living in British-ruled Palestine and centered on the contested territory by two national movements: the Palestinian national movement and the Jewish national movement (Zionism), which strived to bring back Jews to their ancient homeland. For many decades, the two movements have clashed recurrently over the same land, the right of self-determination, statehood, and justice. This conflict has been violent almost from its beginning. At first, economic boycotts, demonstrations, strikes, and occasional violence erupted, which reached a climax in the Arab rebellion of 1936–1939, primarily against the British rule but also against Jewish waves of immigration. Following the UN decision in 1947 to divide the land between

Jews and Palestinians, rejected by the latter as unjust, a full-scale war broke out, which claimed many thousands of lives, including civilians, and hundreds of thousands of Palestinians became refugees. Through the years, both sides (on the interstate level) fought at least four additional wars – 1956, 1967, 1973, and 1982 – and in between them engaged in other violent activities. With the occupation of the West Bank and Gaza Strip in the 1967 war, the conflict moved again to the Jewish-Palestinian focus. Between 1987 and 1991, Palestinians in the areas occupied by Israel in 1967 waged an uprising (Intifada). Although some intractable features are still present, the nature of the Israel-Arab conflict changed with the visit of the Egyptian president Anwar Sadat in Jerusalem in 1977. The peace treaty with Egypt in 1979, the Madrid conference in 1991, agreements between Israelis and Palestinians in 1993 and 1994, and the peace treaty between Israel and Jordan in 1994 – all signed by leaders who changed their views – are watersheds in the peace process, which have greatly affected Arab-Jewish relations. But the Israeli-Palestinian conflict reescalated in September 2000, when Palestinians began their second Intifada, called the Al-Aqsa Intifada. The attempts to resolve it peacefully failed, the negotiations stopped, and the conflict continues.

These brief examples of two intractable conflicts imply that socio-psychological factors play a major role in their eruption, escalation, and maintenance and also in peacemaking, resolution, and reconciliation. Human beings begin the conflicts, carry them out, and then decide to terminate them. Although leaders often make the decisions, society members are an inherent part of these conflicts, as they have to be mobilized for participation and then for the conflict's peaceful settlement. Leaders and their followers thus form a socio-psychological repertoire composed of beliefs, attitudes, values, motivations, emotions, and patterns of behaviors that lead to conflicts and their escalation, and both must change in order to deescalate and terminate the conflicts before pursuing a peacebuilding process.

The formation and modification of the socio-psychological repertoire is a dynamic process that has to be unveiled in the analysis of intractable conflicts. To illuminate these socio-psychological foundations and dynamics in all the phases of the intractable conflict and its resolution, specific questions that stand at the heart of the perspective provided by social and political psychology must be addressed: What is the nature of intractable conflicts, and why do they last for a long time? What are the socio-psychological conditions and processes that lead to the outbreak of intractable conflicts? What are the socio-psychological dynamics that underlie the development of intractable conflict once it breaks out? What makes the conflict a societal (collective) phenomenon? How and why does a conflict escalate and evolve to be intractable? What kind of socio-psychological repertoire evolves in intractable conflict, and why and how does it evolve? How does this repertoire become institutionalized? What are the functions of the socio-psychological infrastructure? What is culture of conflict, and how does it evolve? What kinds of conditions influence the evolution of the culture of conflict? What are the mechanisms and processes that maintain it? What are the consequences of the culture of conflict? How does the socio-psychological infrastructure function during the conflict? Why is it so difficult to resolve intractable conflicts peacefully, and how do socio-psychological barriers that prevent their resolution function? What are the socio-psychological conditions and processes that deescalate intractable conflict and move it toward its peaceful resolution? How can the culture of conflict be changed? What is the peacemaking process? How is peaceful resolution of an intractable conflict achieved, and what is its essence? What is the nature of stable and lasting peace? How can it be achieved? What are the features of reconciliation, and why is needed? What is a culture of peace? What are the processes and conditions that facilitate the building of a stable and lasting peace? The present book attempts to respond to all these questions.

But, before embarking on the detailed responses to these questions, the Introduction first describes the nature of conflicts in general and especially their psychological implications. Then, because more than a few of the intractable intergroup conflicts are interethnic, ethnicity will be considered. Finally, the Introduction presents the socio-psychological perspective with the basic concepts that are used throughout the book and describes different types of intractable conflicts.

DEFINITION OF A CONFLICT

Conflicts are an inherent part of human life. They occur on every level of human interaction, on interpersonal and intergroup levels, in every type of relationship. They take place between friends and allies and, of course, between competitors and rivals. It is hard to think about a relationship without conflict because there always might be a perceived contradiction of goals or interests between individuals and groups, as the definitions of a conflict suggest. In fact, although the study of conflict is one of the central areas of behavioral sciences and much has been written about it, surprisingly there is agreement among the various students of conflict about the definition. Looking on some of the contributions, we find the following definitions.

[A conflict is] any situation in which two or more social entities or "parties" (however defined or structured) perceive that they possess mutually incompatible goals. (Mitchell, 1981, p. 17)

Conflict means perceived divergence of interest, or a belief that the parties' current aspirations cannot be achieved simultaneously. (Pruitt & Rubin, 1986, p. 4)

[Conflict is a] social situation in which there are perceived incompatibilities in goals or values between two (or more) parties, attempts by the parties to control one another, and antagonistic feelings toward each other. (Fisher, 2000, p. 168)

[Conflict is] the experience of incompatible activities (goals, claims, beliefs, values, wishes, actions, feelings, etc.). (Coleman, 2003, p. 6)

A social conflict exists when two or more persons or groups manifest the belief that they have incompatible objectives. (Kriesberg, 2007, p. 2)

The common thread in all these definitions is the emphasis on the contradiction of goals and interests among two or more parties. Thus, a party (an individual or a group), having a goal or goals, thinks that the other party (an individual or a group) prevents or constitutes an obstacle to its achievement. In this situation, the two striving parties cannot achieve their goals because an achievement of a goal by one party precludes this possibility by the other party. For example, if one party aspires to have an independent state on a territory that another party considers to be part of its own homeland, both goals cannot be achieved, as they are in contradiction, and a conflict emerges. This example is based on real conflicts such as between Israeli Jews and Palestinians or between Serbs and Albanians in Kosovo.

I define a conflict as *a situation in which two or more parties perceive their goals, intentions, and actions as being mutually incompatible and act in accordance to this perception.* This definition differentiates between situations of conflictive perception and conflictive behavior that may follow. That is, it suggests that perception of a situation as a conflict does not lead necessarily to a confrontational behavior. A party or parties may perceive a contradiction of goals and decide not to act in accordance with this perception. In such a situation, a conflict may be detected but will not erupt for the time being or will never erupt, but if it does, this will be decided by the involved party or parties. Conflict, as a situation with observable consequences, should be considered only when the perception of the situation is followed by behaviors that reflect this perception (Mack & Snyder, 1957).

In discussing the definition, I begin with the elaboration of goals, which refer to cognitive representations of aspirations. The present conception of the term "goal" is based on goal system theory, advanced by Kruglanski and his colleagues (Kruglanski, 1996; Kruglanski & Kopetz, 2009; Kruglanski, Shah, Fishbach, Friedman, Chun, & Sleeth-Keppler, 2002). They propose to define a goal as a subjectively desirable state of affairs that the individual or group members intend to attain through action. This approach thus views goals as cognitive constructs that are deemed valid and believable. As such, they require appropriate evidence as to their "worthiness" for adoption as objectives. Goals can be personal or collective. In the first case, they reflect personal needs and aspirations. In the latter case, they arise when members of a collective view the goal as either reflecting collective needs (e.g., collective autonomy, religious freedom, or needed collective resources) or reflecting personal needs that are shared by other individuals because of their membership in a collective (e.g., equal treatment). In any event, collective goals do not have to be adopted because of personal needs but can be formed on the basis of mere social identity and identification with the needs of the collective.

The notion that individuals intend to attain a goal implies that it is perceived as both desirable and attainable. Attainability refers to the perceived means that individuals can use in order to achieve their goal. Potentially there are several alternatives to achieve the same goal, and any one of them could potentially be used to advance progress toward several different goals. Eventually, goal attainment is viewed as a positive event warranting a positive affect, and a failure to attain a goal is perceived as a negative event warranting negative affect (Kruglanski & Kopetz, 2009).

In the case of a conflict, group members believe that their group has goals to achieve and that the attainment of these goals is blocked by another group. Both groups may want the same goal (e.g., the same resources), or they may collide over different goals (e.g., different political systems, or a division of resources or values). A goal desired by one group may be under the control of another group, or both groups may not have it and need to strive for it. Goals differ in their generality, tangibility, and importance, or in their remoteness from basic human needs or in the extent they are shared by group members.

Nevertheless, it is clear that when the goals are collective (shared by at least a segment of group members), the conflicts are on a group level and then involve group members. Also, it must be stated that not all the goals that lead to a conflict are expressed explicitly. Some of them may be latent: they are not spelled out openly but exist only in the background and play a role in the emergence of a conflict. Sometimes the latent goals are more important than the explicit goals. For example, American leaders never explicitly stated that one of the reasons to begin the war with Iraq was a desire to control the oil reserves (Klare, 2005).

Some of the goals that appear to be conflictive are not necessarily negative, and thus it should be noted that conflicts are not always negative human phenomena. First, social scientists recognize that conflicts also play a functional role for human beings on individual and collective levels (see, e.g., Coser, 1956). For example, groups achieve solidarity and cohesiveness, as well as clear marking of their boundaries in conflict situations. Of crucial importance is that much of the progress in civilization was achieved through conflicts. In many cases when a new idea appears that contradicts well-established beliefs, it is met with objection and rejection. In this situation, individuals and groups may believe that they are in conflict with those people who propagate these new ideas. But some of these ideas bring useful and valid knowledge, morality, democracy, or other humane values. We can think, for example, about conflicts that erupted in relation to abolishing slavery or colonialism. Without conflicts, it is hard to see how a progress could be achieved on our planet. The fundamental point thus in understanding the dynamics of conflicts is not their eruption but the way they are handled; for example, some conflicts are managed in a destructive way and involve violence, so that a heavy price may be paid, even for positive progress.

PSYCHOLOGICAL IMPLICATIONS OF THE DEFINITION

Of special significance is the psychological perspective that is included in all the presented definitions of conflict. The definitions refer to the perception of contradiction and not to an "objective" state of contradiction. The contradiction has to be perceived in order for the conflict to occur. Thus, the definitions recognize that at least some aspects of a conflict involve psychological processes. Conflicts always begin in our heads. The perception that attainment of a goal by one party precludes the achievement of a goal by another party is a subjective evaluation with which individuals may differ. One of the parties may not even identify a certain situation as a conflict, or may see it as less significant than the other party. In such a situation, the nature of the developed relations between the parties depends more on the party that perceives itself to be in conflict. If this party behaves in a way that leads the other party to recognize the situation as being conflictive, the possibility that the conflict will emerge increases. For example, when Israeli leaders decided to sell parts for unmanned aerial vehicles to China in 2005, they did not think that the United States would see this act as a conflict of interest. But when they realized the U.S. perception, they ended the conflict by quickly canceling the deal with China.

Identification of a Situation as a Conflict

It is possible though, at least theoretically, that one party will not disclose its perception of viewing a situation as a conflict, at least at the beginning. Then, it may take some time until the other party perceives the situation as being conflictive because this perception also depends on the expressed rhetoric and actions of the former party. Even when both parties perceive the situation as being conflictive and act accordingly, they may still differ in the extent to which they perceive their goals as being contradictory and thus differ in the level of experienced conflict. In addition, these differences apply not only between groups but also within a group. Very rarely is there is a uniform view of the level contradiction, the goals to be achieved, or the means to achieve them. Group members as individuals and as members of different subgroups may differ in their opinions, such that a collective may have disagreements and internal conflicts that exceed the intergroup conflict. For example, Catholics in Northern Ireland had a number of views on how to approach and carry out the conflict with Great Britain at the end of the 1960s (Mulholland, 2002). In many cases, formal leaders decide how to view conflict situations and then take a course of action.

While so-called contradicted goals are often real and play a role in the conflict, how the goals are viewed by each of the parties is most important. When the contradicted goals are perceived as central and even existential, then the conflict is of great significance and usually of great intensity. But when the goals are perceived as peripheral, then the conflict is of low importance and low strength. In addition to the ascribed importance to the goals, parties construct justifications and explanations for the goals (called their epistemic basis in Chapter 2). Obviously, rival parties differ in the rationale they use in justifying their goals.

The parties also have to identify the extent of goal contradiction. This dimension indicates how the parties perceive their own goals and the goals of the other party from which they derive the level of contradiction. According to this analysis, the most serious conflicts take place when the parties' most central goals are perceived to be in total contradiction with the goals of another party. This is the case of the Hutu and Tutsi, two ethnic groups in Rwanda that clash recurrently over control of the same resources and power. Both groups view the goals of such control as important, and both view the contradiction as being unbridgeable.

The preceding analysis indicates that an essential condition for the outbreak of a conflict is identification of a situation as a conflict. This identification implies that a given situation is categorized in the cognitive system (i.e., knowledge) of a person, or society member, as a conflict. The presented view is based on an assumption that individuals acquire and hold a general cognitive schema[1] that allows them to identify a particular situation as a conflict (see Bar-Tal, Kruglanski, & Klar, 1989). This schema refers to the incompatibility of goals between parties and indicates what a conflict is. It is acquired by the individuals as a result of their experiences and learning in the particular social setting (e.g., family, neighborhood, school). Once a person acquires a general (prototypic) conflict schema, he or she is able to identify a particular situation as a conflict.

A series of studies by Orr (1995) specifically investigated these premises. First, she found that individuals have cues according to which they identify a situation as a conflict and that they differ in the cues that they use in this identification. Second, in another study she found that priming for conflict with words connoting confrontation significantly increases the identification of an ambiguous situation as a conflict. In a third study, she demonstrated that situational factors may increase or decrease individuals' tendency to identify ambivalent situations as a conflict. Thus, cognitive loads may increase this tendency, while the requirement to avoid mistakes decreases it. In addition, it was found that individuals with strong need for closure tended to identify ambivalent situations as a conflict more than individuals with low need for closure.

In this line, a later study by Golec and Federico (2004) of American foreign policy officials and Polish political activists provides additional support for the presented conception in real-life situations. It shows that officials and activists with a hostile conflict schema in comparison to those with a nonhostile schema sharpened the perception of conflicts (i.e., tended to identify more situations as a conflict) and chose to deal with them in hawkish ways (i.e., to take harsher measures). People differ in their tendency to detect conflicts. While some people (including leaders) are "sharpeners" and tend to view many situations as conflictive, other people are moderators and view fewer situations as being conflictive. Also, while some people (including political leaders) may regard conflict as highly undesirable and try to solve it constructively with mechanisms of peaceful settlement or even avoid it by appeasement, other leaders may view it as positive challenge that requires meeting it with force and firm containment. Obviously, the general cognitive schema is not stable but changes along with the life of the individual as a result of his or her experiences and learning. Thus, with their experiences some people may tend to become sharpeners, whereas others may become moderators. Also, people may

---

[1] A schema is a cognitive structure that represents organized knowledge about a given concept, situation, or type of stimulus (Fiske & Taylor, 1991).

approach conflicts differently depending on their spheres. They, for example, may be sharpeners in national spheres but moderators in economic domains.

Identification of a conflict situation involves and implies different affective states that may range from hatred, frustration, and anger to challenge and joy and also different behavioral implications from flight or appeasement to fight. In addition, the implications may depend on the particular context in which the situation of conflict was identified. These implications, as well as an identification of a conflict situation, are different in various cultures. Cultures differ with regard to the schema indicating conflicts, as well as with the decisions on how to act upon their identification of the situation as a conflict, how to manage a conflict, and then also how to resolve it. Thus, cultural differences in interpretation of a conflict situation may lead to misunderstandings and even disagreements and conflicts. Some cultures may identify a wider range of situations as a conflict than other ones. In addition, cultures may differ in their conflict identification and reaction in different domains of personal and collective life. Also, some cultures may tend to act on a wider scope of identified disagreements and with great intensity, whereas other cultures may be more accommodating and compromising. Finally, some cultures may tend to use more violent ways of action in a conflict situation than other cultures (see, e.g., Avruch, 1998; Avtgis & Rancer, 2010; Eller, 1999).

But although members of a culture may acquire relatively similar general schemata of a conflict, there are still individual differences because of the particular socialization and experiences that each person experiences. These observations have significance for both interpersonal and intergroup conflicts. Even in international, or interethnic, or intersocietal relations, there are individuals who identify situations as conflicts and later reevaluate them. In these cases, individuals who are leaders make these judgments and decisions, and it is not surprising that their personalities, political views, values, and culture influence the way they determine how conflicts are approached and managed (see, e.g., Hamburg, George, & Ballentine, 1999). But in contrast to interpersonal conflicts, decisions made on an intergroup level sometimes have profound implications because they often concern myriad human lives. In these cases, individuals can lead their groups into conflicts, violence, wars, and genocide as well as to peacemaking and reconciliation.

In addition, it is suggested that the identification of a situation as a conflict depends on the clarity of the situation. This factor refers to how well the situation signals a conflict, as situations may differ in their level of ambiguity. Some situations are clear and unequivocal, for example, an attack by a state, as happened on June 21, 1941, when Nazi Germany attacked the Soviet Union. These situations are prototypic and are easily identified. Other situations might be more ambiguous and unclear because no salient and observable cues appear, and society members have to rely on supplied information that suggests the existence of threats. For example, leaders may provide information that another party has an intention to destroy a collective, as did U.S. president George Bush in his claim that Iraq's possession of weapons of mass destruction supported a decision to launch a war. These situations depart from the clear-cut situations of conflict, and the leaders of a party who identify such situations as conflicts need to persuade their own group members and often other groups that the situation indicates a serious conflict.

Decision to Act

The last psychological phase, after identifying the situation as a conflict, is the decision whether to act in accordance with that identification and how to act. Individuals, including leaders, can respond with a range of options, from ignoring the conflict to acting in harsh confrontational way. For example, when Brazil expropriated an American telephone company in 1962, despite popular demand by members of Congress to view this act as a conflict of interest between the United States and Brazil and act accordingly, U.S. president John Kennedy decided to define the dispute as one between the governor of a Brazilian province and an American company over the form and amount of compensation and thus to avoid international conflict (see Bar-Tal, Kruglanski, & Klar, 1989). Brubaker and Laitin (1998) provide two additional examples. In southern Slovakia in 1995, a pair of Hungarian youngsters was pushed from a train by Slovakian youths after a soccer match. Although one of the youngsters was seriously injured and the violence occurred after the Hungarians had been singing Hungarian nationalist songs, the act was interpreted by Hungarian authorities and the press as drunken behavior by soccer fans rather than as interethnic conflict. Similarly, when in 1995 an Estonian secondary school was burned down in a predominantly Russian region, it was interpreted as a Mafia hit and not as reflection of interethnic conflict by Estonians – even though no one could explain why the Mafia might have been interested in a secondary school. These responses prevented the eruption of international or interethnic crisis. By contrast, when Israeli prime minister Ehud Barak blamed Palestinians for the failure to reach an agreement in the Camp David summit in 2000, it contributed to the escalation of the conflict between Israel and the Palestinian Authority, although the Palestinian representative in the summit meeting had defined the process as making progress in the negotiations (Enderlin, 2003; Pressman, 2003; Swisher, 2004).

Before making the sometimes difficult decision on how to respond to a conflict, individuals and especially leaders often consider a range of factors, such as the nature of relations with the party, the history of the relations, the existence of other conflicts, possibilities of a successful line of actions, the reactions of members of the parties, the perceived ability to mobilize participants to the conflict, or the costs and rewards in carrying out various alternatives. Although such decisions can have crucial consequences for the societies involved, including destruction and loss of life, individuals and leaders sometimes respond quickly or intuitively, without going through a comprehensive process of decision making (see Kahneman, 2003).

After laying the groundwork by defining the conflict situation, I can now move on to the theme of the book: violent, serious, harsh, and lasting intergroup conflicts. Although these conflicts can represent different types, we will see that many of them are interethnic. Because ethnicity plays such an important role in many of the conflicts, I would like to begin by elaborating on its nature.

ETHNIC CONFLICTS

The concepts and assumptions presented thus far refer to both interpersonal and intergroup conflicts. This book, however, intends to focus on societal intergroup conflicts only and specifically on severe conflicts that I call intractable conflicts. The reason for focusing on intractable conflicts is that they are often long lasting, hard to resolve, and threatening to the international community. Bercovitch (2005) identified 75 serious interstate conflicts out of 309 occurring in the period of 1945–1995 that are violent, last more than 15 years, and resist peaceful settlement. Many of the severe conflicts are ethnic and involve struggle in which identity plays a crucial role (Gurr & Harff, 1994; Williams, 1994; Worchel, 1999). In fact, Marshall (2002) notes that there is a steady rise in ethnic violence from the end of Second World War. Between 1985 and 1994, he registers 160 cases of ethnic violent conflicts, which account for 67% of all observed cases of political violence. Global Security Organization registers at least 33 violent conflicts going on in the first half of 2011 in which there were at least 1,000 casualties per year.

Ethnic Groups

Ethnic groups are collectives whose membership is determined on the basis of perceived common past, common culture, common language, and common destiny. Scholars of ethnicity are divided between two extreme positions. An essentialist or primordial position emphasizes given and fixed elements of commonality such as ancestry or norms and traditions that were handed down from generation to generation. It stresses the role of lineage and not the actual biological blood connection in creating ethnic consciousness. Thus, it focuses on the continuity of the identity components over the generations and diminishes the value of the changes occurring in these components (Armstrong, 1982; Connor, 1994; Seton-Watson, 1977; van den Berghe, 1981).

In contrast, the constructivist position locates the foundation of the ethnic identity in continual social construction. In this view, ethnicity is the product of an unending process through which people themselves ascribe to being part of an ethnic group or accept such an ascription by others. Individuals construct their social identity on the basis of such socio-psychological processes (Anderson, 1983; Breuilly, 1982; Brubaker, 2004; Gellner, 1983; Hobsbawm, 1992). This is done through construction and reconstruction of narratives that provide rationales to acceptance of a particular social identity.

In this book I adopt Smith's interim approach, which highlights the significant linkage between premodern ethnic communities ("ethnies," in Smith's terminology) and the creation of modern nations. It focuses on the dynamics between continuity and change of nations (Smith, 1986, 1991, 2000, 2008) and the influence of heritage on the present cultural-societal state of affairs and on future aspirations. This position suggests that ethnicity, or ethnic identity, is neither fixed nor given; it is not the result of a pure construction unassociated with bequeathed traditions. Rather, it is based on tangible and intangible cultural products handed down from generation to generation that are interpreted and reinterpreted in line with the particular context in the specific period. Thus, this position corresponds with the fundamental claim according to which social identity in general, and the ethnic one in particular, is to be analyzed using a socio-psychological perspective, one that focuses on the individuals as active, motivated, cognitive, and emotional subjects who are adapting to the social context in which they live (David & Bar-Tal, 2009; Reicher & Hopkins, 2001).

Ethnicity at any given time is based on perception, awareness, or consciousness of shared characteristics and differences from other groups. The social identity of an ethnic group's members underlies the feelings of belongingness, attachment, and distinctiveness. Eller (1999, p. 15) even suggests that "the ideology of cultural continuity and discreteness is the essential distinguishing characteristic of ethnic groups and their permutations, as opposed to other human collectives." The boundaries of ethnic groups are well recognized because of formal and informal rules and symbols that regulate interactions within groups and between groups (Barth, 1969; Connor, 1993). Therefore, members of the ethnic groups perceive their belonging to them as influencing their status and fate in the social-political-economic structure of which they are part (Fenton, 1999; Rex, 1996; Smith, 1986). All these characteristics of ethnicity play a determinative role in interethnic conflicts.

These beliefs are not limited to tribal or national groups; religious groups also hold a common past as an important basis for their membership. In addition, ethnic groups express their common culture in numerous elements such as language, customs, rituals, food, folklore, narratives, writings, or music. Ethnic groups make an effort to maintain their historical and cultural heritage and to transmit it to the next generations. Nevertheless, these elements are created and re-created, invented and reinvented, constructed and reconstructed. They are not stable but are adapted to the needs of the group or society in accordance with the context in which it lives in the present. Thus, for example, a group (e.g., Chechens or Tamils) that lives in the context of lasting violent conflict has different needs from a group living in peace. The former group needs rituals, myth, symbols, folklore, narratives, and other elements of culture that will be functional to the persistent struggle that the group experiences. Moreover, ethnic groups often have to struggle for the right to live by their heritage, express it openly, and transmit it to the next generations (e.g., the Kurds in Turkey).

Ethnic groups that claim sovereignty on a particular territory are called *nations* (Gellner, 1983; Smith, 1986). Nations attempt to create a compelling association between a population, territory, common past, cultural heritage, and destiny (Elcheroth & Spini, 2011). The formation of a nation is a result of various processes over centuries in political, economic, administrative, cultural, and educational spheres. The formation is based not only on an emotional feeling of belongingness but also on rational ideas of citizenship and participation in the economic market. Some national groups live as a collective in their sovereign state (e.g., Jews or Turks). Some nations live as autonomous units in the framework of a state of another nation (e.g., Basques or Scots), and some of the nations still struggle for their right to establish an independent state (e.g., Palestinians or Chechens).

Eruption of Conflicts

In order for a conflict to evolve between ethnic groups, they have to be in some kind of relationship. Interethnic conflicts often appear in states that are multiethnic, in which there is a contradiction of goals between or among ethnic groups (e.g., in the former Nigeria, Congo, or Yugoslavia). But conflicts also occur between ethnic-national groups that do not reside in one state and even in states without common borders (e.g., between Japan and the United States). Seemingly ever present, interethnic conflicts can be over resources, influence, self-determination, autonomy, freedom of religion, statehood, territory, resources, markets, and so on. In the last part of the 20th century, the most serious and violent interethnic conflicts were within one state or between bordering ethnic groups. Many of the interethnic conflicts go on for many years, as the harsh conflicts between Catholics and Protestants in Northern Ireland, between Jews and Palestinians in the Middle East, Chechens and Russians in Chechnya, Tamils and Singhalese in Sri Lanka, or Moslems and Hindus in Kashmir.

Many conflicts break out when one or a few dominant groups (possibly an ethnic group) have power, authority, wealth, control, resources, territory, or another commodity and the other group or groups demand part or all of the commodity (Chapter 2 discusses eruption of conflicts). These demands are always embedded in a constructed rationale that derives from various historical, religious, legal, moral, and cultural epistemic bases. Very seldom does one group yield easily to the demands of another group and thus relinquish power, status, prestige, resources, or other meaningful tangible and intangible goods or commodities. Because these groups also have a well-developed rationale for maintaining their assets and advantages, in these situations, conflicts often break out. Many of the intergroup conflicts are viewed as being related to the identity of the ethnic groups that are involved in them. Thus, the goals that reflect deprivations or the aspirations of the group are defined in terms of needs related to social identity. For example, a particular territory is considered to be part of the homeland and is associated with the group's past (e.g., Palestinians and Kurds); or the demand for statehood, autonomy, or cultural and religious freedom (e.g., Basques and Tamils); or the demand for equal distribution of power and resources (e.g., the Indians in Guatemala) – all are associated with the definition of identity that requires achievement of these goals.

In describing interethnic conflicts, it is important to note that some of the ethnic groups are well established and have a state (e.g., Russians, French), some have ancient roots and once had a state (e.g., Tibetans, Basques), and others never had a state (e.g., Tamils in Sri Lanka). Some groups crystallized in more recent times and also have national aspirations (e.g., Palestinians). Many ethnic groups live in a multiethnic state with varying levels of satisfaction, and many ethnic groups lead interethnic conflicts with different levels of intensity. A conflict may be between two well-established national groups that have their states (e.g., Germans vs. the French) or between a national group that has a state and another national group that evolves or demands its national rights (e.g., Israeli Jews vs. Palestinians). In general, many conflicts, including interethnic ones, involve various economic-social-political-cultural injustices. Some conflicts, though, concern liberation, separation, division of resources, or recognition and autonomy.

A conflict in which ethnic groups are involved is very difficult to win – many of them last for a long time until both groups satisfy their basic needs and agree to end the conflict. The intensity of these conflicts fluctuates, and even when one group successfully wins a battle or even a war, the defeated group may begin the struggle all over again within years. Thus, for example, the Chechens have been fighting for their independence since the 18th century when the conquest of Chechnya by the tsarist Russia began. Poles were continuously rising to fight for their independence since they were divided among the three empires at the end of 18th century, until they achieved it at the end of World War I. Palestinians do not capitulate and abandon their aspirations in spite of the tremendous losses and costs that they have incurred through the years.

But severe intergroup conflicts do not have to be only interethnic. Violent conflicts may break out from time to time also within one ethnic group over values, resources, and other commodities. The domestic war in the United States or the domestic wars in Russia, Spain, Nicaragua, or Nepal are examples of harsh conflicts that took place between parts of the same national group. At present, in conflicts of this type (e.g., in Colombia) polarized societies engage in violent confrontation for many years over basic values, the governing system, and the distribution of resources and wealth. This type of conflict erupts after deep polarization that takes place between at least two segments of a society, within one ethnic group, but along ideological lines. In these cases, the divisive ideology leads to the emergence of two opposite sets of goals. When the two groups evolve a distinctive identity with well-defined institutions, when there do not exist efficient societal mechanisms to regulate the disagreements, and when the goals of the groups are viewed as essential and the grievances of at least one group are ignored, then the groups, or one group, may resort to violence in order to achieve their goals.

All these conflicts are over real issues that have to be addressed in conflict resolution. But because they are accompanied by intense socio-psychological dynamics, they are especially difficult to resolve. These socio-psychological dynamics are especially prominent in intractable conflicts, which are violent and perceived as irreconcilable because they concern essential and existential goals (Azar, 1990; Bar-Tal, 1998a, 2007a; Coleman, 2003; Goertz & Diehl, 1993; Kriesberg 1998a; and Chapter 1 in this book). In addition to the discussed socio-psychological perspective that relates to the definition of a situation as a conflict, long-standing intractable conflicts deeply involve society members, who develop a socio-psychological repertoire of beliefs, attitudes, and emotions about their goals, about the causes of the conflict and its course, about their own group, about the rival, and about the desired solution (see my discussion in Chapters 3, 4, 5, 6, and 7). Eventually, this repertoire becomes an investment in the conflict, because it supports and fuels its continuation. It is frozen and resistant to change and thus inhibits deescalation of the conflict and its peaceful resolution (Bar-Tal & Halperin, 2011; and Chapter 8 in this book).

The analysis of intergroup conflicts can involve historical, political, sociological, economic, or cultural perspectives. Each one offers different concepts, assumptions, theoretical frameworks, or models that provide unique outlooks and emphases. Thus, for example, the historical perspective focuses on the historiography of the outbreak of the conflict and its continuation and tries to describe the course of the events in the most accurate way (e.g., Holmes & Evans, 2006). The present book focuses on the socio-psychological foundations and dynamics of intractable conflicts, discussing their specific contribution to the conflict. This does not mean that other approaches are less relevant or less important. There is no doubt that a political perspective that presents a realistic view of interests can explain well why certain conflicts continue. For example, a superpower may be interested in continuation of a particular conflict or many have a deep interest in supporting one side to the conflict. But even in this political perspective, the socio-psychological aspect cannot be overestimated, because the conflicts involve individuals and groups that hold certain worldviews, ideologies, and beliefs and pursue their interests and goals accordingly (Fitzduff, 2006). We have to remember that these are human beings who decide to engage in such conflicts, to use violence, and to carry out mass killings, and also human beings who agree on solving conflicts peacefully or vehemently resist making peace. All conflicts, including the most viciously violent intergroup conflicts, are man-made.

SOCIO-PSYCHOLOGICAL PERSPECTIVE TO CONFLICTS

Socio-psychological perspective tries to elucidate the socio-psychological factors that affect individuals and collectives in their behaviors in a conflict situation. This perspective does not try to establish what the events in the conflict are, but what people think and feel, as this is extremely important for the understanding of why they act in the particular way they do. As Krech, Crutchfield, and Ballachey (1962, p. 17) noted years ago,

Man acts upon his ideas; his irrational acts no less than his rational acts are guided by what he thinks, what he believes, what he anticipates. However bizarre the behavior of men, tribes, or nations may appear to an outsider, to the men, to the tribes, to the nations their behavior makes sense in terms of their own world views.

Thus, the socio-psychological approach tries to reveal these thoughts and feelings as underlying the evolvement and maintenance of the conflict as well as its later resolution.

The socio-psychological perspective is unique and adds an important aspect in the understanding of conflicts (see also Bar-Tal, 2011a; Christie, Wagner, & Winter, 2001; De Dreu, 2010; Fitzduff & Stout, 2006; Kelman, 2007; Tropp, 2012; Vollhardt & Bilali, 2008). Human beings identify conflicts and act appropriately, behaving according to their repertoire of beliefs, attitudes, emotions, and intentions of behaviors acquired in the course of the conflict or in a different context before the conflict erupted. Past experiences and acquired knowledge also influence how members of a collective may act (see Chapter 4). For the purposes of this discussion, the socio-psychological repertoire consists of beliefs, attitudes, and emotions.

Beliefs

Beliefs are defined as propositions that a person holds with at least a minimal level of confidence in their validity (Bar-Tal, 1990c; Bem, 1970; Fishbein & Ajzen, 1975; Kruglanski, 1989). Proposition refers to an object, relations between objects, or their characteristics. A minimal level of confidence refers to the likelihood that the proposition will be valid and truthful from a personal perspective. Beliefs differ with regard to the level of confidence that is attributed to them. Some beliefs are held as total truth as individuals attribute very high confidence to them, whereas other beliefs may be considered as uncertain or as hypotheses to which individuals attribute a low level of confidence. Thus, for example, for many of the Serbians it is factual knowledge that the Battle of Kosovo took place on June 28, 1389, in which they defended Christian Europe and were defeated. On the other hand, there are Serbs who do not consider information about atrocities carried out by their group members in Bosnia as validated truth.

Beliefs differ also in their centrality. The level of centrality is defined as the extent to which a particular belief is often accessible in the mind and the extent to which it is considered in various decisions that a person makes (Bar-Tal, Raviv, & Freund, 1994). People often think about central beliefs as they are accessible in the human repertoire and use them as consideration in their decisions. In contrast, peripheral beliefs are rarely remembered because they are inaccessible in the human repertoire and rarely used in decisions. For many Jews, the belief that Jerusalem is the cradle of the Jewish nation is a central belief. But the belief in the holiness of Nablus (Shekhem), the traditional site of the tomb of the patriarch Joseph, is peripheral to many Jews.

Attitudes

Attitudes are mostly defined as an evaluation with some degree of favor or disfavor of an object, person, collective, event, or other contents. Thus, attitudes, as an internal state, differ on the dimension of positivity-negativity (Eagly & Chaiken, 1993; Zanna & Rempel, 1988). Individuals may have a positive attitude toward their nation, state, or goals and may have negative attitudes toward their rivals, acts of discriminations, conflict resolution plans, or even their leaders and policies. Public opinion surveys often assess the attitudes of society members toward various issues that stand at the center of the public agenda. Attitudes may last for short or long periods of time, and they differ, as beliefs, on the central-peripheral dimension, as well as on other dimensions, such as the level of commitment or ego involvement (Eagly & Chaiken, 1993). While some attitudes are easy to change, other are resistant to persuasion.

Beliefs and attitudes are organized in structures. They do not normally exist in isolation from one another but are related. Nevertheless, beliefs and attitudes differ in the extent to which they are related. Thus, while some of them are interrelated within large systems that are often called ideologies and encompass many domains of life and dictate a particular life style, others are interrelated into small systems that refer to a very limited subject. Thus, for example, individuals who live under conditions of a harsh conflict for a long time may develop a system of beliefs and attitudes about the conflict, the rival, and one's own group that in some respect may serve as an ideology of the conflict.

Emotions

Emotions are defined as basic psycho-physiological evaluative reactions to stimuli of different kinds (see also Chapter 6). They constitute a multifaceted phenomenon that is based on biochemical, physiological, affective, cognitive, and behavioral processes (Cacioppo & Gardner, 1999; Damasio, 2003; Ekman & Davidson, 1994; Johnson-Laird & Oatley, 1992; Lewis & Haviland, 1993; Manstead, Frijda, & Fischer, 2004). They evolved for their adaptive functions in dealing with basic external challenges (Johnson-Laird & Oatley, 1992; Mandler, 1975), as modes of relating to the changing demands of the environment (Damasio, 2003; Lazarus, 1991). However, they can also lead to maladaptation by eliciting dysfunctional reactions in certain situations, characterized by irrationality and destructiveness. They can be unconscious and conscious (Cacioppo & Gardner, 1999; Damasio, 2003; Ekman & Davidson, 1994; Lewis

& Haviland, 1993). Thus, on the unconscious level they come about through automatic information processing without perception and conscious experience (LeDoux, 2002). On the conscious level they are elicited on the basis of cognitive appraisal and information processing (Lazarus, 1991a). The sensitivity to certain informational cues as well as the expression of emotions can be learned on both individual and collective levels. Emotions play a considerable role in conflicts (Bar-Tal, Halperin, & de Rivera, 2007). They influence decision making, are taken into consideration by the leaders, and motivate individuals to a particular line of actions. Among the most important emotions that play a role in conflicts are hatred, fear, and anger on the negative side and guilt, empathy, pity, and hope on the positive side (Gray, 1989; Halperin, Sharvit, & Gross, 2011; Jarymowicz & Bar-Tal, 2006; Petersen, 2002; Scheff, 1994; Snyder, 2000; Sternberg, 2005).

Shared Repertoire

Of special importance are the beliefs, attitudes, and emotions that are shared by group or society members because they live under the same geopolitical conditions, are exposed to the same information and experiences, and go through similar institutional socialization. In illuminating this phenomenon, it is important to emphasize that individuals form shared views of the world because they are group members who identify with their group (Turner, Hogg, Oakes, Reicher, & Wetherell, 1987).

Sharing beliefs is an integral part of group membership, because individuals who live in groups and societies must form "shared communicative environments" in order to be able to communicate comprehensibly (Krauss & Fussell, 1991; Leung & Bond, 2004; Moscovici, 1988). Only when beliefs are shared can social functioning of planning, coordination, influence, goal setting, and the like take place. Individuals, as members of different groups, hold shared beliefs in their cognitive repertoire. Some of the shared beliefs serve as a basis for group formation, provide meaning to their group membership, and direct as well as justify many of the group actions (Bar-Tal, 2000a; Dougherty, 1985; Fiske, 1991; Geertz, 1973; Lane, 1973; Parsons, 1951). Particular types of shared beliefs are called *societal beliefs*, which are defined as enduring beliefs shared by society members, with contents that are perceived by society members as characterizing their society (Bar-Tal, 2000a).

The contents of societal beliefs, organized around thematic clusters, refer to characteristics, structures, and processes of a society and cover different domains of societal life. In general, they may concern societal goals, self-images, conflicts, aspirations, conditions, norms, values, societal structures, images of outgroups, institutions, obstacles, and problems. The societal beliefs tend to be reflected in language, stereotypes, images, myths, and collective memories. In essence, societal beliefs constitute a shared view of the perceived reality of that society. They provide a basis for efficient communication, common understanding, interdependence, and coordination of social activities, all of which are necessary for the functioning of social systems (Bar-Tal, 2000a). Societal beliefs are often featured on the public agenda, are discussed by society members, serve as relevant references in decisions made by the leaders, and influence courses of action (Gamson, 1988).

This position is well expressed in the sociology of knowledge perspective, which proposes that social knowledge is developed, transmitted, and maintained in social situations and that, as such, it shapes the reality of the society members (Mannheim, 1952). Parsons (1951, p. 352) claims that "the sharing of a common beliefs system is a condition of the full integration of a system of social interactions." The stability of a macrosocial system depends on the degree to which society members internalize the shared beliefs and produce an integrative collective belief system (Bar-Tal, 2000a).

The contents of societal beliefs are based on collective experiences of society members, whether real or imagined, or on implications that are drawn from these experiences, or both. In principle, any collective experience that is meaningful in the eyes of society members can serve as a basis for the formation of beliefs, which may eventually become societal beliefs. Such powerful experiences that may be relevant to group members are wars, conflicts, revolutions, political alliances, disasters, injustices, rebellions, famine, persecutions, hunger, a particular regime, exploitations, victories, economic successes, life in a particular economic or political system, and inequalities. They provide fruitful grounds for constructing societal beliefs. In addition to being based on direct collective experience, societal beliefs can be formed from the implications of such collective experience: they may refer to contents such as evaluations, prescriptive values, aspirations, desirable goals, or learned lessons – all based on the collective experience.

Societal beliefs do not have to be shared by all the members of a society but at least by a portion of them. Some beliefs are shared by most society members, and some are shared only by a segment. Also, societies may hold contradictory themes of societal beliefs, which can often lead to intrasocietal conflicts that can even be violent (e.g., the domestic wars in the United States, Russia, and Spain). Nevertheless, some of the societal beliefs may become hegemonic, implying that that most society members hold them and consider them as valid and central (Moscovici, 1988).

Collective Narratives

Many of these hegemonic societal beliefs present the collective narrative of the society. Following Bruner (1990, p. 76), I define collective narratives as "social constructions that coherently interrelate a sequence of historical and current events; they are accounts of a community's collective experiences, embodied in its belief system and represent the collective's symbolically constructed shared identity." They tell a comprehensive and meaningful story about a single event or events occurring over time that has a plot with a clear starting point and endpoint, provide sequential and causal coherence, are relevant to the experiences of a collective, and illuminate its present reality. Their units are societal beliefs that in their meaningful assembly provide a holistic story. The term "narrative" became popular in social sciences and humanities with the penetration of postmodernism (e.g., Abbott, 2002; Andrews, 2007; Auerbach, 2010; Bruner, 1990; László, 2008). It allows reference to integrative, comprehensive, and holistic stories that societies tell via various channels to facilitate their functioning. The themes of the collective narratives can vary in subject, length, and specificity. They can concern a large-scale master story that establishes the roots of a nation or encompasses a short-term story that tells about the course of a particular event, such as a battle. In general, they can serve as building blocks of the collective identity and a powerful mechanism for mobilization. When they deal with the past, they are part of the collective memory. Societies have many different narratives – some are shared by almost all society members, others by only a segment. They provide meaning to society members' lives (Hammack, 2011). Special events produce narratives, and an intractable conflict as a lasting context for many decades provides a master narrative. In addition, societies produce many short-term narratives that tell stories of specific events that occur in an intractable conflict.

Collective narratives can be divided between dominant narratives and counternarratives. A dominant narrative provides cultural scripts that proliferate in a society and offer its members a way of identifying what is assumed to be a normative experience (Andrews, 2002; Hammack, 2008). The dominant narrative is well embedded into the culture and supplies the foundations for plots to stories of the majority of society members (McAdams, 2006; Polletta, 2002; Rice, 2002). It is viewed by a majority as a valid story that illuminates the reality and therefore provides a hegemonic worldview and serves as guidance to further collective practices. Counternarratives consist of stories that provide alternative social constructions of interrelated sequences of historical and current events with new implications (Andrews, 2007; Bamberg & Andrews,

2004; Lindemann, 2001). They stand in opposition by varying degrees to dominant collective narratives and are in competition with them and often imply resistance, either implicitly or explicitly.

One type of narrative is provided by the *ethos of the society*, which is defined as "the configuration of central societal beliefs that provide dominant characterization to the society and give it a particular orientation" (Bar-Tal, 2000a, p. xiv). An ethos evolves as a result of continuing experiences of the society, and its beliefs lend meaning to societal life (see also Chapter 4). The ethos, furthermore, connects between the society's present and its future goals and aspirations. The society's hegemonic state of consciousness is generated by ethos, equipping members with the justification and motivation to act in accord with the societal system (Bar-Tal 2000a). For example, McClosky and Zaller (1984, p. 1) propose that "two major traditions of belief, capitalism and democracy, have dominated the life of the American nation from its inception," and thus both capitalism and democracy are values (i.e., beliefs) of American ethos.

Shared Emotions

In addition to sharing beliefs, society members may share emotions (Bar-Tal, Halperin, & de Rivera, 2007; de Rivera, 1992; Rime & Christophe, 1997; Stephan & Stephan, 2000; see also Chapter 6 in this book). The concept of *collective emotion* refers to the observation that group members may share an emotion. As a distinction, *group-based emotions* are defined as those felt by individuals as a result of their membership in a certain group or society (Devos, Silver, Mackie, & Smith, 2002; Smith, 1993, 1999). Both concepts suggest that individuals may experience emotions not just as a response to their personal life events but also in reaction to collective or societal experiences in which only a part of the group members has taken part. But while the former concept (collective emotions) suggests that group members may share the same emotions for different reasons, the latter (group-based emotion) refers only to emotions that individuals experience as a result of identifying with their fellow group members (Devos, Silver, Mackie & Smith, 2002; Smith 1993, 1999). However, an accumulation of many group-based emotional responses to societal events can easily turn into a collective emotional orientation, which is defined as a characterizing expression of a particular emotion in a society (Bar-Tal, 2001; Jarymowicz & Bar-Tal, 2006). Noted societal beliefs underlie the development of the collective emotional orientation of a society (Bar-Tal, 2001; Markus & Kitayama, 1994). They are the shared beliefs that evoke emotions; they define the cues for the interpretation and evaluation of information, which in turn evokes the emotions; and they define legitimate ways of expression for these emotions.

Implications of a Collectively Shared Repertoire

Most of the group members can identify shared beliefs, attitudes, and emotions because they are public and, as such, are not only stored in members' minds but are often communicated in channels of communication and presented in educational and cultural products. There is a significant difference for the group or society between the cases in which beliefs, attitudes, or emotions are held by few members or even by all of them but they are not aware of sharing them, and cases in which they are held by at least a portion of society members, or by a majority of them, all of whom are aware of this sharing. The awareness of sharing beliefs, attitudes, or emotions turns sharing into a powerful socio-psychological mechanism that has crucial effects on a group or a society. Shared beliefs, attitudes, and emotions are known to have important cognitive, affective, and behavioral consequences both for group members as individuals and for the group as a whole, especially when their contents concern themes related to the group's life. They serve as a basis for construction of a shared reality among group members, building their sense of belonging, solidarity, and unity; they influence the level of coordination of group activity and intensity of involvement of group members, as well as their mobilization on behalf of the group; they encourage the conformity expected from group members; they exert pressure on leaders; and they direct action taken by the group. Moreover, they often contribute to the sense of uniqueness of society members as a differentiated entity from members of other societies, while at the same time they allow a psychological connection of the society members to their own society. They thus make an important contribution to the formation of social and collective identity of society members by providing knowledge that society members share and can relate to.

The fundamental premise of this book is that, even in large-scale international, interethnic, and intrasocietal conflicts, people (leaders and other society members) are the ones who perceive and evaluate situations as a conflict. They act upon their evaluation and perform various actions in order to mobilize other group members to join them in their evaluation. They propagate their beliefs to society members and try to disseminate them. When these beliefs come to be widely shared, they are potent forces that move the conflict, energize it, maintain it, and prevent its resolution, but they also can inspire peacemaking and reconciliation.

Proposed Socio-Psychological Conception of Conflicts

There is a substantive literature about the socio-psychological foundations of conflict: its nature, evolvement, dynamics, and change (e.g., Chirot & Seligman, 2001; Fitzduff & Stout, 2006; Jervis, 1976; Kelman, 1997b, 2007; Kelman & Fisher, 2003; Mitchell, 1981; Worchel, 1999). Most of these writings focus on a particular socio-psychological phenomenon, such as cognitive and motivational biases in political perceptions and judgments (e.g., Jervis, 1976; Vertzberger, 1991); consider conflicts in generalized terms (e.g., Burton, 1987); report on fragmentary research that investigates only particular aspects of the socio-psychological dynamics (e.g., Cash, 1996; Heradstveit, 1981); or report on survey research, which again captures only part of the socio-psychological dynamics (e.g., Arian, 1995). The present contribution suggests a new macrolevel conceptual framework that illuminates the psyche of society members involved in intractable conflicts (see Bar-Tal, 1998a, 2007b, 2011b). This conception focuses on the socio-psychological dynamics of society members and the shared socio-psychological infrastructure as it evolves during intractable conflict, and it serves as a basis for the development of a culture of conflict. It suggests that this shared socio-psychological infrastructure plays a determinative role in the development of the conflict and its continuation. Shared socio-psychological infrastructure crucially affects every aspect of individual and collective life. It affects how individuals perceive their reality, feel, form attitudes, and act, as well as how a society functions as a whole, selects its course of action, and confronts the rival group. Understanding of these foundations not only may facilitate conflict resolution and the evolution of a peace process but also may help prevent the eruption of destructive conflicts.

This conception has served as a basis for an extensive analysis of Israeli Jewish society involved in Israeli-Arab conflict (e.g., Arviv-Abromovich, 2011; Bar-Tal, 1998a, 1998b, 2001, 2003, 2007a; Bar-Tal & Antebi, 1992; Bar-Tal, Halperin, & Oren, 2010; Bar-Tal, Jacobson, & Klieman, 1998; Bar-Tal, Magal, & Halperin, 2009; Bar-Tal, Raviv, Raviv, & Dgani-Hirsch, 2009; Bar-Tal & Salomon, 2006; Bar-Tal & Sharvit, 2008; Bar-Tal, Sharvit, Halperin, & Zafran, 2012; Bar-Tal & Teichman, 2005; Y. Bar-Tal, Bar-Tal, & Cohen-Hendeles, 2006; Ben-Amos & Bar-Tal, 2004; Ben Shabat, 2010; David, 2007; David & Bar-Tal, 2009; Eldan, 2006; Fuxman, 2012; Gayer, 2012; Gayer, Landman, Halperin, & Bar-Tal, 2009; Golan, 2006; Gopher, 2006; Goren, 2010; Halperin, 2007, 2008, 2011; Halperin & Bar-Tal, 2011; Halperin, Bar-Tal, Nets-Zehngut, & Drori, 2008; Halperin, Bar-Tal, Sharvit, Rosler, & Raviv, 2010; Nahes, 2012; Nets-Zehngut, 2011a, 2011b; Oren, 2005, 2009; Oren & Bar-Tal, 2006, 2007, in press;

Oren, Bar-Tal, & David, 2004; Oren, Nets-Zehngut, Bar-Tal, 2012; Rosler, 2012; Rouhana & Bar-Tal, 1998; Sharvit, 2008; Sharvit & Bar-Tal, 2007; Sharvit, Bar-Tal, Raviv, Raviv, & Gurevich, 2010; Zafran, 2002; Zafran & Bar-Tal, 2003). Part of this work constitutes dissertations and master's theses and other contributions (articles and chapters in books) that were derived directly from the present conception. Also, much of the research done within the Israeli Jewish society can be viewed as supporting this conceptual framework (e.g., Bar-Gal, 1993; Bar-On, 2000; Barzilai, 1996; Ben-Ezer, 1978; Cohen, 1985; Domb, 1982; Firer, 1985; Kelman, 1999a; Lazarus, 1982; Podeh, 2002; Sagy, Adwan, & Kaplan, 2002; Shohat, 1989; Wolfsfeld, 1997; Yadgar, 2004; Zerubavel, 1995). My recent book in Hebrew specifically analyzes the Israeli Jewish society within the framework of this conception (Bar-Tal, 2007a). Nevertheless, the present book does not focus on a particular case but elaborates the general presentation of the conception and draws examples from different intractable conflicts. This is helpful for understanding the socio-psychological dynamics of intractable conflicts and the socio-psychological infrastructure of societies involved in them, and it also makes a contribution to comprehending the socio-psychological changes that are needed on the long process of peace building.

This conceptual framework can be applied to conflicts that are not intractable, including interpersonal ones. In every conflict there is a socio-psychological repertoire that the parties develop, and it greatly influences the nature of the conflict and its course.

TYPES OF INTRACTABLE CONFLICTS

Each intractable conflict has its unique context, contents, and characteristics, and there are different types of intractable conflicts. But it is my belief that, in spite of the differences, similar common processes, themes, and mechanisms appear in all these vicious conflicts. In all of them there is a need to mobilize the society members for participation, to construct a convincing rationale for the goals established in the conflict, and to present the rival in negative light. I do realize that conflicts differ greatly, especially with regard to their context.

First, the context of intractable conflicts differs with regard to their *societal implications*. We can distinguish at least three types of intractable conflicts. A conflict can be intrasocietal when it is clear that both rival parties will eventually need to live in one state (e.g., in Salvador, South Africa, and Rwanda). A conflict can be separatist when one party struggles to part from a state either to form its own state or to join another state (e.g., in the Israeli-Palestinian conflict, Kashmir conflict, or Chechnya conflict). Finally, it can be a conflict between two states that confront each other (e.g., the Syrian-Israeli conflict or Iranian-Iraqi conflict). Nevertheless, this distinction is not stable. A conflict can begin within a political entity and then change into a struggle for separation (e.g., the Jewish-Palestinian conflict), or a conflict can be carried out as an interstate dispute with the attempt of uniting the two states (e.g., the Korean conflict). This distinction has special importance in the phase of peacemaking, settlement of the conflict, and reconciliation because the different types have implications as to how peace has to be secured if it is achieved.

Second, intractable conflicts differ in their *asymmetry* (Geis, 2006; Kriesberg, 2009; Mitchell, 1991; Rouhana, 2004a; Rouhana & Fiske, 1995). Symmetry or asymmetry is usually evaluated on the basis of military and economic capabilities. Some of the intractable conflicts are asymmetrical because one side has a superior military-economic-political capability. This context takes place often when a group with a state, or a group that is dominant in a state, has the needed institutionalized resources to launch a conflict and then to maintain it (e.g., Russia, Turkey, or Israel). On the other side can be found a group that does not have a state as a basis and therefore is at a disadvantage. This group has to build and establish communication channels, organizations, institutions, and resources (e.g., Chechens, Kurds, or Palestinians). In these cases, the different groups have differential access to resources and formal institutions and are using different mobilization practices and different societal mechanisms to maintain the conflict. But asymmetry can be detected also in conflicts between two groups that have a state, as one of the parties may have considerable economic and military advantage over the rival (e.g., in the conflict between Russia and Georgia or between the United States and Iraq). Nevertheless, it has to be recognized in all the cases that the asymmetrical power relationship does not necessarily bring victory to the powerful side. There are various reasons that may prevent the powerful side from winning the conflict militarily or politically (e.g., a strong objection to the conflict in the powerful group, or moral support of the international community, or moral limitations to using military advantage). The asymmetry of conflict is also a matter of psychology, and it happens when both groups perceive themselves as being weaker in the conflict, or when the international community or a powerful third side supports the weaker group, at least morally. For example, the blacks in South Africa viewed themselves as the weaker side in light of the economic, military, and political strength of the whites. But whites in turn looked at the sheer number of blacks and saw themselves as a minority. This also may change within the course of the conflict. The Tutsi felt considerably less powerful, especially during the genocide, until they conquered Rwanda and became the dominant ruling group there.

Also, there are different dimensions to evaluated asymmetry. Often asymmetry can be located in the moral support that one of the two parties involved in a conflict gets from the international community (Geis, 2006). It may happen that a party that is weak economically and militarily gets moral support from the great majority of the international community. Thus, Palestinians, who are weaker in every tangible aspect, get wide support from the international community, which perceives their cause as being morally justified.

Conflicts are often asymmetrical in their moral evaluation (see Rouhana, 2011). Conflicts differ in their causes and goals. Although the parties in conflicts always find them justified, over the years moral criteria to judge them and evaluate them have emerged (e.g., Walzer, 2006). I believe that there are justified conflicts in which society members try to abolish slavery and discrimination or to stop inequality, exploitation, occupation, oppression, colonialism, or genocide. Without these conflicts, important values of equality, justice, or freedom would not be implemented, as individuals and collectives do not usually yield voluntarily their status, prestige, dominance, control, wealth, territories, or resources, even if they have it unjustly. In these conflicts, principles of justice have to be addressed in their peaceful resolution, as took place in the resolution of the Algerian or South African conflicts. In these types of conflicts, the just goals often allow extensive mobilization and support of the international community. Nevertheless, this major issue is also controversial. First, societies involved in the serious and violent conflict view their goals as justified and believe that it is the rival that has unjust goals. Each society in conflict takes a self-righteous perspective in viewing the conflict and produces a narrative that supports this view. Second, if we turn to the international community, we often find disagreement among various bystander societies in their moral evaluation. Moral evaluation is often related to interest, cultural similarity, underlying values, or other reasons. Still, with regard to a few cases, the great majority of the international community formed an agreement about the just position of the one involved party. The boycott of white-dominated South Africa is probably the most salient example of such a consensus.

Third, in discussing these differences, I should note that they lead most of the societies engaged in an intractable conflict to view it as being *unique*. It is probably functional for these societies to perceive their conflict as specific, to which knowledge of other conflicts cannot be applied. This approach usually reflects the inability of society members to see the developed dynamics, the emerged contents, and the consequences of their conflicts in a more impartial way. The view of the conflict as a unique phenomenon with particular dynamics and principles that are difficult to understand places it in spheres beyond the accumulated knowledge. According to this claim, it is difficult to understand it on the basis of observations of other conflicts, as they do not apply to the particular context. Often, adoption of this view implies that the conflict cannot be resolved peacefully because of the specific and extremely difficult conditions and characteristics. In contrast, the position of the present conception is that, irrespective of the nature of the conflict or the power of the parties, or even their moral justification, both parties in the intractable conflict evolve mirror image socio-psychological infrastructures and processes. They need to be described and analyzed, and the conflicts' differences will be noted through the chapters when they are relevant to the analysis. The proposed conception assumes that, although each intractable conflict has its unique context and characteristics, their psychological foundations and dynamics are similar. Thus, the book unveils the general nature and contents of the socio-psychological repertoire, outlines the factors affecting its formation, demonstrates how it is maintained and functions, and describes its consequences.

Finally, conflicts have a long history. Some of them last for centuries and many for decades. It is essential to go to their roots in order to understand their course. Some observers tend to forget this principle and therefore refer mostly to particular periods, events, or processes, forgetting that these types of conflicts have long histories and that the discussed events can be understood only on the basis of the past events. Past events and processes serve as a basis for evolvement of socio-psychological foundations and dynamics that fuel and influence later developments of the conflict. Thus, it is impossible to understand the genocide of the Tutsi that took place in Rwanda in 1994 without knowing the history of the conflict that began decades before. So it is impossible to understand any of the particular events in the Israeli-Palestinian conflict, such as the 1948 war or the outbreak of first Intifada in 1987, without knowing what were the events that preceded their eruption in a long perspective, and not only in the perspective of the preceding months or even year. Intractable conflicts change and fluctuate with time, and as the context changes, so changes the socio-psychological repertoire of the involved societies. There is continuous interaction between the context and the repertoire – each element affects the other one (see Bar-Tal & Halperin, in press).

THE PRESENT BOOK

The present book analyzes the socio-psychological foundation and dynamics of intractable conflicts and their peace building on the basis of a particular conceptual framework that I developed with collaborators over the past 30 years. This framework provides a holistic, comprehensive, and integrative view that sheds an illuminating light on the "psyche" of the society members involved in intractable conflicts as individuals and as a collective. The conception focuses on the shared socio-psychological repertoire that evolves in societies involved in intractable conflict and plays a determinative role in its dynamics. Specifically, this repertoire underlies the evolved culture of conflict and influences the nature of social reality about the conflict that society members construct, the involvement with and mobilization of society members for the conflict, and the direction of action taken by them.

But although this conceptual framework serves as a basis in this book, I am presenting many other theories and empirical evidence to illuminate these complex topics. I draw from every relevant discipline that can help to shed light on many of the issues related to this type of conflict, and in this regard I provide numerous examples through the book that are taken from different cases of intractable conflict.

Thus, the present book begins with the first part defining and characterizing the nature of intractable conflicts and describing the challenges that they pose to societies that must adapt to their conditions. This part also elaborates on the societal process of conflict eruption and then its escalation. Then, the second part presents the socio-psychological infrastructure that develops in order to adapt to the conflict conditions, which includes collective memories, the ethos of conflict, and collective emotional orientations. This infrastructure serves as a pillar of a culture of conflict. In the third part, the book outlines functions that the socio-psychological infrastructure fulfills for a society and later focuses the institutionalization of the socio-psychological infrastructure and development of the culture of conflict. Subsequently, a chapter describes the barriers that hinder peacemaking and then elaborates on the profound consequences of the culture of conflict on socio-psychological behavior on both the individual and societal levels. In the last part the book, one chapter discusses the beginning of the long process of peacemaking that starts sometimes with a minority and gradually may lead to peaceful conflict resolution. Then two chapters describe the long peace-building process that sometimes takes place after the conflict settlement: the first presents the concepts of stable and lasting peace and the culture of peace and reconciliation, and the second outlines various methods that are needed in order to assure its success. Finally, an epilogue provides my thoughts and my lessons from the long journey of learning about intractable conflicts.

PART I

EVOLVEMENT OF INTRACTABLE CONFLICTS

1

Nature of Intractable Conflicts

The particular context in which human beings live as individuals and collectives greatly influences their perceptions, beliefs, attitudes, feelings, motivations, and patterns of behaviors (Lewin, 1942, 1947; Moscovici, 1972; Reicher, 1996; Tajfel, 1972, 1981; Turner, 1999). Thus, because the context of intractable conflict has a determinative influence on society members who take part in it, unveiling the characteristics of that context is the first phase of this analysis.

CONTEXT

Context provides human beings with opportunities, limitations, frames, cues, and stimulations and thus dictates to a large extent the types, range, and scope of human behaviors. In general terms, context in its widest scope refers to *geographic aspects of the environment with material human products; socio-economic-political structures, processes, and conditions; cultural tangible and intangible symbols; a shared socio-psychological repertoire; and intergroup relationships in which a society functions.* In fact, there are multilayer contexts in which society members live. One way to look at context is through a relatively stable geographic perspective that focuses on the physical and meteorological conditions of an area. Other aspects include a general global political-economic-cultural context in which the society is positioned (see Bronfenbrenner, 1977; Lewin, 1951; Reis, 2008; Ross & Nisbett, 1991) and a narrower context via a situational-temporal perspective that considers situations capable of having a profound effect on human beings, such as earthquakes, famines, economic recessions, wars, or conflicts.

The focus of the present book is on a relatively limited situational context – the context of intractable conflict – in which many of the involved societies live for decades and even centuries (Bar-Tal & Halperin, in press). This context can be viewed as long-lasting and man-made. It has determinative, durable effects on those societies involved in it, on both individual and collective levels. This context has relevance to the well-being of the society as a whole and of its society members. It occupies a central position in public discussion and public agenda, supplies information and experiences that force society members to construct an adaptable worldview, continuously shapes the lives of the involved societies, and leaves an imprint on every aspect of individual and collective life. This context even contains a culture of conflict, which develops because of its intensity and durability. But even this relatively lasting context of intractable conflict has sublayers called transitional context (Bar-Tal & Sharvit, 2008).

TRANSITIONAL CONTEXT

Transitional context consists of major events and information that have a profound effect on the experiences of the society members involved in them. *A major event*, as defined, can be experienced either directly (by participation) or indirectly (by watching, hearing, or reading about it) by society members, causes wide resonance, has relevance to the well-being of society members and of society as a whole, involves society members, occupies a central position in public discussion and the public agenda, and presents information that forces society members to consider, and often change, their held socio-psychological repertoire (Oren, 2005). A major event can be a war, a specific battle, a major atrocity, or an act of reconciliation. Thus, the genocide in Rwanda in 1994, Bloody Sunday in the Northern Ireland conflict in 1972, or the visit of the Egyptian president Anwar Sadat in Jerusalem in November 1977 in the Israeli-Arab conflict are all examples of major events.

Similarly, information that can be classifed as major is defined as information supplied by an epistemic authority (i.e., a source that exerts determinative influence on the formation of an individual's knowledge; see Kruglanski, Raviv, Bar-Tal, Raviv, Sharvit, Ellis, Bar, Pierro, & Mannetti, 2005) about a matter of great relevance and importance to a society and its members. It, too, causes wide resonance, involves society members, occupies a central position in public discussion and the public agenda, and forces society members to reconsider their socio-psychological repertoire. *Major information* does not create observable changes in environmental conditions and therefore does not provide experiential participation, but it does change the socio-psychological conditions of the society, influencing society members' thoughts, feelings, and behaviors. Dramatic information about threats or intentions of rivals are examples of major information in conflict. Because society members do not have access to many types of information or ways to validate information they do receive, they tend to accept it as truthful, especially in cases in which leaders are viewed as epistemic authorities or in which the domains of information are viewed as related to personal and collective security. Statements by the Israeli prime minister Ehud Barak to the Israeli Jewish population in 2000 that Arafat is not a partner to the peace process or the announcement by the Russian prime minister Vladimir Putin that Chechens carried out deadly terror attacks in Russian cities, including Moscow, in 1999 provide examples of major information that shaped the dynamics of the intractable conflicts. Intractable conflicts by their nature include major events and disseminate major information that influences the direction of the conflict.

Transitional context suggests that an intractable conflict is not stable but has a dynamic nature. Its intensity and extensity change with the major events and information. Intractable conflict is not eternal, as it may change when the societies involved in the intractable conflict win (or lose) decisively, bringing the conflict to an end, or embark on a long road of peace building. The latter process may continue for years, but it changes the context gradually. Some societies even succeed in constructing a completely new context – a context of living in peace with the former rival – which provides an entirely new experience to society members.

CONTEXT OF CONFLICT

A description of the context of intractable conflict must be based on the recognition that conflicts between societies or nations cannot be viewed as a unitary phenomenon. There are different types of conflicts and different ways to classify them (e.g., on the basis of their goals, durability, level of violence involved, or interest of the international community). One of the more meaningful classifications focuses on their level of severity and longevity. Unlike some short-term and easily solvable conflicts, intractable conflicts are long term and severe and have serious implications for the involved societies and the world community. Some of today's conflicts began decades and even centuries ago, such as the conflict in Chechnya between Russians and Chechens.

To describe these severe and lasting conflicts, Edward Azar and other researchers have advanced the concept of "protracted conflict" (Azar, 1990; Brecher & Wilkenfeld, 1988; Crighton & Mac Iver, 1990). Social scientists have introduced additional concepts, such as enduring rivalries (e.g., Goertz & Diehl, 1993; Huth & Russett, 1993; Mor & Maoz, 1999), malignant conflicts (Deutsch, 1985), and deep-rooted conflicts (e.g., Burton, 1987; Mitchell, 1981). In recent years, following the work of Kriesberg (1993, 1998), the term intractable has become popular to describe a conflict that is in stalemate. According to Webster's dictionary, intractability denotes "hard to manage; unruly or stubborn; hard to work, manipulate, cure, treat." Indeed, in the view of Coleman (2000), this type of conflict is recalcitrant and extremely difficult to resolve. Various contributors elaborated on the meaning of intractability (see, e.g., Coleman, 2000, 2003; Crocker, Hampson, & Aall, 2005a; Gray, Coleman, & Putnam, 2007; Lewicki, Gray, & Elliot, 2003). All of them agreed that these types of conflicts are resistant to peaceful resolution and therefore last a long time, as none of the parties involved in them can win or is willing to compromise in order to reach a peaceful settlement. They thus constitute a special type of conflict that is difficult to resolve. Vallacher, Coleman, Nowak, and Bui-Wrzosinska (2010, p. 262) suggest that "intractable conflict is one that has become entrenched in cognitive, affective, and social-structural mechanisms, a transformation that effectively distances the conflict from the perceived incompatibilities that launched it." Putnam and Wondolleck (2003, p. 38) characterize intractable conflicts as "conflicts that have an extensive past, a turbulent present and murky future."

I intend to elaborate the characteristics of intractable conflict on the basis of Kriesberg's work (Kriesberg, 1993, 1998; Kriesberg, Northrup, & Thorson, 1989), with more emphasis on the nature of its long-lasting context by providing criteria that explain its durability and resistance to peaceful resolution. Specifically, I propose in line with Kriesberg (1993, 1998) to classify conflicts on the intractable-tractable dimension. On the one pole of this dimension are found conflicts that last a short time because the parties in dispute resolve them through negotiation and without rising hostility, whereas on the other pole are found conflicts that are prolonged, involve great animosity and vicious cycles of violence, and seem to be irresolvable and self-perpetuating (see also Kriesberg, Northrup, & Thorson, 1989). The conflicts between Protestants and Catholics in Northern Ireland, Turks and Kurds in Turkey, Moslems and Hindus in India's Kashmir, Tamils and Singhalese in Sri Lanka, Russians and Chechens in Chechnya, Hutu and Tutsi in Rwanda, Greek Cypriots and Turkish Cypriots in Cyprus, and Jews and Arabs in the Middle East conflicts are cases in point.

CHARACTERIZATION OF TRACTABLE CONFLICTS

Tractable conflicts are the least damaging conflicts that may erupt even between allies and groups characterized by cooperative and friendly relations, because conflicts are inescapable as groups have many goals and there always is a possibility that one of them will be contradicted by the allied group.

Tractable conflicts concern goals of low importance that are perceived as peripheral to group interests. Thus, from the start, there is room for compromise, as parties view the situation as being one of mixed motives. Both parties realize that they can win if they compromise and peacefully resolve the conflict, and both can lose if they do not resolve the conflict. In most cases of the tractable conflicts, the parties have institutionalized mechanisms that enable dealing with the contentions of the conflict and then negotiating within this framework a fair solution that will satisfy both parties. Parties in a tractable conflict recognize its mixed motives, do not consider using violence, do not mobilize society members, and do take into account mutual interests, goals, and needs. This implies that the conflict remains low key, often without broad public knowledge and extensive public debate. Such conflicts do not require much investment, as both sides are interested in their fast and just solution. Therefore, tractable conflicts do not involve development of a socio-psychological repertoire or an infrastructure that feeds them. All this does not mean that socio-psychological factors are not involved in tractable conflicts. Individuals who deal directly with the tractable conflicts may develop socio-psychological dynamics and invest in the conflict psychologically, but these investments do not penetrate to the societal repertoire. This category of conflicts can be found between allies such as Germany and France, Canada and the United States, and the French and German communities in Switzerland.

CHARACTERIZATION OF INTRACTABLE CONFLICTS

Kriesberg (1993, 1998) suggests four necessary features that characterize intractable conflicts: they are protracted, involve violence, are perceived as unsolvable, and demand great investments. I add three characteristics to the list: such conflicts are total, central, and viewed as a zero-sum contest. The seven characteristics are described in the order of their importance.

Intractable Conflicts Are Total

The characteristic of totality refers to the goals of a conflict – their nature and their level of contradiction. Intractable conflicts are viewed as existential from the point of view of the participating parties. They are perceived as being about essential and basic goals, needs, or values that are regarded as indispensable for the group's existence or survival. Many of the goals are related to the basic ingredients of social identity, and many also have important symbolic value (Coleman, 2003). They usually concern territory, self-determination, autonomy, statehood, resources, economic equality, cultural freedom, free religious practice, and other central values. Because the goals of the other party stand in direct contradiction to the goals of the ingroup, the level of perceived contradiction is immense. Horowitz (1985) views this perception as deriving from the fear of extinction that dominates intractable conflicts, because the groups fear that if they do not achieve their goals fully, they will have difficulty existing or will even disappear as a distinct entity. This emotion can be defined as a collective angst, which is aroused when group members appraise a situation as potentially harmful to the future of the group (Wohl & Branscombe, 2008a). Because of this perception and feeling, the parties in intractable conflicts resist attempts to resolve it, as conflict resolution always demands compromises in goals. Thus, the characteristic of totality is an important contribution to the intractability of the conflict and often appears very early in its development.

The characteristic of totality is in many respects psychological, as it requires perception of the goals as being of supreme importance for the survival of the group (a belief that without such goals, a group cannot exist) and a perception (i.e., a formation of a belief) that achieving these goals is contradicted by another group. These beliefs may not be so obvious to all the society members and often require construction of a well-developed epistemic basis (i.e., rationale) of why the goals are of supreme importance for the group. For example, already in the second half of the 18th century, Jews set a goal to establish a Jewish state in the area that they considered to be their ancient homeland and have viewed this undertaking to be of existential importance. Thus, they began waves of immigration to this land. But more or less at the same time Palestinians, who lived on this land, began to develop their own nationalism, which sought to realize self-determination on the same land. They also viewed their goals with ultimate importance, and the conflict between these two groups became unavoidable, as the goals of these two parties were in complete contradiction. Also, it should be noted that small segments of both groups at the beginning of the conflict made special efforts to persuade other members of the groups of the importance of the collective goals, as they were not so obvious and salient to many Jews who lived around the world and Arabs who lived in Palestine (Morris, 2001; Tessler, 2009).

If we look to the Indo-Pakistan example, both sides see the possession of Kashmir as existential for the group or for its ruling elite. For Indians, and for the Indian government in particular, ceding Kashmir would result in a second round of partition on religious grounds in the subcontinent, negating India's secular credentials. Furthermore, relinquishing Kashmir could open the gates for separatist movements in other parts of India and could inflame intercommunal violence (Paul, 2005; Schaffer & Schaffer, 2005). For Pakistanis, the acquisition of the entire Jammu and Kashmir is a core national mission and an important part in Pakistan's identity, as it perceives itself as the "homeland for Muslims" in South Asia (Cohen, 2004; Paul, 2005; Schaffer & Schaffer, 2005).

The belief about totality of goals may appear immediately as the conflict develops, or it may develop over time. An example of the first case occurred in Kashmir when the Indian army intervened there in 1947 after Hindu ruler Maharaja Hari Singh ceded Kashmir and Yammu to India. But in many cases goals may evolve, as one group usually crystallizes its own contention for self-determination, independence, or other essential values. It may take years or even decades before a group first shapes its goals and begins to perceive them as existential. This was the case with the Palestinians, who realized only after a number of years how dangerous the immigration of Jews to Palestine was for them and then formulated their goals through the process of nation building (Khalidi, 2010).

Not always has there been symmetry with regard to the perception of goals. Only one side may begin to realize that its major needs or goals are blocked, while the other side does not yet share this perception. But it can be assumed that when one party views a situation as seriously conflictive, the other group will also begin to experience it, because the idea that the conflict exists is always transmitted by the former group and penetrates into the awareness of the other group. Because no group yields easily to satisfy another group's goals, especially when they are of a wide scope and contradict one's own goals because of their totality, both groups eventually experience a total conflict. This was the case with the Afrikaners in South Africa, who realized the intensity and totality of being in conflict only when the black community began to challenge their dominant views and practices in the established apartheid regime (Gerhart, 1978)

The characteristic of totality very often also signals that the conflict involves a number of layers and is multifaceted. Thus, intractable conflict often concerns contradictory goals related to a number of domains, such as territory, economic resources, political power, natural resources, religious disagreements, or cultural collision, as in the cases of the Israeli-Palestinian conflict and the Catholic-Protestant conflict in Northern Ireland.

Intractable Conflicts Are Violent

The second important characteristic of intractable conflicts is their violence. Acts of violence are defined as acts carried out with the intention of harming a rival (see also Baron & Richardson, 1994). Acts of violence may involve not only physical but also psychological harm. The physical violence can involve the killing and wounding of group members in wars, small-scale military engagements, and terroristic attacks. Such violence is an ugly but characteristic expression in many intergroup interactions. It occurs over time in different forms, not necessarily continuously but usually with fluctuating frequency and intensity. Even when its use is dormant, the parties still continue to view the use of violence as a legitimate way to manage the conflict (Crocker, Hampson, & Aall, 2005b). Violence can be carried out by individuals or groups. Although it may appear to be initiated and carried out informally, violence in intractable conflicts is almost always approved formally by a group, including state authorities; is well planned; and is executed as a part of a policy.

Once violence appears, it leaves its mark for years to come and changes the conflict qualitatively. In my view, the use of violence is the most critical characteristic in turning intergroup conflict into intractable conflict. Not only are soldiers wounded or killed, but civilians, including women and children, are also attacked, and civil property is often destroyed. Additionally, such violence can create refugees and sometimes involve atrocities, including mass rape, mass killing, ethnic cleansing, and even genocide (Brubaker & Laitin, 1998; Staub, 1989, 2011; Staub & Bar-Tal, 2003). Obviously the latter types of violence leave a lasting imprint on the victims and the conflict.

The war in Bosnia-Herzegovina in 1992–1995 forced as many as 1 million Muslims to flee their homes. During the acts of violence that were carried out by Serbian forces, 200,000 were killed, including at least 7,000 men and boys who were mass-murdered in Srebrenica in July 1995, in what entered history as the largest massacre since World War II (Mennecke & Markusen, 2004). The protracted conflict between Hutu and Tutsi in Burundi and Rwanda resulted in two mass killings: the 1972 mass killing of Hutus in Burundi that took the lives of 100,000 to 200,000 people (Lemarchand, 1994); and the 1994 genocide of Tutsi in Rwanda, when at least half a million people perished (Des Forges, 1999; Melvern, 2006).

In the case of the Israeli-Palestinian conflict, violence has claimed many lives. Israelis began to count the losses since the second half of the 19th century and by 2011 reached a total of at least 22,000 deaths and many more wounded. The number of Arabs killed, including Palestinians, is probably considerably higher. Just the Israeli-Arab War of 1948, for example, led to many thousands killed and wounded on both sides (Jews had about 6,000 losses, which constituted at that time 1% of their population) and created approximately 700,000 Palestinian refugees, which constituted more than 55% of the total Palestinian population (Morris, 2001).

The characteristic of violence is also well reflected in the Chechen-Russian conflict. Ever since the Russian colonialist expansion project to North Caucasus started, it was faced with indigenous resistance. The resistance was met with harsh and violent reactions, including deportations; mass use of force, which caused Chechens to lose nearly half their population during the 19th century; and destruction of the Chechen economy (Dunlop, 1998; Smith, 2001). But the pivotal and most influential act of violence occurred in 1944, after the Russians accused Chechens of collaborating with the Nazi occupation army and deported the local population to other parts of Asia, causing the death of around 20% to 30% of the Chechen population (ca. 150,000–200,000 people) – "raw genocide by anyone's definition" (Dunlop, 1998, p. 70).

The "troubles" in Northern Ireland claimed 3,600 deaths in the period 1969–1998, a significant number given Northern Ireland's small population of 1.6 million; 53% of the victims were civilians, and 26% were of 21 years of age or under (Fay, Morrissey, & Smyth, 1998). According to the Police Service of Northern Ireland (PSNI), more than 47,000 people were injured in the period 1969–2003, of which 63% were civilians (Police Service of Northern Ireland, 2003). The protracted conflict in Sri Lanka took the lives of an estimated 80,000 to 100,000 people until the defeat of the Tamil rebellion in 2009. According to official estimates, the Sri Lanka armed forces suffered around 13,000 casualties before the cease-fire of 2001 (independent estimates point to a larger number of 25,000), and the LTTE, the Tamil rebel group, lost 14,000 to 18,000 of its men (Bose, 2007; Strategic Foresight Group, 2006).

Other types of violence can also have serious consequences. Destructions, expulsions, or an influx of refugees can cause conflicts to escalate. For example, the Palestinian refugee problem of 1948 and 1967 in the case of the Israeli-Palestinian conflict serves as a major obstacle to its peaceful resolution. Additional acts of violence can include different types of restricting and discriminating orders and the expropriation of land – acts intended to harm the rival group.

Violence does not have to appear at the beginning of conflicts; in some cases it appears only with time. Nor does it have to appear on a large scale. However, violence always has an effect on the development of a conflict, reflecting its most tangible outcomes. It often immediately sets a precedent for aggressive acts and provokes retribution. This situation then fixes the direction of the conflict on its escalating path. Which party begins the use of violence is often an important question that preoccupies both sides and also the international community. With time, however, as the cycles of violence evolve, it is hard follow what constitutes a trigger and what constitutes a response. In general, both sides claim that the violence of the other side is disproportional, vicious, unjust, random, and unprovoked. Soon, it does not matter, as both sides engage in cycles of violence that escalate the conflict and cause its perpetration and the continuation of more violence. Nevertheless, when one side or both perform unacceptable forms of violence (e.g., atrocities, ethnic cleansing, or genocide) that violate international codes and mores, the question of responsibility is raised with great urgency.

Attempts have been made to formulate a conceptual approach and practice by which conflicts can be managed without violence (e.g., Sharp, 2005). Gandhi's approach in the Indian struggle for independence from Great Brittan is well known (Borman, 1986). But, despite Gandhi's attempts to institute nonviolent struggle, even this conflict was accompanied by bloody violence that spread through the subcontinent. It seems that almost every conflict over essential goals leads to violence, as no side is willing to compromise in the initial stages of the conflict. Violence unfortunately is a human signal of power and determination that is used in order to demonstrate the seriousness of a group's contentions.

Even in considering characteristics of violence that may look like an objective component of conflict, there is a need to add a psychological perspective to this analysis. First, there is an aspect of interpretation and attribution. Groups involved in conflict act according to their perception of violence. Both sides view the other side as an initiator of the violence. A group's own violence is considered a reaction or is justified as a necessary means to an end. In contrast, violence from the other side is immoral and unjustified. Second, groups differ in the evaluation of the nature of acts and their seriousness. Thus, for example, Israelis and Palestinians define broadly as violence various acts of the other group: Israelis define a demonstration against a separating security fence being built in 2003 as an act of violence, while Palestinians view it as a legitimate act of nonviolent protest; similarly, Palestinians define violent action by the Israeli military as acts of terror, while Israelis interpret it as the implementation of standard security measures (Shamir & Shikaki, 2002).

The consequences of physical violence, especially the loss of life, have an immense impact on all group members, not only on those directly related to the individuals killed. In addition, particularly important in the context of many of the intergroup conflicts is the fact that, although individuals perform violent acts, the violence is initiated and carried out within a framework of a social system. That is, a social system provides the rationale and the justification for the violence, a system's institutions and organizations train the individuals to carry out violent acts, and social channels and institutions glorify the violent confrontations. Because the consequences of violence are considered as a group problem, the group accepts the obligation to support and legitimize violence carried out by its own group's members; it takes the responsibility of treating and compensating its own victims, trying to prevent the reoccurrence of physical violence by the rival side, and avenging the human losses that have already occurred.

In sum, violence changes the nature of the conflict because the loss of human life and the performance of violent acts have special meaning for society's members. Violence often escalates the level of intergroup conflicts; when it continues for many years, violence has a crucial effect on the society, as the accumulation and sedimentation of such experiences in collective memory penetrate every thread of the societal fabric. The collective memory of physical violence serves as a foundation for the development of a culture of conflict. In turn, the culture of conflict preserves the collective memory of the human losses, as well as the perceived cruelty, mistrust, inhumanity, and evilness of the enemy (Bar-Tal, 2003). By doing so, it rationalizes the continuation of the conflict and makes an imprint on the perception of reality by society members.

Intractable Conflicts Are Perceived as Zero-Sum Contests

Intractable conflicts are all-out conflicts, without compromises and with adherence to all the original goals. Both parties see a zero-sum outcome, in which the conflict resembles a dispute over one pie: the more one side takes, the less the other party will have (Axelrod, 1967). Each side focuses only on its own needs and adheres to the whole set of goals, perceiving them as essential for its survival, and therefore neither side can consider compromise or concessions. Each party has a desire to defeat the rival completely and then take all it wants. Deutsch (1985, p. 263), referring to malignant conflicts, characterizes them as "increasingly dangerous and costly and from which the participants see no way of extracting themselves without becoming vulnerable to an unacceptable loss in a value central to their self identities or self esteem." That is, the involved parties want to achieve the goals in their entirety, do not consider any compromise, and therefore present polarized solutions that are unacceptable to the other party (Zartman, 2005). In fact, they view at least some of their goals as "protected value," which denotes a goal or goals as being so essential that they have been granted protected status against any compromise, concession, or trade-off (Landman, 2010). These protected values have the status of a taboo, violation of which is considered a violation of the society's fundamental rules of ethics (Tetlock, 1999, 2003).

In addition, parties engaged in intractable conflict perceive any loss suffered by the other side as their own gain, and conversely any gains of the other side as their own loss. This characteristic adds special tension and stress. Practically every aspect of life is considered relevant to the conflict, and each group does its best to inflict as much harm as possible on the rival in as many domains as possible and to prevent it from making any gains, even in areas unrelated to military or political struggle (Ordeshook, 1986). This zero-sum competition is not restricted to the bilateral conflict relationship but also affects relations with third parties and fans out into the international arena. That is, each side tries to maximize support and aid from the international community and minimize those extended to the opponent.

This characteristic, which often appears from the beginning of the conflict, is also socio-psychological, as it suggests that the zero-sum nature has to be perceived by the parties involved in the conflict. In essence, this psychological perception requires that no compromises are possible and that there is a need to adhere to the original goals despite the sacrifices and the costs that the group or a society incurs. Once groups set their goals and view them as existential, they also often do not perceive any possibility of compromise, which contributes significantly to the intractability of the intergroup conflict.

The psychology underlying the zero-sum perception of conflict indicates that the rival sides close themselves in an ethnocentric closet. They focus on their own needs and goals, building a psychological fence that prevents them from looking at the rival as a fellow human. The rival is viewed only through the prism of the rifle aimed at a vicious enemy that has to be destroyed. This view limits the perspective of the group from seeing the needs and goals of the rival. The limited zero-sum perspective may continue for a long time, in spite of the fact that it leads to the suffering and misery of both groups. The zero-sum approach by its nature leads to a disconnection between inflicted harm and received harm.

In the conflict between India and Pakistan over Kashmir, we can find an ongoing unwillingness from both sides to compromise on a territorial issue that is overshadowed by the perceptions of the conflict as existentially risking the national identities (Schaffer & Schaffer, 2005). Similarly, the zero-sum approach can be found in the Russian view of the Chechen conflict, as well as in the views of the Singhalese and the Tamils in their conflict in Sri Lanka. In Northern Ireland, Unionists saw any offered change in their traditional practices, such as parading, as a "capitulation to the IRA" and therefore resisted with such slogans as "Not an Inch" and "No Surrender" (Jarman, 1997). Another expression for the fierce objection to any compromises made to Nationalists' goals could be found in the speech that Ian Paisley, as the leader of the second-biggest Protestant party (Democratic Unionist Party), delivered shortly after publication of the 1985 Anglo-Irish agreement:

We pray this night that Thou wouldst deal with the Prime Minister of our country. We remember that the Apostle Paul handed over the enemies of truth to the Devil that they might learn not to blaspheme. In the name of thy blessed Self, Father, Son and Holy Ghost, we hand this woman Margaret Thatcher to the Devil, that she might learn not to blaspheme. We pray that thou'dst make her a monument of Thy divine vengeance.... O God, in wrath take vengeance upon this wicked, treacherous lying woman. (quoted in Tonge, 2002, p. 133)

The extent of discontent and disapproval within the Protestant community to the symbolic concessions that were made by Thatcher in creating the Anglo-Irish Intergovernmental Council were manifested on November 23, 1986, when an overwhelming number of 200,000 protesters attended an "Ulster Says No" demonstration rally in Belfast. The rally was attended by 20% of the entire Protestant population (Tonge, 2002).

Another example for perceiving no option for compromises in intractable conflict could be taken from the famous Gazimestan speech that was given on June 28, 1989, by Slobodan Milošević to mark the 600th anniversary of the Battle of Kosovo:

Even later, when a socialist Yugoslavia was set up, in this new state the Serbian leadership remained divided, prone to compromise to the detriment of its own people. The concessions that many Serbian leaders made at the expense of their people could not be accepted historically and ethically by any nation in the world.... This situation lasted for decades, it lasted for years and here we are now at the field of Kosovo to say that this is no longer the case. (Gazimestan speech, 2008, May 5)

Intractable Conflicts Are Central

Intractable conflicts occupy a central place in the lives of the individual group members and the group as a whole. Thoughts related to the conflict are easily accessible and are relevant to many decisions that society members make for both personal and collective purposes. Members of the society are involved constantly and continuously with the conflict. The centrality of the intractable conflict is further reflected in its high salience on the public agenda. The media, leadership, and other societal institutions are greatly and continuously preoccupied with the intractable conflict. The centrality feature indicates that the considerations about conflict feed into various decisions taken by group members as individuals and into decisions taken by the collective, for example, by the leaders. It suggests that the conflict has an imprinting effect on every area of life and becomes part of the daily personal routine of life, as well as an indispensable part of the collective life in political, social, economic, educational, and cultural spheres. Also, the centrality feature has a sociopsychological element because it indicates an intensive preoccupation with the conflict by society members on both cognitive and emotional levels. This preoccupation leads to an overinvolvement by society members and plays a significant role in the development of the conflict because society members feel that they are part of the conflict. Thus, centrality indicates that society members live a normalized conflicted life, often even without realizing its tremendous effects and without being aware that there are other ways of life. This central preoccupation with the conflict through normalization and routinization contributes to the intractability of the conflict because participants do not feel an urgency to terminate it.

In the Chechen example, the harsh conditions of oppression, discrimination, and periods of warfare and existential threat are common phenomena, which make the conflict a central feature in Chechnya's public life. From the other side, during the past two decades the Chechen conflict has had high salience in the Russian public discourse because of its perception as a major threat to the stability and security of the Russian Federation as a whole (Dunlop, 1998; Smith, 2001). In addition, it existed as a central element in all of Russia's recent election campaigns.

In the Israeli-Palestinian conflict, the centrality is reflected in the fact that almost daily the conflict features in the news of the mass media and often has a focal place (see, e.g., in Israel, Bar-Tal, 2007b; Liebes & Kampf, 2007). The public discourse in the Israeli and Palestinian societies is almost completely dominated by the conflict. The decisions taken in both societies by leaders almost in every sphere of life have imprints of the conflict. In addition, many of the daily conversations among the members of the Jewish and the Palestinian societies are related to the conflict, and many of their personal decisions are directly related to its course. The Palestinian daily life is continuously affected by the state of the conflict (movement from place to place or the ability to work). On the Jewish Israeli side, service in the army greatly preoccupies the society members and sets priorities in many of the families. In addition, terror attacks affect daily routines of life when they take place.

The playwright Brian Friel addressed the centrality of the violent conflict between Protestants and Catholics in the Northern Ireland when he wrote: "The troubles are a pigmentation in our lives here, a constant irritation that detracts from real life" (quoted in Mulholland, 2002, p. 9). Its central place in Northern Irish society could be well illustrated with two examples: the numerous painted murals and parades. Both are visual and dominate the living space of the two rival communities, turning the conflict into a ongoing experience in everyday life and a part of the daily landscape. The practice of painting murals dates before the First World War and is mostly prevalent in the working-class neighborhoods of Belfast and Derry (Jarman, 1997). Most murals are devoted to paramilitary iconography and "represent the most dynamic element in the commemorative political cycle" (Jarman, 1997, p. 212). The parading history in Ireland goes back 300 years and has become a popular expression of identity and a prominent part of the political process. The parades usually commemorate different conflictive historical events, which are of high importance to each community. From the mid-1980s to mid-1990s, there was a steady increase in the number of sectarian parades, from a total of 1,950 in 1986 to 2,883 in 1995. Most parades were loyalist, 1,731 in 1986 and 2,581 in 1995 (Jarman, 1997). Even after the Belfast Agreement was signed in 1998, parades still dominated the streets of Northern Ireland: in 2006, 2,480 loyalist and 185 nationalist parades took place (Police Service of Northern Ireland, 2008). In the view of Ross (2007), murals and parades in Northern Ireland are part of the contesting experiences in everyday expressions and performances that signify the identities of the rival groups in conflict.

Another manifestation of the centrality of the conflict in the life of young people in Northern Ireland, even after a political settlement was reached, can be observed in the work of Barton and McCully (2005): the figures and events with which children mostly identify include categories that focus on conflict and division, such as the hunger striker Bobby Sands and the Easter Rising for Catholics, and King William and the Siege of Derry for Protestants. As one of the girls who participated in the study said: "That's the biggest thing in our lives, and you can't go anywhere without being reminded of that" (Barton & McCully, 2005, p. 99).

Intractable Conflicts Are Perceived as Unsolvable

Society members involved in intractable conflict do not perceive a possibility of resolving the conflict peacefully. It means not only that the parties do not believe that it can be revolved peacefully but also that they cannot overcome the other side militarily. This characteristic, which is a central part of the intractability, usually develops with time, because it evolves with one's perspective on the history of the unresolved conflict. Many different reasons may underlie this perception: among the most notable are a long history of failed attempts to achieve a peaceful resolution or to subdue the rival party, mutual delegitimizing practices by both sides, the resistance of involved societies to changing their conflict's goals and making compromises, or a lack of accommodating leadership. Because neither side can win, both sides expect the conflict to continue and involve violent confrontations. They take all the necessary steps to prepare themselves for a long conflict, and this requires major adjustments on the part of the groups involved. This perception indicates a kind of hopelessness because the prognosis suggests no hope for a normal, peaceful life but rather a continuation of the violent conflict that brings loss of life, destruction, and anguish. Coleman (2000, p. 42) suggests that "the parties become unable to envision any approach to resolving the conflict other than that of continued use of force aimed at annihilating the other."

This characteristic is purely psychological, as it depends on the evolution of a belief that does not necessarily have to be grounded in reality. Resolution of the conflict peacefully depends also on the perceived reality of the rivals; if they believe it is unsolvable, then they act accordingly. They do not trust attempts to resolve it peacefully, do not trust the rival, and think that the conflict will continue for years to come. They prepare themselves for a long conflict, and obviously such beliefs often serve as a self-fulfilling prophecy, because both sides initiate acts of violence on the basis of this belief that provide a confirmation to the established belief.

In spite of the fact that attempts to move to peaceful negotiation between India and Pakistan were initiated in 2000, after three major wars fought between them over Kashmir, the conflict still looks unresolvable. The goals of the involved parties are far apart, and with time there emerged even a third party that advocates independence of Kashmir and withdrawal of both India and Pakistan from this territory (Schaffer & Schaffer, 2005).

The conflict in Sri Lanka saw several failed attempts at its resolution. The first attempt at peace talks between the government and the LTTE occurred in 1985; the second was in 1987, when the government signed a treaty with India that created new councils for Tamil areas and enabled the deployment of the Indian Peacekeeping Force in the northern parts of Sri Lanka (Bose, 2007; Strategic Foresight Group, 2006). The conflict escalated to violence once again in 1990; peace talks were initiated in 1994 but collapsed after one year. The last peace initiative, sponsored by Norway, began when the government and the LTTE signed a cease-fire in February 2002, which led to a series of peace talks during 2002–2003 (Bose, 2007; Strategic Foresight Group, 2006). The peace talks resumed during 2006 in Geneva but failed, and violence mounted once again. In January 2008 the cease-fire officially expired when the government pulled out of the agreement (BBC, 2008; Bose, 2007; Strategic Foresight Group, 2006). Eventually the government defeated the Tamil Tigers militarily in May 2009, conquering the entire area held and controlled by them. However, a complete defeat has not brought an end to the conflict, as many of the grievances of the Tamil population remain. Only time will tell whether the military victory will bring about conditions that will satisfy the basic needs of the Tamils and thus lead to peaceful relations between the two populations.

Similarly, in spite of the total military victory of Russians over Chechens in the last war in May 2000, the conflict still looks to both rival groups as unresolvable. Russians still experience terror attacks that remind them about continuation of the conflict, while many of the Chechens do not accept the present situation of being ruled by a Russian collaborative regime that does not address the goal of establishing an independent state. Despite the cessation of an active conflict, these examples indicate its continuing durability and the sense that it cannot be resolved.

Intractable Conflicts Demand Extensive Investment

Parties engaged in an intractable conflict make vast material (e.g., military, technological, and economic) and psychological investments in order to cope successfully with the conditions of the conflict context. The material investments include mobilization of society members, training the military, development of military industries, acquisition of weapons, and development of supportive infrastructure in all spheres of collective life – in essence, development of the military-societal-economic infrastructure that supports the management of the conflict. The psychological investment refers to building and imparting the epistemic basis that provides the justification for the conflict and the development of the will to maintain the confrontation – all necessary for mobilization. An ethos of conflict eventually develops that serves as a basis for the development of a culture of conflict. The psychological investment also includes development of adaptive beliefs, including attitudes and emotions that facilitate living under the conditions of intractable conflict (see Chapter 3).

All these investments indicate that societies engaged in intractable conflicts make tremendous efforts and sacrifices to maintain the conflict. The costs of the continuation of the conflict are enormous. Societies forgo many opportunities for improving the conditions of life and standards of living and postpone dealing with important problems in order to maintain the conflict. Psychologically, society members are frozen within the evolved socio-psychological repertoire and society becomes dogmatic. These investments eventually have an effect on various tangible and intangible spheres of individual and collective life.

The extensive investment required for the continuation of the conflict is well reflected in the Chechen-Russian conflict. Although the Chechen Republic constitutes only 0.1% of Russia's area, Russia invested significant military and economic resources in the conflict, even during turbulent periods such as World War II. From the Chechen side, the conflict draws repeated readiness for mobilization from the population to confront a highly asymmetrical adversary (Dunlop, 1998; Smith, 2001).

Since its eruption in 1983, the conflict in Sri Lanka has resulted in a sharp increase in military expenditures – up to 6.5% of the GDP and 17% of the government's total expenditure in 1995 (Strategic Foresight Group, 2006). Between 1993 and 2005, annual government spending on the military due to the conflict averaged an additional 25 billion Sri Lanka rupees (roughly US$230 million according to 2006 exchange rates) (Strategic Foresight Group, 2006). Arunatilake, Jayasuriya, and Kelegama (2001) estimate that the accumulated total cost of the conflict in Sri Lanka until 1996 was at least US$20.6 billion (according to 1996 exchange rates).

Of the conflict in Northern Ireland, Ruane and Todd (1996, p. 2) point out:

The cost of maintaining the security forces in Northern Ireland was £1 billion in 1990–1, UK compensation averaged over £33 million per year in the first decades of the conflict; one bomb in the City of London in 1993 cost over £1 billion in insurance payments. The cost of the Northern Ireland conflict to the Irish Republic in the years of the violence is estimated at over £100 million per year.

Hever (2013) calculates the costs of the Israeli occupation in 1967 of the West Bank and Gaza Strip, which is one of the focal reasons for the continuation of the Israeli-Palestinian conflict, as the staggering total of 381 billion shekels, which is more than US$100 billion. He suggests that the annual cost of occupation is about US$6.84 billon and the direct expenses incurred by the occupation currently total 8.72% of Israel's budget. One aspect of the huge material investments needed from the Israeli society due to its conflict with the Palestinians are the funds invested in developing and providing security for the Jewish settlements built on the occupied territories. Civilian cost of settlements was estimated at around 2.4 billion shekels per year in 2003 (about US$530 million), from which 705 million goes to municipalities, 440 million to housing, and 396 to roads (*Haaretz*, September 26, 2003). The expenditures per settler are estimated at 10,000 shekels per year (about US$2,600 in 2011). Just the expenditure for housing since 1970 until 2003 was estimated at around 11 billion shekels (about US$2.4 billion). The total civilian expenditures on the settlements from 1967 to 2003 are estimated at around 45.37 billion shekels – about US$10 billion (*Haaretz*, September 26, 2003). The military costs of protecting the settlements were estimated at around 2 billion shekels per year until the second Intifada, and around 4 billion since then (about US$1 billion). The budget for the Israeli police activity in the occupied territories is estimated at around 406 million shekels per year – about US$90 million (*Haaretz*, September 26, 2003).

Another aspect of the material investment in the Israeli-Palestinian conflict is the military expenditure needed to manage the conflict. Since the beginning of 1988, after first Intifada broke out, until 2005, at least 29 billion shekels (about US$6.5 billion) were added for the defense budget because of "intensified activity in the territories." During the second Intifada years, this excess expenditure reached 12% of the defense budget (Swirski, 2005). Also, although the percentage of Israeli defense expenditure as part of its GDP has been steadily decreasing over the past 30 years (Lifshitz, 2000), Israeli defense expenditure is among the highest among the OECD states. In 2006 Israeli defense expenditure composed more than 16% of the state annual budget and 8.4% of its GDP. When comparing Israeli defense expenditure percentage with other countries, it can be seen that Israeli defense expenditure far exceeds that of France (2.5%), Germany (1.4%), Italy (1.9%), Sweden (1.5%), the United Kingdom (2.7%), or even the United States (4.1%). It also exceeds that of its Arab neighbors: Egypt (2.8%), Syria (5.1%), and even Iran (5.8%) (www.sipri.org/contents/milap/milex/mex_database1.html).

Intractable Conflicts Are Protracted

Longevity is the last characteristic to appear and is a crucial one. Intractable conflicts persist for a long time, at least a generation (about 25 years). Many of them last many decades and even centuries. With some conflicts, it is even difficult to point to their beginning, as they deescalate for a long time and then reescalate with all the features of intractable conflict. The length of the intractable conflict is important. There is a major difference between conflicts that last a short time and conflicts that persist for at least a generation. Long-lasting conflicts have serious implications. The long duration implies that attempts to resolve them have failed, and they often are perceived as irresolvable. Neither side can win, and both sides do not find grounds for its peaceful resolution. Their length also implies that the involved parties in a conflict have had many confrontational experiences and, as a result, have accumulated increasing amounts of prejudice, mistrust, hatred, and animosity.

The duration forces group members to adapt their lives to face the continuously stressful situation, and they learn to live with it often without realizing that there are alternatives to a life with intractable conflict. The important implication of longevity relates to the evolution of a socio-psychological infrastructure that includes collective memory, ethos of conflict, and emotional orientations. This process takes a long time and therefore is one of the dominant characteristics of intractable conflict. Thus, over the years, groups involved in conflict selectively form their narratives about the conflict. On the one hand, they focus mainly on the other side's responsibility for the outbreak and continuation of the conflict and its misdeeds, violence, and atrocities; on the other hand, they concentrate on their own self-justification, self-righteousness, glorification, and victimization. These beliefs are institutionalized and maintained by the groups in prolonged conflict (see Chapters 4, 5, and 7). They transmit them through the political, social, and cultural channels and institutions, and they contribute to the group's social identity (Bar-Tal, 2007a). In addition, through the years emotional orientations of fear, hatred, and anger are evolved, disseminated, and entrenched in the personal and collective repertoire of the society members. This repertoire is also imparted to new generations through the educational system. Of importance is the fact that during 25 years of a conflict a new generation becomes actively involved in it. This generation grows up under conditions of intractable conflict, absorbing the socio-psychological repertoire that feeds its continuation; is socialized within the framework of its themes; and is inspired with the mobilization and the patriotism. In essence, the long duration of conflicts has a determinative effect on the emerging cultures of both societies, which is imprinted by the ongoing hostility and is therefore labeled a culture of conflict. Hadjipavlou (2004, p. 200), in describing the Cyprus conflict between Turkish and Greek Cypriots, notes that time has a determinative effect as "at least two generations have never seen or interacted with the 'other.' They learn about each other through mediated information; they develop deep insecurities, animosities, and negative collective memories about the 'other' whom they have never met."

The list of lasting conflicts is not a short one. For example, the conflict in Ireland and later in Northern Ireland has lasted about 500 years; the Israeli-Arab conflict or, more specifically, the Israeli-Palestinian conflict has lasted more than a century; the Chechen-Russian conflict has existed now for more than 230 years; the conflict in Kashmir began in 1948; the conflict in Rwanda between Tutsi and Hutus began with Belgian colonialism in the 19th century; and the conflict in Sri Lanka between Tamils and Sinhaleses began to evolve at the beginning of the 20th century during the British domination of the island.

IMPLICATIONS OF INTRACTABILITY

Seven characteristics can define intractable conflicts: they are conflicts over existential goals that last for a long time and that neither side can win; they involve violence, are viewed by the parties as a zero-sum dispute, and are unsolvable; and they greatly preoccupy society members of the parties that invest in them in order to manage the conflict successfully.

We need a time perspective to judge whether conflicts are intractable; because they are dynamic, their nature changes with time, and not necessarily in a linear way. Certain characteristics may be salient at a particular time and then fade and then reappear. But many of the characteristics may already be present at the outbreak of the conflict. For example, a conflict may begin with its totality when at least one party formulates far-reaching goals, viewing them as existential (e.g., the Indian-Pakistani conflict over Kashmir). Also, a conflict may begin with violence, such as a sudden military campaign or big terror attack (e.g., the Chechen conflict). Then perception of the conflict as being a zero-sum situation may appear (and a conflict may even be perceived at the early stage as being unsolvable); centrality can also develop, and therefore indicators of potential intractability may emerge. The conflict then is over essential goals, and parties see no possibility of compromising but strive instead to achieve all their goals (owing to its zero-sum nature), as was the case through many years in the Israeli-Palestinian conflict. The last two features suggest that both parties do not want to resolve the conflict peacefully at this stage. But the evolvement of conflicts depends also on persuasion and on mobilization of the masses. For the conflict to evolve with sufficient extensity and intensity, there is a need to persuade society members that the goals are of existential importance and to achieve them. Such mobilization may take time, and therefore the climax of the conflict may develop with time and then last for a long period (e.g., conflicts in South Africa and Algeria). Once many of the society members are mobilized, the conflict becomes central.

Violence may also appear in the later stages of a conflict, but once it appears, it contributes greatly to turning the conflict into a salient and central element for society members (e.g., the conflict between Hutu and Tutsi in Rwanda). Violence plays a crucial role in turning the conflict to become intractable – the more people are killed, the more the society members feel threatened and the more they invest in the conflict (see Chapter 3). Empirical data show that enduring rivalries are prone to lead to war more than short-term rivalries are. Goertz and Diehl (1992) report that lasting conflicts are almost eight times more likely to include a war than conflicts that are isolated. Still, it does not mean that conflicts that do not last 25 years are less violent or vicious. World Wars I and II were among the most vicious conflicts in human history and had millions of casualties and victims. They had all six characteristics of intractable conflicts without the longevity. Eventually both of them ended with the total victory of one side and left their marks on the entire world civilization. The scope of violence is one of the most important indicators (if not the most significant one) of the seriousness of the conflict, the involvement of the society members engaged in the conflict, and the preoccupation of the international community.

In any event, with eruption of violence, the conflict always becomes central, because it preoccupies the society members. Centrality adds considerably to its severity, and therefore it adds to its potential intractability. Other characteristics, investment in conflict and its longevity, evolve with time because of their nature. Investments always take time as they require mobilization of resources, formulation of a strategy and policy, and the setting of plans and their executions. As the conflict lasts, some characteristics may disappear at least for some time. For example, violence may cease for periods of time. But the conflict may still remain to be perceived as total, as a zero-sum situation, and as unsolvable (e.g., the Chechen conflict).

Once all of the characteristics appear, the state of intractability begins, in which each characteristic adds to this chronic reality. But only when all the seven features emerge in their extreme form do the intractable conflicts appear in their most extreme nature. It can be suggested that the Israeli-Arab conflict, during the late 1940s and 1950s, and then with the 1967 war and during the first part of the 1970s, had all the characteristics of the extreme case of intractable conflict. Also, the Algerian conflict in the late 1950s, the Sri Lanka conflict in the 1990s, and the Kashmir conflict in the 1990s had all the features of the prototypical intractable conflict. The seven features are additive, and each characteristic intensifies the conflict. But they have different weight. As was suggested, the characteristics of totality, a zero-sum nature, and violence play a determinative role in its seriousness and viciousness. Also, although each of the characteristics has a unique feature, there is a relationship among them. For example, the characteristic of totality is often related to the conflict's perceptions as being a zero-sum dispute and unsolvable. Also, the violent nature of a conflict is often related to its centrality and one's investment in it.

In reality, intractable conflicts differ in terms of the intensity with which each of the seven features appears. It is possible to evaluate the state of the conflict by assessing where it stands with regard to each of the seven characteristics. The characteristics can be established empirically: the perception of the goals and the view of the conflict by a majority of society members, the level of violence, the level of investment, its centrality, and its durability. I realize that there could be cultural differences in calculating the importance of each of the features. Some groups pay determinative weight to violence performed by the rival group, while other groups may focus on the importance of goals.

Configuration of the seven characteristics changes from case to case and with time. This dynamic is contingent upon the transitional context. The context of intractable conflict, despite its overall stability, changes over time. The changes pertain to the conditions in which the two rival parties live during the conflict, as well as the conditions that the international community creates. Conditions relate to such characteristics as military success in violent confrontations, availability of resources, levels of mobilization for conflict, emergence of alternative goals and their dissemination, and the level of resilience of society members. The international community, or a third party, not only can intervene but also may create a climate that escalates or deescalates the conflict.

Intractable conflicts fluctuate and thus move on the dimension of low-high intractability. The seven characteristics may change independently with time in various directions (see Oren, 2005, 2009). For example, the belief that the Israeli-Palestinian conflict is unsolvable weakened in the 1990s and then reappeared with strength again in the early 2000s. At the same time, in the early 2000s the level of perceiving it as being a zero-sum situation remained low. Another example is the Chechen-Russian conflict, which escalated and deescalated many times. We can find considerable variances in the flames of the conflict during the 20th century, when the conflict escalated in the 1920s, then deescalated and stayed low until World War II. In this period, it escalated dramatically when the mass deportation of Chechens was carried out by the Soviet regime. The conflict then deescalated once again, until the collapse of the Soviet Union, after which the first and second Chechen wars occurred, and it reached one of its peaks again.

PSYCHOLOGICAL BASIS OF THE CHARACTERISTICS

The description of the seven features suggests that the psychological aspect in the characterization of the intractable conflict is essential. Three of the characteristics are psychological: perceiving the conflict as being existential, being irresolvable, and exhibiting a zero-sum nature. Other features are associated with different realms of experience, such as behavioral features in the case of violence and investment, as well as consequential features in the case of centrality and longevity. Nevertheless, even the latter four features have psychological components because individuals evaluate the extent of violence, invest psychologically in the conflict, are involved with it, and form and accumulate the socio-psychological repertoire with time. Thus, intractability of the conflict indicates that the involved societies are in a particular psychological state (which can be called the intractable syndrome), which plays a major role in this type of conflict. Society members perceive and decide that the particular conflict is intractable and, once they decide, they act accordingly.

The preceding point implies that group members involved in an intractable conflict continuously evaluate its state. This important process allows group members to assess their situation in order to plan their strategy and lines of actions. These evaluations and decisions, being psychological, depend on various factors and change with time. They depend, for example, on the perceived conflict situation, the collective memory of the group about the present and past conflicts and other experiences, and the availability of information (especially alternative information) and the willingness of the group members to absorb alternative information, not only about one's own but also about the rival group. More specifically, the perception of the conflict situation depends on the evaluation of one's own goals, the level of the goals' contradiction, the evaluation of rival's ability, and the intentions and severity of actions taken. Traumatic remembered experiences about the present and other conflicts are examples of collective memory that also influence the evaluation of the conflict. Finally, society's access and openness to various alternative opinions and information that shed new light on the conflict, the rival party, and one's own group affect how group members evaluate the conflict situation.

A question then arises of how widely the perceptions about the conflict (at least that it is total, irresolvable, and zero sum) have to be shared before the intractable conflicts will emerge. The present conception gives special attention to the persuasion of society members in the nature of the conflict and their mobilization to act in its framework. These processes are essential. Intractable conflicts can last for a long time only when at least a substantial majority shares the perception that defines the characteristics of the intractable conflict. Nevertheless, it is clear that when leaders view the conflict as being intractable and accept its psychological features, then the conflict is managed in this way at least by them.

NATURE OF INTRACTABILITY

Intractable conflicts by definition are particular types of severe conflicts. They evolve with time because their longevity is one of their main characteristics. Just as important is the difficulty involved in resolving an intractable conflict. Agnew (1989) views intractability as a process rather than as a set of zero-sum conditions. This process evolves in his view on two dimensions: spatial and temporal. The former is related to territorial claims, ritualization of symbolic places, rivalry over spatial-economic resources, and competition over ideological spaces. The latter is related to a continuing and accumulative evolvement of public, social, and cultural elements that feed the conflict and foster its maintenance. These elements develop with time, are institutionalized, and become foundations of developed culture. Once they crystallize as part of culture, intractability becomes a reality for the involved society.

Parties in an intractable conflict cannot disengage because they perceive their goals as existential. This involves a kind of loss of control over the course of the conflict, as it enters the path of intractability. Once it is on this path, it moves on the course of continuing hostility, violence, and animosity, which acts as a *perpetum mobile*. This type of conflict "is intractable if it resists attempts at resolution" (Thorson, 1989, p. 3).

One way to end it in some cases is via a decisive military victory, but this ending cannot always be achieved, because either none of the groups can win or one can but morally cannot use the full force to overcome the rival. In general, the parties involved in intractable conflict cannot win and do not perceive a possibility of resolving it peacefully, but they continue the confrontation for decades until intractability eventually is overturned – that is, either one side wins, or both sides decide to resolve it peacefully. *Of crucial importance for the continuation of an intractable conflict and lack of its peaceful resolution are the shared beliefs of the rival societies' members that their sacred goals cannot be compromised, that the rival cannot be trusted, that they have the human and material resources to continue the conflict, and that time is on their side either to gain a better deal or to create better conditions.* All these master beliefs or even one of them prevents engagement in peacemaking. Each of them provides a determinative argument why the conflict should continue in spite of the losses, suffering, and costs involved (see also Chapter 8). Appearance of all of them is a definite assurance for the conflict's continuity and a determinative factor in preventing a peacemaking process. Brockner and Rubin (1985) call this situation an entrapment because the engaged parties see the losses they suffer, the forgone investments, and the incurred costs, but they cannot terminate the conflict. They need to justify and rationalize all of them as well to try to recoup them, and therefore must continue the conflict.

This is the case with the ongoing intractable conflicts. Some of them continue with violent cycles as in the Middle East, Kashmir, or Turkish Kurdistan. Others continue, even if at a particular stage they are relatively nonviolent and appear stabilized, as, for example, in Rwanda, Chechnya, or Sri Lanka. The victory of one party without satisfying the basic needs of the other party leads not to the end of the conflict but only to a temporal period of dominance by the victorious party until circumstances eventually change.

It is not unusual for intractable conflicts to continue because there are leaders, elites, or segments in the society that profit in the intractable conflict and have vested interest in their continuation (Crocker, Hampson, & Aall, 2005b). The profits can be on material level, such as wealth or territory, or on a more symbolic level, such as ideology. For example, the Jewish settlers as a segment of the Israeli society have profited greatly as a result of the continuation of the conflict in the Middle East. First, they were able to settle in the space of the territory that Palestinians aspired to be their state, and then they got favored living conditions from the government to carry out and expand the Jewish settlements (see Zertal & Eldar, 2007). They constitute a powerful sector that objects to the compromises needed to settle the Israeli-Palestinian conflict peacefully.

When conflicts involve rivals of asymmetrical power, this fact can affect the course of events and the military, economic, and political strategies involved. But it has to be recognized that an asymmetrical power relationship does not necessarily bring victory to the powerful side. Various reasons may prevent the powerful side from winning the conflict decisively, whether militarily or politically, and bringing it to an end.

What is important in the nature of intractable conflicts is that they last for a long time, and in this period a socio-psychological repertoire evolves that includes an ethos of conflict, collective memory, and emotional orientation. Zartman (2005, p. 49) points out that the duration of such conflicts has a deep influence, as they "are folded into the history and mythology of the parties, an ideological explanation for national efforts and problems, and so parties become reliant on them and are loath to part with them." Also, in my view, the uniqueness of intractable conflicts lies both in the lasting socio-psychological aspects that affect the dynamics of the conflict and in the socio-psychological repertoire that emerges and is institutionalized. The evolved socio-psychological repertoire becomes with time an extremely potent factor that prevents any settlement. The evolved socio-psychological infrastructure becomes a blinding barrier that directs society members toward escalation of the conflict, providing unequivocal rationalization for its continuation. This socio-psychological infrastructure serves as a foundation of the culture of conflict that develops in societies that are engaged for so many years in intractable conflict. Also, intractability implies that at least a generation of society members, and often more than one generation, is reared in the conditions of the given conflict and socialized from its earliest days for mobilization and participation in it.

But intractable conflicts are not God-given and doomed to their eternal continuation. Being created by human beings, they can also be peacefully resolved by them (e.g., the conflicts in Northern Ireland, South Africa, or Algeria). Also, the intractability of the conflict can be reduced with time, and it can move beyond the destructive intractability toward manageable tractability. With time, segments of the societies involved in the conflict may change their views on whether the conflict is total, is a zero-sum situation, and is unsolvable by reframing the goals of the conflict and changing the views of the rival. Thus, change of the nature of conflict also requires psychological change that in fact constitutes a major societal change. Reduced intractability begins when parties (at least the leaders and some segments of the society) begin to define the conflict as solvable and begin to negotiate. But the psychological change has to be accompanied by reduced violence. In these cases, as the violent context changes, the views of the society members may change too in the direction of a compromising position. It is also clear that the change of the context may lead to a further change of the conflict views, and therefore both directions of changes have to be implemented if the parties actually strive to change the intractable nature of their conflict. This conception suggests that the socio-psychological aspects of intractable conflict are not necessarily stable and frozen.

Nevertheless, even when the conflict's intractability is reduced, there may be significant segments of a society that continue to view it as a total, zero-sum, and unsolvable conflict. Thus, just as there is a need to mobilize society members for the conflict, there is also a need to mobilize society members for its resolution. Intractable conflicts are eventually terminated not only when the parties' leaders negotiate peaceful settlement but when they go through major societal changes that lead to building a stable and lasting peace.

SUMMARY

Intractable conflicts have specific features that explain their resistance to peaceful settlement. They take place mostly in interethnic relations but also involve states, as in the cases of the Israeli-Palestinian or Kashmir conflict. They may also take place in the context of intrasocietal conflicts, as in El Salvador or Colombia. What is unique in this type of conflict is the stubbornness of the involved groups to carry on with the conflicts without a readiness to make compromises that will allow their settlement, in spite of the parties' difficulty in achieving unequivocal victory. And so these conflicts continue despite the long-term negative effects that they have on the individuals and the collectives, including human losses, suffering, and destruction. But the societies learn to live with them, adapting to their condition without even knowing that there are alternatives. Sometimes it even seems that they prefer to live in the context of conflict rather that to begin a new way of life that requires serious changes and adaptations. Tremendous investments in the continuation of the conflict, turning its goals into sacred values, continuous indoctrinations carried out by agents of conflicts that reject compromises, and closure to information that signals alternatives to conflict are just a few of the factors that lead to its continuation.

I do not intend to imply that all such conflicts are unjust. I believe that at least some of the parties involved in them have just contentions. In many cases, it is the weak side that formulates just goals, but parties with military, political, and economic power ignore these contentions. As time passes, both sides become interlocked in intractable conflict, which can eventually cause the suffering of innocent civilians on both sides. The destructive nature of intractable conflicts is a detrimental phenomenon that contemporary civilization still does not know how to deal with.

In order to understand these obstacles one must consider the psychological dynamics that develop in intractable conflicts, a challenge that this book tries to meet.

2

Eruption of Intractable Conflicts

During the eruption phase of intractable conflicts not only do groups become aware of their deprivation and formulate their goals but they also translate the deprivation and goals into a movement that begins to take active steps to achieve its collective goals. This is an important phase that in many respects imprints the nature of its continuation. Societies begin to mobilize their members for participation in conflict and construct a persuasive epistemic basis, a narrative, with the societal beliefs and attitudes, accompanied with discrete emotions, that will eventually crystallize and serve as a foundation of a culture of conflict. This system provides the rationale for continuation of the conflict, its escalation, and even the prevention of its peaceful resolution. Thus, this chapter describes the development of the conflict goals with their epistemic basis, then expounds on conflicts that are related to social identity, and finally elaborates on the issue of mobilization for participation in the conflict.

In general, conflicts begin when groups (i.e., at least a segment of group members in each group) perceive that their goals or interests are contradicted by the goals or interests of another group and act accordingly. Thus, every conflict begins with at least one of two mutually inclusive ideas (i.e., beliefs), which may appear together: (1) an idea that expresses an aspiration or motivation to achieve a goal that contradicts the goal of another party; (2) an idea that expresses a realization that an intention or behavior of another party contradicts its own goals and interest. Often these ideas complement each other as each of them appears in one of the two parties.

When one or both of these ideas appears in one group, and another group perceives this development as contradicting its own goals, a situation of conflict can emerge. The perception (i.e., awareness) of such a contradiction is a necessary and sufficient condition for believing that a conflict exists. But to move the identification of a conflictive situation into the realm of behavioral conflict, actions on the basis of this perception are required. Once actions by one group or by two rival groups are carried out as a result of this identification, a conflict erupts.

In cases of intractable conflicts, identification of the contradicting goals almost always leads to action and mobilization. When, for example, at least some of the Palestinians recognized that the return of Jews, as a realization of their new national ideology, contradicted their own goals, the seeds of the Jewish-Arab conflict were planted (Morris, 2001). According to Mazur (2012), the earliest known document concerning the opposition of Arabs to Jewish immigration and to the sale of land to Jews is a cable dated June 24, 1891, sent by a group of Arab notables from Jerusalem and then followed by a memorandum signed by 500 Jerusalem notables. This action identified a conflict with Jews. It is thus not surprising that 14 years later Negib Azouri, an Arab assistant to the governor of Jerusalem, observed:

Two important phenomena, of the same nature but opposed, which have still not drawn anyone's attention, are emerging at this moment in the Asiatic Turkey. They are the awakening of the Arab nation and the latent efforts of the Jews to reconstitute on a very large scale of the ancient kingdom of Israel. Both these movements are destined to fight each other continually until one of them wins. The fate of the entire world will depend on the final result of this struggle between these two people representing two contrary principles. (cited in Mandel, 1976, p. 52)

Similarly, when Catholics in the 1960s decided to act in order to change the political-economic system established in Northern Ireland that discriminated against them, it was the beginning of their struggle for equality and civil rights that later served as a basis for national and religious contentions (McGarry & O'Leary, 1995). These acts reignited a conflict in Northern Ireland between Catholics and Protestants that began centuries ago between Irish and English. While the Catholics aspired to unite with the Irish Republic, the Protestants preferred to remain part of Great Britain. Also, the aspiration of tsarist Russia in the 18th and 19th centuries to expand the Russian Empire into Chechnya led to the realization by Chechens that their goal of independence was in danger. In these two campaigns the Chechens forcefully resisted their subjugation and so the conflict with the Russians began and continues today (Dunlop, 1998).

On the basis of the conception proposed by Snow and Benford (1988), it is possible to suggest the following framing for intractable conflict to evolve psychologically: (1) diagnosis of some problematic event, experience, or aspect of life that touches the group life and therefore demands a change in the situation; (2) recognition that another group either is responsible for the problematic situation or condition or has the commodities needed for changing the situation; (3) establishing goals to correct the problem and provide an epistemic basis (i.e., a rationale, a narrative) for it, and suggesting a conflict as a way to achieve it; (4) deciding to act to achieve these goals and constructing well-rationalized arguments for justifying the selected line of action. This framing also includes an assumption that another group will not willingly and easily agree to change the situation because any change would result in unacceptable costs and losses to this group. Thus, this framing indicates that the conflict will erupt because a contradiction of goals is inevitable and actions will follow this recognition. The decision to begin the conflict can be made and carried out by a formal or informal leader and his or her circle, by a collective of individuals who organized themselves to achieve the group goals, or by segments of group members supported by channels of communication. They usually hold beliefs about the necessity of conflict with great confidence and as a central element in their repertoire.

EVOLVEMENT OF GOALS AND THEIR EPISTEMIC BASIS

The ideas that lead to a conflict develop in a particular context and come with a well-organized system of justifications and legitimizations.

Context for Evolvement of the Perception of a Conflict Situation

Although conflicts are an inseparable part of intergroup life and appear in every intergroup relationship, the intractable conflicts tend to evolve in certain contexts. Among the various contexts in which they develop (see Thackrah, 2009) are conditions of unequal divisions of wealth, power, or resources (e.g., El Salvador conflict); social stratification and barriers to mobility (e.g., Rwandan conflict); discrimination (e.g., South African conflict); conquest and colonialism (e.g., Algerian-French conflict); disputes over territories (e.g., Israeli-Palestinian conflict); unfulfilled group aspirations and needs (e.g., Basque conflict); need of territories, resources, or other valued commodities (e.g., Japanese expansion into China); or existence of rival ideologies and dogmas (e.g., Korean conflict). These contexts, which are not mutually exclusive, may be found in interstate relations or intergroup relations within one state.

Since War World II, various conditions that foster conflict evolvement have appeared: new multiethnic states in which a group, or few of them, dominate, discriminate, and control other groups; emergence of new states on the basis of artificially demarcated borders; conflicts and competitions between various superpowers that encourage emergence of various local conflicts;

growing gaps within societies and between states that increase alienation and dissatisfaction; increased resources and means for mobilization; institutionalization and an increased means of mass communication that leads to easy dissemination of ideas and information; globalization processes that enable dissemination of ideas; movement of people across continents and states that changes the composition of national societies; diffusion of various ideologies (religious or political) that provide an epistemic basis for conflict eruption; legitimization of certain goals in intergroup struggles, such as liberation, self-determination, equality, justice, or freedom; growing recognition of injustice in the division of wealth and resources and the demystification of the rationalizations that served as its foundation; external intervention that instigates and maintains confrontations and disagreements; proliferation of the arms trade, which allows easy access to weapons and thus enables violence; and a decrease of certain badly needed resources that frustrates groups (see, e.g., Williams, 1994). These conditions serve as breeding grounds for the development of serious and harsh conflicts, but they all have to begin with the evolution of goals that are perceived as contradicting goals of another group.

Goals in Conflict

According to the approach that views goals as knowledge structure, goals are defined as subjective desirable states of affairs that individuals or groups intend and strive to attain through action (Kruglanski, 1996; Kruglanski & Kopetz, 2009; Kruglanski, Shah, Fishbach, Friedman, Chun, & Sleeth-Keppler, 2002). Like other knowledge structures, goals are governed by the same principles: they can be formulated, activated, validated, and changed. Their special feature lies in their representation of a state or states that have to be achieved through action or actions (Kruglanski & Kopetz, 2009). They can be represented in the form of tangible and intangible goods.

Intractable conflicts can erupt over various desired or deprived goods (goals). Among them are territory, political autonomy, national self-determination, control, statehood, values, economic resources, freedom, equality, wealth, collective recognition, power, cultural goods, religious dogma, and ideology, and often more than one are involved in a particular conflict. Burgess and Burgess (1996) classify the goods that serve as goals in conflicts into three categories. First are moral issues, which refer to fundamental moral, social, cultural, and religious values that allow little room for compromise – for example, the conflicts between Sunni and Shiites in Iraq over religious doctrine. Another prominent example of ideology-based conflict is the one in the Korean Peninsula between the communist Democratic People's Republic of Korea and the capitalist Republic of Korea. A second category includes tangible goals such as territory or resources (e.g., the Israeli-Palestinian conflict or the Chechen-Russian conflict). Goals of this category can be divided, redistributed, and even assessed, but the problem is to establish criteria and justifications for these acts that can be accepted by the rival parties. A third category refers to intangible resources that have materialistic meaning, as well as, for example, issues of status, power, or dominance (e.g., the conflict in Rwanda or the conflict Lebanon). Here, reallocating goals is possible, but in this case establishing criteria for the just redistribution is often difficult, as principles of justice or pragmatism are dependent on subjective judgment. This classification is not mutually exclusive, as the conflicts usually include at least two or even all the three types of the described categories of goals.

For example, the Irish Republican Army (IRA) as the representative of Catholics in the Northern Ireland conflict formulated its goals in a constitution, known as The Green Book, which states its objective "to support the establishment of an Irish socialist republic based on the 1916 Proclamation; to support the establishment of, and uphold, a lawful government in sole and absolute control of the Republic; to secure and defend civil and religious liberties and equal rights and equal opportunities for all citizens; and to promote the revival of the Irish language as the everyday language of the people" (in O'Boyle, 2002, p. 31).

Of special importance in the formation of goals are basic needs that underlie physical survival and safety (Maslow, 1970). They include goods, resources, wealth, and security (World Development Report, 2011). Other needs relate to self-esteem and self-actualization (e.g., positive social identity, or self-determination). Deprivation of these needs (at least one of them) leads naturally to setting goals with the aim to satisfy them. Maslow's seminal theory refers to individual needs, but the present conception focuses more on collective needs. Although the needs are experienced on an individual level, at least some group members may share the same needs and be aware that they experience them because of their group membership. Even group members not experiencing these needs may care about needs that concern the whole collective. Thus, it seems that individual needs proposed by Maslow can be applied to a collective level as well, as, for example, a group's need for security or actualization. Some theories refer directly to collective needs and propose that collectives have to satisfy certain needs. Among the most important collective needs are needs for security, positive identity, equality, justice, freedom, and well-being (Azar, 1986; Burton, 1990, 1987; Galtung, 1996; Staub, 1999, 2011). Deprivation of these needs by another group leads to attempts to change the situation by active behavior, including protracted and vicious conflicts (Azar, 1990; Burton, 1987; Gurr, 1970, 2010; Staub, 2011; Weinstein, 2007; Wickham-Crowley, 1992). For example, an extensive analysis of violent conflicts in Latin America by Wickham-Crowley (1992) shows that wide-scale economic-political deprivations of classes of people (mostly native Indians and peasants) led to crystallization of goals to change this condition of inequality.

When the contradicted goals are perceived by one party or both parties as essential or existential, the conflict may be perceived as severe and has a potential to become intractable. The noted goals may be tangible or intangible, but their achievement requires observable acts that can be perceived and evaluated by group members – for example, a change of institutionalized inequality, as it took place in Northern Ireland. The latter point suggests that in most of the cases group members establish criteria to judge the achievement of their goals. Also, all these goals reflect serious contentions, and therefore there is not a simple way to achieve them. States or even international systems usually do not have institutionalized mechanisms to deal with conflicts that involve these types of goals, as they require major political, social, or economic changes. It is difficult to decide how to implement them and supervise their implementation.

Relative Deprivation and Conflict

Goals that ignite conflicts evolve out of the recognition, first, that there is a deprivation in collective goods (either tangible or intangible), or there is a potential in such deprivation; and, second, that the other party is responsible for the deprivation or has the needed goods. The concept of collective *relative deprivation*, which indicates that groups compare their state with subjective standards and find that in comparison to other parties or the past situation they are deprived, captures this process very well (Carrilo, Corning, Dennehy, & Crosby, 2011; Crosby, 1976; Major, 1994; Olson, Hermann, & Zanna, 1986; Runciman, 1966; Walker & Smith, 2002). The sense of relative deprivation can occur in political, economic, societal, cultural, religious, and other domains of life. It means that this comparison results in an awareness of the disparity between one's own present subjective state of affairs and either the state of another group or one's own past state. One can assume that Chechens, Palestinians and Jews, Kurds, Algerians, Tamils and Singhalese, or Hutu and Tutsi experienced this type of relative deprivation when comparing their state with either their state in the past or the state of the other ethnic group in the present (see experiments by Grant & Brown, 1995; Taylor, Moghaddam, Gamble, & Zeller, 1987; Wright, Taylor, & Moghaddam, 1990).

I would like to add to this equation that groups may also compare their present state to an imaginary state that they believe they deserve. This imaginary state may be formulated on the basis of ideology or other system beliefs. In any event, these comparisons result in recognition that the groups are distanced from a desirable state and therefore are in a situation of deprivation. The most salient examples of this type of deprivation are the Japanese and Germans during the 1930s who constructed an ideology that focused on national needs and eventually led these two nations to enter into a vicious conflict in order satisfy their needs.

Later theorizing differentiated between deprivations due to lack of fairness in the distribution of resources, wealth, and power (distributive injustice) and deprivation due to lack of fairness in decision making and treatment of groups (procedural injustice [Tyler & Smith, 1998]). The first case is often related to satisfaction of basic needs, mostly in the realm of economics and personal safety (Maslow, 1970), as groups may not have the basic means to survive (Ledgerwood, Liviatan, & Carnevale, 2007). Such conditions develop especially in multiethnic communities where the resources are divided to a great extent unequally on the basis of group belonging. For example, the long intrasocietal conflict in Guatemala was based on unequal distribution of wealth and land. Whereas poor indigenous farmers, who constituted a majority, lived in great poverty, the thin layer of powerful landowners lived in wealth (Handy, 1994). When the attempts to carry out social and agrarian reforms failed in the 1960s, a violent conflict began that ended only in 1996, when a peace accord was signed by the rival groups. The second case can be found in Turkey in its conflict with the Kurdish minority, which has been discriminated against politically, economically, and culturally (Kirisci & Winrow, 1997). Nevertheless, both types of deprivations often appear concurrently in intractable conflicts and then sharpen the confrontation.

The basic assumption in this theorizing is that the noted disparities cause states of distress, frustration, and dissatisfaction that are accompanied by beliefs of living amid scarcity, shortage, injustice, unfairness, and inequality, as well as with emotional reactions such as feelings of anger, shame, rage, humiliation, vengeance, or resentment. These psychological reactions energize groups to set new goals and take actions in order to diminish the level of disparity, if not to close the gap completely (Wright & Tropp, 2002). Experiments by Becker, Tausch, and Wagner (2011, p. 1596) are among the few studies that investigated the effect of emotions on participation in collective action to improve the conditions of the ingroup; they showed that outgroup-directed anger and contempt are more important than self-directed positive emotions in predicting a willingness to engage even in radical collective actions in the future. In the view of the researchers, "collective action participation heightens the perception that the ingroup is treated unfairly, which produces corresponding 'negative' outgroup-directed emotions and increases the intention to engage in actions against this type of injustice in the future."

But for intergroup conflict to begin, it is important that the deprivation be group related and not random or related to "God's will" or nature. It has to be perceived in one of the two ways: either one group or its individual members feel deprived because of their membership, or one group lacks a needed commodity that another group has. Without this recognition, the sense of deprivation often remains on an individual level. Thus, before the intergroup conflict will emerge, it is of crucial importance that at least a considerable segment of the group will view the situation of deprivations as being part of the group's fate owing to its dependence on another group's behavior. Under these conditions, even individual group members who do not personally experience deprivation may join the group efforts in pursuit of the new goal because of their identification with the group as a collective and with its fate (De Dreu, 2010). Thus, recognition of group relative deprivation means that members of a group, or groups, become aware that they need something (I'll call it goods) that was taken from them, or that they do not have, but in both cases they want it now. This recognition, which is often accompanied by a feeling of an existential threat, leads to a desire to get the needed group goals.

One more condition is still necessary for eruption of the intergroup conflict: the recognition that another group took or controlled goods unjustly and has done so for a long time or wants the goods unjustly, while one's own demand is based on justified group needs. This condition is important because groups may become aware of their state of deprivation and even recognize the relations between one's own state and another group's state, but also believe that this state is justified or legitimized. For example, in the Hindu caste system, the Harijans, also referred to as untouchables, suffered deprivation for many generations as a result of segregation, discrimination, and exploitation by other castes, but many of them in the past perceived their fate as deriving from Hindu scriptures and therefore as given by God (Flood, 1996). In these cases they may rule out conflictive action against the other group because they view it as being illegitimate. Thus, in the present formulated socio-psychological conception, a fundamental condition for the evolvement of the conflict is the perception that the outgroup's goals, possessions, interests, or values unjustly prevent satisfaction of the ingroup's needs and the attainment of its goals (see also Gamson, 1992; Gurr, 1993; Kriesberg, 1998, 2007; Tajfel & Turner, 1986). It becomes clear that both groups cannot achieve these particular goals because they are viewed as being undivided, or they see no legitimacy, need, or justification to divide them. As a result, the goals of the two groups collide, because only one of them can get the privileged goods and must persuade the other group to change its goals or to share its possessions and interests.

The final condition that leads to the eruption of conflict is the decision to act. At least theoretically, a group will identify all the conditions that are needed for starting a conflict and then decide to do nothing or perhaps to postpone the action. For example, Czechs decided to accept without interference in 1992 the decision of the Slovak parliament to dissolve Czechoslovakia, although it was perceived by many of them as a conflictive act. In some cases, a leader may decide to avoid confrontational behavior, as happens often in international relations (Bar-Tal, Kruglanski, & Klar, 1989). Also, a party may decide to wait for a more suitable situation in order to act in a confrontational way.

The decision to act in order to actualize the conflict is a separate decision that has crucial implications. Many factors may lead to the decision to act after identifying the contradictions between goals and thus to begin a conflict by states or by collectives within a state. This decision may be carried out within a formal framework (e.g., a government) for evaluating a situation and considering various options for action. Among the considered factors are the perceived likelihood of achieving the goal, the evaluation of other party's ability and intentions, the perceived ability to mobilize group members for carrying out the conflict, the history of relations with the rival party, and the existence of conflicts with other parties. In fact, theories of collective action can easily be applied to the present discussion of making a decision for action in the situation of intergroup conflicts. These theories note the importance of such factors as availability of resources, opportunities, and especially a sense of self-collective efficacy (Klandermans, 1997; McAdam, 1982; Van Stekelenburg & Klandermans, 2007; Wright, 2001). The latter factor suggests that collective action begins when group members believe that they have the ability and resources to change the situation (Bandura, 2000).

Nevertheless, history shows that in many cases groups decide not infrequently on the basis of the depth of their grievances, feelings of injustice, emotional load, level of perceived threat, and already experienced harm by the other groups. As a result, they begin a conflict that may sometimes be very costly to the group, at least in the first phase of the struggle. Algerians paid an extremely heavy price for the conflict with France, but the costs are overrated in comparison to the depth of deprivation and humiliation that at least a segment of the society experienced. In these cases, the mere eruption of the conflict serves important functions for the society that cannot be overemphasized (e.g., empowerment). Thus, it is important to deepen our understanding of the role of deprivation in setting goals.

Process of Recognition in Deprivation and Setting Goals

The processes of recognizing deprivation and then of setting goals to change the situation can take various forms and occur in different time frameworks, through different processes and in different contexts: they may rise in a fast or a slow, piecemeal process; they may arise as a reaction to another party's action or as an evolvement of recognition in one's own needs and goals and also in some kind of combined process. These actions can be verbal (e.g., a statement about intentions or a demand) or behavioral (e.g., demonstration or violent attack).

Recognition may take place in situations of sudden change that deprive a group of resources, power, or status when one group decides to take goods from another group. Walsh (1981) and Tarrow (1998) refer to this situation as suddenly imposed grievances. This may happen for instance when a group conquers a territory (the invasion of Kuwait by Iraq), or takes political resources in a coup d'etat (e.g., Chile), revolution (e.g., Bolshevik Revolution in Russia), or change of regime (e.g., ascendance to power of the Islamic forces in Algeria via democratic elections). In these cases, the realization and recognition in deprivation by group members usually take place in a short time.

But a sense of deprivation may also arise gradually in a process of self-collective enlightenment, especially in situations in which an imbalance of power exists between groups and in which the more powerful group exploits, controls, discriminates, and abuses the less powerful groups (Azar & Farah, 1981; Coleman, 2003). Such a situation may last for a long time and be embedded in the existing system. The process of enlightenment may take many years until at least a substantial segment of society members begins to realize that its goals are contradicted and decides to carry out actions in accordance to this perception.

This type of intergroup conflict takes place mostly in multiethnic states. A group may be institutionally deprived of basic rights and victimized in a systematic way. In addition, the deprivation is almost always legitimized by a set of beliefs that provides the epistemic basis for the unequal relations and the deprivation (Sidanius & Pratto, 1999). A deprived group may accept these legitimizing beliefs and see the situation as normal for a long time until it begins to realize that this deprivation is not acceptable. Thus, of importance is the growing awareness of deprivation and the emergence of goals to change the situation. This is often a special challenge, which requires persuasion of group members that the deprivation should and can cease and that the achievement of this goal is a collective mission because the deprivation causes harm to the group as a collective. Because the emergence of the goal(s) and its justification may take a long time, a person, or a group of people, must define the situation as a deprivation, point to the group responsible for the deprivation, and set the goal of changing this situation. This is not a simple process. It took many decades of discrimination, exploitation, and oppression of the black people in South Africa until eventually they developed active resistance and formulated goals of changing the situation. Individuals like Pixley ka Isaka Seme, Richard Msimang, or George Montsioa, who were educated in Great Britain, began the long journey of changing this situation. They formulated the goals, tried to unify the different African groups in South Africa, and eventually founded the South African native National Congress in 1912, which later was renamed as the African National Congress (ANC). This organization engaged in the conflict for many decades until it finally achieved its goals in 1994 (Walshe, 1970).

But the long enlightening process does not have to take place within an exploited and discriminated group that tries to correct an unjust situation. The process of developing recognition in deprivation can also be gradual in groups that construct the idea about needing additional resources and territories that another group or groups have. Also in these cases it is necessary to persuade the group members of their deprivation and then construct new goals. In Japan at the end of 19th century and the first part of the 20th century, beliefs evolved claiming that Japan had essential economic and political needs that could not be satisfied within the space of Japan. The acts that followed this sense of deprivation can be illustrated with the specific case of the conquest of Manchuria. Japan had deep economic and political interests in Manchuria since the beginning of the 19th century and decided that it needed to conquer this territory in order to assure its interests. Eventually a fabricated incident served as a pretext to invade Manchuria in 1931, and Japan opened a violent conflict (Matsusaka, 2003).

Coleman (2003) suggests that the ideas about experiencing deprivations that require setting new goals appear especially when there is change, instability, or anarchy. In these situations, according to Coleman, norms are weakened, there is redefinition of the power balance, and a sense of relative deprivation arises. Thus, in this line, for example, the Russian Revolution and the collapse of the Soviet Union, which caused great instability, both facilitated attempts by the Chechens to gain independence and reinflamed the conflict, which lasted many decades after each of these two points of time (Dunlop, 1998; Russell, 2007). Also, starting in 1920 in Northern Ireland, the Protestants ruled with a one-party government for almost fifty years, with no Catholic representation, and controlled the economy and the civil service. Only in the 1960s, when the waves of struggle to change economic and political rights in

United States and Europe emerged, did the latter group begin systematically to demand equality (Farrell, 1976). Similarly, in the Indian-ruled parts of Kashmir the process of recognition in deprivation took a few decades. The competing nationalist visions of the province together with ethnoreligious economic inequalities and ongoing political decay and repression gradually led to the outbreak of violent ethnic conflict in late 1980s between Hindus and Muslims, with the development of an armed insurgency. This recognition crystallized only after a prolonged process of political mobilization, a result of increasing levels of education, exposure to mass media, and social and physical mobility (Ganguly, 1996).

In the past decades, the sense of deprivations takes place mostly in states of developing nations where there is scarcity of resources, great poverty, huge inequalities, enormous corruption, and acute economic and heath problems, mostly in Africa, Asia, and South America. Many of the beliefs about deprivation evolved a long time ago, but the emerged goals are still not achieved. In addition, there are still today raging interethnic conflicts that focus on fulfillment of self-determination, autonomy, statehood, and various territorial disputes, as well international conflicts about territories and resources, especially petroleum (see Harff & Gurr, 2004; Pfetsch & Rohloff, 2000).

Development of Epistemic Basis

Epistemic basis consists of an elaborated system of beliefs (or messages) that provide explanation, rationalization, legitimization, and justification for a set of societal goals. Epistemic basis also presents ways and means to achieve them and assures high likelihood of achieving them. It serves as a basis for the development of an ethos of conflict with its core theme "justness of the goals" (see Chapter 5). This epistemic basis, as well as an ethos of conflict, can be seen as a narrative. Narrative is a social construction that tells a coherent story about *a sequence of historical and current events* related to collective experiences (Bruner, 1990). Thus, first, the system of beliefs, or the narrative, describes the deprivation of the society – its nature and causes, with special focus on the group that is responsible for the deprivation, or the group that has the resources to end the deprivation, or the group that poses tremendous threat to the existence of the society. Then it refers to the need to change this situation, emphasizes the importance of the new goals, and explains why they are so essential as well as just for the group.

Goals are often framed as moral convictions that stand on a high level and cannot be compromised (Skitka, Bauman, & Sargis, 2005). This framing motivates society members to engage in conflict in order to change the undesirable situation. Violated moral convictions are combined with a relevant social identity to fuel collective action against collective deprivation (van Zomeren, Postmes, & Spears, 2008, 2012). Thus, for example, one of the leaders of the Algerian nationalism who demanded independence, Ferhart Abbas, wrote in 1943 the Algerian People's Manifesto in which the supreme goal of establishing a sovereign Algerian nation was presented (Stone, 1997). It served as an important basis for justifying the struggle for an independent Algeria. In another example, the Federal Party of Tamils in Sri Lanka formed in 1949 spelled out the demands of this ethnic minority in the emerging conflict. At this early stage, the party demanded equal status for the Tamil language and considerable autonomy in the Tamil regions (Wilson, 2000).

The epistemic basis (i.e., narrative) is needed because group members need to know why the goals are important to them individually and to the collective as a whole and whether the goals are of a just nature and realistic. It has to provide an unequivocal, understandable, and meaningful picture that serves as a determinative factor for mobilizing society members. It also arouses the emotions that are needed to motivate and energize society members. The success of their mobilization and level of involvement, and in fact the success in launching a conflict, are at least partially dependent on the persuasiveness of this epistemic basis in terms of the presented arguments, as well as on its motivating strength. This element is essential in every conflict eruption. The epistemic basis thus has to be persuasive to at least a significant segment of society members, irrespective of what other groups and the international community at large think about the goals of the conflict and the outlined rationale. In fact, not infrequently the international community does not accept the goals with the presented epistemic basis, but the group may still launch the conflict.

Nevertheless, the epistemic basis is also important for persuading the international community of the justness of the group's goals, though the set of arguments for internal use and external use may be different. The epistemic basis is context dependent and is constructed on the basis of the dominant norms in the particular period and situation. These norms change. What was normal and accepted as a goal for launching a conflict centuries or even decades ago is not accepted in the present time; on the contrary, what was not accepted in the past may be well approved nowadays. For example, practices of colonialism, occupation, or legal discrimination are not accepted by the present codes of intergroup relations. Thus, for example, conquest for extending territory or getting resources is not accepted any more, although it was when Russia conquered Chechnya in the 18th century or France conquered Algiers in the 19th century. The United States had to provide a well-accepted reason for invading Iraq in 2003. At the same time, terminating oppression or discrimination is a well-supported goal to begin a conflict by the international community today, as in the case of the Egyptian popular revolution in the winter of 2011. Societies must sometimes adapt their epistemic basis to the changing hegemonic international codes of behavior. In any event, without a well-developed and elaborated epistemic basis, it is difficult to mobilize group members to participate in the conflict and receive support from the international community.

The deprivation, the set goals, and the epistemic basis are often related to the identity of society members in cases of intractable conflict – meaning that they are identity based. In the next part, the notions of goals and identity are further elaborated.

IDENTITY-BASED CONFLICT

Most of the intractable conflicts, if not all of them, are defined in terms of social identity. This is one of the main reasons for their resistance to peaceful resolution, as both sides adhere to their contentions. Society members view their deprivation as impinging on the essence of their being identified as a group (Ellemers, 2002). The group perceives that the contradicted goals are essential for the group existence (Korostelina, 2006). Also, identity is related to a sense of justice as moral values are central to a social identity by indicating what is deserved (Clayton & Opotow, 2003; Skitka, 2003). Thus group members on the basis of their identity are able to formulate their needs and demands. According to Rothman (1997, p. 6), these conflicts are "deeply rooted in the underlying human needs and values that together constitute people's social identities." This perception has several different roots that are not mutually exclusive.

At the core of identity stands a number of key issues, which are not necessarily mutually exclusive. First, the most frequent conflicts of this type relate to territory, as groups, especially national groups, relate their identity to a specific country (David & Bar-Tal, 2009; Sack, 1986; Smith, 1991). The specific territory is considered as the homeland of the group, the object of attachment, and the basis of its existence; it is where their ancestors lived and is therefore necessary for group survival. In many cases, a group demands this territory to establish its authority for an expression of collective identity in various forms, such as an independent state, autonomy, or a union with another state because of an affinity with its ethnic group. An example of this type of conflict is the struggle of Kurds to establish their state or at least to achieve autonomy as a nation with an attachment to a particular territory. They were promised to have a sovereign state in the early years of the 20th century, but this promise was never realized, and since then Kurds have carried on a conflict in Iraq and in Turkey to achieve their goals (Kreyenbroek & Sperl, 1992).

Second, groups relate to their identity the type of political-economic structure in which the group lives. Many of the groups try to change the political-economic system in view of their central values and beliefs. This may take place because of ideology that underlies the identity or fulfillment of values that are viewed as essential for group survival. An example of this type of conflict is the Spanish conflict that eventually erupted into a violent civil war. Segments of the society had contradictory visions about the nature of the Spanish political, religious, and economic system (Preston, 1978).

The third category of demands reflects the bases for expression of group culture, heritage, tradition, religion, and language, which are all perceived as reflecting the identity of the group. Groups strive to have freedom and equality in these expressions, believing that it is essential for group existence. Without their free expression, the group believes that its identity is not actualized and the group is severely harmed to the extent that it may lose its particular identity. An example of this type of conflict is in Sri Lanka, where the Tamils demand to get autonomy from the Sinhalese along with recognition of their language and culture. This conflict was energized when a law was passed in 1956 mandating only the Sinhala language as the official language, thus disregarding the needs of the minority (Gamage & Watson, 1999).

Finally, groups may feel that a particular context in which they live threatens their identity. Crighton and Mac Iver (1990) point out that Protestants in Northern Ireland and Maronites in Lebanon view their rivals as being outsiders to their faith and thus feel that they reside in a sea alien to their basic identity and therefore sense a great threat to their existence as a unique group. So the Protestants view themselves as "the last bastion of evangelical Protestantism in Western Europe" (Mac Iver, 1987, p. 368), and the Maronites perceive themselves to be "the last outpost of Western and Christian civilization in the region, encircled by the hostile Islamic forces" (Entelis, 1981, p. 11).

In all these cases, society members experience threats to their identity. When group members perceive that their identity is denied, threatened, harmed, or endangered, this constitutes a basis for developing a strong feeling of deprivation and a collective action of defense. Those are seeds of a serious conflict (Brewer, 2011). Eventually identity-based conflicts are difficult to resolve because the society's demands are viewed as being existential and needed for survival and therefore are total (Bar-Tal, 2007a; Burton, 1987; Rothman, 1997). Some of these demands (e.g., self-determination, cultural autonomy, security, control over one's own life, freedom of religious practice) are difficult to divide, and therefore a compromise is hard to achieve. In fact, they are often considered as sacred values that cannot be negotiated (Atran & Axelrod, 2008). This perception greatly affects the nature and course of conflicts.

In addition, in many of the intractable conflict cases, the described identity-based contentions are inclusive and appear concurrently, although they do not have to appear at the early phase of the conflict but can develop later on. Many of them involve demands that correspond to the different layers of identity. Therefore, intractable conflicts are often multifaceted because various essential goals for the group are at stake (see also Chapter 5). This multilayer identity factor also contributes greatly to a conflict's intractability. For example, the conflict in Sri Lanka or the Kurdish conflict contains different elements of identity that pertain to a territory, autonomy, religious values, cultural freedom, and socio-economic well-being. Similarly, in the Korean case, we can find competing claims for legitimate sovereignty over the whole peninsula, as well as an ideological divide between the North and the South that was perpetuated during the Cold War, leading to an interlocked interstate and intrastate conflict (Snyder, 2005).

One of the basic challenges that groups face at the outbreak of a conflict is to convince group members that the conflict touches on their basic existential group needs and to mobilize them for the causes of the conflict. Meeting this challenge is based on the individual's identification with the group. Indeed, social identity theory posits that individuals may identify with the collective relative deprivation without actually experiencing it themselves. This happens when they feel high identification with the group (Foster & Matheson, 1995; Hinkle et al., 1996). But the process of mobilization is greatly facilitated when group members experience personal deprivation that is attributed to their group membership. When they feel deprivation personally, then it is easy to persuade society members that their goals are existential, but when the conflicts touch on collective ideological issues like self-determination, the case may not be important for all society members. Some may be in a personally prosperous situation and not interested in collective deprivations. It is even possible that participation in conflict may worsen personal life conditions of some group members. Often a person has to sacrifice personal benefits to join the conflict for the collective cause. In any event, in order for the conflict to erupt in great intensity, group members must identify with the group and be mobilized for the posed conflictive goals.

MOBILIZATION FOR THE CONFLICT

As an axiom it can be noted that without participation of group members, conflicts cannot evolve, gain strength, and be maintained. In other words, intractable conflicts require mobilization of the group's members (Williams,

1994) because the number of supporters of the conflict, the number of active participants in them, and the extent of their motivation, devotion, and commitment to the goals are important determinants of conflict eruption, its development, and its course. Thus, the challenge of every society that enters a conflict is to mobilize leaders, elites, and masses. Each of these societal segments is of great importance for managing lasting intractable conflict. Society members, including elites and masses, have to recognize the importance of the goals and participate persistently in the conflict. Because of its unique nature, it requires intensive involvement of society members, as well as active participation and readiness to incur costs, including the sacrifice of life. This is a necessary condition for successfully carrying out an intractable conflict. Conflicts extend in their scope and escalate only when a substantial part of the society's members are mobilized to act. But it should be noted that mobilization is important not only for the first phase of the conflict. Society members have to maintain their participation along its course, even when it lasts for many decades (Klandermans, 2004). Mobilization, in essence, as a social act, can be seen as being based on at least two pillars: one pertains to the messages (i.e., the contents, the epistemic basis, the narrative) that are told by the mobilizers to assure participation of society members in conflict; and the other refers to various tactics, ways, and methods that are used in transmitting the mobilizing messages.

Mobilization means not only that individuals identify with the group but also that they accept the goals related to the conflict, the direction of actions that the group takes, and the means that it takes. They are willing to carry out various needed activities, including military operations, on behalf of the group to begin the conflict and keep it alive (see, e.g., Klandermans, 1988). Mobilization is the deliberate recruitment of society members to be involved in the conflict.[1] It is a process of persuasion, with the goal of convincing group members to join the conflict. Thus, group members may be mobilized by accepting the consensual view about the conflict and, on a higher level, may be mobilized to join the activities related to conflict (action mobilization; see Klandermans, 1984). In the case of conflict, the latter mobilization is more important because intractable conflicts require by their nature active participation of society members and not only consensus mobilization. Klandermans (1997) proposes a four-step model of mobilization that describes movement toward active participation. The first step requires minimal mobilization as it indicates only the potential readiness that is reflected in

---

[1] There is large literature in the social sciences about mobilization into social movements and action, and it is beyond the goals of this book to review it (e.g., Klandermans, 1984; Klandermans, Kriesi, & Tarrow, 1988; Snow, Soule, & Kriesi, 2004; Stryker, Owens, & White, 2000). This book utilizes only some of the propositions and empirical findings that serve the present conception.

sympathizing with the causes of the conflict. Then society members become targets of mobilization attempts by the agents, and in the third step they move to the stage of being motivated to participate in the conflict. The fourth step concerns overcoming concrete barriers (e.g., time, money, or other responsibilities) to actual participation.

Action mobilization represents readiness for collective action, which is seen as behavior that is carried out on behalf of the group to improve its situation or state of affairs – in other words, to help achieve the collective goal (Iyer & van Zomeren, 2009). This is an important challenge because it is difficult to move society members from psychological support of the conflict's goals to active participation (Oegema & Klandermans, 1994). Active participation in intractable conflicts requires tremendous personal sacrifice. Active participants have to leave their normal routine, incur economic costs, and endanger family and personal life and sometimes even the lives of the other people in their social environment (van Zomeren & Iyer, 2009).

Levels of mobilization range from minimal to maximal participation (Tindall, 2002; Wiltfang & McAdam, 1991). The minimal participation is reflected in passive support, feelings of concern, or expressions of interest in the conflict. This minimal level requires certain cognitive, emotional, and even behavioral efforts on behalf of the group that can be detected and observed. It can be viewed as the maximal consensus mobilization proposed by Klandermans (1984) and is necessary for the wider evolvement of the conflict. Maximal participation, called total participation, takes place when a person leaves the route of normal life and becomes fully involved in the conflict, fulfilling various roles in it, as, for example, being a mobilizing agent, an organizer, or fighter. Between the two extremes are various forms of participation, most of them partial, as society members continue to live their normal lives and participate only in limited activities (e.g., donating money for the cause, demonstrating, signing petitions).

Total participation requires full commitment by the participant on cognitive, emotional, and behavioral levels. In these cases, the social identity takes over much of the personal identity, and one's personal life is controlled by the identification with the group causes. This leads to full active involvement in the collective aspirations and goals. Evolvement of a conflict requires that at least a significant number of society members will devote their life to the management of the conflict. Without their total devotion and readiness to sacrifice their lives, the intractable conflicts cannot gain momentum.

In well-established and institutionalized societies within a state framework, usually security and military personnel, such as army subscripts, fulfill these roles. The society actively and formally recruits society members for participation in violent conflicts. These society members serve the role of conflict carrier, being fully recruited to this role. In most societies engaged in intractable conflicts that control a state, mobilizing citizen participation in conflict is anchored in the law requiring mandatory recruitment. Institutions of the state often require mandatory military service with its professional extension and mandatory reserve service. In these societies, service in security forces is glorified, and the active participants in conflict receive tangible and intangible rewards. But even in these cases participation in conflict requires construction and then maintenance of a well-grounded epistemic basis. Thus, for example, the armies in Pakistan, India, Turkey, Israel, Sri Lanka, or Russia, which all involve dominant societies controlling a state and participating in intractable conflict, are able to mobilize citizens for active participation in their conflict and enjoy special status because of their determinative importance in the struggle for achieving the societal goals posed in the conflict.

In other cases in which the society involved in conflict does not have the institutionalized organization of a state, it must form such organizations and recruit society members to fulfill these roles. In these cases, the recruitment is much more difficult because it depends on volunteers. These societies have to not only organize a bureaucratic system that supports the conflict and find material resources to finance it but also organize military wings and recruit, train, and arm participants. Those are great challenges, and indeed Algerians in Algeria, blacks in South Africa, Tamils in Sri Lanka, Tutsi in Rwanda, Kurds in Turkey, and Catholics in Northern Ireland had to make such preparations in order to launch a violent conflict.

This difference is a major source for asymmetry. One party in the conflict is using state resources, security forces, formal institutions, and channels of communication to launch the conflict, whereas the rival party has to find resources, recruit volunteers, structure the institutions, and build the organizations informally and often illegally, while the dominant group often actively prevents and disrupts these processes. Thus, these latter parties require goals and an especially persuasive epistemic basis that will be well accepted by society members. The mobilization process in these societies depends crucially on convincing the members of the need for change via conflict, as these members have to volunteer to participate in it (McGarty, Bliuc, Thomas, & Bongiorno, 2009).

MOBILIZATION AND IDENTITY

The necessary basic precondition for mobilization is that individuals who participate in the conflict will hold the social identity of the group involved in conflict. Social identity denotes this "part of an individual's self-concept which derives from his knowledge of his membership of a social group (or groups) together with the value and emotional significance attached to that membership" (Tajfel, 1978, p. 63). The process of constructing social identity is an individual one (Tajfel, 1978, 1981) and includes a number of basic components: feeling of belonging to the given group, willingness to belong, importance ascribed to this belonging by the person, emotional attachment one feels toward the group, commitment to benefiting the group, belief that the group has highly valued qualities, and deference to the group's norms and cultural symbols (David & Bar-Tal, 2009; Roccas, Sagiv, Schwartz, Halevy, & Eidelson, 2008). Each of these components is unique and adds a layer to the identification's wholeness.

Social identification is a transformation of the self that redefines the meaning of self-interest by focusing on belonging to a group (Brewer, 1991). The process of identification with the group indicates that an individual's sense of self and self-interest becomes inextricably tied to group interests and welfare (Brewer, 2011). When social identity is strong and salient, the survival and welfare of the ingroup – whether it is an ethnic group or a nation – is tantamount to survival of the self as a person. In fact, individuals who strongly identify with their group evaluate outgroup goals and actions in terms of their implications for ingroup interests and are sensitive to challenges to ingroup symbols and values (Smith, Seger, & Mackie, 2007). Reicher, Hopkins, Levine, and Rath (2005, p. 624) argue "that shared social identification is what makes collective action possible." This is so because once individuals see themselves as members of a group, they think, feel, and behave as members of the categorized social category because of the depersonalization process that they go through (Tajfel, 1982; Turner, Hogg, Oakes, Reicher, & Wetherell, 1987). The important implication of this process is that group members sharing social identity also share beliefs (including goals), attitudes, values, and patterns of behavior. In turn, this sharing "enhances the ability to a set of people to ensure that their efforts complement each other and are directed in the most effective way to reach group goals" (Reicher et al., 2005, p. 625).

Identification and Conflict

Mobilization to participate in conflict requires feeling and thinking as being part of the group; viewing that the belongingness is a central part of the individual's being; a conviction that group members have to comply with the group's rules, orders, or calls; and the readiness to contribute to the welfare of the group. Brewer (2011) proposes that in general ingroup identification influences whether intergroup threats are perceived in the first place, and then it determines how much a threat to the ingroup matters to individuals and how likely they are to mobilize in defense of ingroup interests (see also Branscombe, Ellemers, Spears, & Doosje, 1999; Brewer, 2001; Polletta & Jasper, 2001; Reicher, 2004; Roccas & Elster, 2012).

The concept of *identity fusion* is important for understanding the mobilization of society members for participation in dangerous endeavors such as violent conflict. Identity fusion defines those cases in which society members feel that their personal self is merged with a social self (Gómez, Brooks, Buhrmester, Vázquez, Jetten, & Swann, 2011; Swann, Gómez, Seyle, Morales, & Huici, 2009). Such mergers are associated with a profound, familial connection to the society and its members. This type of identification entails feelings of obligation to sacrifice for the group, together with confidence that other group members will feel similarly obligated. Research suggests that fusion with one's nation predicts even willingness to fight and die for the group (e.g., Gómez et al., 2011; Swann, Gómez, Huici, Morales, & Hixon, 2010; Swann et al., 2009) – a behavior that is required for participation in violent conflict. Thus, fusion with the society in need indicates a high commitment and determination to take part in the conflict.

There are empirical indications that social identity becomes a basis for mobilization (see Huddy, 2001). White and Fraser (2000), in their study of Republican Sinn Fein (i.e., the Catholic side), describe individuals who devoted their lives to carrying on the conflict in Northern Ireland. Indeed, many of them were second-generation activists, with very high group identification, who acquired their full commitment from their parents. Also, Muldoon, McLaughlin, Rougier, and Trew (2008, p. 691), in their study about mobilization to paramilitary activities in Northern Ireland, note that "the most prevalent explanations young people perceived for individuals' paramilitary activism were ones which relied on social identification issues, such as patriotism and collective action, emphasizing the position of the group and perceived group inequities and grievances." In her ethnographic study of insurgents in El Salvador, Wood (2003) shows that high identification with the oppressed sectors and with the causes of the movement was the main reason for their moral commitment and emotional engagement to join the insurgence. Goodwin (2001), in an analysis of intrasocietal conflicts, also notes that identification with the group and its cause contributed to successful mobilization of participants in a conflict.

Socio-psychological studies have found that the strength of group identification is related to a mental overlap between the self and the group. That is, the distinction between "I" and "we" is blurred, and events that affect any member of the ingroup are experienced as if they occurred to the self (Coats, Smith, Claypool, & Banner, 2000; Tropp & Wright, 2001). Identification with the group implies having a positive affect toward the group, accepting group goals, and caring about its well-being (Klandermans & de Weerd, 2000). Also, strength of group identification was found to be related to the degree of emotional response to collective threats that a group encounters – whether anger or fear or some combination of both (Smith, Seger, & Mackie, 2007) – and to the willingness to engage in political action (Klandermans & De Weerd, 2000). Also, people who identify with their group feel strong emotions in response to events that have occurred to other group members, even if they themselves were not involved in them (e.g., Seger, Smith, & Mackie, 2009; Wohl & Branscombe, 2009; Yzerbyt Dumont, Wigboldus, & Gordijn, 2003). Other studies found that shared social identity increases perceptions of interdependence and common fate (Brewer & Silver, 2000) and that the harm incurred by any ingroup members is experienced as personal harm (Stenstrom, Lickel, Denson, & Miller, 2008). Furthermore, it leads to solidarity and readiness of action for the benefit of the group, including sacrifice (Brewer & Silver, 2000; Kramer & Brewer, 1986). This occurs through increased trust in the intentions of the group (Kramer, Brewer, & Hanna, 1996). In addition, people who are highly identified with the group are especially prone to the perception of ingroup continuity (Sani et al., 2007; Sani, Herrera, & Bowe, 2009). Because of perceived group continuity, traumatic events that threatened the group in the past can motivate group members to engage in group strengthening behaviors a long time after their occurrence (Wohl, Branscombe, & Reysen, 2010). People who strongly identify with the group hold more aggressive attitudes toward outgroup members (Brown, Maras, Masser, Vivian, & Hewstone, 2001; Struch & Schwartz, 1989), support more aggressive action (Maitner, Mackie, & Smith, 2007), and express more willingness to participate in illegal and violent actions in order to protect their group (Moskalenko & McCauley, 2009).

Of special relevance to understanding the importance of identification in the situation of conflict eruption are studies by Rothbart and Korostelina (2006) that investigate the impact of identity salience on the readiness for conflict with another group in Crimea. They propose that the readiness to begin a conflict with the outgroup reflects the willingness to defend one's own group in situations of real or perceived threat from other groups, or to punish or take revenge on members of the other group. The results show that group members with salient ethnic identity in comparison with other group members with nonsalient ethnic identity considered obedience, loyalty, and social recognition as important values. They also highly valued and adhered to group goals; focused on negative experiences with an outgroup; tended to stereotype the outgroup negatively and especially viewed it as aggressive and antagonistic; and minimized interaction with this group. The concept of *politicized collective identity* proposed by Simon and Klandermans (2001) denotes a mind-set based on high identification with the group that leads to mindful involvement and engagement in the struggle of the group for its goals.

Collective Identity

Nevertheless, in order to mobilize successfully, it is necessary to go beyond the individual construction of social identity to the collective level of the construction of collective identity (Foster, 1999; Hunt & Benford, 2004; Polletta & Jasper, 2001). *Collective identity* indicates the awareness that members share the same social identity and thus share the recognition that they are members of the same group (David & Bar-Tal, 2009; Klandermans & De Weerd 2000; Melucci, 1989). This "shared social identity is the basis of collective social power" (Haslam, Reicher, & Platow, 2010, p. 60). Successful mobilization, which goes beyond the basic characteristics of social identity and the formation of collective identity, depends on the strength of six fundamental generic characteristics of the collective identity (David and Bar-Tal, 2009). The first feature pertains to the *perception of the uniqueness of the collective* and its distinction from other collectives. This factor is an essential mechanism for the consolidation of collective identity, because without it the collective members' perception of themselves as a unique unit is meaningless. The second refers to *a commonality of beliefs, attitudes, norms, and values,* which characterizes group members and provides the basis for their feeling as being unique (Bar-Tal, 2000a; Smith, 1991). The third feature, *continuity and consecutiveness in the dimension of time,* indicates the formulation of a perception that presents the group with its past, present, and future. This view requires the molding of collective identity in a dynamic process involving an interaction and integration among three time dimensions, without complete rejection or absolute adoption of any one of them.

These three features are essential for establishing collective identity, but the following three features are of crucial importance for mobilization. *A sense of a common fate* pertains to the sense of unity and the feelings of mutual dependence that prevail among members of a collective. This is the feeling of "togetherness," the "cement" that bonds individuals and social groups (Brown, 2000) and enables them to define themselves as belonging to the same collective, despite variability in values, beliefs, attitudes, and patterns of behavior. But the significance of shared fate is more extensive and implies that the fate of each one of the collective's individuals is perceived as dependent on the fate of the whole collective. Doosje, Ellemers, and Spears (1999) and Ellemers, Spears, and Doosje (2002) draw connections between common fate and members' commitment – that is, the extent to which group members feel that they have strong emotional ties with the collective – and relate a high level of commitment to behavioral mobilization for the sake of the group.

Concern for the welfare of the collective and mobilization and sacrifice for its sake refers to feeling an interest in the experiences of the collective, a concern for its welfare, and motivation to act on its behalf. The motivation to act is manifested through willingness to join in missions of a collective nature, to contribute personal resources for the benefit of all, to help society members in times of distress, and even to sacrifice one's life for the protection of the collective (Kashti, 1997). Concerns for the well-being, prosperity, and security of society lead to collective mobilization, in which members take risks and invest their own resources on behalf of the collective (Reykowski, 1997).

Finally, mobilization and activities in the conflict require *coordinated activity of the collective's members*. This feature refers to the ability of the different groups and sectors that compose the collective to collaborate with each other to achieve societal goals. The coordinated collective activity stands on two bases: one is the ability to set superordinate goals in a conflict that are shared by the collective's members (i.e., goals that are perceived as promoting collective interests and not the particular interests of one group in a society); and the second is the ability to act in ways that allow for the achievement of these goals (van Zomeren & Iyer, 2009).

These latter three features of collective identity facilitate mobilization. Societies that possess these features can succeed in mobilizing society members with relative ease to participate in conflict if they produce a convincing rationale to carry it out. Other societies have to develop these characteristics in order to mobilize successfully.

After discussing the nature of mobilization and its relationship to identity, we can turn to the process of mobilization, as the recruitment of society members, and elucidate a number of determinative factors that influence it, including the way it is carried out, agents who handle it, messages used, and the context in which it takes place.

DETERMINATIVE FACTORS OF MOBILIZATION

Ways of Mobilization

Messages that are used for mobilization have to reach group members, and therefore using efficient ways of dissemination is the first condition for successful mobilization. Klandermans (1988) provides a long list of ways for mobilization, including public speeches, declarations, leaflets, door-to-door canvassing, use of newspapers and journals, utilizing informal networks, use of radio and television, publicizing the results of public opinion surveys, banners, slogans, symbolic public acts, organizing dramatic events, demonstrations, public events, and small group meetings. Some of them are informal and personal, and others are more formal and institutionalized. The choice depends on the access that the mobilizing agents have to institutions and channels of communication. If they have access, mass media can play an important role. Agents may use various societal institutions, such as the military, schools, and religious institutions. In many cases, though, these institutions and channels are controlled by the dominant party and may be closed to groups that want to challenge the status quo. In these cases, the group may have to mobilize secretly, resorting to various informal methods to disseminate the messages of mobilization. Interpersonal contacts through social networks are a basic way of recruiting supporters and activists. Through interpersonal interaction, activists can persuade other society members to join their cause. The first goal of mobilization in this situation is to construct a primary network of supporters and activists that will carry on the conflict (see Diani, 2004). Later an attempt can be made to extend the initial network and reach the masses of group members. Then methods such as speeches in public places, demonstrations, distribution of written material, or clandestine channels of mass media such as radio or the Internet are often used.

McAdam and his colleagues (Fernandez & McAdam, 1988; McAdam, 1986, 2003; McAdam & Paulsen, 1993) suggest that membership in various social networks facilitates mobilization for collective action. Furthermore, they emphasize the importance of an individual's position within such networks for mobilization and participation. Researchers have claimed that social networks provide information regarding mobilizing opportunities; create commitment to the goals; and enable informal social pressure, sanctions, and rewards in order to facilitate participation (McAdam, 2003; Passy, 2001).

Mobilization of Catholics in Northern Ireland was done mostly through social networks of political parties and nongovernmental organizations (NGOs). In view of the incompetence of the Catholic Nationalist Party that was established in the 1920s to represent Catholic interests, a new Social Democratic and Labour Party (SDLP) was established in 1970. This party made a special effort to organize at the grass-roots level to form a political body with mass support. In addition, in the early 1960s were established new NGOs, including the Campaign for Social Justice and Northern Ireland Civil Rights Association, which sought to end the discrimination against the

Catholic population (Bew, Gibbon, & Patterson, 1985; Bosi, 2008). All these organizations also used networking methods to mobilize supporters to take an active part in the struggle.

On the other side, Protestants also used various ways to mobilize. One unique way was to organize Orange marches, which symbolized their dominance and resistance. The main marches were held on July 12, and during the years when the Stormont parliament ruled (1921–1972), they were granted the status of a state ceremony. Protestant marching bands were practicing all year long for the "marching season," which included in 1984 not less than 2,400 marches, the vast number of them loyalist. The marches were highly ritualized and included speeches, music, banners, and slogans designed to "affirm the validity of the Protestant faith, the settler experience of siege and victory, and Ulster Protestant loyalty to the Crown and empire in times of war and peace" (Ruane & Todd, 1996, p. 109).

Stokke and Ryntveit (2000) note that the mobilization of the Tamils for their violent conflict with the Sinhalese in Sri Lanka was done through informal networking in higher-educational institutions in Sri Lana and London via student informal networks and student associations and through the fishing port of Valvettithurai, where there resided a caste of fishermen who traditionally opposed the state and were identified as potential participants in the conflict.

Messages of Mobilization

Principles. Mobilization requires messages that delineate goals and provide the epistemic basis for them. The content has to refer to the deprivation of the society, the need to change the deprived state, and the responsibility of the other party for this situation. They must be clear and meaningful and motivate the receivers to join the cause of the conflict. To be successful, the messages should first be comprehensible to group members (see Sniderman, 1975). Comprehension facilitates their acquisition and storage in the repertoire (Bransford, 1979). The implication is that group members can relate to the messages on the basis of their stored knowledge (Winograd, 1972). If the messages are not understood and meaningful to society members, they do not respond to the mobilization efforts.

Second, the messages have to be perceived as valid in order to be effective for mobilization. Group members have to attribute high confidence to them, perceiving them as verities (see Kruglanski, 1989). This is a necessary condition because the messages define the reality of group members, and this reality has to be firm and certain. Group members have to rely on them in making their judgments and decisions about mobilization. Reduced confidence in the messages could shatter their support for the conflict.

A third feature that is necessary for turning the message into a powerful tool of mobilization is its perceived relevance to the society (Sperber, 1996). Relevance implies that the messages are perceived by group members as having implications for personal and societal life (Bar-Tal & Saxe, 1990). In other words, the messages have to fulfill certain needs of the group members; according to Smith (1968, p. 86), "A person acquires and maintains attitudes and other learned psychological structures to the extent that they are useful to him in his inner economy of adjustment and outer economy of adaptation." The messages have to refer to needs or threats, and group members have to be able to relate to them personally, even if they relate only to the group level. Research in social psychology showed that individuals pay special attention to relevant messages, as well as acquire them and store them more easily than irrelevant ones (Wyer & Srull, 1980, 1986).

Group members have to be able to find interest in messages and think that they also concern them, as part of the group. Sometimes the conflict becomes relevant to every society member as it breaks out. An attack of one state signals danger and becomes of immediate personal relevancy to every member of the attacked society, as happened in the case of the Japanese conquest of Manchuria or the Iraqi conquest of Kuwait. Relevancy may also be achieved when the rival strikes the symbol of the group, and every society member feels hurt and experiences personally the conflict, as happened to Palestinians with the demonstrative visit of the Israeli opposition leader in 2001 in the Temple Mountain, where there are holy mosques of the Muslims. In other cases, the relevancy is not so obvious, and the society members have to be persuaded that eruption of the conflict is in their interest and they have to mobilize to participate in it. This is not a simple task, as individuals have a basic interest in carrying on their normal lives and usually experience fear when a threat to this way of life appears. They try to avoid negative events that may affect them personally or their family.

Skitka and Bauman (2008) propose that mobilization for collective action becomes effective when the goals of the conflict and the causes for its eruption are presented as moral convictions and then accepted by society members. Moral convictions denote the "strong and absolute belief that something is right or wrong, moral or immoral" (Skitka & Bauman, 2008, p. 31). These types of beliefs compel action more than other strongly held beliefs, because they describe what one "ought" to do. Thus, when society members understand the message as implying moral conviction, they tend to mobilize for the cause. For example, Kirisci and Winrow (1997, p. 109) describe the moral conviction that stood at the core of Kurdish contentions: "The political discourse that has once stressed under-development as a source of the problems of eastern Anatolia had begun by the 1970s to focus on Kurdish ethnicity and discrimination." That is, Kurds formulated a set of grievances that all referred to moral transgressions of the Turkish regime – denial of self-determination, economic-political discrimination, and cultural oppression regarding use of Kurdish language, Kurdish tradition, and collective memory.

Contents. Mobilization efforts have to be based on a well-prepared epistemic basis with persuasive arguments that explain the reasons for the collective participation in the conflict. These sets of arguments in mobilizing messages are taken from different realms of knowledge. In general, to be persuasive they have to utilize cultural categories and contents defining an identity to which group members can easily relate. The use of identity symbols is important to persuade society members that the goals relate to the group's genuine interests and to every group member (Haslam, Reicher, & Platow, 2010; Reicher, Hopkins, Levine, & Raksi, 2005). These symbols may include concerns, myths, values, and collective memories – for example, specific heroes and glorious events as well as defeats and losses. Another frequently used theme relates to feelings of collective victimhood. It suggests that the group is right not only in seeking the goals but also in labeling itself as a victim because of unfair treatment by the other group. This theme frames the state of deprivation in terms of victimhood, which can be related to similar themes in the collective memory unrelated to the present state.

Contents of messages can also be drawn from the universal themes of knowledge that pertain to human rights, democracy, or equality. They can describe the deprivation in these universal terms as in the case of Algerians or of blacks in South Africa. But there is no one specific content that can motivate all the group members. On the contrary, different contents touch different group members. Nevertheless, there are often hegemonic group symbols that are relevant to at least a majority of group members. They can be easily found in the speeches and in written material distributed during conflict eruption.

Thus, the Russian authorities provided a number of messages along the years that enlighten the conflict with the Chechens. During the tsarist period, the need to expand the Russian domination and especially the fear of Muslim expansion from the south constructed the contents justifying conquest of Chechnya as well as other parts of the Caucasus. Later on, Chechnya was presented as an integral part of Russia, and therefore Chechen separatism was considered a threat to the Russian nation as whole (Dunlop, 1998; Smith, 2001). In addition, accusations of collaborating with Nazi Germany during the 1940s and the "war against terror" argument in the 2000s were also used as justification for the continuation of the conflict.

In another example, the goals set by the Sinhalese community, as a majority ethnic group in the island known as Ceylon, led eventually to the eruption of a bloody and protracted conflict with the minority group of Tamils. The Sinhalese leaders decided to correct the situation established by the British colonial rule, which in self-interest practiced a "divide and rule" principle, by providing Tamils with preferential status for their service within the system. Sinhalese leaders from the majority, which viewed itself also as an indigenous group, constructed messages that propagated change in the status of the group and appealed to its identity. Eventually in 1956, a Sinhalese leader S. W. R. D. Bandaranaike won a massive electoral victory by appealing with a very relevant message, promising to implement Sinhala as the sole official language of government affairs (Spencer, 1990).

In constructing the message of mobilization for the conflict, a group may also use an entrenched narrative that could be dormant through the years. The new conflict can be energized with motivating forces that are implanted in old narratives. The use of the old narratives can help to mobilize the society members for the new conflict. These narratives usually touch on themes that raise patriotic feelings, threats, old fears, or sometimes hatred. They are very effective, as they are well-accepted and easily evoked themes that are well understood because they are part of the culture.

An example of use of dormant narrative is the case of the Serbs. In the 1980s a discontent was developing among Serbian nationalists who anticipated the loss of Serbian hegemony and privilege through the economic and political strengthening of individual Yugoslav republics (Gagnon, 2004). With his ascendance to power, Slobodan Milošević tried to preserve Serbian domination and historic hegemony within Yugoslavia (Gagnon, 2004). When he realized that this was not feasible, he opted to pursue an old Serbian dream of the creation of a Greater Serbia, which in essence reflected an aspiration for an exclusive identity (Gow, 2003; Judah, 2000; Little & Silber, 1996). Milošević utilized Serbian nationalist sentiment as a tool to unify all Serbs in one state under the notion that anywhere Serbs live or have lived was essentially Serbian territory (Gow, 2003; Ramet, 1996; Thomas, 1999).

The commemoration of the 600th anniversary of the military defeat of Serbians by the Turks at the Battle of Kosovo on June 28, 1989, was a very important event, which facilitated the resurgence of an exclusive Serbian national identity (Glenny, 1993). In a pivotal speech in Kosovo, which many believed to be a warning signal of the violence to come, Milošević sent shockwaves through the other Yugoslav republics with a clear message to non-Serbs.

"Six centuries after the battle of Kosovo Polje, we are again engaged in battles and quarrels. There are not armed battles but the latter cannot be ruled out yet" (National Technical Information Service of the Department of Commerce of the U.S., 2009). The Serbs' chosen trauma, the Battle of Kosovo, had been passed on from generation to generation and kept effectively alive, though dormant at times. The reactivation of the "psychological DNA of Kosovo" awakened the traumatized self-image of the Serbs' ancestors: never again would they allow such a defeat to occur (Volkan, 1997).

Another crucial element that appeared in the construction of the messages for mass mobilization by the Milošević regime was use of old traumatic events during World War II, when thousands of Serbs were massacred and others sent to concentration camps (Anzulovic, 1999; Gagnon, 2004; MacDonald, 2002; Ramet, 1996). Milošević's state-run Serbian media became a tool of war, consistently and systematically engraving fear into the hearts and minds of many Serbs who believed that *they* were under threat from Croatian Ustashe (Croatian fascists who were allies of Nazis in the World War II) and Islamic fundamentalists (referring to Bosnian Muslims) (Denitch, 1994; Malcolm, 1994).

Oberschal (2000, pp. 989, 998–999) summarizes these developments with the following observations: "Yugoslavs experienced ethnic relations through two frames: normal frame and a crisis frame. People processed both frames in their minds: in peaceful times crisis frame was dormant and in crisis and war the normal frame was suppressed.... In the waning days of communism, nationalists activated the crisis frame on ethnicity by playing on fears of ethnic annihilation and oppression in the mass media, in popular culture, in social movements, and in the election campaigns." This observation indicates that old national elements of collective memory and other national credos do not disappear but can lie dormant, ready to be reawakened when the societal-political-cultural forces need them. According to Sekulic (in press), they especially come to life when the violence begins and provides unequivocal evidence to malintention.

Thus, a traumatic reenactment and exploitation of old fears and hatreds, as well as the emphasis on Serbs' victimization in the past and the delegitimization of the opponents, allowed the construction of new goals and the epistemic basis that led to the eruption of conflict, its escalation, and subsequently horrendous acts of revenge, mass killings, and ethnic cleansing in the former Yugoslavia (Bar-Tal & Čehajić-Clancy, in press). This campaign redefined the national identity of Serbs by placing the goals of the conflict in its center and thus facilitated mobilization of ordinary Serbs to participate in the conflict.

Agents of Conflict

In all these cases, mobilization is performed mostly by agents of the conflict who actively mobilize group members for the cause. Agents of conflict are individuals, groups, and organizations that support and propagate the view that the goals are essential; they justify them and claim that the conflict is necessary and unavoidable. They also are called entrepreneurs because they invest their efforts and sometimes other resources to mobilize society members. Reicher and his colleagues, who suggested this term, focused on entrepreneurs' use of identity in the epistemic basis as the dominant way of mobilizing participants for social action (Reicher & Hopkins, 2001; Reicher, Hopkins, Levine, & Rath, 2005). They develop and use the epistemic basis that rationalizes and justifies the conflict. In this function, they also try to structure the social identity and thus shape the reality of society members (Reicher, Hopkins, Levine, & Rath, 2005). Also, their primary goal is to structure unity, solidarity, and patriotism, which are essential for any collective action.

In addition, the agents often suggest ways to manage the conflict and sometimes, at least some of them, propagate the use of violence to achieve their goals. The latter call does not have to appear at the beginning of the conflict but often appears with time, especially if the contentions raised are rejected by the other party or parties. Cases of the Algerian, South African, or Sri Lankan conflicts show that in the first stage of the conflict the groups that raised contentions did not resort to violence. Only when their grievances were not addressed did groups began to move to violent struggle. An extensive study by Wickham-Crowley (1992) about violent conflicts in Latin America in the second half of the 20th century shows that agents of conflict were mostly males, highly educated offspring of rural elites, and urban middle and upper classes. Observing the deprivation of other classes of citizens, they sought to mobilize other sectors within the society through the articulation of grievances and the setting of goals according to the well-formulated epistemic basis.

Individuals – agents of conflict – who are or become leaders play an important role in the mobilization for conflict. They can be elected leaders of states or organizations or informal leaders who build their standing via their activity to advance the causes of the conflict. Leaders can make a difference in mobilization of the group members (Morris, 2004). If they function as epistemic authorities[2] for the group members, leaders have great influence. Charisma is

---

[2] Epistemic authority denotes a source on whom individuals rely in their attempts to acquire knowledge on various topics. If they view such a source as valid and truthful, they tend to accept it (Kruglanski, Raviv, Bar-Tal, Raviv, Sharvit, Ellis, Bar, Pierro, & Mannetti, 2005).

a term often associated with leaders who successfully mobilize. Charismatic leaders can identify the needs of the group members, know what kind of rhetoric to use in persuasion, and have the ability to outline a course of action and implement it (Shamir, Arthur, & House, 1994). Charismatic leaders can persuade group members in the justness of the conflict's goals and the chosen way to achieve them. They know how to elicit identification with the group and specifically with the goals that lead to conflict (Haslam, Reicher, & Platow, 2010). Included among charismatic leaders who led their societies to conflict is Nelson Mandela, who was a pivotal leader in the African National Congress and then a leader of its armed wing. He exercised tremendous influence on the way ANC managed the conflict with the government of South Africa.

Collective Efficacy

Mobilization is successful when group members have collective self-efficacy – that is, when they believe that collective action can achieve the posed goals (Bandura, 2000; Klandermans, 1984). In some respects, this condition reflects the rational approach to mobilization that suggests that society members seek to maximize subjective utility and thus mobilize after they calculate the costs and benefits of their participation in conflict (McCarthy & Zald, 1977; Olson, 1968). Bandura (2000, p. 76) posits, "People's shared beliefs in their collective efficacy influence the types of future they seek to achieve through collective action, how well they use their resources, how much effort they put into their group endeavor, their staying power when collective efforts fail to produce quick results or meet forcible opposition, and their vulnerability to the discouragement that can beset people taking on tough social problems." This is an important belief and often a crucial condition in the successful attempt to launch a conflict. Society members have to believe that there is at least some likelihood that their line of action will be successful. People do not usually invest efforts in a lost cause. They may be mobilized in such a situation only when the situation is so hopeless that they have nothing to lose as individuals and as a collective (e.g., launching a rebellion in the Warsaw Ghetto). In other cases of launching a conflict, the messages have to persuade the society members that they have the ability to change the situation and achieve at least some positive outcomes. Reading documents or interviews of participants in various conflicts makes clear that they began the conflict with the belief that they could achieve their goals, even if it might be a long and bloody confrontation. For example, Wood (2003) conducted numerous interviews among peasants who joined the insurgent forces in El Salvador (Farabundo Marti Front of National Liberation, or FMLN) that confronted the government violently. She found that they were convinced in their ability to bring a major change in redividing the land that was concentrated in the hands of very few landlords.

Acts Facilitating Mobilization

Mobilization is dependent not only on the contents of messages but also on motivating acts that are performed by agents of the conflict to provide a powerful energizing factor. The acts can raise the level of awareness and group consciousness by having a strong meaning, arousing emotions, and strengthening identity. These acts may transform mobilization from passive consensual support to active participation in the group struggle.

Acts in mobilization should present the goals clearly and demonstrate not only adherence to them but a determination to achieve them, even if it involves personal losses. Losses of life are viewed as the highest level of sacrifice on behalf of the group cause and often are viewed with great sympathy, causing others to mobilize. The hunger strikes of Catholic prisoners that took place during 1980 and 1981 are a prominent example of mobilizing social action. The strikers became symbols of the Catholic resistance to the British rule, while resonating to Christian traditions of martyrdom. The endurance and conviction that the strikers demonstrated, along with the indifference demonstrated by the British, and the subsequent deaths of ten of them inflamed large political protests and riots, while drawing internal and international attention and sympathy to the Catholic struggle (Ruane & Todd, 1996).

Mobilization and Emotions

Successful messages also arouse emotions (see also Chapter 6). Emotions energize society members and guide them to take action (Goodwin, Jasper, & Polletta, 2004; Halperin, Sharvit, & Gross, 2011; Petersen, 2002). They may be aroused not only by messages but also by experiences. Emotions such as anger, resentment, and fear are crucial for channeling perceptions of deprivation and injustice into motivation to mobilize on behalf of the group (Smith & Ortiz, 2002; van Zomeren, Postmes, & Spears, 2008).

For example, anger is evoked by the recognition that the rival group performed, or is performing, unjust and unfair acts that deviate from acceptable societal norms (Averill, 1982). This framing is an essential part of messages in many conflicts that aim at mobilization, because in these conflicts at least one party and often both begin the conflict with the recognition of an unjustice that is blamed on the other group. The aroused anger thus leads to the wish to correct the situation and therefore fits well the objective of mobilization (Sturmer & Simon, 2009; van Zomeren, Spears, Fischer, & Leach, 2004).

Another well-used emotion is fear, defined as an aversive emotion that is evoked by a perception and interpretation of information as threatening (Gray, 1987; Jarymowicz & Bar-Tal, 2006). An extensive body of research indicates that messages triggering moderate fear levels are most effective for persuasion (see, e.g., Dillard, 1994; Rachman, 1978; Rogers, 1975). Thus, in a situation involving eruption of conflict, focus on threat is an inseparable part of the mobilizing message (Lake & Rothchild, 1996; Petersen, 2002). The message elaborates first that continuation of the deprivation constitutes danger to the collective and then it points to the threats coming from the rival that prevent the satisfaction of the needs and achievement of the goals. A threat in one's environment can make an individual reconsider his or her current views and open him or her to persuasion to participate in the conflict in order to remove the threats (Marcus & MacKuen, 1993; Marcus, Neuman, MacKuen, & Sullivan, 1996).

Humiliation is another important emotion that appears in situations of group deprivation. Humiliation, as a complex and multiply determined emotion, is experienced in intergroup relations. It is defined as "enforced lowering of any person or group by a process of subjugation that damages their dignity; 'to be humiliated' is to be placed in a situation that is against one's interest (although sadly not always against one's will) in a demeaning and damaging way; 'to humiliate' is to transgress the rightful expectation of every human being and of all humanity that basic rights will be respected" (Lindner, 2006a, p. xiv). In other words, humiliation is experienced in cases in which a group carries out intentionally demeaning treatment of another group that transgresses established expectations of what is appropriate. It creates rifts between groups and breaks relationships (Lindner, 2001). A humiliated group then may also feel frustration, distress, and even trauma, which all underlie a sense of deprivation and the desire to stop this treatment. Lindner (2002) suggests that humiliation often motivates aggressive behavior. Her study in Somalia, Rwanda, and Burundi provides an example of how humiliation served as both an antecedent and a consequence to fuel the cycles of violence and intractable conflict. In a four-year study, Lindner interviewed 216 individuals who had been involved in violent, deadly conflict in Somalia, Rwanda, and Burundi either as parties to the conflict or as interveners. She found experiences of humiliation to be central in the perpetuation of conflict in these settings. She describes how humiliation begot humiliation when parties who were once underlings rose up and rebelled against their oppressors, only to commit the very same humiliating atrocities on them. In this way, humiliation may fuel intractable conflicts, maintaining cycles of violence for a long period of time.

Also, hatred is a powerful emotion that facilitates mobilization and therefore is used often in messages of mobilization (Reicher et al., 2005). It motivates society members to move to action and harm the rival (Halperin, 2008; Reicher et al., 2005; Royzman, McCauley, & Rosin, 2005; Sternberg & Sternberg, 2008). Hatred is evoked when society members focus on the harm done to them and when it is framed as carried out by evil people who intentionally performed it because of their innate malevolent disposition (Halperin, 2008). This framing leads to a feeling of hate that energizes society members to punish the rival and revenge the harm done to them (Staub, 2005). This is so because hatred focusing on the destructive acts in the past also alerts society members to future malintentions of the rival, implies low expectations for positive change, and thus leads to the recognition of the need to act in order to change the situation (Halperin, Sharvit, & Gross, 2011).

Characteristics of Context

In our discussion of context, at least two variables play a determinative role in influencing the mobilization process: clarity of the situation and the threat implied.

Clarity of the Situation. Clarity of the situation indicates the extent to which the conditions imply the deprivation to group members and its great importance, as well as indicates that the other group is responsible for the deprivation or has the goods that are badly needed. The clearer is the conflict situation, the easier it is to mobilize group members to take part in a conflict. In fact, classifying the situations of conflict on a dimension of clarity is possible. On the one end of this dimension are situations that clearly indicate the situation of conflict, including the deprivation and the responsibility of the rival group, as, for example, an attack by a state. No American had to be convinced that there was a conflict with Japan on December 7, 1941, when the Japanese planes attacked Pearl Harbor. On the other end are ambiguous situations. The ambiguity takes place when the deprivation is not clear to society members, when the deprivation is not saliently related to another group, or when the goals are not well defined. In all these cases, the situation of a conflict is not self-evident but depends on provided information and enlightenment of society members. In fact, many of the intractable conflicts took many years to evolve as it took time for the societies to realize that they lived in deep deprivation and to develop a social consciousness that led to the eruption of open conflict (see, e.g., the cases of Algerians, Kurds, Palestinians, Catholics, and Native Indians in Guatemala). Those are the challenging cases that require special efforts for mobilization. In these situations, agents make intensive efforts to persuade the public of the need of the conflict, by elucidating the conditions of deprivation and constructing a convincing epistemic basis that shows society members that their goals are contradicted by another group. That is, as was shown in the case of the ANC in South Africa, the mobilization process requires persuasion to recognize unjustified deprivation and to show the relevance of the conflicts' goals to the life of group members.

The harsh conflict in Cyprus, as another example, did not evolve overnight but developed through decades, as the Greek and Turkish populations in the island were gradually mobilized to the opposing goals that crystallized at the beginning of the 20th century, after Cyprus was declared as a British colony. This move was at first perceived positively by the Turkish Cypriots, but with the strengthening of the goal to unite with Greece (Enosis) by Greek Cypriots following mobilization, they realized that the conflict between the residing population was inevitable (Mallinson, 2005).

In general, research has shown that there is a relationship between the level of context clarity and identifications with the group. Hogg and his colleagues propose that group identity meets fundamental needs for reducing uncertainty and achieving meaning and clarity in social contexts (Hogg & Abrams, 1993; Hogg & Mullin, 1999). It is thus possible that one function that group memberships and identities serve for individuals is that of providing self-definition and guidance for behavior in otherwise ambiguous social situations (Deaux, Reid, Mizrahi, & Cotting, 1999; Vignoles, Chryssochoou, & Breakwell, 2000).

Perceived Threat. The other important variable that affects mobilization is the level of perceived threat as a result of potential behavior or behavior of another group. Perceived threat, as the key experience leading to a conflict, is defined as perceived probability that harm is already taking place or will occur. Experiencing threat means not only perception of potential harm by another group but also the understanding that the harm cannot be completely prevented, and therefore some of the harm may potentially occur. Threats can be perceived on a collective level as society members may perceive that their group is in danger of being harmed. This harm does not have to be viewed as being aimed at a person but can be perceived as harming other ingroup members, blocking the ingroup's goals or needs, or causing deprivation. By identifying with the group, society members may perceive that their group is under threat. Stephan and his colleagues (Stephan & Renfro, 2002; Stephan,

Renfro, & Davis, 2008) propose that two types of threats play a major role in intergroup relations – realistic and symbolic. The realistic threats refer to a group's beliefs about potential or already occurred human losses, or about losses of a territory, resources, economy, power, status, or general welfare, while the symbolic threats refer to group's worldviews about harms in religious, political, moral, or cultural systems of beliefs, attitudes, and values. Perception of threats can occur not only as a result of concrete experiences but also on the basis of, for example, provided information, learning, imagination, and past memory. Once the threat is detected, from the psychological perspective it exists for the collective, although it may be viewed by other groups and even by segments of the ingroup as absolutely unfounded and imaginative (Cohen, 1979; Knorr, 1976).

Perceived threats imply that another group may harm the collective or the society members as individuals. This perception indicates eruption of a conflict because no group wishes to be harmed. Perception of threat is dependent on attribution of intentions and ability to the rival. When there is attribution of a high ability of harm and an intention to carry out this harm with low ability to prevent it, then group members experience a high level of threat. The more threat the society members feel, the more of them are mobilized.

Perception of threat is related to different psychological factors that all facilitate mobilization. Theory of terror management specifically elaborates on various consequences of threat identification to one's own well-being (salience of mortality) in situations of conflict (Greenberg, Pyszczynski, & Solomon, 1997; Greenberg, Solomon, & Arndt, 2008). The accumulated research shows that this type of threat strengthens adherence to values of one's own group, magnifies extreme reaction toward the rival, and increases support for use of violence in conflicts (see also Chapter 3). In addition, it facilitates the exaggeration of differences between good and evil, dehumanizes the opponent, and in general reinforces structure of a simplistic worldview (Hirschberger & Pyszczynski, 2010, in press). Fritsche, Jonas, and Kessler (2011) propose that perception of threat leads to attempts to control restoration, which is greatly diminished in situations of threat. The restoration is done via adherence to group membership. In turn, collective threats in times of intergroup conflict not only increase identification with the group but also foster ethnocentric behavior expressed in favoritism and support of ingroups and intolerance and derogation of the rival group.

Threat is often increased with acts of violence performed by the rival group. These actions not only provide clear indication of already done harm but also signal the potential for harm and the evil intention of the other group. They then anger group members, lead to emotional involvement, and increase the level of mobilization. Brutal acts of the other group, which are viewed as unjustified and immoral, serve as traumatic turning points for group members when they succeed in evoking group outrage, feelings of being a victim, and empathy for the hurt co-patriots. They then increase the identification of group members and their readiness to act for the group cause.

It is assumed that the events in Northern Ireland on Bloody Sunday in 1972 and in South Africa in Sharpeville in 1960 served as major events that increased the readiness of the respective communities of Catholics and blacks to join actively their different conflicts. In the first case, British troops shot at the peaceful marchers of the Northern Ireland Civil Right Association, killing 14 Catholics (7 of them were teenagers) and injuring 13 others. In the latter case, South African police opened fire on a crowd of black protesters, killing 69 of them (including 10 children) and injuring more than 180.

As the number of human losses grows, groups develop beliefs about being victimized by the opponent. These beliefs focus on the losses, the deaths, the harm, the evil, and the atrocities committed by the adversary and delegate the responsibility for the violence solely to the "other." This self-perception focuses on the gloomy and wretched fate of the group and frames its victims as martyrs, who are representatives of the society and not just individuals. The dead and wounded become the salient, concrete evidence of the group's status as a victim. All these acts and the accompanied beliefs are crucial for mobilization. They motivate the group members to support their own group by increasing their sense of interdependence, solidarity, social responsibility, and concern for the well-being of the group. In this state of mind and collective conditions, conflict will become a reality. Once it erupts, it is very difficult to terminate it.

IMPLICATIONS

The process of experiencing and thinking is part of human functioning, for humans are reflecting and creating ideas about their situation all the time, especially in reference to their needs and goals. A complementary determinant to this process is the ever-changing context that instigates new reflections and new thoughts. The continuous interaction between the two factors creates all the situations of intergroup conflict because it leads to realization that the goals of the two groups are in complete contradiction. In some cases, when the context provides unequivocal evidence of the deprivation caused by another group, then the realization of the conflict situation is fast and clear. In other cases, the enlightening process about the conflict is a long one, as the context either is well habituated or does not provide unambiguous cues about the contradiction of goals and needs by another group. Thus, relating one's own collective deprivation to another group is the first condition for conflict eruption. But mobilization for participation by at least a segment of society members is the necessary condition for the activation of the conflict. Mobilization also depends on the two previously noted factors: the realization of society members in the necessity to take part in the conflict, and the clarity of the conflict situation that touches society members. When such clarity of the context is salient, it is easy to mobilize society members for participation in a conflict. Mobilization for participation in the conflict depends at least on the context in which both groups live, the perception of relative deprivation, the resources that groups have, organizational abilities, the construction of the persuasive epistemic basis, leading figures, use of mobilizing methods, and the state of mind of the society members.

In this early stage, societies formulate their beliefs (i.e., epistemic basis), attitudes, and emotions, which eventually crystallize into well-developed sociopsychological infrastructures that underlie for many coming years the rationale, justification, and explanation for carrying on the conflict. This developed repertoire plays a crucial role in eruption of the conflict and especially in the mobilization of society members to carry it out with active participation that includes use of violence. This repertoire sows the seeds not only for the development of a well-elaborated, comprehensive, and extensive system of conflict-supporting beliefs, but also for their entrenchment deep into the evolved culture of conflict, which eventually serves as a major obstacle to peacemaking and thus aids the long continuation of the intractable conflicts.

This is the place to remind ourselves that different conflicts have different moral foundations. It is impossible to aggregate them into one category. The moral bases of conflicts differ, and also the parties differ in their contentions, as judged with established moral codes of intergroup behavior, although all the parties form a well-formulated epistemic basis that provides justification for carrying out violent conflict. There are collectives that, without realization in their deprivation, would continue to be disadvantaged because of continuous discrimination, exploitation, or oppression. Thus, their realization in deprivation leads them to attempt to correct an unjust and immoral situation that is most often expressed in eruption of a conflict. In contrast, there are groups that experience deprivation because of various reasons, sometimes even unrelated to the other group, and decide to satisfy their needs at the expense of another group, which then experiences deprivation. In these cases, steps taken by the former group lead to eruption of a conflict. There are also ambiguous situations in which two groups or even more feel that they need to satisfy a deprivation that concerns the same or similar needs and therefore initiate a conflict. Those general schemata probably do not exhaust all the foundations for an eruption of a conflict, but they indicate that there are differences, though eventually they all lead at some point to violence and durability of the conflict.

Also, the eruption of the conflict in most of the cases is not a one-time event. Even when an instigating event leads to the eruption of the conflict, such as the murder of Archduke Ferdinand of Austria in Sarajevo on June 28, 1914, it is clear that this event was only an instigating event in the sense that it served to light the dynamite, while evolving conditions over the preceding years constituted the real foundations for the eruption of the conflict. Sometimes identifying these instigating events is possible, and sometimes they do not even exist, but the conflict evolves in the development of the parties' needs, feelings of deprivation, and formulation of goals according to their epistemic basis. Eventually this process leads to mobilization of the group members.

Hypothetically, situations of deprivation and their appearance on the public agenda could lead to the recognition of the situation of injustice by the powerful group, and then this group could attempt to change the situation by correcting the injustice, by dividing goods in an equal way, granting autonomy, or compensating for the victim's suffering. But, in reality, this situation almost never happens. *In serious cases, almost no group voluntarily relinquishes goods in terms of power, status, privileges, wealth, resources, or territories.* As a rule, in almost all these cases, the demand itself and the steps that are taken to achieve it are perceived by the dominating group as contradicting its goals and interests, and the conflict erupts. Thus, satisfaction of the deprivation usually takes place within the framework of a conflict, after a long struggle, often violent, which may lead eventually to the victory of one side or to a peaceful settlement of the conflict. But some of these conflicts last for decades or centuries without either peaceful resolution or victory of one side or the other. They escalate and intensify with violence. The next chapter discusses the escalation of intergroup conflicts as the next phase of their development.

3

Escalation of Intractable Conflicts

Once a conflict erupts and spreads, as both sides mobilize group members, the conflict often escalates because the goals of the rival parties seem to be existential to both sides. Escalation indicates that the raised grievances, objections, and contentions, as well as the aspirations, claims, and desires, are not considered but are rejected and even countered with stronger actions. As a reaction, the side that raised the grievances or objections or claims resorts with more serious steps in order to make the conflict more salient and more costly to the rival. Both sides thus raise the level of confrontation, entering into cycles of reactions and counterreactions. Escalation also means that each side is determined to achieve all its goals, and neither side is ready to compromise – thus turning the dispute at this early stage into a zero-sum, unsolvable conflict.

Finally, further escalation takes place when a party or both parties resort to severe violence. Escalation is observed with the intensification of hostile acts that include verbal rhetoric but are primarily a variety of behavioral acts that indicate an adherence to original goals and an attempt to overcome the rival by harming him. Pruit and Kim (2004) suggest that the parties transform their orientation, as they move from the wish to achieve goals to the desire to harm the opponent. Elcheroth and Spini (2011) argue that the introduction of violence not only produces intense animosity and hatred that feeds into the escalation of the conflict but also transforms the ingroup into a confrontational society. Therefore I would like to extend the discussion about violence.

VIOLENCE

Although violence may appear already in the early stage of the conflict, even with its eruption, it is the most salient feature of escalation. In all the conflicts, the use of violence is a very influential element that changes the nature of the conflict. Indeed, as Brubaker and Laitin (1998, p. 426) observe, "Violence is not a quantitative degree of conflict but a qualitative form of conflict, with its own dynamics." Although I give special emphasis to physical violence in intractable conflicts, as noted in Chapter 1 violence has many faces and forms that result in different types of harms.

Violence has not only concrete effects as the involved societies lose their members but also symbolic meaning as it signals that the rival party has neither deterrent power nor control; that the ingroup has a strong will, commitment, and determination to achieve its goal; that it is not frightened and even expects retribution; and that it has the power to use violence and therefore will resort to extreme means. The use of violence is thus a powerful message that is well understood by the parties in conflict. It transforms the nature of the conflict by meaningfully sowing the seeds for the emergence of vicious cycles of violence.

In many of the conflicts, the use of violence is perceived as necessary to achieve one's goals. Scholars have counted at least 240 armed conflicts between 1946 and 2008 (Harbom & Wallensteen, 2009). Between 1990 and 1996 alone, more than 90 armed conflicts took place (Jentleson, 1996). In conflicts that are over existential goals related to the social identity of the group and which are viewed as a zero-sum dispute, the use of violence is almost inevitable, as the contentions are on such a large scale that very rarely can they be satisfied with goodwill when they emerge. Violence also erupts often in conflicts in which one party is not recognized as a legitimate contender, when there is a great disparity of power and one side believes that it can ignore the demands of the other, when there is no institutionalized ways to deal with the grievances, or when a party believes that using violence is the best way to achieve its goals.

Violence erupts in cases where a strong party decides to use it or when a weak party decides that only with violence can it demonstrate its determination and harm the strong rival. An example of the former case is the attack of Manchuria by Japan in September 1931. The latter case can be exemplified with the antiapartheid organizations of the African National Congress (ANC) and the Pan Africanist Congress (PAC), which were both prohibited from having a legal operation in South Africa and therefore established underground organizations in 1961 to carry out their struggle with violence against the government. Nevertheless, in all the cases violence erupts when a party believes that it can speed the achievement of its goals by making the conflict salient and costly to the other party. Also, in all these cases society members participating in collective violence believe that their participation eventually advances collective well-being and goals (Ginges & Atran, 2009). Thus, in some cases the violence appears in the very early stages of the conflict when a party decides to win the conflict quickly or to signal its serious intentions. In all these situations, the dominant belief that the other party will yield only under the pressure of violence is very central in the group that initiates it.

In most of the cases, initial acts of violence by one side immediately evoke a violent response from the other side. From this point, violence becomes part of the conflict, and the meaning of initiation and retribution for specific acts is lost. For example, Israeli Jews begin to count the beginning of the violence in the Israeli-Arab conflict from 1860 when Jews began to leave the walls of the city of Jerusalem and build the first Jewish neighborhood beyond them. The Israeli Ministry of Defense, which records fallen Jewish soldiers, begins with a Jew who was killed by Arabs on January 1, 1873, defending his home against robbers in the new neighborhood of Jerusalem. Morris (2001) begins to attribute the killings of Jews to nationalistic circumstances only at the start of the 20th century when Arabs resented Jewish Zionist immigration to Palestine and its settling practices, viewing it as an act of violence. Specifically, according to Beeri (1985) the violence in spring 1908 in Jaffa between Jews and Arabs and the murder of three Jews in Segera (a Jewish settlement) in April 1909 signaled the beginning of the new phase in the Jewish-Arab conflict when it moved to its violent stage. With time, these violent acts became more prevalent and led of course to Jewish defensive actions and to retributions. By the 1920s the conflict became fully violent and led to severe losses of life on both sides. As of May 9, 2011, Israeli Jews count a total of 22,867 fighters and 2,443 civilians who have lost their lives in the conflict (*Maariv*, May 9, 2011).

Activities related to violence are among the major underlying causes for the asymmetry of conflicts. Parties with state power have the ability to use organized military forces and other formal institutions (Ball, Kobrak, & Spirer, 1999). This fact allows the normal recruitment of military personnel and investment in military activities. In contrast, when a party does not have a state, all these acts are done on a voluntary basis, often illegally and without formal resources, which have to be done by the group or done externally. Violence carried out by a party without a state, however, often takes different forms than state violence. The former is often used in a more conventional way and through the use of terror, while the latter is characterized more often by the use of more sophisticated and modern weapons, including military ships, planes, and missiles.

Violence does not always appear on the same level throughout a conflict. In intractable conflicts that last for a long time, violence may fluctuate and appear in different forms and with variable intensity. It may involve full-scale wars, military encounters, terror attacks, attacks on civilian population, destruction, discrimination, and denial of various rights and liberties, among other measures. The Israeli-Palestinian conflict, as an example, involved at first sporadic acts of violence, then spontaneous massive violent pogroms and retributions, then more organized communal confrontations between Jews and Arabs in the British era of the mandate. Full war between Jews and Arabs with the involvement of Arab states broke out in 1947–1949. This war was followed by full-scale interstate wars between Arab states and the State of Israel, with continuous military encounters and terror attacks. The violence still continues today in various forms (Morris, 2001).

Groups differ greatly in defining violence, doing so according to their own goals and needs and, at the same time, disregarding the views of the rival. In fact, one of the more important psychological warfare techniques concerns framing one's own violence and the violence of the opposed groups. Each group in the conflict tries to present the violence of the rival group as illegitimate, immoral, planned, malintentioned, and inherently evil. At the same time, it tries to hide its own violence, to minimize its consequences, to present it as a result of situational circumstances and as relatively acceptable to existing moral codes and needed because of the behavior of the opponent (Bar-Tal, Oren, & Nets-Zehngut, 2012; Staub, 1989; Wohl & Reeder, 2004).

Violence has an imprinting effect on the society that contributes to the escalation of the conflict (Elcheroth & Spini, 2011). Sekulic (in press) provides as a case study evidence showing that once the violence began in the former Yugoslavia in the 1990s it had a dramatic effect on the course of the conflict. The violence had a profound detrimental influence on the deterioration of the interethnic relations and the appearance of an extreme negative sociopsychological repertoire that intensified the brutal violence in the conflict. Thus, I assume that there is a major difference between conflicts that involve violence and those which do not. Once it erupts, violence changes the nature of the conflict. The following discussion indicates why violence is such a determinative part of intractable conflicts.

Sanctity of Life

The maintenance of life is perhaps one of the most sacred and universal values in human culture. Alternatively, killing or severely physically hurting another human being is considered with some exceptions the most serious violation of the moral code (Donagan, 1979; Kleinig, 1991). The commandment "Thou shalt not kill" is of great importance for most, if not all, societies (Feldman, 1992). Societies tend to adhere to this commandment devoutly through norms and laws. In modern times, the right to life has become a fundamental moral principle; under most circumstances, no person is allowed to take the life of another person. Taking a human life, especially the life of an innocent, is an unforgivable sin, in almost all situations. Those who violate the moral and legal codes regarding the sanctity of life are severely punished. Some societies even take the life of the killers, which is viewed to be the most severe punishment that can be meted out to the transgressor. Other societies avoid taking the life of even the most notorious criminals because of the sanctity of life.

As long as the conflict is limited to verbal statements and even hostile acts without loss of life, it remains on a lower level of confrontation. However, once one party in a conflict wounds or kills a member of the other group, or both sides suffer losses, the conflict moves to another phase. In this context, even taking the lives of soldiers, despite their being trained to kill and prepared to be killed, is perceived as a violation of a moral code (Osgood & Tucker, 1967). Thus, the killing or wounding of military personnel leads to the escalation of a conflict.

Harming of innocent civilians is viewed by the parties as particularly painful and harsh because it is considered as the ultimate violation of moral conduct. These cases fuel the conflict, forcing the parties to take special action to prevent further violence and to punish the perpetrators. The described dynamics are well reflected in the Israeli-Palestinian conflict. Both sides are sensitive to human losses when inflicted by the other side, and they mutually delegitimize each other by claiming that the other side does not respect sanctity of life, especially when it harms civilians.

Collective Emotional Involvement

Violence increases the emotional involvement of the parties engaged in intergroup conflict. Group members are deeply, emotionally touched when compatriots are killed and wounded, especially when the loss is sudden, untimely, and intentionally inflicted by the rival. In principle, the closer the relationship to the injured or deceased, the more intense is the emotional reaction. But, in the case of violent, intergroup conflict, even when those killed are not personally known, the personal relevance of these losses is intensified. Those killed or wounded are perceived as compatriots and kin, as group members who have been harmed.

In modern societies, this perception and the subsequent emotional involvement are consequences of socialization processes, which extend the concepts of kinship (i.e., patriotism, nationalism) toward personally unknown society members (e.g., Billig, 1995; Fox, 1994; Johnson, 1997). More specifically, societies make special efforts to inculcate patriotic and nationalistic feelings through methods that include the use of fictive kin terms such as "sons," "brothers and sisters," "brotherhood," "motherland," and "fatherland" in reference to members of the society and the land (see, e.g., Halliday, 1915; Johnson, Ratwik, & Sawyer, 1987). Through this method, members of a society are encouraged to form a sense of belonging, feelings of closeness, and a sense of mutual responsibility and solidarity. All these elements reflect collective identity (David & Bar-Tal, 2009). Indeed, social categorization theory specifically proposed that group members not only form a sense of belonging with their group but also experience group events personally (Turner, Hogg, Oakes, Recher, & Wetherell, 1987). Individuals are personally touched when members of their society fall as a consequence of violence in the context of intergroup conflict. They feel that the inflicted harm is an act of violence against the collective.

In most cases, the whole society mourns those killed in intergroup conflict. They are considered as society's martyrs, because they fell as a result of a societal cause. Their death, thus, is viewed as the group's loss, and therefore group members feel emotional involvement. The loss of compatriots frequently turns the conflict into a relevant experience for many society members. It is so, because many issues of disagreement between the parties in conflict are difficult to understand and are irrelevant to the lives of society members, but death of compatriots is an experience that concerns every society member and turns the conflict into concrete reality. The conflict then becomes a relevant part of society members' lives and absorbs a new personal meaning.

This description is well founded in the case of the Israeli-Palestinian conflict. Almost every human loss, if caused by the other side, causes Israeli Jews and Palestinians to be greatly emotionally involved. The death touches every group member, and those killed in the conflict are considered to be sacrificed for the benefit of the collective (Bar-Tal, 2007b). Also, the deaths of Chechens caused by the Russians during their protracted conflict are well embedded in the Chechen collective and private memory. As Caucasus specialist Sergei Arutiunov (1995, pp. 16–17) points out:

For a Chechen... to be a man is to remember the names of seven generations of paternal ancestors... and not only their names, but the circumstances of their deaths and the places of their tombstones. This constitutes an enormous depth of historic memory, and in many cases the remembered deaths occurred at the hands of Russian soldiers – under Catherine the Great; under Nicholas the First; under Stalin.

Irreversibility of the Situation

Loss of life has particular importance in the conflict process because of its irreversibility. That is, while suitable compensations and compromised solutions can be found for various disagreements and even for destruction of properties or the displacement of people, nothing can compensate for the dead. Therefore, the conflict escalates in tandem with the human costs incurred. The parties involved in the conflict find it difficult to justify compromises in view of human losses. Although sometimes compromises could be possible before the losses, the parties following the ultimate loss find it difficult to justify such an option. It is impossible to bring to life those who were killed in conflict, and therefore the society members adhere to the original far-fetched goals. Their death is an experience that cannot be reversed. Families of those killed and the whole society have to continue to live without the fallen, who can only be remembered as victims of the conflict. The fallen change positions into intransigent ones, a situation that perpetrates the conflict.

The Desire for Vengeance

Killings within the context of intergroup conflict serve as a basis for vengeful acts. The losses in intergroup conflict are almost always perceived as unjustified; moreover, there is an identified, concrete, and specific perpetrator (from the other party in conflict) who has to be punished for his act. "An eye for an eye" is a basic norm in many societies and may even be considered a moral requirement. That is, the society's members feel an obligation to harm physically members of the group in conflict, in retribution for the inflicted violence. Thus, once group members are killed, it is difficult to settle the conflict peacefully, before avenging those killed.

Turney-High (1949, pp. 149–150), in analyzing the causes of primitive warfare, points out that

> revenge is so consistently reported as one of the principal causes of war that it requires detailed analysis. Why should the human personality yearn to compensate for its humiliation in the blood of enemies? The tension-release motive plays a part here: Revenge loosens the taut feeling caused by the slaying or despoiling of one's self, clan, tribe, nation. Even the hope for revenge helps the humiliated human to bear up, enables him to continue to function in a socially unfavorable environment.... Revenge, or the hope of revenge, restores the deflated ego, and is a conflict motive with which mankind must reckon with universally.

As Turney-High implies, the call for vengeance is not unique to primitive societies but is a universal phenomenon. Scheff (1994) suggests that vengeance is one of the most important psychological bases for international conflict. In his view, vengeance is a result of the denial of emotions such as shame, guilt, or alienation. These emotions are especially aroused in situations when parties in conflict incur human loss. According to Scheff, in most cases the parties deny these emotions and raise their voices for vengeance. This wish is often underscored by hatred, which is a direct reaction to protracted harm to the "hater" or members of his or her group. The hater perceives this harm as deliberate, unjust, and a situation that he or she cannot cope with. Behaviorally, hatred leads people to a desire to harm the hated group (Halperin, 2008; White, 1996).

Vengeance is perceived as a matter of national or ethnic obligation, an expression of responsibility to those killed. It is, therefore, seen even as a matter of national honor to punish the opponent, an expression to "prevent" future losses by showing the perpetrator that violence against the group will not be tolerated. It is thus not surprising that members of a society demand vengeance when society suffers human loss as a result of intergroup conflict (Kim, 2005). For example, Rutkoff (1981, p. 161) quotes French poems that call for revenge written during the Franco-Prussian War of 1870–1871. One of them reads:

> Revenge will come, perhaps slowly
> Perhaps with fragility, yet a strength that is sure
> For bitterness is already born and force will flow
> And cowards only the battle will ignore.

Indeed, Minow (1998) observes that in the cases of Rwanda and Bosnia vengeance played a major role in escalating and perpetuating these conflicts. A review by Lickel, Miller, Stenstrom, Denson, and Schmader (2006) describes the psychological mechanisms that underlie acts of violence carried out as vengeance by ingroup members. They suggest that factors such as initial construal of the event as a harmful act, identification with the ingroup, generation of emotion and motivation for revenge, homogenized perception of the rival, and legitimized perception of all outgroup members as responsible for the harm done lead to "vicarious retribution." In this frame it is not surprising that society members who were not directly hurt will harm members of the rival group who themselves did not perform any act of harm.

Need for Rationalization

Physical violence against human beings requires explanation for those who carry it out, as well as for its victims (e.g., Grundy & Weinstein, 1974). It stems from the basic need to live in a meaningful and predictable world, as well as in a just world (Heine, Proulx, & Vohs, 2006; Katz, 1960; Lerner, 1980; Reykowski, 1982). In view of the ascribed sanctity to life and its violation, which takes place in physical violence, the participants need to explain and justify these acts. They need to explain and justify why they kill and why the co-patriots are killed. The performers require reasons to carry out the violent acts, and the victims need reasons why they incurred their losses. McFarlane (1986), for example, provides an anthropological analysis of the explanations used by people in rural areas of Northern Ireland for the violence in the Catholic-Protestant conflict. They tended to explain the abnormal acts of violence such as murders, bombings, and so forth by insisting that they were aberrations performed by outsiders. Also, the explanation for violence by the perpetrator and victim groups almost always involves delegitimization of the other (i.e., devaluation). Grossman (1995) notes delegitimization as one of the psychological mechanisms that allows combatants to kill combatants of the rival group. It is delegitimization of the rivals that provides a moral permit to kill them because they are reduced to social categories that can be exterminated (Bar-Tal & Hammack, 2012). The perpetrators need this delegitimization in order to carry out the violence against human beings, and the victims need it in order to explain the injustice done from their perspective. In addition, both sides always view their goals as essential and worthy of the sacrifice of life. The consequences of these explanations and justifications are the perpetuation of violence, because both sides have a clear rationalization. As "the victims" retaliate and become perpetrators of physical violence against their adversary, a cycle of victimization and rationalization begins (see Chapter 5).

Botcharova (2001) delineates this circle of revenge that illuminates the feelings and processes stemming from personal and ethnonational trauma. The original feelings of suffering, injustice, anger, and frustration may lead to the desire "to do justice" and then directly to violent acts of "justified aggression." This desire also explains and justifies the sacrifice of the ingroup members. Eventually both sides engage in cycles of violence that reinforce the delegitimization of the other and perpetuate the continuation of the bloodshed. Similarly, Staub (2006) proposes that the sense of collective victimhood is related to negative affective consequences of fear, reduced empathy, and anger; to cognitive biases such as interpretation of ambiguous information as hostile and threatening; to the emergence of the belief that the violent action taken is morally justified; to reduced moral accountability; and, finally, to a tendency to seek revenge.

Bandura (1999) suggests psychological mechanisms that serve as facilitators of moral disengagement leading to acts of violence. Among them, he notes moral justification, euphemistic labeling, advantageous comparison between the groups, disregard or distortion of the severe consequences of violence, and dehumanization of the rival. This analysis can be easily applied to the victims' state of mind that facilitates the harm they inflict in turn. Ramanathapillai (2006) describes how this process led Tamils, who had themselves experienced continuous atrocities, to perform acts of indiscriminate violence that killed many innocent Sinhalese. As Tamils began their protest activities in the 1950s against the discriminating laws and policies of the Sinhalese governments, they were met with violence. The periodic rounds of violence eventually led to reconstruction of a new Tamil identity and strengthened the determination of Tamils to resist the discriminating acts, to demand autonomy, and to use their own systematic and well-organized violence to achieve their goals.

The genocide in Rwanda is one of the most poignant examples of the victim-to-victimizer cycle between Tutsi and Hutu. In a book about this horrendous event that took place during 1994, Mamdani (2001, p. 34) poses a series of questions that shed light on elements of the process that locks victims into the cycle of victim-turned-perpetrator:

What happens when yesterday's victims act out of a determination that they must never again be victimized, *never again*? What happens when yesterday's victims act out of a conviction that power is the only guarantee against victimhood, so that the only dignified alternative to power is death? What happens when they are convinced that the taking of life is really noble because it signifies the willingness to risk one's own life, and is thus, in the final analysis, proof of one's own humanity?

Once violence begins and enters into its vicious cycles, society members develop new norms toward killings that go well beyond the defined codes of moral behavior. First, together with the delegitimization of the rival and one's own perception as the victim there develops a rationale that "permits" physically harming the enemy. Then performance of acts of violence desensitizes the performers and leads to moral disengagement, so that they become capable and motivated to carry out violence on a wider scope (Bandura, 1990). It becomes a more habitual and routinized activity, and the involved societies can tolerate and even encourage it (Archer & Gartner, 1987).

In Central America, Guatemala experienced four decades (1960s–1996) of internal armed conflict and massive political repression (Ball, Kobrak, & Spirer, 1999). Nearly 12,000 people were assassinated between 1966 and 1970. Overall, between 50,000 and 100,000 people (including women, children, and the elderly) were killed during the nearly 40 years of conflict, and approximately 83% of them were Maya. More than half of those killed were assassinated in group massacres aimed at destroying a community (CEH,

1999). For example, during the 1970s and 1980s, the Guatemalan army developed a "scorched earth" policy and burned more than 400 villages of the Highland indigenous population. This policy led to the displacement of hundreds of thousands of peasants and the militarization of the countryside (ODHAG, 1998). According to the Commission for Historical Clarification (1999), 1 million people – approximately 25% of the population of the Guatemalan Highlands – were displaced between 1981 and 1983. The guerrilla forces that fought the government also attacked not only the army but also civilians.

Cohrs and Boehnke (2008) have summarized general findings that bear on public support for violence. Generally, public attitudes toward use of violence are more supportive if society members perceive that an adversary poses a collective threat, feel angry and outraged, and suffer harm. In regard to framing and presenting violence Gavriely-Nuri (in press) proposes that societies involved in intractable conflict develop a war-normalizing dialogue with the goal of blurring the anomalous character of violent conflict by transforming it into an event perceived as a "normal" part of life. She further proposes that this function of the war-normalizing dialogue is done in four different ways: through euphemization, it gives to violence a positive appearance, as, for example, presenting it as leading to bravery and brotherhood; through naturalization, it represents violence as a natural event; through legitimation, it represents violence as just, rational, and moral; and through symbolic annihilation, it omits or blurs its basic negative characteristics (death, destruction, immoral acts).

In the present time, with the change in the international climate and the emergence of new international moral codes, parties that care about international reactions weigh the use of violence carefully. They try to establish and then justify the use of violence (see, e.g., Walzer, 2006). This justification is used for the persuasion of the members of their own group, outgroups of positive reference, and then the international community at large. As an example, few studies explicitly investigated the justification and legitimization of violence carried out by Basque organization ETA (Basque Homeland and Freedom), which struggled in Spain to achieve independence following repressive measures against Basques during Franco's dictatorship (Pena-Martin & Opotow, 2011; Sabucedo, Blanco, & De la Corte, 2003; Van den Broek, 2004). Over its five decades of history, ETA has been responsible for killing more than 850 people, many of them not related to the military forces or government of Spain. The studies analyzed statements of ETA (in either interviews or newspapers) and found that the organization had a campaign of justification before terrorist actions as a preparation. In this attempt, it tried to remove doubts by explaining the need for violent acts. After a terror act, the organization used a variety of reasons such as justification of the goal, attribution of blame and responsibility to the enemy, depersonalization of the victim, euphemisms for violent acts, and overemphasis of Basque suffering. For example, in one incident the organization declared, "As long as the rights of the Basque Country are not respected or recognized, resistance against oppression will continue" (quoted in Pena-Martin & Opotow, 2011, p. 142).

Still, very strong groups may decide to take violent actions without receiving broad support from the international community, as, for example, the United States did when it invaded Iraq in 2003 or Russia did when attacked Georgia in 2008. Nevertheless, in these cases even a superpower cares for the support of ingroup members. But disregard of the international community may be also found among weak groups, which perceive violence as the only way to express grievances, as the IRA did during the violent part of the Northern Ireland conflict or Tamils in the Sri Lanka conflict, or Palestinians who in 1965 began terror attacks in Israel. But even in these cases, the organizations responsible for the violence weigh their action in view of the support that they may receive from their constituent supporters. For example, a study reports that Palestinian militant groups increased their use of terrorism against Israeli targets following increases in Palestinian public support for a violent struggle between 2000 and 2006 (Sharvit, Kruglanski, Wang, Sheveland, Ganor, & Azani, 2010). In any event, although use of violence is often censored by the international community, it continues in different conflicts.

Over time, the violent struggle is fought separately from the course of the conflict, as the goals of violence become somewhat separated from the goals of the conflict. Each side wants revenge for the harm inflicted but wants to stop the violence of the other side as a goal in itself. In long conflicts, groups may use a range of violent acts to try to stop the violence of the other group. This goal often leads to escalation, as many parties increase the level of violence considerably, assuming that its increase will lead to the cessation of violence by the rival group. In reality, escalation frequently causes increases in violence on both sides. This in turn leads to continuous violence, which can be called direct violence (Galtung, 1990). In the continuous cycles of violence, it is often difficult to differentiate between the trigger and the reaction, although the rival sides continue to view every violent act by the other side as being performed as an initiative without a cause and its own violence as a reaction to the violence of the rival (Lickel, 2012). Poole (1995, p. 43), in analyzing the distribution of violence in Northern Ireland, concludes that the vicious circle is a continuous process, having no end. "Lulls may occur, but they come to an end: . . . when the killing recommenced, it was concentrated in exactly the same places as before. The local social reproduction of a culture of political violence can apparently lie dormant for many years, even well into the next generations. However, it merely disappears from immediate view – and only until the next time."

In his analysis of cycles of violence in the 1950s during the Israeli-Arab conflict, Morris (1993) suggests that the retributive actions by the Israeli army, which are often perceived by Israeli Jews as having an effect on the decrease of Arab violence, in fact had an opposite effect. Morris reports that they not only increased the level of violence but also served as an instigator of the full war in 1956.

In interethnic conflicts, which sometimes are asymmetrical because one side has considerably more military and economic power, the strong side may crush the other side militarily. It has occurred throughout history, as in the cases of the second Chechnya war in 2000 and more recently in Sri Lanka, when the Tamils where fully defeated in 2009. But in interethnic conflicts, military victories usually do not end the conflict when there is continuous significant deprivation of individual and collective needs. These conflicts may be controlled for the time being but then may reescalate again after years of relative calm, as happened with the Chechens in the past. Ethnic groups continue their conflicts for many years until their basic needs are satisfied, or at least until a majority of the members think so, as happened in the case of the Basques' struggle in Spain. Only complete, or considerable, elimination of the ethnic group ends an interethnic conflict completely without satisfying the needs of the deprived group. Cases of genocide in Australia, North America, or South America regarding the native inhabitants testify to this principle. In other cases, the violent struggles go on, as we can see in many places in the world (see, e.g., the cases of the Kurds in Turkey, Hutus in Rwanda, or Muslims in Kashmir).

PROCESS AND CONDITIONS OF ESCALATION

A process of escalation may take place as a result of an evaluation of the state of the conflict that leads to a decision to enhance its intensity (Pruitt & Rubin, 1986). Escalations are sometimes a result of a formal decision-making process. Groups in many cases evaluate continuously the state of their conflict, either to adapt courses of actions to the changing conditions of the conflict or to plan the next steps. In this case, one side or both may decide to escalate the conflict by using more severe acts of confrontation. These acts can be verbal or violent. Escalation is not necessarily based on an "objective" evaluation but can depend on various psychological judgments. For example, the decision of India in 1947 to send military forces to help the Maharaja of Kashmir, Hari Singh, who tried to repulse the rebel forces, was a planned act that had to lead to the escalation of the conflict (Schofield, 2000). Also, the decision of the FLN in Algeria to launch well-organized attacks in various parts of country on November 1, 1954 (Bloody All-Saints Day), was a decision to push the conflict into a war. The French overreaction resulted in indiscriminate arrests of suspected rebels, many of them innocent Algerians (Horne, 2006).

Escalation may also take place because of planned action but without that intent. Such escalation often takes place because of misjudgment that leads to an escalation that neither side may want or plan. For example, on September 28, 2000, the Israeli opposition leader Ariel Sharon, together with a Likud party delegation surrounded by hundreds of Israeli riot police, visited the Temple Mount compound, which is considered the third holiest site in Islam. This act was considered by some as the trigger that led to the reescalation of the Israeli-Palestinian conflict and the eruption of the second Palestinian Intifada (Pressman, 2003; Swisher, 2004).

Many question these cases as well others because they may be viewed like the shots in Sarajevo in 1914, which only ignited an already existing situation. Major events and major information often change the context of conflict dramatically and cause group members to react (Bar-Tal & Sharvit, 2008). It is hard to believe that Israeli prime minister Ehud Barak, who unsuccessfully negotiated with the Palestinian leader Yasser Arafat, knew what would be the consequences of his framing the failure of the Camp David meeting in the summer of 2000. By providing the major information without any hard evidence about "exposing" the motivation of the Palestinian leader Yasser Arafat to destroy Israel, he greatly influenced the severe escalation of the Israeli-Palestinian conflict (Halperin & Bar-Tal, 2007). Also, various acts serve as important escalating events because of their intensity and symbolic meaning – for example, Bloody Sunday in 1972 in Northern Ireland when British troops shot at the peaceful marchers of the Northern Ireland Civil Right Association; or the Sharpeville riots in South Africa in in 1960 when police opened fire on a crowd of black protesters; or the Setif massacre in Algeria in 1945 when thousands of Algerians were killed by the French forces.

In this section, some of the factors and conditions that influence the escalation of a conflict are considered.

Sense of Deprivation

The higher the sense of deprivation and the refusal of the parties or one party to satisfy its needs, the more escalated the conflict will become. In fact, a sense of deprivation indicates the level of contradicted goals, as a high sense of deprivation suggests that the level of contradiction between the goals of the two parties is also high. Lack of progress in the attempts to achieve goals indicates that the sense of deprivation remains high, and the two groups or one group need to escalate the conflict to demonstrate resolution to achieve its goals. In cases of symmetry, escalation is needed because neither of the two groups achieved victory over the other, and neither is interested in negotiating a settlement of the conflict. Both groups are determined to achieve their goals and therefore escalate their conflict. This is the case of the Indian-Pakistani dispute over Kashmir that has led already to three wars (in 1947, 1965, and 1999) in an attempt to escalate it. Also, in asymmetrical conflicts each of the groups may escalate the conflict in later stages. The deprived group or a segment of it can raise the level of struggle to show its determination, while the dominant group may also escalate the conflict because of the contradiction of goals, trying to show its willpower to stand by its position without any intention to yield to the demands of the weaker side. Examples include the deadly Tamil ambush in July 1983 on a Sri Lanka army patrol. In response, President Jayewardene organized massacres of Tamils in various cities of Sri Lanka. Both acts reflected a deep sense of deprivation without any progress to meet the raised grievances.

Perception of the Ability and Intentions of the Rival

The perceived ability of the rival to inflict harm is compared to one's own ability to cope with the opponent and withstand the conflict. This perception is often based on an objective calculation of manpower and weapons that each side has for the conflict. But perception of ability also relates to psychological elements of motivation and determination of each side to pursue its own goals, which is more subjectively determined. Perception of ability does not have unequivocal consequences. A perceived strong ability of the rival may inhibit the escalation of the conflict because of the fear of being harmed. But it also may instigate the will to hurt the rival by initiating ways of violence in order to demonstrate lack of deterrence. A perception of weakness, however, instigates an escalation because the party may think that by using excessive force against the rival it may improve its position in the conflict. Such a perception leads to a belief that success is nearing and the party has to exert increased efforts and abilities to overcome the rival. In this line, some analysts suggest that the outbreak of the second Palestinian Intifada in the fall of 2000 was at least partially instigated by the Israeli retreat from Lebanon in May 2000, which was perceived as a sign of Israeli weakness (Pressman, 2003).

The perceived intentions of the rival are purely psychologically based, as they depend on the attribution of intention that a party ascribes to the rival. In this part, the process is often based on going beyond the objective data because the intentions have to be inferred from verbal and behavioral actions. The intentions refer to the evaluation of how important the stated goals are for the rival, how does the rival intend to achieve them, and what is the level of determination. Perception of malintentions toward one's own group always escalates the conflict. This perception indicates that the rival intends to harm and hurt the group, and therefore the group attempts to prevent it. The perceived ability and intentions of the rival are reflected in the level of threat that the group experiences. The perceived threat has important implications not only for the mobilization but also for the escalation of the conflict. Threat in general escalates the conflict. Groups usually do not easily go for slaughter but try to prevent it, if they can. The threat experienced by both sides in the Rwandan conflict as a result of the perceived intentions and ability had been fueling the conflict continuously. Already in the 1950s both sides attributed malintentions to each other. While the Hutu viewed the intention of the Tutsi to continue their dominance, the Tutsi saw a threat to their longtime superior standing. These perceptions led to continuing reciprocal violence that culminated in the attempted genocide of the Tutsi in 1994.

Actions Taken by the Rival

The level of perceived threat is related to the actions taken by the rival. Conflicts escalate when the groups take harsh and violent measures with the intention to harm the opponent. Usually these types of actions lead to mobilization or retaliation that escalates the conflict. But in the short term harsh and severe lines of actions may restrain and even overcome the rival. Nevertheless, the histories of long conflicts show that they usually cause only a temporary overpowering, because with time the rival recovers and comes back to the conflict with more determination and power. Harsh actions motivate the group members to achieve both prevention and retribution. They often raise the motivation of the group members and increase the mobilization. In almost every conflict it is possible to identify this factor: when one side takes a harsh violent action, in most cases it is met with a harsh reaction, and then both acts lead to serious escalation. The rebellious violent acts by Tamils, Tutsi, Algerians, Palestinians, Kurds, or Chechens were always met with harsh reactions of their rivals. This is a rule in cases in which a group challenges a state, because a society that controls a state cannot allow itself to ignore violence of a minority group. But the acts of the dominant group also often are met with retribution. Harsh repression by the dominant groups often leads to radicalization and more extreme acts of violence by the minority groups.

Successful Mobilization of Group Members

Successful mobilization of group members often escalates a conflict. It adds participants with high motivation who are ready to sacrifice much for achieving group goals. Lasting conflicts require persistent participation of group members who manage the conflict on a chronic level without exhaustion and desperation. This factor applies especially to groups that do not have a state but rely on the volunteering mobilization. In these groups, mobilization based on free will is an important condition for escalation of their conflict. Thus, for example, in the cases of Catholics in Northern Ireland (in the early 1970s) or of Muslims in Kashmir (in the late 1980s), the conflicts escalated greatly after these groups succeeded in mobilizing their members to violent struggle. But also in democratic states the support of the society members in the escalation and continuation of the conflict is of importance. Leaders have to persuade them that escalating steps are needed and are benefiting the society. In the cases of Turkey, Israel, and both sides in Cyprus, the leaders mobilize society members when they intend to escalate the conflict.

Resources

Conflicts require not only human but also material resources to feed the fighters, to shelter them, to buy weapons, and so on. It is difficult to manage a protracted and severe conflict without money. Resources thus determine to a large extent the escalation of the conflict (McCarthy & Zald, 1977). When a party or both parties have resources, they can often escalate the conflict in hopes of winning it. Mobilization of resources depend on the parties involved. While some parties can use the resources of a state (e.g., India and Pakistan or Turkey or Israel), other parties have to seek resources informally and often illegally.

External Support

Resources are often related to external support from another group or groups or from the international community. Third parties may provide tangible support that allows management and even escalation of the conflict. This support may come in various forms beginning with money and food and ending with weapons and fighters. Such a support adds a new dimension to a conflict. The armed insurgency in Kashmir could not have escalated the conflict in the 1990s without material support from Pakistan. Also, the financial support that the IRA got from the Irish diaspora in the United States and also from Libya was crucial in financing violent actions in Northern Ireland.

The external support may come also in an intangible way as moral support. In these cases, the group's belief in the justness of its own goals increases, which strengthens its motivation to continue the struggle. This type of support is important especially if it comes from a world power or a respected world organization. A salient case of moral support was the international boycott of South Africa's apartheid system. Between 1970s and 1994, many of the states and international organizations imposed embargoes on military supplies, trade, cultural exchanges, and sport participation in competitions. The boycott had the objective of isolating white South Africa.

Past Experiences

Past experience is another factor that can influence escalation. Groups come to a conflict situation with their collective memories, which provide perspective about the present conflict. Collective memories serve as lenses through which group members evaluate the level of threat and their ability to cope with the rival. A group with a history of intergroup conflicts often raises the sense of threat, and the ability to cope with it will escalate it in order to withstand the opponent. Indeed, the reactions of Israeli Jews and Serbs are greatly influenced by their respective collective memory. Both societies are sensitive to existential threats that have appeared in their histories, and therefore they react violently when such a threat is perceived again (Bar-Tal & Antebi, 1992; MacDonald, 2002). A history of past failures, however, may inhibit escalation to prevent another disastrous outcome. Thus, for example, after the very harsh reaction of the Israeli army in putting down their uprising in 2000–2005, Palestinians are careful in escalating the conflict violently again.

COLLECTIVE EXPERIENCES IN INTRACTABLE CONFLICT

Once escalation takes place, the conflict becomes more severe and moves toward its intractable extreme end. The escalation and the accompanying experiences lead to the emergence of various psychological process and outcomes. It is possible to propose that *the more the conflict is intractable, the more psychological implications it has for the involved society members as individuals and the collective alike.* The next part of the chapter will focus on these implications.

In order to understand the dynamics of intractable conflicts, we have to consider the psychology of society members involved in these conflicts, which is largely determined by their individual and collective experiences. These harsh conflicts last a long time, and even after the initial excitement and positive feelings about the need for conflict, there are always accompanying negative experiences. It hardly needs repeating that violence has a serious effect on human beings. In addition to violence, though, intractable conflicts always involve economic hardship through direct and indirect destruction of the society's infrastructure. Conflicts also require tangible investments in the military. Thus, they may lead to a decrease in economic growth and an increase in poverty and sometimes unemployment. Even when societies live a "normal life," they bear damages and use resources for conflict that could be otherwise directed to other constructive spending for the benefit of the societies. Also, for many groups, the conflict is related to limitations of freedom with regard to movement, organization, the practice of religion, expression of cultural identity, and support for a particular ideology. Exposure to the costs and experiences of the conflict in most cases is negative. Violent acts, future threats, negative economic prognoses, and restrictions on freedom become part of an encapsulated environment in which the participating society members must live. They hear daily about the conflict and its effects and implications in all spheres of life. Thus, the salience of this information not only increases identification with the group experiences but also makes it the focus of public and private discourse. All these descriptions mean that individual and collective life under conditions of intractable conflict necessarily affects the experiences of all the participants.

A representative intractable conflict is the Chechen conflict with Russia, which began with great intensity in the 18th century as Russian tsars extended their empire southward. But only in the early 19th century did Russia embark on a full-scale conquest of the Chechens' territory, using "scorched earth" tactics and deportations. Chechens were eventually defeated in the mid-19th century, and then many of them became refugees or were deported to the Ottoman Empire. Since then, they suffered from oppression and discrimination, as their various rebellions against the Russians were put down. In 1944 their oppression reached its apogee as all Chechens, together with several other peoples of the Caucasus, were accused of collaboration with the Nazis and ordered by Joseph Stalin to be deported to Kazakhstan and Siberia. In this deportation, between one-quarter and one-half of the entire Chechen nation perished. In 1956, after their rehabilitation, they were allowed to return, though still suffering discrimination. They had a low rate of employment, as well as a low quality of housing, health care, social services, and educational benefits, placing them at or close to the bottom among the peoples of the Soviet Union. With the collapse of the Soviet Union, they tried to regain independence and waged two devastating wars with the new Russian state. In the first war in 1994–1996, an estimated 40,000 Chechens were killed, more than 200,000 injured (mostly civilians), and more than 500,000 displaced. During the second war in 1999–2000, the unofficial estimate is that at least 30,000 Chechens were killed, most of them civilians (Dunlop, 1998; Jaimoukha, 2005).

This description of personal and collective daily life in intractable conflicts implies that society members experience harsh negative psychological effects and suffer threats, pain, exhaustion, grief, traumas, misery, insecurity, fear, hardship, and costs in both human and material terms (see, e.g., Collier, 1999; de Jong, 2002; Hobfoll, Lomranz, Bridges, Eyal, & Tzemach, 1989; Kalyvas, 2007; Milgram, 1986; World Development Report, 2011). Probably the key experience is the chronic sense of threat that touches everyone. The two types of threat proposed by Stephan and his colleagues (Stephan & Renfro, 2002; Stephan, Renfro, & Davis, 2008) – realistic and symbolic, on both the group and individual levels – play a major role in intergroup relations. Realistic threats refer to beliefs about possible human losses, as well as losses of territory, resources, wealth, power, status, or general welfare. Symbolic threats refer to worldviews about possible harm in one's religious, political, moral, or cultural system of beliefs, attitudes, and values.

Intractable conflicts by definition involve threats to basic existential needs, values that are perceived as essential for survival, or both. Members of groups involved in intractable conflict often experience difficulties in satisfying these needs and values. Because intractable conflicts can last for many years, these threats involve specific chronic personal stressors, such as constant fear of being harmed by violence, concern about family members who may be hurt, and worries about economic repercussions. An additional characteristic of intractable conflicts is the extensive psychological investment in their continuation, which could lead to states of chronic fatigue and exhaustion. Thus, experiences of threat are a dominant factor that has major implications on societies involved in intractable conflict (Canetti, Rapaport, Wayne, Hall, & Hobfoll, in press).

These experiences also affect the active carriers of the violence – the soldiers, fighters, security personnel, and other related groups. They live under hardship, witness the death and injuries of their comrades, are sometimes injured themselves, and experience tremendous stress. They also actively take part in violent actions themselves. In such conflicts, they not only injure opposing military personnel but also harm the civilian population, including women and children. These acts leave their marks on individuals, who have to live with the outcome of deeds that may be immoral by their own standards and who possibly suffer psychological distress as a result (see, e.g., Greenbaum & Elizur, 2013).

Milgram (1986, 1993) proposes that the effects of these experiences on participants in violent conflicts should be evaluated on the basis of their duration, intensity, multiplicity, palpability, probability, and personal relevance. The more durable the negative experiences in conflict are, the more intense they are, the more often they occur, the more repeatedly they take place on a wide scale, the more likely their occurrence is, and the more relevant they are for the individuals, then the greater effect they have on participating society members. In cases of intractable conflict, all these parameters exist. The negative experiences are not limited to a defined period of time but can last for years. In most of the cases, society members cannot predict when the conflict will end or even when it will deescalate. Thus, the negative experiences in intractable conflict are chronic and, from time to time, are of very high intensity, and there is no member who does not experience them at least vicariously. Almost every society member is hurt, suffers economic hardship, observes violence at least through mass media and personal stories, or has someone close who suffered or experienced the violence. Thus, the negative experiences are relevant to almost all, if not all, society members involved in intractable conflict.

Stress

The most notable effect of living under the conditions of intractable conflict with direct and indirect exposures to violence and hardships is the experience of stress. There are at least three categories of approaches to the definition of stress, and all of them shed light on the situation of intractable conflict: the accumulated changes in the environment as sources of stress (Dohrenwend & Dohrenwend, 1981; Holmes & Rahe, 1967); the adaptive reaction to noxious stimuli or demands upon the body (Selye, 1956, 1993); and environmental conditions and individuals' reactions to those conditions (Hobfoll, 1988, 1998; Lazarus, 1999; Lazarus & Folkman, 1984). On the basis of the well-accepted approach propagated by Lazarus (1999) that emphasizes the importance of cognitive appraisals of stressful situations, stress is defined here as "a particular relationship between the person and the environment that is appraised by the person as taxing or exceeding his or her resources and endangering his or her well-being" (Lazarus & Folkman, 1984, p. 19). Conversely, the theory of conservation of resources (COR) (Hobfoll, 1988, 1998) places less emphasis on individual differences in appraisals and posits that the most important factor contributing to stress is loss of personal and social resources. This cycle of resource loss may itself be a multistep process. Violence may result in loss of objective resources. Hence, people may lose friends and family and employment opportunities or the ability to work due to destruction of workplace settings, the possible danger of going to work, and downturns in the economy. The degree to which these losses lead to stress reactions depends on the availability of key management resources, such as generalized self-efficacy and perceived social support. As violence continues, management resources may also be depleted and the likelihood of extreme stress responses such as post-traumatic stress disorder (PTSD) increases. As Coleman (2003, p. 29) describes in his analysis of the outcomes of intractable conflicts, "Trauma is a loss of trust in a safe and predictable world. In response, individuals suffer from a variety of symptoms, including recurrent nightmares, suicidal thoughts, demoralization, helplessness, hopelessness, anxiety, depression, somatic illnesses, sleeplessness, and feelings of isolation and meaninglessness."

Stress and its various effects are the most investigated topics of intractable conflict. Numerous studies conducted in various conflict settings around the world have documented the prevalence of stressful experiences that such conflicts entail, as well as the adverse effects of these experiences on the mental health of the members of the societies involved in such conflicts (e.g., Breznitz, 1983; de Jong, 2002; Milgram, 1986; Silove, 1999; Solomon, 1995; Zomer & Bleich, 2005). Slone and Hallis (1999) developed a scale for measuring exposure to political life events, most of which are events that occur in the context of war or conflict, and report a correlation between exposure to these events and symptoms of distress among Israeli children. Bleich, Gelkopf, and Solomon (2003, p. 612), in a study of the effects of exposure to violence among an Israeli national sample during the escalation of the Israeli-Palestinian conflict throughout the second Intifada between September 2000 and April 2002, report that "472 persons (318 civilians) had been killed in terrorist attacks and 3846 persons (2708 civilians) had been injured (totaling 0.067% of the population of 6.4 million). Five hundred sixty of the terrorist attacks (out of more than 13,000), with a death toll of 185, had been carried out within Israel's 1967 borders." The researchers found that 16% of Israelis were directly exposed to terrorist attack and about 37% reported that a family member or friend had been so exposed. A majority of Israelis felt unsafe (60%) and expressed fears for themselves and about two-thirds expressed fears for themselves and relatives. Of importance is that 76.7% of the respondents reported at least one symptom of traumatic stress (TSR), 9.4% reported PTSD, and 58.6% reported feelings of depression (see also Canetti, Halperin, Sharvit, & Hobfoll, 2009).

On the other side of the conflict, Canetti et al. (2010) conducted face-to-face interviews with a national sample of adult Palestinians in the Gaza Strip, West Bank, and East Jerusalem in September–October 2007 and asked about exposure to violence and about PTSD symptoms. The study was done in view of Palestinians' continuous experiences of violence in the frame of the Israeli-Palestinian conflict. According to Canetti et al., since 1987 "during the first and second Intifadas (uprisings) more than 6,200 Palestinians were killed, more than 60,000 wounded, and more than 65,000 detained. Over 590 individuals have been killed in internecine warfare between Palestinian political factions" (p. 220). The results show a chronic exposure to various violent events; specifically, "men commonly reported being exposed to witnessing violence, death or injury of loved one, and being forced to leave their home, having their home demolished or being harassed and having themselves imprisoned, injured or tortured. Women were most commonly exposed to witnessing violence, death or injury of a loved one, and being forced to leave their home, having their home demolished, or being harassed" (p. 225). Roughly 25% of the interviewees had at least one severe symptom of PTSD (see also Hobfoll, Hall, & Canetti, in press).

In a study by Muldoon and Downes (2007) in Northern Ireland and in the border counties of the Irish Republic in 2004, a representative sample of respondents was asked about encountering distressing events during the "troubles" (the violent conflict), and those who reported witnessing such an event were asked to complete the 17-item PTSD Checklist. The results show that 42% of the respondents reported experience of a distressing event during the violent conflict. Of these respondents, 10% had symptoms severe enough to warrant a diagnosis of PTSD, even six years after the Good Friday agreement was signed ending the violent conflict. In this conflict there were 3,500 fatalities between 1969 and 1998 in a population of 1.68 million citizens. Other studies conducted in other settings of intractable conflict also reveal the adverse effects of exposure to conflict-related stressful life events on the mental health of the members of the involved societies (de Jong, 2002).

Deprivation of Needs

The harsh experiences of intractable conflicts indicate that group members living under such conditions necessarily experience at least some deprivation of their needs, and in many cases this deprivation is on a deep scale. Innate psychological needs are also important for human functioning whether as individuals or as a part of a collective; Deci and Ryan (2000, p. 229) define them as "nutrients that are essential for ongoing psychological growth, integrity, and well being." Indeed, intractable conflicts cause a state of deprivation and the threat of further deprivation (Azar, 1986; Burton, 1990; Galtung, 1996; Lederer, 1980; Staub, 1989, 1996, 1999; Staub & Bar-Tal, 2003). People experience epistemic, mastery, and safety needs; needs to be right (justice needs); and positive personal and social identity needs. Thus, in times of intractable conflict, society members live under a continuous situation of uncertainty and ambiguity. They do not know when the next round of violence will take place, when an act of violence will occur, when something bad will happen to them or to someone dear to them. They live in a world that does not always have a meaning to them. Questions regarding the goals of the rival and its violent behavior arise, as well as questions regarding goals of the group own group and its wisdom in engaging in the conflict. In such a context, individuals often feel that they do not have control over the situation or mastery over their fate and have a sense of helplessness and even hopelessness.

The context of intractable conflict often leads to loss of personal and collective safety. Society members feel that their existence is insecure because of various threats, which may pertain to loss of life, health, housing, or employment. Many of these threats are continuous and disturb the flow of normal life. Because the context of intractable conflict often leads to behaviors that violate moral codes, society members may experience distress as result of moral emotions (e.g., guilt, shame, moral outrage). These feelings pose a threat to positive social identity as well as to personal esteem. Society members do not have to perform immoral acts themselves in order to feel threats to their identity; it is enough to be members of the group in which other members carry out these acts. All these deprivations lead to negative psychological reactions, such as feelings of distress, exhaustions, hardship, misery, and suffering. At the same time, the context of intractable conflict also raises feelings of resentment, striving for justice, feelings of determination, and a sense of solidarity. These experiences may be called positive, as they play a major role in energizing and mobilizing society members to take part in the intractable conflict. These experiences lead to the achievement of goals, a collective self-efficacy, and a sense of accomplishment. They underlie a feeling of pride and satisfaction that enhances motivation and mobilization.

Challenges

In general, psychological experiences and reactions are prevalent among group members involved in intractable conflict. They are mostly negative, emotional, powerful, and attributed to the conflict. In view of these experiences and their consequences, societies involved in intractable conflict face three psychological challenges on both individual and collective levels (see, e.g., Hobfoll & deVries, 1995; Shalev, Yehuda, & McFarlane, 2000).

First, they must learn to *cope* with the stress, fears, and other negative psychological phenomena that accompany intractable conflict situations (Mitchell, 1981). Societies involved in intractable conflicts are required to live for an extended time under difficult conditions of violence, human loss, threat and danger, demands for resources, and other hardships. Therefore, one of the challenges that societies face is the development of appropriate mechanisms for coping with these difficult conditions.

Second, societies must *satisfy* psychological needs that are absent during intractable conflicts, such as needs of knowing, confidence, mastery, safety, and positive identity (Burton, 1990; Lederer, 1980; Staub, 1999, 2003). If people are to function properly as individuals and society members, these needs must be fulfilled (Maslow, 1970). Of special importance is the epistemic need for a comprehensive understanding of the conflict, providing a coherent, organized, meaningful, and reliable picture of the situation and creating predictability. Individuals try to reduce uncertainty and ambiguity by creating a comprehensible environment. Therefore, they strive to perceive and structure their world in a way that events and people can be understood (Baumeister, 1991; Berkowitz, 1968; Heine, Proulx, & Vohs, 2006; Maddi, 1971; Reykowski, 1982). This understanding has to justify the conflict situation, as it often involves violence and even atrocities. The need for safety is also of great importance as individuals strive for security, stability, protection, and freedom from fear and anxiety (Maslow, 1970). They also have a need for mastery that leads them to strive for predictability and a sense of self-control. In addition, individuals have a need for positive self-evaluation, respect, and esteem as individuals and members of a society, which is well represented in their personal and social identity (Maslow, 1970; Tajfel, 1981).

Third, adaptation requires development of socio-psychological conditions that will be conducive to successfully withstanding the rival group; that is, they must attempt to try to *win the conflict* or, at least, not to lose it. Successfully withstanding enables groups to maintain an intensive conflict with an opponent over time, with all the concomitant challenges and adjustments, on both personal and societal levels, that this context entails. Groups have to prepare themselves for a long struggle, and this requires recruitment and mobilization of society members and immense investment in material resources. For these purposes, they need to develop well-grounded justifications for the conflict as well as a system of socio-psychological conditions, such as care, loyalty, commitment to a society and country, adherence to the society's goals, high motivation to contribute, persistence, readiness for personal sacrifice, unity, solidarity, determination, courage, and endurance.

EVOLVEMENT OF FUNCTIONAL SOCIO-PSYCHOLOGICAL REPERTOIRE

In view of the challenges presented in the preceding section, I would like to propose a fundamental proposition: *Societies involved in intractable conflict evolve a functional socio-psychological repertoire in order to meet the psychological challenges.* The repertoire includes shared beliefs, attitudes, affect, and emotions that provide the necessary ingredients for successful adaptation to the context of intractable conflict (of special importance in this repertoire are functional societal beliefs discussed in the Introduction). But this development is not a beginning. The developing socio-psychological repertoire is based on the goals, epistemic basis, and emotions that evolved in the very early stage of the conflict (see Chapter 2). These early-developed beliefs, attitudes, and emotions provide the foundation for the development of a more elaborate, extensive repertoire. This extended repertoire allows meeting the three challenges: coping with the stress, satisfying basic needs, and facilitating the confrontation with the enemy by constructing a meaningful, coherent, and systematic perspective on the conflict and on all the related issues.

This view on the functioning of the constructed societal beliefs is based on extensive work in psychology that points out that in times of stress and deprivation there is a need to form a worldview that provides meaning. The concept of "finding meaning" is commonly defined as an ability to construct a worldview that integrates the experiences into a system of societal beliefs that is coherent, is comprehensible, and make senses of the situation (Davis, Nolen-Hoeksema, & Larson, 1998). Numerous theories have addressed the role of meaning in the coping process and its relationship to an organizing worldview. Some have provided very general definitions of the concept of meaning and of worldviews that provide coherent understanding, whereas others have developed and elaborated about more particular worldviews that contribute to meaningful coping.

Victor Frankl (1963, 1978), who developed his approach partly on the basis of his experiences in a concentration camp during the Holocaust, observes that a central characteristic of individuals who were able to cope and survive under extremely difficult conditions was the ability to transcend their immediate survival concerns and find meaning and purpose in their struggles and suffering. According to his approach, believing that there is a person, idea, or value that is worth fighting for and being able to identify a promise and an opportunity in given situations are the most important factors that facilitate both survival under extremely difficult conditions and a high quality of life in more normal circumstances.

Similarly, according to Antonovsky (1987), who worked in Israel on stressful conflict experiences, the most important factor that contributes to successful coping with traumatic events and prevents their adverse effects on health is a "sense of coherence." In his view, the sense of coherence is a general cognitive orientation comprising three themes: comprehensibility, manageability, and meaningfulness. *Comprehensibility* is defined as the extent to which individuals perceive information that they encounter as making sense as well as being consistent, structured, clear, and predictable. *Manageability* refers to the extent to which individuals perceive the resources at their disposal, or at the disposal of legitimate others, as adequate for meeting the demands posed by stimuli in their environment. *Meaningfulness* refers to the extent to which individuals experience life emotionally as making sense and believe that certain life domains are worthy of an investment of effort, energy, and commitment even if they pose difficulties and demands. In other words, a sense of meaningfulness involves seeing difficult stressful situations as a challenge rather than burden.

The cognitive adaptation approach developed by Taylor (1983) is based on the postulate that most people are capable of adapting and coping successfully with difficult, threatening events. The theory identifies the psychological mechanisms that enable such adaptation. According to Taylor, coping with threatening events requires a process of cognitive adaptation, which involves three component processes. The first process is *a search for meaning* in the threatening event, which involves attempts to understand the causes of the event, its significance, its symbolism for the individual, and its implications for the individual's life in the present and future. Finding meaning facilitates the second process of cognitive adaptation, which is *a sense of mastery* and control over the threatening event and a belief that it can be prevented from recurring. The third process involved in cognitive adaptation is *self-enhancement*. Threatening events often take a toll on individuals' self-esteem, and therefore the process of adaptation involves the restoration of positive self-esteem. Self-enhancement is achieved by focusing on the positive consequences of the threatening events and by making downward comparisons, that is, comparing one's own condition to the conditions of those who are even less fortunate.

Of direct relevance for the situation of intractable conflict is terror management theory (TMT), which proposes that humans have developed sophisticated intellectual capacities that enable self-awareness and recognition of the inevitability of death (Greenberg, Solomon, & Arndt, 2008; Greenberg, Solomon, & Pyszczynski, 1997; Solomon, Greenberg, & Pyszczynski, 1991). This recognition gives rise to the terror of death but also encourages creation of a mechanism for managing and controlling this terror. According to TMT, one of the human mechanisms of terror management is culture, which includes beliefs about the world, nature, and reality that are shared by humans belonging to a particular group within a culture. The worldview constructed in a culture allows individuals to perceive the world and human existence as meaningful, orderly, and stable and instills standards of significant values that give one reasons to live. Living up to these standards contributes to individuals' sense of self-esteem by means of a cultural promise of literal or symbolic immortality. Symbolic immortality is provided by identifying with collectives that are larger and longer-lasting than the individual, as well as with their system of beliefs. Indeed, meta-analysis of 277 experiments on the effects of mortality salience showed unequivocally that an experienced threat as a result of salience of potential death leads to increased adoption of cultural worldviews that serve as a buffer for death anxiety (Burke, Martens, & Faucher, 2010). Hirschberger and Pyszczynski (2010, in press) apply this line of thought to situations of violent conflicts and point out that in times of threat individuals tend to support coherent and simplistic militaristic views that fuel the continuation of the intergroup conflict. In this line, a study by Landau et al. (2004) shows that increased salience of mortality in view of threats (e.g., the 9/11 terror attack) led the United States to bolster its adherence to symbols and policies that constitute the dominant cultural worldview, propagating a patriotic position. Similarly Canetti, Guy, Lavi, Bar-Tal, and Hobfoll (2012) find among representative samples of Israeli Jews and Palestinians in the occupied territories a strong relationship between the perception of threat and an adherence to the ethos of conflict, indicating that the higher the perception of threat, the higher the adherence to the ethos.

Lavi, Canetti, Sharvit, Bar-Tal, and Hobfoll (in press) examined the effect of adherence of the ethos of conflict on psychological distress among a representative sample of Israeli Jews. The study shows that among those society members who strongly adhered to the ethos of conflict elaborated in Chapter 5, the relationship between exposure to conflict-related violence and psychological distress (reported depression) was found to be weaker than among those who adhered mildly. According to the researchers, these results show that an ethos of conflict in a violent and stressful context of intractable conflict has a protective function (see also Milgram, 1993). As a kind of ideology, it enables society members to find predictability and meaningfulness, even when they are confronted with harsh events of violence (Jost & Hunyady, 2003). In addition, it may reduce the experience of stress because it may affect the primary appraisal of violent events (Lazarus & Folkman, 1984) – that is, society members who adhere to an ethos of conflict tend to believe that the conflict is mandatory and cannot be avoided, and therefore they accept the violence as consequences of the unavoidable conflict. Finally, adherence to an ethos of conflict may also effect a secondary appraisal (Jost & Hunyady, 2003; Lazarus & Folkman, 1984), by fostering determination and a sense of control, that assists in making postevent coping decisions. When exposed to violent events, society members with a high ethos endorsement may believe that they are a part of a nation that has been coping with hardships for centuries and thus has the stamina to continue coping.

Sharvit (2008), using the present conceptual framework, shows experimentally that exposure to stress-activated societal beliefs of an ethos of conflict occurs among Israeli Jews (members of a society involved in an intractable conflict), even if this activation was not consciously acknowledged. She suggests that the reasons for this high accessibility and easy activation of the ethos beliefs among Israeli Jews are its acquisition at an early developmental stage and the constant exposure to it because of its frequent expressions in societal channels of communication. These findings hold across all the sectors of the Jewish Israeli society, including supporters of peace process. Similarly, Canetti, Rapaport, Wayne, Hall, and Hobfoll (in press), on the basis of extensive empirical literature, propose a stress-based model of political extremism. Specifically, they suggest that during protracted violent conflicts society members exposed to continuous violence develop psychological distress and threat perception. As a coping mechanism, they tend to adhere to hawkish ideologies (such as the ethos of conflict) and support an increase in hostile action against the rival group.

Thus, in line with these approaches it is suggested that society members develop a specific socio-psychological repertoire that allows them to view the conflict situation in a comprehensive, coherent, and meaningful way. They can understand what the conflict is about, why it erupted, why the rival opposes the goals of the ingroup and resorts to violence, why the ingroup has to struggle violently for the goals, what the difference is between the ingroup and the rival, why the conflict continues for such a long time, why it is important to mobilize for the conflict, and what the conditions are that facilitate coping with the rival. This repertoire enables society members to satisfy various needs during escalation of violent conflict, such as needs for mastery, security, positive self-collective view, and positive social identity. At the same time this repertoire plays a crucial role for the challenge to confront the rival, as it is essential for mobilization of the society members and development of their readiness to make great sacrifices on behalf of their society.

CONCEPTUAL SOCIO-PSYCHOLOGICAL FRAMEWORK OF THE INTRACTABLE CONFLICT

Figure 1 presents the conceptual framework of the socio-psychological dynamics of intractable conflicts. The description of this model will be extensively expanded in the next five chapters. As Figure 1 indicates, any society that lives under the shadow of intractable conflict needs to adapt to the life under this stressful, threatening, uncertain, and harsh context. It has to satisfy the needs of society members as individuals and the needs of the collective as a whole, it needs to cope successfully with the chronic stress, and it has to withstand the enemy in order not to lose the conflict.

Figure 1 further shows that, as the intractable conflicts continue, the societies involved develop a shared repertoire of societal beliefs, attitudes, and emotions, which is functional to the challenges that the context poses on the basis of the repertoire formed in the early phase of the conflict. With time this reformed shared repertoire turns into a socio-psychological infrastructure,[1] and the shared repertoire gradually crystallizes into a well-organized system of societal beliefs, attitudes, and emotions that penetrates into the institutions and communication channels of the society. This socio-psychological infrastructure consists of three central elements: collective memories, ethos of conflicts, and collective emotional orientation, which are mutually interrelated. *Collective memory* consists of societal beliefs that present the history of the conflict to society members (Cairns & Roe, 2003; Connerton, 1989; Halbwachs, 1992; Wertsch, 2002). This narrative develops over time, and the societal beliefs describe the conflict's eruption and its course, providing a coherent and meaningful picture (Devine-Wright, 2003). *Ethos of conflict* is defined as the configuration of central societal shared beliefs that provide particular dominant orientation to a society and give meaning to the societal life, under the conditions of intractable conflict (Bar-Tal, 2000a). It supplies the epistemic basis for the hegemonic social consciousness of the society and

---

[1] Throughout the book I use a number of concepts regularly. Socio-psychological infrastructure, defined here, is one. Another is societal beliefs, which are shared propositions and constitute building blocks of narratives, ethos, or collective memory (see Introduction); narratives refer to stories that have a plot. Socio-psychological repertoire refers to a collection of beliefs, attitudes, and emotions held by an individual or a collective.

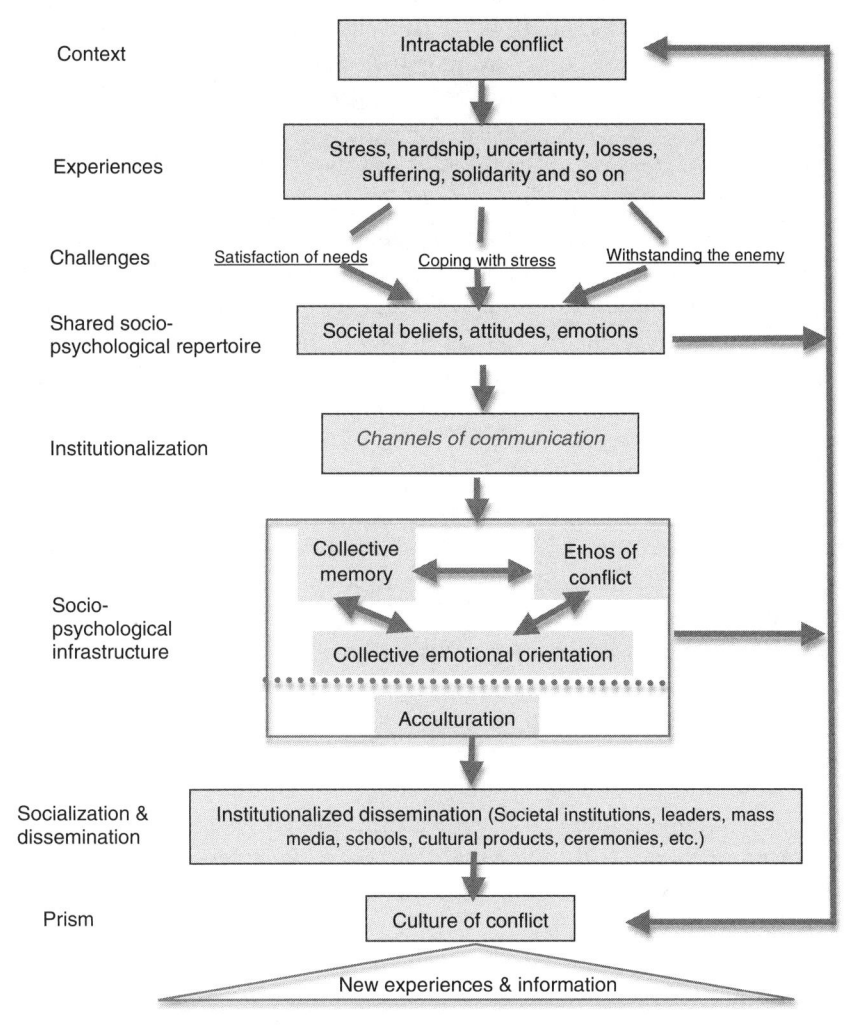

FIGURE 1. Conceptual Model of the Socio-psychological Foundations of Intractable Conflicts

serves as one of the foundations of societal life in times of intractable conflict. *Collective emotional orientation* refers to the characterizing expression of one emotion, or a number of particular emotions in a society, under the conditions of intractable conflict (Bar-Tal, 2001; Halperin, Sharvit, & Gross, 2011). After this infrastructure becomes well institutionalized and disseminated, it serves as a foundation for the development of a culture of conflict that dominates societies engaged in intractable conflicts. A culture of conflict develops when societies saliently integrate into their culture tangible and intangible symbols, which are created to communicate a particular meaning about the prolonged and continuous experiences of living in the context of conflict (Geertz, 1973; Ross, 1998). Symbols of conflict become hegemonic elements in the culture of societies involved in intractable conflict: they provide a dominant meaning about the present reality, about the past, and about future goals, and serve as guides for practice.

Solidification of the socio-psychological infrastructure, as an indication of the development of a culture of conflict, includes four features. First, through *extensive sharing*, the beliefs of the socio-psychological infrastructure and the accompanying emotions are familiar to society members,[2] who acquire and store this repertoire as part of their socialization from an early age. They share it as members of the society who identify with societal goals, experiences, history, and narratives. Second, the repertoire has *wide application*; it is not only held by society members but also put into active use by them in their daily conversations, being chronically accessible. In addition, it appears to be dominant in public discourse via societal channels of mass communication. It is often used for justification and explanation of decisions, policies, and courses of actions taken by the leaders. Finally, it is also expressed in institutional ceremonies, commemorations, and memorials. Third, *expression in cultural products* indicates that the socio-psychological infrastructure is also expressed through cultural products, such as literary books, TV programs, films, theater, visual arts, and monuments. It becomes a society's cultural repertoire, relaying societal views and shaping society members' beliefs, attitudes, and emotions. Through these channels, it can be disseminated to every sector of the public. Fourth, the availability of *educational materials* ensures that the socio-psychological infrastructure is introduced in schools and even in higher education as central themes of socialization.

Eventually the learned, absorbed, shared, and institutionalized repertoire of ethos of conflict, collective memory, and collective emotional orientation serves as a prism through which society members collect information and interpret new experiences. In this way, the vicious cycle of intractable conflict is established because the new experiences and information are interpreted in light of the held repertoire and then they validate the held beliefs of ethos of conflict, collective memory, and shared emotions, which in turn lead to courses of action in the conflict that trigger only the same cycle with the rival.

---

[2] It is recognized that not all members of societies involved in intractable conflict share the repertoire equally. Societies differ in the extent of sharing the societal beliefs of ethos and collective memory. Moreover, there are societies that hold contradicting views of ethos even at the height of the conflict, and others may develop it with time. Ethos is more fully described in Chapter 5.

Considering that this process occurs simultaneously with the two parties in the conflict, it is obvious how the vicious cycle of violence operates. As the conflict evolves, each of the opponents develops a culture of conflict with the socio-psychological infrastructure, which initially fulfills important functional roles, on both the individual and collective levels. This development leads to the emergence of a "mirror image," which indicates a great similarity of negative general beliefs and attitudes that each side holds about the conflict, about the other side, and about one's own group (Bronfenbrenner, 1961; Kelman, 2007). With time, however, this infrastructure comes to serve as the major motivating, justifying, and rationalizing factor of the conflict. Any negative actions taken by one side in the conflict then serve as information validating the existing socio-psychological infrastructure for the other side and, in turn, magnify its motivation and readiness to engage in conflict. The behaviors of each side confirm the held socio-psychological infrastructure and justify harming the opponent.

Now it is possible to elaborate in detail the proposed conceptual framework depicted in Figure 1. The collective memory will be presented in Chapter 4, the ethos of conflict in Chapter 5, and the collective emotional orientation in Chapter 6. Chapter 7 will then elaborate on the development of culture of conflict.

PART II

SOCIETAL PSYCHOLOGICAL REPERTOIRE OF CONFLICTS

4

Collective Memory of Intractable Conflicts

An important part of crystallizing the socio-psychological infrastructure of intractable conflict is the collective memory of the conflict. It plays a major role in maintaining and fueling the conflict. Collective memory necessarily develops because intractable conflicts last at least 25 years, a period that enables their solidification. Before elaborating on the special functions of the collective memory in intractable conflicts, I first describe its general conception and meaning.

GENERAL CONCEPTION OF COLLECTIVE MEMORY

Definition of Collective Memory

Every nation or ethnic group needs to have a common past. Told in a shared narrative (or narratives), a common past provides a commonality and a continuation of experiences across time, which are crucial ingredients for group formation, survival, and identity constructions. This narrative, or a number of narratives, called collective memory, tells the story or stories of the group's past as adopted by the group's members and institutions (Kansteiner, 2002; Olick & Robbins, 1998; Olick, Vinitzky-Seroussi, & Levy, 2011). The interest in the collective memory has been steadily growing among social scientists and historians, as a result of the seminal work by the French sociologist Maurice Halbwachs (1992), who unveiled its crucial importance in the life of a collective (see, e.g., Ben-Ze'ev, Ginio, & Winter, 2010; Cairns & Roe, 2003; Connerton, 1989, 2009; Middleton & Edwards, 1990; Pennebaker, Paez, & Rime, 1997; Zerubavel, 1995).

Kansteiner (2002) defines collective memory as representations of the past that are remembered by society members as the history of the group. These representations compile a complete, meaningful, and comprehensive story about the past that can be also called a narrative, of which societal beliefs serve as the building blocks. But this narrative of the past is not necessarily based on researched historiography, as presented by a historian. It consists of a construction of the past by a collective with the symbols, myths, models, major events, and plots that are part of the group culture. It is remembered by the group members; reported by the group's institutions, channels, and cultural products; and transmitted to group members (Carmines & Stimson, 1989; Olick, Vinitzky-Seroussi, & Levy, 2011). Therefore, as Winter and Sivan (1999, p. 8) point out, it is "apparently too important a subject to be left to the historians" because of its cultural and political importance. Thus, although it may include parts that are supported by historical facts, its goal is not to establish factual truth but to serve societal needs. Indeed, the developed conceptions and empirical investigations show that the study of collective memory is necessary not only for revealing how society views its past but mostly for understanding societal functioning and activity in the present, as well as societal aspirations and goals for the future. In fact, collective memory can be conceptualized as a shared narrative with societal beliefs on particular themes regarding the remembered past of the society that provide an epistemic foundation for the group's belonging, solidarity, existence, mobilization, and courses of action.

Types of Collective Memory

We can differentiate between at least two types of collective memory: popular and official. Popular memory refers to the narratives of collective memories held by society members in their repertoire. In some societies, they may be imparted by formal institutions such as schools and mass media but can also be presented orally by family members, friends, and other agents, as well as transmitted through ceremonies and rituals. Popular memory constitutes the narratives accepted by the public as valid and is reflected in oral accounts of the society members, as well as in their customs, traditions, and social practices (Alonso, 1988; Middleton & Edwards, 1997). Also, its expression in mass media and cultural products is often free of governmental control. The official memory represents the narrative that the formal representatives of the society hold and which they present through formal channels and institutions (Alonso, 1988; Nets-Zehngut, 2011a, 2011b; Rosoux, 2001; Zheng, 2008). It is presented in the publications of the governmental institutions, formal organizations of the society, and in school textbooks, when they are under the control of the formal authorities.

These two types of collective memories can correspond or be in divergence but are always in continuous interaction and communication. That is, sometimes the popular collective memory of society members can be similar to the official collective memory presented by the formal institutions of the society, as, for example, during the 1950s and 1960s these two types of collective memory of Jews in Israel regarding the Israeli-Arab conflict were very similar (Nets-Zehngut, 2012b). But in some cases there might be divergence between the two, as, for example, in Poland, Hungary, and Czechoslovakia regarding the Cold War during the communist regimes that governed these states. Then, the popular collective memory was different from the one propagated by the formal institutions and the ruling communist parties of these states (see, e.g., Benziger, 2010).

This classification recalls a distinction proposed by Assmann (1995) between communicative and cultural memory. From this perspective, communicative memory, which is part of popular memory, is mainly related to the oral transmission of vivid "firsthand" information about an event or events, whereas cultural memory is accumulated in the cultural products that maintain and transmit it. Cultural memory may be at least partially related to the official narrative, because often the formal institutions encourage the expression and transmission of the official memory through cultural means, as, for example, typically happened in the states of the East bloc during the Cold War. Nevertheless, popular memory can also be carried via cultural products, even when they are not supported or even approved by the authorities. A good example of this case was the publication of the book about gulags in the Soviet Union during the communist era by Alexander Solzhenitsyn (1979), which was not in line with the presented official memory.

Schuman and Scott (1989) propose a communicative memory span of about 80–100 years, as it depends on living grandparents who tell the story of the events and, in many cases, on their own autobiographical collective memory. This type of memory has great influence on society members, as they tend to trust the sources and view the narratives as valid and truthful. Communicative memory is of great importance in certain situations, especially when for various reasons cultural transmission is not possible or forbidden and the official memory is not trusted. Thus, for example, in the case of the Palestinian citizens of Israel, their collective memory of what happened to them in the 1948 war has been transmitted mainly via communicative channels from one generation to another, despite suppression of this information in official and unofficial Israeli channels (Nahhes, 2012; Nets-Zehngut, 2011c).

Another proposed distinction is between mental remembering and active remembering (Connerton, 1989; Devine-Wright, 2003). The former refers to the cognitive repertoire, the contents, that society members remember, whereas the latter refers to actions that are performed in the course of remembering (e.g., ceremonies to commemorate a war). These actions are performed in the framework of commemoration of past events, which require patterns of behaviors (Frijda, 1997). Performed behaviors strengthen the existing memories and routinize them into rituals that maintain them. For example, Nahhes (2012) reports that Palestinian citizens of Israel visit regularly, and especially on commemoration days, the sites of their villages that were destroyed by Jews during and after the 1948 war. These acts serve an important function of strengthening and solidifying their popular collective memory.

Also, a society does not necessarily maintain only one narrative of a collective memory. A polarized society may maintain two competing narratives, or even more. The competing narratives of memories appear on the popular level because formal institutions usually do not hold two competing narratives. The competing narratives of popular memories may arise because of a schism in a society over ideological disagreements or as counternarratives to the dominant one. Also, a society may hold competing collective narratives regarding major events of the past that signified a major polarization at that time. But more common reasons are related to the presence of multiethnic populations that have different, sometimes even contradictory, collective memories. The contradiction may be a result of conflict, discrimination, or oppression.

An example of two competing popular memories can be found in the Spanish society that holds at least two popular collective memories regarding the civil war of 1936–1939, from either the Republican or the Nationalist side (Aguilar, 2002). Also, Israeli Jewish society has at least two different popular collective memories regarding events related to the Israeli-Palestinian conflict since the Lebanese war in 1982 (Nets-Zehngut & Bar-Tal, 2009), one part believing that it was necessary, another that the war was unjustly orchestrated (Nets-Zehngut & Bar-Tal, 2009; Raviv, Bar-Tal, & Arviv-Abromovich, in preparation). Also in the Israeli society, the majority Jews and the minority Arabs often have contradictory popular memories regarding the history of the country and the Israeli-Arab conflict (Nets-Zehngut, 2011c). The same divergent collective memories regarding conflict can be found in Rwanda as held by Hutu and Tutsi and in Sri Lanka as held by Tamils and Singhalese.

Characteristics of Collective Memory

Collective memory does not intend to provide an objective history of the past; rather, it tells a story about the past that is functional and relevant to the society's present existence and future aspirations. Thus, it provides a socially constructed narrative that has some basis in events but is biased, selective, and distorted in ways that meet present societal needs (Hobsbawm & Ranger, 1983; Liu & Hilton, 2005; Southgate, 2005). It is entrenched in the particular socio-political-cultural context that imprints its meaning. Connerton (1989, p. 2) points out that "our experience of the present very largely depends upon our knowledge of the past. We experience our present world in the context which is causally connected with the past event and objects."

The memory of the past is always concrete and certain, whereas the future is imagined and doubtful; and because the present always needs a frame, the past is an excellent candidate to fulfill this task. In short, the societal beliefs encased in collective memory help to make sense of the past, illuminate the present, and serves as a basis for aspirations, vision, and plans for the future. This is their raison d'être, and thus they had to be adapted, reconstructed, and reappropriated to serve changing conditions as well as societal needs and goals (Halbwachs, 1992; Hilton & Liu, 2008; Kammen, 1991). That is, collective memory omits certain facts, adds doubtful ones, changes the accounts of events, makes biased inferences, and offers a purposive interpretation of the events that took place in order to be functional, which is the fundamental criterion for acceptance and adoption. When a society relies on the past chronically and centrally, collective memory directs the focus on the past without providing an ability to evaluate properly the present and plan the future. It clouds judgment and evaluation of the present and preparation for the future.

Second, societal beliefs of collective memory are shared by group members and are treated by many of them as truthful accounts of the past and a valid history of the group. They hold them in their repertoires, rely on them in constructing a political worldview, express them in intrasocietal public discourse and as major arguments in intergroup debates, and use them as a rationale in justifying their line of action. The narratives are not unitary because of individual differences that characterize human beings even when they hold the same narrative. Societal beliefs take different forms, contents, and emphases, but when they construct the same narrative, they encompass very similar themes. This almost always applies to popular collective memory that is held by the whole society or only a segment of it. Official memory, however, may not be accepted as truthful by some segments of society members or even by a majority.

Third, collective memory serves as a foundation for experiencing shared emotions (see Chapters 2 and 6). The societal beliefs of the narrative elicit various emotions that society members experience as individuals and as a collective. These emotions are part of the collective emotional orientation and serve various societal functions. Thus, collective memory may raise fear because of past traumatic events, or anger because of a remembered unjust act carried out by another group, or pride because of the memorialized victory and heroic acts performed by group members. The emotions provide a particular meaning to the remembered events and facilitate their memorializing (see, e.g., Bar-Tal, 2001; Kouttab, 2007).

Fourth, collective memory provides the foundations of contents for various cultural symbols such as literature, films, monuments, and ceremonies. The remembered past with its events, heroes, and myths serves as a basic source for creation of cultural symbols and narratives. For example, the national museums are filled with pictures that depict various scenes from collective memory and the national literature describes stories based on this narrative (e.g., Crane, 1997).

Fifth, collective memory should be viewed as a multilayer narrative because a new major event or prolonged experience is interpreted and understood on the basis of the held collective memory of the previous events, even if they are unrelated, as long as it serves the needs and goals of the society. Then, it is integrated into the narrative and serves as evidence for the general representation of the group.

Sixth, collective memory is dynamic and changeable. Through the years, it may change not only its focuses, heroes, commemorated events, or particular narratives but also its general outlook, by changing its orientation. It depends very much on the political and cultural context in which new needs, goals, values, or practices appear. The case of such change is well illustrated in Poland with regard to remembering its communist past.

Seventh, collective memory serves the political-societal and economic decisions on the societal level and is used to justify societal actions in the past and present and plans for the future. It serves as a kind of rationale by the authorities for making policies and decisions (Langenbacher, 2010). But it may also serve as a basis for individual decisions as well.

Finally, collective memory is perceived by group members as characterizing the collective in a unique, distinctive, and exclusive way. It tells the particular narrative of the group's past and thus outlines the boundaries for the group's description and characterization. In this way, it makes a major contribution to the formation, maintenance, and strengthening of the social identity.

Collective Memory and Identity

Construction of social identity is a crucial requirement in the formation of any society or group, because individuals have to identify themselves as group members in order for the group to exist (e.g., Abrams & Hogg, 1990; Calhoun, 1994; Cohen, 1986; Dunn, 1988; Jenkins, 1996; Lactau, 1994; Tajfel, 1981; Turner, 1999; Worchel, Morales, Paez, & Deschamps, 1998). As already noted in the Introduction, the formation of social identity is based on a self-categorization process in which individuals group themselves cognitively as belonging to the same group, in contrast to some other classes of collectives (Turner et al., 1987). On this basis, a sense of similarity, uniformity, unity, interdependence, and coordination of group behavior emerge. But while self-categorization is fundamental for self-definition as a society member, additional societal beliefs must provide meaning to social identity (Bar-Tal, 1998c; Turner, 1991, 1999). Societal beliefs of collective memory fulfill this role. They outline a common origin, describe common past events, and thus illuminate present experiences. They provide a basis for a feeling of commonality, cohesiveness, belonging, uniqueness, and solidarity – all necessary elements for the evolvement of social identity. Sharing the same societal beliefs of collective memory, therefore, shapes society members' identity. These beliefs allow differentiation among societies, drawing boundaries between those who hold them with great confidence and those who do not even know them. Thus, societal beliefs of collective memory, in addition to other elements such as territory, language, customs, or physical features, characterize the particular collective and contribute to its uniqueness and to the formation of a well-defined collective with clear social identity (see David & Bar-Tal, 2009). They are an essential ingredient in constructing and maintaining the "imagined community" of the nationhood (e.g., Anderson, 1983; Hobsbawm, 1990; Kohl & Fawcett, 1996; Reicher & Hopkins, 2001; Southgate, 2005; Wertsch, 2002). Corkalo et al. (2004, pp. 157–158) talk about the "ethnization of memory," where "memory itself and interpretation of the past become ethnically exclusive, creating subjective, psychological realities and different symbolic meanings of common events in people who belong to different ethnic groups." Because of their critical role in identity politics, social representations of history are strongly linked to their state production and control, through such institutions as the public education system and official ceremonies and commemorations (LeGoff, 1992; Olick, 2003).

For example, in Northern Ireland, as in other places, collective memory has played a major role in the construction of identity as well as in feeding the conflict. Protestants emphasize historical events that have established Northern Ireland as an inseparable part of Great Britain or that represent assaults on them. Catholics, on the other hand, focus on Irish cultural and political autonomy and on injustices suffered by them and other Irish natives. This politicized representation of history is found not only in political discourse, school textbooks, and the media but also in ever-present visual symbols – gable walls, flags, arches, banners, and even graffiti (Gallagher, 1989; Jarman, 1997; McBride, 1997; Walker, 1996). With more detailed analysis, Ruane and Todd (1996, p. 87) describe the ethnic identity of Irish Catholics in Northern Ireland:

At the centre of this nationalism was a narrative construction of the history of the Irish nation. This narrative posited a golden age, a fall and a process of rebirth. Ireland was the home of an ancient and independent people with its own distinctive language and culture. In this period of freedom the Irish lived in peace and harmony, the arts and industries flourished. The unique potential of this civilization was cut short first by Viking attacks, later by the Anglo-Norman invasion which prepared the way for centuries of English rule. With foreign domination came division, decline and decay. The English re-conquest in the sixteenth and seventeenth centuries combined religious oppression, political domination and economic exploitation, and a sustained effort was made to destroy Ireland's distinctive culture and language. Following the challenge to English rule by the Irish parliament and United Irishmen at the end of the eighteenth century, the British government forced through the Act of Union by bribery and threats. With union came the destruction of Irish industry, the decline of the Irish language and a devastating famine. But the will to resist remained, growing stronger in the knowledge that only freedom would bring national recovery, the rebuilding of the economy, the halting of the decline in the native language and culture. The 1916 rebellion and the war of independence were the culmination of this long struggle.

As another example, Papadakis (2003) shows how formal political institutions stage commemorations of different historical events in order to solidify contested historical narratives that are parts of the identities of the two rival ethnic communities in Cyprus, the Greek and the Turkish communities. In both cases, the narratives of the collective memory have the beginning of a story, a plot, certain categories of actors, the spatial location where history unfolds, the moral criteria through which events are to be evaluated, and an end. However, according to Papadakis, "each narrative suggests a different story through which issues of identity and 'otherness,' self-justification and blame are negotiated in order to define the 'imagined community' of the nation, its enemies and its pertinent history" (p. 253). Thus, for instance, Greek Cypriots commemorate the 1821 Greek revolution against Turks and the achievement of Independent Cyprus in 1960, whereas the Turkish Cypriots commemorate the victory of Turks over the Greeks in 1922 and the violence perpetrated by the Greeks in the island that caused losses to Turkish Cypriots (called martyrs).

THE NATURE OF THE COLLECTIVE MEMORY OF INTRACTABLE CONFLICTS

In the case of intractable conflicts, societal beliefs of collective memory evolve to present the history of the conflict to society members (Cairns & Roe, 2003; Connerton, 1989; Halbwachs, 1992; Middleton & Edwards, 1990; Olick & Robbins, 1998; Papadakis, Peristianis, & Welz, 2006a; Pennebaker, Paez, & Rimé, 1997; Wertsch, 2002). This narrative develops over time, and it describes the outbreak of the conflict and its course, providing a coherent and meaningful picture of what has happened from the societal perspective (Devine-Wright, 2003; Papadakis, Peristianis, & Welz, 2006b; Tint, 2010). Also in this case there is a distinction between the popular and official memories that very often in the context of intractable conflict are almost identical. In most societies involved in conflict, as long as no chance for peacemaking appears, society members are usually united under the umbrella of the official narrative.

Of special uniqueness in the case of intractable conflict is the fact that the rival societies form a collective memory about the same events, because any intergroup conflict involves always at least two sides. Nevertheless, the two narratives about the collective memory differ dramatically from each other (see, e.g., Adwan, Bar-On, & Naveh, 2012, presenting Israeli Jewish and Palestinian historical narratives). They look like two completely different stories because they come to fulfill goals and needs of two rival societies, many of which are opposing (Bar-Tal & Geva, 1986; Winter, 2010).

In every intractable conflict, the involved parties construct a conflict-supporting *collective master narrative* that focuses on its entirety. It explains the causes of the conflict, describes its nature, refers to major events, presents the image of the rival, portrays its own presentation, and makes major attributions of responsibility for the eruption of the conflict, its continuation, and the violence used (see, e.g., French collective memory about the Algerian war in Prost, 1999). It provides a complete and meaningful picture of the conflict. In addition to this general master narrative about the conflict in its totality, there are also more specific narratives that concern major events in the conflict, such as wars, and mini narratives that refer to a specific incident, such as a battle and even specific events in a battle, or personalities involved in the conflict (Auerbach, 2010). Most of these narratives tell about extraordinary and exceptional events that have influence on the well-being of the society, and many of them refer to violence. Violent events are core behaviors in intractable conflicts that greatly preoccupy the society members involved (Bar-Tal, 2003; see also Chapters 1 and 3 in this book). Thus, the collective memories usually refer to wars, occupation, major battles, and atrocities performed by the rival group, as well as to the revered ingroup heroes who took an active part in the conflict, usually in the military role, and performed courageous acts or were commanders in the violent confrontations. Paez and Liu (2011) propose that society maintains those narratives that fit dominant cultural values, that are relevant for current social issues, that enhance collective self-esteem, that are based on direct and vivid experience of the society, and that are supported by institutional and informal acts of remembering.

Major events contribute to a determinative repertoire (beliefs, attitudes, and emotions) for the social identity and provide the prism through which the present is judged (see Chapter 1). Each society has major events that become symbolic events, which are remembered by the group and commemorated. Groups encode important experiences, especially extensive suffering, in their collective memory, which can maintain a sense of woundedness and past injustice through generations. These events can be part of the ongoing intractable conflict or events unrelated to the conflict that took place in a distant past. In both cases, they provide the key evaluative measure that enables assessment of other events in the group history. But they always serve the needs and goals of the present, and therefore their content and attributed meaning are in the service of the ongoing conflict. Still, they may change with time, as the needs and goals change, too. The society eternalizes these events and keeps referring to them in public discourse, cultural products, ceremonies, and commemorations. These events constitute a major symbol in the educational system, as the young generation of group members is required to learn about them over and over again and grasp their significance for the group.

Volkan (1997) proposes that societies especially remember major events that he calls "*chosen traumas*" and "*chosen glories.*" Chosen trauma is defined as shared societal mental representations of a historical event in which the group suffered a catastrophic and traumatic defeat, loss, or humiliation at the hands of its enemy. It has determinative effect on the shared societal feeling of being a victim by society members. Of importance is the fact that the group did not allow this experience to heal and is unable to properly mourn it. Therefore, the event becomes something externalized, leaving an indelible imprint upon the psyche of the group, marking its memory and even shaping the collective identity (Alexander, 2004). It is embedded into the culture, passed from generation to generation, and thus can be "reactivated" during times of threat and stress to ensure the continued support of its members (Svasek, 2005; Volkan, 2001). In contrast, chosen glory refers to a mental representation of an event that has had positive determinative effect on the shared societal feeling of success and triumph. It also contributes greatly to the definition of group identity and therefore is maintained in the culture and transmitted to new generations. Psychological literature suggests that society members tend to be more affected by the chosen trauma than by the chosen glory. First, negative events have lasting effects when they are not healed. They continue to plague the ethnic groups and nations especially in the context of continuing intractable conflict because this context, with its violence and threats, brings back an awareness of the experiences of the chosen trauma. Second, there is consistent evidence in psychology that individuals tend to remember and be affected more by negative events than by positive ones (Cacioppo & Berntson, 1994; Cacioppo, Gardner, & Berntson, 1997, 1999). Thus, chosen trauma, as a master negative event, continues to have tremendous effect not only on the fixating collective memory but also on worldviews, values, norms, and practices, especially in the realm of the intergroup relations of the society.

Examples of chosen traumas are the Serbian defeat by Turkish forces in the Battle of Kosovo in 1389, the Holocaust of Jews in War World II, or the Palestinian Nakba (in Arabic, "the disaster") in the 1948 war against the Jews. Examples of chosen glories are the victory of England over France in Agincourt in 1415, or the Soviet victory over the German Nazis in the Stalingrad battle in 1943. Each of these events is viewed with great societal significance, is well maintained, observed, and used for various purposes in many different ways to provide an important lesson for the society that holds it. For example, the Palestinian catastrophe (Nakba), which refers to the loss of the 1948 war with Jews, especially to the destruction of the villages and of Palestinian society and the dispersion of the Palestinian people, is a master tragic event in the Israeli-Palestinian conflict. As Abu-Lughod and Sa'di (2007, p. 3) wrote, "For Palestinians, the 1948 War led indeed to a 'catastrophe.' A society disintegrated, a people were dispersed, and a complex and historically changing but taken for granted communal life was ended violently. The Nakba has thus become in Palestinian memory and history, the demarcation line between two qualitatively opposing periods. After 1948, the lives of the Palestinians at the individual, community, and national level were dramatically and irreversibly changed." Nakba thus not only feeds into the Palestinian identity but also stands as a key issue that has to be resolved in the peaceful settlement of the Israeli-Palestinian conflict (Sa'di, 2002).

Chosen trauma is often used to rationalize a completely different conflict. For example, Serbs used their chosen trauma, a battle with Turks in 1389, to rationalize the conflict with Bosnia 600 years later; as Volkan (2001, p. 95) pointed out, the "fact and fantasy, past and present were intimately and violently intermingled." Serb propaganda before the ethnic cleansing evoked the Kosovo battle with the fear that the Ottomans would return and reclaim

Serbia and rape its women; as a result, this fear was transferred to modern Muslim Bosniacs, who were labeled as Turks (Gerolymatos, 2002; MacDonald, 2002; Volkan, 2001). Also, the lessons of Holocaust that took place in Europe are used often in a very particular way by Jews in Israel to rationalize their way of managing the Israeli-Arab/Palestinian conflict (see Klar, Schori, Pave, & Klar, in press). Similarly, in the framework of the Northern Ireland conflict, the iconic Battle of Boyne fought in 1690 between Protestants and Catholics turned out to be for the latter the chosen trauma, and at the same it serves for the former as the chosen glory, which still today has great symbolic value. Jabri (1996) observes that many of the today's present conflicts revolve around stories of the past, where the traditions and territorial claims of forebears are relived, and then in their names violent conflicts are legitimized.

Empirical studies about popular collective memory indicate that society members tend to remember better recent and fundamental events that are also central to their construction of national identity (Liu, Lawrence, Ward, & Abraham, 2002; Liu, Wilson, McClure, & Higgins, 1999). These findings have implications for remembering ongoing intractable conflicts because they imply that society members tend to maintain their memories about intractable conflicts that are related to social identity (Papadakis, 1998; Tint, 2010). This memory goes beyond specific events to periods that have importance and can be characterized distinctively. In general, collective memory of intractable conflict is often accessible and becomes chronically available because it is relevant to present experiences of society members. It thus appears often in the public discourse and various institutionalized channels. It paints the present, providing a prism to comprehend and evaluate current experiences and information.

Thus, any attempts to understand present dynamics between Hutu and Tutsi in the Rwandan conflict has to take in to account that the Hutu well remember that during the colonial time the Tutsi were granted privileges and that widespread discrimination was practiced against them with the help of the Tutsi-dominated administration. Also, they remember that once independence was granted, the Tutsi began ongoing violent guerrilla activities to destabilize the new state. In contrast, the Tutsi collective memory focuses on the discrimination that they suffered with the ascendance of the Hutu to power and the ongoing violence against them that culminated in the attempted genocide by the Hutu in 1994 (Prunier, 1998; Slocum-Bradley, 2008).

Contents of the Collective Memory of Conflicts

In terms of particular contents, the societal beliefs of collective memory of an intractable conflict touch on at least four important themes that will be described at length in the next chapter. First, they justify the outbreak of the conflict and the course of its development. They outline the reasons for the supreme and existential importance of the conflicting goals, stressing that failure to achieve them may threaten the very existence of the group. In addition, they disregard the goals of the other side, describing them as unjustified and unreasonable.

Second, the societal beliefs of collective memory delegitimize the opponent. They describe the adversary's inhuman and immoral behavior through the course of the conflict and present him as intransigent, irrational, extreme, and irreconcilable. Because societies involved in intractable conflicts view their own goals as justified and perceive themselves in a positive light, they attribute all responsibility for the outbreak of the conflict and its continuation to the opponent (Bar-Tal, 1990a; Bar-Tal & Hammack, 2012; Oren & Bar-Tal, 2007). That is, it is the adversary who prevents a possible peaceful settlement of the conflict. This is an important theme that enlightens the conflict in a particular way. In addition, the narrative focuses on the other side's violence, atrocities, cruelty, lack of concern for human life, and viciousness. All these societal beliefs present the opponent as an existential threat to the ingroup's survival.

Third, the societal beliefs of collective memory of intractable conflict present a positive glorifying image of the ingroup (e.g., Baumeister & Hastings, 1997). They describe events that reflect well on the society and exhibit its positive characteristics. Of special emphasis are usually events that present the humane and moral side of the society that can be contrasted with the evil nature of the rival. Another line of description usually focuses on the bravery and heroism of the society that enables it to withstand the enemy.

Fourth, the beliefs of collective memory present one's own group as the sole victim of the conflict and of the opponent. This view is formed over a long period of violence as a result of the society's sufferings and losses (Bar-Tal, 2003; Mack, 1990). Its formation is based on beliefs about the justness of the goals of one's group and on one's positive self-image, while emphasizing the wickedness of the opponent's goals and characteristics (Bar-Tal, Chernyak-Hai, Schori, & Gundar, 2009; Frank, 1967; Vollhardt, 2012). In other words, focusing on the injustice, harm, evil, and atrocities associated with the adversary, while emphasizing one's own society as being just, moral, and humane, leads society members to present themselves as victims. Beliefs about victimhood imply that the conflict was imposed by an adversary, who not only fights for unjust goals but also uses immoral means to achieve them.

While these four themes appear also in the ethos of conflict and will be further elaborated, collective memory contains two additional very specific themes: one referring to violent confrontations with the rival; and another that focuses on the fallen members of the ingroup, and especially the fighters, with an emphasis on heroes. These two themes are central components of the culture of conflict and evolve as result of the violence that is a significant part of intractable conflicts.

With regard to the events of violent confrontations, societies retain their memories independently of their outcomes. The violence of intractable conflicts by its nature traumatizes the involved societies with enduring effects and is well remembered by society members (Winter & Sivan, 1999). On a popular level, society members remember the general personal misery and the suffering. But the formal collective memory focuses more on the victories and defeats. Victories are remembered for providing exemplary events and for honoring the heroes and leaders who lead to them. They arouse feelings of pride and glory that provide the inspiration for their repetition. They play an important role in showing society members that they can cope successfully with the rival; that the conflict can be won; and that investments in the conflict are paid off. Defeats are remembered for the lessons that societies can learn. They arouse grief, sorrow, and frustration, which often lead to cries for vengeance. They show to society members that they are victims in the conflict and provide conformation to the evil nature of the rival (see, e.g., Bar-Tal, 2007a, describing the collective memory of the Israeli Jewish society; Papadakis, 1998, describing the collective memory of the Greek Cypriots; and Ramanathapillai, 2006, describing the collective memory of Tamils).

The second theme focuses on society members who fell in the conflict. Most often it refers to the fallen active participants in the violent confrontations with the rival (e.g., in battles), but it also may refer to the civilian population that is victimized in the conflict as, for example, fatalities suffered in terror attacks (Sivan, 1999). All the fallen are remembered and commemorated, as they constitute the highest price that society pays for the conflict (Winter, 1995). Their deaths are viewed as being untimely and unjustified because the fallen could have lived if not for the evildoings of the rival who malintentionally caused the harm. The performed harm is irreversible, as no compensation can bring back to life the fallen. It is thus not surprising that society members view themselves as victims in the conflict. Of special concern, though, are the fighters, who either volunteered or were sent in society's name. Usually the fighters are young men, who at the beginning of their adulthood fall for the sake of their fellow society members. Their fall is especially painful, because they are considered as being sent by the society to fulfill the most dangerous role in the conflict. Thus, their death is seen as a societal loss. Among the fallen, so-called heroes are especially remembered – those fighters who performed extraordinary acts that also often led to their death. Some of them literarily sacrificed their lives by performing heroic acts.

Mosse (1990, p. 35) points out the importance of commemorating of the fallen: "War monuments commemorating the fallen, symbolize the strength and manliness of the nation's youth and provided an example for other generations to follow." Indeed, memorials fulfill important functions of perpetuating the memory of the fallen and inspiring the remaining society members with the will to continue the conflict and fight the enemy. But society's members remember not only the fallen but also why they fell, and their unfinished mission. With time, these memories are institutionalized in rituals and ceremonies and thus are maintained and reinforced (Connerton, 1989; Halbwachs, 1992). The monuments and cemeteries, then, are constant and enduring reminders about the losses suffered in conflict, the sacrifices made by patriots and heroes, and the malevolence of the opponent. In one sense, and during certain periods, they represent concrete investments in the continuation of the conflict (Kasabova, 2008).

These contents provide the major themes of collective memory that appear in the context of intractable conflict. These themes are general, and during the escalation of the conflict they are dominant. Nevertheless, there are individual and group differences with regard to the particular contents that individuals and groups hold and emphasize.

The narratives of Tamils (supporters of the Liberation Tigers of Tamil Eelam–LTTE) and Sinhalese in Sri Lanka provide an illustration of the preceding six themes. Both societies had collective memories of intractable conflict that lasted for decades before turning into continuous war between 1983 and 2009. As a distinguished ethnic minority, the Tamils struggled to end their discrimination and to establish an independent state. Their collective memory of the conflict focuses on the violence that was inflicted on them, such as the massacres in 1956, 1976, or 1987, and later during the war in which thousands of Tamils were killed and a significant portion was displaced. The collective memory views the Sinhalese as brutal murderers and one's own group as brave victims who were able to withstand the stronger army through many years. In contrast, the Sinhalese as the majority believe that they have just goals to solidify the dominance of the Sinhalese culture, especially in view of the fact that they were discriminated against for many years during the colonial period. They viewed themselves as victims and Tamil supporters of LTTE as terrorists who carried out more than 170 suicide attacks in which many civilians lost their lives. Violence and especially the civil war constitute a major part of the collective memory of both groups with regard to the conflict, with the focus on the violence and the fallen, as at least 80,000 people were killed during the civil war (De Mel, 2007; Little, 1994).

Unfortunately, few large-scale studies about popular collective memory have been conducted in the world in general and specifically in the societies involved in intractable conflict. One of the few studies was done in Israel (Nets-Zehngut & Bar-Tal, 2009). A representative sample of Israeli Jews was asked in a survey conducted in 2008 about their general views of the Israel-Arab/Palestinian conflict and about specific events. Although responses of the majority of Jews in most of the questions corresponded to the official narrative perpetuated by the Israeli authorities, a minority view was detected that advanced a counternarrative. In late 2008, after an attempted peace process that created relative openness, information penetrated the society that served as a basis for the formation of alternative narratives regarding specific events, as well as regarding the master Zionist narrative. For example, 57.4% of the respondents thought Israel was sincere or somewhat sincere in its efforts to achieve peace throughout the conflict but Arabs were not sincere; 58.4% thought that only or mostly Palestinians were responsible for violence between Jews and Palestinians from the end of the 19th century until 1948; 59.8% believed that Jews carried on the conflict with either very high or high morality; but less than half (43.4%) thought that Arabs are primarily responsible for the outbreak of the conflict and its continuation, and 46% attributed equal responsibility to Jews and Arabs. With regard to more specific events as examples, the survey showed the following: 66% of the respondents thought that Palestinians consisted of at least a majority in Palestine before the arrival of the Jewish Zionists in the 19th century (21.8% thought that they were a minority); 49.6% of Jews thought that, according to the 1947 UN resolution on dividing the land into two states, Palestinians were supposed to get an equal or bigger part relative to their representation in total population (in reality, Palestinians who constituted 67% of the total population got 43% of the land); 47.2% of the respondents acknowledged that at least some of the Palestinian residents were expelled by Jews in the 1948 war; 58.6% thought that the Sinai War in 1956 was a defensive war, 71.6% thought the same about the 1967 war, but only 46.8% thought so about the Lebanon war in 1982. A minority of 16.2% thought that the Jewish settlements in the West Bank and Gaza were established only or mainly because of security reasons, and 44% thought that they were established equally because of security and ideological reasons; 40.8% thought that the Palestinian uprising in 1987 erupted mainly or somewhat because of hatred, and 32% thought that it erupted equally because of hatred and unwillingness to be occupied; 50.6% believe that Palestinians bear at least primary if not total responsibility for the failure of the peace process in the 1990s; and 55.6% of the respondents accepted the official version propagated by Israel that, in the Camp David summit meeting in 2000, Israeli prime minister "Barak offered Arafat a very generous peace agreement but Arafat declined mainly because he did not want peace." This study shows that collective memory of conflict focuses mostly on wars, failed peacemaking attempts, and other major processes. In all of them, the focal issue is the attribution of responsibility for the violence.

Contents Not Related to the Conflict

Collective memory of the conflict is not isolated from the society's previous experiences that preceded the conflict. On the contrary, the collective memory of the society regarding periods preceding the conflict is very often embedded in the new narrative. This is so because the intractable conflict is a major experience for society members and is of major importance both individually and collectively. The intractable conflict requires a concentration of major efforts and energies of the societies involved in order to adapt to the continuous confrontational situation and to successfully cope with its challenges. Collective memory is useful for these missions because it plays a functional role in fulfilling the needs and goals of the society. In this context, the distant past, not related to the intractable conflict, is an expropriated memory for the ongoing major struggle, which stands at the center of the societal experience. Past collective memory often provides contents that can serve well the present situation, especially when it reopens ancient and festering wounds (Wertsch, 2002). Memories can include major events, perhaps chosen traumas and chosen glories that have a special ability to illuminate the present reality and serve the present needs. Events that are frequently related to wars and conflicts have relevance to the current intractable conflict, which is always violent.

Thus, any analysis of an intractable conflict must also be familiar with the collective memory that preceded the conflict or with the collective memory of events that took place simultaneously with the conflict, but are not related to the relations with the enemy. These collective memories are often adapted, reconstructed, and reinvented to serve the needs and goals of the challenges that the intractable conflict poses. Eventually they play a major role in the psyche of the societies that live with the intractable conflict. Schwartz (1996) considers this memory as important because distant memories can be "brought back to life" through politically motivated dialogue and action. As an example, it is possible to bring back a memory similar to the way Ian Paisley, the leader of the extremist Protestants in Northern Ireland, reminded his audience about the massacre of Protestants by Catholics that was carried out in 1641 during the Irish rebellion and compared this event with the St. Bartholomew's massacre of Huguenots in France by Catholics in 1572

(Mac Iver, 1987). In the same way, Jones (2006) argues that the activation of a centuries-old conflict in the Balkan Wars was achieved by linking the situation of the late 1980s and early 1990s with the narrative of the old conflict with Turks and with vivid memories of ethnic and religious wars, including especially the atrocities committed during World War II (Denitch, 1994; MacDonald, 2002).

An example of an event of the past that is removed from the conflict context but whose collective memory has a major influence on the present is the Holocaust of the Jews, their chosen trauma. This crystallizing and major traumatic event took place in Europe during the War World II, but it has had a major effect on the psyche of Jews in Israel involved in the Israeli-Arab conflict and has influenced their decision making and the course of action. It has served as a major lesson for Israeli Jews on how to manage their conflict (e.g., the slogan "never again" is a major one; see Bar-Tal & Antebi, 1992; Klar, Schori, Pave, & Klar, in press; Segev, 2000; Weiss, 1997; Zertal, 2005). Specifically, it affected the suspicious and mistrustful view of Arabs, as well as the opinion that Jews cannot rely on support of the international community and must rely on their own strong military forces to prevent another national disaster. Years ago, a well-known Israeli writer and a publicist noted:

The Holocaust remains a basic trauma of Israeli society. It is impossible to exaggerate its effect on the process of nation-building.... There is a latent hysteria in Israeli life that stems directly from this source.... The trauma of the Holocaust leaves an indelible mark on the national psychology, the tenor and content of public life, the conduct of foreign affairs, on politics, education, literature and the arts. (Elon, 1971, pp. 198–199)

His observation a few decades later is now even more valid. The Nazi German enemy with its evil characteristics and intentions became a symbol that was transformed to the view of Arabs (Bar-Tal & Teichman, 2005).

Another example can be drawn from the Serbian view of the conflict in former Yugoslavia. The chosen trauma of the Serbs, the defeat by Turks centuries ago in Kosovo, served as a prism to look at the reality of the later 1980s (Bar-Tal & Čehajić-Clancy, in press; Bozic-Roberson, 2004; Mertus, 1999). Their leader Slobodan Milošević in his famous Gazimestan speech on June 28, 1989, expressed this view, as he justified the conflict over Kosovo:

By the force of social circumstances this great 600th anniversary of the Battle of Kosovo is taking place in a year in which Serbia, after many years, after many decades, has regained its state, national, and spiritual integrity. Therefore, it is not difficult for us to answer today the old question: how are we going to face Milos [Milos Obilic, legendary Serb hero of the Battle of Kosovo]. Through the play of history and life, it seems as if Serbia has, precisely in this year, in 1989, regained its state and its dignity and thus has celebrated an event of the distant past which has a great historical and symbolic significance for its future. (http://www.slobodan-milosevic.org/spch-kosovo1989.htm)

Another example is the case of Arabs' memory of Salah Adin's success in his battles with the Crusaders. His victory inspires hope that eventually Arabs will be able to win the conflict with Jews (who are compared to Crusaders) even if decades will pass. This story is adapted to the new circumstances of the Israeli-Arab conflict (Birnbaum, 2009).

In times of intractable conflict, societies may evoke forgotten events in order to meet the conflict's challenges. A society may transform them into major events that serve the needs of the present intractable conflict. For example, Jews did not refer through generations to the Bar Kochva rebellion against Romans during the time of Hadrian (A.D. 132–136), which ended in defeat that led to dispersal of the remaining Jews across the Roman Empire. But the contemporary Jewish leaders understood that the event can be functional for the needs that arose in the context of the intractable conflict with Arabs. It can inspire heroism and the readiness to sacrifice, as well as love for the independent homeland. Therefore, this event told in a particular narrative that meets the needs of the present conflict has been incorporated into the culture and tradition of Jews living in Israel (Harkabi, 1983; Zerubavel, 1995).

Another example illustrating how a narrative of an event can be invented and reinvented to serve the present needs of a society is the collective memory of Masada (Liebman & Don-Yehiya, 1983; Zerubavel, 1995). Israeli Jews constructed the events on Masada in the spirit of the present needs, in spite of the fact that the only account of the story was provided by Josephus Flavius, who did not describe the event complimentarily. Josephus Flavius tells about 960 Jewish rebels[1] against the Roman occupation in A.D. 73, who left Jerusalem for the desert fortress of Masada, where they fought Roman legions under siege. Seeing that Masada's fall was inevitable, its defenders committed collective suicide in order not to surrender. Ben-Yehuda (1995) investigates how this narrative has become a primary myth for the reviving nation, symbolizing heroism, patriotism, self-determination, and lonely struggle in the context of the Israeli-Arab conflict. This was done consciously and intentionally, as the political leadership realized the need for this type of myth in a society engaged

---

[1] According to Josephus Flavius, these rebels were Sicarii – a band of Jewish extremists known for their embrace of political assassination in their struggle against those Jews who promoted a more pragmatic line against Rome. They fled Jerusalem before its fall, escaping the fighting, and while encamped in the Herodian fortress, they raided the nearby Jewish settlement of Ein Gedi, killing hundreds of its inhabitants and stealing their food.

in violent struggle to achieve independence and later in the violent conflict with the Palestinians and the Arab states.

Another study by Zerubavel (1995, p. 202) shows the changes in the use of this myth in Israeli culture. In the first phase, Masada represented Jewish military valor and the "culmination of the ancient Jewish spirit that contemporary Jews should venerate and attempt to revive." The mass suicide that culminated the story was ignored or glossed over as a form of "fighting until the end." In this narrative, the Masada myth provided a potent antidote to the internalized anti-Semitic images of an exilic Jew who cowered in the face of persecution and, most notoriously, went "like a sheep to slaughter" during the Holocaust. But according to Zerubavel, following the disastrous Yom Kippur war in 1973, Masada narratives took on a different emphasis because of the new societal experiences. The renewed sense of vulnerability in Israeli society led the myth to continue the exilic past narrative about the continuity of persecution and Jewish suffering: "Whereas the activist commemorative narrative emphasized the contrast between Masada and the Holocaust, the new narrative highlights the analogy between the two events. . . . In this framework, the situation, not the act of suicide, is strongly condemned" (Zerubavel, 1995, p. 193). Although to an extent in competition with one another, the two alternative narratives contributed to a higher-order synthesis. Both narratives "contribute to Israelis' commitment to be powerful and ready to sacrifice themselves for their nation to ensure that the Masada/Holocaust situation does not recur" (p. 196). In a phrase, the two competing Masada narratives promoted the common slogan, "Masada shall not fall again!" (*Shenit Masada lo Tipol*).

Collective Memory of Conflict and Emotions

In addition to its cognitive part, the collective memory of conflict is greatly related to emotions, which are aroused in view of the accessible specific contents (see also Chapter 6). This is an important relationship because the elicited emotions are usually negative. Collective memories are often linked to feelings of anger, fear, sadness, and hatred. On the one hand, collective memory once it has achieved public awareness as a result of a specific event or reminder may arouse a particular emotion or emotions. On the other hand, the continuous availability of the collective memory in the mind and its availability in the culture can cause a crystallization of a stable emotion (sentiment) that is well reflected in the collective emotional orientation (Bar-Tal, 2001; Halperin, Sharvit, & Gross, 2011; Lake & Rothchild, 1998; Petersen, 2002). Thus, the argument suggests that the narratives of collective memory of conflict are linked mostly to negative emotions and continuously maintain such emotions. Even victories do not lead to complete pride and joy, because in spite of the particular victory the conflict still continues, and as always victories also require human losses that arouse negative emotions. Of importance for understanding the dynamics of intractable conflict are findings that the aroused emotions have implications for the dominating beliefs and attitudes as well as for lines of performed behaviors (Halperin, 2012). For example, the emotions may lead to a willingness for revenge, continuation of the conflict, and avoidance of contact with the rival.

Halperin, Bar-Tal, Nets-Zehngut, and Drori (2008) report that collective memory influences the experience of collective fear. Individuals who tend to remember the very negative experiences of the Jewish people tend also to experience fear about the future of the Jewish collective. This finding shows that remembering traumatic Jewish experiences that took place in the distant past affects collective fear related to the Israeli-Arab conflict. It confirms long-standing observations by social scientists and historians who suggest that remembrance of the distant Jewish past and especially the Holocaust experience, as actively propagated and fostered in Israel, feeds into Israeli citizens' fear of Arabs (Bar-Tal, 2007a; Segev, 2000; Zertal, 2005). Wohl and Branscombe (2004) show that reminding Israeli respondents about the Holocaust led them to reject collective guilt for Israeli wrongdoings to Palestinians and to endorse views that exonerated the Israelis (e.g., a focus on Palestinian terrorism) and to reject views that laid blame at their door (e.g., Israeli oppression of Palestinians).

Functions of Collective Memory

Collective memory in general plays essential functions in the life of every ethnic group, being a fundamental ingredient for collective identity and a pillar of culture, but in times of intractable conflict its role is greatly augmented. This key premise can explain much about the remembered and maintained contents of the collective memory of intractable conflict. Although the collective memory tells the story of the past, it is directed toward the present. It has to be functional for the present struggle in intractable conflict on the individual and collective levels. Thus, various functional parts are well remembered and rehearsed, whereas the dysfunctional parts of the collective memory disappear or are modified.

The general functions of the repertoire that evolves during intractable conflict are multiple, but only a few of these general functions of the collective memory are noted here. First, collective memory of conflict supplies the needed contents from which collective identity is constructed. Second, collective memory satisfies basic needs that are deprived during intractable conflicts, such as psychological needs of knowing, mastery, and positive identity (Burton, 1990; Lederer, 1980; Staub, 1999, 2003). It does not try to reach the truth; rather, the major criterion for its construction is to fulfill the needs and goals of the society that is engaged in harsh, serious, and violent conflict that may last many years. This is an existential requirement to produce collective memory that will help meet the challenges of the present conflict.

Collective memory provides a coherent and meaningful narrative about the past history that allows comprehensive, coherent, and meaningful understanding of the conflict for society members. Within this narrative, it explains why the conflict erupted, why it still continues, why it is violent, and why it was necessary to carry out even immoral acts against the rival. As an epistemic basis, the narrative of the collective memory provides major rationalization and justification for the present decisions and lines of actions. The story of the past explains why it is necessary to adhere to the original goals without compromise and why it is necessary to carry out violent and even immoral acts against the enemy. Also, the narrative of the past plays a role in satisfying the basic need for collective positive self-esteem. It focuses on the positive features and acts of the ingroup and differentiates between one's own group and the rival group, portraying the latter as evil and immoral. Collective memory also provides a basis for a sense of unity and solidarity by emphasizing these themes.

Third, the collective memory supplies the motivational tool for mobilization of society members to be involved in the conflict because it suggests a comprehensive rationale for the conflict. There is the need to mobilize society members who will be ready to sacrifice their lives on behalf of the group. This function is essential for continuation of the struggle, which must be perceived as existential and just. Collective memory outlines the reasons for the mobilization and portrays heroes who serve as models willing to sacrifice themselves.

Few of these functions are unique to collective memory. The collective memory, in telling the story, forms a shared past as society members acquire the common narrative and hold it. As a shared narrative, collective memory provides a sense of continuity that is crucial for the construction of a meaningful social identity. It indicates to society members that the common present is a continuation of the common past, and thus the society is a consequence of common past experiences and events that unite the destiny of the society members.

Transmission and Dissemination of Narratives of Collective Memory

The collective memory is perceived by societies involved in intractable conflict as a powerful source of capital that strengthens the society in its struggle against the enemy, provides the needed justification and legitimization for the continuation of the conflict, and satisfies many of the needs the society in intractable conflict is facing. Therefore, major efforts are made to transmit it to the new generations and then maintain it. Collective memory thus appears continuously in the public discourse and therefore is continuously accessible in the repertoire of society members.

In this mission, families and the immediate social environment, through channels of social communication and cultural mechanisms, fulfill an important role in the transmission of popular memory. In this environment, the young generation listens to the stories about national history and personal experiences of the family members as autobiographical and biographical memory. This way is especially important in societies in which the formal authorities do not allow the transmission of popular collective memory of the group and in some cases may even use active means to suppress it, as in the case of the Hutu in present Rwanda or in the case of Chechens in Chechnya. But in every society, the older family members tell about their personal involvement (autobiographical memory) in the conflict and wrap it within the framework of the national popular narrative. In this framework, society members could either be personal witness to various acts (such as terror) or be vicarious participants by being exposed to the media reports. Members of the family not only may take an active part in the conflict by participating in wars, army service, guerrilla groups, or underground activities but also may incur losses by having members killed or injured (all this may be part of the social environment beyond the family – with friends or acquaintances). All the personal stories may be accompanied by other modes of transmission, such as family commemorations, ceremonies, or holidays (Hackett & Rolston, 2009).

An example of transmission of collective memory in families is found in a study by Nahhes (2012), who interviewed three generations (grandfathers, fathers, sons) in Palestinian families living in Israel about the events of the 1948 war, which is viewed by Palestinians as a major trauma (see also Yahya, 1999). She reports that family members take a responsibility for transferring Palestinian history, as well as the history of the family, to the next generations. They carry on the mission of the collective through personal stories about the events of the past, transmission of the collective experiences with their commentaries, and the use of ceremonies and trips to related sites. For them this is a national obligation, because Israeli institutions suppress the Palestinian national narrative and do not allow formal institutions, such as public schools, to transmit it (Nasser & Nasser, 2008). But the findings also reveal that besides having one unifying transgenerational popular collective memory narrated by all three generations, each generation selected certain contents to remember, others to forget, and certain parts to be added or distorted, forming a "unique portrait" for each generation. The observed intergenerational differences are a result of the different context in which each generation lived. Each context supplied information and experiences that compelled the collective to construct adaptable worldviews.

The use of other agents for transmission of collective memory accepted by the specific group depends on the openness of the authorities. Because narratives of collective memory are the burning coals that keep the flames of the conflict alive by maintaining the goals and encouraging mobilization, in cases where one party has control over the formal institutions it tries to prevent the transmission and dissemination of the popular collective memory of the rival party and also the transmission of a counternarrative that may contradict the official collective memory. But, in general, it can be argued that the acceptance of collective memory transmitted by agents other than family depends on the level of trust attributed to them. Thus, if some society members (e.g., segments of the society in Chechnya, Rwanda, Sri Lanka, or Kashmir) do not trust the agents or do not see the transmitted contents as valid, then they do not accept the disseminated collective memory. In these cases, groups develop various ways to maintain their collective memory and rely especially on familial oral transmission.

Another informal way of disseminating the conflict's narratives is through direct experience, but this time not in the private family context but in the public one. This is done via memoirs, testimonies, and interviews of those society members who took or still take an active part in the conflict (such as soldiers or victims). The versions of these participants are usually significant because they are often viewed as being knowledgeable about the events, and their versions have a wide circulation (Hackett & Rolston, 2009; Moeller, 2001; Nets-Zehngut, 2011c).

In principle, nevertheless, in many groups transmission of collective memory can also take place via cultural products, societal institutions, and practices, ranging from books and films to museums and ceremonies (Kössler, 2007; Winter, 2010; Winter & Sivan, 1999). Cultural products and practices transmit collective memory with different contents. In some of these products, the entire narrative of the conflict may appear, often produced by the formal authorities of the collective. In other cultural products, only part of the conflict may be presented, with a focus on specific heroic figures, particular events, or with use of the conflict as a background to a specific story.

On the formal level, the most important agent for transmitting the narrative of collective memory is school. In this case, the presented narrative consists of the official collective memory because schools almost always are part of the governmental system and school textbooks are written in line with the governmental supervision or guidance. Through the discipline of history and other subject matters, schools impart the narrative of the official collective memory. This is a golden opportunity to present the national story in line with the national doctrine, providing an institutionalized basis for creating shared perception of the past, a united view, and a crystallization of national identity. For example, the Ministry of Education in Israel published in 1956 a new curriculum of history for the elementary schools with the objective of helping "the nation to stand against all its enemies and maintain its independence" (Porat, 2001, p. 39). It is not a rare case that the system of higher education, including its research, serves the purpose of transmitting and disseminating collective memory. These processes take place definitely in the authoritarian regimes but also in democratic states. For example, in a study of the role of the Israeli Jewish research community (both academic and independent scholars) in carrying out and transmitting the Zionist historical memory regarding the exodus of Palestinians during the 1948 war, Nets-Zehngut (2011a) reports that until 1976 the Israeli Jewish academics almost exclusively presented the Zionist narrative, which blamed Palestinians for the exodus. Only from 1977 did the Zionist narrative begin to change significantly with the adoption by 1988 almost exclusively of a narrative that admitted incidents of expulsions of Palestinians by Jewish military forces in the 1948 war.

Studies in Cyprus found that the schoolbooks played an important role in transmitting the collective memory of the Greek and Turkish communities. As such, one of the main characteristics of Greek Cypriot textbooks was the construction of the concept of the continuity of Hellenism in Cyprus since the time of the ancient Greeks, to the virtual exclusion of all other political and cultural links with other eastern Mediterranean countries. Additionally the term "Cypriots" was reserved exclusively for Greek Cypriots, creating the impression that all Cypriots ethnically are Greeks, ignoring the existence of the Turkish Cypriot community. This latter community was described negatively in relation to the intervention by the Turkish army in 1974, which led to the division of Cyprus. In general, this pattern appeared also in the Turkish Cypriot national narrative presented in the school textbooks. These books also disregarded the existence of the other group by erasing Greek identity in the island. Sentences like "Cyprus is Turkish," "Greeks never ruled Cyprus,"

"Greeks living in Cyprus are not Greeks," and "Turkish Cypriots are the ones who suffered from Greek and Greek Cypriot barbarism" were common. With this outlook, the books presented as modern history that after the Ottoman rule was replaced by British control, the Greek Cypriots started a campaign for the unification of the island with Greece, and when the Republic of Cyprus was established in 1960, the Greeks prepared a plan of genocide to massacre all the Turks, in order to realize Enosis (unity with Greece). The books explicitly delegitimized Greek Cypriots, presenting them as barbaric and cruel. To support this stereotyping, they graphically described atrocities committed against the Turkish community (Kızılyurek, 1999; Papadakis, 2008).

Other formal institutions that disseminate narratives of collective memory are national information centers that may hold various titles (e.g., for Turkey with regard to the World War I Armenian genocide, see Dixon, 2010; for Israel, see Nets-Zehngut, 2008, in press; or for Russia, in the context of its war with Chechnya, see Koltsova, 2000). Also, in many of the states that are involved in intractable conflict, the military actively forms and disseminates to members of its own society and also to the international community narratives of the collective memory (e.g., in Israel, see Nets-Zehngut, 2011a; and in Russia, see Caryl, 2000).

In addition to the noted channels, society members are continuously reminded about the themes of collective memory via yearly routines in which the society commemorates various people and events that are the core of the collective memory (Frijda, 1997). Societies tend to present specific wars, battles, events, and personalities, especially heroes and leaders who played a significant role in the intractable conflict. Thus, throughout the year, various themes of the collective memory appear on the public agenda (Wertsch, 2002). Also, mass media, which transmit speeches of leaders and report about commemorations of events and people, publicize stories related to the conflict, and sometimes conduct investigations and research about various events of the conflict, remind society members continuously about the themes of collective memory (Gillis, 1994; Hutt, 2006; Wolfsfeld, Frosh, & Awabdy, 2008). Mass media are powerful agents because they can reach so many society members and also in many cases are viewed as trusted sources of information. Mertus (1999) shows how a well-orchestrated campaign in Serbia based on official collective memory was used to start a violent confrontation with Albanians in Kosovo. The campaign, drawing on various events throughout the history of Serbs, was carried out by mass media, leaders, and social-political institutions.

Collective memory is also transmitted via the physical environment by naming streets and settlements with names of events and individual role models. In addition, monuments and cemeteries often serve as formal socialization places where students are brought and taught, and later as adults they may come themselves with their families (Schramm, 2011). A project initiated by the Israeli Ministry of Education that instructs high schools to adopt cemeteries of fallen soldiers to take care of them is an example of this type of socialization.

Selectivity of the Collective Memory

Collective memory in general is selective, biased, and distortive, but in times of intractable conflict these features are greatly magnified. During intractable conflict, because society experiences many basic needs, their satisfaction is of existential importance. This challenge causes society to be more selective than ever, so it chooses to remember certain contents but forget others, and to add certain parts but distort others. The selection depends on what function the particular event fulfills, and what its lessons and implications are. It is not surprising that a society makes special effort to maintain functional collective memory, trying to prevent the appearance and dissemination of counternarratives that may undermine it. Thus, a society may select victories as well as defeats, prosperous times as well sufferings, successes as well as failures, brave acts as well as cowardly ones, and even immoral as well as moral acts, as long as they satisfy various psychological needs (see, e.g., Bar-Tal, 1990b, describing how Israeli Jews and Palestinians present their history). In short, the narratives of the collective memory relating to an intractable conflict are functional and provide a black-and-white picture, which enables parsimonious, fast, unequivocal, and simple understanding of the "history" of the conflict. These narratives reflect mobilization of the collective memory for the conflict.

Societies involved in intractable conflicts maintain narratives about conflict justification, delegitimization of the rival, self-collective glorification, and self-collective perception as the victim. But they refrain from including content that does not serve the needs and goals of the present or has negative implications for the society and its relation with the international community (e.g., Baumeister & Hastings, 1997; Fishman & Marvin, 2003; Pratto & Glasford, 2008). Revelations about immoral acts may undermine the belief in the justness of the conflict, damage the self-collective perception and self-presentation as being the victim, hurt the motivation to take an active part in the struggle, and diminish support from the international community, while at the time they may increase the empathy and support for the rival group.

Thus, atrocities, mass killings of civilians, killings of war prisoners, torture, ethnic cleansing, or genocide are omitted from the collective memory. For the sake of their image, societies experience collective amnesia about these types of events (Branscombe and Doosje, 2004; Halperin, Bar-Tal, Sharvit, Rosler, & Raviv, 2010; Leidner, Castono, Zaiser, & Giner-Sorolla, 2010; Roccas, Klar, Liviatan, 2006; Trouillot, 1995). They try to deny wrongdoing, censor information, or sanction those who bring such information to light. When these stories do enter the collective memory, societies attempt to rationalize them, justify them, and minimize their effects. They are almost always presented as being exceptional and due to external circumstances. In contrast, in order to motivate their own society and to mobilize support and empathy from the other groups, societies are more than ready to remember the immoral acts of the rival toward members of their own group and eager to pass the reports on to the international community, and even to greatly exaggerate them. These acts are presented as random, intentional, and reflecting stable dispositions. This tendency is part of the competition between the rival parties to darken and delegitimize the rival and present one's own side as a moral and law-abiding society (see Bar-Tal, Oren, & Nets-Zehngut, 2012; Tint, 2011).

Baumeister and Hastings (1997) suggest a number of mechanisms and strategies that groups may use to maintain a positive view of themselves. *Selective omissions* refer to deleting and erasing certain facts. *Fabrication* refers to inventing a false memory. *Exaggeration and embellishment* refer to taking a particular minor event and extending considerably its scope, importance, and implications to glorify the deeds of one's own group. *Manipulating associations* means either linking the event to particular desirable events or consequences or, on the contrary, disconnecting the remembered facts from particular events or implications in order to save face for the group. *Blaming the enemy* refers to focusing on the actual or presumptive wrongdoing of the rival in order present one's own misdeed as a reaction to the acts of the rival. *Blaming the context* refers to the attempt to minimize one's own responsibility for the wrongdoing by attributing it to the circumstances. *Contextual framing* refers to illuminating the whole event in a particular light that has positive bearings on the group or at least avoids negative implications. To this list can be added additional mechanisms and strategies, such as minimizing the effect of the group's own wrongdoing by downplaying its scope and consequences; blaming marginal individuals and outcasts from the ingroup for the immoral behavior; denial, which means rejection of the information about one's own wrongdoing; projection, which means attributing the wrongdoing to the rival; and delegitimization, which suggests that the rival deserves the maltreatment because of innate evil dispositions. The list is inexhaustible, and additional mechanisms and strategies can be added.

For example, the Russian government blocks information about immoral acts in Chechnya, including atrocities committed by the Russian army, at the same time that it magnifies information about Chechens terrorism (Caryl, 2000; Harding, 2011; Koltsova, 2000). A study by Nets-Zehngut (2008, in press) demonstrates the functioning of the Israeli National Information Center, the main Israeli institution for disseminating information to the Israeli public. The center refrained from providing information about the past that may present the State of Israel in a negative light and damage its reputation. As one of the directors said about refusal to publish a book about the 1948 war that contradicted the propagated Zionist narrative:

Because of all kinds of interpretations... we had a feeling that we, as far as I remember, that we as a governmental organ can not print what he wrote... you can not, because you are a civil servant, you, you can not... we did not want to go over mines... in general I would say that the policy then was very tough and not so open as today. (Nets-Zehngut, 2008, p. 664)

In a study of historical memories of the Armenian genocide at the beginning of the 20th century, Bilali (2010) reports that Turkish participants viewed Turkish perpetration as a response to provocation by Armenians (i.e., the victims) and third parties (e.g., the European powers or American missionaries). They even delegitimized the victim to explain the immoral act in order to "psychologically escape" from the consequences of the act (Castano & Giner-Sorolla, 2006).

Of special interest is an observation that societies use many of these mechanisms long after the conflict ends. Many of the groups continue to deny wrongdoing and block information about it for decades. This human characteristic can be found at every level of human behavior. In addition, societies defend consistently the positive collective self-view, assuming that exposure to information that has negative implications hurts collective self-worth, collective identity, and the society's standing in the international community (Lundy & McGovern, 2001; Metsola, 2010).

Liu and Atsumi (2008) describe the difficulties that Japan has been facing in dealing with wrongdoing during the years of war and violent conflict with China. It has tried to hide the atrocities performed, including the 1937–1938 Nanking massacre of some 300,000 Chinese by the Japanese soldiers, the mass killings of civilians and prisoners of war, destruction, and the rape and forced prostitution of Chinese and other Asian nations' women. For example, the Japanese Ministry of Education, controlling school textbook certification, omitted contents that describe the immoral acts performed by Japanese during the war years, even long after the conflict ended. A similar line has been taken by Turkey, which after almost a century continues to deny the Armenian genocide carried out by the Ottoman Empire during War World I (Dixon, 2010a). Also, until the late 1990s, French media, cultural channels, and studies did not expose the widely used tortures and executions of the Algerians during the 1954–1962 France-Algeria War (Branche & House, 2010; Macmaster, 2002).

Contradiction and Struggle between the Collective Memories of the Rivals

Each narrative, by definition, is unique, distinctive, and exclusive (Baumeister & Gastings, 1997; Irwin-Zarecka, 1994). The special case of narratives of collective memory of conflicts is that at least two societies have a collective memory regarding the same history, and it follows that opposing groups in a conflict will often entertain contradictory and selective historical collective memories. Contradiction and clash between narratives are likely (Bar-Tal & Geva, 1986).

The negation and contradiction are expressed in various ways. Each side blames the other for the outbreak of the conflict and its continuation. Each side stresses the importance of its own goals and their existential and moral foundations and at the same time disregards and delegitimizes the goals of the rival. Those are important points to justify eruption of the conflict and its continuation as well as present the evil nature and the narrow-mindedness of the rival. Each side describes the violence of the other side, blames the other for the moral misdeeds, and stresses various negative characteristics in order to delegitimize it. They are almost always attributed to genetic makeup and disposition, indicating stability and intentionality. Also, each side focuses on the irrationality and intransigence of the other side to continue the conflict, presenting itself as wanting peace, being rational, and compromising. These discrepancies enhance the magnitude of the conflict and complicate the possibilities of resolving it. Each narrative entrenches the society in its own rightness regarding the causes of the conflict and adherence to the original goals. The delegitimization of the other side and the sense of being the victim serve as major obstacles to the evolution of trust, which is a necessary condition for development of a readiness to compromise and begin a peace process (see, e.g., Rotberg, 2006, for an analysis of the Israeli and Palestinian narratives of their conflict). This contradiction characterizes every intractable conflict.

To illustrate the discrepancy between the narratives of two rival societies, consider what Israeli Jews and Palestinians present as the historical background of their conflict (see also, e.g., Bar-On, 2006, and Pingel, 2003, who describe the disputes over the presented narratives of Israelis and Palestinians in their school textbooks). The Israeli version is taken from the booklet *History from 1880* (1973) distributed by the Israeli Information Center (an institution of the Israeli government that propagated the official collective memory), which consists of material originally published in the *Encyclopedia Judaica*:

The merging of two trends – the rationally intellectual and emotionally traditional – gave birth not only to Zionism as an organized political effort, but also to the beginning of the pioneering movement of the late 19th century, which laid the foundations, on the soil of Erez Israel, for the economic, social and cultural rebirth of the Jewish nation. The land itself seemed eminently suitable for the purpose: a marginal province of the weak Ottoman Empire, sparsely inhabited by a population consisting of various religious groups and seemingly lacking any national consciousness or ambitions of it sown; a motherland waiting to be redeemed from centuries of neglect and decay by its legitimate sons. (pp. 1–2)

In contrast, Sami Hadawi (1968) writes the following in his book *Palestine Occupied*, which was published by the Arab Information Center:

The basic issue in the Palestine Problem is the uprooting and dispossession in 1948 of an entire nation to make room for the "ingathering" in Palestine of Jews from all parts of the world. This build-up of the Jewish population in Palestine was not inspired by humanitarian considerations for the oppressed and persecuted Jews of Europe as was made to believe. It was achieved mainly in order to fulfill the political aspirations of a major ideological movement called Zionism. (p. 8)

Similarly, in a study examining historical memories of conflict between Tutsis and Hutus in Burundi, when asked about the history of the violent conflict in Burundi, each group blamed the outgroup for provoking the violence and described the ingroup's violent actions as self-defense (Bilali, 2010).

Collective memories of the rivals in conflict collide and serve as one of the battlegrounds between the sides. The two sides in conflict struggle to impose their collective memory regarding the account of the whole conflict as well as specific events (see Bar-Tal, Oren, & Nets-Zehngut, 2012). This battle is carried on three fronts. First, each society involved in intractable conflict attempts to maintain a unitary view of the collective memory among its members. Thus, it imparts the narrative to society members and persuades them in its exclusive validity. A change in the collective memory that questions the national narrative is viewed as weakening the ability to withstand the enemy, and therefore the societies not only propagate the national narrative but also use their formal and informal mechanisms to suppress attempts to introduce alternative narratives that may undermine presented collective memory (Paez & Liu, 2011; Tint, 2010).

In addition, each society makes an effort to convince the international community that its narrative is exclusively truthful and validated. This struggle, which is conducted within the psychological domain, is as intensive as some of the violent confrontations. The outcome of this struggle may even determine the course of the conflict, because the international community usually tries to help morally and materially the side that is viewed as the victim in the conflict. Each party in conflict makes an effort to persuade the international community about being just, as well as being unjustly and immorally harmed in the conflict, while the other party not only carries on the unjust conflict but also uses immoral methods and violates principles of conducting warfare (Barkan, 2000; Langenbacher, 2010; Mor, 2007). Finally, a society involved in intractable conflict even tries to persuade the rival group in the falsehood and untruthfulness of its account of what happened in the conflict. This is part of the psychological confrontation between the groups (Jowett & O'Donnell, 2006; Schleifer, 2009).

In the dissemination of the collective memory of any conflict as well as in the struggle on all the three levels, societies that have a state have an advantage over societies that need to establish their institutions. This advantage expresses the asymmetry in conflicts. Turkish, Russian, Singhalese, or Jewish societies, for example, have organs, institutions, and organizations with well-trained staff to plan, form, transmit, control, and disseminate their official narrative. This line of action pertains to the master-conflict-supporting narrative and various specific narratives that appear continuously during the conflict.

Change of Collective Memory

Collective memory rarely changes dramatically during the conflict because it has to continue serving the needs and goals of the conflict. In general, society members have great difficulty changing collective memory (see, e.g., Hein & Selden, 2000), but in times of intractable conflict this difficulty is intensified considerably. As long as both sides engage in violent confrontations without any possibility of resolution, collective memory plays a crucial role in reminding the society members about various themes that are functional for adapting to the conditions of conflict and withstanding the enemy.

Still, collective memory is not static, even during the conflict. Some changes do not touch the hegemonic themes of the collective memory of conflict but lead to new particular contents. Within this framework, there may be needs that require new emphases concerning particular contents, lessons, and implications. Also, changes within the society may raise new contents of collective memory, minimizing or maximizing some and suppressing others. Thus, for example, in Israel the rise to power of Menachem Begin in 1977, the leader of Etzel (an underground organization that took an active part in the struggle against the British and Arabs in the prestate period), changed the presentation of the collective memory by the official organs. The new account gave more prominence and a greater share to nationalistic undergrounds (Etzel and Lehi) in the national narrative about the struggle against the British and the Palestinians before the establishment of the State of Israel (Lebel, 2007). Nevertheless, there is a possibility also of major changes in the themes of collective memory of conflict even before the resolution of the conflict.

Nets-Zehngut and Bar-Tal (2012) propose a model that describes and explains the change of collective memory. According to the suggested model, the change goes through six stages, from a search for new primary information that supports an alternative narrative to the full acceptance of this narrative. Between these stages there is disclosure of the found new primary information and alternative narratives to the public sphere; dissemination of the new information and alternative narrative through various channels of communication, and especially via mass media and cultural products; a contest between the supporters of the dominant narrative and those of the alternative one, regarding which narrative is truthful; and a process of change that is determined by the characteristics of the conflict (e.g., the level of intractability, whether the rival's collective memory of the conflict also underwent a transformation), intrasocietal characteristics (e.g., societal homogeneity, political tolerance), memory (e.g., its importance, centrality), characteristics of the core institutions of the transformation process (e.g., their climate, their products), and the international context (e.g., attitudes of the international community toward critical historiography, relativism, postmodernism, and reconciliation). In general, the process of transformation of memory is thorny, because such a change requires often "looking into a mirror," which can lead to the recognition of negative deeds in a way that impinges upon self-image. Therefore, it is prolonged, gradual, and nonlinear and can stop at any phase.

As an example of the transformation of collective memory, Nets-Zehngut and Bar-Tal report a study about changes that took place in Israel regarding creation of the Palestinian refugee problem in the 1948 war (Nets-Zehngut & Bar-Tal, 2012; and see also Nets-Zehngut, 2012b). This is one of the major historical issues in the Israeli-Palestinian conflict, and it concerns mainly the question whether the Palestinian refugees left voluntarily for various reasons (the Zionist narrative), or whether some left voluntarily, while others were expelled by the Jewish and later the Israeli security forces (the critical narrative). The study showed that during the first decades after the 1948 war the Zionist narrative was hegemonic and dominated all the channels of communication and institutions, informal and formal. But beginning in the 1970s, a change was gradually introduced by individuals in the informal institutions, mostly of the research community and mass media, as well as in cultural products. But the formal institutions (i.e., the Israeli army [IDF], the national Information Center, and the Ministry of Education) have had great difficulty accepting this change that had negative implications for the State of Israel and its Jewish society, because they are the gatekeepers of the official presentation. Only a few history textbooks that were approved by the Ministry of Education since 2000 have adjusted their content to the well-solidified evidence provided by the Israeli research community and Jewish 1948 war veterans about the occurrence of Palestinian expulsion by Jews. This modification happened more than two decades after informal institutions started significantly adopting the critical narrative.

However, the publication of the new textbooks evoked heated debates in the Israeli Jewish society, including in the Israeli parliament, the Knesset. In November 2000 the Education Committee of the Knesset decided to disqualify use of one of the history textbooks – an act that shows that part of the society and its representatives have difficulty accepting changes in school textbooks that question the Zionist narrative. This decision may have reflected a regressive trend in the Israeli society that began with the reescalation of the Israeli-Palestinian conflict – the outbreak of the second Palestinian uprising (Intifada) in fall of 2000 (Nave & Yogev, 2002).

Another study, by Podeh (2002), examines history school textbooks used in the Israeli Jewish educational system. He analyzes them on various focal topics related to the Israeli-Palestinian conflict and found that these textbooks were transformed over time. While until 1970s they presented the Zionist one-sided narrative, later their contents began to change. They began to acknowledge the existence of Palestinian nationalism and to use less pejorative terminology in their description of Arabs and Palestinians. In late 1990s, the textbooks, written in line with the new curriculum in history and civics, went through another change. Some of these books used newly released archival material and were based on new and critical historical research that shed a more balanced light on the Arab-Jewish conflict. Arabs and Palestinians were presented "not only as mere spectators or as aggressors but also as victims of the conflict. For the first time, there appeared to be a genuine attempt to formulate a narrative that not only glorifies Zionist history but also touches on certain shadows in this history. Additionally, in some cases there is a discussion of controversial questions, such as the Palestinian refugee problem, Israel's presence in Lebanon, the desirability of establishing a Palestinian State, and so on" (Podeh, 2002, pp. 149–150). Many of these textbooks referred to the Palestinian nation, recognized the role of Palestinian nationalism in the development of the conflict, described in a more balanced way the violent acts of Palestinians against Jews, and provided a more balanced description of the wars. In general, they provided a new perspective to the conflict and presented in a more complex, multidimensional, and differentiated way Arabs and particularly Palestinians.

The described changes that began to take place in the 1970s reflected changes in the state of the conflict as well as changes in the Israeli Jewish society and in the international community. In 1979 Israel signed a peace treaty with Egypt, the most powerful enemy, after the 1977 historical visit of the Egyptian president Anwar Sadat in Jerusalem. Also, the Israeli Jewish society went through a process of democratization, decentralization, privatization, and diversification, which allowed more openness, pluralism, and self-criticism (Bar-Tal & Oren, 2000). These processes intensified as a result of globalization and emergence of a new zeitgeist in the world regarding reconciliation and transitional justice. All these developments affected the research community, various informal institutions, and the educational system in Israel.

Another example of collective memory transformation is the conflict in Cyprus. Papadakis (2008) reports on significant changes of the Turkish Cypriot history textbooks in 2003 following the ascendance to power of a new government in Turkish Cyprus, which had a more accommodating view toward resolution of the Cyprus conflict. The changes were reflected first in new objectives that advocated showing "the place of Cyprus in world history... creating thinking, questioning, responsible and active citizens... getting students interested in researching influences between different cultures and communities... viewing history from different sources, perspectives and facts... creating peace-loving citizens" (Papadakis, 2008, p. 17). According to the study, the new textbooks referred differently to the concepts of nation, nationalism, and identity. For example, they began to use terms such as "our island" or "our country" for Cyprus instead of the term "motherland," which was used for Turkey. In addition, they began to use the more generic identities of "Cypriots" and "people," which can include both Greek Cypriots and Turkish Cypriots. They also began to describe Greek Cypriots and Turkish Cypriots as subgroups that have many similarities but were divided by forces of nationalism and the British "divide and rule" policies.

SUMMARY

Groups need to have a past, as it is an important element in their collective identity, showing that there is continuity in their existence and that they have a firm foundation for their uniqueness and solidarity. But in times of intractable conflict, collective memory receives a special place and focus because the challenges that stand before the involved societies are enormous. They need continuous mobilization of society members for support and participation in conflict in various capacities. Society members have to be ready to die for their group; if they stop this readiness, conflicts will have to be terminated. Also, they need resilience in coping with various hardships, stresses, and other negative experiences that are an integral part of intractable conflict in which violence plays a major role. In this context, the involved society members have to believe that the conflict is just and the sacrifices are worthwhile. Collective memory provides crucial testimony to these needed convictions. It depicts the reasons for the conflict's eruption, describes the events that took place, and explains why it did not end. This is done always in a selective, biased, distortive, and simplistic way with the goal of putting all the blame on the rival and portraying the other side with the most negative characteristics, which stand in clear contrast to the glorification and moralization of the ingroup.

Of course, societies involved in intractable conflicts do not have equal responsibilities for its eruption or for the level of violence. Intractable conflicts can erupt because of continuous immoral practices by one group in conflict. These groups need more selection, biases, and distortions in order to cover the injustice. They need to find justifications and explanations that will rationalize the behaviors that led to the eruption of the conflict. Also, while all the groups during the conflict use immoral acts, some of them distinctively perform more atrocities on a wider scale. These groups also need justifications and explanations for the inhuman treatment of the enemy. In all these cases, collective memory serves these needs.

Thus, in many cases collective memory functions as an obstacle and barrier to a peace process because it crystallizes a self-righteous and ethnocentric narrative that not only hides one's own misdeeds and deficiencies but also blocks information about the humaneness of the rival group and especially about its just needs and goals. Blind adherence to a collective memory of conflict assures its continuation, and collective memory of intractable conflict becomes a compass for the future. As such, society is unable to pursue the opportunities of peace. But collective memory does not stand alone in its functioning. It is well integrated with and supported by an ethos of conflict and emotional collective orientations that are part of ongoing interactions. Together they are part of the socio-psychological infrastructure that serves as a pillar of the culture of conflict.

5

Ethos of Conflict

In addition to the narrative of the collective memory of conflict, societies involved in intractable conflicts evolve another part of the socio-psychological infrastructure, a narrative called an ethos of conflict.

NATURE OF ETHOS

I view ethos as the configuration of shared central societal beliefs that provide a dominant orientation to a society; these beliefs illuminate the present state of affairs and conditions and set goals for the future (Bar-Tal, 2000a). Ethos binds the members of society together, along with the goals and aspirations that impel them toward the future (see, e.g., McClosky & Zaller, 1984), and provides the key characteristics of a society in a holistic perspective. This perspective allows an understanding that cannot be achieved when the societal beliefs are described separately and provides a comprehensive picture.

In other words, ethos provides the epistemic basis for the hegemonic social consciousness of the society and for the future direction it takes. It gives meaning and predictability to societal life and provides a coherent view of societal institutions – their structure, history, visions, concerns, and courses of action. Ethos indicates to society members that their behavior is not based on random beliefs but represents a coherent and systematic pattern of knowledge. This narrative implies that the decisions of society's leaders, the behavior of the members of society, and the structure and functioning of the society are all based on coherent and comprehensive beliefs that justify and motivate members of society to act in a coordinated manner within an accepted system. Ethos provides legitimacy to the societal order and fosters integration among society members and thus serves as a crucial mechanism for organizing a collective of individuals as a society.

Societal beliefs constitute an ethos if the following criteria are met. First, the beliefs are well known to almost all society members, even if all do not agree with them. In most cases, the hegemonic ethos provides an orientation to most society members, who acquire societal beliefs of ethos at an early age as the epistemic foundation that gives meaning to society's goals and direction. Second, they appear often in public debates as arguments of justification and explanation and often in mass media and other channels of communication. Third, they serve as an influencing basis for policies and decisions taken by the leaders of the society and various institutions. Fourth, they appear as major themes in various cultural products such as literature, films, and theatrical plays. Fifth, they constitute major themes in contents transmitted to the younger generation. Sixth, they appear in various societal expressions, including ceremonies and rituals. Eventually, societal beliefs of ethos constitute the building blocks of the contents that characterize a culture.

A well-founded ethos evolves over a long time on the basis of society's experiences as a whole and its accumulated culture. Under conditions and experiences of a prolonged intractable conflict, societies develop a particular ethos that provides a clear picture of the conflict – its goals, conditions, and requirements – and images of their own group and of the rival (Bar-Tal, 2000a, 2007b). The narrative of this ethos reflects the society members' accumulated and continuous experiences in conflict. Themes can appear in times of conflict but also in times of peace; in intractable conflict, their contents adapt to new conditions. The narrative of the ethos of conflict is supported by the narrative of collective memory, and in both narratives similar themes appear. During intractable conflict, societies can also hold other ethoses that are a result of major historical experiences or adherence to religious dogma, as well as the result of political, economic, and cultural conditions.

THEMES OF THE ETHOS OF CONFLICT

I have proposed that the challenges of the intractable conflict lead to the development of eight themes of societal beliefs in the ethos of conflict (Bar-Tal, 1998a, 2000a, 2007b):[1] the justness of one's own goals, opponent delegitimization, self-victimhood, positive self-image, security, patriotism, unity,

---

[1] The detection of the eight themes is based on extensive systematic studies in the Israeli Jewish society involved in intractable conflict (see Bar-Tal, 2007a; Oren, 2009). In addition, these themes were found to be dominant in other societies engaged in intractable conflict, including those of the Serbs, Kosovars, Albanians, Croats, and Bosnians (MacDonald, 2002), Hutus in Rwanda (Slocum-Bradley, 2008), and Greek and Turkish Cypriots (Hadjipavlou, 2007; Papadakis, 1998, 2008).

and peace. When the ethos of conflict evolves, these themes gain master status in the society's culture and can be viewed as Gamson's (1988, p. 220) cultural themes that refer to "frames and related symbols that transcend specific issues and suggest larger world views."

The first three themes – the justness of one's own goals, opponent delegitimization, and self-victimhood – develop in times of intractable conflict and are the key themes that feed and maintain it. Without their change, it is difficult to reach conflict resolution. The other five societal beliefs of the ethos of conflict are not unique to the situation of conflict, as they are necessary ingredients for the existence of every ethnic group or nations. But in times of intractable conflict, contents and directions of beliefs about of positive self-image, patriotism, unity, security, and peace are adapted to the needs and requirements of the conflict context. In any event, all the themes are crucial in the functioning, mobilization, and struggle of the group during intractable conflict.

Societal Beliefs about the Justness of One's Own Goals

Every society holds beliefs that relate to the justness of its own goals; the assumption is that human beings will not be prepared to carry out activities, particularly collective ones, if they believe that these are unjustified and unsuitable. Without such societal motivation, mobilization would be impossible.

Societies in intractable conflict always pose goals that they intend to achieve, and beliefs about the justness of one's own group's goals outline, explain, and justify these goals. As Chapter 2 indicated, adoption of these beliefs signals the beginning of the conflict. They provide a meaningful and coherent picture as to why the conflict erupted and why it is important to continue the conflict and make sacrifices for its goals. Often, the goals for launching the conflict are presented as being of supreme and existential importance and stress that failure to achieve them may threaten the existence of the group. The focal emphasis of the societal beliefs about the justness of goals is elaboration about their justification, or their epistemic basis, as presented in Chapter 2. This part needs to be persuasive because it plays a major role in mobilization of society members to take active part in the conflict.

According to a theory of system justification (Jost & Banaji, 1994; Jost, Banaji, & Nosek, 2004), society members cannot accept conflict goals as being random and unjustified. They need justification of the goals as they seek their coherent meaning, legitimacy, and explanation, sometimes even "at the expense of personal and group interest" (Jost & Banaji, 1994, p. 2). This need reflects the desire to develop and maintain favorable images of one's own group and to defend and justify its actions (Tajfel, 1981; Tajfel & Turner, 1986).

The reasons provided as justifications for the goals can be of different categories, drawn from historical, economic, national, theological, cultural, or economic spheres, and they are frequently embodied in national or ethnic ideology, which plays a vital role in the society's life. Thus, the epistemic base of reasons and justifications provides a crucial foundation for continued successful coping with the rival. Conversely, negation of goals or a lack of faith in their justice, however slight, can lead to a weakened resolve with regard to the willingness to mobilize, struggle, and sacrifice. Such trends can have destructive consequences for the society, especially if the adversary is not open to a peaceful resolution of the intractable conflict and continues violent struggle.

Some of the goals are viewed as reflecting sacred values, defined by Tetlock (2003, p. 320) as "those values that a moral community treats as possessing transcendental significance that precludes comparisons, tradeoffs, or indeed any mingling with secular values." Goals that are based on sacred values are viewed as "moral mandates" (Skitka, 2002), and accordingly it is impossible to use rational tools in measuring their utility or substitution. Therefore, these goals are regarded as protected, and compromising them implies moral bankruptcy and violation of the fundamental rules of ethics (Landman, 2010). Society members thus adhere to these goals stubbornly and try to achieve them even with violence (Ginges & Atran, 2011). Obviously goals presented as sacred need special justification. Often their status is based on religious or national-historic beliefs, or both, that provide contents to collective identity (David & Bar-Tal, 2009). They frequently concern holy sites, "homeland" territories, or even a resource such as water. But goals reflecting supreme aspirations may also receive "sacred" status, as, for example, self-determination, equality, freedom, or justice (Skitka, 2002). Indeed, a study by Ginges, Atran, Medin, and Shikaki (2007) shows that neither Israeli Jewish settlers nor Palestinian students were willing to compromise over issues that they considered sacred: for Jewish settlers, ceding the occupied territory, which they considered as their ancient homeland; and for Palestinians, compromising over the sovereignty of Jerusalem, because of its sacred status. Jerusalem is one of the three most important religious cities to Sunni Muslims, primarily because of Muhammad's Night of Ascension, in which he is believed to have ascended to Heaven from the Temple Mount to meet previous prophets of Islam. Today, Temple Mount is the location of two Islamic landmarks intended to commemorate the event: Al-Aqsa and the Dome of the Rock mosques. In viewing Jerusalem as sacred, Palestinians presented uncompromising positions about the future of Jerusalem during the Camp David summit in 2000. Eventually, the issue of Jerusalem, the future of the city (and the Temple Mount in particular), has been considered as the primary reason for the failure of the summit; for both sides, Jerusalem in general and the Temple Mount specifically are related to the realm of sacred values (Druker, 2002; Klein, 2001; Sher, 2001).

In general, societal beliefs about the justness of conflict serve as a major force in a group's mobilization and struggle as well as in its readiness to use violence (Ginges & Atran, 2011). Thus, they have to be held confidently by society members, and because they come to justify the major sacrifices that are required, including that of human life, their significance cannot be exaggerated. They also allow positive self-perception because they provide a justifying basis for adherence to the goals. They indicate to society members that their goals are in line with the group's moral codes. These beliefs can then be used in presenting the group to the international community, an important function in the contemporary world. Decades ago and definitely centuries ago, international codes were completely different and permitted goals and their justification that would be unacceptable today.

Of course, not every society involved in intractable conflict even today can claim that its goals are moral and justified according to the international codes that have been developed. Some societies are still proposing immoral goals and yet provide a well-developed justifying system of societal beliefs to their members. The present analysis focuses on the socio-psychological dynamics of posing goals and justifying them with the implications and consequences of all societies involved in intractable conflict.

Thus, for example, in Cyprus the Turkish Cypriots and the Greek Cypriots have had opposite goals. The Greek Cypriot children learned that the island was and "will always be Greek" and the Turkish Cypriots that "the island is Turkish and should go back to Turkey" (Hadjipavlou-Trigeorgis, 1987; Papadakis, 2005). Even after independence, each ethnic group showed more loyalty to its own "motherland" than to the state of Cyprus and its state symbols (the Greek and Turkish flags were and still are more visible than the Cyprus flag).

In the Chechen conflict, we can find beliefs about the justness of goals on both sides. From the Russian side, the justifying belief for considering Chechnya as an integral part of Russia is that Chechnya acquiescently joined Russia after reaching agreement with the tsarist regime. After the collapse of the Soviet Union, Russia's invasion was based on the dominant belief that political stability and law and order must be achieved, while the Chechen separatist actions were considered as contradicting that goal (Smith, 2001). From the Chechen side, freedom and independence are highly motivating values, which serve as a basis for formulating goals in the conflict (Arutiunov, 1995).

In the conflict that violently erupted during the 1990s between the different ethnic groups in former Yugoslavia, we can find few manifestations for Serbia's belief about the justness of its own goals. During the 1980s, 16 members of the prestigious Serbian Academy of Sciences and Arts wrote "the Academy Memorandum," a manifesto of Serbian nationalism that later served as the ideological platform for Slobodan Milošević's policy. The memorandum justified the goal of creating a Greater Serbia that would bring all Serbs into one state:

The establishment of full national and cultural integrity of the Serbian people, regardless of which republic or province they live in, is their historical and democratic right. The achievement of equal status and independent development has a deeper sense for the Serbian people. In less than fifty years, during two successive generations, [it was] twice exposed to physical annihilation, forced assimilation, conversion, cultural genocide, ideological indoctrination, devaluation and rejection of its own tradition under an imposed guilt complex, [and was] intellectually and politically disarmed. (quoted in Anzulovic, 1999, p. 116)

We can discern another example in the conflict in Sri Lanka between Sinhalese and Tamils, where S. J. V. Chelvanayakam, leader of the Tamil United Liberation Front, made the following statement on February 7, 1975, concerning the justness of the Tamils' claims for independent sovereignty, after winning a huge majority of the Tamils' votes:

Throughout the ages the Sinhalese and Tamils in the country lived as distinct sovereign people till they were brought under foreign domination. It should be remembered that the Tamils were in the vanguard of the struggle for independence in the full confidence that they also will regain their freedom. We have for the last 25 years made every effort to secure our political rights on the basis of equality with the Sinhalese in a united Ceylon. It is a regrettable fact that successive Sinhalese governments have used the power that flows from independence to deny us our fundamental rights and reduce us to the position of a subject people. These governments have been able to do so only by using against the Tamils the sovereignty common to the Sinhalese and the Tamils. (Chelvanayakam, 1975, p. 1; http://tamilnation.co/selfdetermination/tamileelam/7504sjvstatement.htm, October 4, 2011)

While the presentation and justification of one's own goals are major parts of the theme, another part tries to negate and discredit the goals of the other side in the conflict, the enemy. Societies involved in intractable conflict attempt to refute the goals of the rival and their justifications by disseminating contradictory information through various channels. Claims that the enemy's arguments are unreasonable, unfair, baseless, and unjustified are used for internal purposes to strengthen the epistemic basis of the ingroup, but are also distributed outside the group to wage psychological warfare against the rival and to attract support from the international community.

For example, the French denied the need for self-determination of Algerians and viewed Algeria as an integral part of France. Prime Minister Pierre Mendès-France spoke to the French Assembly on November 12, 1954, saying "One does not compromise when it comes to defending the internal peace of the nation, the unity and the integrity of the Republic. The Algerian departments are part of the French Republic. They have been French for a long time and they are irrevocably French" (quoted in Horne, 2006, p. 98). This was his way of denying the Algerians' arguments to end French colonialism and achieve independence. In a similar way, Turks at the beginning of the 20th century denied the unique identity of the Kurds, who attempted to secede from Turkey and establish their own state. They viewed Kurds as "mountain Turks" who changed their language and therefore did not need self-determination because they were not a national entity (Kirisci & Winrow, 1997).

Societal Beliefs about the Delegitimization of the Opponent

Societies in intractable conflict develop societal beliefs that portray the opponent in delegitimizing terms (Bar-Tal, 1989, 1990a; Bar-Tal & Hammack, 2012; Bar-Tal & Teichman, 2005; Stagner, 1967; White, 1970). "Delegitimization" is defined as "the categorization of a group, or groups, into extremely negative social categories that exclude it, or them, from the sphere of human groups that act within the limits of acceptable norms and/or values, since these groups are viewed as violating basic human norms or values and therefore deserve maltreatment" (Bar-Tal & Hammack, 2012, p. 30). In essence, delegitimization denies the adversary's humanity and morality, providing a kind of psychological permit to harm the delegitimized group (Bar-Tal & Teichman, 2005; Holt & Silverstein, 1989; Kelman, 2001; Moses, 1990; Opotow, 1990; Rieber, 1991). It magnifies the difference between the groups in conflict; homogenizes and deindividuates the adversary as an evil entity without a human face; directs against the adversary intense negative emotions of rejection, such as hatred, anger, scorn, fear, or disgust; encourages deep mistrust and animosity; implies the adversary's potential for negative behavior, which could endanger the delegitimizing group; and has behavioral implications for the delegitimizing group, suggesting that the adversary does not deserve being treated humanely and that measures should be taken to prevent the harm that it might inflict. The last two features provide the key implication for societies involved in intractable conflict because delegitimization psychologically legitimizes harming the rival group. This implication is the essence of delegitimization and grants to this societal phenomenon its unique meaning: psychological authorization to perform negative violent acts against the delegitimized group, including mass killing, ethnic cleansing, and even genocide.

In the past, various forms of delegitimization were proposed (Bar-Tal, 1989, 1990a, 2000a), categorizations that authorize harm of the delegitimized group. The first such form is *dehumanization*. It can involve using subhuman epithets such as "uncivilized savages" or "primitives" (see, e.g., Constantine, 1966; Jahoda, 1999); using biological, zoological, or medical labels such as "monkeys," "snakes," "worms," "cancer," or "microbes" (Boccato, Capozza, Falvo, & Durante, 2008; Goff, Eberhardt, Williams, & Jackson, 2008; Savage, 2006, 2007); or using demonizing terms (categories that have supernatural power) such as "demons," "monsters," "devils," or ones who control the world economy or even drink human blood (see Wistrich, 1999); or mechanistic terms such as being without emotions or cognitive openness (Haslam, 2006). *Outcasting*, the second form, is characterized by categorization of the rival into groups that are considered as violators of pivotal social norms. Outcasts include such categories as murderers, thieves, psychopaths, terrorists, or maniacs (Bar-Tal, 1988). *Trait characterization*, as a third form, consists of attributing traits that are considered extremely negative and unacceptable in a given society. Traits such as aggressors, idiots, or parasites exemplify this type of delegitimization (Bialer, 1985; English & Halperin, 1987; Ugolnik, 1983). A fourth form of delegitimization involves the use of *political labels*, which denote political groups that are absolutely rejected by the values of the delegitimizing group. These labels are culturally bound and their use depends on society's cultural ideology. The labels are mainly drawn from the repertoire of political goals, ideology, or values. Nazis, fascists, imperialists, colonialists, capitalists, Zionists, and communists are examples of this type of delegitimization (Bronfenbrenner, 1961; White, 1984). Finally, delegitimization by *group comparison* occurs when the delegitimized group is labeled by a name of a group that traditionally serves as an example of negativity in the delegitimizing group. Uses of such categories as "Vandals" or "Huns" are examples of this type of delegitimization. These forms may not be exhaustive, and they are clearly culturally bound, but they provide illustrative examples of what kind of categories can be used by societies in delegitimizing categorization.

Delegitimization, as an extreme social categorization, does not appear in every intergroup conflict. It tends to appear when the negated goals of the outgroup are perceived as far-reaching, unjustified, and endangering the fundamental goals of the ingroup and when threats to take violent steps are expressed. These conditions indicate that intractable conflicts almost always involve delegitimization. The conflictive context in which delegitimization evolves is stable and salient in its threatening and violent nature (Rothbart & Korostelina, 2006).

In times of intractable conflict, the term "enemy" also has the same features and consequences as other delegitimizing terms (e.g., Alexander, Brewer, & Herrmann, 1999; Frank, 1967; Herrmann, 1985; Holt & Silverstein, 1989; Kelman, 1997). A social category defined as an enemy is seen as a group that threatens to do harm and therefore arouses feelings of hostility (Silverstein & Flamenbaum, 1989). This label not only implies attribution of negative characteristics to the opponent but also describes the confrontational and hostile relations between the two groups. It indicates that another group intends to harm one's own group or has already carried out such acts. It is a stable label used during the intractable conflict that is difficult to change (Kelman, 1997). The concept "enemy" was found to arouse extremely negative associations, such as war, destruction, killing, hatred, anger, evilness, danger, or aggression (Szalay & Mir-Djalali, 1991). Indeed, Keen (1986), who examines how the enemy images are portrayed in posters, leaflets, caricatures, comics, photographs, drawings, paintings, and illustrations appearing in books from different countries, suggests that the prototype has certain delegitimizing features. The enemy is a stranger; a faceless, barbarous, greedy criminal; and a sadistic and immoral aggressor. The enemy is often presented in depersonalized abstract terms as a torturer, rapist, desecrator, beast, reptile, insect, germ, or devil. White (1970, 1984, p. 133) in analyzing various violent conflicts used the term "diabolical enemy-image" to depict the delegitimizing content that refers to the "obvious guilt of the enemy, unchangeableness of the enemy's evil nature, the efficacy of force in dealing with such an opponent, and the inefficacy of anything but force."

In analyzing delegitimization in intractable conflict, we need to recognize that the two engaged groups are psychologically and socially separated, even if they live in the same geographic area as, for example, Protestants and Catholics in Northern Ireland or Jews and Palestinians in the Middle East. There is usually little social contact between members of the two groups, and sometimes they are actually separated by real borders. Most of the information that they receive about each other is dominated by conflict themes that present the malevolent acts of the other side. In such contexts, it is not surprising that the persistent use of delegitimization evolves. This was the case in Cyprus where education played a role in promoting delegitimizing beliefs. Historically, the educational curriculum, textbooks, and methodologies came from the respective "motherlands," and to a great extent they still do. The Cypriot schools, being either Greek or Turkish, celebrate to this day the "chosen glories" and "chosen traumas," and the national holidays of Greece and Turkey, respectively. Thus, the children grow up with Greek or Turkish identity, not Cypriot one. The narrative about the "chosen past" and the antagonistic interpretations of events have been important aspects of their socialization, which promoted the "enemy image" as it centered around nationalism and the perception of what constitutes a "bad Turk" or a "bad Greek" without much differentiation between Turks and Turkish Cypriots and between Greeks and Greek Cypriots (Hadjipavlou-Trigeorgis, 1987; Spyrou, 2002).

Once delegitimization evolves, it plays a major role in the conflict. Without delegitimization, it would have been difficult to carry out the major violence, cruelty, and atrocities involved in conflicts. First, delegitimizing stereotypes explain the nature of the conflict, why it erupted, why it continues, and why it is violent. Because societies involved in intractable conflicts view their own goals as justified and perceive themselves in a positive light, they attribute all responsibility for the conflict to the dispositional characteristics of the opponent: the enemy. Delegitimization labels (i.e., bloodthirsty, murderer, terrorist, cruel, oppressive, savage, Vandal, or Nazi) help explain the opponent's goals and present them as "far reaching," "irrational," and "malevolent," which threaten to negate the goals of the delegitimizing society. They also explain why the adversary is intransigent and irreconcilable and precludes any possible peaceful solution; therefore, the conflict cannot be resolved (Bar-Tal, 1990a). In addition, delegitimizing beliefs provide an explanation for the opponent's violence, aggression, cruelty, lack of concern for human life, and viciousness (Finlay, Holsti, & Fagen, 1967). They help explain how an adversary can behave in such an inhumane and immoral way.

Second, in their epistemic function, delegitimizing beliefs also serve to justify the violence and destruction inflicted on the adversary by the delegitimizing group (Tajfel, 1981a). They provide justification for the individuals and for the social system as a whole to intentionally harm the rival, and for continuing to institutionalize aggression toward the enemy (Jost & Banaji, 1994). This is an important function that resolves feelings of dissonance, guilt, and shame. Third, delegitimizing beliefs create a sense of differentiation and superiority (Tajfel, 1978a, 1981) to the extent of totally excluding the delegitimized group from the community of groups considered as acting within the accepted range of norms and values. Because the rival group is perceived not only as an enemy but also as delegitimized and belonging to a lower category, the demarcated boundaries between the groups are not penetrable. The delegitimized group is perceived as completely different, especially in view of the fact that the ingroup ascribes to itself positive characteristics. Baumeister (1997, pp. 68–69) explains the logic of the differentiation:

The... important implication of the view of evil as the adversary of the good is that it seems tailor-made to increase hostilities between rival nations, ethnic groups, and other social units. One of the most powerful and universal human tendencies is to identify with a group of people similar to oneself, and to square off against rival groups. Moreover, people automatically and inevitably begin to think that their group is good. But if we are good, and you are our opponents, and evil is the opponent of the good, then you must be evil. Groups of people everywhere will come to that same conclusion, even groups on opposite sides of the same conflict.... Such views may then be used to provide easy justification for treating one's enemies harshly, because there is no point in being patient, tolerant, and understanding when one is dealing with evil.

Finally, delegitimizing beliefs have a motivating and mobilizing function. On the one hand they indicate to group members that the delegitimizing group should be avenged for the violent acts performed against them, and on the other hand they imply a need to initiate violent acts to prevent the perceived potential danger and threat. Withstanding the enemy and averting the danger of delegitimized groups such as "murderers," "Nazis," "terrorists," or "psychopaths" require full mobilization. In intractable conflicts, delegitimizing labels serve as cues to remind the ingroup about the threats and the mobilizing steps that have to be taken to counter the threatening enemy.

An example of mutual delegitimization can be found in the case of the long conflict between Protestants and Catholics in Northern Ireland. Through the years, both societies developed mutual negative stereotypes, including the use of delegitimizing characteristics (see Darby, 1976; Harris, 1972). Cecil (1993, p. 152) reports that Protestants view Catholics as "lazy, priest-ridden, untidy and potentially treacherous," whereas Catholics perceive Protestants as "bigoted, mean, and lacking in culture."

Another example of mutual delegitimization is provided by Oren and Bar-Tal (2007) in the case of the Israeli-Palestinian conflict. Already at the beginning of the conflict, Jews arriving in Palestine during the waves of Zionist immigrations initially viewed Arabs in the region as primitive, dirty, stupid, easily agitated, and aggressive. As the conflict evolved and became violent, Arabs were perceived as killers, bloodthirsty, treacherous, untrustworthy, cowardly, cruel, and wicked (Bar-Tal & Teichman, 2005). A special effort was made over the decades to delegitimize the Palestinian Liberation Organization (PLO), established in 1964, which eventually came to express the aspiration of the great majority of Palestinians. It was viewed as a bloodthirsty terror organization (Bar-Tal, 1988). In many aspects, the Palestinian delegitimization of Jews is a mirror image in terms of its content to the Israeli delegitimization of Palestinians (Bar-Tal, 1988). In general, Jews were viewed almost from the start of the Zionist immigration as colonialists who came to settle Palestinian land and expel the Palestinian population. They were stereotyped as strangers, crusaders, and enemies. Also, Jews were labeled as deceitful, treacherous, and disloyal and were seen as aggressors and robbers. In addition, they were perceived as colonialists, racists, fascists, and imperialists and were even compared to the Nazis. The term Zionism itself became a delegitimizing label as it was considered a colonialist ideology. This line of delegitimization continued through the decades. The national Covenant of the Palestine Liberation Organization, approved in 1964, stated in its article 19: "Zionism is a colonialist movement in its inception, aggressive and expansionist in is goals, racist and segregationist in its configuration and fascist in its means and aims." The mutual formal delegitimization continued until the Oslo Agreement in 1993, when the PLO and Israel struck an agreement of mutual recognition. Nevertheless, the unsuccessful peace process led to the renewal of the mutual formal delegitimization that still today plays a major role in preventing a peaceful settlement of the conflict.

Hadjipavlou (2007) found in Cyprus mirror-image perceptions among Turkish and Greek Cypriots in a survey with a representative sample of each. Most Greek Cypriots (95.1%) think that the intransigence of the Turkish Cypriots has contributed to the perpetuation of the conflict, attribute full responsibility to the other side, and have a tendency to demonize the other and label themselves as victims. At the same time a substantial majority of Turkish Cypriots (78.5%) viewed the intransigence of the Greek Cypriots similarly.

In his analysis of Russian delegitimization of the Chechens, Russell (2002, 2005, 2007) reports prevailing uses of categories such as "savages," "wolves," "thieves," "bandits," and "mafia types." During the Second World War, Chechens were accused of collaborating with the Nazis, an accusation that was used to legitimize their mass deportation in 1944 (Dunlop, 1998). When in the late 1990s some Chechens began to conduct bloody terror attacks against Russians civilians, they were in addition delegitimized as merciless Islamic fundamentalist terrorists and viewed as uniquely criminal, a conception that provided an epistemic basis for use of massive military force by Russian president Vladimir Putin against them (Wood, 2007). From the other side, and in accordance with the Chechen collective memory of Russian atrocities, Russians were delegitimized as cruel and inhuman people who put no constraints on their brutal acts against the Chechens.

Serbian leader Radovan Karadžić used delegitimizing labels against non-Serbs, especially Muslims in Bosnia. He stated that the Serbian fight was against "Asiatic darkness" in order to protect Europe by making sure "Islamic fundamentalism doesn't infect Europe from the south" (Cigar, 1995, p. 100).

Serbian nationalist rallies organized by Slobodan Milošević in the late 1980s used a slogan depicting Muslims as nonhumans: "Oh Muslims, you black crows, Tito is no longer around to protect you!" (Cigar, 1995).

Further examples can be found in the conflict in Rwanda between Hutus and Tutsis. Tutsis were portrayed as foreigners, committed to stealing power from Hutus by changing their identities and deviously infiltrating positions of power in the state, the economy, and religious institutions, positions that rightfully belonged to Hutus. (Klinghoffer, 1998). They were depicted as "the enemy," as seeking to kill Hutus on a massive scale and hoping to conquer lands of the genuine Rwandans (Hutus). The hate radio during the genocide in 1994 called for the killing of the cockroaches (the word used to describe Tutsis), who otherwise would destroy the Hutus (Melvern, 2006). *Kangura*, an influential anti-Tutsi propaganda newspaper, published such a charge in an article of March 1993:

> We began by saying that a cockroach cannot give birth to a butterfly. It is true. A cockroach gives birth to another cockroach.... The history of Rwanda shows us clearly that a Tutsi stays always exactly the same, that he has never changed. The malice, the evil are just as we knew them in the history of our country. We are not wrong in saying that a cockroach gives birth to another cockroach. Who could tell the difference between the Inyenzi [i.e., cockroaches, a scornful term for members of Rwandan Patriotic Front] who attacked in October 1990 and those of the 1960s? They are all linked... their evilness is the same. The unspeakable crimes of the Inyenzi of today... recall those of their elders: killing, pillaging, raping girls and women, etc. (quoted in Des Forges, 1999, pp. 73–74)

Delegitimizing labels exclude negotiations with the rival because of the lasting expectations that the rival intends and is able to harm the ingroup, and therefore no risk can be taken. Indeed, Maoz and McCauley (2008) report that, among a representative sample of Jews in Israel, dehumanization of Palestinians predicted support for their severe harm, including population transfer and violation of their human rights. Also, Čehajić, Brown, and Gonzalez (2009) show that dehumanization of victims allows avoidance of a feeling of empathy. Serbian adolescents who were reminded about their group misdeeds felt less responsibility for these acts if they dehumanized the victim groups.

Societal Beliefs about Victimization

Societal beliefs about being a victim in a conflict (Mack, 1990; Volkan, 1997; Vollhardt, 2012) are based on having suffered violence, viewing one's own goals as just, having a positive collective self-image, emphasizing the wickedness of the opponent's goals, and delegitimizing the opponent's characteristics (Frank, 1967). Bar-Tal, Chernyak-Hai, Schori, and Gundar (2009, p. 238) define self-perceived collective victimhood as "a mindset shared by group members that results from a perceived intentional harm with severe and lasting consequences inflicted on a collective by another group or groups, a harm that is viewed as undeserved, unjust, and immoral and one that the group was not able to prevent." In other words, focusing on injustice, harm, evil, and the atrocities of the adversary, while emphasizing one's own society as being just, moral, and human, leads society members to conclude that they are the victims in the conflict. Feelings of being victimized mean that a society believes that the conflict was imposed by an adversary, who not only fights for unjust goals but also uses immoral means to achieve them (Eidelson & Eidelson, 2003). With time, as a result of prolonged sufferings and losses, these beliefs become well entrenched in the society's repertoire and are held on both individual and collective levels. During the intractable conflict almost every society member incurs some loss, including the personal loss of a family member, a friend, or an acquaintance. But even if a society member does not know the killed or a wounded personally, he or she identifies with the loss, seeing it as a loss to the society, because society members must take a collective responsibility. In addition, intractable conflicts often lead to other types of costs, such as damage, destruction, or a refugee problem. These types of experiences also contribute to the feeling of being a victim (Vollhardt, 2012).

For example, a study by Cairns, Mallet, Lewis, and Wilson (2003) provides an estimate of the extent of a reported sense of being a victim in the conflict of Northern Ireland in the 26 council areas that had experienced most of the "troubles" during the violent confrontations. In a random survey sample of 1,000 adults (Protestants and Catholics), 12% reported that they often or very often thought of themselves as victims of the troubles, while 16% were classified as being direct victims (injured in a sectarian incident, home damaged by a bomb, or intimidated outside their home) and 30% as indirect victims (family member or close friend injured, intimidated, or home damaged by a bomb). In another study, one of the Protestants observed, "I think we're all victims of the conflict" (Ferguson, Burgess, & Hollywood, 2010, p. 870). In addition, not surprisingly, those seeing themselves as victims or reporting direct or indirect victimization showed lower levels of psychological well-being as measured by a general health questionnaire (Cairns et al., 2003).

But a collective sense of victimhood in a conflict can also have roots in the distant past, as noted by Staub and Bar-Tal (2003, p. 722): "Groups encode important experiences, especially extensive suffering, in their collective memory, which can maintain a sense of woundedness and past injustice through generations." This encoding fulfills various functions, just as Liu and Liu (2003) believe that cultures shape their collective memories according to a "historical affordance." They preserve those narratives which can be functional in the life of the collective. Events in times of intractable conflict, even if they took place in a different context, feed the feeling of being a victim in the present confrontation. A salient example of this case is Jews' collective sense of self-victimhood in the Israeli-Arab conflict, which has been fueled by their collective memory of the 2,000-year Jewish diaspora, characterized as a continuous period of persecutions culminating in the Holocaust, the genocide (Bar-Tal 2007a). In another study, a nationwide representative survey of Israeli Jews shows that the more group members experience a general sense of collective victimhood based on the long history of persecution in the Diaspora, the more they view themselves as victims in the ongoing conflict with Palestinians (Schori, Halperin, & Bar-Tal, 2011[study 1]). Another nationwide representative survey of Israeli Jews indicates that the more group members view themselves as victims in the protracted conflict with Palestinians, the more they viewed themselves as victims in the particular major event of the conflict: the war in Gaza in 2009 (Schori, Halperin, & Bar-Tal, 2011 [study 2]). Interestingly, in the first study the self-view as a collective victim was highly related to noncompromising views regarding the solution of the Israeli-Palestinian conflict, and in the second study this self-perception was related to supporting the use of extreme violence against Palestinians.

Indeed, societal beliefs of self-collective victimhood redirect the focus to the society's own suffering and reduce the capacity for empathy. A collective state of victimhood impedes seeing things from the rival group's perspective, empathizing with its suffering, and accepting responsibility for harm inflicted by one's own group (Čehajić & Brown, 2008; Chaitin & Steinberg, 2008; Mack, 1990; Staub, 2006). A collective sense of victimhood has a basis in reality, but embedding it into the social fabric and psyche turns it into a paralyzing force (Roe & Cairns, 2003). For example, in a study by Schori-Eyal, Klar, and Roccas (2011), the sense of self-perceived collective victimhood in Israel is found to be strongly positively associated with the willingness to continue the military operations at all costs, even allowing for great losses to either the Israeli or Palestinian side, and with the wish to continue punishing the enemy group, even if such punishment means retaliation and suffering inflicted upon the ingroup – the Israelis. Victimhood thus becomes a chronic psychological state to which nations in conflict adhere often without drawing moral lessons.

During intractable conflict, it is functional to perceive one's own society as being the victimized party. This perception delegates responsibility for the outbreak of the conflict and the subsequent violence to the opponent. It sharpens intergroup differences because while it describes the opponent in delegitimizing terms and, at the same time, as responsible for the unjust and immoral acts, it presents one's own society as the sole victim of the conflict. In addition, belief in victimization provides the moral weight to look for justice and oppose the adversary. In this respect, these beliefs provide a rationale for continuing the struggle. The sense of self-victimhood does not preclude self-collective perceptions regarding the heroic and brave struggle that is necessary to withstand the enemy.

But self-presentation as the victim is especially important with regard to the international community. Victims are viewed with much more empathy and support and are not blamed for the continuation of the conflict and the violence. The perception of being the victim in the conflict is crucial in obtaining the backing of worldwide public opinion and increasing the likelihood of moral, political, and material support. As pointed out, "The status of victim renders the victim deserving of sympathy, support, outside help. Victims, by definition, are vulnerable, and any violence on their part can be construed as the consequences of their victimization. The acquisition of the status of victim becomes an institutionalized way of escaping guilt, shame or responsibility" (Smyth, 2001, p. 126).

Thus it is not surprising that in probably all intractable conflicts both groups perceive themselves as victims of the rival. As examples, this is the case of Israeli Jews and Palestinians in the Israeli-Arab conflict (Bar-Tal, 2007a; Caplan, 1999; Khalili, 2007; Rouhana & Bar-Tal, 1998; Vollhardt, 2012); Serbs and Croats in the conflict following Croatia's declaration of independence in June 1991 (Volkan, 1997, p. 54); Greek Cypriots and Turkish Cypriots (Hadjipavlou, 2007); Tamils and Sinhalese in Sri Lanka (Ramanathapillai, 2006); Catholics and Protestants in Northern Ireland (Hunter, Stringer, & Watson, 1991; Wichert, 1994); and Russians and Chechens in the context of the Chechen conflict (Wood, 2007). Because intractable conflicts involve violence in which civilians are also hurt, each party has enough evidence to perceive itself as the victim in the conflict. Each party construes the other as the cause of its suffering and perceives its own side as not responsible. The label of "victim" is a role that both sides in an intractable conflict try to claim. Thus, the self-view as being the victim in the conflict leads to competition to claim victimhood (see Noor, Brown, & Prentice, 2008).

The side that wins this status is assured of international support and often gets financial aid (Bar-Tal, Oren, & Nets-Zehngut, 2012). Nadler and Liviatan (2006) argue that the "victimhood competition" between Palestinians and Israelis is actually a fight over moral social identity. Palestinians portray Israel as an imperialist power, sometimes comparing Jewish soldiers to Nazis (Oren

& Bar Tal, 2007). Israeli Jews, on the other hand, insist they are the victims of Arab aggression (Bar Tal, 2007b). These two groups are striving to achieve a moral social identity by favoring their own group tragedies over those of the other. Similarly, Noor et al. (2008) report that Catholics and Protestants in Northern Ireland not only focus on their own ingroup's victimhood but also engage in competition about which group's suffering is greater (see also Sullivan, Landau, Branscombe, & Rothschild, 2012).

Societal Beliefs about Positive Collective Self-Image

Societies engaged in intractable conflicts develop and maintain societal beliefs that formulate and support a positive collective self-image (Sande, Goethals, Ferrari, & Worth, 1989; White, 1969). The contents of such beliefs can pertain to a variety of positive traits, values, or skills that characterize the society but also to positive actions performed in the past and positive contributions to mankind and civilization (Hirshberg, 1993; Kaplowitz, 1990). Eidelson and Eidelson (2003, p. 184) speak about "shared conviction of moral superiority, chosenness, entitlement and special destiny" that groups in conflict hold about themselves. These beliefs reflect the general tendency toward ethnocentrism documented in different groups (LeVine & Campbell, 1972; Sumner, 1906) and the striving for positive social identity assumed by Tajfel (1981) that characterizes group members. But in times of intractable conflict, they gain special importance. The amount of effort demanded, the need for mobilization, the reliance on violence, and the perpetration of aggressive, immoral acts (sometimes even atrocities) all require the maintenance of a stable positive self-image and positive social identity. This task is very challenging because by their nature intractable conflicts involve behaviors that violate moral norms such as the killings of human beings involved in fighting (i.e., soldiers, fighters). But all intractable conflicts include serious immoral transgressions because they also involve harming civilians who are not engaged in violent confrontations. These acts include killing, raping, injuring, expulsion, and torturing, as well as such violations of basic human rights as preventing free movement, humiliation, and destruction that often can extend to massacres, ethnic cleansing, or other atrocities. Society members who carry out these acts have a strong need to view themselves as human beings of good nature. Thus, groups involved in intractable conflicts engage in intense self-justification, self-glorification, and self-praise, as well as moral disengagement.

In view of the nature of intractable conflict, it is not surprising that some characteristics are especially propagated: humanness, civility, morality, fairness, and trustworthiness on the one hand, and competence, courage, heroism, and endurance on the other hand. Special efforts are made to contrast these characteristics with the adversary (Frank, 1967; Stagner, 1967). The objective is to form a self-image that is superior in comparison to the enemy and to make a salient differentiation between "them" and "us." The first category of positive self-image beliefs gives moral strength: it presents the society as humane and one that observes universal codes of morality. In fact, Leach, Ellemers, and Barreto (2007) demonstrate that morality is most important to ingroup evaluation, and Schwartz (1992) shows that people in different parts of the world highly value moral standards and consider them among the most important "guiding principles" in their lives. In large-scale studies across the world, Campbell and his colleagues found that morality was the only characteristic that ingroups consistently ascribed to themselves more than to outgroups (Brewer & Campbell, 1979; Levine & Campbell, 1972). This tendency, as explained, is greatly magnified in situations of intractable conflict, where violent acts are performed by the ingroup.

These beliefs also play an important role in self-presentation before the international community, which judges acts from a moral perspective. Often this judgment is a precondition for receiving support, both politically and materially. Thus, even when members of a society commit immoral acts, a special effort is made to minimize them by suggesting their exceptionality and their insignificance when compared to the immoral acts of the adversary or in comparison to immoral acts of other societies. In a study of Israeli Jews presented with evidence of violent actions committed by Israelis against Palestinians, Roccas, Klar, and Liviatan (2006) show that that self-glorification negatively predicted collective guilt and positively predicted exonerating cognitions (e.g., consideration that the accounts about immoral acts are exaggerated). Also, Leidner, Castano, Zaiser, and Giner-Sorolla (2010) report that ingroup glorification leads to disregard of the suffering of the victims through minimization of the emotional suffering of the victims and explicit dehumanization of the victim group.

The second category of characteristics boosts group morale and serves as a basis for hope and encouragement. These beliefs are directly relevant to the protracted violent struggle in that they suggest that the society has the ability to contain the enemy and even to win the conflict. They focus on competence, heroism, and determination. It is the competence in its general meaning that is considered "status-defining" – the basis of a status distinction that favors the ingroup over an outgroup (for reviews, see Bettencourt, Dorr, Charlton, & Hume, 2001). Arafat, in a speech on December 10, 1987, referred to these Palestinian qualities: "O heroes who are defending Jerusalem, the most sacred place in our holy land, you have proved and continue to prove to the enemy and to the whole world that our people daily extricate their existence and freedom from the aggressor's paws and that they offer dear sacrifices through their souls and blood for the homeland" (Daily report of the Foreign Broadcast Information Service).

Unionists in Northern Ireland, for example, saw themselves, according to Ruane and Todd (1996, p. 105), as "outward looking, industrial, urban, religiously and politically liberal, culturally pluralist, modernizing." The Serbian positive self-image is well expressed in these excerpts from the Gazimestan speech that was delivered by Milošević on June 28, 1989, and can serve as prototypical speech expressing the ethos of conflict:

The Kosovo heroism has been inspiring our creativity for 6 centuries, and has been feeding our pride and does not allow us to forget that at one time we were an army great, brave, and proud, one of the few that remained undefeated when losing.

... Serbs have never in the whole of their history conquered and exploited others. Their national and historical being has been liberational throughout the whole of history and through two world wars, as it is today. They liberated themselves and when they could they also helped others to liberate themselves.

In the Israeli case, it is often presented to the public by the leaders that the Israeli army is the most moral army in the world and the society meets all the standards of moral international codes (Bar-Tal, 2007a; Oren, Nets-Zehngut, & Bar-Tal, in press).

Societal Beliefs about Security

Beliefs about security point out the nature of threats that emerge in times of intractable conflict, stress the importance of personal and collective safety, and outline the necessary conditions for their achievement. Security is an essential precondition of an ordered existence for an individual and for a collective and a societal system. This objective reflects one of the basic human needs and involves a desire for protection, safety, and survival (Maslow, 1970). Both as individuals and as society members, humans strive to fulfill these needs because they are the prerequisites for managing normal life.

People form beliefs about being insecure when they detect dangers or threats and see difficulty in coping with them (Lazarus, 1991; Smith & Lazarus, 1993). In essence, security and insecurity touch on many different issues that preoccupy societies, including war, international conflicts, nuclear threats, arms races, development of weapons, terrorism, hunger, economic depressions, unemployment, proliferation of weapons, discriminations, lack of religious freedom, and oppression (Bar-Tal & Jacobson, 1998; Buzan, 1991, 1997; Krause & Williams, 1996; Ney & Lynn-Jones, 1988). In most cases, it is the role of the societal system to provide security to its members, on both internal and external levels. The theme of security appears in every society all the time, but in times of intractable conflict it becomes of vital importance. Intractable conflicts by their nature raise many different security issues for society members as individuals and for the society as a whole. Society members worry about personal ability to live under hardship and even about survival, group existence, the collective's losses, the opponent's military and political gains, economic hardship, threats to cultural values, and so on. Thus, maintaining security becomes one of the central societal objectives. In many cases, the state through its institutions and organizations as well as its resources and personnel has the responsibility to assure security (e.g., in the cases of Russians, Israeli Jews, Turks, or Singhalese). But in many other cases, when a distinct society challenges the society that controls the state, this role is performed by informal systems that have to be developed. In these societies, the established system through its military keeps society members secure while trying to establish economic, social, and cultural security (e.g., Kurds, Palestinians, or Tamils).

In all the cases of intractable conflict, the involved societies are obligated to focus on the existential aspects of the concept of security, that is, preserving the mere existence of the individuals and the collective. Thus, security issues are found at the top of the agenda of a society involved in an intractable conflict, and beliefs about security play a more central part in its collective identity. In this context, the societal beliefs about security refer mostly to the sources of the insecurity and the conditions that can secure personal and national survival. They identify the various threats that cause insecurity and outline the conditions that strengthen and even establish a secure existence. With regard to identifying a threat, the beliefs point to the rival in conflict as the most dangerous source of insecurity. The intention, the ability, and threatening acts already performed are sufficient to indicate serious jeopardy in security. Then comes elaboration of those conditions, which can change the present unacceptable state of insecurity. Almost always, they point to the necessity to win the conflict or at least to withstand the rival. In this realm, the beliefs outline the conditions that are necessary to achieve this goal. Mobilization for conflict (including resources) and material investments are the elementary conditions. In addition, they outline other necessary conditions that are needed for securing the existence of the collective. These conditions are related to the goals of conflict. Examples on the collective level would include the boundaries that can ensure security, the type of political system, industries that can produce military equipment, the manpower that is needed to maintain security, education that facilitates mobilization, and laws that facilitate the establishment of security. Each society in an intractable conflict specifies its own conditions for security, and these are influenced by various factors, such as the nature of intractable conflict, characteristics of the enemy, its own society's culture, and legal considerations. Also, almost every society engaged in intractable conflict creates societal beliefs devoted to the glorification of those security organizations and institutions (as well of their members) that are instrumental in assuring and maintaining security. Thus, for example, the fighters are revered, and their acts of sacrifice are worshiped.

All these societal beliefs related to the security theme fulfill important functions. They not only provide knowledge about security concerns but most of all set the basis for successful coping (Brown, 1983). The beliefs themselves serve as an important rationale for the legitimization of policies, decisions, and actions in the society. They also provide guidelines for the development of the desired psychological conditions needed to maintain security. In general, they serve a motivating role in mobilizing society members to take an active part in the conflict and consolidate security.

The question of how to secure the personal life of Jews and the existence of the Jewish collective in Israel has been the fundamental problem that has preoccupied every Israeli Jew and all the Jewish authorities of this collective for more than a century (Arian, 1995; Bar-Tal, Jacobson, & Klieman, 1998; Horowitz, 1984, 1993; Inbar, 1991; Yaniv, 1993a). This challenge has become the single most critical factor that has shaped the personal and societal life in Israel and has had a determinative effect on the possible resolution of the Israeli-Arab conflict in the Middle East. The continuous violent conflict turned the Israeli society into "a nation in arms" or "a nation in uniform," which has lived in a situation that has been called a "dormant war" (Yaniv, 1993b). As a result, security, which symbolizes the existence of the State of Israel as well as personal safety, has become a key concept in Hebrew vocabulary and a master symbol in the Jewish culture in Israel (Bar-Tal, Jacobson, & Klieman, 1998; Liebman & Don-Yehiya, 1983).

Through the years, security has been used continuously as an important justification and explanation for many governmental decisions, even if they do not have direct implications for security; it has become a rationale for initiating actions and for reacting in military, political, societal, and even educational and cultural domains; it has become an excuse for undemocratic, immoral, or even illegal practices done by the Israelis; and it has been used to mobilize human and material resources (Bar-Tal & Schnell, 2013a; Sheffer & Barak, 2009, 2010). Professional opinions of experts of the military, intelligence organizations, the police, or counterterrorism units have disproportionate influence and a great deal of respect, to the point that their recommendations are adopted almost unquestionably by broad sections of society. Party leaders and political candidates compete against each other on the basis of their contributions to the national security throughout their careers. In political platforms the concept of "security" is used as a convenient code word in order to differentiate between one party and another, in an attempt to convince an anxious and eager public that this party's proposal is the best solution for the dilemma of insecurity, while raising the argument that its opponents will only expose Israel to greater dangers and even to calamity. The television broadcasts and the news reports only intensify this preoccupation by allotting ample space and time for the daily evaluation of the security situation because the public must satisfy its basic need for the sense of knowing and understanding and for the ability to predict the future. Security has also been used as the most important objective in the negotiations with Arabs, because this is the only legitimate consideration accepted by the international community and by the great majority of Israeli Jews. Such central and intensive preoccupation with security turned it, as some social scientists suggest, into a civil religion, whose beliefs dominate the Israeli ethos (Liebman & Don-Yehiya, 1983). Bar-Tal, Magal, and Halperin (2009) define this centrality as a state of *securatism* where security becomes the major determinant of policies and decisions in many spheres of collective life, where society members view security as a central issue in societal life with all its implications, and where security forces have major determinative power in the society.

An expression for the great importance that the Protestant community in Northern Ireland attached to security can be found in the high number of members in the Ulster Defence Association (UDA – the largest Protestant paramilitary organization), which at its peak in the early 1970s claimed to have around 30,000 active members (Tonge, 2002). These large numbers should be added to those of the police force (RUC), which had 8,489 regular full-time police, 3,202 full-time reservists (RUCR), and 1,765 part-time reservists during the 1990s, with only 8% of the whole police force being Catholic (Hainsworth, 1996). Issues of security played a major role during the active conflict, and the Protestant community was recruited to secure normal life for its members.

But the two presented illustrations can be generalized to all the societies engaged in intractable conflict, without exceptions. As noted, intractable conflicts by their nature involve violence that causes insecurity in every domain of life. Not only are society members concerned about their physical safety, but intractable conflicts frequently cause the displacement of the population, economic hardship, and cultural or religious restrictions, which all are related to securing individual and collective life. In addition, in many of the conflicts minority groups suffer discrimination and oppression, which underlie insecurity. Thus, some societies – for example, Russians and Chechens, Tutsis and Hutus, or Muslims and Hindus in Kashmir – are greatly preoccupied with security, and societal beliefs about this theme are central in the collective repertoire.

Societal Beliefs about Patriotism

Somewhat related to societal beliefs about security are societal beliefs about patriotism. But while the former focus on the threats and the conditions to eliminate them, the latter focus on the particular bond between the society members and their collective that is essential for participation in conflict. Patriotism lingers on people's desire to belong to a society that society members evaluate positively. That is, patriots want to be part of their society and define themselves as members of it (De Figueiredo & Elkins, 2003; Huddy & Khatib, 2007). Patriotism is always found in ethnic groups and nations because it implies attachment of group members to the society and the country that is accompanied by senses of belonging, affection, and concern (Bar-Tal, 1993). Beliefs about love, care, and loyalty toward the people and the country create crucial bonds that keep the members of society together. They increase a sense of belonging and enhance integration and solidarity. Societal beliefs in fostering patriotism motivate nation members to act on behalf of the group, by providing the explanation and justification for giving up personal comfort so as to contribute time, efforts, or money for the benefit of their collective. Without them a group cannot exist. It is thus not surprising that after studying nationwide samples Rose (1985, p. 86) concludes: "Patriotism is the norm in every country surveyed: the differences in national pride are a matter of degree, not of kind." Staub (1997) proposes a distinction among different types of patriotism, underscoring the possible reactions to one's nation's virtues and faults. Whereas *conventional* patriotism refers to mere attachment, *blind* patriotism refers to rigid and inflexible attachment through total identification with the group. It reflects unquestionable acceptance of group goals, means, ideology, policies, norms, practices, and formal leadership, without tolerating criticism of possible failings or violations of moral codes. It closes the way to reflective thinking and openness. In contrast, *constructive* patriotism refers to an attachment with critical loyalty that reflects care and concern when the group loses moral ground or makes mistakes, and it leads to criticism thought necessary to change the way (Schatz, Staub, & Levine, 1999).

In times of intractable conflict, beliefs about patriotism are of major importance because of the heavy costs in terms of human and material resources (Bar-Tal, 2003). In the name of patriotism, society members are asked to give up their personal comforts, desires, or even basic needs to help to achieve society's goals (Somerville, 1981). Patriots who actively participate in violent conflict are honored, and patriots who lose their lives are especially revered. Heroes are glorified and publicly presented as models. Events from the past that indicate exceptional patriotic acts serve as examples for the society members to act in the present conflict. In this respect, patriotic beliefs outline the required route for action, portray the desired models of patriotism, and serve as explanation and justification for sacrifices made (Bar-Tal & Staub, 1997). Societies invest efforts to socialize the society members toward patriotism in general, but in times of conflict this socialization is essential. Without patriotism it is impossible to maintain a conflict that requires so much investment, deprivation, mobilization, and sacrifice on behalf of the society by its members (Stagner, 1967). In the ultimate patriotic acts, society members have to be ready to kill and to die for their collective in order to continue the conflict. For example, this readiness is expressed in numerous ways in Palestinian society. Already in the early phases of the violent struggle after the 1948 war, militant Palestinians sent into Israel *fedayin* (self-sacrificers), who carried out deadly attacks on Israeli targets (mostly civilian), and many of them were killed by the Israeli military forces. In the late 1980s the term *shahid* (martyr) appeared and replaced the term *fedayin*; it refers to a person who sacrificed his or her life on behalf of the Palestinian cause, including in acts of suicide-homicide bombing. *Shahids* are revered by every layer of Palestinian society and are commemorated with posters, poems, films, children's plays, street names, ceremonies, and speeches (Hafez, 2006; Khalili, 2007). Arafat said on March 9, 1988: "Blessed are the martyrs who are immortal in the final abode. Blessed are their souls in heaven because they sacrificed themselves for the most sacred and most noble aim" (Foreign Broadcast Information Service).

Sacrifice needed from the Serbs as the required route for action can be also found in Milošević's already noted Gazimestan speech:

Six centuries later, now, we are being again engaged in battles and are facing battles. They are not armed battles, although such things cannot be excluded yet. However, regardless of what kind of battles they are, they cannot be won without resolve, bravery, and sacrifice, without the noble qualities that were present here in the field of Kosovo in the days past. (http://en.wikisource.org/wiki/Gazimestan_speech)

This speech is not unique. Its essence can be found in the speeches of all political and military leaders who lead their society into violent and prolonged conflict and know that patriotic feelings with all their implications are the necessary conditions for mobilization and readiness for sacrifice.

Of special significance in times of intractable conflict is the tendency to demand and practice blind patriotism. Society members are encouraged to mobilize but discouraged from asking questions and voicing criticism regarding the goals of conflict, which are positioned as supreme and often sacred. Individuals and groups who voice their disapproval of the goals of the violent conflict are sanctioned and often viewed as traitors. In fact, during intractable conflict, societies practice *monopolization of patriotism*, which denotes demands for unquestioning loyalty not only to the group but also to the aims of the conflict (Bar-Tal, 1997). In such times, in an attempt to maintain the societal beliefs of the ethos of conflict and collective memory, societies view the conflict as being of supreme importance and define patriotism as supporting exclusively the narratives of the culture of conflict. The society views as patriots only those who support the goals of conflict and its continuation with the accompanied themes of the ethos of conflict and collective memory. Society members who have different goals or promote alternative narratives with their societal beliefs, or do both, are considered as nonpatriots. Thus, in monopolizing patriotism those who are agents of conflict view calls for peacemaking and compromises as disloyally weakening the struggle of the collective and breaking its efforts to achieve the goals. Monopolization of patriotism has been observed in the various societies involved in intractable conflict. In the Israeli Jewish society, it was practiced in the 1980s and 1990s. In 1995 Israeli prime minister Itzhak Rabin, who initiated a recognition agreement with the Palestinian Liberation Organization, was assassinated by a Jewish extremist. It has also been observed in the 2000s (Oren & Bar-Tal, 2004) and continues still today. Monopolization of patriotism has been identified in other societies involved in violent conflicts such as Tamils, Singhalese, Hutus, Tutsis, Irish Protestants, and Irish Catholics.

Societal Beliefs about Unity

Beliefs about unity are viewed as a special addition to patriotic beliefs. They refer to the importance of maintaining unity, by ignoring internal discords and disagreements, in the face of an external threat. Such beliefs about unity refer to common origins, history, and traditions and stress consensus about goals, values, and norms. The emphasis on consensus demarcates the boundaries of agreements and applies pressure to conform. The beliefs emphasize that internal conflict can harm the common cause (Moscovici & Doise, 1994).

Conflict situations raise the need for unity and solidarity, whereas societies that exist in peaceful conditions may tolerate deviation from social norms and criticism about the collective (Coser, 1956). Societies in intractable conflicts tend to demand more conformism from their members and find it more difficult to accept subgroups that do not conform. They try to eliminate or postpone internal conflicts in order to diminish disagreements and schism within a society whose superordinate goal is confronting the enemy. It is essential that such societies be united. The purpose of beliefs about unity is to provide a sense that all society members, or at least a great majority, support the goals of the conflict and the course of its management. They play a role in increasing the solidarity and cohesiveness necessary for mobilization. According to Horne (2006, p. 134), recalling Dorothy Pickles's observation about the Algerian war, "Up to 1956 the only point on which virtually the whole of France was united was that Algerian independence was unthinkable and unmentionable." This fact indeed brought much strength to the French standing against the developing war against the FLN. But later, with the development of support for Algerian independence in French society, the lack of unity weakened the French struggle to keep Algeria French.

Lack of unity leads to societal polarization and internal tension that can impede the struggle with the enemy. When it occurs during the climax of the intractable conflict, when there is still no sign of a peace process, disagreements within a society especially about the goals and ways to manage the conflict or about personal intrigues and schisms can cause great damage to the societal cause. For example, in the Iraqi-Kurd conflict, fought between 1994 and 1998, the Kurdish Democratic Party, led by Massoud Barzani, and the Patriotic Union of Kurdistan, led by Jalal Talabani, fought a bloody war for power over northern Iraq, which ended in September 1998 when the two sides agreed to a power-sharing arrangement. This schism significantly harmed the common cause of fighting Iraqis (Entessar, 2010).

A major part of Milošević's already noted Gazimestan speech was dedicated to stressing the importance of Serbian unity and the harsh implications that Serbs suffered from disunity in the past:

The lack of unity and betrayal in Kosovo will continue to follow the Serbian people like an evil fate through the whole of its history. Even in the last war, this lack of unity and betrayal led the Serbian people and Serbia into agony, the consequences of which in the historical and moral sense exceeded fascist aggression....

Disunity among Serb officials made Serbia lag behind and their inferiority humiliated Serbia. Therefore, no place in Serbia is better suited for saying this than the field of Kosovo and no place in Serbia is better suited than the field of Kosovo for saying that unity in Serbia will bring prosperity to the Serbian people in Serbia and each one of its citizens, irrespective of his national or religious affiliation. (http://en.wikisource.org/wiki/Gazimestan_speech)

The social importance attached to unity in order to overcome the enemy and the dangers of internal divisions were also expressed in the Rwandese conflict by the dominant Hutu Kangura newspaper: "Your unity, your mutual understanding, your solidarity are the certain weapons of your victory, . . . you understand that when the majority people is divided, [then] the minority becomes the majority" (quoted in Des Forges, 1999, p. 82).

The sense of unity is almost always broken when at least a segment of society detects signs of a possible peace process and begins to change its goals and views of the rival. This process often leads to harsh sanctions by the majority, which perceives this disagreement in a negative way (see Chapter 9).

Societal Beliefs about Peace

Societies engaged in intractable conflict need a light at the end of the tunnel that provides them with some kind of positive expectations during periods of bloodshed and suffering. Presentation of peace, as a supreme goal for society, satisfies this need. The beliefs indicate that if a society can achieve the goals of the conflict, peace will be achieved. The beliefs about peace almost never refer to specific and concrete steps that can resolve the conflict through compromises but present it in general, utopian, and vague terms, often in the form of an aspiration, a wish, or a dream. This theme also presents society members as peace loving and peace seeking both to the outside world and to themselves. By describing themselves as peace loving, members of the society can strengthen their positive self-image and try to convince the international community that the pursuit of peace is their ultimate goal.

Ironically, Milošević's Gazimestan speech, which is often interpreted as the first rhetorical threat to use force to reshape Yugoslavia and to create a "cult of revenge and the promise of a new Serbian empire" (Anzulovic, 1999, p. 113), concluded with the call: "Long live peace and brotherhood among peoples!" In Sri Lanka as well, when President Kumaratunga shifted from a dovish to hawkish position during 1995–1996, deciding to crackdown on the Tamils' LTTE, she repeatedly pledged to wage a "war for peace" (Bose, 2007). On an empirical level, in a study that was conducted in Israel in 2002, 36 popular songs were detected between 1948 and 2000 (26 during the active conflict 1948–1992 and 10 during the peace process 1993–2000) that had a major theme about peace. Of these songs, 33 described a very amorphic view of peace, as a dream, wish, or a prayer; 33 of them presented Israeli Jews as peace loving; 27 of them had an ethnocentric self-view without any reference to the other; and 26, especially during the height of the conflict (1948–1992), projected an optimistic outlook (Bar-Tal, Ofek, & Shachar, 2002).

RESEARCH ON THE ETHOS OF CONFLICT

Various studies investigate the societal beliefs of the ethos of conflict and how they have changed in the Israeli Jewish society.

Bar-Tal, Sharvit, Halperin, and Zafran (2012) demonstrate that the eight themes of the ethos of conflict constitute a coherent and gestaltist view of conflict conditions. Each of the themes has unique content and adds to the holistic orientation, but they complement each other and are interrelated in forming a core societal outlook about the conflict. These results are in line with other studies that show similar findings. Gopher (2006) investigated the views of the Israeli-Palestinian conflict by adults of the Israeli Jewish mainstream with an original scale of the ethos of conflict that consists of 48 items (see the items of the scale in Table 1). Factor analysis yielded a master core factor that contained major themes of the ethos of conflict: societal beliefs in the justness of their own goals, delegitimization of the enemy, self-collective perception as the victim, self-collective glorification, and the abstract pursuit of peace. Similarly, in an investigation of socialization to the ethos of conflict by soldiers during their basic military training, Borovski-Sapir (2004) reports that a factor analysis using the items scale yielded one major factor on which were loaded the principal themes of the ethos of conflict.

An additional study reported by Bar-Tal, Sharvit, Halperin, and Zafran (2012) with a national sample of Jews in Israel verifies the ideological functioning of the ethos of conflict as a prism through which individuals evaluate the ongoing major events or major information presented throughout the protracted conflict. The results show that the ethos of conflict measured with a 16-item scale is related to noncompromising views of the particular proposed solutions to settle the conflict peacefully (see the scale in Table 2). That is, the more society members adhere to the ethos of conflict, the less they support solutions that could be accepted as an agreed settlement of the conflict. Thus, the last study supports the notion that the ethos of conflict is a unique cognitive ideological element that provides a particular outlook on the conflict. Both scales can be easily adapted to the context of any intractable intergroup conflict, with few modifications.

Oren (2005, 2009) analyzes Israeli Jewish public opinion polls, cultural products, and political platforms to find out their extent of dominance between 1967 and 2000. The analysis reveals that until 1977 the eight themes of societal beliefs were hegemonic in the Israeli Jewish culture (see Chapter 7).

TABLE 1. *Questionnaire on the Ethos of Conflict*

	Item	Societal Belief Theme
1	The need for a Jewish state, which resulted from anti-Semitism in the Diaspora, does not contradict the Palestinians' right for a national state in part of the Land of Israel.	Justness of goals
2	Nowadays the Israeli people should no longer be a "Nation in Arms."	Security
3	The Arabs are not war seeking by nature.	Delegitimization
4	Paying taxes and military service are not sufficient for expressing one's loyalty to the homeland.	Patriotism
5	We should not let the Arabs see any signs of disagreement among us concerning the desirable political solution to the Arab-Israeli conflict.	Unity
6	Jews have always been known for their wisdom.	Positive collective self-image
7	During the 100 years of Arab-Israeli conflict, Jews were usually victims of Arab aggression.	Victimhood
8	Most Israeli Jews have always aspired to resolve the conflict with the Arabs peacefully.	Peace
9	The claim that unlike the Jewish people, Palestinians did not have any strong attachment to the land of Israel, denies Palestinian people the right for a part of this land.	Justness of goals
10	Security concerns should not be superior to other concerns in government decisions.	Security
11	Arabs have always been characterized by untrustworthiness.	Delegitimization
12	It is possible to understand Israelis who immigrate to other countries during crises.	Patriotism
13	The goal of education is to encourage critical thinking even if it leads to major controversies in society.	Unity
14	The ability of Jews to defend themselves against Arab countries is a testimony to their incredible quality.	Positive collective self-image
15	Israel has not always done its best to achieve a peaceful agreement with the Arabs.	Peace
16	The exclusive right of Jews for the land of Israel stems from it being their historical homeland.	Justness of goals
17	Enforcing military actions is a most efficient means for eliminating threats to the country's security.	Security
18	Among the Arabs human life is not a supreme value.	Delegitimization

	Item	Societal Belief Theme
19	Fostering a feeling of loyalty to one's homeland should be one of the most important goals of the educational system.	Patriotism
20	Unless united, the Jewish people are in danger of extinction.	Unity
21	Jews are the chosen people.	Positive collective self-image
22	The belief that "the whole world is against us" does not accurately reflect international reality	Victimhood
23	Without compromise, peace cannot be achieved.	Peace
24	Since it was only after the British conquest of Palestine that Palestinians began to view it as their national homeland, they do not have real historical rights for the land as much as Jews.	Justness of goals
25	Military force is not enough to ensure real security for the State of Israel.	Security
26	The mistake made by Palestinian leadership when it rejected the partition plan is just one example of the shortsightedness of the Arabs.	Delegitimization
27	There are values no less important than self-sacrifice for homeland.	Patriotism
28	Despite Israel's will for peace, Arabs kept enforcing wars.	Victimhood
29	The strength of the State of Israel lies in a pluralism of viewpoints.	Unity
30	Jews have just as many negative characteristics as Arabs.	Positive collective self-image
31	The history of Jews teaches us that "in every generation they rise up to destroy us."	Victimhood
32	The negotiations for ending the Arab-Israeli conflict will not end in the near future. Conflict resolution is a matter of generations.	Peace
33	Arabs' declarations of peace are insincere.	Delegitimization
34	The fact that Jews kept living in the land of Israel during the Diaspora does not give them an exclusive right for this land.	Justness of goals
35	All means are legitimate for ensuring the security of the State of Israel.	Security
36	The moral level of Israelis is no different from that of other nations.	Positive collective self-image
37	Loyalty to one's homeland should be more important than other values.	Patriotism
38	Criticism of Israel by the international community is usually not a result of anti-Semitism.	Victimhood

(continued)

TABLE 1 *(continued)*

	Item	Societal Belief Theme
39	Expression of different opinions in times of conflict weakens national strength.	Unity
40	The aspiration for peace should be measured by willingness to compromise.	Peace
41	The fact that when Jews returned to the land of Israel, a Palestinian population had been living there, attests to the right of the latter to establish their homeland there.	Justness of goals
42	We should make sure that the best of the young generation remain in regular army service.	Security
43	It is possible to find among the Palestinians a moderate segment that wants to end the conflict.	Delegitimization
44	The saying "it is good to die for our country" should not serve as a guide for education.	Patriotism
45	In the Israeli democracy, it is a civic duty to express opinions, even if they oppose the opinions of the government and majority.	Unity
46	Israelis did not act differently from Arabs in the Arab-Israeli wars.	Positive collective self-image
47	Peace will be achieved only after "grounding facts in reality."	Peace
48	The Palestinians are just as much victims of the conflict as Jews are.	Victimhood

Note: Responses are given on a 5-point scale between "absolutely agree" and "absolutely disagree."

But after 1977 some of the societal beliefs that composed the Israeli ethos of conflict lost their status as widely held societal beliefs (e.g., beliefs rejecting the Palestinians' claims to self-determination and their own statehood). Other beliefs retained their place in the conflict ethos, but their support in the Israeli public diminished (e.g., beliefs that glorify the morality of the Jewish nation or beliefs that present Jews as sole victims of the conflict). Still other beliefs, specifically about peace and about the nature of the existential threat to Israel, significantly changed their content. Similar results were found in studies that investigated the contents of school textbooks (Bar-Tal, 1998a, 1998b; Podeh, 2002), in a study that examined societal beliefs of the ethos of conflict that appeared between 1948 and 2006 in the state ceremonies of Memorial Day and Independence Day (Arviv-Abromovich, 2011), and in a study that investigated the appearance of these beliefs in the Israeli youth weekly magazines (Golan, 2006).

In a large-scale interview study conducted by Raviv, Bar-Tal, and Arviv-Abromovich (in preparation), similar results about the ideological societal

TABLE 2. *Items Selected for the Shortened Scale*

Item	Theme	Factor Loading[a]	Corrected Item-Total Correlation
1. The fact that an Arab population was living in the Land of Israel at the time of the Jews' return attests to the Palestinians' right to establish their homeland there as well.[b]	Justness of goals	.78	.67*
2. We should not let the Arabs see that there are disagreements among us regarding the resolution of the Arab-Israeli conflict.	Unity	.48	.36*
3. Despite Israel's desire for peace, the Arabs have repeatedly forced war.	Ingroup victimization	.59	.50*
4. The exclusive right of Jews to the Land of Israel stems from its status as their historical homeland.	Justness of goals	.56	.47*
5. One can find broad moderate segments among the Arab public that wish to end the conflict.[b]	Delegitimization	.58	.54*
6. There are values no less important than self-sacrifice for the homeland.[b]	Patriotism	.35	.23*
7. The intentional exercise of military force is the most efficient means for eliminating security threats to the country.	Security	.58	.50*
8. The Jews have no fewer negative qualities than do the Arabs.[b]	Positive collective self-image	.63	.54*
9. Without compromise, there can be no peace.[b]	Peace	.62	.50*
10. The strength of the State of Israel lies in the diversity of opinions within it.[b]	Unity	.37	.07
11. The Jewish people's ability to defend themselves against the Arab states is a testimony to their incredible quality.	Positive collective self-image	.56	.44*
12. Encouraging loyalty to the Land of Israel should be one of the education system's most important goals.	Patriotism	.74	.55*
13. Peace will be achieved only after "the facts are set on the ground."	Peace	.37	.36*
14. Military force alone is not enough to truly ensure the security of the State of Israel.[b]	Security	.17	.17*
15. Untrustworthiness has always characterized the Arabs.	Delegitimization	.70	.62*
16. The Palestinians were victims of the Israeli-Arab conflict just as the Jews were.[b]	Ingroup victimization	.61	.49*

[a] The presented loadings were obtained in confirmatory factor analysis of the interim list of 48 items, with each item loading on one of eight themes and all themes loading on a single second-order factor.
[b] These items were reverse scored.
* $p = .001$.
Source: Bar-Tal, Sharvit, Halperin, & Zafran, 2012.

beliefs of the ethos of conflict were found. In this study 100 Israeli Jews were interviewed in depth (November 2003–June 2003) about their views on the Israeli Arab conflict. The interviewees had been at least 17 years old in the 1967 war and proportionally represented all segments of the Jewish population in Israel (according to political orientation, socio-economic status, religiosity, gender, and geographic residence). In general, the study showed that the ethos of conflict is well entrenched among the interviewees, independent of their self-categorization on the dimension of hawks versus doves. Many of them believe that Jews have an exclusive right to the land between the Mediterranean Sea and the Jordan River, and in 1967 this land was completely liberated. Only a small percentage of them recognized some kind of rights to this land by Palestinians. Although the majority of the interviewees understood that the idea of "Greater Israel" was unrealistic and accepted the principle of dividing the land between the two nations, they objected to a complete dismantling of the Jewish settlements in the Palestinian occupied territories. The majority of them agreed to dismantle only isolated Jewish settlements. In addition, the great majority of them viewed Jerusalem as the reunited capital of the State of Israel and objected to its division. Almost all of them rejected acceptance of any refugees and did not see any Jewish responsibility for the creation of the problem. The vast majority of respondents, including those who viewed themselves as doves, expressed extreme mistrust of Arabs and, in particular, of Palestinians and attributed negative characteristics to them. This stands in contrast to their self-view in a positive light and as being the main victim of the conflict. They did not believe that peace was near and saw Palestinian intransigence as responsible for this situation (see also a review of public polls among Jews in Israel by Bar-Tal, Halperin, & Oren, 2010).

In an analysis of interviews with high school students in Israel, Fuxman (2012) shows that the most dominant group of societal beliefs of the ethos of conflict related to security and patriotism. Many of the students spoke about the importance of serving in the military to defend the state and contribute to its well-being as part of the collective (Israeli) identity and also to serve for those who fought and died before them. This suggests that in a society undergoing an intractable conflict, special attention is directed to motivating young people – those nearing military age – about the importance of military service. Other dominant beliefs delegitimize Arabs with the conviction that Palestinians are the main culprits for the lack of peace and hold that Jews have the right to settle in their homeland and are victims throughout their history (see also Hammack, 2009; Sagy, Adwan, & Kaplan, 2002). In a related study involving several hundreds of high school students from different parts of Israel, Fuxman (2012) reports that students who strongly adhere to the beliefs that constitute the ethos of conflict are more likely to trust information that confirms these beliefs (e.g., information that comes from military sources, Israeli government sources, and the Israeli media).

Bar-Tal, Raviv, Raviv, and Dgani-Hirsch (2009) supply a clear-cut demonstration of how the ethos of conflict influences the perception of the conflict. They first assessed the level of adherence to the ethos of conflict, and then participants were exposed to four photographs of daily situations that are relevant to conflictive life in Israel and portray Jewish and Palestinian characters. Three of the pictures contained aggressive interactions between the Jewish and Palestinian characters. In the first photograph of the three, the Jew appears to be more aggressive than the Palestinian, in the second photograph the Palestinian appears as more aggressive, while in the third photograph it is unclear who is more aggressive. In the fourth photograph a Jew and a Palestinian walk side by side with no sign of violence toward each other. Seeing each of the photographs separately, the participants were asked to make up a story that explains what happens in each of them. This indirect assessment and procedure is based on the projective Thematic Apperception Test (TAT). The purpose of the TAT test is to reveal personality conflicts, motives, emotions, and inclinations of which the examinees are not necessarily aware, or whose existence they are not willing to admit (Murray 1971).

The findings showed that in general Jewish Israeli participants with a high level of the ethos of conflict tended to perceive photos depicting encounters between Jews and Palestinians differently from those with a low level of the ethos of conflict. Specifically, the former tended to perceive Palestinians as more aggressive, to blame them more for attributed aggressiveness, and to explain this perceived aggressiveness more in terms of internal and stable causes. This latter finding means that they viewed Palestinians as having stable and unchanging negative dispositions. They also tended to stereotype Palestinians more negatively and Jews more positively.

Using the translated scale of the ethos of conflict with minor adaptation in Serbia, Medjedovic and Petrovic (2011) report that individuals who adhere to the ethos of conflict supported confrontational attitudes toward Kosovo and supported nationalistic political parties that hold noncompromising views regarding the conflict with Kosovo. In another study, Gayer (2012) employs the ethos of conflict as a conceptual framework to analyze national identity constructions in Israel and Palestine, using Q methodology. She compares the content, meaning, and importance of the 48 societal beliefs of the eight themes reflecting the ethos of conflict on the intra- and intersocietal levels and showed which of these beliefs are consensual, characteristic, or contested within and across both societies at the particular stage of the Israeli-Palestinian conflict that she studied. According to her findings, the *consensus beliefs* reflect those beliefs that all society members hold and which represent a kind of monolithic nucleus of national identity construction. The results showed that on the Jewish side in Israel the consensus beliefs focused on the threat that Jews experienced in 1948 and the need for solidarity to cope with possible threats because of their ethnicity, as well as a pronounced positive collective self-image and extreme forms of rival delegitimization by unequivocally associating the other's national ideology with terrorism, militarism, or racism. The last two themes reflect mirror images as they also appeared on the Palestinian side as consensus beliefs. In addition, on the Palestinian side the consensus beliefs focused on themes of justness of the goals to establish an independent Palestinian state on the land beyond the 1967 Israeli borders, on collective self-perception of being the victims in this conflict, and on the need for loyalty to the Palestinian cause.

In addition, the *characteristic beliefs* show that there are competing constructions of national identity, and they reflect societal beliefs that are important for one part of the society but much less central for another segment. Also, she found that the *contested beliefs* display those beliefs that are highly endorsed in one part of the society and extremely refuted in another part. The contested societal beliefs pertain to particularistic and liberalistic national identity that can be found in both societies. The most decisive similarities can be found in Israeli and Palestinian particularistic national identity constructions – which also reflect many items of the ethos of conflict scale. In this case, Israelis and Palestinians rely on eight mirror-inverted societal beliefs, whereby four evolve around societal beliefs about security and use of violence; two are concerned with blind nationalism or patriotism and the remaining two with the justness of the ingroup's goals and the delegitimization of the rival. In contrast, the liberalistic national identity constructions in Israel and Palestine emphasize the need for a free and critical evaluation of the conflict situation and for launching peace education, as well as for recognition that there is a partner on the other side of the peace process.

Gayer's research also illustrates that the analysis of societal beliefs in intractable conflicts must take into account the gendered dimensions and implications of the ethos of conflict – both within and across the adversarial societies. She reports that particularistic and liberalistic national identity constructions are significantly intertwined with regressive and progressive gender-role ideologies, respectively. As such, the oppressive, hierarchical, and invidious aspects of societal beliefs underlying particularistic national identity constructions directed at the outgroup also favor an oppressive, hierarchical, and violent organization of the ingroup's society. In turn, the more equitable conative, cognitive, and affective aspects of liberalistic national identity constructions are strongly related to a more egalitarian gender organization within the society.

In another study that also used Q methodology, Ulug and Cohrs (2012) examine various representations of the Turkish-Kurdish conflict by different involved groups. They report that, in spite of the different emphases expressed by different groups, almost all conveyed viewpoints seem to be quite compatible with the themes of the ethos of conflict. Thus, the researchers argue that, although there are variations within a conflict party about how the conflict is represented, the different representations underlie the ethos of conflict.

Nasie and Bar-Tal (2012) investigate themes of the ethos of conflict as expressed by Palestinian children and adolescents in their writings in a youth newspaper with a content analysis method. The timeline focused on three distinct periods: the peace process (1996–1997), the reemergence of the violent conflict (2001–2002), and a relatively calm period (2005–2007). The key findings show that about a third of the writings of Palestinian children and youth focused on the conflict and demonstrated the existence of the themes of the ethos of conflict. In particular, the writings reflect the themes of victimization and patriotism, while other themes are less frequently expressed. Also, the findings show that when the violent conflict reemerged, the preoccupation with the Israeli-Palestinian conflict in the writings of the children and adolescents is more extensive than at the time of the peace process and in the relatively calm period. This shows that at times of conflict escalation, the involvement with the conflict becomes more salient.

Finally, Bar-Tal, Zoran, Cohen, and Magal (2010) investigated the themes of the ethos of conflict as they appeared in Sabbath leaflets (about the weekly Torah portion) distributed in Israeli synagogues on the Sabbath during Gaza war in 2009. These leaflets are a prism through which one can learn about the perspectives of the religious Zionist ideology regarding the Israeli-Palestinian conflict. The content analysis revealed that themes of the collective self-view of victimhood, justness of goals, delegitimization of the opponent, and positive view of the collective self were very dominant. These findings indicate that Sabbath leaflets, as informal channels of communication for the religious public, preserve and maintain the societal beliefs of the ethos of conflict that fuel the continuation of the conflict.

IMPLICATIONS

The presented conception suggests that the ethos of conflict consists of central societal beliefs that form a holistic perspective of the conflict context. The ethos represents a societal view as a whole and is "similar to the concept personality as used by psychologists to describe the total characteristics of an individual or the concept climate to describe the total characteristics of an organizational environment" (Bar-Tal, 2000a, p. 139). This view corresponds well to Adorno et al.'s (1950) theorizing about the "structural unity" that exists between underlying psychological needs and the ideological manifestations of those needs – in our case, between the needs that appear in times of intractable conflict and the ethos of conflict that satisfies them psychologically, by providing holistic orientation about the reality of the conflict situation.

All the themes fulfill the same function of facilitating adaptation to the conflict context and creating the psychological conditions that allow the society to live under the conditions of conflict with meaning and predictability. They all contribute to the same orientation, suggesting that the conflict is just and essential for the societal life and that the rival is vicious and outside the boundaries of normative groups in contrast to the ingroup, which is the victim and is characterized by virtues. Therefore, the beliefs focus on the needed conditions for full mobilization of the society members not only to support the conflict but also to actively take part in it with a readiness for sacrificing life. The societal beliefs of the ethos of conflict do not refer to specific issues or topics that are raised in particular situations but constitute together a general ideological system that serves as a general prism to evaluate and judge them. In this respect, it is proposed that the view of the ethos of conflict corresponds well to the conception of ideology developed by Jost and his colleagues (Jost, 2006; Jost, Federico, & Napier, 2009; Jost, Glaser, Kruglanski, & Sulloway, 2003; Jost, Nosek, & Gosling, 2008). Ideology can be defined as an organized construct of beliefs, attitudes, and values that provide a general worldview about a present and future reality, with the aim to create a conceptual framework that allows human beings to organize and comprehend the world in which they live and to act toward its preservation or alteration in accordance with this standpoint (Eagleton, 1991; Jost, Federico, & Napier, 2009; McClosky & Zaller, 1984; Shils, 1968; Van Dijk, 1998). It reflects a top-down cognitive process that provides meaning and order to the absorbed information coming from experiences and external sources (Nosek, Graham, & Hawkins, 2010). It also strengthens unity, interdependence, and solidarity as it creates a shared view of the conflict reality because of common experiences that include common socialization.

The ethos of conflict, as an ideology, describes, interprets, and explains the conflict and the related issues by making assertions and assumptions about the nature of the conflict, the conditions related to it, the goals that are needed to win the conflict, and the image of the rival and one's own group. It addresses well the most challenging problems of individual and collective life that society members encounter in the harsh reality. Accordingly, it functions as a system of interpretations that is well accepted in times of conflict because it satisfies basic human motives to understand the world and to avoid existential threat (Jost et al., 2009; Jost et al., 2008). It reflects not only genuine attempts to give meaning and organize the experiences and the provided information that are part of life in the context of intractable conflict but also conscious or unconscious tendencies to rationalize the way things are or, alternatively, the wishes of how they should be (e.g., Jost et al., 2003). People need a frame of understanding social reality with direction, orientation, and perspective, and the ethos of conflict provides them with all these. It is a determinative factor in affecting the evaluation and judgment of the issues and topics that are conflict related. It affects the way society members view events of the conflict, interpret their experiences, and judge various issues that appear over time, including different proposed solutions to resolve the conflict.

From another perspective, the ethos of conflict is in line also with the system justification theory, which proposes that people form a system of beliefs that justifies the socio-political system, the collective needs, or the societal structure – or all three – which maintains the status quo. This justification occurs even if the status quo leads to negative consequences (Jost, Banaji, & Nosek, 2004). The ethos of conflict is thus a construct with special implications for social systems and structure. It specifically provides an ideological system of description, explanation, and justification that supports the status quo – the ongoing intractable conflict. As a linguistic system of description, it provides information about the conflict, including the goals, reasons, and contexts of one's own group and of the rival's. As a system of explanation, it clarifies the causes of its eruption and maintenance. Finally, as a system of justification, it rationalizes the importance of its continuation and the rejection of compromising.

In this conception, the ethos of conflict provides a conservative ideological outlook on the reality of intractable conflict (Krochik & Jost, 2011). Indeed, Hogg (2005) proposes that ideologies that tend to develop under extreme uncertainty (such as intractable conflict) resist change. In this line, the ethos of conflict as a conservative ideology seeks to preserve the existing order of continuing the conflict and thus to maintain the known and familiar without taking any risks by moving into unknown and ambiguous areas that peacemaking would require. It focuses on potential threats and losses in moving toward compromises with the rival and emphasizes stability of the present situation and its security (Jost et al., 2003). It expresses fear of change – as Thórisdóttir and Jost (2011, p. 789) notes, "the status quo, no matter how aversive, is a known condition and is therefore easier to predict and imagine than a potentially different state of affairs that could be either better or worse." It is thus not surprising that we found that a general conservative outlook, reflected in right-wing authoritarianism (RWA) developed by Altemeyer (1981), predicted adherence to the ethos of conflict (Bar-Tal, Sharvit, Halperin, & Zafran, 2012). A close relationship between the ethos of conflict and RWA as worldviews mirrors a conservative orientation of adhering to traditional goals and known situations, closure to new ideas, and mistrust of the other, which lead to the detection of threats and dangers in possible changes. This study also shows that adherence to ideology of the ethos of conflict is related to holding noncompromising views about conflict. Individuals who have worldviews of the ethos of conflict tend to object to specific compromises that are needed for peaceful resolution. Their ideology about the conflict causes them to be intransigent (see also Halperin & Bar-Tal, 2011).

In sum, societal beliefs of collective memory and the ethos of conflict complement each other, although each of them constitutes a solid and holistic narrative that society members share. Each of the two narratives includes themes that contain a cluster of societal beliefs referring to the same topic. Some of the themes appear in both narratives, especially justness of the conflict's goals, positive collective self-image, self-view as a victim, and delegitimization of the rival. They provide the contents that contribute to the continuation of the conflict by constituting its epistemic basis. In addition to the described cognitive elements – societal beliefs of collective memory and the ethos of conflict – the socio-psychological infrastructure in situations of intractable conflicts includes also an emotional element – the collective emotional orientation– that is discussed in the next chapter.

6

Collective Emotional Orientations in Intractable Conflicts

Societies living for a long time under the shadow of intractable conflict develop characteristic collective emotional orientations, with an emphasis on one or more particular emotions. This process develops because the conditions of intractable conflict provide the experiences, information, models, and instructions that serve as stimulators and facilitators for the arousal of such emotions as fear, hatred, and anger by society members. These aroused emotional experiences become a societal phenomenon, taking the form of a collective emotional orientation as society members identify with their group. Because these emotions play a pivotal role in the behavior of society members, they are an important socio-psychological determinant of the way an intractable conflict develops (see also Barbalet, 1998; de Rivera & Paez, 2007; Harré, 1986; Kemper, 1990; Mackie & Smith, 2002; Petersen, 2002; Rimé & Christophe, 1997; Scheff, 1994). "For the group, emotion processes seem necessary for the creation and maintenance of group viability and for long-term commitment to actions that achieve the goals of the group" (Niedenthal & Brauer, 2012, p. 269). The shared emotions are the stimulator, interpreter, motivator, energizer, director, and controller of various socio-psychological processes related to the dynamics of the intractable conflict. It is thus not surprising that many students of such conflicts observe that not infrequently the negative emotions have an intense motivating energy that leads participants of the intractable conflict into dark spaces (e.g., Horowitz, 1985, 2001; Lake & Rothchild, 1998; Petersen, 2002). They not only feed the continuation of conflict but serve as potent barriers that prevent the peacemaking process.

The process of development of the collective emotional orientation is strongly interrelated to the other pillars of socio-psychological infrastructure – the collective memory of conflict and the ethos of conflict. On the one hand, the societal beliefs of the collective memory of conflict and the ethos of conflict, as the cognitive part of the socio-psychological infrastructure, provide the narrative, or the stories, that evoke particular emotions. They serve as a framing directive to the arousal of a particular emotion. These societal beliefs provide the criteria and sensitivity for selection of information that evokes emotions. These beliefs also influence the interpretation and evaluation of situations in terms of the particular emotion. They signal what emotions should be felt and how they should be expressed. Eventually, these societal beliefs guide both what kinds of behaviors are expressed and how these behaviors should be performed as reactions to the particular emotion.

On the other hand, the developed collective emotional orientation evokes the prevalent societal beliefs of the socio-psychological infrastructure. That is, aroused emotions bring to mind held societal beliefs because of the well-established association between emotions and beliefs, and they provide enlightenment and a framework for the experienced feeling. In this process, society members have an acceptable explanation of why the emotion appeared. Thus, the three elements of the socio-psychological infrastructure should be seen as complementary, standing in constant interaction and reinforcing each other. These interactive processes show that emotions facilitate the eruption of the conflict, as was suggested in Chapter 2; fuel its escalation; and inhibit the development of the peace process and the peaceful settlement of the conflict. But they also may facilitate peace building and then play a crucial role in the reconciliation process. Yet, despite being so meaningful, emotions are relatively neglected in the traditional literature about intergroup conflicts, so in this chapter I will extend the discussion about them, beginning with their general nature.

THE NATURE OF EMOTIONS

Emotions are fundamental psycho-physiological evaluative reactions to various kinds of stimulations and therefore play a crucial role as a base for motivation and direction on every level of human functioning, especially in the context of intractable conflicts, which by their nature provide a range of stimulations for their arousal. These reactions are elicited as a consequence of an encounter of stimuli with biological and/or cognitive standards (Cacioppo & Gardner, 1999; Jarymowicz, 2009a; Manstead, Frijda, & Fischer, 2004), evaluated with particular meaning, and eventually provide limitations and/or opportunities for the person to behave (Frijda, 1986; Tooby & Cosmides, 1990). Their major role is to decode the meaning of stimulation, either unconsciously or consciously, and then to transform a concrete stimulation into a concrete behavioral motivation (Bargh, 1997; Berridge & Winkielman, 2003; Cacioppo, Larsen, Smith, & Berntson, 2004). This decoding not only occurs through subception or perception but is based also on social learning and memory, because of which individuals respond with the same emotional reactions when they encounter the same or similar events or objects (Bandura, 1986; Christianson, 1992; Damasio, 2003; LeDoux, 2002; Oatley & Jenkins, 1996). Thus, individuals do not have to experience an event that leads to arousal of an emotion before they are motivated to behave. They can learn about the meaning and consequences of an event or an object and develop an emotion on the basis of this learning. Individuals may be socialized or learn to respond to various cues in their social world with strong emotion without ever personally encountering the cue. For example, although a society member may never have met a member of the adversary group, he or she may hate or fear a member of the rival group only on the basis of learning. Emotions are related to patterns of actions, as each emotion evokes a specific tendency of behaviors (Arnold, 1960; Frijda, 1986). Emotions such as fear, hatred, or anger may lead to destructive behaviors, whereas empathy or guilt may lead to behaviors that facilitate peace making.

Primary and Secondary Emotions

Of the two general categories of emotions (Cacioppo & Gardner, 1999; LeDoux, 1996), primary emotions have a clear physiological basis, are reactive, and can be elicited unconsciously, whereas secondary emotions are based on cognitive processes of identification and evaluation (Reykowski, 1968, 1985). Because with the primary emotion, the basic processes leading to emotional reaction are biochemical and neurological (Damasio, 2004), their functioning is spontaneous, fast, uncontrolled, and unintentional in the early stage of evaluation (Ekman & Davidson, 1994; Jarymowicz, 1997, 2009a; LeDoux, 1996; Zajonc, 1980). They may not be reflected in feelings or perceptions and, as a result, may not require updating of the conscious standards of evaluation (Damasio, 2004; Zajonc, 1980). In fact, the majority of emotions are evoked automatically as a result of stimuli unconsciously detected and evaluated on the subcortical level (within the thalamus and amygdala). Cacioppo, Larsen, Smith, and Berntson (2004, p. 224) note that "conscious experiences provide a glimpse of only a small subset of the cognitive structures and operations that needed to be explored and understood." Thus, in many cases emotional reactions are unconscious and come about through automatic information processing without perception and conscious experience (Killgore & Yurgelun-Todd, 2004). Any subtle signal can relate to an important category (like the label "enemy," which leads to an immediate reaction without any reflection). Furthermore, these processes directly activate effectors leading to uncontrolled behavior without mediation of cognitive appraisal (Bargh, 2001; Damasio, 2003). Only under certain conditions does stimulation of primary emotions reach cortical structures and generate conscious feeling and even cognitive appraisal (Buck, 1999; Cacioppo et al., 2004; Damasio, 2004; LeDoux, 2000). Thus, fear may also be elicited unconsciously in conflicts without information processing and lead to reactions that may be destructive. Primary emotions, though, may also be evoked not as a result of an external stimulation but as a consequence of cognitive activity, such as recalling, analyzing, interpreting, evaluating, or planning (Jarymowicz, 2001a). Thus, in situations of intractable conflict they also may be evoked by the societal beliefs of collective memory and the ethos of conflict.

In order to appraise the complexity of human emotional functioning, one has to consider the "low-high" distinction between subcortical (unconscious) and cortical (conscious) reactions. This distinction is basic for understanding mechanisms of primary and secondary types of regulation and emotions (Buck, 1999; Damasio, 1994; Jarymowicz, 2001b; LeDoux, 1996; Pavlov, 1930), and it indicates that the functioning of secondary emotions is based on a cognitive appraisal of a situation. That is, evaluations based on an appraisal process – related to deliberative thinking, intellectual operations, and use of cognitive evaluative standards – are relatively independent of basic primary affective mechanisms (Piaget, 1970; Jarymowicz, 2001b, 2009a, 2009b; Reykowski, 1989). This process is significant because it uses other bases of evaluation (not primary affect), namely articulated standards (Reykowski, 1989). It has to be noted that the cognitive standards (articulated criteria for behaviors) can vary on the basis of individual values and ideology. Therefore, according to Jarymowicz (2009a, 2009b; Jarymowicz & Imbir, 2010) they lead to a distinction between at least two types of standards. One type refers to standards focused on the affective base of the egocentric-ethnocentric perspective and the understanding of what is good or bad for oneself and for the ingroup members. These types of standards may fuel continuation of the violent conflicts because they focus on the ethnocentric values grounded in the ideological societal beliefs of collective memory and the ethos of conflict. For example, hatred as a secondary emotion is based in these types of standards and can lead to destructive behavioral consequences.

The other standards are reflective (based on deliberative thinking), transgressive, general, and abstract. These standards refer to universal axiological rules of behavior based on superior values accepted by different cultures (Kohlberg, 1984). They refer to moral codes of behavior such as freedom, humanity, justice, and equality. Jarymowicz (2009a, 2009b) suggests at least three conditions for the development of these types of standards:

understanding the meaning of the noted evaluative universal concepts; connecting these abstract concepts with specific conditions in the real world; and experiencing positive feelings for particular states of reality coherent with axiological concepts. These types of emotions are a result of mental activity that requires an investment of time and effort (also inhibited by the ego/ethnocentric affects). It provides a basis to prevent conflict and also to evoke motivation to resolve conflict peacefully. Experimental findings suggest that concentration on axiological concepts decreases the influence of the primary negative affect on evaluation (Jarymowicz, 2006).

In sum, emotions in general serve as data for processes of feeling, impression formation, interpretation, judgment, evaluation, and decision making that may then lead to particular behaviors (Averill, 1980; Carver & Scheier, 1990; Elster, 1999; Frijda, 1986). In conscious processes, emotions automatically guide attention to particular cues and information, influence the organization of memory schemas, give differential weight to specific stored knowledge, activate relevant associative networks in memory, influence the order of cognitive processing priorities, provide interpretative frameworks to perceived situations, and on this basis drive toward certain objects, situations, individuals, or groups, while abstaining from others (Berridge & Winkielman, 2003; Blaney, 1986; Bower, 1992; Cacioppo & Gardner, 1999; Clore, Schwarz, & Conway, 1994; Isen, 1984; Jarymowicz, 2009a; Murphy & Zajonc, 1993; Niedenthal & Kitayama, 1994; Öhman & Wiens, 2001; Ohme & Jarymowicz, 1999, 2001; Schwarz, 1990; Wyer & Srull, 1989). Also, emotions lead to a particular line of behaviors (Frijda, 1986). This analysis points out the potential destructive effects of emotions such as fear and anger in conflict that are automatically evoked or are based on egocentric/ethnocentric evaluative standards. They may have chronic influence not only on information processing because of the persistent availability of internal (i.e., beliefs, attitudes, and so on) and external (i.e., violence, rhetoric, and so on) cues that elicit them in the context of intractable conflict but also on the level of aggressive behaviors, discrimination practices, and other lines of negative actions.

Negative Asymmetry

In addition, various conceptions postulate that evaluation and action are based on an input from two separate and specialized channels: one is related to negative and the other to positive information processing (see Cacioppo & Gardner, 1999; Carver & Scheier, 1990; Isen, 1990). The first one is threat related; the second is appetitive. Some neurobiologists suggest a different anatomic localization of the negative and positive emotions: the former are linked with the right hemisphere, and the latter with the left one (e.g., Grabowska, 1999; Heller, Nitschke, & Miller, 1998; Kobylińska, 2003; Ornstein, 1997; Springer & Deutsch, 1998). The functioning of the right hemisphere is presented in terms of intuitive and holistic modes of information processing, whereas the left hemisphere serves as a basis for specific human processes such as articulation and analytic thinking (Davidson & Fox, 1982; Grabowska, 1999; Ornstein, 1997). This differential localization seems to be consistent with psychological findings indicating that many negative emotions, of which fear is a prototypical example, tend to function in a way that is specific to the right hemisphere – that is, without mediation of analytic conscious insight and appraisal (LeDoux, 1996). They come evolutionarily to protect the individual, and this superior mission disregards truthful evaluations and tolerates exaggerations or distortions. In contrast, the secondary, positive emotions, such as hope, are manifested with the involvement of conscious cognition and anticipation (Snyder, 2000a), specific to the left hemisphere. This process includes an evaluation of the reality and future states, and sometimes has to be based on abstract ideas, especially when these ideas do not have a basis in experiences.

The functions of the two hemispheres in this respect are asymmetrical (Baas, Aleman, & Kahn, 2004) and described in a way that seems to be coherent with the robust psychological findings about the so-called positive-negative asymmetry (Cacioppo & Gardner, 1999; Czapinski, 1985, 1988; Peeters & Czapinski, 1990; Peeters, 1991). The primary negativity-positivity dissociation may lead either to integration or to dominance of the negative type of activation. This asymmetry comes to emphasize the importance and even dominance of the negative emotions in the context of intractable conflict. This context elicits chronically negative emotions that are hegemonic. They dominate individuals as they are spontaneously, automatically, and even unconsciously activated. They thus overflow individuals' conscious, leading to particular experiences, which in turn have an influence on cognitive functioning.

Emotions were studied for many years as an individual psychological phenomenon, but extrapolation from accumulated knowledge on the individual's emotional functioning to collective functioning on a societal level in situations of intractable conflicts can be assumed. This latter assumption is based on the fact that individuals experience these emotions, although in the macrosocietal analysis the focus is on socially shared emotions. However, the shared emotional orientation of society members does not amount to a mere addition of individual emotions but indicates unique qualities of the society as a whole with serious social implications. Macrosocial conditions allow the operation of various factors of social influence that are absent in the individual cases. Thus, the analysis of emotions cannot be limited to an understanding of the emotional functioning on the individual level but has to move to the group level and then we can discuss collective emotional orientation.

FOUNDATIONS OF COLLECTIVE EMOTIONAL ORIENTATION

Shared Emotions

In the discussion of shared emotions, there is a need to differentiate among socio-psychological phenomena. First, emotions called *collective emotions* can be shared by large numbers of individuals in a certain society, being evoked more or less simultaneously in group members (Stephan & Stephan, 2000). This phenomenon can happen because of exposure to the same experience or information. A further development of this observation is a claim that a society, or specifically society's culture, shapes individuals' emotions (see, e.g., Averill, 1980; Gordon, 1990; Harré, 1986; Kitayama & Markus, 1994; Lazarus, 1991; Mackie & Smith, 2002; Mesquita & Frijda, 1992; Smith, 1999). This process occurs as a result of particular common experiences, socialization, and conditions in a society, which include exposure to common information, discourses, symbols, models, epistemic authorities, emphases, values, norms, narratives, beliefs, attitudes, influences, and learning. By recognizing this societal phenomenon, it is possible to assume that like individuals, who may be characterized by a dominant emotion, societies too may develop collective emotions. As a result, society members form a similar cognitive basis that tunes them toward expression of particular emotions. Markus and Kitayama (1994, pp. 341, 343) point out that

> every cultural group has some key ideas that have been traditionally and collectively held in place and that are used to select and organize their own socio-psychological processes. These *core cultural ideas* can influence the nature of the group's habitual emotional tendencies through constraining and affording particular, relatively culture-specific sets of immediate and everyday life realities, in which members of the cultural group are socialized or "trained" to think, act, and feel in a more or less adaptive fashion.

Society members share central beliefs (see Bar-Tal, 2000) that provide the prism through which they view their world and relate to it. This prism not only organizes society's outlook or directs intentional forms of action but also determines collective emotions. A society may be characterized by sensitization to and evaluation and expression of a particular emotion. This shared emotion thus reflects norms, values, and expectations of the society (Smith-Lovin, 1990).

Smith (1993) goes one step farther and defines *group-based emotions* as emotions that are felt by individuals as a result of their membership in a certain group or society. He and his colleagues (Devos, Silver, Mackie, & Smith, 2002; Mackie, Devos, & Smith, 2000; Smith, 1993, 1999; Smith & Mackie, 2008) capitalize on the theorizing of Turner, Hogg, Oakes, Recher, and Wetherell (1987) about evolvement of group behaviors within the framework of their self-categorization theory and propose a theory of intergroup emotions on the basis of group members' feelings of social identity. According to the theory, individuals may interpret specific events or conditions as group members (i.e., when social identity is salient and relevant). As a result, they may experience a particular emotion that is derived from the situation, even if they did not attend the situation personally. That is, "when appraisals occur on a group basis, emotions are experienced on behalf of the ingroup" (Devos et al., 2002, p. 113). The strength of the experienced group-based emotions is dependent, according to Iyer and Leach (2008), on whether the event that arouses the emotions is relevant to the group member, on self-categorization as an ingroup member, and on identification with the ingroup. Furthermore, the group-based emotions that follow from the cognitive appraisal of the situation play an important role in shaping intergroup behaviors. An impressive line of research supports various hypotheses derived from the previously described theory (see reviews of Devos et al., 2002; Smith, Seger, & Mackie, 2007; Wohl, Branscombe, & Klar, 2006; Yzerbyt, Dumont, Gordijn, & Wigboldus, 2002). All these studies show that people experience differential emotions on the basis of the situation confronted by their own group as a whole or by subgroups or individual ingroup members.

The initial work by de Rivera (1992) focuses on the context in which collective emotions are evoked. He suggests that it is important to differentiate emotional atmosphere from emotional climate and emotional culture. *Emotional climate* refers to collective emotions that arise when members of a group focus their attention on a specific short-term event that affects them as a group (e.g., major terror attack as occurred in New York on September 11, 2001). In turn, *emotional culture* refers to the emotional expressions that are socialized in any specific cultures because of the particular practices (see also de Rivera & Paez, 2007). In both cases, nevertheless, the focus is on shared emotions.

Halperin, Sharvit, and Gross (2011) propose to differentiate among shared short-term emotions and shared chronic emotions, which they call long-term sentiments. Whereas short-term emotions are multicomponential responses to specific events, chronic emotions are an enduring and stable emotional disposition toward a person, group, or symbol (Arnold, 1960; Ekman, 1992; Frijda, 1986; Halperin, 2008b, 2011; Halperin & Gross, 2011a). In their view, the nature of long-term intractable conflicts creates a fertile ground for the continuation and aggregation of emotions beyond the immediate time frame. Some major conflict-related events, which may be accompanied by repeated dissemination of specific information about the conflict, may produce stable group-based emotional sentiments toward the opponent and the conflict. As a result, stable negative intergroup emotions such as fear, anger, and hatred become an inherent part of the stable socio-psychological repertoire of society members in such conflicts.

Halperin et al. (2011) propose and Halperin and Gross (2011a) demonstrate empirically that particular chronic emotions influence the discrete emotional reactions to specific events that take place in conflict via their impact on cognitive appraisal (Lerner & Keltner, 2000). Thus, according to the following example, long-term external threats to one's group are likely to cause bouts of discrete fear and insecurity, and these emotions in turn encourage longer-term emotional sentiments that cause group members to be more sensitive to potentially threatening cues, and therefore they more frequently and easily elicited responses of fear. Long-term emotional sentiments bias the cognitive appraisals of specific events in the particular direction of evoking specific discrete emotions (see Halperin, 2011; Halperin & Gross, 2011a). This premise is based on the *appraisal tendency* framework (Lerner & Keltner, 2000), according to which each emotion activates a cognitive predisposition to interpret events in line with the central appraisal dimensions that triggered the emotion. In this process, the well-established and institutionalized chronic emotion has the determinative effect on the appraisal process in a particular situation, leading to its evocation and not that of another emotion (see Halperin & Gross, 2011a, for empirical support).

Elaborating further these ideas, Halperin (in press) describes the sequence of processes by which enduring emotional sentiments and short-term emotions contribute to the formation of specific attitudinal and behavioral responses to conflict-related events. In his view, the processes begin with the occurrence of, either together or separately, a new event, the appearance of new information related to the conflict, or recollection of a past conflict-related event that has either positive or negative meaning (e.g., war, terror attack, rejection of a peace offer, or peace gesture). In most cases, the events are experienced directly by only a few society members and later transmitted to other members through the mass media or other channels of communication. In these cases, if individuals identify with the same collective as the directly exposed society members, they experience short-term group-based emotions, depending on the manner in which they are appraised. (Mackie et al., 2000; Smith, 1993). For example, a violent act committed by rival group members against the ingroup would induce anger if it is appraised as unjust and is accompanied by the evaluation of the ingroup as strong (Halperin, 2008; Huddy, Feldman, & Cassese, 2007). According to Halperin (in press), in the context of long-term conflicts the appraisal of events is influenced by three main factors: the event may be framed by the agents who transmit the information about the event in a certain way, which influences society members' appraisal; the event's appraisal may be influenced by the system of beliefs, which serves as a prism to process information and may include the collective memory and the ethos of conflict as well as other values and ideological views; and, finally, the appraisal-based framework assumes that long-term emotional sentiments bias the cognitive appraisals of specific events (e.g., according to Halperin and Gross [2011b] Israelis' angry reactions to Palestinians during the war in Gaza were influenced, to a large extent, by Israelis' enduring sentiment of anger toward Palestinians, measured more than a year before the war).

Of special importance is the cycle of thoughts and emotions in which each element is interrelated and affects the other in times of intractable conflicts. That is, on the one hand, emotions are evoked by the information that transmits societal beliefs of collective memory and the ethos of conflict as well as information about current events. On the other hand, when emotions are evoked, they draw their meaning from societal beliefs of the ethos of conflict and collective memory. This system is self-sustaining and self-reinforcing. In these processes, evaluations are simplistic, homogeneous, and diffusive, with nonrelated aspects. The ways in which emotions are socially constructed influences how emotions are experienced, recalled, and then acted upon. Eventually, these experiences, actions, and recollections directly influence the degree to which conflicts escalate and become engulfed in cycles of violence.

For example, a long-term external threat to the group makes society members develop a chronic emotion (i.e., sentiment) of fear. In turn, this chronic fear emotion, together with the repertoire of societal beliefs of collective memory and the ethos of conflict, attunes them to threatening cues and leads to a higher appraisal of danger that subsequently elicits more frequent fear. In this continuously repeated process, the chronic emotion is further solidified in the repertoire of the society members and, in turn, strengthens the validity and centrality of collective memory and the ethos of conflict. In understanding the emotions in conflict, it is necessary not only to look at the emotions evoked as a result of the particular event but also to elucidate the long-term dominant chronic emotions that have crucial effect on the total emotional, cognitive, and behavioral reactions of society members involved in intractable conflict.

Collective Emotional Orientation

Important in this perspective is the concept *collective emotional orientation*, which refers to the characterizing expression of a particular emotion or a number of emotions (Bar-Tal, 2001). The expression is evident not only on the individual level but also in various channels of communication, institutions, and products. Collective emotional orientation refers to societal characterization of an emotion that is reflected on individual and collective levels in the socio-psychological repertoire, as well as in tangible and intangible societal symbols, such as cultural products or ceremonies. Collective emotional orientation evolves as a result of living under particular durable conditions (see also Bar-Tal, Halperin, & de Rivera, 2007). These conditions involve prolonged experiences that often lead to the dominance of an emotion or even a few emotions that became part of the psychological and cultural-societal repertoire.

An intractable conflict as a context provides prolonged conditions that contain cues and signals for the appearance of a particular emotion. That is, society members appraise the conflict context through salient cues and signals that appear as threatening and stressful (see Lazarus & Folkman, 1984). On the basis of this appraisal is evoked a particular emotion (see also Halperin, Sharvit, & Gross, 2011). When such a context lasts for a long time, society members who live in this context experience the emotion again and again. With time, they learn the cues and signals and become predisposed to respond emotionally to them. They themselves develop many different cues in the societal-cultural institutions and products to maintain this emotion. As a result, this emotion as a sentiment becomes dominant and chronically evoked. In this way, a collective emotional orientation develops.

The salience of a particular emotion in a particular society does not necessarily imply that this society is characterized by collective emotional orientation. Years ago I proposed the following criteria for identifying collective emotional orientation (Bar-Tal, 2001):

1. Society members experience a particular emotion, and they report on experiencing this emotion.
2. The emotion appears frequently in the society's public discourse: it is expressed and discussed often in public debates by societal channels of communication. There is direct reference to this emotion as well

as to the cues and signals that evoke it. It can be found, for example, in speeches of leaders or in mass media that provide information and knowledge.
3. Cultural products, such as books, films, or theater, directly express the particular emotion and the beliefs that trigger it and refer to the cues and signals that evoke it.
4. The educational system is greatly responsible for the formation of the collective emotional orientation as it imparts the emotion from a very early age. It teaches the children and the adolescents about the emotion and the cues that lead to its expression. The students learn about the importance of the emotion, as well as when and how to express it. In general, the educational system, through school textbooks, ceremonies, and teachers, transmits beliefs that reflect and evoke the particular emotion.
5. The emotion and the beliefs that evoke this emotion are embedded in the society's collective memory. The learning of the emotion by society members is often based on past experiences of the collectives. The collective memory of conflict provides unequivocal basis for the evolvement of particular emotions. But then other, often unrelated collective experiences may also serve as a basis for the development of a particular collective emotional orientation that is viewed as being relevant to the ongoing intractable conflict.
6. The emotion and beliefs evoking the particular emotional orientation play a role in decision making by the society's institutions and influence policy and courses of action. That is, the emotion eventually directs and energizes the decision makers to take a particular line of action as a result of their own emotion or as a result of emotional pressure from the constituents.

Thus, a collective emotional orientation may have nonmutually exclusive origins. It can originate in the common direct and personal experience of society members as, for example, occurs in situations of conflict when society members personally experience threat and danger. In addition, without having personal experience, society members may receive information that can facilitate the development of the collective emotional orientation. Such information can be transmitted via mass media or by educational, cultural, and social channels of communication, including various epistemic authorities, such as leaders, teachers, and parents. This conception implies that collective emotional orientation can be investigated not only by interviewing or surveying society members, but also by examining the contents of channels of communication and cultural products. Thus, for example, Nasie and Bar-Tal (2012) studied the expression of emotions as they appeared in the eyes of Palestinian children and adolescents via an analysis of their written pieces in a Palestinian newspaper. Focusing on the emotions of fear, hatred, anger, revenge, and hope, they found that in the sampled articles half of the references concerned the collective emotion of hope (46%), a substantial portion touched upon the emotions of fear (22%) and revenge (16%), while the emotions of hatred (10%) and anger (7%) received fewer references. The expressions that reflected the dominant hope in the writings of Palestinian children and adolescents include descriptions of longing for freedom, victory, liberation from the occupation, return of refugees to their homeland, emancipation of Jerusalem, avenging the blood of the *shahids*, and yearning for a bright future. An elaborated example of a collective emotional orientation of fear is presented in the next section in which the emotion of fear is described.

In sum, when beliefs and reaction patterns are disseminated and shared, they constitute a major influence on the emotional functioning of society members. They evoke the particular emotion(s). Then they supply the criteria and sensitivity necessary for the selection of information, which, in turn, evokes emotion. Finally, they affect the interpretation and evaluation of situations in terms of particular emotions, signal what emotions are appropriate in general and especially in particular situations, direct how these emotions should be expressed, and guide the behaviors performed in reaction to the emotions (Armon-Jones, 1986; Hochschild, 1983; Wallbott & Scherer, 1986; Zajonc, 1998).

Society members share central societal beliefs (see Bar-Tal, 2000a) that provide the prism through which they view their world and relate to it. This prism not only organizes society's outlook or directs intentional forms of action but also serves as an appraisal framework and thus determines collective emotional orientation. A society may be characterized by sensitization to and evaluation and expression of a particular emotion. This shared emotion thus reflects norms, values, and expectations of the society (Smith-Lovin, 1990). It permeates the societal-cultural channels, institutions, and products that maintain and express it. Society members are socialized to acquire the socially approved emotional orientation from an early age. They learn what cues to attend to in order to feel a particular emotion, how to appraise these cues, how to express the emotion, and how to behave in accordance with it (Averill, 1980; Lewis & Saarni, 1985; Saarni & Harris, 1989). This learning is also done, beyond the family setting, via political, educational, and cultural mechanisms. The shared emotion of the collective becomes one of the influencing factors in decision making by society members in their own personal decisions and also by leaders who set the policies and lines of action for the collective. These decisions determine the course of the intractable conflict.

Now, after presenting general descriptions of emotions and of collective, emotional orientation, I analyze a few collective emotional orientations that are prevalent in societies engaged in intractable conflicts. I begin with a description of collective fear, which is one of the dominating emotions in intractable conflict and also has been extensively researched.

COLLECTIVE FEAR

Fear as a primary aversive emotion arises in situations of threat and danger to the organism (the person) and his or her environment (the society), and it enables that person to respond adaptively (Gray, 1989; Öhman, 1993; Plutchik, 1980; Rachman, 1978). It constitutes combined physiological and psychological reactions with an objective to maximize the probability of surviving in a dangerous situation. Behaviorally, it is usually associated with the avoidance of taking risks and the motivation to create a safer environment (Frijda, Kuipers, & ter Schure, 1989; Halperin, Bar-Tal, Nets-Zehngut, & Drori, 2008). It is possible to differentiate between two mechanisms of fear arousal: one via automatic and unconscious reactions and the other via conscious appraisal of the situation as threatening and dangerous (Goleman, 1995; LeDoux, 1996; Oatley & Jenkins, 1996; Zajonc, 1980). The former way is based on automatic stimulus-reaction relations; the latter is based on cognitive evaluation but is associated with an appraisal of low strength and low control over the situation (Roseman, 1984), as well as with increased risk estimates and pessimistic predictions (Lerner & Keltner, 2001). Also, the emotion of fear is related to cognitive evaluation of insecurity, which also implies reasoning that the situation signals threats (Bar-Tal & Jacobson, 1998). Threats and dangers, which can be detected in present situations, or generalized from past experiences, can be related specifically to a particular individual (e.g., being in a bombed house or being arrested) or be evoked indirectly in collective situations (e.g., being a member of a society that is involved in intractable conflict, political persecution, or war). In addition, as demonstrated by Grings and Dawson (1978), fear can be acquired by information received about certain objects, events, people, or situations that are supposed to threaten the person or his or her society (see Rachman, 1978). Societal institutions and channels of communication can create, disseminate, and maintain information about threats and dangers.

Once the information about threatening or potentially threatening stimuli is acquired through different modes of learning, it is stored in a memory about emotional situations and influences appraisal of a particular situation (Lazarus, 1991). The stored information provides a basis for further generalization of fearful situations to additional situations and conditions. Fear may operate irrationally and destructively because defensive reactions are evoked not only as a result of cues that directly imply threat and danger but also by conditioned stimuli that are nonthreatening in their nature (LeDoux, 1996; Mowrer, 1960; Öhman, 1993; Rachman, 1978). Once fear on a high level is evoked, it limits the activation of other mechanisms of regulation and stalls consideration of various alternatives because of its egocentric and maladaptive patterns of reactions to situations that require creative and novel solutions for coping. Finally, fear motivates defense and protection from events that are perceived as threatening. When defense and protection are not efficient, fear may lead to aggressive acts against the perceived source of threat (Bandura & Walters, 1959). That is, when in fear, human beings sometimes tend to cope by initiating a fight, even when there is little or nothing to be achieved by doing so (Blanchard & Blanchard, 1984; Eibl-Eibesfeldt & Sutterlin, 1990; Jarymowicz, 2002; Lazarus, 1991b; Plutchik, 1990).

Growing knowledge in social sciences has established that groups can be characterized by collective fear. For example, Corradi, Fagen, and Garreton (1992) analyze the formation of the collective fear in the 1970s in four South American societies: Argentina, Brazil, Chile, and Uruguay. In these cases, the collective fear developed in reaction to certain threatening societal conditions. Members of these four societies were subjected to systematic and consistent terror, and as a result they perceived the political system as the source of life-threatening dangers. This perception was shared by a substantial segment in each society, resulting in a "fear culture," as the researchers called it.

It is assumed that societies involved in intractable conflict develop collective fear orientation, as such situations are usually characterized by continuous threat and danger to society members and to society as a whole (Bar-Tal, 2001; Jarymowicz & Bar-Tal, 2006). Intractable conflicts involve physical violence in which soldiers and civilians are killed and wounded, civil property is destroyed, refugees suffer, and often atrocities are carried out. The prolonged experience of violence affects the personal life of society members and marks their behavior. Indeed, analyses of real conflicts provide unequivocally strong evidence for the emergence of fear in conflict situations (Bar-Tal, 2001, 2006; Brubaker & Laitin, 1998; Horowitz, 2001; Jarymowicz & Bar-Tal, 2006; Lake & Rothchild, 1996, 1998; Petersen, 2002; White, 1984).

In stressful situations of intractable conflict that last for a long time, society members tend to process information selectively, focusing on the evil and malintentional acts of the adversary, which are threatening and full of danger. These experiences become embedded in the collective memory, get incorporated into cultural products, and then are disseminated via society's channels of communication (Bar-Tal, 2003; Paez, Basabe, & Gonazales, 1997; Ross, 1995). In addition, fear also spreads via social contagion as group members empathetically absorb the fearful reaction of their co-patriots, as group members influence each other via modeling and imitation in various public situations. Eventually, they serve as a fertile ground for the formation of the collective fear orientation (Bar-Tal, 2001).

A collective fear orientation cuts deeply into the psychic fabric of society and becomes linked with a collective memory of conflict and the ethos of conflict. The collective fear orientation becomes embedded in the societal culture of conflict simply because fear is functional and adaptive. Fear prepares society members to cope better with the stressful situation on a very primary level (Collins, 1975; Lazarus & Folkman, 1984). This preparation is achieved in a number of ways: it mobilizes constant readiness for potential threats against unwished surprises; it directs attention and sensitizes society to cues that signal danger and to information that implies threat; it increases affiliation, solidarity, and cohesiveness among society members in view of the threat to individuals and to society at large; and it mobilizes society members to act on behalf of the society, to cope with the threat, to act against the enemy, and to defend the country and society. But in addition to the functions of the collective fear orientation, there are also other consequences. It may lead when it is at a high level to a collective freezing of beliefs, as will be explained later. The empirical evidence shows that a high level of fear has limiting effects on cognitive processing.

In the context of high fear, a society in intractable conflict tends to stick to certain beliefs about the causes of threat, about the conflict, about the adversary, and about ways of coping with the dangers. It has difficulty entertaining alternative ideas, solutions, or courses of actions. Maslow (1963, p. 124) notes that "all those psychological and social factors that increase fear cut impulse to know." This line of behaviors in the context of threat was also demonstrated in experimental social psychological research (e.g., Corneille, Yzerbyt, Rogier, & Boudin, 2001; Mackie, Devos, & Smith, 2000; Rothgerber, 1997).

Furthermore, on a high level the collective fear orientation tends to limit society members' perspective by building expectations for the present and future exclusively on the past when disassociation from the past may allow creative thinking about new alternatives to resolve the conflict peacefully. A society oversensitized by fear tends to misinterpret cues and information as signs of threat and danger, searching for the smallest indication in this direction, even in situations that signal good intentions. The fear also causes great mistrust and delegitimization of the adversary (Bar-Tal, 2001; Maoz & McCauley, 2008). Thus, it may prevent launching a peacemaking process, cause stabilization of the violent context, or even escalate the conflict. In addition, political research shows that fear leads people to increased conservatism and ethnocentrism, as well as prejudice and intolerance toward outgroups (Feldman & Stenner, 1997; Jost, Glaser, Kruglanski, & Sulloway, 2003; Marcus, Sullivan, Theiss-Morse, & Wood, 1995; Stephan & Stephan, 2000). Finally, the collective fear orientation is a major cause of violence. A society in fear tends to fight when it copes with threatening conditions. Fight is a habituated course of action, based on past experience, causing a society to fixate on coping with threats in a conflictive way, without trying new avenues of behavior that might break the cycle of violence (see Brubaker & Laitin, 1998; Lake & Rothchild, 1998; Petersen, 2002). Thus, fear feeds the continuation of the intractable conflict. This feeding is powerful because the collective orientation of fear is not only maintained by the experiences of society members but often reinforced by society's channels of communication and its institutions.

Nevertheless, because fear is associated with the emotional goal of reducing the threat (Halperin, 2008), the primary goal of fearful people is to protect themselves and avoid threats and dangers. Thus, fear, when it is not accompanied with hatred, may even lead to support of compromises that reduce threat (Halperin, 2011). But it can be assumed that fearful individuals will not be supportive of compromise that involves a perceived security risk because they do not support risk taking (Rydell, Mackie, Maitner, Claypool, & Smith, 2008). Under some circumstances fear may restrain military actions and aggression in order to prevent further threats (Huddy, Feldman, & Cassese, 2007; Lerner, Gonzalez, Small, & Fischhoff, 2003; Skitka, Bauman, Aramovich, & Morgan, 2006; Spanovic, Lickel, Denson, & Petrovic, 2010).

Fear as an emotion is often accompanied by insecurity, which is a cognitive element that is a response to a perceived danger in the environment as the result of a threat (Jacobson, 1991a). In essence, two beliefs are essential in the formation of beliefs about insecurity: the appraisal of one or more events, conditions, or situations that indicate a threat or danger ("primary appraisal"); and beliefs about available defenses and the ability to cope with the perceived threat or danger ("secondary appraisal"). Only when individuals believe they will have difficulty in coping with the threat are insecurity beliefs formed (Lazarus, 1991a; Smith & Lazarus, 1993). Beliefs of insecurity that have affective implications, being accompanied with feelings of fear, unpleasantness, anger, or frustration, are often labeled as feelings of insecurity. Thus, beliefs of insecurity can be triggered by one or more events that are perceived as indicators of threat and are dependent entirely on the individual's interpretations and evaluations of the diverse information coming from the environment (Jacobson, 1991b). Because this process of appraisal depends on a person's repertoire of beliefs (i.e., stored knowledge) concerning different contents such as goals, ideology, or coping capability (Bar-Tal & Jacobson, 1998a), in a society that endures constant threat, security beliefs can turn into societal beliefs, lend society their unique traits, prevail in the heart of the ongoing public discourse, and act as a crucial factor which dictates social action (Bar-Tal, 2000a). In the cases of an intractable conflict, they even become a part of the conflict's ethos, as was discussed in Chapter 5 (Bar-Tal, 2007b).

Studies conducted in Guatemala showed how massacres performed during the conflict led to the evolvement of a collective emotional orientation of fear (Beristain, Pérez-Armiñan, & Lykes, 2007). According to the researchers, during four decades of internal armed conflict, political repression, and political violence, thousands of civilians were killed, many of them in atrocities, and about a million people were displaced, mostly Mayans. The studies found that human rights violations affected the emotional climate of Maya communities by increasing fear, sadness, and distrust, all of which led to decreased ability to talk to others about the experiences, particularly the terror and repression. The responses that constituted the emotional climate encompassed cognitive responses (negative thinking such as "nothing can be done"); negative feelings, such as sadness and loneliness; and certain behaviors, such as self-isolation and failure to participate in community processes. The fear penetrated well into the societal fabric and was expressed in cultural symbols.

Israeli Collective Emotional Orientation of Fear

In 2000 I analyzed the Israeli Jewish society's collective emotional orientation of fear (Bar-Tal, 2001). Already in the early 1960s, fear was one of the dominant emotions expressed by Jews in Israel (Antonovsky & Arian, 1972). Years later, but still at the height of the intractable conflict, Israeli polls began to gauge Israeli Jews' fears. Unsurprisingly, they showed that Israeli Jews felt threatened and expressed worries about the security situation. In 1970–1971 about 70% of Israeli Jews expressed security worries, and in 1972 about 60%; after the 1973 war, this percentage rose to 90% (Stone, 1982). Surveys conducted in the past decade found that a large majority of Israelis believes that ongoing terror attacks might cause a strategic and even existential threat to the state of Israel (www.nssc.haifa.ac.il): 85.5% of Israelis expressed this feeling in 2000, 86.6% in 2002, and 83% in 2006 (Ben-Dor, Canetti-Nisim, & Halperin, 2007). In addition, 80% of the Israeli public expressed in 2006 high levels of fear from a nuclear attack by Iran that would destroy the state of Israel (Peace Index,

August 2006). Finally, more than 25% of the Israeli public has reported in 2003–2005 on high levels of fear that Arabs will drive Israeli's Jewish population to the sea (www.nssc.haifa.ac.il). In late 2000, approximately 80% of the respondents expressed concern that they or a member of their family might become a victim of a terrorist attack, reaching a height of 92% in 2002. Subsequently, this indicator dropped to 83% in 2003, 78% in 2004 and 2005, 72% in 2006, 69% in 2007, and 70% in 2009 (Ben Meir & Bagno-Moldavsky, 2010).

These findings are not surprising in the view of the Israeli-Palestinian conflict and the Israeli-Arab conflict that have raged for about a century. During this period, from the Jewish perspective Arabs including Palestinians not only have vowed to destroy the Jewish community and the State of Israel but also have launched ongoing violence against Jews and later against the State of Israel when it was established. This violence not only included sporadic attacks but also major wars. Many thousands of Jews were killed during this lasting conflict and more were injured.

Nevertheless, the Jewish fear in Israel has additional roots as well. It is also fed by the societal and cultural institutions and channels of communication that disseminate societal beliefs that instigate and maintain fear, forming a collective emotional orientation. The study demonstrated the appearance of stimulation of fear in Israeli school books, literature, films, press, and leaders' speeches (Bar-Tal, 2001; Bar-Tal, Jacobson, & Klieman, 1998). Thus, as an example Ben-Ezer (1992, p. 36) writes that Israeli literature in the 1950–1970s turned

the Arab into a nightmare, into something essentially sinister, into that dark part of existence onto which we project our own fear, our dread and terror.... the Arab has no existence – for himself – a social, national, everyday existence. He is a scary projection born from the soul of the Israeli hero. And even more than he instills fear, the Arab is a nuisance who doesn't allow the Israeli person to get on with his life as he would like to, away from his ongoing troubles with the conflict and the wars it has caused.

Similarly, negative and threatening portrayals of Arabs could also be found in Israeli children's literature. In an extensive study, Cohen (1985) analyzes the image of the Arab in children's books from the 1950s until the early 1980s. He found that Arabs were consistently dehumanized as a threatening entity, beginning with the description of their external appearance (e.g., "having a scar," "an angry and evil face," "horrifying eyes") and ending with characterizations (e.g., murderous, villainous, ruthless, cruel).

The creation of the collective emotional orientation of fear in Israel was not based only on the experiences of Jews in the course of the Israeli-Arab conflict but also on the collective memory of Jews (Bar-Tal, Magal, & Halperin, 2009). According to this collective memory, throughout the centuries Jews were exposed to continuous threats: from the Greek and Roman eras, through the Islamic conquests, the Middle Ages, the Reformation, and the Industrial Revolution up to the present time (Poliakov, 1974). The threats took the form of anti-Jewish tracts, libels, the imposition of distinctive dress, the levying of special taxes, social and economic restrictions, forced conversions and other religious attacks, deportations, expulsions, and pogroms (Grosser & Halperin, 1979). These experiences were transmitted between the generations throughout the centuries, becoming part of the Jewish culture (Liebman, 1978; Stein, 1978). Their peak took place between 1941 and 1945, when six million Jews – one-third of the Jewish people – were exterminated in an organized and systematic genocide, the Holocaust (Bauer, 1983; Dawidowicz, 1975). The Holocaust has a special imprinting effect on the Israeli society, raising the existential chronic fears of Jews to play a major role in the Middle Eastern context (Elon, 1971).

Studies by Zafran and Bar-Tal (2002) are unique as they investigate the antecedents and effects of collective fear. The results show that so-called hawks, who object to the compromises required by the peace process owing to mistrust of Arabs, are characterized by a higher collective fear orientation than doves, who support the compromises required by the peace process and are ready to try peaceful relations with Arabs. The former are more fearful regarding the fate of the Jewish people and Israel than the latter. They also are more preoccupied than doves with collective memories implying fear. Also, the study reports that preoccupation with collective memory is an important predictor of fear orientations independent of the political orientation. High preoccupation with collective memory implying threat and fear leads to a high collective fear orientation. Finally, the study shows that doves and hawks have different ways of processing information drawn from collective memory and learn different lessons. Specifically, it finds that hawks reported that events in Jewish history related to fear (such as pogroms of Jews, the Holocaust, Israeli-Arab wars, or Arab terror) influenced their personal lives more than they did for doves. In addition, hawks thought that events in Jewish history related to fear should affect the decisions of the Israeli government more than did doves.

Similarly, Halperin, Bar-Tal, Nets-Zehngut, and Drori (2008) report in a study involving Jewish students that individuals who tend to remember the negative experiences of the Jewish people in the distant past tend also to experience fear about the future of the Jewish collective. Thus, remembering traumatic Jewish experiences that took place in the remote past affects collective fear related to the Israeli-Arab conflict. Moreover, the results indicate that remembering the negative experiences in the Jewish distant past highly influences the results of interethnic meetings. For those who greatly remembered these experiences, meetings with an Arab triggered feelings of collective fear. This suggests that for them an Arab serves as a generalized negative stimulus who elicits memories of past persecution. On the other hand, it appears that for people who are less flooded by traumatic national memories, interaction with the "other" has actually managed to reduce perception of collective threat and feelings of fear. The results also show that delegitimization of Arabs was closely related to fear. The more a person delegitimized Arabs, the more he or she experienced collective fear.

Studies on a larger scale provide similar results. The findings indicate a robust relationship between threat perception and conciliatory positions regarding the solution of the Israeli-Arab conflict. Arian (1989) reports that among a representative sample of Israeli Jews the more they believe that they are alone in a hostile world the less they are ready to withdraw from the territories occupied in the 1967 war; also, the more Jews perceived Arabs as a threat, the less ready they were to withdraw from the occupied territories. The latter results were replicated in 1996–1999 with national samples of Israeli Jews (Gordon & Arian, 2001). Studies by Maoz and McCauley show similar results. On the basis of a nationwide representative sample of Jews in Israel, Maoz and McCauley (2005) report that two of the most powerful predictors of opposition to making compromises for peace are the long-term belief in the zero-sum nature of the conflict and the levels of perceived threat from Palestinians. These results were replicated in another study based on a representative sample (Maoz & McCauley, 2009). In addition, a study by Maoz and McCauley (2008) reports that threat perception was highly related to dehumanization of Palestinians and support for harsh aggressive retaliatory policies against them. Halperin (2011) reports that fear is an emotional antecedent fostering an opposition to taking risks during negotiations. This factor can be a crucial obstacle to any progress toward peace, which inherently requires mutual risk taking. In addition, he found that fear reduced the support for making territorial compromises that might lead to security problems and also induced support for initiating militant actions against Palestinians. All these studies observed the detrimental role that fear plays in intractable conflicts.

But, as noted earlier, fear with its motivation to avoid and prevent dangers also induced other results. Maoz and McCauley (2009) argue that, in contrast to collective fear that is aroused as a reaction to threats to the well-being of the group, personal fear leads to moderate support for compromises with Palestinians. Also, Halperin (2011) reports that while fear reduced the support for making territorial compromises that imply serious risk taking ("support for Israeli withdrawal to the 1967 borders and evacuation of all settlements"), it also increased support for symbolic compromises (declaring the Arab neighborhoods and villages in Jerusalem as the capital of the future Palestinian state), which did not involve any serious concrete risk taking.

Collective Angst

Wohl and his collaborators propose that very serious perceptions of threat – one that indicates to the perceivers that there is a possibility of group extinction – leads to the appearance of a group-based emotional response of collective angst (Wohl & Branscombe, 2008a; Wohl, Branscombe, & Reysen, 2010). Collective angst is aversive because it reflects the belief that a possible negative event or a more prolonged process may befall the ingroup in the future and cause its destruction. In an attempt to prevent the expected destruction, society members who experience collective angst express a desire to act in ways that will allow full mobilization and strengthening of the ingroup. Crighton and Mac Iver (1990) describe the fear of extinction (collective angst) of the Maronites in Lebanon and Protestants of Northern Ireland, who felt isolated in a sea of enemies, believing that they constituted an outpost in a hostile population that intends to eliminate their dominant position and presence. This fear led them to strengthen their domination and inflict violence on the rival group.

Nevertheless, the specific manifestations of collective angst may vary across contexts. Thus, feelings of collective angst may be manifested also in constructive responses that are aimed at strengthening the ingroup's vitality. For example, in order to retrieve the sense of security, during intergroup conflict some collective-angst-inducing contexts might lead group members to support constructive responses (e.g., negotiation), whereas in another context it may lead to support for destructive responses (e.g., refusal to compromise or even militant actions). Thus, for instance, in one study in Israel, Halperin, Wohl, and Porat (2011) report that when angst was raised by emphasizing the Iranian nuclear threat to Israel, Israeli Jews were less willing to negotiate with Palestinian Hamas in the Gaza Strip, believing that this negotiation cannot contribute to the reduction of the Iranian threat. But the second study showed that the same threat and angst resulted in the willingness to negotiate with the Palestinian Authority, under the assumption that this agreement would allow better chance to cope with the Iranian threat.

Siege Mentality

In the 1990s, together with Dikla Antebi, I proposed another source of the feeling of threat that can develop into fear. We suggested that groups may form and adopt a societal belief that the whole world has highly negative intentions toward them and develop a mind-set of siege mentality (Bar-Tal, 2000; Bar-Tal & Antebi, 1992a). It always has strong affective implications, being accompanied with negative affect and specific negative emotions. The focus of the core societal belief is on "negative intentions" and "the rest of the world." "Negative intentions" refers to the desire and motivation of the world to inflict harm or to hurt the society; such intentions imply a threat to the society's well-being. The crucial part of the belief relates to the "rest of the world." This element is unique to siege mentality beliefs; many societies probably believe that at least one other society has negative intentions toward them, but in this case the situation is far more extreme and serious. Members of the society believe not only that their society is in conflict with another group, or surrounded by hostile neighbors, but that the rest of the world, as a whole, is hostile toward them. Situations of intractable conflict provide a fertile ground for the development of a siege mentality. The chronic threat, hardship, and criticism of the international community may lead to a deep conviction of living in a hostile world. The recent past and the present offer examples of such societies: the South African white society before the elimination of apartheid and the Jewish society in Israel are examples of societies with a siege mentality (see Bar-Tal, 2000).

In the former case, in view of the imposed sanctions by the international community, and especially following the expulsion of South Africa from the British Commonwealth, white South Africans began to perceive themselves as a nation with its back to the wall, singled out by a hostile world (see, e.g., Brown, 1966). Legum and Legum (1964) cite numerous expressions of the South African political leadership that demonstrate this perception, that "the world is against us. But we have stood before – belied, slandered and spied upon" (Dr. Hertzog, minister of Post and Telegraphs, *The Star*, December 16, 1960). In the empirical investigation of the phenomenon in Israel, Bar-Tal and Antebi (1992b) constructed scales to assess the view of siege mentality: the General Siege Mentality Scale (GSMS) and the Israeli Siege Mentality Scale (ISMS). The correlation between these two scales was found to be very high (.70) among 376 Israeli students. Both concepts were found to be very different than individual paranoia and ethnocentrism. They were well predicted by political orientation – that is, hawkish individuals who object to compromises of resolving the Israeli-Arab conflict were found to also have a high level of siege mentality. This latter result was also obtained in the study carried out among the national representative sample of the Jewish population in Israel (Arian, 1989).

COLLECTIVE HATRED

Hatred is a powerful emotion that has immense impact on individual and collective behavior. It is a hostile feeling directed toward another person or group that consists of malice, repugnance, and willingness to harm and even annihilate (Sternberg, 2005). It is a secondary emotion that is based on fear and anger, with the accompaniment of cognitive appraisal (Johnson-Laird & Oatley, 1989; Quillian, 1995; Sternberg, 2003; Sternberg & Sternberg, 2008). Hatred is viewed as a cold chronic, emotional sentiment that can last for a long time (Royzman, McCauley, & Rosin, 2005). According to Allport (1954, p. 363), hate has behavioral implications as it is an "enduring organization of aggressive impulses toward a person or class of persons. Since it is composed of habitual bitter feelings and accusatory thoughts, it constitutes a stubborn structure in the mental-emotional life of the individual." In his view, hatred toward another group can be both rational and irrational and is associated with both the prejudice and the worldview of the person. Sternberg (2005) proposes that hate is composed of three components: negation of intimacy, which is related to repulsion and disgust; passion as the result of a threat, which is expressed in anger and fear; and devaluation of the target through feelings of contempt. Opotow and McClelland (2007) are more general in their approach and suggest that hate is aroused as a result of real and imagined experiences, including shared stories in a group situation, that are related to affect (anger, fear, frustration, disgust, etc.), cognitions (labels, stereotypes, and social representations that are relevant to intergroup relations), and morals (norms, rights, and duties that guide the behavior). Eventually hate may lead to destructive behavior.

A study by Halperin (2008, p. 718) found through in-depth interviews among lay Israeli Jews that hatred is defined as

> a powerful, extreme and persistent emotion that rejects the group towards which it is directed in a generalized and totalistic fashion. Group-based hatred is provoked in consequence to recurrent offenses committed against the individual or his or her group. These offenses are perceived as intentional, unjust, threatening the person or his or her group, and of a nature with which in practice the individual has difficulty coping. This hatred includes cognitive elements which make a clear ideological, moral and cultural differentiation between the in-group and the out-group while de-legitimizing the out-group. The affective element of hatred is

secondary and it is manifested in unpleasant physical symptoms as well as in anger, fear, and a strong negative feeling toward the out-group to the point of a desire to harm and even destroy it. In the majority of cases, this desire is not realized and therefore is channeled to other behavioral directions such as isolation from the object of the hatred, delight at the expense of the hated other, or taking part in political action against him or her.

Halperin (2008) reports that hatred can also be hot as a result of immediate cues that arouse it. His findings also show that it arises under conditions of continuing harm by an outgroup, which is viewed as being intentional and unjustified and attributed to stable negative dispositions of outgroup members. The outgroup is viewed as being innately evil (Elster, 1999). The evil group will not change its disposition and thus harm will continue – and there is a need to prevent it. Thus, hate leads to desire to harm, humiliate, and even kill, as a wish to vengeance is part of the reaction (White, 1996). But actions do not necessarily have to follow.

Group members may share hatred toward another group, and in fact it was suggested that hate can easily be collectively experienced because it is fairly easy to disseminate and communicate (Volkan, 1988; Yanay, 2002). Hate can be learned by society members at an early age or in adulthood. It may be acquired on the basis of personal experience or information provided by external sources, without any contact with the other group (Staub, 2005). Once group members form hatred toward another group, it may last for a long time. When hatred toward a particular group is acquired, it becomes a powerful collective psychological force that is easily evoked, even by the mere encounter with a hated group label (Halperin, 2011; Yanay, 2002). It not only affects thoughts but is also a potent motivating force, because it may lead to the most violent acts against the hated group, including extreme forms of terrorism, ethnic cleansing, and even genocide (Kressel, 1996; Sternberg, 2003).

Intractable conflict situations provide a fertile breeding ground for hatred, because the rival group threatens the basic existence of the group and over time performs harmful violent acts, which are viewed as unjust (Baumeister & Butz, 2005). Moreover, these acts of harm are attributed to the delegitimized stable characteristics of the rival (Bar-Tal, 1990a; Berkowitz, 2005). Thus, the situations of intractable conflict have all the basic ingredients that arouse hatred. White (1984) identifies shared hate in cases of conflict and sees it as a cold, deep, and steady negative emotion, lasting a long time as a result of a long accumulation of objectionable, harmful acts by the rival group. It leads to immoral behaviors by ingroup members while sustaining another societal belief – positive self-image. It appears that deep-rooted intergroup hatred might moderate potential development of moral emotions, like guilt, regret, or shame, which in some situations might have a positive effect on resolving conflicts (Wohl and Branscombe, 2005). Hatred might have a determinative influence on the development of the perception of self-victimhood (Volkan, 1997) among ingroup members and in the creation of blindness toward any claims of countervictimhood raised by the outgroup. In fact, hatred is the affective complementary force to delegitimization (which is a cognitive element) and thus is a major psychological factor that feeds the continuation of the intractable conflict and underlies much of the violence that takes place, including the worst atrocities. Together with delegitimization, it serves as a legitimizing psychological force, leading to moral disengagement that enables harming the rival in the most vicious ways.

Halperin (2008) reports that among a national sample of Israeli Jews group-based hatred is related to a very specific emotional goal – to do evil to, remove, and even eliminate the outgroup. On the other hand, its related action tendencies are not so absolute. The problematic nature of the emotional goals seems to turn the more practical tendencies into more diverse phenomena. In some situations, haters desire to move away from the outgroup; in others, they aspire to hurt the outgroup members and, in more extreme events, they even support or take part in a destructive process. A study conducted in Israel on the eve of the Annapolis peace summit in 2007 found that, above and beyond any other emotion, sentimental hatred increased the tendency of Israelis to support extreme military action against the Palestinians and reduced support for symbolic compromise and reconciliation. It was found that it stands as an obstacle to every attempt to acquire positive knowledge about the Palestinians (Halperin, 2011). Another study (Halperin, Russell, Dweck, & Gross, 2011) shows that hatred moderates the effects of another common emotion, anger, on support for making compromises for peace. More specifically, it shows that inducing anger toward Palestinians several weeks before the Annapolis summit increased support for making compromises in upcoming negotiations among those with low levels of hatred but decreased support for compromise among those with high levels of hatred.

COLLECTIVE ANGER

Other emotions, such as anger, guilt, or shame, may also appear collectively in situations of intractable conflict. Lazarus (1991) mentions anger as one of the powerful emotions aroused when demeaning offenses are committed, that is, when threats or damage lead to the erosion of identity. Specifically, he suggests that anger is evoked in response to a negative event that frustrates a personally relevant or desired goal and is intensified when the event is caused by a specific agent and viewed as unjust or illegitimate. In recent years, it became clear that anger can be shared collectively even when the negative event was not experienced personally but harmed a group (Halperin, 2008, 2011). Accordingly, the emotional goal of anger has been defined as a desire to correct perceived wrongdoing, injustice, or unfairness (Halperin, 2008a). Berkowitz (1990) extends the definition of anger to include the frustration of expected gratification. He also acknowledges that arbitrariness, inconsiderateness, and malevolence – all present in conflict – are factors that also influence the arousal of anger. Along these lines, Averill (1982) analyzed anger and related it to aggression. In his view, anger is socially construed and arises in situations when individuals or groups appraise what another person or group does as an unjustified and unfair violation of social norms. They will then seek to correct the wrongs done to them. Intense emotions of anger usually involve feelings of threat, attributions of blame, and a desire for revenge. Averill points out that anger is often expressed in aggressive behavior, an observation also made earlier in the theory of frustration and aggression that proposes anger as a mediating emotion in this relationship (Dollard, Doob, Miller, Mowrer, & Sears, 1939). In prolonged intractable conflicts, people view the acts of the rival as evil and the harm done by the enemy as unjustified. This generates chronic anger, which in turn leads to acts of aggressive revenge.

Indeed, anger has been shown to be an emotion that makes people eager to act (Davidson, Jackson, & Kalin, 2000; Harmon-Jones & Seligman, 2001; Mackie, Devos, & Smith, 2000). As such, it involves appraisals of relative strength and high coping ability (Mackie et al., 2000). It has been demonstrated that the integration of these two characteristics leads, in many cases, to the tendency to confront (Berkowitz, 1993; Mackie et al., 2000), hit, kill, or attack the anger-evoking target (Frijda, 1986; Roseman, Wiest, & Swartz, 1994). Anger is linked to indiscriminant optimism about one's own chances of success (Fischhoff, Gonzalez, Lerner, & Small, 2005) and to increased willingness to engage in risky behavior (Lerner & Keltner, 2001; Rydell, Mackie, Maitner, Claypool, Ryan, & Smith, 2008).

In line with anger's characteristics, studies conducted in the context of real-world conflicts consistently find clear and direct associations between anger and attribution of blame to the outgroup (Halperin, 2008; Small, Lerner, & Fischhoff, 2006). Other studies find that individuals who feel angry appraise future military attack as less risky (Lerner & Keltner, 2001) and forecast more positive consequences of such attack (Huddy, Feldman, & Cassese, 2007). Accordingly, studies conducted in the United States following the 9/11 attacks found that angry individuals were highly supportive of an American militant response in Iraq and elsewhere, reflecting more willingness to engage in risk (Cheung-Blunden & Blunden, 2008; Huddy et al., 2007; Lerner, Gonzalez, Small, & Fischhoff, 2003). Halperin suggests that the support for aggressive acts in cases of conflict depends on the perception whether the ingroup can overpower the rival group (Halperin, 2010). In addition, he suggests that public support for an aggressive response to an outgroup's provocation is highly dependent on believing that the outgroup action stemmed from a stable, irreversible, and evil disposition central to the outgroup members' character (Halperin, 2010). Thus, in his view when anger appears with hatred, then it is very destructive, often leading to aggressive acts. Studies performed in Israel with the Jewish population confirm this proposition (Halperin, 2010).

But anger can sometimes lead to constructive action (Fischer & Roseman, 2007; Halperin, 2008; Halperin, Russell, Dweck, & Gross, 2011) and can thereby potentially contribute to a peaceful resolution of intergroup conflicts. In the view of Halperin and his colleagues, anger is targeted at specific actions taken by individuals or groups but does not necessarily imply any negative internal characteristics of these groups or individuals. Therefore, "angry" people may differ in the way they translate that general goal into specific response tendencies. While some angry individuals gravitate toward achieving the required improvement using aggressive means, others with similar levels of anger may channel the anger into more constructive solutions, such as education, negotiation, and even compromises. Clearly, the responses are dependent on the framing of the group that causes anger by the various channels of communication and by the leadership. They may frame the rival as having a stable evil disposition that leads to harmful and unjust behavior or present the angering acts as being part of the circumstances of the conflict context (see also Reifen, Halperin, & Federico, 2011). In this line, Halperin, Russell, Dweck, and Gross (2011) demonstrate with the Israeli Jewish population that when anger was not accompanied with high levels of hatred, it led to support for making compromises in upcoming negotiations. In a more general perspective, this study shows that cognitive appraisals play a central role not just in determining the kind of emotion that will occur in response to a conflict-related event but also in influencing the specific response tendency that will be developed as a result of this emotion (see also Halperin, 2010; Halperin, Sharvit, & Gross, 2011).

COLLECTIVE HUMILIATION

Another collective emotion that often functions in intractable conflicts as a chronic sentiment is humiliation. Humiliation, as noted in Chapter 2, is defined as feelings of subjugation and damaged dignity. A person feels unjustly downgraded and devalued as a result of intentional behavior of the other (Hartling & Luchetta, 1999; Lindner, 2001, 2002, 2006; Statman, 2002). Humiliation is thought to belong to the family of secondary emotions based on self-conscious awareness (Tangney and Fischer, 1995) and moral views (Margalit, 2002), and thus the construction of events as being humiliating is part of this experience (Goldman & Coleman, 2011). Society members do not have to experience humiliation personally but can be affected by humiliation of a collective or some of its members. It is a negative emotion that individuals avoid if possible, but in a conflict situation it is imposed by the rival. Humiliation is evoked as a result of a series of acts or even one act. In the first case, it is a result of continuous negative behaviors imposed by another group, such as discrimination, oppression, or occupation in the conflict situation. In these cases, acts that cause humiliation are inflicted because the other group has more power. Examples of this type of humiliation are experienced by Chechens and Palestinians, as a result of prolonged occupation and oppression (see, e.g., Lacey, 2011, discussing Palestinian humiliation). In these cases of asymmetrical conflict, one group has the power to carry out acts of humiliation that intentionally demean, damage, subjugate, or downgrade the rival group.

But humiliation can also be experienced as a result of a particular act that hurts a group. In this case, a strong group can also be humiliated, meaning that it can lose its dignity and self-respect by the acts of another group. It can be a loss in battle or a harsh terror attack that hits the center of another group. These acts are unpredictable, and the society may feel that it lost its dignity unjustly. An example of this type of humiliation was experienced by Russians when between 40 and 50 Chechens seized a crowded Moscow theater on October 23, 2002. They took hostages and demanded the withdrawal of Russian forces from Chechnya. At the end of this dramatic terror attack, more than 130 hostages were killed together with most of the attackers (Giligan, 2010).

Lindner (2002) suggests that humiliation leads to a wish for retribution and therefore motivates violence; her study in Somalia, Rwanda, and Burundi validates this assumption. In two studies among Palestinians residing in the West Bank and Gaza Strip in 2005 and 2006, however, Ginges and Atran (2008) report that a high percentage of Palestinians described being humiliated by Israelis but that the humiliation produces an *inertia effect* – a tendency to inaction that suppresses rebellious or violent action, which in turn paradoxically suppresses support for acts of intergroup compromise. Palestinians who felt more humiliated by the Israeli occupation were less likely to support suicide attacks against Israelis but also expressed high reservations about the peacemaking process. The effects of humiliation may depend on the particular context of intractable conflict and can lead to different reactions.

COLLECTIVE PRIDE

Pride, which is a salient emotion that appears in the context of intergroup conflict, has not received much attention in the study of this context. Pride is a positive feeling that appears as a consequence of a successful evaluation of either action or performance, or a line of actions. The phenomenological experience of pride is joy, pleasure, and satisfaction as a result of praise by others or independent self-reflection (Lewis, 1993; Tracy & Robins, 2004). It is a secondary emotion that requires the development of a sense of self or social identity and then a positive evaluation of the self or of one's own collective following the performance of a specific act or of a continuous line of behavior (Lewis, Takai-Kawakami, Kawakami, & Sullivan, 2010; Tracy, Robins, & Schriber, 2009). Weiner (1985) emphasizes that pride is felt when the successful performance is appraised as having been caused by the individual and, I can also add, by the group. Pride can be considered as a group emotion because society members may feel pride though identification with the collective and by observing the successful group's performance. In fact, pride was often included in the assessment of patriotic feelings of society members (De Figueiredo & Elkins, 2003; Mumendey, Klink, & Brown, 2001; Smith & Kim, 2006).

The context of intergroup conflict, including intractable conflicts, also provides opportunities to experience pride (Brewer, 2001). During long-lasting intractable conflicts, involved societies may experience pride either in periods of successful coping with the enemy or as a result of a specific successful performance in either a battle or even a war. Performances characterized as victories, heroism, resilience, successful persistence, sacrifice, or extensive mobilization are examples of successes that may result in collective pride. Intractable conflicts provide these events because societies engage in prolonged violent behavior that may have successful consequences. For example, the unequivocal and very fast Israeli victory in the Six-Day War in June 1967 over the Egyptian, Syrian, and Jordanian armies led to exhilarated feelings of pride among Israeli Jews. Similarly, Singhalese felt much pride when finally the Sri Lanka army succeeded in defeating the Tamil insurgent forces and conquering all of their strongholds in May 2009 to conclude a civil war that lasted 37 years. Devine-Wright (2001) reports that in the Northern Ireland context Protestants who commemorate their past victories in parades view them with great pride, seeing them as symbolic reminders of successful historical events that fuel their sense of social identity. Pride may also be experienced as a result of the ability to withstand a stronger rival in the conflict, one that has military and economic superiority. Palestinians succeed in challenging Jews in their desire to establish Palestinian state when they receive the support of many nations in the international community, despite their being defeated militarily in 1948 and during the uprisings.

COLLECTIVE HOPE

One of the distinguishing emotions in situations of intractable conflict is hope. Hope involves expectations and aspirations in pursuing a goal, as well as positive feelings about the anticipated outcome (Staats & Stassen, 1985). It is a secondary emotion that is accompanied with goal setting, planning, use of imagery, creativity, mental exploration of novel situations, and even risk taking (Breznitz, 1986; Snyder, 1994). In most of the literature about violent and prolonged conflict, this emotion appears in a positive context as expressing a yearning for peace. This is because Snyder (2000a), as well as Averill, Catlin, and Chon (1990), limits the definition of hope to positive and moral aspirations and desires. But it seems to me that this limiting approach omits important hopes that members of such societies may have. Society members may hope to win the conflict or at least withstand the enemy with the hope to punish the rival, to revenge losses, and to harm him in general. In addition, society members may experience hope that focuses on yearning for relief from negative conditions (Lazarus, 1991b). I assume that such strong hopes appear during the intractable conflict especially at its eruption and escalation phases. An example of this type of hope can be found in the study by Nasie and Bar-Tal (2012) that investigated expressions of emotions as they appeared in the eyes of Palestinian children and adolescents via an analysis of their written pieces in a Palestinian newspaper. The expressions of hope include descriptions of longing for freedom, victory, liberation from the occupation, return of refugees to their homeland, emancipation of Jerusalem, avenging the blood of the *shahids*, and yearning for a bright future.

Society members who initiate a conflict in its initial stages have to hope that their acts will lead to an achievement of the stated goals of the conflict. Because deprivation is the important force that leads to eruption of conflicts, those who set the goals hope that the deprivation will be relieved when the goals are achieved. They also have to inspire other society members with this hope in order to conduct a wide-scale mobilization. Those who are mobilized to take part in conflict likewise have to hope that the goals will be achieved. Then, as intractable conflicts escalate and violence becomes a way of conflict management, it is just normal that the participating societies hope that they will inflict harm on the rival to terminate the conflict. They also hope to avenge the losses and the harm done at the hands of the rival.

It also possible that at least a segment of society members experiences a positive emotion of hoping to achieve peace in different phases of the intractable conflict. This type of hope is an important determinant to move to conflict toward the peacemaking process. Nevertheless, in all these cases the reference is not to amorphic wishes but to affective feelings that accompany the concrete expectation of achieving a goal, together with planning how to achieve it.

In sum, intergroup emotions play a critical role in intractable conflict. Any analysis of the socio-psychological dynamics of intractable conflict has to include this powerful force. Many of the negative intergroup emotions maintain the intractable conflict and serve as energizing factors that not only fuel its continuation but also prevent the opportunity for peacemaking. They appear on the collective level, spread deeply into the fabric of the society, and become an inseparable part of the infrastructure, as they function as an emotional collective orientation within the framework of a culture of conflict.

PART III

MAINTAINING CONFLICTS

7

Institutionalization of the Culture of Conflict

The three preceding chapters described the socio-psychological infrastructure that develops within the context of intractable conflict that may last for many decades and thus contribute to its protracted nature. The present chapter elaborates on the further evolution of the infrastructure into a culture of conflict. But first it begins with the fundamental premise suggesting that the socio-psychological infrastructure plays a functional role – through collective memory, the ethos of conflict, and collective emotional orientation – in helping society members on the individual and collective level to adapt to the harsh, stressful, and demanding conditions of the intractable conflict. Obviously, the described functions play a role for society members who hold the societal beliefs and emotions of the socio-psychological infrastructure, although there are individual differences in every society with regard to adherence to this repertoire. It can be assumed, however, that during the climax of intractable conflict a significant portion of a society involved in the conflict shares the socio-psychological infrastructure that supports the continuation of the conflict.

FUNCTIONS OF THE SOCIO-PSYCHOLOGICAL INFRASTRUCTURE

The socio-psychological infrastructure meets at least three challenges. First, it facilitates coping with stress that develops under the conditions of intractable conflict. Second, it helps to satisfy various needs during intractable conflict. Finally, it is supposed to create conditions that help to achieve the conflict's goals in the confrontation with the rival. I will now delineate five functions that the socio-psychological infrastructure fulfills in reference to the three challenges.[1] The first three functions and the last one respond mainly to the second challenge of satisfying needs, while the first function also refers to coping with stress. The fourth and the fifth functions are related to the challenge of withstanding the enemy.

Illumination of the Conflict Situation

One of the most important functions that the socio-psychological infrastructure (especially the societal beliefs of collective memory and of the ethos of conflict) fulfills is the epistemic function of illuminating the conflict situation (see also Chapter 3). The context of intractable conflict is extremely threatening and is accompanied by stress, vulnerability, uncertainty, and fear (Cohen, 1979; Lieberman, 1964). Therefore, society members try to satisfy the epistemic need for a meaningful understanding of the conflict situation. This is one of the fundamental human needs that motivates individuals to have a coherent, organized, and predictable picture of the world in which they live (Baumeister, 1991; Burton, 1990; Maddi, 1971; Reykowski, 1982). Furthermore, there is a need to cope with the stress created by the harsh conditions of intractable conflict. Successful coping with stress requires making sense of, and finding order and meaning in, the stressful conditions within existing schemes and the existing worldview, or integration between the events and the existing worldview (Antonovsky, 1987; Frankl, 1963; Horowitz, 1986; Janoff-Bulman, 1992; Kobasa, 1985; Taylor, 1983). For both of these challenges, collective memory and the ethos of conflict, as holistic narratives, fulfill this demand, providing clear-cut, simple, and comprehensive knowledge about the conflict. The narratives of these two components of the socio-psychological infrastructure explain very meaningfully and holistically the nature of the conflict to group members: Why is the group in conflict? What are the goals in the conflict, and why they are existential? What are the challenges that the society is facing? How did the conflict erupt? What was the course of the conflict? Why is it so violent? Why does it still continue, and why can it not be resolved peacefully? What is the enemy's responsibility for and contribution to the conflict? How has the ingroup acted in the conflict? Certain themes of the societal beliefs, such as well-defined goals, positive collective self-view, recognition of being a victim, and seeing difficult conditions as a challenge to be overcome with patriotism and unity, are especially functional for coping with

---

[1] Through the chapters of the book I also outlined how different parts of the infrastructure (e.g., collective memory or specific themes of the ethos of conflict or particular emotions) are critical to the functioning of the individuals and collectives in intractable conflict. This provides a holistic picture of the functions of the socio-psychological infrastructure.

stress (Antonovsky, 1987; Janoff-Bulman, 1992; Kobasa, 1985; Taylor, 1983). They portray a coherent and predictable world so the society members know what to expect and can understand the reality of the conflict in a meaningful way. They explain the reasons for the experienced stress and thus can serve as a factor that contributes to the resilience of society members, serving as a buffer to negative consequences.

Investigations in Israel directly confirm this premise. Two experimental studies reported by Sharvit (2008) show that the ethos of conflict is automatically activated in the face of stressful information, even among Israeli Jews who support peaceful resolution of the conflict. The activation of the ethos is assumed to facilitate coping with the stressful experience as it presents a clear illumination of the situation. Another study shows that the ethos of conflict functions in the Israeli population as a protective factor that reduces the negative psychological effects of exposure to the violent situation (Lavi, Canetti, Bar-Tal, & Hobfoll, in press). By offering a meaningful, simple picture of the conflict, the ethos serves as a buffer that alleviates the negative consequences of stress. These findings are consistent with Milgram's (1993) analysis suggesting that one of the unique features of the Israeli Jewish society, which protect its members from the deleterious effects of conflict-related stressful events, is socialization into a belief system that emphasizes the importance of the Jewish state, its positive characteristics, and the value of defending it – all themes of the ethos of conflict.

Justification of the Ingroup's Behavior

In its moral function, the socio-psychological infrastructure serves to justify the negative acts of the ingroup toward the enemy, including violence against humans and destruction of property (see, e.g., Apter, 1997; Jost & Major, 2001). It also provides justification for group members to commit misdeeds, perform intentional harm, and institutionalize aggression toward the enemy. Human beings do not usually willingly harm other humans. The sanctity of life is perhaps the most sacred value in modern societies. Killing or even hurting other human beings is considered the most serious violation of the moral code (Donagan, 1979; Kleinig, 1991). However, in intractable conflict, groups hurt each other most grievously, even resorting to atrocities, ethnic cleansing, and even genocide. Harming the other side is viewed as justified in light of the key societal beliefs of the narrative that present one's own goals as justified, portray one's own group as a victim, and at the same time view one's own group in a positive light as being moral, virtuous, and righteous. In contrast, they present the goals of the other group as unfounded, and they delegitimize the rival, which in essence denies the humanity of the rival and allows the intent to harm him. This black-and-white narrative focuses on the violence, atrocities, cruelty, lack of concern for human life, evilness, and viciousness of the rival. Thus, because societies involved in intractable conflicts view themselves in a positive light, they attribute all responsibility for the outbreak of the conflict and its continuation to the opponent. They use all kinds of justification and explanations for their own violence, presenting it as prevention, containment, and retribution. These beliefs about the ingroup and about the rival position the ingroup on high moral ground (e.g., Staub, 1999), thus clearing one's own side of any responsibility for acts of violence toward the other side (Waller, 2002). They provide the moral weight to seek justice and oppose the adversary, and thus serve to rationalize and legitimize the harmful acts of the ingroup toward the enemy (see Apter, 1997; Jost & Major, 2001).

Indeed, the beliefs reduce activation of psychological mechanisms that usually prevent individuals and groups from committing harmful acts. This is an important function of societal beliefs of the ethos of conflict and collective memory that resolves feelings of dissonance, guilt, and shame for group members. Feelings of guilt and shame, moral considerations, or the motivations to hold positive collective self-view are the human safeguards of humane conduct, but they often fail to operate when individuals perceive themselves as being victims and delegitimize their opponent (see Bar-Tal, Chernyak-Hai, Schori, & Gundar, 2009; Bar-Tal & Hammack, 2012; Branscombe, 2004; Branscombe, Ellemers, Spears, & Doosje, 1999; Branscombe, Schmitt, & Schiffhauer, 2007; Grossman, 1995; Wohl & Branscombe, 2008). The themes of the socio-psychological infrastructure thus have great psychological value; they serve as a buffer against group-based negative thoughts and feelings regarding the ingroup. They allow what Bandura (1999) calls moral disengagement, a psychological separation from moral considerations and other human safeguards that prevent acts of violence. In this respect the infrastructure fulfills an important function of allowing society members to maintain a positive self-image as well as a positive personal and collective identity in spite of the violence perpetrated by the ingroup against the rival. This function is important because society members have great difficulty accepting a negative image of their own group.

For example, in the Israeli-Palestinian conflict, a strong association exists between holding a societal belief of collective victimhood (which is part of collective memory and the ethos of conflict) among Israeli Jewish respondents and reduced group-based guilt over Israel's actions against the Palestinians (Schori-Eyal, Klar, & Roccas, 2011). Those who had a high sense of collective victimhood expressed less guilt, less moral accountability, and less willingness to compensate Palestinians for harmful acts inflicted on them by Israel. They also used more exonerating cognitions, or justifications, such as "under the circumstances, any other state would treat the Palestinians in the same way" and "I believe the Palestinians brought their current situations upon themselves." Čehajić and Brown (2008) report that in Serbia viewing one's own group as a victim also serves the function of justifying the ingroup's negative behavior after it has occurred and, as such, undermines one's readiness to acknowledge the ingroup's responsibility for misdeeds. Serbian adolescents who believe that their group is actually the true victim (in the 1991–1995 war) or has suffered more than members of the other groups are less willing to acknowledge their group's responsibility for atrocities committed against others. Similarly, studies on the Israeli-Palestinian conflict show that Israeli soldiers who used substantive violence against the Palestinian population tended also to delegitimize this population considerably more than soldiers who refrained from violent behavior (see Elizur & Yishay-Krien, 2009; Kimhi & Sagy, 2008; Kolonimus & Bar-Tal, 2011).

Differentiation between the Ingroup and the Rival

The socio-psychological infrastructure creates a sense of differentiation between the ingroup and the rival and a particularly superior position for the ingroup over the rival (Sidanius & Pratto, 1999). It sharpens intergroup differences because it describes the opponent in delegitimizing terms on the one hand, while on the other hand it glorifies and praises one's own society, as well as presenting it as a sole victim of the conflict (Baumeister, 1997). Because societies involved in intractable conflict view their own goals as justified and perceive themselves in a positive light, they attribute all responsibility for the outbreak of the conflict and its continuation to the opponent. The repertoire of beliefs embedded in the infrastructure focuses on the unjust goals of the rival and especially on the misdeeds, hostility, atrocities, meanness, disregard of human life, and brutality of the other side. The rival is presented as breaking moral codes and therefore is located beyond the boundaries of the international moral community. Societal beliefs of delegitimization push the rival to such an extreme that it amounts to a denial of humanity. These beliefs stand in contrast to societal beliefs of a positive collective self-image, which portray the ingroup in glorifying terms. In addition, in contrast to the portrayal of the rival as a chronic perpetrator, one's own group is presented as the victim in the conflict. This view allows a rigid psychological separation between the ingroup and the rival and creates such social distance that the rival is relegated to inferior spheres of inhumanity.

Thus, whereas the ingroup is associated with emotions such as pride, empathy, or pity, the outgroup is presented in a way to arouse negative emotions such as hatred, fear, or anger. This differentiation allows maintenance of the needed positive collective self-esteem, positive social identity, and feelings of superiority, which can justify immoral acts of violence performed by the ingroup (Sandole, 2002). For example, Hunter, Stringer, and Watson (1991) report that Catholics and Protestants in Northern Ireland tended to attribute their own group's violence to external causes, whereas they ascribed the opponent's violence to internal delegitimizing characteristics, with descriptors such as "psychopaths" or "bloodthirsty." This differentiation enabled individuals to perceive their own group in a positive way and even to view their own violence as an unwanted, unintentional result of circumstances and as legitimate acts of self-defense, while the other group was viewed as being innately evil.

Preparedness for the Conflict

The socio-psychological infrastructure prepares the society to be alert and ready for the threatening and violent acts of the enemy, as well as for difficult life conditions. The narratives of collective memory and ethos and the collective emotional orientations tune the society to information that signals potential harm and continuing violent confrontations, allowing psychological preparations for the lasting conflict and immunization against negative experiences. The society becomes attentive and sensitive to cues about threats so that no sudden surprises can arise. Also, the society easily absorbs information that signals possible threats and danger. The socio-psychological infrastructure also allows economic predictability, which is one of the basic conditions for coping successfully with stress (e.g., Antonovsky, 1987; Lazarus & Folkman, 1984). Human beings need to live in a world whose future can, to some extent, be predicted, and they have to feel a sense of mastery over their fate. Unpredictable events, especially when harmful, may cause negative psychological reactions. Given, however, that some degree of unpredictability is unavoidable, people prefer to be positively surprised, rather than to face threats unprepared. In this way, expectations of negative events prevent disappointments.

Themes such as the opponent's delegitimization and one's own victimhood and insecurity, as well as fear, hatred, and anger, serve as a basis for these expectations and for perceptual tuning as preparation for the challenges of the conflict. For example, Podeh (2002, p. 177), after an analysis of Israeli history school textbooks, notes that during the climax of the Israeli-Arab conflict in the 1950s through 1970s these books reflected "a genuine sense of fear of the enemy, which may, with hindsight, seem exaggerated. The sense of being a state under siege (euphemistically depicted by the biblical phrase *'am levadad yishkon'* – 'a people that shall dwell alone') was perceived as relevant until 1967, and for some it continued in the post-1967 period as well. The fear of another round of war with Arabs was genuine and not theoretical."

Participation in the Conflict

The socio-psychological infrastructure has the function of motivating in support of unity, solidarity, mobilization, and readiness for sacrifice on behalf of the group (Bar-Tal & Staub, 1997). Collective memory and the ethos of conflict together with fear, hatred, and anger imply a threat to the society's well-being and even to its survival. They raise the security needs as a core value and indicate a situation of emergency, which requires creating conditions that will allow, on the one hand, adaptation to the conflict situation and, on the other hand, successful managing of the confrontation with the rival. Unity and solidarity are crucial for lessening the threat. Moreover, by justifying the goals of the conflict – by focusing on the delegitimization and the intransigence and violence of the opponent, as well as on self-victimhood, fear, hatred, and anger – the repertoire implies the necessity to exert all the efforts and resources of the group in the struggle against the enemy. All these societal beliefs and emotions play a central role in nourishing patriotism, which leads to a readiness for various sacrifices in order to defend the group and the country and to avenge acts of past violence by the enemy. Reminders of past violent acts by the rival indicate that such acts could recur. The implication is that society members should be united and mobilized in view of the threat and should carry out violent acts to prevent possible harm. This function therefore is crucial to meet the challenge of withstanding the enemy. In the case of Sri Lanka, for example, victimhood narratives were used by militant groups to recruit the Tamil people and induce them to commit violent acts. As Ramanathapillai (2006, p. 1) notes, "Stories about the traumatic events became both a powerful symbol and an effective tool to create new combatants."

Before turning to the detailed description of the development of culture of conflict (based on the socio-psychological infrastructure) that develops in times of intractable conflict, we should consider the construction of collective memory and ethos of conflict, which are the conflict-supporting master narratives (see Bar-Tal, Oren, & Nets-Zehngut, 2012).

CONSTRUCTION OF THE CONFLICT-SUPPORTING NARRATIVES

Because the socio-psychological infrastructure has been shown to fulfill very important functions with its narrative, it is appropriate now to describe the principles and the methods of the narratives' construction that is embedded in this infrastructure. Master narratives provide the general outlook on the conflict. In addition to these general narratives, societies may construct many more specific narratives about particular events, such as battles or individual deeds, that contain themes of the ethos of conflict. All these narratives are supposed to fulfill functions to meet the challenges that the conditions of the conflict pose and contribute to the epistemic basis in support of the conflict. Agents of conflict (also called entrepreneurs) are responsible for constructing the repertoire of the socio-psychological infrastructure with its narratives. The most important agents are the society's leaders, who prepare their society for conflict and need to formulate the epistemic basis of the eruption of the conflict and later its protracted continuation. They are supported by various institutions, organizations, cultural products, and channels of communication represented by journalists, writers, artists, school curricula developers, teachers, and others.

Because both the master narratives and the other more specific narratives must contain functional themes, they have to be constructed according to certain principles. First, the narratives are constructed in a *selective* way, consistent with the themes of the conflict-supporting narratives; inconsistent contents are omitted (Brandenberger, 2009; Tint, 2010; Wertsch, 2002). Second, the narratives are constructed in a *biased* way, with the motivation to reach the particular conclusion that supports them. Therefore, the processing of the information such as evidence and experiences is guided by this motivation (i.e., their interpretations, evaluations, inferences) (Boyd, 2008; Brandenberger, 2009; Wertsch, 2002). Third, the narratives are constructed through *distortion* because they either omit contents that are inconsistent with the themes of the narrative or add contents that do not have any support in evidence but relate to these themes (Anderson, 1983; Baker, 2006; Baumeister & Hastings, 1997; Heisler, 2008; Tint, 2010). Fourth, the principle of *simplification* suggests that the narratives contain uncomplicated and general arguments that support their major themes. They are constructed as black-and-white stories in which the rival is portrayed in negative and evil terms, while the ingroup is viewed in a positive and glorifying frame (Auerbach, 2010; Baker, 2006; Gonzalez-Allende, 2010; Papadakis, 2008; Torsti, 2007).

These general principles serve as guidelines that allow construction of narratives in line with the dominant themes of the ethos of conflict and collective memory (see also Bar-Tal, Oren, & Nets-Zehngut, 2012). Methods used to achieve these narratives include:

1. *Reliance on supportive sources.* In using this method, the construction of the conflict-supportive narratives is based on sources that provide information that is consistent with this narrative's themes. In their construction, documents, testimonies, materials, historians, and leaders that support the major themes of the master narrative are used, while sources that provide contents contradicting these themes are intentionally disregarded or minimized (Havel, 2005; Papadakis, 2008; Podeh, 2002).

2. *Magnification of supportive themes.* Themes of the conflict-supporting narratives are exaggerated, salient, and central (Kelman, 2007), especially ones that concern the justness of the goals, self-collective presentation, delegitimization of the rival, and patriotism. They can be repeated in different minor specific narratives. Every event in the past that supports the narrative receives special emphasis (Deutsch & Merritt, 1965; Sears, 2002). In addition, every new information or experience that is in line with the narrative gets prominence (Barnard, 2001; Baumeister & Hastings, 1997). A specific example of magnifying themes of the master narrative is to deliberately and consistently present the rival very negatively as a homogeneous entity with an innate evil disposition as a threat to the ingroup (Bar-Tal & Teichman, 2005; Papadakis, 2008; White, 1970).

3. *Marginalization of contradictory information.* In general, conflict-supportive narratives marginalize contents that contradict their major themes. These contents are presented with minimized importance, are often hidden, and are not repeated. Their appearance provides credibility to the narrative because the narratives include some contradicting elements, but at the same time their influence is not significant. This method is used especially to minimize exposure to information that impinges negatively on the justness of group goals or a positive collective self-image.

4. *Skewed interpretations.* Inferences, evaluations, judgments, and causal explanations of events and processes are provided in a way that upholds the themes of the conflict-supporting narratives (Baumeister & Hastings, 1997; Tint, 2010). This method is used especially with regard to

ambiguous information and knowledge that is open to different interpretations. But it also is used with unambiguous unsupportive contents as human beings have motivated cognition to support their claims in the narrative (Kruglanski, 1989, 2004).

5. *Fabrication of supportive contents.* Contents (details and even events) are used in the narratives that do not have any support in evidence in order to create a coherent and meaningful story to promote its major themes (Baumeister & Hastings, 1997; Hobsbawm, 1990; Podeh, 2002; Sibley, Liu, Duckitt, & Khan, 2008).

6. *Omission of contradictory contents.* Conflict-supporting narratives omit contents (e.g., events, processes, or individuals) that have a firm evidential basis but contradict their themes. This method is sometimes entitled "silence" or "collective amnesia" (Baumeister & Hastings, 1997; Maksudyan, 2009; Tint, 2010; Winter, 2010). Groups in intractable conflict use this method to suppress evidence that shatters the presumed justness of the goals in the conflict and that undermines the moral image of the group.

7. *Use of framing language.* Terms, concepts, and wordings are used to frame the story in a way that is in line with the themes of the conflict-supportive narratives. It is based on the assumption that the language used dictates the way the reality is perceived by people. The language also triggers existing emotions, memory, cognition, and motivations, and it nurtures and shapes them in line with conflict-supporting narrative (Bozic-Roberson, 2004; Hrvatin, 2000; Riskedahl, 2007; Tsur, 2013). Euphemism is also used to present milder, indirect, or vague expressions to diminish the damaging impact of aspects that do not support the themes of the narrative (Harkabi, 1974; Maksudyan, 2009; Tsur, 2013; Winter, 2010).

Although every society in conflict uses these methods in constructing its master narrative of intractable conflict and more specific narratives, societies differ with regard to the extent of their use. One important reason is that societies involved in intractable conflict differ with regard to the justness of their own goals according to the prevailing international codes of morality and justice and therefore differ in their need to excuse immoral goals (see, e.g., Amstutz, 2005; Lauren, 2011; Walzer, 1994, 2006). Also, in each conflict, and at different periods of its duration, various combinations of these methods can be used. These methods can also be used in different degrees. Some of the specific methods relate to *what* aspects are discussed, while others relate to the *ways* in which these aspects are discussed in order to increase their preferred impact. The use of these methods may be carried out automatically, because society members who produce the narrative are involved in intractable conflicts and characterized, inter alia, by selective, biased, and distorted information processing (Isen, 1999; Jost, Glaser, Kruglanski, & Sulloway, 2003; Rouhana & Bar-Tal, 1998). These methods, however, are also deliberately used by gatekeepers in the ingroup, who try to prevent the society from attaining knowledge and information that contradicts the themes of the master narrative, which support the continuation of the conflict (Baumeister & Hastings, 1997; Langenbacher, 2010; Nets-Zehngut, Pliskin, & Bar-Tal, 2012; Tint, 2010).

The master conflict-supporting narratives as well as more specific narratives provide a "good story" that is well understood and meaningful. The plot of the story is simple and clear, elaborated in a black-and-white form with unambiguous villains, victims, and heroes. It provides a flawless beginning and then follows the events or the processes, or both. The narratives also provide stories that are relevant and related to the society members' identity. Thus, the stories not only elicit emotional involvement but also evoke strong identification. Finally, the narratives are moralizing (White, 1987). They provide criteria for judging the events and the processes of the conflict. These three characteristics of the conflict-supporting narratives help explain why they are so well absorbed by society members. In general, human beings like these types of stories, remember them well, and assimilate them easily.

Eventually, the constructed master narratives of collective memory of conflict and the ethos of conflict with many other specific narratives serve as the foundations of the culture of conflict.

EVOLVEMENT OF THE CULTURE OF CONFLICT

After the socio-psychological infrastructure crystallizes into a well-organized system of societal beliefs of collective memory and the ethos of conflict with the emotions of the collective emotional orientation and penetrates into the institutions and communication channels of the society, in the next phase a culture of conflict develops (the process is depicted in Figure 1 and described also in Chapter 3).

A *culture of conflict develops when societies saliently integrate the elements of the socio-psychological infrastructure into their cultural symbols, which then communicate a particular meaning about the prolonged and continuous experiences of living in the context of conflict.* This outlook is based on Geertz's (1973, p. 89) definition of culture as "a historically transmitted pattern of meaning embodied in symbols, a system of inherited conceptions expressed in symbolic forms by means of which men communicate, perpetuate, and develop their knowledge about and attitudes towards life." Here culture is viewed as publicly shared meanings in which worldviews, behaviors, institutions, and cultural products are understood as culturally constituted phenomena (Spiro, 1984). Ann Swidler's (1986, p. 273) discussion of culture as "a 'tool kit' of rituals, symbols, stories, and world views" that people use to construct "strategies of action" is an important addition and can serve as a foundation for the present discussion. These approaches place a focal emphasis on evolved tangible and intangible symbols that provide meaning to life under the conditions in which the society lives. These symbols, representing the prolonged experiences and their meaning, provide a hegemonic worldview. Bond (2004, p. 62) defines culture psychologically as "a shared system of beliefs (what is true), values (what is important), expectations, especially about scripted behavioral sequences, and behavioral meanings (what is implied by engaging in a given action) developed by a group over time to provide the requirement of living.... This shared system enhances communication of meaning and coordination of actions among culture's members by reducing uncertainty and anxiety through making its members' behavior predictable, understandable, and valued." In a similar way, Ross (1993, 1998) directs attention to the way beliefs reflect the culture of society members about social reality and in turn lead to particular courses of action. These elaborations fit perfectly into the present attempt to describe the development of the culture of conflict.

My basic premise is that the prolonged experiences of living under the conditions of intractable conflict lead to the development and crystallization of the culture of conflict, which becomes interwoven into the fabric of the societal life on every level and in every domain. Ross (1998, pp. 157–158) points out that "the culture of conflict defines what people consider valuable and worth fighting over, investing particular goods, statuses, positions or actions with meaning; it suggests appropriate ways to wage disputes, identifies suitable targets of conflict; it supports institutions in which disputes are processes; and it determines how conflict are likely to end."

In this line, Bond (2007, p. 27) more specifically elaborates that the culture of conflict serves "as educator, as motivator, as roadmap, as coordinator and as legitimizer of the evil we do in the name of good. Culture provides the plausibility structures... for these essential supports to the collective violence we wreak upon one another, but culture is not the agent of the carnage; it is we as social agents acting in concert who provide the daily, proximal supports for the orchestration of collective violence. We reward and we punish those who act with us or against us or who by-stand, thereby motivating ourselves and others to act in accordance with those plausibility structures." Essentially when a culture of conflict becomes dominant, intractable conflicts come to be way of life, affecting its every aspect.

We can diagnose the existence of a culture of conflict with four criteria that were briefly noted in Chapter 3.

1. *Extensive sharing.* The beliefs of the socio-psychological infrastructure pertain to the eight themes that appear in the ethos of conflict and collective memory, and the accompanying emotions are widely shared by society members. Society members are deeply convinced in the justness of their own group's goals; they view the rival in an extremely negative way with delegitimizing categories that deny humanness and legitimize his harming; they view their own group in glorifying terms, emphasizing their own moral qualities, but at the same time view their own group as a sole victim in the conflict; they identify great threats originating from the rival and develop ways to cope with them; they believe in the need for patriotic mobilization for the conflict and for the need to be united; and finally they believe that they are lovers of peace, which will eventually be achieved. Also, they share group emotions such as anger, fear, and hatred that characterize societies involved in intractable conflict. They acquire and store this repertoire, as part of their socialization, from an early age and carry it through their lives. They learn the repertoire from agents of socialization, such as family, teachers, or mass media. It is impossible to live in an intractable conflict without being exposed to the contents of societal beliefs of the ethos of conflict and collective memory. Thus every member of the society acquires them. But societies do differ with the extent of their consensus regarding this repertoire, and it changes over time. In some societies schisms about societal beliefs may even develop in some stages of the conflict. But at the climax of the intractable conflict a high consensus usually develops about these beliefs in many of the societies involved. Nevertheless, in all the societies involved in intractable conflict, they are readily available, and therefore exposure to them is unavoidable. Once they are acquired, they are stored and even unconsciously become accessible in situations of stress (see Sharvit, 2008).

2. *Wide application.* The repertoire of the societal beliefs of collective memory and the ethos of conflict as well as of shared emotions is not only held by society members but also used in their daily conversations. This repertoire is chronically accessible and therefore often features in interpersonal communications, because the conflict is part of the daily

lives of society members. Many of the personal judgments, evaluations, and decisions are influenced by the conflict repertoire. Moreover, in societies involved in intractable conflict that do not have access to media and formal societal institutions, interpersonal networks serve as means to disseminate elements of the socio-psychological infrastructure. In addition, in many other societies themes of socio-psychological infrastructure appear to be dominant in public discourse via societal channels of mass communication. They deal with the conflict almost daily, and the socio-psychological infrastructure serves as a frame for interpretation and assessment of the situation and events. It is often used for justification and explanation of decisions, policies, and courses of actions taken by the leaders at different levels. Finally, it is also expressed in institutional and civil ceremonies, commemorations, rituals, and memorials.

3. *Expression in cultural products.* The socio-psychological infrastructure also appears in cultural products, such as literary books, TV programs, films, theater plays, and visual arts. It becomes a society's cultural repertoire, relaying themes of collective memory and the ethos of conflict, as well as emotions promoted by the dominant group. The cultural products focus on them, and they constitute major themes in artworks. Through these cultural products, societal beliefs and emotions of the socio-psychological infrastructure are disseminated and can reach every sector of the public. Many of these products portray the ingroup's suffering or heroism and depict the brutality and inhumanness of the adversary.

4. *Appearance in educational systems.* The societal beliefs of collective memory and the ethos of conflict appear also in the educational system, including even in higher education. They are used as a major venue of collective socialization. They appear in different modes. First, the societal beliefs appear in school textbooks and other written materials that serve as an epistemic authority and are viewed usually as sources that provide a truthful and valid account of the past and present. Societal beliefs are also propagated by teachers on different occasions in formal instruction and informal encounters. Finally, they are transmitted in various curricula and extracurricular activities, such as art classes and field trips. All these modes have an influence because education is compulsory in almost all societies and therefore whole new generations are exposed to the contents of the ethos of conflict and collective memory, and it can be assumed that many of the students also acquire them.

Thus, as the culture of conflict develops, the processes of institutionalization, socialization, and diffusion transmit, disseminate, and maintain the societal beliefs of collective memory and the ethos of conflict, as well as group-based emotions, among society members and society's institutions. They become easily accessible, solidified, and dominant.

The development of a culture of conflict seems to be unavoidable because of the intensive psychological experiences that society members go through during intractable conflict, which lasts at least a few dozen years. These powerful experiences leave their mark on every aspect of societal life. They eventually shape the system of societal beliefs, attitudes, values, norms, and practices of society members, who produce tangible and intangible symbols that reflect them. Nevertheless, societies differ with regard to the level of dominance of the culture of conflict. While in some societies during the climax of intractable conflict a culture of conflict can be absolutely hegemonic (as in the Jewish and Palestinian societies), in other societies its dominance can be more limited, being restricted to certain segments of the society (e.g., in Northern Ireland). Factors that determine the level of dominance of a culture of conflict include the level of threat, level of homogeneity of the society involved, level of agreement on the goals of the conflict and its management, level of a society's tolerance to deviant views, level of openness of the society to alternative information, strength of the segments of the society that oppose the conflict, level of indoctrination through a mobilized educational system and the mass media, types of violent experiences, level of trust in the channels of communication, and the extent of the use of societal mechanisms to enforce consensual thinking. When there is a high level of threat perception, a high level of homogeneity, a consensus regarding the conflict in society, a high level of closure to alternative information, high indoctrination through mobilized mass media and the educational system, high trust in leaders who are agents of conflict, and high use of societal sanctions to enforce consensus, then in such a society the culture of conflict would achieve hegemonic status. Under these conditions, a society evolves with a single-minded agenda directed toward continuation of the conflict. The presented list of factors is not exhaustive, but it provides the general view that the hegemonic status of a culture of conflict depends on the conditions of the intractable conflict, characteristics of the societal system and its channels of communication, characteristics of the leadership, and characteristics of society members. The factors operate from the beginning of the intractable conflict and influence its development. Some have linear influence, and some curvilinear. These factors change over time and may affect the maintenance of the culture of conflict at any point in time.

This analysis indicates that a culture of conflict may not be hegemonic during the long period of intractable conflict; its level of dominance is dynamic and may change, as its development and maintenance are not linear. It may even compete with a culture that provides alternative symbols that cherish peace and value practices of peacemaking. It may even lose its dominance, as the majority of the society members may embrace an alternative culture that promotes peace building.

The Israeli Jewish culture of conflict has been thoroughly investigated, partly in the framework of the described conception (Bar-Tal, 2007a). Thus, we can use this research in order to provide a concrete example of a culture of conflict.

THE CULTURE OF CONFLICT: THE CASE OF ISRAELI JEWISH SOCIETY

The Israeli-Arab conflict, and specifically the Israeli-Palestinian conflict, was a prototypical case of extreme intractable conflict, being violent, perceived as unsolvable, fought over goals considered existential, and perceived as a zero-sum conflict between 1948 and 1977. The conflict greatly preoccupies society members, and the parties involved invest much in its continuation (see Bar-Tal, 1998, 2007a, 2007b; Kriesberg, 1993, 2007). Although some of the intractable features are still intact, between 1977 and 2000 the conflict began to move toward the tractable end of the dimension. The peace treaty with Egypt in 1979, the Madrid convention in 1991, the Oslo agreements in 1993 and 1995, and the peace treaty with Jordan in 1994 are hallmarks of the peace process that changed the relations between Jews and Arabs in the Middle East (see detailed descriptions in Caplan, 2009; Dowty, 2005; Morris, 2001; Tessler, 2009; Wasserstein, 2003). A reescalation of the Israeli-Palestinian conflict began with the failure of the Camp David summit meeting between Israeli and Palestinian leaders in July 2000. After violent encounters that lasted a few years, both sides attempted to continue negotiations with the help of third parties, mostly the United States, but these efforts did not yield a peaceful settlement of the conflict. On the contrary, in recent years since the ascendance to power in Israel of Prime Minister Benjamin Netanyahu there has been an intensification of the conflict, without any negotiations. Nevertheless, even the state of the present conflict is far removed from the extreme level of intractability that characterized it in the 1950s or 1960s.

With this background, and focusing only on the climax of the Israeli-Palestinian intractable conflict (which was in this period part of the more general Israeli-Arab conflict) during late 1940s, 1950s, and 1960s until the visit of the Egyptian president Anwar Sadat in Jerusalem in November 1977, one can detect all the features of the culture of conflict in Jewish Israeli society.

Public Opinion and Public Discourse

Although there are no systematic studies about Israeli public opinion during Israel's first two decades, Oren (2005) provides a glimpse into the shared beliefs (i.e., societal beliefs), at least in the late 1960s and later. She assembled an extensive database of various Israeli Jewish public opinion polls that were conducted from 1967 to 2000 and which asked questions regarding different themes of societal beliefs of the ethos of conflict. Analysis of the responses to these surveys that often constituted time series shows that during the late 1960s and early 1970s until the 1973 war the Israeli Jewish public at large held the eight core themes of beliefs of the ethos of conflict consensually. They not only emphasized the Zionist goals of creating a Jewish state in Israel but also supported (at least 75% of them) holding the territories conquered in the 1967 war, especially the West Bank, Gaza Strip, and Golan Heights. Thus for example, during the years 1967–1970 more than 75% of the respondents in public polls conducted by the Guttmann Institute thought that Israel should keep the West Bank. Israeli Jews also perceived high threats and almost all considered security as their primary concern. For example, an international study from 1962 of the main hopes and fears in 13 nations, including Israel, revealed that only the Israelis and the Americans expressed concern about war as a personal worry (none of the Egyptians, one of Israel's main adversaries, expressed such fear on a personal level). As for fears on the national level, 49% of the Israelis worried about war with Arabs (again, none of the Egyptians expressed concern about war with Israel) (Antonovsky & Arian, 1972). Numerous questions in Israeli public polls also indicate that between 1973 and 1989 most Israeli respondents (more than 80%) thought that war was probable between Israel and the Arab states sometime in the future.

Most Jews in Israel did not recognize the Palestinian identity; for example, most of the respondents (more than 60%) thought during the years 1974–1977 that Palestinians did not constitute a separate people but were rather a part of the Arab nation and that Jordan already fulfills the role of a state for the Palestinians. Also, during these years most Israeli respondents in public polls (more than 70%) agreed with the statement that "The Palestinian Arab Nation" is an artificial concept that has emerged only in the recent years owing to developments in the area. Israeli Jews viewed Arabs as one homogeneous entity with negative intentions toward Jews and the State of Israel. During the years 1973–1977 more than 75% of the respondents thought that Arabs' true intentions were to destroy the State of Israel. The image of Arabs was dominated by negative stereotypes, as they were viewed as backward, violent, primitive, and treacherous (Bar-Tal & Teichman, 2005). At the same time, most Israeli Jews perceived themselves to be intelligent, progressive, modern, and of high moral superiority. In 1968, for example, 60% of Israeli Jews in a public poll agreed with the sentence "The Arabs can improve much but will never become as advanced as the Jews."

Also, Jews viewed themselves as the victims of the conflict (Bar-Tal & Antebi, 1992). They downplayed sectarian societal conflicts and depicted the Israeli Jewish society as united. In a survey from 1970, 74% thought that the Israeli public should identify with the government, more than the public in other democratic countries. They also expressed strong patriotic feelings by taking pride in Israel and expressing readiness to make sacrifices on behalf of the country. During the 1970s most of the respondents (usually more than 80%) indicated that they would not want to live their lives outside of Israel, even if they had the chance. As for sacrifice, polls showed that during the years 1967–1977 most respondents (more than 60%) thought that there is a need for personal sacrifice for the state. Finally, peace was considered as a core value in the society; for example, the international study from 1962 of the main hopes and fears in 13 nations mentioned previously revealed that 55% of the Israelis pointed to "peace with the Arabs" as the main hope on a national level (none of the Egyptians expressed such hope on a national level). A 1975 follow-up study indicated that 14% of the Israelis chose "peace with the Arab" as their main hope and 58% chose "peace." Nevertheless, during these years, peace was perceived as a dream or a wish and not as a tangible possibility in the foreseeable future. Indeed, between 80% and 90% of Jews in Israel would not consider far-reaching compromises to achieve peace. Even the slogan "Peace for Territories" appeared only in the late 1970s.

The hegemonic beliefs of the ethos of conflict were commonly expressed in the public discourse. For example, studies by Gavriely-Nuri (2008, 2009, 2010, in press) illustrate how Israel developed a war-normalizing dialogue that presented the Jewish-Arab wars and violence in a positive, natural, and legitimate way. Beliefs of ethos were disseminated by the mass media and expressed by the leaders (see, e.g., Barzilai, 1996; Caspi & Limor, 1992; Nosek & Limor, 1994). In this period, all the media outlets operated under the influence and supervision of the political echelon, and censorship was well institutionalized. The political and the military establishments viewed the media as a branch of the establishment that could be used to promote ideological and national goals, especially with regard to the issue of security and the Jewish-Arab conflict (see

Barzilai, 1992, 1996; Caspi & Limor, 1992; Nosek & Limor, 1994; Peri, 1998). The dominance of the ethos of conflict was also reflected in the political arena. For example, a study of the formal platforms of the political parties showed that the societal beliefs of the ethos of conflict appeared in them prominently in the 1960s and 1970s (Magal, Oren, Bar-Tal, & Halperin, 2010; Oren, 2005, 2010). Tsur (2013) illustrates how the Hebrew language reflected the dominant ethos of conflict by incorporating expressions, sayings, and words that denote and connote this particular worldview. Similarly, in a study of the central governmental ceremonies of the Remembrance Day commemoration for fallen soldiers and Independence Day between 1948 and 2006, Arviv-Abromovich (2011) found that until the 1970s all eight themes of the societal beliefs of the ethos of conflict were central in the national state ceremonies of Memorial Day and Independence Day, expressed in symbols, in speeches by the Israeli formal leaders, and in rituals.

Adult Hebrew Literature

Ben Ezer (1992) notes that following the war of independence, during the first decades of the State of Israel, Hebrew literature presented the Israeli-Arab conflict as existential, one that has to be determined on the battlefield. It greatly justified the return of Jews to their homeland and presented them in a glorifying way as they struggle to live a normal life and at the same time are forced to hold a gun for self-defense. Thus, writers described Israeli Jews as the victims in the conflict, forced to defend themselves in the violent lines of actions, and also glorified their patriotic readiness to sacrifice life. At least until the 1967 war, the writers expressed a deep sense of shared danger in Israeli society. During this period, the literature presented Arabs' intentions to annihilate the Jewish presence in various ways. Arabs were often delegitimized and viewed not as individuals but as an abstract sinister force in nightmarish terms (Ben-Ezer, 1978, 1992; Govrin, 1989; Shaked, 1989).

For example, in *Nomad and Viper* (1999), published in 1963, Amos Oz writes about a young woman in a kibbutz. She meets a Bedouin shepherd, a nomad, portrayed as primitive, bestial, ugly, and wretched. Eventually, the invasion of nomads into the kibbutz area has brought devastation – foot-and-mouth disease, destruction of cultivated fields, and theft. In this story, according to Ben- Ezer (1977, p. 100), "The Arab symbolizes the dark, instinctual side of life.... The Arab exists in the dark part of her soul, just as bestial lust, irrationality and abandon-death do. The Arab is also the desert, and disease."

Children's Literature

The most extensive studies analyzing the presentation of the climax of the Israeli-Arab conflict in children's Hebrew literature are by Adir Cohen (1985) and Fouzi El Asmar (1986). Cohen (1985) points out that many of the books published in 1960–1970 dealt with the Arab-Jewish conflict. In these books the conflict is usually described in a simplistic and one-sided way. They not only provide national, historical, and political justifications for the Zionist enterprise, which is understandable, but also negate a basis for Arabs' claims. The country is presented as uninhabited and desolate. Jews are presented in these books as heroes who are attacked by Arabs and thus fight them with great determination and courage. Arabs are often delegitimized with labels such as thieves, murderers, robbers, spies, arsonists, violent mob, terrorists, kidnappers, "cruel enemy," war lovers, devious, monsters, bloodthirsty, dogs, prey wolves, and vipers. Also, the books characterize Arabs with delegitimizing traits such as brutality, violence, malignity, cruelty, and treacherousness. These descriptions transmit feelings of eternal fear, horror, hatred, and animosity. For example, in one popular book series, about Danidin by On Sarig (*Danidin in a Kidnapped Plane*, 1972), the captain of the plane asks the terrorists not to wave with their guns because they may go off. The terrorists respond, "We are the commanders here and not you, and soon we will be the commanders in all your Israel, and then we will annihilate all of you together with your state until a sign or trace will not remain... we will finish what Hitler began to do and did not succeed in completing" (quoted in Cohen, 1985, p. 146).

Teff-Seker (2012) investigates the representation of the Arab-Israeli conflict in Israeli children's literature between 1967 and 1987. While on the one hand these books patronize and even delegitimize Arabs, on the other hand they also reflect the interest of Jewish ingroup members in individual (Arab) outgroup members. In this case, Israeli Jews occasionally even exhibit an attraction, social and erotic-romantic, toward Arabs. Furthermore, the study shows that while war is prominent on the Arab-Jewish group level reality, peace and friendship are (favorably) shown to exist on an individual level between Arab and Jewish group members. Additionally, many (though not all) books depict the Arab outgroup as heterogeneous, and some even promote personalization and decategorization of Arabs, presenting them as (positive and negative) individuals or as a group that also contains innocent civilians – rather than only members of a homogeneous hostile enemy group. But at the same time, though war against Arabs is viewed negatively, it is seen as being justified because it will eventually bring peace. The Arab-Israeli conflict is presented as a continuation of the historic persecutions in which Jews are the victims and the rivals are cruel oppressors. But even if the conflict is forced upon the Jews, they will prevail.

Hebrew Drama

In an analysis of the portrayal of Arabs through the years in the Hebrew plays, Urian (1997) finds that while Jews are presented positively, with glorification, Arabs figures rarely appear in plays of the 1950s and 1960s. In a few plays, Jewish playwrights view Arabs as the enemy with whom either a peaceful solution will be achieved or violent confrontation will take place. According to Ofrat (1979), in almost all plays of this early period, Arabs are portrayed as an external threat and a military danger, but rarely do their characters appear on the stage. When they do appear, they have no individual identity and are presented just as "Arabs" (e.g., in *They'll Arrive Tomorrow* written by Nathan Shaham in 1950). Violent confrontations are presented as resulting from the Arabs' irreconcilable standpoint, which means that the Israeli fighters have no choice but to kill the attackers. In the play *In the Desert Plains of the Negev* (1949) by Yigal Mossinsohn, an Israeli woman fighter says, "You don't want to kill, you don't want war, you don't want to kill poor fellahin from Palestine or Egypt, but you have to" (quoted in Urian, 1997, p. 23).

Israeli Films

After the independence war, the Israeli filmmakers concentrated on the presentation of the Zionist ideology (Shohat, 1989). They often portrayed the heroic Jewish struggle against the hostile Arabs, for example, *Faithful City*, 1952; *Hill 24 Doesn't Answer*, 1955; *Pillars of Fire*, 1959; and *Rebels against Light*, 1964. In these films Arabs are presented in a negative way, and the struggle with them is a justified existential conflict. Later, the victorious 1967 war brought a series of heroic films, nearly all of which are about Arabs' violent intentions and their aggressive behavior, which had to be contained by the heroism of the Israeli fighters (e.g., *60 Hours to Suez*, 1967; *Target Tiran*, 1968; *Five Days in Sinai*, 1969; *The Great Escape*, 1971; and *Operation Thunderbolt*, 1976). In these films Arab soldiers are often portrayed as being cowards, ignorant, stupid, lazy, and cruel. Gross and Gross (1991) note that about 50 war films were produced in Israel in the first 30 years after 1948 and all have a similar narrative that focuses on Israeli security problems; justified, existential, and violent confrontations with Arabs; an intransigent Arab position; and the heroism of the Israeli army.

Schoolbooks

During the climax of the conflict, the Israeli school system was mobilized for the challenge of coping with the Arab threat and indoctrinating students with themes of the ethos of conflict. The leaders explicitly expressed the need to develop an education system that is functional for this national mission. Deputy Minister of Education Aaron Yadlin said in 1967, "It would appear that today the younger generation needs a special vaccination concerning the historic and moral implications of Arab-Israeli relations. One encounters young people who are unaware of the immense gulf that lies between us and our anti-Semitic Arab neighbors. The Arabs' aim of destroying the state of Israel has not adequately permeated our consciousness" (cited in Podeh, 2002, p. 40).

Thus, according to Podeh (2002), history textbooks written between 1948 and the 1970s (the so-called first-generation textbooks) had the objective of strengthening national Jewish ideology with the ethos of conflict (see also Firer, 1985; Mathias, 2002, 2005; Yogev, 2010). Thus, when referring to the first waves of Jewish immigrations, these books depicted the country to which Jews arrived as desolated and uninhabited (see also Bar-Gal, 1993). These ideas were used, on the one hand, to justify the return of the Jews to their homeland, implying that they cared about it and successfully turned the swamps and the desert into blossoming land; and, on the other hand, to delegitimize Arabs' claims to the same land. The schoolbooks focused on the exclusive rights of the Jewish people for the ownership on the country and provided justifications for these rights. At the same time, the books disregarded Arabs' rights for such ownership, not recognizing their national entity and rights (Bezalel, 1989; Firer, 1985; Podeh, 2002). In addition, the history books avoided calling the country Palestine, when referring to the period of the British Mandate, and used the name Israel or Eretz Israel (the land of Israel). This way of writing negated Arab claims to Palestine. The Arab residents were mentioned only in negative terms. The negative descriptions referred to their backwardness and primitivism and to their cowardice, treacherousness, and violence. According to Firer (1985), the Jewish-Arab conflict was described with emotive concepts taken from the history of Jews in the Diaspora (i.e., pogroms, massacre, riots, disturbances, attacks of terror by bloodthirsty murderers, or bloody outbursts). Arabs were stereotyped negatively with delegitimizing terms such as "robbers," "wicked ones," "bloodthirsty mob," "killers," "gangs," or "rioters" (Zohar, 1972). In contrast, the history textbooks emphasized a positive image of the Jewish people, presenting them as peace loving. The books also stressed the moral and cultural superiority of the Jewish people over other nations and the exceptionality of the Zionist nationalist movement. Some books referred to the Jewish people as "the chosen people," the "special people," and even the "pure race." Firer's (1985) analysis also shows that during the intractable conflict the history textbooks made special efforts to impart patriotism, by glorifying the pioneers and the soldiers (Bar-Gal, 1993; Firer, 1985). At the same time, the books also presented a picture of the Jewish people as victims. There was overwhelming emphasis on Jewish suffering through the centuries as a result of anti-Semitism, with its climax during the Holocaust, and then Jews were presented as victims in the Israeli-Arab conflict (Bar-Gal, 1993; Firer, 1985; Podeh, 2002).

Commemoration of the Events and of the Fallen

Israel has a rich history of commemoration (see Almog, 1992; Azaryahu, 1995; Bar-Tal, 2007a; Handelman, 1990; Shamir, 1976; Sivan, 1991, 1999; Witztum & Malkinson, 1993) and a range of policies that support these practices. Military cemeteries are constructed for the fallen soldiers; the Ministry of Defense has been publishing books presenting the biographies of the fallen, as well as their literary and artistic contributions; the fallen soldiers are also memorialized through books, films, and songs; Jewish settlements and many streets are named after the fallen heroes; every Jewish city has a building to commemorate its fallen soldiers; almost every Israeli institution or place of work has a corner commemorating the fallen soldiers who were associated with the institution; throughout Israel are dispersed war monuments to immortalize fallen soldiers – by 1990 there were 900 (Levinger, 1993); every major war is commemorated formally by the government; the official Remembrance Day to honor the fallen soldiers is one of the most sacred days in the Israeli calendar, and the commemoration takes place on the governmental and municipal levels and in every school; the mass media together with other public institutions play a major role in commemoration by observing dates of important battles and wars and by referring extensively to the fallen soldiers; and the fallen, between 1950 and the 1970s, were presented in cultural products as ultimate heroes of the nation. All the noted cultural symbols have continued up to the present since the late 1970s; however, critical expositions of the conflict also appear prominently.

Obviously, the culture of conflict is not static but changes over time in different ways. It changes its forms, emphases, contents, symbols, and even direction. But while the culture of conflict was absolutely hegemonic and consensual during the first decades of the state, beginning in the 1970s the Jewish population exhibited the development of alternative beliefs that recognized the rights of Palestinians to their state, that legitimized and humanized Arabs, that began to question the exclusivity of Jewish victimhood in the conflict, and even began to present immoral acts of Jews and thus question their moral superiority (Arian, 1995; Bar-Tal, 2007a; Bar-Tal & Schnell, 2013a; Bornstein, 2008; Oren, 2005, 2009; Oren & Bar-Tal, 2006; Shohat, 1989; Urian, 1998; 2010; Zertal & Eldar, 2007). In fact, in Israel there is at present an alternative culture that is in competition with the dominant culture of conflict. It is not only expressed in the shared views of segments of the Israeli population but also reflected in cultural products such as films, literary books, theatrical plays, and visual arts, as well as in new ceremonies, symbols, narratives, and language (see Bar-Tal, 2007a).

CHARACTERISTICS OF THE CULTURE OF CONFLICT

The culture of conflict has various characteristics, the first of which is that its general themes, as reflected in collective memory and the ethos of conflict, are universal. Themes about the justness of one's own goals, the importance of security, self-collective glorification, self-collective presentation as a victim in the conflict, delegitimization of the rival, emphasis on patriotism and on unity, and valuing peace can be found in the culture of societies that are involved in intractable conflict. These eight themes serve as an organizing framework to view the reality of the conflict and even beyond; they form part of the general worldview – an ideology – that influences information processing.

Second, one theme that receives particular significance in the culture of conflict and therefore needs a specific note is glorification of violence. It praises the personnel, organizations, and the institutions that carry out the violence. Because many of the societal activities in the frame of the intractable conflict are related to violence and because violent acts stand at the core of the dynamics of intractable conflict, it is thus natural that those society members who perform the violence on behalf of the society and the organizations and the institutions that are responsible for its performance receive focal attention, a large part of the societal resources, and glory. The fighters and the supportive staff are the front runners of the society. They are considered as the ultimate patriots who are ready to sacrifice their lives. It is thus not surprising that they are the desirable societal models, and their acts are viewed with reverence and glorification. This focus is reflected in many different ways. The violent events, such as battles or wars, and the fallen are noted in mass media; leaders talk about them; they are commemorated in ceremonies, rituals, and monuments, and eternalized in different cultural products (songs, poems, visual arts, films, or literature); and they figure saliently in educational materials and curricula. They communicate particular meaning by symbolically reflecting beliefs, values, and attitudes toward the violent conflict that eternalize the collective memory of conflict, granting hegemony to the beliefs of the ethos of conflict, and by expressing emotions of conflict. Specifically, they glorify battles and wars and the heroism of those who participated in the events, recall the martyrdom of those who fell, cultivate the sense of collective victimhood, and emphasize the malevolence of the enemy and the necessity to continue the struggle in fulfillment of the patriotic "will" of the fallen in order to achieve their sacred goals. As such, they serve as an important socializing and cultural factor (all this stands in complete contrast to disapproving, negating, condemning, and delegitimizing the violence used by the rival). The reverence toward violent events and those involved in them creates symbols that fuel the continuation of the violence. Thus, these elements contribute greatly to what is also sometimes referred as the culture of violence (Bar-Tal, 2003; Rupesinghe & Rubio, 1994).

Third, each society has particular contents that fill out the general themes with narratives that concern its specific symbols, including experiences, history, conditions, events, heroes, and myths (see an example of the Israeli society by Bar-Tal, 2007a). Thus, each society accumulates through its history in general and especially during years of the intractable conflict in particular specific contents that fill out the eight general themes and provide cultural meaning to the given conflict. For example, Palestinians draw the particular contents of their cultures, such as a key (the symbol of returning back to their homes), the notion of *shahid*, and the olive tree, as a symbol of their deep-rootedness in the country from their unique experiences and symbols of other ethoses.

Fourth, the specific symbols of the culture of conflict (e.g., sacrifice, heroism, sacred value of the goals, suffering, or victimhood) are expressed through different contents (e.g., stories about heroes, old myths, aspirations, prescriptions, narratives about major events). The same symbols appear and reappear in different narratives. Thus, for example, the narrative of heroism can appear in Israel in the story about Masada, which tells about the heroic act of Jews about 2000 years ago who defended a fortress against Romans and eventually committed suicide in order not to fall in the enemy hands; in the story of Bar Kokhba, who rebelled against Rome in the second century during Hadrian's reign and bravely fought the superior legions; in the story of the Warsaw Ghetto uprising, which tells about a hopeless uprising of few hundred Jews who decided to put up a fight against the Nazis, who sent millions of Jews to their death; in the story of Joseph Trumpeldor, who together with his few friends fought a battle against hundreds of Arabs in 1920 and, after being injured and while dying, said that "it is good to die for our country"; and in the stories of heroic battles fought by Israeli Jews in many wars against Arabs.

Fifth, some contents of the culture of conflict are expressed through different cultural modes and channels, such as books, ceremonies, art, films, speeches, and monuments. That is, various institutions and channels take an active part in the dissemination of the contents among society members and their socialization, and they do so in different ways. Thus, for example, memory of the heroic act of Joseph Trumpeldor is maintained with a museum in the place where the battle took place, a monument built in this area, ceremonies held to commemorate this event, and a description in the school textbooks and in the stories, songs, and poems that were written about this event and its hero.

Sixth, symbols of the conflict and of the culture of conflict become routinized into everyday life experience (see Bar-Tal, Abutbul, & Raviv, in press). There are at least four aspects of this routinization process. First, society members regularly engage in practices that are related to the conflict situation. These practices are a result of the constraints of the conflict conditions and can be formally or informally imposed. For example, Israelis go through a security search in the entrance to every public space, such as a bank, mall, or public office. Second, society members are exposed to images and symbols of the conflict in public spaces such as streets and parks and even private residences. For example, in many of the societies it is part of the daily experiences to see soldiers and weapons. Also, the symbols and objects can be statues, sculptures, names of streets, shelters, and gas masks. This exposure is an inescapable part of living in the context of intractable conflict. Third, part of the everyday life experience is to be exposed to information about the conflict, which is very central in the public discourse. The exposure can be to news and commentaries presented in the newspapers or on radio, television, or the Internet. Also, many of the private discourses touch on the conflict. Fourth, words and expressions that portray the conflict with their meaning become part of the daily language. These words and expressions become a slang that describes events unrelated to conflict. All these aspects are responsible for the routinization and even ritualization of the culture of conflict. That is, the physical and social spaces are fully saturated with expressions of the conflict. In other words, a whole complex of "beliefs, assumptions, habits, representations and practices" are reproduced in a "banally mundane way" (Billig, 1995, p. 6), because the intractable conflict is part of everyday life.

All these reflections regularly charge the climate of individual and collective life with a particular orientation that strengthens the conflict-supporting ideology. For example, Ross (2007) investigated the role of murals and parades in Northern Ireland where both elements appear in daily life. He suggests that they are part of contests over everyday cultural expressions and performance that signify identities of the rival groups in conflict. Indeed, hundreds of murals appear on many of the buildings and walls depicting divisive events, slogans, and persons in the past and present history of Northern Ireland. Parades are an important part of the Northern Irish culture especially for the Unionist (Protestant) side, which holds well over 1,000 parades during a year. Nationalists (Catholics) organize over 100 parades every year. Both groups use the parades to solidify their own identity and secure continuous mobilization of society members. Also, Hadjipavlou (2004, p. 200) notes that everywhere in Cyprus are visible images of "barbed wire, the military posts, the blue berets, and the blue and green posters that read 'Buffer UN Zone,' 'Beware Mine Fields,' 'No Entry-Occupied Zone,' 'Dead Zone,' and 'No Photographs-Security Zone.' Flags of all kinds wave together or apart." In addition, on the Turkish side were displayed photographs of atrocities performed by the Greek Cypriots as well as photographs of Turkish Cypriots who were killed. According to Hadjipavlou, these everyday symbols of conflict helped "to adapt to the conflict and the status quo, especially when there is no daily interethnic violence."

Indeed, the routinization has a number of important functions. First, it normalizes what is an unusual life by turning conflict-related experiences into everyday routines. In addition, this way of life prepares society members to cope with life characterized by threats and dangers. In some ways, it strengthens the psychological resilience that allows overcoming stress. Routinization also reinforces solidarity, cohesiveness, and fate interdependence. Society members live daily in a particular way, one that is different from normal life without a conflict. They are aware of their uniqueness that creates a bond and also boundaries of belonging. Thus, these daily experiences contribute to the formation of a unique collective identity. Finally, this way of life solidifies support for the ethos of conflict because the routines of life are based on an ideology of conflict.

As an additional characteristic, the culture of conflict evolves through a long process that takes years and decades. It takes time to construct the symbols and to institutionalize them via processes of dissemination and socialization until they become dominant parts of the culture that is shared by at least a majority of society members. Therefore, intractable conflicts that last for at least 25 years are special candidates for the evolvement of the culture of conflict.

Finally, the culture of conflict is not static but changes dynamically in accordance with prolonged experiences that the society goes through. The changes are usually gradual because culture changes not overnight but in a long process that can be observed from the perspective of time. Intractable conflicts can escalate, deescalate, and change their form. These different phases of conflict can last years and thus have effects on the culture of conflict. Also, in societies involved in intractable conflict, there may slowly emerge an alternative culture with symbols propagating peace. Thus, new societal beliefs may be formed, new symbols may appear, new narratives, new ceremonies, new cultural products, and even new schoolbooks. These developments are dependent not only on the changes in the nature of the conflict but also on the nature and development of the society. In societies that are closed or not tolerant to alternative views, or use mechanisms that prevent dissemination of alternative information, alternative culture has difficulty developing. But when the new culture develops, it competes with the culture of conflict. The competition may last for many years, and sometimes one of them becomes more dominant. It is important to note, though, that an alternative culture may exist all the time, even during the climax of intractable conflict, as was the case in Northern Ireland, when the two cultures competed.

In addition to the culture of conflict, another important societal component that also is greatly affected by the lasting intractable conflict and plays an important role in its continuation is collective identity. Collective identity and the culture of conflict are in a complementary relationship. On the one hand, the culture of conflict feeds its contents into the collective identity and, on the other hand, collective identity serves as a supporting foundation of the culture of conflict.

IDENTITY AND CONFLICT

Last, but not least, the described narratives of collective memory and ethos not only serve as foundations of the culture of conflict but also fulfill the unique role of contributing to the formation, maintenance, and strengthening of collective identity that reflects the lasting conditions and experiences of intractable conflict (Auerbach, 2010). Collective identity "indicates a joint awareness and recognition that members of a group share the same social identity" (David & Bar-Tal, 2009, p. 356). This definition puts an emphasis not only on the identification with the collective but also on awareness that other members of the collective share this identification and hold similar beliefs and feelings and act in a similar fashion. This macroapproach has two major foundations: generic features that are found in every collective and characterize it on a general level (see Chapters 2 and 3), and specific contents that provide the collective with features that endow it with unique and particular characteristics (Barthel, 1996; Cairns, Lewis, Mumcu, & Waddell, 1998; Gillis, 1994; Oren, Bar-Tal, & David, 2004). Clearly, self-categorization and identification are fundamental for self-definition as a society member, but that is only an initial phase, which has to be followed by acceptance of additional societal beliefs that provide meaning to the collective identity (Bar-Tal & Oren, 2000; Turner, 1991, 1999). Society members, as thinking human beings, need an elaborated system of societal beliefs that justifies and explains their belonging, describes their characteristics and concerns as society members, and explains the meaning of their social identity (Oren & Bar-Tal, in press).

Thus, the contents (also called narratives or societal beliefs), defined by Ashmore, Deaux, and McLaughlin-Volpe (2004, p. 94) as "the semantic space in which identity resides – a space that can include self-attributed characteristics, political ideology, and developmental narratives," provide the particular epistemic basis for the collective identity (see Andrews, 2007; Tilly, 2002). They portray the specific meaning of a particular collective and draw from at least three sources: a tradition that refers to memories, cultural products, symbols, and institutions that have formed a collective identity in the past (these may be religious, cultural, national, or some fusion of these); ideology that articulates the right to self-determination and self-definition in a certain territory and that provides a general orientation to the members of the collective; and crucial experiences, based on important events that have taken place in the society and that have been experienced by its members, either directly (through participation) or indirectly (by observation, hearing, or reading) (Eriksen, 2001).

This conception implies that collective identity is charged with the contents of the culture of conflict. In other words, it is proposed that when intractable conflict lasts for a long time, the collective identity of the involved societies is filled with contents of collective memory and the ethos of conflict (see Oren & Bar-Tal, in press; also Bar-Tal, 1998c; Oren, Bar-Tal & David, 2004). These contents provide the meaning to the particular collective identity. Obviously, the culture, as well as identity, of every collective involved in intractable conflict has other elements that provide the epistemic content to their foundation (e.g., national, religious, or economic). But the intensity of the conflict experiences, their durability, and their major role in the life of the society members as individuals and as the collective turn them into a dominant part of the culture and identity (Cash, 1996; Northrup, 1989; Ross, 2001; Worchel, 1999). Members of societies involved in intractable conflicts view themselves in a particular way, with a unique identity that gives special place to the conflict. They perceive the experiences of the conflict as marking boundaries that differentiate them from other collectives. Often they even see themselves as so unique in their conflict experiences that they differentiate themselves even from other societies involved in intractable conflicts as well. This view contributes to the collective identity by strengthening their *sense of a common fate* and *perception of the uniqueness* – both generic features of the collective identity (see David & Bar-Tal, 2009). The former feature pertains to feelings of mutual dependence in view of the conflict, implying that the fate of each one of the collective's members is perceived as dependent on the fate of the whole collective. The latter refers to the definition of the collective's selfhood as a unique entity that is different from that of other collectives. Both features are shaped by the experiences of intractable conflict. Members of the collective realize that their fate as a result of the conflict is interdependent. They also believe that these experiences, as well as the conditions of the conflict, do not resemble conditions and experiences of other collectives involved in intractable conflict.

The conditions of intractable conflict and the accompanied experiences have additional effects on the collective identity of society members. First, in times of intractable conflict there is an increase in saliency of identity. It becomes an important feature that marks who is in and who is out (Kelman, 2001; Northrup, 1989). This differentiation is often used within a society to distinguish supporters and opponents of continuing the conflict. Also, it becomes useful in cases where the intractable conflict is intrasocietal in one state. Second, in times of intractable conflict society members tend to increase their sense of identification with the society in order to fulfill their need of belonging and security. Third, participation in collective action leads to politicized identification that indicates greater involvement, increased readiness to participate, and commitment to the conflict goals (De Weerd & Klandermans, 1999; Drury & Reicher, 1999; Reicher, 1996; Simon & Klandermans, 2001; Turner, Oakes, Haslam, & McGarty, 1994). Finally, Kelman (1999) proposes that identities of parties in some of the intractable conflicts become negatively interdependent, such that a key component of each group's identity is based on negation of the other. As a result, often for one group to maintain its legitimacy, it must not only delegitimize the other but also cannot accept compromising solutions. As a case in point, Kelman (1999, p. 588) describes the "psychological core" of the Israeli-Palestinian conflict as "the perception by both parties that it is a zero-sum conflict, not only with respect to territory, but, most importantly, with respect to national identity and national existence." Under such a zero-sum conceptualization, each party holds the perception that only one can be legitimately recognized as a nation, which means that one can sustain national identity only at the expense of the other's claim to nationhood.

Much of the Pakistani national identity was formed around the rivalry with India. The need to justify Muslim communalism in face of the Indian Hindu-secular identity was evident from the beginning of the Pakistani nationalism led by Mohammad Ali Jinnah (Nasr, 2005). The fear of Hindu domination in the formative years of Muslim nationalism and the rejection of Indian secularism and of Hindu cultural and political domination in the postpartition era were underpinning the Pakistani-Islamic ideology. The military, which is a major power in Pakistan, held similar views, while fortifying nationalism as opposition to India and maintaining the flames of the conflict until the late 1990s (Nasr, 2005). Alongside proximity in religious identity, many Pakistanis, especially those from Punjab province, hold ethnic kinship with Kashmir's inhabitants (Saideman, 2005).

A study by Bar-Tal, Sharvit, Halperin, and Zafran (2012) shows that the ethos of conflict, being a distinct construct, is related to identity. Members of the Israeli Jewish society who identified closely with their nation also adhered to the ethos of conflict. This study suggests that while social identity reflects the extent of identification with the society on the individual level, ethos as the dominant orientation provides contents that give meaning to the identity (Oren, Bar-Tal, & David, 2004).

Of special interest is the study by Kreidie and Monroe (2002) that has direct implication on the understanding of the nature and effects of social identity in societies torn by intractable conflict. Specifically, the researchers investigate what turns ordinary individuals into the perpetrators who performed atrocities in the Lebanese civil war. In-depth interviews of five Lebanese with different backgrounds, who all were involved in different ethnic massacres, killing members of the other ethnic groups, show in all the cases that identity was the key factor that influenced their choices of behavior. Their identification with their ethnic group with clear boundaries differentiating "us" from "them," with clear delegitimization of "them" as being a threat to "us," led ordinary human beings to perform the most horrible acts of violence. The researchers note that "what triggered the violence was the way our subjects situated themselves within the ingroup in the Lebanese multiethnic society and how each one, as a group member, perceived the other group and their relations between groups. The identity described in the narrative analysis thus is as follows. The fighters first see themselves as victims of the sectarian political arrangement. They then see themselves either as subordinates and victims of an unjust distribution of power and resources or as members of the dominant group that must protect its existence against larger threatening populations, who might destroy the group's existence. It is at the moment when a perpetrator feels a threat to his existence that he resorts to the use of force" (p. 28). This analysis suggests that the culture of conflict and the new shaped identity have a tremendous critical influence on the way societies engulfed in intractable conflict function.

CONCLUSIONS AND IMPLICATIONS

This chapter suggests that intractable conflicts lead to prolonged continuous imprinting of experiences that serve as a fertile ground for the evolvement of the culture of conflict. The culture of conflict evolves especially in response to continuous physical violence, which claims human losses of compatriots and motivates mobilization and continuation of the conflict. Its major societal beliefs concern the justness of one's own goals, security considerations, delegitimization of the opponent, group's victimization and glorification, and patriotism and unity, as well as peace as a desired aim. In the context of protracted violent conflict, all eight themes of societal beliefs flourish intensively and extensively. That is, these beliefs preoccupy a central place in the societal repertoire; are used often in the public discourse; appear in various societal, cultural, and educational products and channels; and are disseminated as the violence continues over an increasing number of years. Within the culture of conflict, on the one hand, various tangible and intangible symbols (e.g., memorial sites, books, or ceremonies) help to maintain the societal beliefs, making them more accessible, relevant, and concrete; and, on the other hand, the societal beliefs provide the conceptual framing for the creation of these symbols. That is, the societal beliefs of the culture of conflict, which serve as a prism through which society members attach meaning to the acts and the artifacts, provide the contents elaborated in the symbols.

From another perspective, societal beliefs of the culture of conflict serve as the cognitive and affective foundations of the conflict by providing explanations and justifications for its continuation. They constitute the comprehensive narrative in its entirety that provides a simplistic and one-sided picture of the conflict with all the related themes. In fact, this narrative constitutes *experienced and imagined reality* for the society members participating in intractable conflict. It is experienced because intractable conflicts by their nature have direct and indirect effects on the lives of the society members as individuals and collectives. They witness the falling members, see the destruction, and experience stress and hardship. But it is also imagined because societies and society members also rely in the construction of their narrative on misinformation, exaggerations, and myths. In turn, the societal beliefs of the narrative arouse emotions (fear, hatred, and anger toward the opponent, and feelings of self-pride, esteem, and pity) and also lead to behaviors that are consistent with them, such as acts geared to persevering one's own goals, avenging losses, hurting the opponent, and sacrificing one's own life for the group. Society members who hold these beliefs (i.e., the narrative) and accept their rationale are compelled to continue the violent conflict. Furthermore, once these beliefs become embedded in the culture, it is difficult to change them.

The fundamental premise is that every society needs the narratives of the societal beliefs of the culture of conflict because they enable successful adaptation to the conditions of conflict and to withstanding the rival. Specifically, as an example, every society engaged in intractable conflict needs justification of its own goals and patriotism for mobilization of their members. Thus, in every society engaged in intractable conflict at least the leading agents of conflict and segments in the society believe that their goals exclusively are justified. But this observation does not imply that all these societies have a similar underlying moral basis in the justness of the goals according to prevailing contemporary moral intergroup codes. In some of them, there is a moral gap between the prevalent moral codes and posed goals as well as practices during the conflict. That is, some of the societies involved in intractable conflict try to achieve goals that are unacceptable by the present codes of intergroup behavior. Societies such as whites in South Africa or French in the case of Algeria tried to maintain systems that negated the emerged moral norms. But even these societies had a well-elaborated system of societal beliefs that not only justified goals of colonialism or apartheid but also presented themselves as being the victims in the conflict.

The basic thesis of this chapter suggests that when intractable conflict, with its violence, continues throughout decades, then violence and the accompanied experiences constitute a determinative factor in intergroup conflict. Therefore, it is of special importance to understand not only the specific acts of violence but also the socio-psychological and cultural bases that evolve and then underlie these acts. These bases play a crucial role in violent conflicts because human beings have various needs, aspirations, and drives that have to be satisfied in every human society.

A question, though, that can be asked is whether the developed bases with the socio-psychological infrastructure are indeed functional and adaptive, as they fuel continuation of the conflict. It is important in answering this question to take into account that the analysis is done from the perspective of the involved societies in intractable conflict, which try to adapt to the harsh conditions of the conflict context, achieve their goals, withstand the rival, and survive the violent period in the best way possible. Those are the aspirations and objectives during the climax of intractable conflict, when there is no light at the end of the tunnel – when neither side can win the conflict and achieve its conflict goals, and neither party thinks about compromises in order to settle it peacefully. That is, the analysis applies to the situation when both societies are engulfed in violent confrontation, without seeing any possibility of engaging in a peace process. In this situation, human beings involved in intractable conflict develop a socio-psychological repertoire that is functional to their individual and collective needs and goals. It fulfills many functions that greatly facilitate the adaptation of the society. When the prospect of a peace process appears and the indications for constructive negotiations become salient, however, then the same socio-psychological repertoire embedded in the culture of conflict that was functional during the period of intense confrontation without signs of peace becomes a barrier to conflict resolution and detrimental to peacemaking, as will be discussed in Chapter 8.

The present chapter attempts to elaborate on the evolvement of the culture of conflict with its components, which has the determinative role in the dynamics of intractable conflict. This culture comes to serve as the major motivating, justifying, and rationalizing factor of the conflict. It is underlined by epistemic motivation for specific content and resistant to change during the intractable conflict. Any negative actions taken then serve as information validating the existing psychological repertoire and, in turn, magnify the motivation and readiness to engage in conflict. The behaviors of each side confirm the held expectations and justify harming the opponent. In this way, cycles of conflict develop that often lead not only to its escalation and blind continuation but also to the solidification of the culture of conflict. It is the hegemonic culture of conflict that serves as a major factor for the continuation of the conflict and a barrier for resolving it, being part of the vicious cycle of the intractable conflict. In the next chapter I elaborate further on the barriers to peaceful conflict settlement, discussing their nature on societal and individual levels.

8

Socio-Psychological Barriers to Peaceful Conflict Resolution

Socio-psychological barriers play a major role in peacefully resolving intractable conflict.[1] These barriers develop in a society involved in intractable conflict on individual and collective levels within the dominant culture of conflict, with its pillars of societal beliefs of collective memory of conflict, the ethos of conflict, and collective emotions. The culture of conflict has tremendous effect on the collective when the societal beliefs of the culture of conflict are shared among society members; they are often used by the leaders as the major epistemic basis for the decision to continue the conflict; they appear continuously in the public discourse, mass communication channels, and cultural products; and they are imparted in socialization practices (see Figure 2). In fact, in this case the society (at least in some cases) becomes to some extent closed in a bubble of conflict walls, without encountering and processing major alternative information that may shed new light on the situation, the rival's or one's own society. This may happen when, in addition to the dominance of the culture, a society is closed as a result of active prevention of alternative information by authorities, as, for example, takes place in the extreme case of North Korea, but also in Russia or Pakistan. This closure takes place to varying degrees also in societies that in practice are open to new information but are psychologically closed. In such a political climate alternative information is available, but its availability merely serves to create a positive self-image of the society as being open and pluralistic. In reality, though, the indoctrinating practices close the society from actually entertaining alternative information.

---

[1] I recognize that other powerful barriers also prevent peaceful resolution of every intractable conflict; among them it is possible to find political, cultural, economic, and other reasons. But the present book focuses on the socio-psychological dynamics and foundations of the intractable conflict and therefore deals only with the socio-psychological barriers.

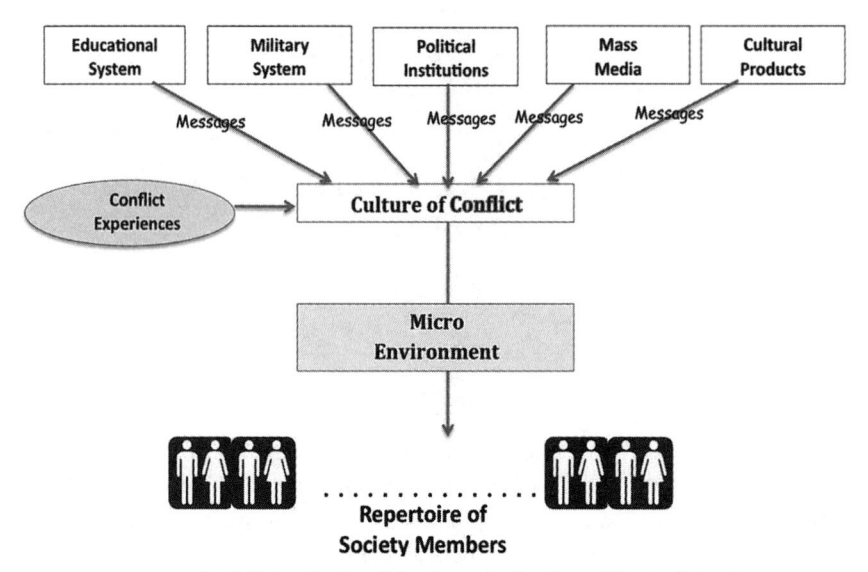

FIGURE 2. Socializing Society Members: Activation of Societal Barriers

In general, I recognize that each society may differ in its need to close itself because it differs with regard to its moral responsibility for waging an intractable conflict as it is perceived by the international community and by segments of the ingroup. It may differ with regard to formal closure by societal institutions and with regard to the psychological closure, which society members with the help of the societal institutions impose upon themselves. My basic premise is that in order for intractable conflict to last, there is a need to practice some level of closure that will allow the dominant themes that propagate continuation of the conflict to prevail. Extensive dissemination and eventual dominance of alternative ideas about peaceful resolution of the conflict may lead eventually to its termination in a democratic society. Northern Ireland is an example where even in the 1970s there was a well-established movement that promoted peaceful resolution of the conflict. Organizations such as Women Together and Women Caring propagated messages that called for peaceful resolution of the conflict when the country was dominated by violent confrontations between Catholics and Protestants. The existence of these voices played a determinative influence on the agreement that was achieved years later in 1998 (Fitzduff, 2002; Frazer & Fitzduff, 1986). Nevertheless, in many societies involved in intractable conflict the culture of conflict is hegemonic and its components constitute major barriers to its peaceful resolution.

My discussion of the socio-psychological barriers is divided into two parts. The first part concerns the societal mechanisms that actively play a role in setting barriers for preventing the flow of alternative information that contradicts the major themes of the ethos of conflict and collective memory and indicate a way for a possible resolution of the conflict peacefully. The second part, the larger one, describes the nature and functioning of the barriers on the individual level by society members who are involved in intractable conflicts and support it. The main argument advanced in this chapter is that, although socio-psychological barriers function on the individual level, this functioning is greatly affected by the dominant political culture of conflict, which provides opportunities and restrictions to the flow of information about the conflict. They provide the social environment in which individual society members collect information and then process it. Societies involved in intractable conflict very often make efforts to maintain the dominant societal beliefs of the conflict-supporting narrative and prevent penetration of alternative beliefs that may undermine this dominance. They use various societal mechanisms to block the appearance and dissemination of such information that promotes these beliefs. Such alternative information may humanize the rival and shed a new light on the conflict; suggest that goals can be compromised; identify a partner on the other side with whom it is possible to achieve peaceful settlement of the conflict; argue that peace is rewarding, while the conflict is costly; claim that continuation of the conflict is detrimental to the society; and even provide evidence that the ingroup is also responsible for the continuation of the conflict and has been carrying out immoral acts.

SOCIETAL MECHANISMS AS BARRIERS

Societal mechanisms are used to block alternative information and narratives from entering social spheres. When they do penetrate, they are often rejected before society members might be persuaded by their evidence and arguments (Bar-Tal, 2007b; Horowitz, 2000; Kelman, 2007). The use of societal mechanisms can be activated by the formal authorities of the ingroup – in some cases, of the state – or by other agents of conflict, who have a vested interest in preventing dissemination of alternative information. The former agents can be governments, leaders, and societal institutions, while the latter can be NGOs and various organization, as well as individuals, who play the role of the gatekeeper. (For detailed descriptions of the mechanisms and for examples from various conflicts, see Bar-Tal, Oren, & Nets-Zehngut, 2012;

Burns-Bisogno, 1997; Miller, 1994; Morris, 2000; Oren, Nets-Zehngut, & Bar-Tal, 2012; and Wolfsfeld, 2004.)

These societal mechanisms are used against individuals as well as organizations and groups. In the category of individuals are often found mass media journalists, academic experts, and artists, as well as individuals who saw and experienced events that in their essence contradict the societal beliefs of the culture of conflict and want to make them known to a wider public. Organizations may also collect and provide alternative information. Some are established to provide information, some monitor the behavior of the ingroup to prevent violations of human rights, and others try to build relations with the rival groups.

Control of information is practiced when the dissemination of information, including for the mass media, is controlled by the formal authorities and other agents of conflict. Then, sources that are supposed to provide information for the most part just report what is provided to them. In this situation of control, the authorities try to provide information that is in line with the dominant narrative of the culture of conflict and avoid providing information that may challenge this narrative. In principle the authorities may use a different method to control the information as, for example, providing selective information, limiting or even closing access to particular areas in order to prevent collection of information, or controlling who is allowed to get information. This list of possible control methods is partial. But the control does not have to be formal or institutional; it can also be done by controlling the flow of information, by rewarding those who adhere to the desired narrative, or by punishing those who deviate from preferred methods. The control of mass media is not necessarily by state leaders and its institutions; it can also be done by groups and organizations that function as agents of conflict or even by those without the support of the state. The control comes to assure that society members adhere to the societal belief of the culture of conflict and accept a group narrative about major specific events that occur in the course of the conflict. The way the Russian authorities dealt with the media during the second Russia-Chechnya war illustrates use of this mechanism. They established the Russian Information Center with the objective to disseminate the Russian narrative. This Information Center briefed journalists, but Russian officials were instructed on what to tell the media. In addition, Russians exercised tight control of journalists' movement in Chechnya. Even when journalists were allowed to enter war zones, they were accompanied by Russian officials, who decided where they could go and what they could see (Caryl, 2000).

Academia may also be controlled. Academics may seek new information, examine innovative research questions, provide creative new knowledge, and shed new and critical light on various issues. Thus, by this nature, it is the role of the academic to provide knowledge that may contradict the societal beliefs of the culture of conflict. Formal authorities of a state or authorities of the academic institutions may try to prevent researchers from carrying out their mission. They may practice selective hiring, censor research findings, prevent promotions, provide awards to conformists, not award grants, and even close departments. They may also directly prevent investigation of research questions that contradict the dominant conflict-supporting worldview. Nets-Zehngut (2011a, 2011b) analyzes the way the Israeli research community dealt with the information about the Palestinian exodus during the 1948 war. He found that during 1949–1957 almost all the studies disregarded the available information, indicating that the exodus at least partially happened because of the organized expulsion of Palestinians by the Jewish military forces. He found that the Israeli higher-educational institutions refrained from hiring historians who challenged the formal Zionist narrative and provided alternative information and interpretations about the history of Israel and especially about the history of the Israeli-Arab conflict (see also Zand, 2004).

Censorship on information occurs when the authorities practice formal control over information and decide what can be published. In contrast to the previous mechanism, this formal mechanism assures that contradicted information does not appear in the media and other channels. The censorship office can be related to government, formal leaders, or military institutions (De Baets, 2002). It can be limited to certain themes or be general. In any case, when censorship is practiced, information about the conflict has to be submitted for approval by an authority. This mechanism exercises formal power to assure that no alternative, unwanted information will be presented. This method is used by almost every society involved in intractable conflict. As one example, the government of Sri Lanka in its struggle against the Tamil minority enacted in 1973 the Press Council bill that formed a censoring council. Its members authorized considerable limitation on public debates in the mass media about issues related to the way the conflict was handled (Tyerman, 1973). Also, Harrison (1964) describes various acts of the French government during the Algeria war to censor and limit freedom of press.

Delegitimization of alternative sources of information is done in an attempt to discourage its distribution to prevent the shedding of positive light on the rival, negative light on the ingroup, and news about the concrete possibilities of peacemaking. The delegitimization is usually done by presenting the sources of alternative information as being traitorous, harmful to the cause of the group, and disloyal. It implies that the source of information is not among society's compatriots but also signals that the source can be harmed formally or informally. This mechanism is a socially powerful one because society members do not want be excluded and potentially punished or harmed. The price paid for providing alternative information is high and serves well the mechanism of preventing the collection and dissemination of information that contradicts the narrative provided by the societal beliefs of the culture of conflict. Also, this mechanism is practiced in many of the societies involved in intractable conflict. The Greek society in Cyprus exemplifies extensive use of this mechanism. Conflict-supporting governments as well as political parties, NGOs, and individuals have tried, continuously and systematically, to discredit and even delegitimize individuals, groups, and organizations that have engaged in dissemination of information that counters the prevailing official societal beliefs about the conflict, the rival, and the Greek society (Papadakis, Peristianis, & Welz, 2006).

Monitoring is a mechanism of following and supervising information provided by specific individuals and organizations that have a role in providing enlightening alternative information. This mechanism is often applied to academic experts who study research questions regarding the conflict or the societies involved and then publish this knowledge. Also, it is used against media sources and their correspondents or NGOs that are active in the conflict, as, for example, peace organizations or human rights NGOs. Using this mechanism, government or other agents of conflict monitor what is written, published, or aired and then single out the alternative information and its source, presenting them as harming the causes of the ingroup. This method is used by organizations in Israel that monitor information that in their view is harmful to the Israeli Jewish society in conflict with Palestinians. Israel Academia Monitor systematically documents academics, from students to professors, who the Web site operators believe "undermines Jewish Zionist interests," including signing petitions, attending conferences, speaking to the media, and writing articles that criticize government policy toward Palestinians. Based on that monitoring, the organization submits an annual report to the Israeli universities' boards of trustees, with the warning "this is what people do with your money." Another monitoring organization is NGO Monitor, which tracks organizations that "claim to promote moral agendas, such as humanitarian aid and human rights." The description of the mission says, "The aim of NGO Monitor, as outlined in the mission statement, is to generate and distribute critical analysis and reports on the output of the international NGO community for the benefit of government policy makers, journalists, philanthropic organizations and the general public. We intend to publicize distortions of human rights issues in the Arab-Israeli conflict and provide information and context for the benefit of NGOs working in the Middle East. We hope this will lead to an informed public debate on the role of humanitarian NGOs" (http://www.mgo_monitor.org?articles.php?type=about, November 24, 2011). An NGO named The Legal Forum for the Land of Israel even called students in schools "to provide information about teachers who introduce anti-Zionist contents into schools" (http://www.haforum.org.il/newsite/cat.asp?id=1146, December 7, 2011).

Punishment is through formal and informal sanctions, both social and physical, for providers of alternative information in an attempt to silence these sources that may contradict the dominant narrative. In extreme cases, the carrier of the alternative information may be even eliminated. Elimination usually is done unofficially and never admitted. But in many cases the carrier may be tried and then sentenced to a term in prison. Also, the punishment can involve intimidation and restrictions. This mechanism was used extensively in El Salvador during the civil war. Journalists, scholars, and students who criticized the government were constantly labeled as "destabilizing" and traitors; they were harassed, arrested, and physically attacked; their residences and offices were bombed, and some were even murdered. In addition, harsh measures were taken also against the institutions themselves, such as newspapers and even the National University of El Salvador (Matheson, 1986).

Closure of archives is done either completely or for a long time by the authorities with the aim of preventing the appearance of information that may contradict the societal beliefs of the dominant narrative. This mechanism is most often exercised by states, which have archives as a formal institutions, but a closure can also be practiced by informal groups. The closure can last many decades and thus prevent the appearance of information that may shed a negative light. Usually such information pertains to misdeeds of the ingroup, including performed atrocities or missed opportunities to make peace, or to positive deeds of the rival, which might present him in a new favorable light. For example, since War World I the Ottoman and later the Turkish archives were closed to the public with regard to documents that pertain to the Armenian genocide. State officials had access to such documents but only to search for documents that supported the Turkish "no genocide" narrative. In 1985 the archives were partially opened, but even then the access to the documents was very selective (Dixon, 2010; Safarian, 1999).

An encouragement and rewarding mechanism uses a "carrot" for those sources, channels, agents, and products that support the psychological repertoire of conflict. In the case of mass media, for example, the particular correspondent may receive exclusive information or permission to conduct an interview. In the case of cultural products, the writer or painter may get a prize for a creative work that supports the culture of conflict. The goal is to show that those who follow the line have benefits and rewards. They should serve as models for others. The Israeli Minister of Culture, for example, decided to give an annual prize for cultural work in the area of Zionism that gives "an expression to values of Zionism, to the history of the Zionist movement and to the return of the Jewish people to its historical homeland" (http://www.mcs.gov.il/Culture/Professional_Information/CallforScholarshipAward/Pages/PrasZionut2011.aspx).

The described societal barriers provide illumination on the context in which society members function on the individual level. Nevertheless, although in every society these mechanisms appear on at least some level, societies involved in intractable conflict differ with regard to their use. Their appearance depends on various cultural, political, societal, and even international determinants. Among the important categories of variables that influence the development of these processes are structural characteristics of the society and especially its political culture (Almond & Verba, 1989). Of special importance is its level of openness, pluralism, tolerance, and freedom of speech, which have determinative influence on control of information, freedom of expression, openness to consider alterative information, the free flow of information, availability of free agents of information, and access to global sources of information. The higher the level of control the society exercises over its members, the less freedom of expression there is to consider alternative information and the more closure there is. A society that has these characteristics prevents pluralism, skepticism, or criticism – emergence of alternative ideas that may push for peaceful resolution of the conflict (e.g., Russian society in the case of the conflict with the Chechens).

Also, societies in conflict differ with regard to the need to use societal mechanisms to obstruct the flow of alternative information. In asymmetrical conflicts, one society may have a more solidified moral epistemic basis in line with international moral codes. This epistemic basis requires less use of societal censoring mechanisms, as, for example, in the case of blacks in South Africa or Algerians in Algeria demanding an end of legal discrimination and end of colonialism, respectively. Other societies may need to construct an epistemic basis that negates moral codes of intergroup behavior and also to use societal mechanisms in order to uphold this narrative, as in the case of whites in South Africa and the French during the Algerian crisis.

The described societal processes and mechanisms influence the way society members think, process information, and act. Individuals' behavior is embedded within the societal context with its special conditions. This context provides not only the space in which society members can act cognitively, emotionally, and behaviorally but also the stimulations, opportunities, and limitations of these actions. The more open the space is, with more stimulations and opportunities and fewer limitations, the more society members can flourish and provide new, creative, and innovative ideas. Now I can turn to the discussion of the functioning of the socio-psychological barriers on the individual level.

SOCIO-PSYCHOLOGICAL BARRIERS ON THE INDIVIDUAL LEVEL: FREEZING

In all the societies involved in intractable conflicts, in their climax, all societies' members acquire the societal beliefs of the ethos of conflict and of collective memory, and at least a significant portion of the society's members see these beliefs as central and hold them with high confidence. These societal beliefs, which can be also called conflict-supporting beliefs, are the pillars of the culture of conflict and provide the narrative that is used in the society. Theoretically, the societal beliefs could be easily changed with persuasive arguments that provide information about costs of the conflict, humane characteristics of the rival, the rival's willingness to negotiate a peaceful resolution, or immoral acts of the ingroup. But in reality this change rarely happens in a short time;[2] even when society members are presented with alternative valid information that refutes their beliefs, they continue to adhere to them. One of the reasons for this functioning is the presence of socio-psychological barriers that are defined as "an integrated operation of cognitive, emotional and motivational processes, combined with a pre-existing repertoire of rigid conflict-supporting beliefs, world views and emotions that result in selective, biased and distorting information processing" (Bar-Tal & Halperin, 2011, p. 220). Thus, the individual functioning of the barriers results in one-sided information processing that obstructs and inhibits a penetration of new information that can contribute to the facilitation of the development of the peace process. That is, individuals are not interested even in exposure to alternative information that may contradict their held societal beliefs about the conflict.

The reason for this closure before alternative information is *freezing* of the societal beliefs of the narrative, which is the essence of barriers' functioning (Kruglanski, 2004; Kruglanski & Webster, 1996). The state of freezing is reflected in continuous reliance on the held societal beliefs that support the conflict, the reluctance to search for alternative information, and resistance to persuasive arguments that contradict held positions (Kruglanski, 2004; Kruglanski & Webster, 1996; Kunda, 1990). The freezing of the societal beliefs

---

[2] Still, the process of change may take place (see Chapter 9) with great difficulty.

of the culture of conflict is based on the operation of cognitive, motivational, and emotional processes and a number of socio-psychological factors (see also the integrative model of socio-psychological barriers to peacemaking in Bar-Tal & Halperin, 2011, for elaboration). In analyzing the cognitive processes, which I consider first, I focus on the rigid structure of societal beliefs.

Cognitive-Structural Factor

Freezing as a cognitive process is fed by the rigid structure of the societal conflict-supporting beliefs as they are held by many of society's members. Rigidity implies that these societal beliefs are resistant to change, being organized in a coherent manner with little complexity and great differentiation from alternative beliefs (Rokeach, 1960; Tetlock, 1989). Several reasons cause this rigid structure. First, societal beliefs about the conflict are often interrelated in an ideological structure. (In fact, they can be considered as a conservative ideology, as was suggested in Chapter 5 in the discussion about the ethos of conflict.) These beliefs subscribe to all the criteria for being an ideology, and as such they provide a well-organized system that stands against counterarguments and new information and is difficult to change (Jost et al., 2003). Second, as already indicated, these beliefs satisfy important human needs, such as needs for certainty, meaningful understanding, predictability, feeling of safety and mastery, positive self-esteem and identity, differentiation, and justice (Burton, 1990; Kelman & Fisher, 2003; Staub & Bar-Tal, 2003). As a result, by fulfilling such primary needs, they are relatively resistant to change. Finally, they also are held by many society members with high confidence, have central importance, and are ego-involving, which implies their stability. All these reasons contribute to the rigid structure of the societal beliefs of the ethos of conflict and collective memory, which as a result do not change easily but are maintained even when the most convincing alternative arguments that suggest peaceful resolution of the conflict are presented (Eagly & Chaiken, 1993, 1998; Fazio, 1995; Jost, Glaser, Kruglanski, & Sulloway, 2003; Krosnick, 1989; Lavine, Borgida, & Sullivan, 2000; Petrocelli, Tormala, & Rucker, 2007).

Closure is also affected by *general worldviews*, which are systems of beliefs that are not related to the particular conflict but provide orientations that contribute to its continuation because of the perspectives, norms, and values that they propagate (Bar-Tal & Halperin, 2011; Halperin & Bar-Tal, 2011). The list of these general views is a long one, but among the more distinctive systems it is possible to note as examples political ideology (such as authoritarianism or conservatism) (Adorno, Frenkel-Brunswick, Levinson, & Sanford, 1950; Altemeyer, 1981; Jost, 2006; Sidanius & Pratto, 1999), specific values such as those related to power or conservatism (Schwartz, 1992), religious beliefs (Kimball, 2002), and entity theory about the nature of human qualities (Dweck, 1999). All these worldviews influence how society members perceive the conflict disagreements and form their other beliefs about the nature of the conflict, the rival, and their own group (see, e.g., Beit-Hallahmi & Argyle, 1997; Dweck & Ehrlinger, 2006; Golec & Federico, 2004; Halperin, Russell, Trzesniewski, Gross, & Dweck, 2011; Jost, Glaser, Kruglanski, & Sulloway, 2003; Maoz & Eidelson, 2007; Sibley & Duckitt, 2008).

Motivational Factor

A second factor leading to freezing is motivation because the held societal beliefs are assumed to be underlined by specific closure needs (see Kruglanski, 1989, 2004). That is, society members are motivated to view the held beliefs of the ethos of conflict and collective memory as being truthful and valid because they fulfill for them different needs (see, e.g., Burton, 1990). Therefore, society members use various cognitive strategies to increase the likelihood of reaching particular conclusions that are in line with this knowledge (Kunda, 1990). In this motivational process, they reject information that contradicts the held conflict-supporting beliefs but accept information that validates their desired conclusion.

Emotional Factor

The third factor that affects freezing involves enduring negative intergroup emotions such as fear or hatred (see Chapter 6). They function to close the psychological repertoire of society members and strengthen the rigidity of the societal beliefs. The link that connects them and the societal beliefs is the appraisal component of the emotions. Each and every emotion is related to a unique configuration of comprehensive (conscious or unconscious) evaluations of the emotional stimulus (Roseman, 1984), and emotions are interpreted in view of the societal beliefs, and they also instigate them once they are evoked. Hence, emotions and beliefs are closely related and reinforce each other steadily. In the case of the societal beliefs of the culture of conflict, they are well related to negative emotions such as fear, hatred, and anger. They concern the particular worldview that the societal beliefs provide, and once they are established and maintained as lasting sentiments, they activate thoughts in line with the societal beliefs supporting continuation of the conflict to appraise various situations related to the conflict (Halperin, Sharvit, & Gross, 2011).

A typical example of a negative emotion that has in many cases an obstructing effect on the peacemaking process is chronic fear, which is an inherent part of the psychological repertoire of society members involved in an intractable conflict (Jarymowicz & Bar-Tal, 2006). In many cases, fear in this violent context may even lead to the development of angst that indicates perception of possible group extinction (Wohl & Branscombe, 2008a; Wohl, Branscombe, & Reysen, 2010). The prolonged experience of severe fear leads to observed cognitive effects that intensify freezing. It sensitizes the organism and the cognitive system to certain threatening cues. It prioritizes information about potential threats and causes extension of the associative networks of information about threat. It causes overestimation of danger and threat. It facilitates the selective retrieval of information related to fear. It increases expectations of threat and dangers, and it increases accessibility of procedural knowledge that was effective in coping with threatening situations in the past (Clore et al., 1994; Gray, 1989; Isen, 1990; Lazarus & Folkman, 1984; LeDoux, 1995, 1996; Öhman, 1993). It may also lead to repression and – as a consequence – to uncontrolled influence of unconscious affect on behavior (Czapinski, 1988; Jarymowicz, 1997).

Once fear is evoked, it limits the activation of other mechanisms of regulation and stalls consideration of various alternatives because of its egocentric and maladaptive patterns of reactions to situations that require creative and novel solutions for coping. The empirical evidence shows that fear has limiting effects on cognitive processing. It tends to cause adherence to known situations and avoidance of risky, uncertain, and novel ones; it tends to cause cognitive freezing, which reduces openness to new ideas and resistance to change (Clore et al., 1994; Isen, 1990; Jost, Glaser, Kruglanski, & Sulloway, 2003; LeDoux, 1995, 1996; Öhman, 1993).

On a societal level, the collective fear orientation tends to limit society members' perspective by binding the present to past experiences related to the conflict and by building expectations for the future exclusively on the basis of the past (Bar-Tal, 2001). This seriously hinders the disassociation from the past needed to allow creative thinking about new alternatives that may resolve the conflict peacefully. Being deeply entrenched in the psyche of society members, as well as in the culture, it inhibits the evolvement of the hope for peace by spontaneously and automatically flooding the consciousness. Society members then have difficulty freeing themselves from the domination of fear to construct hope for peace (Jarymowicz & Bar-Tal, 2006). This dominance of fear over hope is well documented in previously presented studies of negativity bias.

An example of the functioning of negative emotions is an experimental survey conducted among a representative nationwide sample of Jewish Israelis in the week before the Annapolis peace summit in which Halperin (2011) found that fear and hatred function as clear barriers to the peacemaking process. Fear was found to reduce the support for making territorial compromises that might lead to security problems. Hatred was found to be even a stronger major emotional barrier to peace. It is the only emotion that reduces support for symbolic compromise and reconciliation and even stands as an obstacle to every attempt to acquire positive knowledge about the Palestinians. In addition, hatred was found to lead to the support for halting negotiations and, when coupled with fear, induced support for military action (see also Bar-Tal, 2001; Baumeister & Butz, 2005; Lake & Rothchild, 1998; Petersen, 2002).

The magnified effect of negative emotions as well as of the negative information on a human being is a well-known phenomenon in psychology coined as *negativity bias* or *negative asymmetry* (see also Chapter 6). The bulk of psychological writings and empirical studies suggests that human beings are more sensitive to themes (beliefs and emotions) that activate the negative motivational system than those activating the positive motivational system (Cacioppo & Berntson, 1994; Cacioppo, Gardner, & Berntson, 1997, 1999; Jordan, 1965; Kanouse & Hanson, 1972; Lewick, Czapinski, & Peeters, 1992; Peeters, 1971; Peeters & Czapinski, 1990; Rozin & Royzman, 2001; Taylor, 1991). A negative motivational system operates automatically at the evaluative-categorization stage in which negative events tend to be more closely attended to and better remembered, thus eliciting more cognitive work. It is also structured to respond more intensely than the positive motivational system does to comparable levels of motivational activation (Cacioppo & Gardner, 1999).

In terms of judgment and decision making, there are solid indications that negative information strongly impacts evaluation, judgment, and action tendencies (see reviews by Cacioppo & Berntson, 1994; Christianson, 1992; Lau, 1982; Peeters & Czapinski, 1990; and studies by Ito, Larsen, Smith, & Cacioppo, 1998; Waganaar & Groeneweg, 1990). A similar bias has also been noted within the literature on persuasion: negative events and information tend to be more closely attended, better remembered, and more able to produce attitude change than positive events and information (Bar-Tal & Halperin, 2009; Brehm, 1956; Cacioppo & Berntson, 1994; Patchen, Hofman, & Davidson, 1976). Rozin and Royzman (2001) provide extensive evidence to the greater weight given to negative entities (events, information, etc.) in historical, religious, and cultural sources, as well as in psychological processes such as learning, attention, memory, and impression formation.

These ideas are also supported by the prospect theory (Kahneman & Tversky, 1979), according to which people are more reluctant to lose what they already have than they are motivated to gain what they do not have (Tversky & Kahneman, 1986). If we formulate this principle differently, it suggests that the value function is steeper on the loss side than on the gain side. Consequently, the negative bias has two implications: during evaluation of new opportunities, information about potential harm is weighted more heavily than positive information about peace opportunities (Baumeister, Bratslavsky, Finkenauer, & Vohs, 2001; Cacioppo, Gardner, & Berntson, 1997); and when making a decision under risky conditions, potential costs are more heavily weighted than potential gains (Kanouse & Hanson, 1971).

All these accumulated findings about negativity bias indicate that human beings are more attuned to negative information about violent conflicts than they are to positive information of peacemaking. The negative information strengthened by negative emotions has more weight; is more attended, remembered, and considered; and eventually influences the decision to continue the conflict. Required compromises to make peace imply losses, and possible peace looks as though it is distanced and unrealistic, while the possible positive gains in peacemaking look risky and uncertain.

Threatening Context

A fourth factor that leads to freezing is related to the chronic threats implied by the context of intractable conflicts. It is well established that threatening conditions lead to closure and limit information processing (Driskell & Salas, 1996; Staal, 2004). Indeed, numerous studies provide empirical evidence about the effect of the perception of threat and stress on cognitive functioning (see the extensive review of Staal, 2004). For example, the effect can be reflected in premature closure of decision alternatives, restricted consideration of the number and quality of alternatives, sole reliance on previously stored knowledge, more errors on cognitive tasks, persistence in the use of previous methods to solve problems even after they cease to be useful and helpful, and increased use of schematic or stereotyped judgments (Y. Bar-Tal, Raviv, & Spitzer, 1999; Hamilton, 1982; Janis, Defares, & Grossman, 1983; Keinan, 1987; Keinan, Friedland, & Arad, 1991; Keinan, Friedland, & Even-Haim, 2000; Pally, 1955; Staw, Sandelands, & Dutton, 1981; Svenson & Maule, 1993). Various explanations are offered for this detrimental effect of threat and stress. One proposal suggests that emotional arousal as a result of stress reduces the range of information that individuals use (Easterbrook, 1959). The most widely cited explanation in the literature is derived from capacity resource theory (CRT), which posits that stressor identification and appraisal, emotional and physiological reaction, and coping efforts all take up cognitive capacity (Hamilton, 1982; Mandler, 1993). Given that attentional resources are limited (Eysenck, 1982; Kahneman, 1973), their consumption by stress leaves less attention for task performance. To overcome the overload, people shift to the effortless and less resource-taxing approach of cognitive structuring, and this shift results in deficient performance. Recently, in contrast, Bar-Tal and his colleagues proposed that, rather than limited capacity effect, cognitive reaction to stress is explained by the motivational processes connected with coping processes (Bar-Tal, Raviv, & Spitzer, 1999; Bar-Tal, Shrira, & Keinan, in press). According to their cognitive motivational model, the effect of stress on cognition is mediated by the increased desire for certainty because of its essential role in achieving a sense of control, which is crucial for the coping processes. Achieving certainty, however, requires cognitive structuring. Cognitive structuring, in turn, is a function of the interaction between a person's epistemic needs and efficacy in meeting these needs (Y. Bar-Tal, 1994, 2010; Bar-Tal, Kishon-Rabin, & Tabak, 1997; Kossowska & Bar-Tal, in press). Thus, according to this explanation, the heuristic processing instances found very often under stress judgments can be viewed as manifestations of cognitive structuring aimed to achieve certainty.

In the context of conflict, studies found that perception of threat is causing closure of the societal beliefs of the conflict, which means support for continuation of the conflict, use of violence, and opposition to compromises (Arian, 1995; Gordon & Arian, 2001; Halperin, Bar-Tal, Nets, & Drori, 2008; Maoz & McCauley, 2008). Leaders know that creating a threat is the most profitable investment in getting support for continuation of the conflict. They therefore do not hesitate to use this powerful tool. Indeed, perceptions of threats also have a significant impact on the negative attitudes toward the rival outgroup. These tendencies reflect adaptive behavior because threats may require immediate functional reactions to the new situation (Fox, 1992; Gil-White, 2001). It is thus not surprising that perception of threats leads to aggression (Eibl-Eibesfeldt, 1979), increased intolerance and ethnocentrism (Bettencourt, Dorr, Charlton, & Hume, 2001; Halperin, Canetti-Nisim, & Hirsch-Hoefler, 2009), and enhanced ingroup solidarity and cohesion (Grant & Brown, 1995; Wohl, Branscombe, & Reysen, 2010). Thus, experience of threat elicits automatically, as part of the evolutionary reactions, lines of functional violent behaviors that are needed for group survival and, at the same time, lead to the continuation of the conflict. More direct evidence regarding the role of threat in preserving conflicts is presented by Maoz and McCauly (2008), who found that perceived threat by Israeli Jews in the context of the Israeli-Arab/Palestinian conflict led Israelis to higher support of retaliatory aggressive policies against the Palestinians, either transfer or coercive operations.

Another approach explaining the central role of threat and fear in the process of freezing and their role as socio-psychological barriers to peacemaking comes from the social psychological terror management theory (TMT) (Pyszczynski, Greenberg, & Solomon, 1997; Solomon, Greenberg, & Pyszczynski, 1991; see also Chapter 3). According to this theory, innate anxiety of annihilation, combined with the human knowledge of inevitable death, creates an ever-present potential for terror. A central defense mechanism in this situation is the validation and maintenance of cultural worldviews that instill meaning, order, permanence, stability, and the promise of literal and/or symbolic immortality to those who meet the prescriptions of the worldviews and adhere to the values of the culture. Indeed, meta-analysis of studies investigating the effect of morality salience found that people are motivated to affirm cultural meaning systems, including political ideologies, to avoid the awareness of mortality. The same analysis also found that mortality salience leads to a general shift toward conservatism, regardless of preexisting ideology (Burke, Kosloff, & Landau, in press).

In the case of intractable conflict, signals of threats increase the salience of mortality, which causes adherence to conflict-supporting societal beliefs (ethos of conflict and collective memory) that are hegemonic worldviews as part of the culture of conflict. In addition, collectives may turn to violent means in order to defeat or annihilate those who hold competing worldviews (Hirschberger & Pyszczynski, 2010). Thus, conditions of heightened mortality salience, such as intractable conflict, lead to a desire to bolster societal beliefs in the need to defend and select behaviors that uphold those beliefs, as well as to readiness to reject and even annihilate outsiders who are viewed as threatening the society.

In sum, threat and fear play a role in every intractable conflict because of its prevailing violence. Every intractable conflict involves killings, inquiries, and destruction not only of the military personnel but also of civilians. Also, many of the intractable conflicts involve terror attacks as well as state terror, which adds considerably to the chronic threat during the conflict. This perception of threat can be found, for example, on both rival sides in Kashmir, Northern Ireland, Sri Lanka, Rwanda, and elsewhere. Eventually perception of threats and resulting fears fuel continuation of the conflicts and inhibit their possible peaceful resolution. The view of the Chechens by the Russians in the context of their conflict provides a specific example to the effect of threat. Since the beginning of the fighting in the mid-1990s, Russians suffered casualties not only on the battlefields but also and most significantly at home as a result of terror attacks against the civilian population. Such terror incidents included, for example, the taking of hostages at Budennovsk (1995) and Kizlyar (1996), the "Black September" bombings in various cities (1999), the Nord-Ost theater siege (2002), and the "Black Widow" suicide bombings throughout 2003. These traumatic threatening events caused fear, alarmed the majority of Russians, and swung their public mood decisively against the Chechens. This was manifested, for example, by intensified feelings of insecurity, an intolerance of any opposition to sometimes quite drastic counterinsurgency measures, and an ambiguous attitude to both the norms of international law and the reaction of world public opinion. The Chechens have been dehumanized and perceived as terrorists, bandits, spooks, thieves, wild, dangerous, and mad (Russell, 2002, 2005). As a result, many Russians are resistant to resolve the conflict peacefully and instead favor military means.

Mistrust

Another important element that contributes to freezing and closure is mistrust (see Bar-Tal, Kahn, Raviv, & Halperin, 2010). Mistrust is an integral part of any intractable conflict, at least in its initial escalating phase. It can develop without eruption of violence, on the basis of the deteriorating relations during the outbreak of the conflict. It develops because the parties do not see any possibility to reach an agreement and embark on the path of serious violent confrontations (Webb & Worchel, 1986). In fact, violence continuously validates mistrust of the rival because of the intentional harm inflicted on the group.

Mistrust denotes lasting expectations about future behaviors of the rival group that affect the welfare of one's own group and does not allow risk taking in various lines of behaviors (Bar-Tal et al., 2010; Deutsch, 1958; Kydd, 2005). The expectations refer to the *intentional negative behaviors* of the rival group that have an effect on the welfare (well-being) of the ingroup, as well as to the *capability* that the rival group has to carry out these negative behaviors. Complete mistrust means that the ingroup has absolutely negative expectations and a lack of positive expectations about future behaviors of the rival regarding all behaviors that determine the welfare of the ingroup. Because these two lines of expectation are orthogonal, in cases of severe conflict the ingroup expects only harming acts and not any positive behaviors by the rival. Attribution of the rival's malintentions to stable disposition with high capability leads to very high levels of mistrust.

Mistrust has a number of consequences. Society members who mistrust the rival have negative feelings about him, live under continuous threat that the rival may cause harm, and therefore must exercise continuous readiness to absorb information about the potential harm (Kramer, 2004). In this respect, mistrust is functional in constructing a chronic preparedness for possible harm by the rival group. At the same time, mistrust forces carrying out negative, violent, defensive behaviors as retribution for the harm already done. But it also may lead to preemptive violent acts to deter the rival, with the intention of preventing harm. In fact, these lines of action can be seen as steps of building and reinforcing mistrust. It is mistrust that reduces the possibility of opening any meaningful channel of communication that can advance peaceful solution to the conflict. Without minimal trust, it is almost impossible to begin moves toward peacemaking.

Habituation

Another factor that increases freezing and thus leads to closure is habituation. It indicates adaptation to the conflict situation and difficulty in creating a new situation of peacemaking. Individuals as well as collectives learn through years of protracted conflict how to deal with the situations and conditions of violent confrontations and how to adapt to them. Eventually this learning leads to the perception that the conflict situation is understandable and meaningful. Peacemaking requires changes of well-established ways of coping and adaptation. By its nature peacemaking requires risk taking and moving into unpredictable and unfamiliar territory. Thus, with its changes, peacemaking arouses uncertainty, unpredictability, and ambiguity. Society members prefer to suffer with the known, familiar, certain, and predictable than to risk what might come with possible relief.

Mitzen (2006) proposes that the situation of conflict, which is full of threats, paradoxically leads to ontological security. That is, in times of intractable conflict, society members seek to satisfy the need to live in certainty and stability, as part of identity fulfillment. This need is achieved by the establishment of routines that are familiar, trusted, and well practiced. The established routines become embedded into the culture of conflict (see also Bar-Tal, Abutbul, & Raviv, in press). But this integration perpetuates and eternalizes the conflict because it prevents movement toward a different situation – a situation of peacemaking, which requires risk taking and uncertainty. This analysis suggests that society members involved in intractable conflict develop a mind-set that allows them to live relatively adaptively, knowing what is going on, what is accepted, and how to cope with the conditions. They have difficulty imagining a peaceful situation after living through years in a conflict, in which the patterns of thoughts and behavior became well established and continuously used, and thus they continue dogmatically to pursue the familiar line of societal conflict beliefs and behaviors, without examining the alternatives.

This analysis is illustrated in the conflict between the Greek Cypriots and the Turkish Cypriots. In the recent referendum, Greek Cypriots rejected the UN proposal to resolve the conflict. Various explanations can be given for this result, but one of them pertains to the habituation process. A majority of Greek Cypriots felt that the conflictive situation is more acceptable to them than the proposed new situation of peace. Being habituated to the conflict situation, refusing to accept the proposed compromises, led to continuation of the conflict (Michael, 2007; Yilmaz, 2005).

Investments

Another psychological reason that upholds freezing is tangible and psychological investments that individuals and groups participating in conflict have made in it. Once the investment is done, it is difficult to change the view and take an opposite direction that contradicts support for the continuation of the conflict. A salient example of investment is the losses that societies in intractable conflicts encounter. The sanctity of life is a universal value that is considered sacred in human culture. Therefore, killing is considered as the most serious violation of the moral code (Donagan, 1979; Kleinig, 1991). Societies engaged in intractable conflict frequently suffer heavy human losses of both soldiers and civilians. The death of an individual is perceived as the group's loss and increases the emotional involvement of the parties engaged in the conflict (Bar-Tal, 2003; Nets-Zehngut, 2009).

Human losses generate rituals, ceremonies, and monuments that are dedicated to preserving the collective memories. They glorify battles and wars, the heroism of the fallen, the malevolence of the enemy, and the necessity to continue the struggle in fulfillment of the patriotic "will" of the fallen. Thus, they inspire the remaining society members to continue the conflict and fight the enemy (Arviv-Abromovich, 2011). A vivid example of this feeling is found in the words of a young Israeli who explained his objection to withdrawal from the occupied territories by Israel in the 1967 war: "Now, I . . . I'm not in favor to give up territories for . . . for peace. It pains me because people fought, people died there for that territory, so why are you returning them? Do you know how much Jewish blood there is there?" (Fuxman, 2011). Furthermore, society's members feel obliged to avenge these losses in retribution for the inflicted violence (Silke, 2006; Turner-High, 1949) because they know that it is impossible to compensate society members and their loved ones for the loss of a life (Bar-Tal, 2003; Scheff, 1994).

In addition, society members who lost their dear ones often urge the society to adhere to its original goals and object to any peace move that results in compromise. This stand is motivated by the feeling that by compromising the goals, the sacrifice was in vain. In a similar line, a peace settlement now raises a feeling that, if made earlier, it may have been possible to avoid the sacrifice. They assume that early compromises could have saved lives, but because the society has decided to adhere to its original goals, which involved sacrificing compatriots in the conflict, there should be continuation of this adherence (see examples in Bar-Tal, 2007a). Particularly, supporting peace might cause a cognitive dissonance, because adhering to new goals is inconsistent with the sacrifice made in continuing the conflict. Playing a significant role in the society as members who lost their dear ones, they have a strong influence over the decision to continue the conflict and to reject reaching a compromise that could settle the conflict peacefully.

Empirical data from Israeli society show that those who were personally exposed to or suffered from terrorism expressed more radical positions toward Palestinians (Canetti-Nisim, Halperin, Sharvit, & Hobfoll, 2009). Specifically, for example, the Israeli Jewish hawkish NGO Almagor was founded by relatives of victims of Palestinian terror attacks. It conducts activities in opposition to the Palestinians, such as demonstrations, lobbying in the Israeli Parliament and abroad, and giving lectures, all about delegitimizing the Palestinians and trying to prevent peaceful conflict resolution (Almagor, 2011).

Similarly, relatives of Nationalist victims in the conflict in Northern Ireland demanded during the 1990s peace negotiations that the responsibility of the British army for the death of their beloved ones be investigated and that, in the case of illegal killings, the responsible soldiers be prosecuted. This demand was rejected by the British and presented an obstacle in the peace process (Lundy & McGovern, 2010).

Another type of investment that is on a collective level but also has direct influence on the psychology of the individual society members is the vast material investments (i.e., military, technological, and economic) that societies involved in intractable conflict make in order to cope successfully with the situation. These investments include mobilization of society members, training the military, development of military industries, acquisition of weapons, and development of supportive infrastructure in all spheres of collective life (see, e.g., Mintz, 1983). The investments eventually constitute obstacles to peacemaking because they provide particular lines of developments, rationale, organizational frameworks, trained personnel, budgets, resources, and systems that by their nature continue the course of conflict for which they were established (Koistinen, 1980). These tangible investments are always accompanied with a psychological investment that provides a rationale and a justification taken from the repertoire of societal beliefs of the culture of conflict. It is thus not surprising that society members who are the investors freeze their societal beliefs of the culture of conflict because they have a well-defined rationale for continuing the line of investments. Having a well-developed system of justifications, they do not see alternatives and often are threatened by the possibilities of changes that will imply peacemaking and thus cessation of the line of work they do.

Additionally, in every intractable conflict there are segments in the involved society that profit from the continuation of the conflict. Those are investors in the military-industrial complex, military personnel who gain status and prestige, and sectors that profit in the conflict territories or gain other resources. These sectors become the agents of conflict during its management and spoilers of the peace process when this possibility appears. The ethos of conflict serves for them as an ideology that provides a clear justification for their approach. It provides a meaningful and coherent view of the situation of conflict, one that negates any alternative ideas that may promote peacemaking.

For example, Jewish settlers who received land to build their houses from the Israeli government on settlements in the West Bank gained much from the conflict. Thus, a peaceful resolution of the conflict that would necessitate dismantling many of these settlements could lead to the loss of these gains. Many settlers thus are part of a well-orchestrated campaign to prevent peaceful resolution of the Israeli-Palestinian conflict (Hever, 2013; Zertal & Eldar, 2007).

Another example relates to the conflict in El Salvador between the military-led government of El Salvador and the Farabundo Martí National Liberation Front (FMLN). The Salvadorian army had significant gains from the continuation of the conflict. It acquired major power and status in the state's administration and elite as their protector from the revolutionaries. In addition, senior officers gained wealth from acts of extortion they conducted during the war and from payments received from the elite. Consequently, they had an interest in the continuation of the conflict (Deane, 1996; Huge, 1996).

Finally, leaders of intractable conflicts who make coherent and well-elaborated justifications for their continuation later have great difficulty changing their minds and persuading the same audience of the need for peacemaking. On the individual level, leaders who support continuation of the conflict have psychological difficulty in absorbing information indicating that they are wrong (Bar-Siman-Tov, 1996). On the social level, their previous political and ideological commitments, as well as their fears of political and electoral criticism, further enhance their tendency to avoid major changes in policy (Auerbach, 1980; Janis & Mann, 1977). In societies engulfed by intractable conflict, a change of view that modifies a leader's previous public commitments may lead to loss of public support and legitimacy, and even to the perception of the leader as a traitor (Bar-Siman-Tov, 1996; Kelman & Fisher, 2003). Thus, in many cases leaders stubbornly uphold the views of the public, often without offering an alternative outlook that may lead to change. They use the themes of the culture of conflict repeatedly, committing themselves to the conflict's continuation and, at the same time, contributing to the freezing of public opinion.

This practice leads to a circle of interactions between the leaders and their followers. On the one hand, a leader constructs and reconstructs the worldview that supports the continuation of the conflict, and then, on the other hand, maintenance of this worldview by society members limits the ability of the leaders to maneuver or engage in peacemaking efforts. Each side is reinforcing and investing in the conflict. The leaders often sense the needs of society members in times of conflict and satisfy them with the rhetoric and actions that eventually result in support for the continuation of the conflict. Society members, not seeing any alternative, insist that leaders continue the conflict according to the hegemonic culture of conflict. Thus, leaders may at certain points lose their freedom to make decisions and become captives to the views of the masses (see Mintz, 2004). They cannot allow themselves to be perceived as weak, or traitors, who change the course of action by compromising on the sacred goals with the delegitimized rival. Of interest are studies by Suedfeld and his colleagues that analyze the public speeches of leaders in two cases of intractable conflict – the Israeli-Arab conflict (Suedfeld, Tetlock, & Ramirez, 1977) and the Indian-Pakistani conflict (Suedfeld & Jhangiani, 2009). They found that, especially before military encounters in both conflicts, leaders exhibited low cognitive complexity. They considered fewer alternative strategies, made fewer attempts to take the perspective of the rival, and gathered less information in general. Thus, the leaders provided a narrower view, with more limited options, to the audience. As a specific example, W. P. Botha as the leader of South African white National Party was elected to keep the system of apartheid. He kept his promise by initiating various new steps to fight the African National Congress and by refusing to open negotiation with the rival side, as shown by his commitment to a harsh line in his 1985 "Crossing the Rubicon" speech, in which Botha was expected to announce new reforms. Pursuing these polices led to severe political and economic consequences for South Africa, including further isolation of the state and deterioration of the economic situation. Only de Clerk, the next leader of the National Party, initiated a dramatic shift in handling the conflict, which led to its termination

(Barber, 1999). Still, there are leaders who change their policies dramatically and move management of violent conflict to its termination. In France between 1958 and 1962, de Gaulle moved from support of French Algeria to a peace agreement with Algeria's National Liberation Front (FLN) (Horne, 2006).

Research and Summary

Freezing is the dominant cause for the societal beliefs of the culture of conflict to function as socio-psychological barriers. The barriers lead to the selective collection of information, as society members involved in intractable conflict tend to search for and absorb information that validates the societal beliefs of the repertoire, while ignoring and omitting contradictory information (Kelman, 2007; Kruglanski, 2004; Kruglanski & Webster, 1996; Kunda, 1990). But even when ambiguous or contradictory information is absorbed, it is encoded and cognitively processed in accordance with the held repertoire through bias, addition, and distortion. Experiments by Klar and Baram demonstrate that exposure to the narrative of the other side is an ego-depleting experience, meaning that it requires use of energy and mental resources, as it is a psychological burden. They also illustrate how rival groups process information about competing narratives. Their study with Jewish and Arab participants presents to each group one of two identical stories – about either a real Jewish or a Palestinian leader of a paramilitary group. Participants were asked to reconstruct the story 90 minutes later. The results showed that Jews and Arabs added positive details and omitted negative ones to the stories of their heroes, while adding negative details and omitting positive ones from the stories about the rival leaders (Klar, 2011; Klar & Baram, 2011). Other studies have found that cognitive processes are so biased in favor of the initial narratives that people realize that it is hard for them to change these narratives, even when these narratives are proved to be wrong (Ecker, Lewandowsky, & Tang, 2010; Lewandowsky, Stritzke, Oberauer, & Morales, 2009).

Because indoctrination of the repertoire occurs in the early years of childhood via societal institutions and channels of communications, one can assume that almost the entire young generation absorbs the contents of the societal beliefs of the culture of conflict. Indeed, a study by Ben Shabat (2010) finds that young Israeli children at the ages of 6–8 years old tend to hold societal beliefs of the ethos of conflict even when their parents support peacemaking. During childhood probably most of this generation holds the conflict-supporting beliefs as valid and truthful, if they are systematically presented in educational institutions. When the peace process begins and progresses, at least some of them acquire alternative beliefs that promote the peace process. But important empirical findings in Israel reveal that even when society members acquire alternative beliefs and attitudes that support peacemaking, the repertoire learned at an early age continues to be stored as implicit beliefs and attitudes and has automatic influence on information-processing functioning in times of stress (Sharvit, 2008).

Bar-Tal, Halperin, and Oren (2010) use ideas about the functioning of the socio-psychological barriers in an analysis of Jewish Israeli society in the stalemate of the negotiations between the State of Israel and the Palestinian Authority. The analysis shows that Jews in Israel continue to hold many of the societal beliefs of the culture of conflict, and these societal beliefs eventually are related to rejection of compromises that potentially could lead to peaceful settlement of the conflict with the Palestinians. Also, a study by Halperin and Bar-Tal (2011) demonstrates the functioning of the barriers. It shows in a nationwide representative sample of Israeli Jews that the ideological conflict-supporting beliefs lead to rejection of information that may shed light on the rival and that this closure in turn played a crucial role in the maintenance of noncompromising views of society members. Also, the results of the study show that that people with hawkish political orientation, those who tend to delegitimize Palestinians, and those who see Israel as the ultimate victim are less supportive of compromises.

Porat, Halperin, and Bar-Tal (2012) specifically investigated the effect of the ethos of conflict on information processing about the Israeli-Palestinian conflict. In the study, Israeli Jewish participants, after assessing their level of adherence to the ethos of conflict, were presented with a supposedly new peace proposal submitted by the Palestinians. They were asked to decide how they think the government of Israel should respond to this proposal. They were presented with a decision matrix that consisted of new information relevant to the decision that has to be taken and were told that they could acquire additional information that might help them in making their decision. Using Decision Board software (Mintz, Geva, Redd, & Carnes, 1997), we were able to trace the general processing tendencies of participants (i.e., the time spent on the search for new information, the amount of information processed) as well as the type of information processed (information in favor of or against the proposal). The results show clearly that the ethos of conflict had a determinative effect on the search for information and the final decision. Specifically, individuals with high levels of ethos spent less time in searching information, looked at fewer themes of new information, and considered less alternative information than individuals with low levels of the ethos of conflict did. This behavior led eventually to the rejection of the proposal by participants adhering to a high level of the ethos of conflict.

Socio-Psychological Barriers to Peaceful Conflict Resolution 305

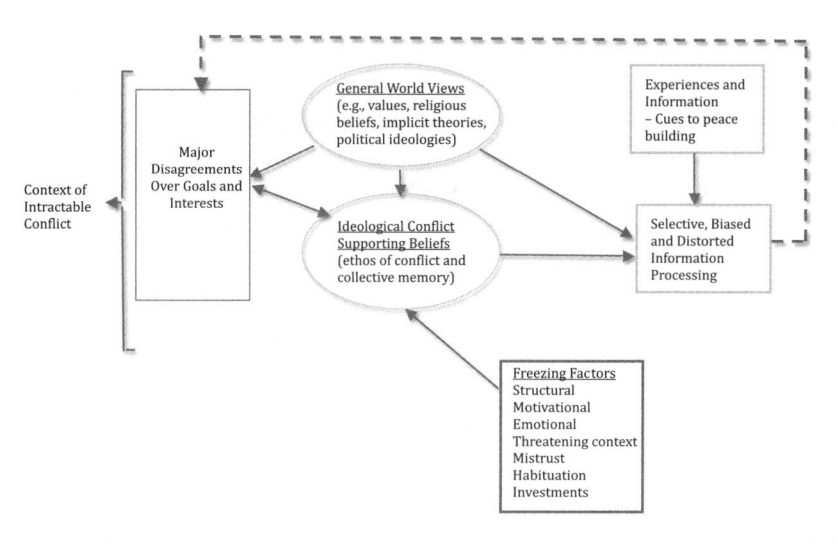

FIGURE 3. Individual Socio-Psychological Barriers to Peaceful Conflict Resolution

These findings are not surprising because societal beliefs of collective memory of conflict and of the ethos of conflict constitute ideological beliefs. Ideological beliefs are well entrenched and stable as a system of beliefs. They contribute to the automatic process that provides meaning and order to the absorbed information and experiences (Nosek, Graham, & Hawkins, 2010). They lead to particular behavioral practices in searching for information. Society members who hold them block alternative information and do not search for a new understanding of the conflict situation (Figure 3).

Society members involved in any intractable conflict differ with regard to the adherence to the socio-psychological repertoire supporting the conflict. It can be assumed that in a consensual society there is a minority, even if marginal, that holds alternative views. Klar and Baram developed a scale called Firmly Entrenched Narrative Closure (FENCE) that measures adherence to the group conflict narrative. In a study conducted in Israel, they found that individuals differ in the extent of their adherence to the Israeli narrative. They also found that antecedents of this adherence are cognitive closure, glorification of the ingroup, authoritarianism, and hawkish ideology. In addition, it was found that this adherence was related to various specific measures that limit exposure to rival narrative as well as to alternative knowledge (Klar, 2011; Klar & Baram, 2011).

In the next section I describe some of the more specific psychological consequences of freezing as a reflection of the functioning of the socio-psychological barriers.

CONSEQUENCES OF THE FREEZING

The repertoire of the culture of conflict with its narratives, which is shared by many segments of the society involved in intractable conflict, serves as a prism through which group members view the world in general and view specifically all the issues related to conflict. The prism influences how society members construe their reality, collect new information, interpret their experiences, and then make decisions about their course of action. This is selective, biased, and distorting information processing, which reflects functioning of the socio-psychological barriers. There is selection of information, biased interpretation of information, addition of one's own knowledge for evaluation, and distortion of available information – all in order to inhibit the exposure, consideration, and acquisition of the alternative new information that sheds light on the conflict and the participating parties. On the psychological level, the held repertoire affects the way incoming information is anticipated, selectively attended to, encoded, interpreted, recalled, and acted upon. A series of specific consequences of freezing occurs on the individual level.[3]

Automatic activation of conflict-supporting beliefs of the culture of conflict tends to occur when cues about the conflict become salient (see, e.g., studies by Bargh, Chen, & Burrows, 1996, and Devine, 1989, which demonstrate automatic activation in a nonconflict situation). Being often used and maintained by public discourse and societal channels of information, these beliefs are readily accessible in the minds of group members. As they become accessible, they paint the absorbed information in line with their content. Moreover, accessibility of one theme of these beliefs serves to activate other themes even without society members' awareness. In turn, the activated beliefs can then influence not only the specific information and stimuli one attends but also the ways in which this person interprets and reacts to subsequently encountered stimuli in a more general way (Bargh, 2007).

Selective attention affects society members who adhere to conflict-supporting beliefs because they are more sensitive to information that confirms these beliefs; in other words, they are selectively attentive in their information processing. They are actively searching for confirmatory information

---

[3] This analysis is based on the robust findings in social and political psychology that demonstrate the influence that stored important beliefs have (e.g., ideology or stereotypes) on human cognitive functioning (e.g., Cohen, 1981; De Dreu & Carnevale, 2003; Dovidio & Gaertner, 2010; Fiske & Taylor, 2007; Iyengar & Ottati, 1994; Lau & Sears, 1986; Markus & Zajonc, 1985; McGraw, 2003; Ottati & Wyer, 1993; Rothbart, Evans, & Fulero, 1979; Silverstein & Flamenbaum, 1989; Smith, 1998; Taber, 2003). In fact, relatively few studies involve a conflict situation. It is nevertheless assumed that society members in a conflict context function very similarly with their held societal beliefs, accompanied by emotions.

that provides validation to their views about the conflict and the rival group, identify it easily, and tend to absorb this information, being less open to alternative information (see, e.g., studies by Fiske, 1998; Macrae, Milne, & Bodenhausen, 1994; Stephan, 1989; Sweeney & Gruber, 1984; Vallone, Ross, & Lepper, 1985, which demonstrates this selectivity in nonconflict situation). Sharvit (2008) demonstrates that individuals spend a longer time viewing the ethos-contradicting information than the ethos-consistent information and that this difference is greater in the high-stress than in the low-stress conditions, supporting the hypothesis that activation of the ethos in response to stress would hinder the processing of ethos-contradictory information.

Memorization is another consequence according to which information that is consistent with conflict-supporting beliefs is more likely to be remembered, whereas inconsistent information is often neglected (see, e.g., Macrae, Milne, & Bodenhausen, 1994; reviews by Rojahn & Pettigrew, 1992, and Stangor & McMillan, 1992; and studies by De Dreu & Carnevale, 2003).

Search of information that confirms their conflict-supporting beliefs is actively conducted by society members who hold conflict-supporting beliefs (see, e.g., Schultz-Hardt, Frey, Luthgens, & Moscovici, 2000); in addition, they examine information that confirms these beliefs less critically (see, e.g., Ditto & Lopez, 1992; Edwards & Smith, 1996). Thus, society members tend to accept more easily information that is consistent with the societal beliefs supporting the conflict without making efforts to validate it.

Interpretation and organization of new information by society members tend to be based on a framework that uses their conflict-supporting beliefs. (see, e.g., Feldman, 1988; Kimhi, Canetti-Nisim, & Hirschberger, 2009; Pfeifer & Ogloff, 1991; Rosenberg & Wolfsfeld, 1977; Shamir & Shikaki, 2002; Sommers & Ellsworth, 2000). Group members use a theory-driven strategy to absorb new information about the conflict in line with the dominant societal beliefs of the culture of conflict. Specifically, society members tend to use their conflict-supporting beliefs in making attributions, evaluations, judgments, or decisions about the conflict (see, e.g., Bartels, 2002; Sibley, Liu, Duckitt, Khan, 2008; Skitka, Mullen, Griffin, Hutchinson, & Chamberlin, 2002). In situations of intractable conflict, information is absorbed in specific ways: group members not only encode it in line with the view of the conflict but also tend to make inferences that go far beyond the data. They make evaluations, interpretations, and attributions that, for example, shed negative light on the rival group, in line with their held view. This tendency reflects biased and distorting information processing in which group members change and add elements to construct images that are consistent with their societal beliefs and emotions. The influence of their held repertoire on information processing is especially pronounced in situations in which the information is ambiguous. But when the repertoire is well established and institutionalized, as is the case in intractable conflicts, biased and distorting information processing also occurs even when information is unequivocal.

A study testing the interpretation and organization framework performed in the context of the Cold War demonstrates how group members go beyond the information they have and add interpretations that are in line with their psychological intergroup repertoire. In a study by Burn and Oskamp (1989), American students were asked to stereotype Soviet and American citizens and their governments. In addition, they were asked to explain four comparable acts by the Soviet Union or the United States in the international arena (e.g., the Soviet invasion of Afghanistan and American invasion of Grenada, the Soviet presences in Poland and American support of Nicaraguan contras). They were supplied with four different reasons, which varied in terms of how favorable they were. The results first showed that the Soviets were evaluated negatively in absolute terms. Then, they showed that all four Soviet actions were evaluated negatively, whereas the actions of the United States, with one exception, were evaluated positively.

A similar study by Bar-Tal, Raviv, Raviv, and Degani-Hirsch (2009) described in Chapter 5 clearly demonstrated how adherence to the ethos of conflict influences interpretation and organization of the new information. In this study, Israeli Jewish participants were shown four photos that depicted different Israeli-Palestinian encounters and were asked to evaluate the extent of aggressiveness of each side and then make attributions about the causes of the aggression. The results indicate that participants who hold a high level of societal belief of the ethos of conflict perceived Israeli Jews to be less aggressive and Palestinians to be more aggressive than participants who hold a low level of societal belief of the ethos of conflict. Also, participants with a higher ethos of conflict attributed in general more negative qualities to Palestinians and more positive qualities to Jews than participants with a lower ethos of conflict. Finally, more participants with a high level of ethos of conflict than participants with a low level of ethos of conflict attributed external causes to the Israeli Jews' aggression, internal causes to the Palestinians' aggression, unstable-circumstantial causes to the Israeli Jews' aggression, uncontrollable causes to the Israeli Jews' aggression, and controllable causes to the Palestinians' aggression.

Expectations are based on the conflict-supporting beliefs of society members, who tend to expect particular events, behaviors of the rival and other groups, and experiences – all associated with the conflict (see, e.g., Darley & Gross, 1983; Hamilton, Sherman, & Ruvolo, 1990). Such expectations may cause the self-fulfilling-prophecy phenomenon. In expecting negative intentions and behavior, society members themselves behave toward the rival group in a negative way (Kelman, 1997). This behavior instigates hostile reactions by the rival. In turn, the hostile behavior of the rival confirms the initial expectations. In effect, this circle of mutual expectations and behaviors leads to a vicious hostile cycle and validates the societal beliefs of the culture of conflict (see the analysis of Hamilton et al., 1990, and Jussim & Fleming, 1996).

Behavioral guidance indicates that society members tend to be guided by the conflict-supporting beliefs in their behavior (Jost, 2006). This guidance means that societal beliefs of the culture of conflict play a determinative role in the decision about courses of action taken by the society on an individual and collective level. Being ideological, they provide the direction for action. This particular premise serves as a basis of numerous case studies that present how leaders determine policies and implement them in line with their ideological beliefs, which supported continuation of the conflict even when their decisions were detrimental to their groups (see, e.g., Barber, 1999, in the case of the policies of the National Party in the South African conflict; Horne, 2006, in the case of French policies in the war in Algeria; and Maoz, 2009, in the case of the Israeli policies regarding the Israeli-Arab conflict).

In addition to these consequences of freezing, various specific phenomena elucidated by social and political psychologists take place in conflict situations and illustrate the selective, biased, and distortive information processing (see also Fisher & Kelman, 2011).

False polarization indicates that groups in conflict tend to exaggerate their disagreements, especially on key issues (Chambers, Baron, & Inman, 2006; Keltner & Robinson, 1993; Thompson & Nadler, 2000). This notable example of cognitive bias is based on a held psychological repertoire about the ingroup, the outgroup, and the nature of the relations between them. It gives expression to exaggerated disparity in the basic goals, values, beliefs, and positions, and therefore it increases the perception of the level of disagreement, with serious implications. With this perception, societies in conflict and their leaders may not begin negotiations because they assume a disparity that cannot be easily closed. Rouhana and his colleagues (Rouhana, O'Dwyer, Morrison, & Vaso, 1997) found in a study conducted among Jews and Arabs in the Middle-East that this tendency is much more common among supporters of less conciliatory political parties (i.e., hawks) than among supporters of more conciliatory political parties (i.e., doves).

Bias perception is part of a larger set of biases Ross and Ward (1995, 1996) originally defined as "naïve realism" and reflects a tendency for people to assume that their perceptions and judgments are more objective and attuned to reality than the differing perceptions and judgments of their peers. This tendency may be amplified in conflict situations in which people tend to perceive their opponents as being biased, and this perception causes them to act in a violent way, which escalates the confrontations (Pronin, Gilovich, & Ross, 2004). Three studies by Kennedy and Pronin (2008) demonstrate that people perceive those who disagree with them as biased, use conflict-escalating approaches, and eventually act toward them in a conflictive way.

Double standard indicates that a judgment or an evaluation of similar acts by the ingroup and by the rival is done with two different standards favoring the ingroup. This bias is well demonstrated in the study by Sande et al. (1989) done during the Cold War in 1985, in which American high school and college students gave opposing explanations of similar acts performed by either the Soviet Union or the United States (a positive act of smashing ice fields to allow whales to reach an open sea and a negative act of building a new fleet of nuclear-powered submarines). The results indicate that the positive act was evaluated as more typical of Americans than of Soviets and different attributions were put forward. While the actions of the United States were attributed to the positive moral characteristics of the Americans, the same acts of the Soviet Union were attributed to the self-serving and negative motives of the Russians in line with their enemy image (e.g., Ashmore, Bird, Del-Boca, & Vanderet, 1979; Burn & Oskamp, 1989; Oskamp, 1965; Oskamp & Levenson, 1968).

Moral amplification refers to "the motivated separation and exaggeration of good and evil in the explanation of behavior" (Haidt & Algoe, 2004, p. 323). This cognitive motivation implies that members of societies involved in violent conflicts tend to view their conflict as a confrontation between good and evil (White, 2004). They maximize the differences between them and the rival group and polarize the entire view of the conflict as a battle of benevolence against malevolence in which their group is the guardian of the goodness and righteousness and the rival represents wickedness and malice.

Correspondence bias is found in cases in which the negative behavior of the rival group is attributed to personal characteristics, while situational factors are disregarded. This bias reflects the tendency of perceivers to draw correspondent depositional inferences from other people's behaviors even when the observed behavior is highly constrained by situational factors (Gawronksi, 2004). This tendency is even more profound because the attribution to the personal characteristics is often made to innate dispositions (Dweck, 1999). This attribution implies that the rival group will not change but will remain evil. This perception precludes making peace with the rival because nobody negotiates with a collective that is evil (Dweck & Ehrlinger, 2006). A study by Hunter, Stringer, and Watson (1991) demonstrates this misperception. The researchers approached Catholic and Protestant students in Northern Ireland, presented them newsreel footage showing scenes of violence performed by Protestants and Catholics, and asked them to explain why the involved people behaved in the depicted way. The results showed clearly that the violence of the ingroup was attributed to external causes such as "retaliation" or "fear of being attacked," whereas the violence of the outgroup was attributed to internal dispositions such as being a "psychopath" or having "blood lust." A study by Bar-Tal, Raviv, Raviv, and Dgani-Hirsch (2009) noted earlier found that the attribution of violence to innate dispositions of Arabs is much more prevalent among Jews who adhere the societal belief of the ethos of conflict than among those who do not (see also Taylor & Jaggi, 1974).

Homogenizing the rival is another misperception that leads to intensification of the conflict. It indicates viewing the rival group as being a homogeneous collective entity with uniform goals, values, beliefs, or needs – all united with the intention of carrying on the conflict and harming the ingroup (see Linville, Fischer, & Salavoy, 1989; Quattrone & Jones, 1980). In reality, in many of the cases, groups have at least some disagreements and sometimes even have major differences regarding the how to manage and resolve the conflict. Also, the societies participating in intractable conflict are by their nature heterogeneous with subgroups that differ with regard to many characteristics. The misperceived homogenization not only justifies generalized harm of the rival but also inhibits peacemaking because rival subgroups that potentially can be partners are not detected.

Biased assimilation plays an important role in the conflict situation as it leads society members to evaluate beliefs-consistent information more positively than beliefs-inconsistent information (Greitemeyer, Fischer, Frey, & Schulz-Hardt, 2009). This bias reinforces adherence to societal beliefs feeding the conflict and prevents their replacement with new beliefs that support peacemaking.

Self-focus is another bias in information processing, which emphasizes one's own needs and goals and disregards empathetic information about the rival. Society members focus on the goals of the conflict and conditions that are functional to their achievement as well as to the survival of the group. They view themselves as victims of the conflict who are unjustly and intentionally harmed. Mack (1990) observes that a society engulfed by the deep sense of being a victim narrows its perspective to its own needs and goals, focuses on its own fate, and is completely preoccupied with its own suffering, developing what he called an "egoism of victimhood." A collective in this state is unable to see things from the rival group's perspective, empathize with its suffering, and accept responsibility for harm inflicted by its own group (Čehajić & Brown, 2008; Chaitin & Steinberg, 2008; Staub, 2006).

Moral entitlement, defined as a conviction that the society is allowed to use whatever means necessary to ensure its safety, with little regard to moral norms, is another consequence of the way society members involved in intractable conflict process information. This perspective develops in view of the conflict-supporting repertoire that focuses on the justness of conflict goals, collective victimhood, and delegitimization of the rival. It is the combination of these core societal beliefs that indicates to society members that they have just goals, they are the victims, and the opponent is evil and not only is trying to prevent the achievement of just goals but also commits immoral acts of violence. It is thus not surprising that this framing frees the society from the limitations of moral considerations that usually limit its scope of action. It allows some freedom of action because the society believes that it needs to defend itself to prevent immoral and destructive behavior of the rival. Survival is the overriding consideration.

An example of moral entitlement is the memorandum of the Serbian Academy of Sciences and Arts, which in 1986 argued that "Serbia must not be passive and wait and see what the others will say, as it has done so often in the past." Similarly, in 1973 Israel's prime minister Golda Meir responded to international criticism by making a statement to "those who are trying to preach to us now.... You didn't come to the help of millions of Jews in the Holocaust... you don't have the right to preach" (*Haaretz*, April 29, 1973). Recently, Israel justified the harm inflicted on the Palestinians in Gaza by referring to the continuous bombardment with Palestinian rockets. A society may thus use the sense of being the victim in a conflict as a reason for rejecting pressures from the international community and to justify taking unrestrained courses of action. According to Schori-Eyal, Klar, and Roccas (2011), the sense of self-perceived collective victimhood is positively associated with the feeling of moral entitlement and negatively associated with group-based guilt over Israel's actions in the occupied territories. It is also related to a willingness to continue military operations and other actions punishing the enemy group.

Moral disengagement frees society members from feelings of guilt and other thoughts and emotions that are usually felt when a group acts immorally. Bandura (1990, 1999) called this reaction moral disengagement because harm and violence against the rival do not activate empathetic reactions that usually make it difficult to mistreat a group without risking personal distress. As with moral entitlement, the core societal beliefs of the conflict-supporting repertoire – justness of one's own goals, perception of self-collective victimhood, and delegitimization of the rival – serve as a buffer against group-based negative thoughts and feelings. In other words, feelings of guilt and shame, moral considerations, or a positive collective self-view as human safeguards of humane conduct fails to operate (see Castano, 2008; Wohl & Branscombe, 2008).

Studies show that delegitimization of a target is related to moral disengagement and increases aggressive behavior (e.g., Bandura, Caprara, Barbaranelli, Pastorelli, & Regalia, 2001; Bandura, Underwood, & Fromson, 1975). Castano and Giner-Sorolla (2006) report that individuals tend to delegitimize even group members who are considered victims as a method to morally disengage and relieve the distress of cognitive confrontation with immoral acts performed by one's own group. Bernard, Ottenberg, and Redl (2003, p. 64) propose that dehumanization should also be seen as a defense mechanism against overwhelming emotions that lead to bad feelings and thus allow maltreatment and even destruction of other groups; then negative and even evil behaviors "may be carried out or acquiesced in with relative freedom for restraints of conscience or feeling of brotherhood." Grossman (1995) notes that delegitimization is one of the psychological mechanisms that allows soldiers to kill soldiers of the rival group. It is delegitimization of the rival that provides a moral permit to kill them because they are reduced to social categories that can be exterminated (Bar-Tal & Hammack, 2012). Similarly, the sense of victimhood also allows moral disengagement to protect the group members' self-esteem and prevent feelings of guilt for committing harmful acts against the other group, acts that take place regularly in intractable conflict (Bar-Tal, Chernyak-Hai, Schori, & Gundar, 2009; Branscombe, 2004; Branscombe, Schmitt, & Schiffhauer, 2007; Branscombe, Ellemers, Spears, & Doosje, 1999). When the ingroup's victimization is made salient, individuals reported less group-based guilt in response to violence perpetrated by their ingroup against the rival.

Čehajić and Brown (2008) argue that through moral disengagement the perception of victimhood serves the function of justifying ingroup negative behavior after it has occurred and as such undermines one's readiness to acknowledge ingroup responsibility for committed misdeeds. Serbian adolescents who believe that their group is the victim (in the 1991–1995 war) and has suffered more than members of the other groups are less willing to acknowledge their group's responsibility for atrocities committed against others. Also, another study conducted in connection with the Israeli-Palestinian conflict indicates a strong association between a sense of victimhood among Israeli Jewish respondents and reduced group-based guilt over Israel's actions against the Palestinians (Schori-Eyal, Klar, & Roccas, 2011). Those who had a high sense of victimhood expressed less guilt, less moral accountability, and less willingness to compensate Palestinians for harmful acts by Israel. They also used more exonerating cognitions, or justifications, such as "Under the circumstances, any other state would treat the Palestinians in the same way" and "I believe the Palestinians brought their current situations upon themselves." Finally, a work of Greenbaum and Elizur (2013) about psychological effects of occupation on the Israeli society reviews studies that show a clear moral disengagement phenomenon. That is, soldiers in the Israeli army who were able to disconnect themselves from moral considerations were the ones who did not experience guilt and therefore were able to carry out immoral acts against the Palestinian civilian population.

Perception of ingroup uniqueness is another consequence of focus on the dominant societal beliefs of the culture of conflict. Society members in intractable conflict tend to believe that their conflict is unique: society members believe that people who are not ingroup members cannot understand the particular conflict context of the ingroup; and it is impossible to learn anything about their own conflict from other conflicts. This view leads them to focus on their own fate and causes them to limit their view of the context. This uniqueness prevents society members from learning about other conflicts, their negative outcomes, and destructive processes, as well as ways to advance peacemaking. Merom (1998) analyzes this perception by Israeli Jews and noted its negative consequences.

Reactive devaluation is another consequence of the way society members involved in conflict process information. Reactive devaluation suggests that a specific package deal or compromise offer is evaluated in accordance to what side proposed it. When the offer is proposed by one's own side, it is accepted, but when the same offer is proposed by the rival, it is rejected (Maoz, 2006; Ross, 1995). Maoz, Ward, Katz, and Ross (2002) shows that Israeli Jews evaluated an actual Israeli-authored peace plan less favorably when it was presented as being a Palestinian plan. They also showed that the evaluation of the proposal was much more negative among extremist Jews and Arabs (hawks) than among doves from the same sides, implying interaction between enduring political positions and the process of reactive devaluation.

Two additional relevant cognitive biases are *optimistic overconfidence* (Kahneman & Tversky, 1995), which means that parties involved in conflicts tend to overestimate the chances of prevailing in the absence of a negotiated settlement; and *loss aversion* (Kahneman & Tversky, 1984), whereby parties tend to reject resolution proposals because they attach greater weight to prospective losses than to prospective gains.

At present, there is a relative lack of systematic empirical research that examines comprehensively various societal beliefs of the repertoire of conflict, their rigidity, and their functioning in real-life contexts. But there are numerous references to beliefs and emotions, as well as to deficient information processing, that fuel continuation of the conflict and prevent its peaceful resolution (see, e.g., Chirot & Seligman, 2001; Frank, 1967; Heradstveit, 1981; Kriesberg, 2007; Lake & Rothchild, 1998; Petersen, 2002; Sandole, 1999; Vertzberger, 1991; Volkan, 1997; White, 1970, 1984). For example, Jervis (1976) provides numerous case studies that demonstrate the selective, biased, and distortive information in the realm of international relations, including many conflict situations.

In sum, this description of the psychological functioning of the socio-psychological barriers suggests that the handling of the information by society members involved in intractable conflict is characterized by top-down processing. This process is affected more by information that fits the contents of the conflict-supporting beliefs and less by information that contradicts these beliefs. That is to say, in harsh conflicts socio-psychological barriers that tend to "close minds" and facilitate tunnel vision evolve, precluding the contemplation of incongruent information and alternative approaches to the conflict. They often prevent even an entertainment of ideas that may initiate a peacemaking process.

To conclude this discussion, I present some additional socio-psychological processes of closure – the phenomena of conformity, obedience, and self-censorship.

SOCIO-PSYCHOLOGICAL PROCESSES OF CLOSURE

Conformity

Conformity may be defined in various ways, but for the present case I am interested in the public expression of opinion that is not in line with privately held views (Cialdini & Trost, 1998). In other words, society members prefer to express in public views that are in line with the opinions of the majority and do not express their own opinion if it is different. In the context of intractable conflict, conformity takes place when society members who hold views that contradict the dominant societal beliefs of the culture of conflict express publicly the views of the majority (Mitchell, 1981), In these cases, voices providing alternative views are not heard. Thus, the conformists contribute to the continuing dominance of the societal beliefs that support the conflict.

Social psychologists explain that this kind of conformity exists to avoid negative sanctions that the society may use to punish the deviants (Deutsch & Gerard, 1955). In this way the person gets the positive sanction of approval. In addition, social psychologists propose that society members may accept the view of the majority and even internalize it (Allen, 1965; Kelman, 1961). This type of conformity indicates in essence a process of persuasion or socialization. It happens when individuals accept the view of the majority to construct their own reality. This conformity reflects the considerable influence that society has on adoption of views, through either compliance, internalization, or identification process (Kelman, 1958).

Obedience

Obedience, which refers to blind execution of orders without any consideration of their meaning or implication, was demonstrated in seminal studies by Stanley Milgram (1974, p. 1). It "is the psychological mechanism that links individual behavior to political purpose. It is the dispositional cement that blinds men to systems of authority. Facts of recent history and observation in daily life suggest that for many people obedience may be a deeply ingrained behavior tendency, indeed, a proponent impulse overriding training in ethics, sympathy and moral conduct." Obedience leads often to severe consequences, especially in the cases of intractable conflicts as involved society members may carry out acts of violence, including severe violations of moral codes and human rights, by blindly following given orders (Benjamin & Simpson, 2009). Soldiers, fighters, and sometimes even civilians, without contemplating the moral meaning of the order or even its legality, carry out orders to kill (even murder), destroy, and humiliate. This is one of the plagues of human beings, and its imprinting effects can be found in most of the atrocities, massacres, ethnic cleanings, and genocides. Intractable conflicts, being violent, provide numerous opportunities for human beings to exhibit this human characteristic with all its inhumane implications. They follow obediently the orders in line with the delegitimizing beliefs without considering their moral implications. This socio-psychological mechanism is carried out especially by active fighters in the conflict, whose role is to fight and withstand the enemy, but it is also practiced by the society members who fulfill different roles in a well-developed system that is responsible for maintaining the conflict.

Self-Censorship

Self-censorship is another socio-psychological phenomenon that contributes to freezing and closure. Self-censorship is defined as an act of voluntarily and intentionally withholding information from others on the basis of a belief that it may have negative implications for an individual or a collective. It encompasses cases in which there is no formal censorship but in which the withholding information depends on individual decision without violation of a formal rule or law. In cases of intractable conflicts, self-censorship takes place when society members, as individuals, intentionally withhold information that they think may shed negative light on the ingroup or challenge its dominant narratives. In fact, this phenomenon should be seen as one of the socio-psychological barriers that prevent information from society members.

Two types of individuals may practice self-censorship: gatekeepers and ordinary individuals. Gatekeepers serve the role of disseminating information, and often work in institutions that provide and transmit information (e.g., in mass media and in governmental and educational institutions). Ordinary individuals who do not fulfill such roles may also be in possession of information. Both may decide not to reveal information they possess. Also, there are at least three ways to receive information that may impinge negatively on the ingroup and therefore may be self-censored. A person may get it firsthand through an experience (e.g., participating in the event and observing what happened); a person may find information through reading (e.g., finding a document); or a person may get the information from another person. In the case of intractable conflict, the possessed information may harm the positive image or the goals of the ingroup or may provide an alternative view to the conflict. In general, this information can negate the dominant beliefs. Thus, the dominant motivation to practice self-censorship is the wish not to harm society's cause. Also, a person may try to avoid negative sanctions that may be applied against him or her if the information was exposed. This socio-psychological mechanism is practiced by society members involved in intractable conflict, especially among those who participated in, observed, or heard about immoral acts done by their own groups.

Nets–Zehngut, Pliskin, and Bar-Tal (2012) conducted a study to show how gatekeepers in the Israeli state institutions carried out self-censorship by preventing dissemination of information that sheds negative light on Israel. Specifically, these gatekeepers in the governmental Publications Agency of the National Information Center, the Information Branch in the Israeli army Education Corps and the Ministry of Education self-censored information about the causes of the Palestinian exodus in the 1948 war in which approximately 700,000 Palestinians left the area in which the State of Israel was established. In spite of the fact that even Israeli historians provided unequivocal evidence about partial expulsion of Palestinians in 1948, the gatekeepers, confessing to self-censorship, continued to publish the Israeli Jewish Zionist narrative that takes no responsibility for the exodus but attributes it solely to Arabs and Palestinians. Ben-Ze'ev (2010, 2011) interviewed Jewish soldiers who participated in the 1948 war and claims that many of them practiced self-censorship in order to block information about immoral acts during this war that may shed a negative light on Jews.

IMPLICATIONS

On a macrosocietal level, when the culture of conflict evolves to be hegemonic, then its societal beliefs are held centrally by society members and shared by them. These beliefs are then chronically accessible, which allows functional structure and organization of reality. The result of these tendencies is freezing, closure, resistance to new ideas, and fixation on the societal beliefs of the culture of conflict. Eventually the societal beliefs of the culture of conflict become lenses though which society members view the reality of the conflict.

On a general psychological level, this processing leads to selective collection of information, as group members tend to search for and absorb information that is in line with the repertoire and omit contradictory information, which is viewed as invalid. But even when ambiguous or contradictory information is absorbed, it is encoded and cognitively processed in accordance with the held repertoire through bias, addition, and distortion. Bias leads to a focus on the consistent part of the absorbed information that disregards the inconsistent part, or to interpretation of ambiguous information in line with the held repertoire. Addition occurs when society members go beyond the acquired information and supplement it to be consistent with the repertoire. Distortion indicates a change of the absorbed information, even when it is unambiguous, to adapt it to the contents of the held repertoire. It is thus not surprising that information processing can lead to such phenomena as double standards, reactive evaluation, perception of self-uniqueness, self-focus, false consensus, and disregard of empathy for the rival. The information processing construes the conflict situation in black-and-white terms as threatening, dangerous, explosive, and menacing. The rival group is perceived in delegitimizing terms. In general, this view of reality results in complete self-focus, self-positive image, and concentration on one's own needs in coping successfully with the conflict situation. The dominant view of reality disregards any sensitivity, consideration, or empathy to the needs of the rival. Even meeting the rival's basic needs is considered as opposing the supreme goal of containing the enemy.

Thus, it is not surprising that the hegemonic culture of conflict feeds the continuation of the conflict and at the same time is its consequence. A vicious cycle is formed. This is the socio-psychological essence of the intractable conflicts, as both sides evolve opposing socio-psychological infrastructures – opposing worldviews, opposing narratives – which consist of collective memories and societal beliefs, so that both sides view the same events very differently. They also view each other negatively in a mirror image. These views underlie the decision to carry out more violence, which in turn serves as evidence to the other group for the validity of its view, and thus the experiences strengthen the view of the conflict.

This view of the conflict is held not only by individual society members but also by societies, which make an effort to maintain it as a repertoire of society members. To achieve this goal they often employ various societal mechanisms to assure that the hegemonic narrative will remain, to impart it to the new generations, and to repeatedly use it in various societal socialization practices such as ceremonies and speeches. In such a climate, society members themselves not only spread the message of the conflict but also, being aware of the consequences of bringing alternative ideas, exercise psychological methods to avoid doing so.

From a more microlevel perspective, one can look on the elaborated barriers as characterizing different society members. That is, the list of different obstacles to peacemaking elucidated here is not intended to suggest that all of them function in one individual. The list outlines salient obstacles, and we can infer that they operate differently in different society members. Thus, for example, while some can be greatly affected by the dogmatic adherence to the ethos of conflict and especially by the societal beliefs of collective victimhood, others may be affected by perceptions of threat, which causes fear and insecurity, and still others may be motivated by profiting in various ways from the continuation of the conflict. Clearly, those socio-psychological obstacles are not mutually exclusive, and some society members may be blocked in their freezing by a number of them. This conception suggests that society members have different underlying foundations to their rigid and dogmatic view of the conflict and to their objection to its peaceful settlement. Some can be guided more by an ideological motivational vector, others by an emotional vector, still others by a utilitarian one. Thus, although these society members who object to peaceful resolution of the conflict are united in their view, their needs and motivations to this position are different. This observation has important implications for attempts to change the view of society members in order to persuade them to support a peacemaking process.

The questions thus that can always be raised are to what extent the repertoire supporting the conflict is hegemonic and held by a great majority of society members. What is its psychological basis? How strongly do they adhere to it? What layers of a society support it firmly? What are the alternative views in a society? How prevalent are alternative views? Who is holding them, and how much influence do they have? What factors that facilitate development of alternative views about the conflict support its peaceful resolution with the necessary compromises? These questions come to examine the extent, intensity, and dominance of views that feed the continuation of the conflict.

I realize that this macroanalysis is a pessimistic view of intractable conflicts. But it is necessary to realize that these conflicts last many decades, at least partially because of the described socio-psychological dynamics, which over many years play an important role in their continuation. Obviously, they do not characterize all society members in all the intractable conflicts. Conflicts differ with the dominance of these processes. But when we take into account the durability of these conflicts at their peaks, these dynamics are dominant and characterize the leaders involved. Nevertheless, some societies develop openness and also examine their conflict-supporting beliefs, and some may even move toward peaceful resolution of the intractable conflict. The crucial question, then, is how to break the cycles of violence of intractable conflict and launch a peacemaking process that will bring about a compromising settlement that satisfies the basic, justified needs of both rival societies. The next chapter begins to tell the story of peace building, which is most often a long and complex process.

PART IV

DEESCALATION AND PEACE BUILDING

9

Breaking the Cycles of Intractable Conflicts

Eight chapters were devoted to the description of evolvement of intractable conflicts, their escalation, and their maintenance. This chapter begins to consider the key question of when and how these conflicts end peacefully. The process of resolving intractable conflicts is not only something to be imagined, as intractable conflicts have been resolved peacefully; rival sides may even move into a reconciliation phase. The conflicts between Israel and Egypt, the Algerian conflict, and the conflicts in South Africa, El Salvador, and Guatemala are examples of intractable conflicts that were resolved peacefully. We will now look at these issues regarding peace building in intractable conflicts from a macrolevel perspective, analyzing the socio-psychological processes that take place in those societies that embark on the road of peace.

MAJOR CONCEPTS

Embarking on the road of peace building often begins when at least some society members begin to think that the conflict should be resolved peacefully and also take actions to realize this idea. Once such an idea emerges and is propagated by society members, a process of moving the society to resolve the conflict begins. There are various ways to illuminate this long process (see Galtung, 1975; Rouhana, 2004a). The societal change is needed to build a new repertoire that allows reaching an agreement with the past rival and then may also continue in constructing a new ethos that serves as a foundation in the emerging culture of peace. This process involves all society members, from the grass roots to leaders, and its success depends on a change of their conflict-supporting repertoire. Society members have to change their basic premises, assumptions, and aspirations – in fact, to change their worldview, the ideology that dominated the life of society members for many years. More specifically, they have to change their fundamental views about the conflict, the goals, the rival, the relationship with the rival, their own group, their past – just to name the major elements. This process is gradual and complex because societal change is not a simple matter, as ideologies, cultures, and identity-related beliefs are well entrenched in the society, and powerful forces guard them. This process is not necessarily linear but may have fluctuations that sometimes lead to reescalation of the conflict and then again to its deescalation. The process is a major societal change that may begin, but not necessarily end, with the new peace-supporting repertoire or with the act of peaceful conflict settlement. It does not have a particular, necessary ending, as it may stop at certain points for a long time without progressing to the next phase.

Reaching a peaceful settlement of the conflict does not indicate the end of the process of peace building. Even without peaceful settlement of the conflict, rivals may learn to coexist with each other, negotiate limited agreements, and stop carrying out violent attacks. Nevertheless, only a peaceful settlement provides the formal and legal act of ending the conflict. Negotiations to settle the conflict peacefully may last for many years, and when the goal is achieved, it still lacks the cement that transfers the relations between the past rivals into completely new lasting, cooperative, and peaceful relations. It is obvious that lasting and stable peace requires very often a long process of reconciliation and always an evolvement of the culture of peace. The lasting and stable peace not only changes the nature of relations between two rivals but also transforms the nature of the societies that lived under the shadow of intractable conflict, sometimes through many generations. A new context of peace has influence on many different aspects of life in different domains and may lead to many other meaningful developments, including a change of relations and power structures between different segments of the society.

Thus, to describe this long process, several concepts can be offered to introduce some order into this wide domain. The *peace-building process* is defined as continuous efforts exerted by society members, society's institutions, agents, channels of communications, and the international community to realize lasting peaceful relations with the past rival within the framework of the culture of peace. Peace building thus includes all the acts that are done to facilitate the achievement of this goal (see also de Rivera, 2009; Lederach, 1997). It includes acts of peacemaking, peaceful conflict resolution, and reconciliation. It involves major societal change; on the socio-psychological level, it involves information processing, persuasion, learning, reframing, recategorization, and eventually acquisition of new societal beliefs, attitudes, emotions, motivations, and patterns of behavior. Thus it is a long, slow, complex, multifaceted, arduous, and general process that can last for many decades. It consists of psychological, social, political, and cultural changes that eventually transform the nature of the relations between two societies completely, from a hostile and violent rivalry to an allied relationship. The most salient example of the peace-building process is between France and Germany, which were considered chronic rivals through centuries and were involved in a number of major wars.

Peacemaking, as an important phase within the peace-building process, focuses only on the societal acts toward reaching an official settlement of the conflict, which is a formal agreement between the rival sides to end the confrontation (see Zartman, 2007). The acts are real and concrete, but the essence of peacemaking is psychological, as it requires changing the societal repertoire that fueled the conflict into a new one that is in line with the new goal of resolving the conflict peacefully. The change has to occur with the leaders who negotiate the peaceful settlement and sign it. But in most of the cases, in order to pave the route to the settlement of the conflict, new societal beliefs have to be constructed, disseminated, and accepted by society members who need to support the negotiated peaceful settlement.

The new repertoire should include ideas about the need to resolve the conflict peacefully, personalization and legitimization of the rival, changing the view that it is a zero-sum conflict and unsolvable, changing goals that fueled the conflict, accepting compromises, building trust, constructing beliefs that the agreement can be implemented, developing goals about new peaceful relations with the rival, and eventually recognition of the need to reconcile and construct a new climate that promotes new ideas about peacemaking and peace building (Gawerc, 2006). These ideas have to be adopted by society members, who must be mobilized for the peace process, if it is to be successful. In addition, on a behavioral level there is a need to decrease considerably and even cease violence, initiate compromises, perform concrete acts of confidence building and conflict deescalation, formulate optimal solutions for conflict resolution that could be accepted by the other side, and begin negotiations in good faith. Thus, in principle the society must move from what is known and well established in the minds of society members and well practiced for many years to new ideas that portray an unknown, uncertain, and unpredictable future that is dependent on the delegitimized rival. Sometimes this process ends with peaceful settlement of the conflict that is a result of *conflict resolution*. Conflict resolution refers to the negotiation process in all its phases and modes that takes place between representatives of the rival parties to reach formal peaceful settlement of the conflict. The conflict resolution process is often well discussed in the literature and therefore is beyond the scope of the present book (see De Dreu, 2010; Handelman, 2011; Pruitt, 2011;

Reykowski & Cislak, 2011; Wallensteen, 2002). Worthy of note, however, is that the negotiated peaceful settlement of the conflict, as it appears with its provisions in the formal accord, has to satisfy the basic needs and goals of the involved parties in order to serve as a basis for peace building. In other words, the majority of the society members who participated in the conflict have to see the settlement as providing a fair and just solution. It is almost inevitable, however, that there will be groups that will not be satisfied by a peaceful settlement of the conflict and will be prepared to continue the conflict. But if these groups are relatively marginal and most society members are determined to embark on the peace-building road with the feeling of need satisfaction, then the involved societies may successfully begin the journey, as the developments in the Spanish-Basque and Northern Irish peace process show.

Although resolving the conflict peacefully is a great achievement that may bring an end to the bloodshed, it does not necessarily indicate that the two societies will continue the process of transforming their relationship and accept deep societal changes. They may not continue the process of peace building with reconciliation but rather stop at the end of the peacemaking process. Then, after stopping the process, they will manage a cold peace for various reasons, as is the case with the Israeli-Egyptian peaceful settlement of the conflict.

Having introduced some major concepts, I now turn to the peacemaking process that stands at the core of this chapter.

PEACEMAKING

In most of the cases, peacemaking involves, on the one hand, bottom-up processes in which groups, grass-roots organizations, and civil society members support the ideas of peace building and act to disseminate them among leaders; on the other hand, it also needs top-down processes in which emerging leaders join such efforts or initiate the peacemaking process, which includes persuading society members of the necessity for a peaceful settlement of the conflict.

The peacemaking process must also get support from the elites and institutions and eventually must be shared by at least a substantial portion of society, especially in democratic societies (see, e.g., Bar-Siman-Tov, 2004; Knox & Quirk, 2000; Weiner, 1998). The mass media and other societal channels of communication, including the school system, can buttress the formation of a peace orientation and then transmit and disseminate the new system of beliefs among the society members. The presentation of new beliefs that provide the goals, plans, information, images, considerations, arguments, and justifications for peace building subscribes to the principles of persuasion. These new beliefs should form a prism for understanding the processing of new information. Obviously, the challenge of the peacemaking process is to change the dominant repertoire that supports continuation of the conflict. This goal sometimes seems to be an impossible mission when one realizes that the dominant repertoire is well anchored into the hegemonic culture of conflict. It is maintained by the political, societal, cultural, and educational channels and institutions that often have a vested interest in resisting change. Also, leaders frequently reject any idea that can open the way to peaceful resolution of the conflict. They habitually get the support of the great majority of society members; in many cases, in fact, they are elected by them to carry on the conflict to achieve their goals. This way is considered to be patriotic and nationalistic, and to be the only one that benefits the society. The goals are viewed as sacred and existential without options of compromise, because compromises are viewed as harming the heart of the society. The rival who threatens the existential basis of the society is delegitimized and viewed as malevolent, and therefore no peaceful settlement of the conflict is considered. As presented in the previous chapter, this view serves as a prism to collect new information and interpret experiences. Societies involved in intractable conflict employ various societal mechanisms to preserve the repertoire and use all the needed steps to prevent penetration of new ideas that propagate peacemaking with the rival.

The Unfreezing Process

According to the classic conception offered by Lewin (1947), every process of societal change has to begin with the cognitive change, in individuals and groups, that indicates unfreezing. Hence, a precondition for the acceptance and internalization of any alternative beliefs about the conflict or peace building depends on the ability to destabilize the rigid structure of the dominant socio-psychological repertoire about the conflict that was described in the previous chapters of this book. This endeavor is especially challenging because in many of the conflict situations, this process begins with a minority that also needs to have courage in order to present the alternative ideas to society members.

In this social climate, in order to begin the long journey of peace building, an idea about the need to pursue the peace process must emerge. Indeed, on the psychological individual level, the process of unfreezing usually begins as a result of the appearance of a new idea (or ideas) that is inconsistent with the held beliefs and attitudes and causes some tension, dilemmas, or even intrapersonal conflict, which may stimulate people to move from their basic position and look for alternative ones (e.g., Abelson, Aronson, McGuire, Newcomb, Rosenberg, & Tannenbaum, 1968; Bartunek, 1993; Kruglanski, 1989). This new idea is called *instigating belief*, because it motivates society members who construct it to evaluate the held societal beliefs of the culture of conflict, and in fact it may lead to their unfreezing and eventually to the seizing (i.e., adoption) of alternative beliefs that sow the seeds for the emergence of the ethos of peace (see elaboration in Bar-Tal & Halperin, 2009). The content of the instigating belief may come from domains that may pertain to the image of the rival, image of the ingroup, the history of the conflict, the goals, or new threats. What is important is that the content of the instigating belief has to contradict at least some of the beliefs in the system. Thus, it may suggest that the rival is human and can be a partner to negotiations, or that the ingroup performed misdeeds that violated moral codes, or that the goals are unachievable, or that the costs of the conflict are extremely high and cause critical damage to the society, or that in the long run the society may pay an immense price in the future for not resolving the conflict.

What is important in this process is that the instigating belief has to be of high validity and come from a credible source, so it will not be rejected easily. The instigating belief has to be strong enough to cause dissonance, in the words of Festinger (1954). This belief has to force society members to pause and think in order to reconcile between the colliding belief. It does not mean that every society member may consider the instigating beliefs, but at least a few will absorb the belief and be motivated to consider it. The belief can come on the basis of personal experience or from an external source, but once it is absorbed and considered, it may eventually lead to the unfreezing process in which at least some of the held beliefs are rejected and a new *mediating belief* emerges that calls for changing the context of intractable conflict. The mediating belief is the logical outcome of the dissonance, if it is resolved in the direction of accepting the instigating belief as providing valid information (see the intrapersonal socio-psychological process described by Kruglanski, 1989). Mediating beliefs are usually stated in the form of arguments: "We must change the strategy, or we are going to suffer further losses"; "Some kind of change is inevitable"; "We have been going down a self-destructive path and must alter our goals and strategies"; "The proposed change is clearly in the national interest and necessary for national security" (Bar-Siman-Tov, 1996). These inducements open a discussion of alternatives and thereby deepen the process of unfreezing begun by the instigating beliefs. At least one alternative that may emerge in this process is suggesting that peaceful settlement of the conflict may change the direction in which the society is going. The emergence of this idea is the beginning of the march toward peacemaking. The description may sound too sketchy, but in essence the idea has to emerge, be seized, and be disseminated among society members. As an example, already in the early 1980s Pieter Willem Botha, the conservative leader of the National Party in South Africa who came to power in 1978, began to realize, in view of the streaming information about a number of unequivocal indicators (internal violence, deterioration in the South African economy, demographic growth of the blacks, and South African isolation, all of which served as instigating beliefs), that the situation could not continue as it had in past and that there was a need to begin to make reforms and start negotiation with the African National Congress. This logic indicates the appearance of mediating beliefs (Beinart, 2001).

This process may look simple in this description, but it is not. The fact is that many societies involved in intractable conflict have great difficulty raising these simple ideas. The described process begins on an individual level, often with a very small group of society members, who either develop it together or assemble it on the basis of their separate understanding of the situation, although in some intractable conflicts there might be a portion of the society members who already at the early stage of the conflict may object to its eruption and support nonviolent resolution. Nevertheless, in many intractable conflicts the existing or evolved minority has to persuade the society members of the need to solve the conflict peacefully, which almost always requires compromise over the far-fetched conflict goals that were posed in the society. Eventually this process may lead to evolvement of a peace-supporting repertoire and even to the development of the ethos of peace (see Figure 4). Thus, the process that begins on an individual level moves to a group level and then proceeds to a societal level.

From another perspective, it is possible to look at the process of change as relating directly to the socio-psychological repertoire that society members hold about the conflict and rival – that is, the narrative in the culture of conflict as described in Chapter 7. This narrative is one-sided and simplistic, being selective, biased, and distortive. In this situation, society members refuse to accept any alternative information because of the functioning of the socio-psychological barriers, as described in Chapter 8. In this psychological situation, the first step for any change is reaching a recognition that one's own narrative does not reflect absolute truth but is selective, biased, and distortive. The achievement of this recognition may move society members beyond this phase into the state of readiness to be exposed and receive alternative information that will shed a new light on the conflict and the rival. But of crucial importance is the last phase in which society members are open

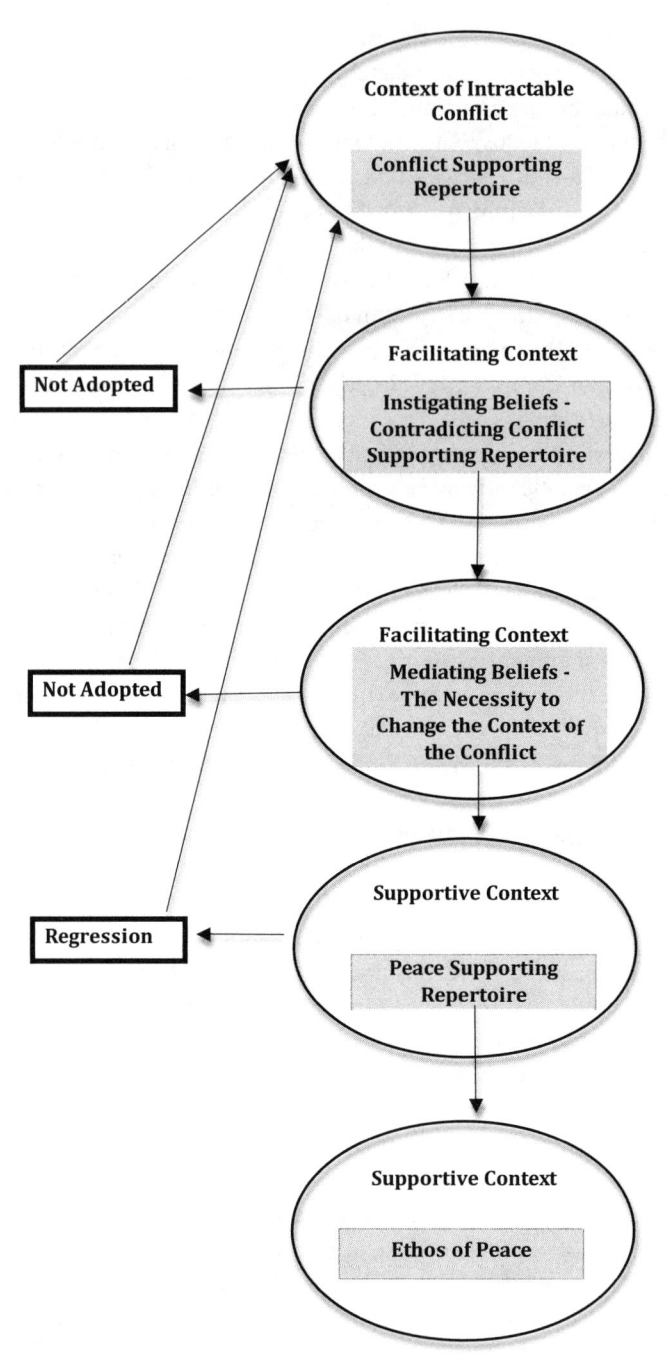

FIGURE 4. Process of Overcoming the Socio-Psychological Barriers

to seizing and adopting the new information and thus changing their held beliefs and attitudes. This is the necessary phase for any meaningful change that opens the way for the peacemaking process. Thus, the ultimate test for openness and the ability to overcome the barriers is the willingness to absorb new information that creates ways for peace building. This is the core challenge for anyone promoting societal change – to motivate society members to be open to new information and be willing to accept it.

Conditions for Change

Some scholars of conflict resolution argue that the success of the peacemaking process and then of conflict resolution is dependent on specific conditions. For example, Zartman (2000, pp. 228–229) proposes, "If the (two) parties to a conflict (a) perceive themselves to be in a hurting stalemate and (b) perceive the possibility of a negotiated solution (a way out), the conflict is ripe for resolution (i.e., for negotiations toward resolution to begin)." Pruitt (2007) offers a psychological perspective on the ripeness theory, testing it with the analysis of the Northern Ireland case. In his view, ripeness reflects each party's readiness to enter and stay engaged in negotiations. Antecedents of readiness include motivation to escape the situation, together with optimism about the prospect of reaching a mutually beneficial outcome. When readiness is present, a subtle conciliatory signal may be offered. If the other party reciprocates, optimism ought to increase on both sides. Reaching this stage, however, is not a natural process but a result of continuous and consistent persuasion by those who begin the peacemaking moves. In other words, individuals and groups are the ones who advocate and propagate the process of peacemaking. They seize the new ideas, adhere to them, and disseminate them among society members, trying to mobilize them for the cause.

Nevertheless, the ideas about terminating the conflict peacefully often emerge and are successfully disseminated when changes in the context of the conflict are observed. These changes pertain to major events or information, or both, that may facilitate the process of peacemaking and therefore can be called the emergence of the facilitating conditions (see Figure 4). The appearance of the facilitating conditions in this context can happen at any point during the peacemaking process. They can appear at its beginning, contributing to the emergence of the first instigating beliefs, or in more advanced stages, when a substantial minority already supports the peace process. The list of such facilitating conditions is inexhaustible, as different societies may be influenced by different experiences. Also, they probably do not sway the whole society to support peacemaking, but they serve as evidence to at least some society members of the need to resolve the conflict peacefully, and thus they contribute to the unfreezing process.

One of the most salient facilitating conditions as a major event or as information is *trust-building actions by the rival*, which lead to perceived change regarding the opponents' character, intentions, and goals. The information about this line of action or even direct experience may begin to change the view of the rival as being evil and intransigent. The best example to illustrate this factor is Sadat's arrival to Jerusalem on November 20, 1977, in the midst of the Israeli-Egyptian intractable conflict, meeting with Israeli prime minister Begin and other leaders and elites, and saying in the Israeli parliament (Knesset), "I come to you today on solid ground to shape a new life and to establish peace. We all love this land, the land of God, we all, Moslems, Christians and Jews, all worship God. . . . I have come to you so that together we should build a durable peace based on justice to avoid the shedding of one single drop of blood by both sides. It is for this reason that I have proclaimed my readiness to go to the farthest corner of the earth. . . . Allow me to address my call from this rostrum to the people of Israel. I pledge myself with true and sincere words to every man, woman and child in Israel. I tell them, from the Egyptian people who bless this sacred mission of peace, I convey to you the message of peace of the Egyptian people, who do not harbor fanaticism and whose sons, Moslems, Christians and Jews, live together in a state of cordiality, love and tolerance" (http://www.jewishvirtuallibrary.org/jsource/Peace/sadat_speech.html, September 9, 2011). Following this dramatic visit, Oren (2005) argues that Israeli Jews reduced substantially their support for the major beliefs of the ethos of conflict. For example, while before the visit more than 70% of Israeli Jews attributed to Arabs the goal to annihilate Israel, after the visit the percentage was reduced to less than 50%.

Another facilitating condition pertains to major information about the state of the society. *The realization of the costs that a society is paying* in continuing the conflict may lead to crystallization of beliefs in the need to change the view of the conflict and the rival, reconsider the intransigent policy, and even adopt compromising positions that allow resolution of the conflict peacefully. An example of this factor can be seen the view of de Gaulle, who came to power in 1958 with the intention of keeping Algeria as part of France. In spite of the fact that in 1958–1959 the French army had a series of military successes and gained a clear upper hand in the war of Algeria, de Gaulle dramatically changed his position and began to speak about "self-determination," which signaled readiness to resolve the conflict peacefully. This change came as a result of the realization that France was paying tremendous intrasocietal costs, with high losses in human life and property destruction; on the military level, with overextension of the French army; and then in the international arena, where France became criticized and isolated (Horne, 2006).

Sometimes *intervention of a third powerful party* that demands peaceful resolution of the conflict may also be a determining condition in changing the view about the conflict. In this context a third party that has the resources and prestige may even use force to influence the position of the party or parties involved in violent conflict to accept the demand. The example that illustrates this context is the intervention of the United States in case of the conflict in Yugoslavia. Between August 30 and September 20, 1995, NATO carried out an air bombing operation mainly against the Army of the Republika Srpska to impose an end to the war. Indeed, the air campaign constituted a determinative final pressure on Milošević to change his views and agree to negotiate the Dayton Peace Agreement in November 1995, which brought an end to the war (Holbrooke, 1999).

In some cases, in contrast, a *proposed mega incentive by a third party* that is highly valued by at least one party to a conflict may affect the views of this party regarding an intractable conflict and move it toward more conciliatory views. As an example, Goren (2009) analyzed the case of Turkey, which was involved in two protracted and violent conflicts, one in Cyprus and one with the Kurds. Turkey had membership in the European Union as an important national goal, and in 1987 it submitted its application. The EU responded by imposing certain conditions that included a change in its policies regarding the two conflicts in which Turkey was involved. Indeed, the EU pressure led the Turkish government to put pressure on the Turkish-Cypriot leadership to accept the UN peace proposal to resolve the Cyprus conflict. In addition, the Turkish government approved a set of major reforms regarding the abolition of the death penalty, granting of cultural rights to the Kurds, and limiting military activities in Kurdish area.

In addition, a change of beliefs regarding a conflict may be a result of *global geopolitical processes and events* that are unrelated directly to the conflict (e.g., realignments or collapse of a superpower). In this case, global change as a facilitating condition may affect a party in conflict and move it to compromise. An example of the effect of this change is a movement by Arafat and the PLO that allowed the signing of the Oslo Agreement in 1993, following the collapse of USSR, which played a major supportive role of the PLO in its conflict with Israel (Tessler, 2009).

In addition, a traumatic war or battle can raise the *costs of the conflict* and lead to recalculations of the benefits of continuing it. Such events may also indicate that the rival is strong and the likelihood of winning the conflict is slim. An example of this kind of event can be the disastrous battle in Dien

Bien Phu in 1954, which had a dramatic effect on the French decision to reach a Geneva accord to end the conflict with the Vietnamese communists. Also, major events and information about the *emergence of a new enemy* that may be more threatening can lead to the need to resolve a conflict peacefully in order to cope with the new rival. As an example, an often-raised argument in Israel is that peace must be made with the Palestinians in order to manage the conflict with Iran. Finally, major *information about one's own misdeeds and atrocities* may have an influence on the readiness and willingness to continue a conflict. An example is the My Lai massacre carried out by a U.S. army unit in 1968 that increased the opposition to the Vietnam War after it became public knowledge in 1969.

The noted conditions are neither exhaustive nor exclusive. Each of them, as well as combinations of some of them, may arouse new needs or new goals that are more important than those which led to conflict. As a result, a set of beliefs may appear that can contribute to the unfreezing of the held repertoires that support the continuation of the conflict. Different beliefs can lead to unfreezing, but probably one of the more influential ideas that has considerable effect on unfreezing is a recognition that *the losses that will be incurred if the conflict continues are greater than the losses that are incurred with the acceptance of the particular peaceful solution* (Bar-Tal & Halperin, 2009). This recognition is a powerful idea that may move the peacemaking process to its successful ending. In essence, it focuses on the losses that the society may incur if it does not resolve the conflict peacefully under the present conditions.

Effects of Information about Losses as a Facilitating Condition

Theorizing about the importance of losses is based partly on Kahneman and Tversky's (1979) prospect theory, which has been adapted to apply to conflict situations (e.g., Boettcher, 2004; Levy, 1996; Geva & Mintz, 1997). According to prospect theory, people are more reluctant to lose what they already have than they are motivated to gain what they do not have (Tversky & Kahneman, 1986). In the language of prospect theory, the value function is steeper on the loss side than on the gain side. The theory's claim about the larger impact of imagined losses than of imagined gains has also been part of other theories. One example is conservation of resources theory (Hobfoll, 1989), which states that losing resources through a traumatic event evokes greater distress than an equivalent failure to gain new resources. A similar negativity bias has been noted within the literature on persuasion (see Chapter 8): negative events and information tend to be more closely attended, better remembered, and more able to produce attitude change than positive events and information (see

Cacioppo & Berntson, 1994, for a review). In many cases, societies engaged in intractable conflict (especially the stronger) do not want to lose what they already have, tend to adhere to their negative memories that the actions of the rival produced, and have great difficulty imagining potential gains resulting from peaceful settlement of the conflict.

One way to emphasize the potential losses associated with continuing a conflict and to reduce the emphasis on losses associated with a peaceful settlement is to reframe the *reference point*. Prospect theory proposes that people react more strongly to changes in assets than to net asset levels; that is, they react to *gains* and *losses* from a reference point rather than to the absolute values of gains or losses (e.g., Kahneman & Tversky, 1979; Tversky & Kahneman, 1986). In most cases, the reference point is the status quo, but in some situations it can be an "aspiration level" (Payne, Laughhunn, & Crum, 1981) or a desired goal (Heath, Larrick, & Wu, 1999). Very often, members of societies involved in a conflict are socialized to believe in the feasibility of future gains from the conflict or even the victory of their group over the rival (Bar-Tal, 2007a). The alternative possibility of paying a high price for continuing the conflict or being defeated is often ignored. As a result, when the compromises required by a peaceful settlement of the conflict are compared with the society's aspirations, or even the status quo (mostly for the stronger group), they are perceived as requiring an enormous loss. In other words, motivation to reevaluate firmly held beliefs and to consider alternatives is based on realizing that continuation of the conflict will not lead to a better or desired future but may drastically reduce the chances of achieving it (Bartunek, 1993). The continuation of the conflict may lead to losses that are greater than the losses that are needed in order to achieve the peaceful resolution of the conflict via compromises.

We tested the proposed process among Jews in Israel (Gayer, Landman, Halperin, & Bar-Tal, 2009). Our main assumption was that instigating beliefs that include information about future losses in various aspects of life (e.g., economic and demographic aspects, as well as potential negotiations with Palestinians) will unfreeze Israelis' predispositions about the peace process with the Palestinians. In line with that assumption, we found in a correlated study (see study 1) based on a nationwide representative sample of Jews in Israel that Jewish Israelis who believe that time is *not* on their side, that is, that the continuation of the Israeli-Palestinian conflict will bring about losses to Israeli Jewish society, showed greater tendencies to look for alternative information about the conflict. In addition, people who held these beliefs regarding future losses also showed a higher willingness to make compromises for the sake of a peaceful resolution of the conflict.

In the second and third studies of that research, we used existing information to induce perceived future losses among Jews in Israel and examine its effect on the levels of openness to new information and support for compromises. The results of study 2 showed that information about possible future losses deriving from the possibility of the implementation of a one-state solution to the Israeli-Palestinian conflict led to attitudinal unfreezing and to higher levels of support for compromises among members of all political groups. Furthermore, corresponding with the original assumptions of the prospect theory, the results of a third study showed that the effect of instigating beliefs about losses on cognitive unfreezing and support for compromises was significantly higher than the same instigating beliefs formulated as future gains. In other words, the same information framed as a possible loss led to more unfreezing and support for compromises than when it was framed as a possible gain.

Nevertheless, a study that we conducted on the basis of Peace Index of January 2012 among a representative sample of Jews in Israel showed that there is no unitary agreement to solve the conflict in order to avoid the cost. In a response to the question, "If you knew that continued Israeli control of the West Bank would lead to one state for Jews and Arabs in the entire Land of Israel that would not have a Jewish majority, would you support or oppose continued Israeli rule in the territories?" it was found that Jews differ in their opinion according to their political orientation: hawks supported more than doves continued Israeli rule in the territories in spite of the delineated cost. Also it was found that religious Jews and those with low income were more ready to accept the costs than were secular Jews and those with high income. Still these results show that in all the groups the mean is skewed toward the opposition, which indicates that Jews in Israel oppose continued Israeli rule in the territories, knowing that it would lead to one state for Jews and Arabs in the entire Land of Israel that would not have a Jewish majority. These results mean that Israeli Jewish society accepts the principle of a two-state solution mainly because of "the demographic threat," which suggests that the much higher population growth of Palestinian communities in Israel and in the Palestinian Authority will soon affect the balance of proportion between the two largest ethno-religious communities in the region. This "demographic threat" or "cost" is expected to lead to the creation of a Palestinian majority within the next few decades.

Two notable examples for changes that were driven, at least to some extent, by the described processes can be drawn from the peacemaking process in Northern Ireland and South Africa. In Northern Ireland, MacGinty and Darby (2002) argue that in the early 1990s the understanding that future change is inevitable, and that such change might consist of fundamental losses to the Unionist side in the conflict, was one of the most central motivations to reconsider its position and finally to join the negotiations in order to gain influence over a possible agreement. The writers quote a statement by a senior Orangeman, which according to them reflected a common view shared by the Unionists: "Every time something comes along it is worse than what came before" (MacGinty & Darby, 2002, p. 23). Within the context of the South African conflict, Mufson (1991, p. 124) points to similar views of the unfreezing process when he suggests that, because de Klerk and his people realized that "White South Africans' bargaining position would only grow weaker with time," they opened negotiations and made every effort to move as quickly as they could toward a viable agreement. In addition, this consideration was clearly influential in the change of views of the Israeli prime minister Ehud Olmert (and also other Israeli leaders). Although he objected to territorial compromises for many years, in the 2000s he realized that in the territories between the Mediterranean Sea and the Jordan River (that include the State of Israel and the occupied territory) Palestinians could constitute a majority and then Israel would lose either its democratic nature or its Jewish nature. This realization led him to adopt comprising beliefs about a solution to the conflict and to initiate negotiation with the Palestinian president Abu Mazen. In line with his new views, he said:

The existence of a Jewish majority in the state of Israel does not coincide with the continued domination over the Palestinian population of Judea, Samaria, and Gaza. We insist on the historical right of the Jewish people over the whole of Eretz Israel.... However, the choice between the aspiration to enable every Jew to live anywhere within Eretz Israel, and the existence of the state of Israel as a Jewish state – necessitates relinquishing parts of Eretz Israel. (Olmert, 2006)

In the attempt to mobilize public support for his peace process, he said later, "A day will come in which the solution of two states will collapse and we will face struggle in the South African style for the right of equal vote. In the moment it will happen, the state of Israel will be finished" (*Haaretz*, November 29, 2007).

Reaching this conclusion signals unfreezing. The ultimate outcome of the unfreezing is cessation of adherence to the repertoire that supports the continuation of the conflict, its evaluation, and consideration of the readiness to entertain alternative beliefs (Bar-Tal & Halperin, 2009). The goal is seizing of alternative societal beliefs that promote a peaceful resolution of the conflict (Kruglanski & Webster, 1996). These examples illustrate more than unfreezing. In all the examples, the leaders reached the point of being able to formulate a coherent set of compromising beliefs that served as a holistic plan acceptable to the rival party. Indeed, the ultimate objective is to go beyond a plan that settles the conflict peacefully to evolving, accepting, and internalizing a new ethos of peace (see Chapter 10). This ethos must act as the opposite equivalent of the repertoire of conflict, in terms of content and structure, in a way that will successfully fulfill the same needs and aspirations of the ingroup members (see Figure 4). But, in the absence of peace and reconciliation, it seems that the attempt to form the new socio-psychological repertoire that will fulfill those needs and aspirations is a great challenge for every society that strives to end the conflict peacefully. Fulfilling those needs in the two clear-cut situations – intractable violent conflict or viable peace – looks much easier than doing so in the "transformational" period between violent conflict and peace, full of uncertainty and often with continuing violence and active opposition groups.

The process of unfreezing and formation of a new system of beliefs that enables peaceful relocation of the conflict may potentially stem from two observations that are not mutually excusive: the peaceful resolution of the conflict will prevent harm of the ingroup and/or benefit it; and the peaceful resolution will stop harm of the rival and/or do justice to its claims. The first observation is based on utilitarian considerations, the second at least partly on moral considerations. I think that the first consideration guides most of the leaders and society members who support peacemaking and resolution of the conflict. Society members (including leaders) are rarely guided by moral considerations that require universal values, high moral codes, perspective taking, and empathetic feelings, because not only do they indicate rare high human development but also they are viewed in times of conflict as reflections of weakness, naiveté, and even treason. Predominantly, society members are moved by considerations that pertain to what is good for their own society in tangible terms.

Any meaningful change of the conflict-supportive socio-psychological beliefs, attitudes, emotions, and patterns of behaviors within the culture of conflict that may eventually lead to peaceful resolution of the conflict is greatly facilitated by the socio-psychological elements that include a new view of the rival, trust, hope, a modified perspective, and guilt. I believe that in order to begin the peace process it is necessary to change the view of the rival. A minimum of legitimization and trust of the rival is needed to permit the idea that there is a partner on the other side of the peacemaking process. Then there must be hope that the process is not in vain but eventually will bring a peaceful resolution of the conflict. Finally, it is necessary to have a wider perspective that allows recognizing that the rival also has needs that have to be satisfied in the peaceful settlement of the conflict. All these elements do not require a moral position but can develop on the basis of utilitarian considerations that suggest that the peaceful resolution of the conflict serves the needs and goals of the ingroup. Guilt in this respect is different because it relates to moral emotions: it is based on the recognition that the ingroup engaged in immoral goals and acts. In this case, a moral consideration suggests that the conflict is at least harming the moral values and norms of the group but also is immorally hurting the rival and therefore it has to be terminated. Each of these elements plays a role in the unfreezing process.

REQUIREMENTS OF THE NEW REPERTOIRE

A New View of the Rival

Peace building can begin when at least a segment of a society thinks that the delegitimized rival is a potential partner in peacemaking. Even the idea that it is worth testing the intentions of the rival is a sign that lessens the notion of his total delegitimization. Viewing the rival as a potential partner is based on at least a minimal legitimizing view. The recognition of the rival as a partner with whom one could negotiate peaceful settlement of the conflict is based on fully legitimizing, equalizing, differentiating, and personalizing him (see Bar-Tal & Teichman, 2005).

Legitimization allows viewing the opponent as belonging to an acceptable category of groups behaving within the boundaries of international norms, with which it is possible and even desired to terminate the conflict and construct positive relations. It ends an exclusion of the group by including it in groups of the international community, which are entitled to moral treatment. This allows recognition of the legitimate existence of the other group with its differences, which may be in the realm of goals, values, ideology, religion, race, nationality, ethnicity, culture, and other domains. Legitimization implies that the other group has the same right to exist and live in peace as one's own group and has the right to raise contentions and grievances that are then to be resolved in nonviolent ways. As such, it provides the basis for trust, which is an essential condition for starting the process of conflict resolution, leading eventually to the construction of peaceful relations.

Equalization turns the rival into an equal partner with whom one can establish new relations. It ends the propagated delegitimizing differentiation between the two groups that was psychological and practical. Equalization implies perception of members of the other group first and foremost as equals, without superiority, and then treating them accordingly. This process requires recognition of the principle of status equality between the groups, a principle that is brought to bear first in negotiations and later in all types and levels of intergroup interactions.

Differentiation leads to heterogenization of the rival group. It enables a new perception of the rival that has hitherto been viewed as a homogeneous and monolithic hostile entity. The new perception implies that the other group is made up of various subgroups, which differ in their views and ideologies. Differentiation thus also makes it possible to see that members of the rival group differ in their opinions regarding the conflict and its resolution. That is, it enables distinguishing between those who do and do not support the peace and, as a result, establishing differential relations with these two groups. It allows a dialogue to open negotiations with this group or other groups that show signs of readiness to negotiate a peaceful settlement.

Personalization allows viewing the rival group not as a depersonalized entity but as a group of individuals with ordinary human characteristics, concerns, needs, and goals. This process of individuation consists of a further step after differentiation – a process of humanization of the rival society members who were viewed not only as a monolithic entity but also as one that is not humane, with a predisposition to be evil. Personalization is a qualitatively significant upgrading of the rival group, which allows one to look at the group via transgroup categories such as mothers, civilians, and physicians. It is personalization that not only enables a different view of the rival group members but also opens a way for trust and contact.

Trust

Trust is one of the most basic ingredients in successful conflict resolution, but it already plays a major role in deescalating intractable conflicts. Eventually it is needed "to transform the relationship between enemies into a relationship characterized by stable peace and cooperation" (Kelman, 2005, p. 640). Trust denotes lasting expectations about future behaviors of the rival group that affect the welfare of one's own group and allows taking risks in various lines of behaviors (Bar-Tal et al., 2010). These expectations refer to the intentional positive behaviors of the rival group that have an effect on the welfare (well-being) of the ingroup, as well as to the capability that the rival groups have to carry out these positive behaviors. Complete trust means that the ingroup has absolutely positive expectations and lack of negative expectations about future behaviors of the rival – all behaviors that determine the welfare of the ingroup. Because these two lines of expectation are orthogonal, the ingroup expects only positive acts and does not expect any negative behaviors by the rival. Attribution of positive intentions to the rival's stable dispositions with his high capability leads to a high level of trust (see also Barber, 1983; Deutsch, 1973; Kramer & Carnevale, 2001; Lewicki, 2006). In fact, the study by Tam, Hewstone, Kenworthy, and Cairns (2009) in Northern Ireland argues that trust is a key aspect of positive intergroup relations. The results of this study indicate that it is a powerful predictor of behavioral tendencies toward the outgroup, even more so than the attitudes toward the outgroup. Similarly, in Israel a study by Maoz and McCauley (2011) among a representative sample of Israeli Jews reports that trust toward Palestinians lowers support for violating their human rights. Trust, in turn, increased as a result of contact with Palestinians.

Minimal trust needs to be developed in the initial phases of the peacemaking process, at least by a segment of the society, because readiness to carry negotiation toward peaceful resolution of the conflict is by its nature risky. This trust has to be based not on an emotional basis but on the reasoning that leads to the realization that the interests of the other side also guide its motivation to resolve the conflict peacefully (Lewicki & McAllister, 1998; Möllering, 2001). Trust allows society members to take the risk of being vulnerable and to make conciliatory initiatives to the other party with some degree of confidence that they will not be exploited (Larson, 1997). Because of these reasons, Osgood (1962) proposes construction of trust through graduated and reciprocated initiatives in tension reduction (GRIT). This proposal refers to a sequence of carefully calibrated and graduated unilateral initiatives that induce the other side to reciprocate with a tension-reducing action, which in turn leads to a sequence of reciprocations. It assumes that unilateral actions initiated by one of the parties to a dispute may eventually reduce mistrust and build trust (Linskold, 1978).

Hope

Development of a new peace-supporting repertoire requires the emergence of hope. Hope that consists of concrete positive goal expectation (Lazarus, 1991; Snyder, 1994, 2000a; Stotland, 1969) in cases of conflict, as hope for peace, reflects expectation to achieve at least peaceful conflict resolution and yearning for relief from the terrible situation of intractable conflict (Jarymowicz & Bar-Tal, 2006). Accompanied by affective reaction, it requires positively valued, realistic, and concrete goals and directed thinking with pragmatic ways on how to achieve it (Snyder, 1994, 2000a; Staats & Stassen, 1985). That is, it is based on higher cognitive processing of mental representations of abstract future situations and more specifically on setting goals, planning how to achieve them, use of imagery and creativity, cognitive flexibility, mental exploration of novel situations, and even risk taking (Breznitz, 1986; Clore, et al., 1994; Fromm, 1968; Isen, 1990; Lazarus, 1991; Snyder, 1994, 2000a). Thus, the affective component is complex and may contain positive and negative elements, because individuals may realize that the achievement of their final goal may involve struggles, costs, and endurance. Hope can be seen as a state of mind that requires development of new "scripts": programs about future actions. According to Fromm (1968), hope requires conviction about what is not yet proved and the courage to resist temptation to compromise one's view of present reality for a better future.

It is hope that liberates people from their fixating beliefs about the irreconcilability of the conflict to find creative ways to resolve it. It enables people to imagine a future that is different from the past and present and motivates society members to change their situation by acts that were unthinkable for a long time, such as, for example, negotiating with the enemy and making compromises. Without hope for peace, it is impossible to embark successfully on the road to peace. But hope has to override other negative emotions described in Chapter 6 and especially the fear that often dominates conditions of intractable conflict (Bar-Tal, 2001; Jarymowicz & Bar-Tal, 2006). Indeed, a study conducted in Northern Ireland found that hope was positively related to the dissipation of the desire to retaliate, which, in turn, was positively related to willingness to forgive the adversary (Moeschberger, Dixon, Niens, & Cairns, 2005). Another study in Israel by Halperin, Bar-Tal, Nets-Zehngut, and Drori (2008) reports that the less Jewish participants delegitimized Arabs, the more hope they had of peaceful relations with them; in addition, individuals who were less dominated by a central sense of Jewish collective memory, which emphasizes persecutions of Jews through centuries, were observed to have higher hopes. Another study conducted in Israel found that hope was the most powerful emotional predictor of Israelis' support for compromises with the Palestinians (Rosler, Gross, & Halperin, 2009). These results indicate that delegitimization of the rival and reliance on threatening collective memory hampers development of hope to resolve successfully an intractable conflict.

Recently Cohen-Chen with her colleagues attempted to evoke hope by changing the view of the intractable conflict (Cohen-Chen, 2012; Cohen-Chen, Crisp, Lehman, & Halperin, 2012). In their opinion, one of the critical reasons for the lack of hope is the deeply rooted view that the conflict is unsolvable and thus provides a pessimistic, stable, and uncontrolled orientation. Therefore, they proposed that there is need to change this mind-set, by imparting a view that the reality is dynamic and the conflict situation can change. In experimental studies, they found that participants who learned that social and political realities are dynamic and change over time experienced increased levels of hope compared to those participants who learned that political and social situations do not change and that reality is stable over time. Moreover the results showed that this manipulation further increased the willingness of the former groups to support concessions on the core issues of the Israeli-Palestinian conflict.

Perspective Taking and Empathy

Perspective taking and empathy are two important factors that have an effect on the way society members view the rival group. In general, they complement each other because psychologists tend to view perspective taking as a cognitive aspect of empathy that is dominant by affect. Perspective taking thus refers to cognitive awareness and recognition of another person's or group's goals, intentions, aspirations, needs, feelings, and perceptions, while empathy as an affect is considered to be the vicarious affective response to another person or a group, meaning the ability to vicariously experience what the other feels (Batson & Ahmad, 2009; Eisenberg, 2000; Hoffman, 2000). Thus, perspective taking in this meaning refers to imagining how the other person is thinking and feeling in the particular situation. According to Batson (1991, 2009), empathy is an affective response that stems from the apprehension or comprehension of another's emotional state or condition and refers to the ability to elicit emotional reactions that are congruent with the perceived welfare of the other person. It is an emotional response to others' distress, suffering, or pain but not necessarily with the same content. Feeling empathy means perceiving that others are in need and being emotionally moved by their suffering; it can often result in feeling compassion, sympathy, or consideration for the other (Batson, Ahmad, Lishner, & Tsang, 2005; Zhou, Valiente, & Eisenberg, 2003). In addition, Batson and his colleagues provide evidence that empathy may also originate as a result of intrinsic valuing of the others' welfare together with a perception of their being in need (Batson, Eklund, Chermok, Hoyt, & Ortiz, 2007). Nevertheless, as it is possible to take the perspective of the other by imagining what this person would feel in a particular situation, it is also possible to make such a differentiation with regard to empathy (Batson & Ahmad, 2009). Stephan and Finlay (1999) suggest that by being emotionally moved, one can experience the same feelings as the sufferer – hence, one can experience the same or similar emotions as those who are experiencing some form of pain (called parallel empathy), or one can simply feel emotions as a reaction to the sufferings of others, which do not necessarily have to resemble those of the sufferer (called reactive empathy).

Empirical evidence shows that empathy can take place only on the basis of perspective taking. First, individuals have to be able to be aware that others have their own reasons, goals, and intentions and have to try to grasp them. If they go through this cognitive process with good intentions, they may find out that others have reasonable thoughts, ideas, and feelings that underlie their line of behaviors. This process of personalization has the potential to make others seem less alien and frightening and thus to break down the perceived barriers between the ingroup and the outgroup. Perspective taking and empathy may reduce prejudice because they lead people to see that they are less different from members of the other group than they thought they were. Perspective taking and empathy may also lead both to perceive that they share a common humanity, as well as common values, concerns, and needs (Stephan & Finlay, 1999).

In cases when the other was harmed, Batson et al. (1997) argue that there is a three-stage process by which attitudes change in response to reactive empathy. First, people experience empathic concern for the individual who is suffering. Second, empathizing with the individual who is suffering leads people to value the welfare of this person. Third, concern for the welfare of this person generalizes to the group of which this person is a member, leading to more "positive beliefs about, feelings toward, and concern for the group" (p. 106) as a kind of *ethnopathy*. As Stephan and Finlay (1999, p. 735) explained, "Learning about suffering and discrimination while empathizing with the victims may lead people to . . . come to believe that the victims do not deserve the mistreatment. . . . If the victims do not deserve this unjust treatment, it may no longer be tenable to hold such negative attitudes toward them."

At the intergroup level, taking the perspective of a member of another group might produce a more inclusive category representation that leads to a major change of view of the other (Dovidio et al., 2004). Indeed, studies found that when individuals are induced to try perspective taking, they reduce bias toward the outgroup members and increase their positive evaluation (Batson et al., 1997; Dovidio et al., 2004; Galinsky & Moskowitz, 2000; Vescio, Sechrist, & Paolucci, 2003). This change takes place because imagining oneself in another person's situation increases the salience of self-attributes, leading one to see the other as more self-like.

In situations of conflict, perspective taking and empathy are key skills that can change the socio-psychological repertoire that supports continuation of the conflict. They enable one to look at the situation from another's point of view. They open a window to see the suffering of the rival, to view him also as a victim, and to understand his needs and goals. This outlook enables one to move from the zero-sum approach to a mixed-motive strategy that eventually allows an achievement of peaceful settlement of the conflict. Perspective taking and empathy indicate that moral considerations become part of the individual's socio-psychological repertoire, and they force one to take into account the outcomes of these processes (Hoffman, 2000). Seeing the suffering of the rival is an important step in the reorganization of one's own socio-psychological repertoire. It causes personal distress and may lead to the wish to change this situation by peacefully resolving the conflict.

Indeed, when empathy is translated into action, it can instigate very powerful and important behavioral processes in real intergroup conflict settings. For example, Brown and Čehajić (2008) report that Serbian adolescents who felt empathy for the suffering of Bosnian Muslims that was caused by their own group were more ready to support reparation policies to be offered by their group, such as issuing an apology or providing material compensations to the victims. Also, in other conflict settings, Nadler and Liviatan (2006) find that empathy felt for Palestinian suffering increased the readiness of Israeli Jewish participants toward reconciliation. Another study conducted in Israel found that empathy felt by Arab children toward Jewish children was negatively related to support for violence (Shechtman & Basheer, 2005). In general, it can be noted that induction of empathy is used in various facilitating methods to advance peacemaking, such as conflict resolution workshops, peace workshops, encounter groups, or peace camps (Batson & Ahmad, 2009; Stephan & Finlay, 1999). The challenge is how to turn one's own real suffering into a transforming constructive force that not only allows empathy for the suffering of the other but also serves as a mechanism for stopping and preventing harm doing. As noted before, it is not easy to develop perspective taking and empathy with a rival that has been viewed in delegitimizing terms for along period of time and has caused considerable harm to the ingroup. Nevertheless, it not an impossible development on the individual and group levels, as empirical studies show and as various cases in societies involved in intractable conflict indicate (e.g., in France, South Africa, and Israel, individuals, organizations, and groups were able to take perspective and feel empathy with the rival group).

Group Guilt

Appearance of collective guilt indicates some kind of rapprochement to the rival side, a recognition of the wrongdoing by one's own group, which undermines the self-collective positive view and the monopoly over the collective victimhood. It rarely appears at the phase of conflict eruption but may appear later as the conflict escalates and at least a small minority of the society members realizes that the intractable conflict involves also immoral acts by the ingroup. It is one of the moral emotions that may lead eventually to the peacemaking process.

Guilt is a secondary emotional experience that is aroused on the basis of one's appraisal that he or she is responsible for actions that violate dominant norms or values, especially moral codes (Branscombe, 2004). Guilt focuses on the wrongdoing itself and not on the characteristics of the violator (Tangney, Wagner, Fletcher, & Gramzow, 1992). This distressful emotion signals that relationships between oneself and another have been damaged and that steps need to be taken to repair them, and often it leads individuals to take corrective action for the harm done. Thus, when a person experiences guilt, it can motivate transgressors to offer an apology, or even reparations, and thereby guilt serves an important social function that enables restoration of social relationships.

Much research on this particular emotion takes place in the context of intergroup relation and especially in situations of conflict. Studies demonstrate that people can feel guilty for the harmful, illegitimate actions of their ingroup, even if they were not directly responsible for those actions (see Branscombe & Doosje, 2004; Doosje, Branscombe, Spears, & Manstead, 1998). These findings established the existence of collective guilt. Appearance of collective guilt not only demonstrates its aversive experiences but supports taking responsibility for having committed illegitimate harm and increased support for a variety of forms of reparations (Branscombe, 2004). It motivates group members to rectify the wrongdoing and to compensate the victims (Doosje et al., 1998; Iyer, Leach, & Crosby, 2003).

This emotion is especially important in intergroup conflicts in which at least one party acts in a way that violates basic moral norms (Barkan, 2000). In fact, almost all, if not all, of the intractable conflicts involve violence that violates human rights and moral codes. But not in all conflicts are these violations symmetrical. There are asymmetrical conflicts in which one party commits more violations (e.g., in the case of Guatemala), and also some of the conflicts are based on severe deprivations that are underlined also by gross violations of moral codes (e.g., in the case of South Africa). In all these cases, at least a small fraction of society members can experience guilt even when the conflict is raging in an escalating phase because of the acts of their group, even if they themselves did not carry out any harmful acts.

During the eruption and escalation of the intractable conflict, involved groups try to provide psychological tools to prevent guilt from appearing. It is viewed as an emotion that weakens the group determination. The evolvement of socio-psychological infrastructure comes to fulfill this function because guilt is perceived as reducing the ability of the group members to adhere to the goals of conflict and withstand the enemy. The societal beliefs that perpetuate the view of the rival in delegitimizing terms and that portray one's own group in glorifying and moral ways, and especially as the sole victim in the conflict, serve this function well. In addition, society members may use various psychological mechanisms, such as denial, repression, or projection, in order to avoid feelings of guilt (Miron & Branscombe, 2008). Halperin and his colleagues analyzed specifically how Israeli Jews cope psychologically with the fact that Israel maintains occupations for many decades, which necessarily leads to oppressive acts against the Palestinians under occupation (Halperin, Bar-Tal, Sharvit, Rosler, & Raviv, 2010; see also Bar-Tal & Schnell, 2013b). Thus, if guilt appears in the escalating stage of the conflict, it is experienced by a minority of society members. It may appear in its wider scope in the later phases of the conflict – during the peacemaking process and especially in the process of reconciliation that will be discussed in Chapter 10. Collective guilt, in fact, is essential to the reconciliation process because it motivates the perpetrators to seek reparation and to support a just relationship with their victims (Branscombe, Doosje, & McGarty, 2002; Čehajić, Brown, & Castano, 2008; Čehajić, Effron, Halperin, Liberman, & Ross, 2011; Miron & Branscombe, 2008).

Wohl, Branscombe, and Klar (2006) propose that when society members are confronted with harmful actions of their ingroup, the degree to which collective guilt will be experienced depends on the following factors: society members have to categorize themselves as members of the group that committed the harm; then they have to perceive their group to be responsible for the actions deemed to be harmful to another social group; these harmful acts have to be perceived as being performed intentionally, as being illegitimate, or as immoral; and the degree of collective guilt experienced depends on the perceived difficulty and costs to the ingroup of correcting the wrongs committed.

Numerous studies conducted in the contexts of various conflicts (e.g., in Bosnia, South Africa, and the Middle East) have demonstrated that individuals who recognize their own group's responsibility for the harm caused to the opponents and experience collective guilt are motivated to compensate and offer reparations to the victims of their own group's actions (Brown & Čehajić, 2008; Brown, González, Zagefka, & Čehajić, 2008; Čehajić et al., 2011; Roccas, Klar, & Liviatan, 2006; Sharvit, Halperin, & Rosler, 2011; Wohl et al., 2006). As such, guilt may contribute to improving the relations between opponent groups and facilitate the process of conflict resolution. Roccas, Klar, and Liviatan (2006) report that different types of identification with one's own group can affect feelings of collective guilt differently. While Israeli Jews with a defensive form of identification felt less collective guilt because of the Israeli actions against Palestinians, Israeli Jews with more affective identification felt more collective guilt. In South Africa, white South Africans who felt collective guilt regarding the past injustices their group inflicted on black South Africans were also more supportive of redistributive policies, such as affirmative action (Klandermans, Wener, & van Doorn, 2008); this study also found that those whites who held conservative ideology did not experience guilt, because the ideology served as a buffer and justification for the wrongdoing.

Together with guilt, the secondary emotion of shame is also associated with an appraisal of improper behavior on the part of ingroup members. Yet, unlike guilt, shame implies that the wrongdoing reflects on the general character of the perpetrators (Tangney et al., 1992). Consequently, the response tendencies associated with shame are targeted toward the self. As a result, individuals who experience shame try to reestablish a self-positive image with various psychological mechanisms. Cases of collective shame are associated with psychological actions that aim to defend and restore the ingroup's image rather than alleviate the damage inflicted on the outgroup (Branscombe, Slugoski, & Kappen, 2004). This includes distancing the ingroup from the shame-invoking situation (Sharvit et al., 2011), although there is also evidence for effects of shame on constructive political tendencies (Brown & Čehajić, 2008; Brown et al., 2008).

After having described the facilitating repertoire for initiating and carrying out the peacemaking process, we can now discuss the societal process through which the new alternative ideas about conflict emerge and are disseminated, legitimized, and eventually institutionalized in the society if peace making is to succeed (the discussion is based on ideas developed by Bar-Tal, Landman, Magal, and Rosler, 2009).

SOCIETAL PROCESS OF PEACEMAKING

In many cases of peacemaking, it is possible to identify three main phases that involve the gradual mobilization of society members and allow their support for peaceful settlement of the conflict: *an emergence* of an alternative socio-psychological repertoire supporting peacemaking; *legitimization* of an alternative socio-psychological repertoire supporting peacemaking; and *institutionalization* of an alternative socio-psychological repertoire supporting peacemaking. The last two phases are characterized by a competition

Breaking the Cycles of Intractable Conflicts

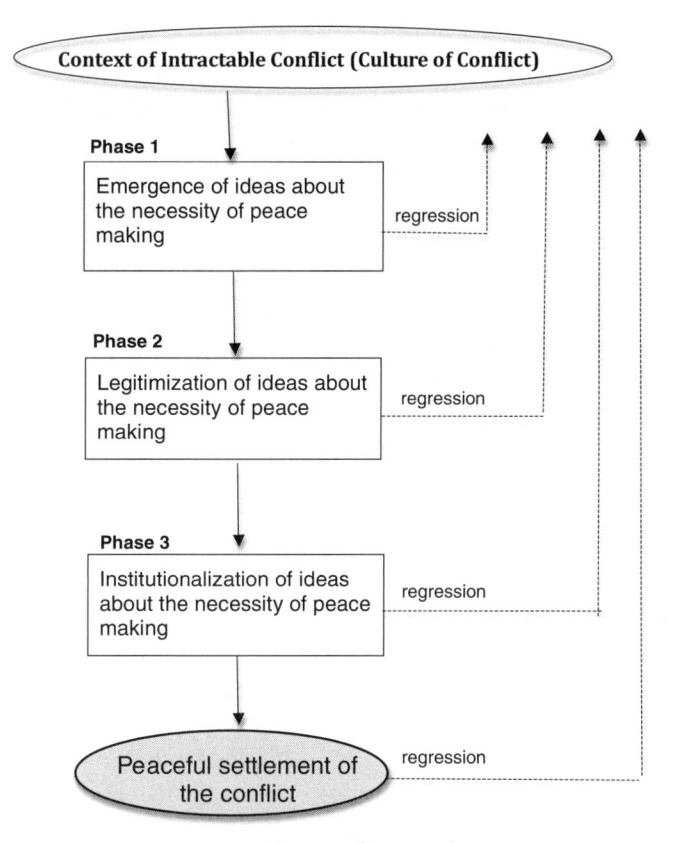

```
┌─────────────────────────────────────────────────┐
│  Context of Intractable Conflict (Culture of Conflict) │
└─────────────────────────────────────────────────┘
                    │
        Phase 1     ▼
        ┌──────────────────────┐
        │ Emergence of ideas   │    regression
        │ about the necessity  │─────────────
        │ of peace making      │
        └──────────────────────┘
                    │
        Phase 2     ▼
        ┌──────────────────────┐
        │ Legitimization of    │    regression
        │ ideas about the      │─────────────
        │ necessity of peace   │
        │ making               │
        └──────────────────────┘
                    │
        Phase 3     ▼
        ┌──────────────────────┐
        │ Institutionalization │    regression
        │ of ideas about the   │─────────────
        │ necessity of peace   │
        │ making               │
        └──────────────────────┘
                    │
                    ▼
        ╭──────────────────────╮    regression
        │ Peaceful settlement  │─────────────
        │   of the conflict    │
        ╰──────────────────────╯
```

FIGURE 5. Process of Peacemaking

between, on the one hand, societal beliefs embedded in the culture of conflict that suggest adherence to the goals, delegitimization of the rival, and therefore continuation of the conflict and, on the other hand, societal beliefs that advocate an alternative course, which suggest a new goal to settle the conflict peacefully by compromising on the new goals and by legitimizing the rival as a partner to the peaceful settlement. Only when the alternative socio-psychological repertoire supporting peacemaking evolves to be institutionalized, dominant, and even hegemonic is the road to peace opened in its significant meaning.

This process is often gradual and nonlinear, and it does not always end with a peaceful settlement to the conflict (see Figure 5). Not every peacemaking process goes through the described phases, and some may begin with a more advanced phase. Also, in a very few cases the peace process takes place overnight, but these cases are rare. The peaceful settlement of the conflict between Egypt and Israel provides such an example when Egyptian president Anwar Sadat arrived to Jerusalem in November 1977 in the midst of the intractable conflict, almost without any public preparation, but this an exception. In some respect the process depends on the type of regime that governs the society involved in intractable conflict. In authoritarian societies, the process would depend more on the whim and will of the leadership. But in general it is a long process, and this analysis describes its challenges.

As outlined in the detailed description of the phases, in many cases the first phase begins when the conflict is still going on – sometimes even in its violent form. This means that the socio-psychological repertoire supporting the continuation of the conflict is hegemonic (being consensual) and well institutionalized. Leaders support this repertoire as well as the political establishment, and the elites and the society are fully mobilized to support the continuation of the conflict.

Process of Emergence

The phase of emergence begins with sporadic ideas by individuals about the need to resolve the conflict peacefully. Very rarely do the ruling societal leaders who manage the conflict initiate these ideas. They are raised by "early risers," who are often educated society members with universal orientation and sensitivity (Tarrow, 1998). These ideas are instigated by their own accumulated experiences, certain major events, or by information that these society members received. The process of emergence can be gradual, but of importance for the success of this phase is development of awareness that the "early risers" are not alone but there are other society members who think similarly. This realization leads to formation of a group, which begins the long journey. The formed group not only fulfills the function of mobilizing the society members for peacemaking but also serves as a support group for those members who commit themselves to the challenging mission of bringing peace. The establishment of a cohesive and active group enables the development of a new social identity for the peace activists. The development of the reference group with membership identity, solidarity, and coordinated action is important for the dissident society members because the developed ideas about peacemaking are viewed by the great majority of the society members and the authorities at best as naive and detached from reality but more often as subversive and dangerous to the goals of wining the conflict. They are viewed as hurting the society's standing, breaking up its unity and solidarity, and obstructing the mobilization for supporting and participating in the conflict. They are viewed often as traitors because their acts are perceived as signaling weakness to the rival and helping him to win the conflict. Therefore, those who promote the mission of peacemaking are often sanctioned and in some cases even ostracized and persecuted. In view of this tendency, society members who decide to disseminate ideas about peacemaking must be courageous and expect being at best marginalized but also delegitimized (McAdam, 1986, 1989). When they organize themselves in a group, they have better chances of withstanding the attacks. With time, this small minority may gain support, and its persistence may serve as a basis for a movement and a change of the context that eventually may open the possibilities to launch an effective campaign for resolving the conflict peacefully. Indeed, social psychological literature about minority influence suggests that a group with a minority opinion can eventually persuade the majority (Crano & Prislin, 2006; De Dreu & De Vries, 2001; Moscovici & Faucheux, 1972; Nemeth, 1986; Prislin & Christensen, 2005; Prislin & Wood, 2005).

When ideas about peacemaking emerge, most society members still hold the central societal beliefs of the culture of conflict, support trying to achieve the maximal goals that were set, and view the rival with delegitimizing terms. Nevertheless, the emergence of this minority is important not only for its own society but also for the rival group. The emergence of a peace-supporting group may ignite a similar process in the rival group or reinforce it. A parallel development of the emergence of the ideas about peacemaking in the rival group is of great importance. It does not have to be completely symmetrical, but the development of groups on both sides provides evidence to each group that the ideas are valid.

The message at this early stage of the process of peacemaking refers often to the general idea of the need to stop the conflict and embark on a process that will eventually lead to a peaceful settlement. In some cases, the emergent group may be more specific and propagate possible solutions to settle the conflict. In addition, the emergence of the general ideas about the necessity to make peace or the specific ideas about the contours of the peaceful solution require construction of an epistemic basis for the new goals that suggest peaceful resolution of the conflict. In some cases, the evolved minority is motivated by universal moral codes that negate violence, seek justice, and promote values that are violated by the continuation of the conflict. Nevertheless, most society members are not moved by moral arguments. Instead, they need to see utilitarian considerations and arguments that point out the costs that the society will incur if the conflict is to be continued or the benefits that the society will gain if it will resolve the conflict peacefully.

The success of the first phase – that is, of the establishment of the minority group and the beginning of the peace process – depends on factors that have been well presented in the socio-psychological literature about minority influence (see De Dreu & De Vries, 2001; Moscovici & Faucheux, 1972; Nemeth, 1986; Prislin & Christensen, 2005). First, it helps if the members of the minority come from the elite groups (such as intellectual elites), have access to resources, and maintain contact with the political mainstream. Second, they need to be determined and strong to survive the initial campaign against them because their lives may become miserable and even dangerous, and not every person is ready for total commitment to the cause. Then, in order to move the group to be active, time and energy are required. The minority group members have to make an investment in peacemaking, which could mean changing their way of life. Some may even be completely devoted to the cause. Members of the minority group need to have a deep conviction of the importance of the mission, self-efficacy, and a belief in its eventual success in order to mobilize the societal change that they aspire to make. In terms of contents, the minority group must formulate persuading messages that will be at least accepted by some of the society members. The group has to be persistent in propagating the message and consistent in the contents. In many respects, this phase is similar to the principles of mobilization for conflicts that were described in Chapter 2. In both cases, there is a need to mobilize society members to support ideas about societal change and also to move them to collective action.

This analysis can be illustrated with an example. During the early phase of the Israeli-Arab conflict, there appeared on the Jewish side intellectual groups that advocated Arab-Jewish reconciliation and the establishment of a binational state, such as Brit Shalom (Peace Covenant) and Ihud (Union), but their influence was negligible, and these groups disappeared (Kotzin, 2004; Ratzabi, 2002). Thus the analysis of the emergence of the Jewish peace moment has to begin with the establishment of the Israeli state after the 1948 war, when the conflict reached its climax and almost all the Jewish population was mobilized to take an active part. During the 1950s and 1960s appeared the "early risers" that propagated various compromising ideas to resolve peacefully the Israeli-Arab conflict (e.g., Matzpen), but in most cases they were heavily delegitimized and mostly marginalized (Greenstein, 2009). They had a hard time disseminating their unpopular ideas, which did not succeed in penetrating Israeli society, except in very marginal, small circles. After the 1967 war, a few very small peace-supporting groups (e.g., the Peace and Security organization) appeared, but only with the establishment of the Israeli Council for Israeli-Palestinian Peace (ICIPP) in 1976 was it possible to identify a meaningful turning point. The council was formed by 100 well-known public figures, including a former general in the army, director of the finance ministry, and a former member of the Israeli parliament (Knesset).

The council propagated direct negotiations with the PLO, based on a two-state solution, and initiated dialogue with official PLO representatives (Hall-Cathala, 1990). At that time, those were unacceptable ideas to the society, but because of the prominence of the ICIPP members, it was hard for the public and the establishment to delegitimize the group and ignore them completely (Kaminer, 1996).

Legitimization

The next phase in the process of peacemaking is legitimization, defined as a stage in which ideas, actions, or agents become morally acceptable in view of the norms and values of the group (Jost & Major, 2001; Kelman, 2001). Legitimization provides a firm basis for the peacemaking process (Bar-Siman-Tov, 1994). In this phase, the minority group moves to a position where the ideas about peacemaking become accepted as part of the legitimate public discourse and justified as a reflection of "freedom of expression." At least by some segments of the society, these messages about the necessity of peacemaking are not seen as threatening but as providing a legitimate alternative for societal goals and means.

The minority group in this phase grows and "late comers" join the minority group, which at this phase may take the form of a peace movement, with a few peace organizations that have different goals (they will be described further in Chapter 11). Although they share the same general approach to and definition of the problem, they may differ with regard to the proposed solution and chosen strategy for its promotion (Gamson, 1992). In this phase, there develops a leadership of peace supporters, which can cooperate and also compete for the somewhat different goals and means of peacemaking.

In fact, the legitimization phase is complex as it consists of the legitimization not only of the messages but also of the minority group. First, the messages that were viewed very negatively become legitimate and begin to contest the hegemonic conflict-supporting repertoire. This new status of the messages implies that the ideas about the necessity of peacemaking become more prevalent and accepted as part of the legitimate public discourse. They appear in the mass media and often become more central in certain social circles, such as the intellectual elite or cultural elite. Thus, in this phase the conviction that the present situation is costly and that the conflict must be ended peacefully begins to be disseminated, and the self-utilitarian epistemic basis becomes well grounded with well-established arguments. Often in this phase already specific proposals appear that detail the plan of a peaceful settlement of the conflict. In addition, the messages may be extended to the evolution of an alternative narrative that refers not only to future goals and aspirations but also to the new illumination of the course of the conflict. The evolved narrative usually takes a more balanced view in describing the course of the conflict and includes a more humane view of the rival as well as a more critical presentation of the ingroup.

Second, this phase also legitimizes the group or groups that carry the message. The mainstream of society, even if it disagrees with the presented ideas, at least recognizes the right of the peace groups to be part of the legitimate social and political system. The groups supporting peacemaking may even find a way into the formal political system and be in contact with some representatives of the government (Gamson, 1975). In many cases, though this group is still viewed by much of society as breaking solidarity and obstructing mobilization for the continuation of the conflict, and by some segments as traitors.

In fact, the success of the peace movement can lead to polarization. While the dominant side tries to uphold the support of society members to continue the conflict and to prevent changes in the conflict-supporting repertoire, the minority tries to disseminate ideas about the need for peacemaking. Polarization not only is reflected in persuasion and in campaigns but also may be accompanied by harsh tactics on both sides and sometimes even violence.

The development of this phase, reflected in the strengthening of the peace movement, is dependent on the numerous factors. First, the noted changes in the context obviously can facilitate this process. Of crucial importance as a necessary condition is a similar development in the rival group. Without this development, the peace movement cannot take off. The development of peace proponents on both sides vitalizes the movement and provides evidence that there is a partner and peace is a viable possibility. Opened meetings and coordination between the developed peace movements can help the cause and facilitate the peace process. Also, deescalation of the conflict with the reduced level of violence may provide the appropriate background to the strengthening of the peace camp. Finally, involvement of the international community in the evolving peace movement may provide the needed moral support and also resources for the activities of the minority.

Political psychology contributes to facilitation of the peacemaking process in this phase. As one example, building on the pioneering work of Burton (e.g., 1969), Herb Kelman and others (e.g., Fisher, 1997; Rouhana & Kelman, 1994) developed a method with the goal of facilitating a peaceful solution of intergroup conflicts called *interactive problem solving* (Chigas, 1997). It is designed as an unofficial, academically based, third-party approach, suited to protracted conflicts (Kelman, 2005). The central mechanism involves problem-solving workshops to which are invited politically influential representatives of the rival societies involved in the conflict. In these workshops, participants are exposed with the help of the facilitator to the repertoire of the rival group – needs, goals, beliefs, motivations, and so on. On the basis of the acquired knowledge and possible transformation, they begin to create ideas about conflict resolution. The workshops create a process that serves as a vehicle for promoting change in the societies by influencing the political debate and the policy-making process in their respective societies (Kelman, 2005). The method has been applied in many conflicts, including Northern Ireland (Hall, 1999), Cyprus (Fisher, 2001), Israel/Palestine (Kelman, 1995; Rouhana & Kelman, 1994), and Sri Lanka (Hicks & Weisberg, 2004). Outcomes of the interactive problem-solving method have included a deepening of mutual understanding between parties, more empathy on the views of the rival group, stronger intergroup relationships, new perspectives on old problems, and a loosening of intransigent and polarized positions (Fisher, 2005; Kelman, 2008).

Legitimization of the peace organizations in the Israeli Jewish society took place in the late 1970s and early 1982. Two major events facilitated greatly the development of this phase: the historical visit of Egyptian president Anwar Sadat in Jerusalem in 1977, which signaled the beginning of the formal peace process; and the outbreak of the Lebanon War in 1982, which was considered by many Jews as the first Israeli "choice war" and which also led to the massacres of Palestinians by the Lebanese Christian militia, which acted in this war in coordination with the Israeli army. In 1978 the Peace Now organization directed its activity to the mainstream of Jewish society and propagated territorial compromises with the neighboring Arab countries and the Palestinians (Bar-On, 1996). In addition, in this period additional peace organizations such as Parents against Salience, Women against the War in Lebanon, Committee against the War in Lebanon, or Yesh Gvul appeared (Hermann, 2009). Legitimization of the minority groups that advocated peacemaking with the Palestinians was apparent, as their messages penetrated into the Israeli public discourse; some of the groups, such as Peace Now, became a legitimate part of the political landscape; some members of a coalition party supported the peace movement, and it turned into a legitimate grass-roots movement (Magal, 2012).

Institutionalization

Institutionalization indicates penetration of the alternative beliefs supporting peacemaking into societal institutions and channels of communication, such as the formal political system, educational system, cultural products, and mass media. These beliefs are then expressed and reflected by these agents.

This phase indicates that the ideas about peacemaking become accepted by a significant segment of the society and dealing with them becomes an inherent part of the public discourse on every societal level. In fact, at this phase an alternative narrative about the necessity of peacemaking becomes well established. It contains beliefs that contradict the ethos of conflict and serve as seeds for building the ethos of peace. Thus, the new narrative establishes new societal goals that include achieving a peaceful resolution of the conflict. It also portrays the rival in a legitimizing and humanizing manner as someone who can be trusted as a partner to peacemaking. In addition, among part of the ingroup members, depending on the context of the conflict, a recognition begins that the rival group is also a victim in the conflict, and sometimes this recognition is accompanied by an acknowledgment that the ingroup also carried out immoral acts during the conflict. This leads also to a new image of the ingroup – a more complex one, which also contains a negative portrayal.

Formal leaders may now express their support for the idea of peacemaking, and in a state entity there may even appear political parties that advocate in their platform a peaceful settlement of the conflict. The peace organizations become institutionalized, and their actions become part of the normative activities of the civil society. Also during the institutionalization phase, there are signs that the societal institutions, including formal institutions, begin to change the well-entrenched one-sided narrative. This trend can be exhibited, for example, in changes of the collective memory, which begins to accommodate the perspective of the rival (Nets-Zehngut & Bar-Tal, 2012).

The competition between the two camps in society becomes central, and often the polarization becomes intense. The two camps propagate opposite ideas – one camp supports continuation of the conflict, and the other camp propagates its peaceful termination. Both struggle to attract the support of the society, and both try to exert influence on the leaders. Sometimes this polarization is even accompanied by violence.

The phase of institutionalization can be achieved in at least two cases that are not mutually exclusive. In the first unilateral case, a significant segment of the society either recognizes the high cost that the ingroup pays or will pay for the continuation of the conflict or loses its confidence in the justness of the goals of its own group (as, e.g., in the case of the Vietnam War, when American society began to object to the United States' conflict goals and the continuation to the conflict). Then this segment may develop unilaterally an institutionalized movement to terminate the conflict. Many of the colonial societies of Europe that exploited other countries eventually realized that the era of colonialism was over and a new standard of international behavior had emerged. Under these conditions, especially when there developed violent resistance, the costs of maintaining the conflict became high, and support developed for the termination of the conflict.

The second case is reciprocal and mutual and takes place when the rival parties develop significant pro-peace movements that energize both societies as in Northern Ireland. Members of the movements realize the need to compromise and settle the conflict peacefully. The reasons also may concern the high costs of the conflict or other arguments. This realization is usually a long process through which the movements carry out a process of persuasion and struggle for the peaceful resolution of the conflict. Eventually the movements become institutionalized as legitimate political forces that propagate alternative ideas in their societies.

The phase of institutionalization is a crucial one. If the process of peacemaking develops gradually, the phase of institutionalization is a precondition to move it to its successful ending with the peaceful settlement of the conflict. The ending requires conviction of the top formal leaders in need of peacemaking. They are the ones who lead the society and negotiate the agreement. Thus, they eventually have to be mobilized to accept the peace process and then mobilize the whole society to support it (Rosler, 2012). In fact, although leaders often talk about peacemaking, these talks are sometimes empty slogans for creating a self-image as one pursuing peace and self-presentation before the international community. It is relatively easy to examine the objectives of these talks when one looks at the policies, acts, or other rhetoric, which imply the real direction leaders take. As an example of serious intentions, Frederik de Klerk, leader of the National Party, which maintained the apartheid system, said on February 2, 1990, after being elected as the president of South Africa in September 1989: "The general elections on September 6th, 1989, placed our country irrevocably on the road of drastic change. Underlying this is the growing realization by an increasing number of South Africans that only a negotiated understanding among the representative leaders of the entire population is able to ensure lasting peace.... Our country and all its people have been embroiled in conflict, tension and violent struggle for decades. It is time for us to break out of the cycle of violence and break through to peace and reconciliation" (http://www.nelsonmandela.org/omalley/index.php/site/q/03lv02039/04lv02103/05lv02104/06lv02105.htm). A few months later he released Nelson Mandela, the leader of the African National Congress, and began negotiations with him that led to the end of the conflict in 1992.

The phase of institutionalization may lead to the beginning of negotiations between the rival parties, which signals significant progress in the process of peacemaking. Representatives of both parties begin to negotiate an agreement on a peaceful settlement of the conflict. This period is by definition a very complex stage in the life of every society that reaches it. In this period, society members are moving from the well-known and familiar context into an uncertain, ambiguous, and risky one.

In the Israeli Jewish example, the phase of institutionalization came relatively quickly after the phase of legitimization. In the second half of the 1980s, the idea of making peace with the Palestinians penetrated deep into the society as about 50% of Jews in Israel expressed willingness to withdraw from the occupied territories of the West Bank and Gaza Strip in return for peace, and 30% began to support the establishment of a Palestinian state. Also, beliefs regarding delegitimization of the opponent decreased significantly, with a differentiation between different Arab nations and the ascription of positive qualities to Arabs in general, and specifically to Palestinians (Bar-Tal & Teichman, 2005; Magal, Oren, Bar-Tal, & Halperin, 2013; Oren et al., 2004). During this phase, new peace organizations were established, including in 1988 the Council for Peace and Security, formed by a group of retired army generals and senior members of academia who were supporters of the Labor Party (Bar-On, 1996; Hermann, 2009; Magal, 2012). Nevertheless, the most significant development in the 1980s was recognition by the Labor Party of the need to resolve the conflict with the Palestinians, while still objecting to the establishment of the Palestinian state (Magal et al.,2013). Knesset members, including some from the Labor Party, expressed openly their views about the necessity of peacemaking and supported peace organizations. However, only the elections of July 1992 and the victory of the Labor leader Yitzhak Rabin brought substantial and concrete progress in the peacemaking process, reflected in the Oslo Accords in September 1993, which brought recognition between State of Israel and the Palestine Liberation Organization (PLO) and served as a framework for future negotiations. This accord led to major polarization in the Israeli society, as political parties of the right, including Likud, fervently objected to the accord and saw it as causing great harm to the Jewish state and even as treasonous.

This example provides evidence for the difficulty of carrying out the peacemaking process. After years of living under conditions of intractable conflict, with the hegemonic culture of conflict that provides a clear outlook on reality, a new context that requires a new repertoire develops, without a complete change of the conditions of the intractable conflict. Society members living with the intractable conflict through many years adapted psychologically to the condition by evolving a repertoire that is functional to the lasting context. It provided an unequivocal ideological picture about the reality. This picture guided views, impressions, information processing, explanations of experiences, judgments, and decision making. At least on the psychological level, society members learned to live with the situation and became habituated to it. It is thus possible to conceptualize institutionalization of the peacemaking process as a development of a new context that is characterized by duality (Rosler, 2012).

Duality of the Peace-Building Context

Duality implies that while the context of intractable conflict is still intact and many of the characteristics of conflict remain, at the same time signs of the new emerging context of peace begin to appear. Thus, on the one hand, at least some level of violence still continues, and it evokes beliefs and emotions supporting the conflict. Also, there are still investments in the continuation of the conflict, and the culture of conflict has a strong hold on the society. Themes about the justness of conflict goals, self-collective victimhood, and the delegitimization of the rival are prevalent, as they were hegemonic and institutionalized over decades.

But on the other hand, there is an attempt to frame the conflict in a different way. Instead of seeing it over existential and sacred goals, it is presented now by significant segments of the society as being over new goals that can be achieved via peaceful settlement of the conflict. The rival is presented as the partner to peacemaking that can be trusted. The conflict is perceived by at least part of the involved societies as being solvable peacefully and presented as being a situation with mixed motives, in which there is a need to compromise and to take into account the legitimate goals of the rival.

When negotiations between the rival parties are taking place and successfully progressing, both sides develop interdependent goals. Both parties can lose if the peace efforts fail, and both will have much to win if the process succeeds. In this mutual phase, both sides begin to make investments to reach a successful peaceful settlement of the conflict. They try to reduce the level of violence and change the context to reflect the new emerging context, by taking visible and concrete steps to advance the peacemaking process (e.g., meetings between the rivals, coordination of some activities, moderation of the violence). These steps, when taken by both sides, signal their seriousness to leave the road of conflict and embark on the road of peace. They signal the beginning of the new era. Both societies begin to adopt a new repertoire that is conducive to the evolving peace process and also to cope with the polarization that disrupts societal functioning. This transitional process requires major societal-cultural change.

The presented context of duality is well reflected in the developments of the peacemaking process in the following cases: in the Israeli-Palestinian conflict in the 1990s after the Oslo Agreement, when the Israeli prime minister signed a mutual recognition agreement between the State of Israel and the PLO and the societies became polarized; in the conflict in Sri Lanka during the negotiations between Tamils and Singhalese in the 2000s; in the Algerian conflict during the negotiations between the French government and the FLN in Avian; or during the negotiations between the South African government and the ANC. All these cases provide exemplary illustrations of the complexity of peacemaking situations.

These examples show that the period of peacemaking is challenging to the societies involved. In this period, the society not only faces the continuous challenges of satisfying the basic needs and coping with stress but also must mobilize itself for peacemaking. This latter challenge is very much related to the satisfaction of the need to provide a meaningful and comprehensive view of the new reality that also will satisfy security needs and needs of predictability. This is the challenge that the agents of conflict (entrepreneurs) of peace face. They have to construct the new reality and explain and justify the dramatic change of direction.

The new evolving repertoire suggests building a new future that cannot be guaranteed, that is based on unvalidated assumptions, and that negates the pillars of the still-dominant ideological societal beliefs. It is thus not surprising that many society members have difficulty adapting to the emerging situation. Many society members still live with the old images and at the same time are encouraged to accept new beliefs. Even when they are ready to support the peace process, they still feel that they cannot abandon completely the repertoire that has been so functional during the climax of the intractable conflict and which allowed them to cope with the challenges of the conflict. During this period the psychological roots of conflict are not easily eliminated. The collective memories of conflict and the ethos of conflict that are well organized in the memory system are automatically activated when threats, real or symbolic, are perceived. Thus, the orientation for peace needs not only to inhibit the automatic activation of thoughts associated with conflict but also to replace them with new beliefs and behaviors. These new beliefs must be attended, comprehended, accepted, and practiced before they can serve as an alternative to the automatically activated repertoire of conflict. These society members live in a duality. The new emerging context offers new goals, a new view of the conflict, and a new alternative for the future, but at the same time it sows dissonance, uncertainty, unpredictability, and incoherence in the worldview.

Also, in the period of negotiations and even after peaceful settlement, both rival parties often do not take great risks, still considering the possibility that they will have to return to the path of violent confrontation. Therefore, even when the peace-building process is progressing, leaders often keep the material and psychological infrastructure of conflict ready for the worst possibility. They have to continue the conflict until peaceful settlement will be achieved. Thus, the challenges that were described in Chapter 3 are still in place. There is a need to withstand the rival in order not to lose the conflict. This challenge is accompanied with the challenges to satisfy the need of society members and to cope with the stress. These challenges are even increased because of uncertainty and ambiguity, which also increase stress.

Arafat in his speech in April 1995 expresses well these challenges:

> We signed that agreement in the name of the PLO, the sole legitimate representative of the Palestinian people everywhere, here inside the homeland and outside the homeland. We must respect that agreement.
>
> I remind you and remind all of our people and Arab and Islamic nations that when the Prophet Muhammad, God's blessings and peace be upon him, signed the al-Hudaybiyah truce agreement, Quraysh refused to have the Prophet sign his name as "Muhammad the Prophet of God." ... Umar Bin-al-Khattab called that agreement the humiliating agreement, and said: Prophet of God, how can we agree to have our religion humiliated?
>
> We signed that agreement in Oslo, and if any of you has one objection to it, I have one hundred objections. (Arafat, Gaza Rally, April 16, 1994, in Rosler, 2012)

In most cases, peacemaking is not accepted willingly by all segments of society. Spoilers often make every effort to stop the process, using various tactics of persuasion and even incitement. There are groups on the rival side that propagate the continuation of the conflict, and there are groups within the ingroup that object vehemently to the peace process. Thus, societies making peace are often polarized with intrasocietal schism between those who support peacemaking and those who refuse to compromise and reach a peaceful solution. The latter group views peacemaking as a traitorous process that harms society. It delegitimizes the idea of settling the conflict peacefully, as well as those who support that approach. This group may even resort to violent means to prevent the process of making peace by carrying out violence against the rival group and also toward the ingroup members who support it.

Cases in France and Israel provide a good example of these processes. In both states powerful spoilers to the peace process appeared and made considerable efforts to stop it. In France, the French settlers in Algeria, pieds-noirs, who viewed Algeria as part of France, with the support of various political and military forces (e.g., OAS – Secret Armed Organization), acted as an underground in France trying to stop the peacemaking process, using political efforts as well as violence (Horne, 2006). Eventually, French president de Gaulle (who was a target of assassination attempts and even of a military putsch) signed the peace treaty (Evian Accord) in 1962 and terminated the conflict (Shepard, 2006). In contrast in Israel, the well-organized campaign by Jewish settlers in the West Bank and Gaza Strip, with the support of the major right-wing political parties that objected to the peace process with the Palestinians, succeeded in stalling the peacemaking process. Israeli prime minister Yitzhak Rabin was murdered by an Israeli Jew who rejected any compromises, and the newly elected prime minister Benjamin Netanyahu who objected to the Oslo Accords made efforts to slow the process (Karpin & Friedman, 1998; Peri, 2000).

Although during the peacemaking process the conflict may stop being intractable, it still continues to exist and may have violent expressions, such as terror attacks on civilians, military encounters, aggressive rhetoric, or agitation. Hostile and aggressive acts do not stop at once, even after achieving formal agreement to settle the conflict. When signs of conflict still occur, this is a challenging task, because not only does the conflict repertoire become accessible but these signs are also used by spoilers of the peacemaking process, who wait for these types of events and know how to inflame animosity, fear, and hatred. In such a situation, the reaction of leaders and the media to the threatening cues is crucial. Also, in this context leaders make a difference. They are supposed to lead the society in this transition. If they accept the new goals of peacemaking, they need to satisfy the needs of the society members (Rosler, 2012).

When they frame the events in support of the conflict orientation, then the peace process has very low chances to evolve. But when, in contrast, the leaders and media on both sides explicitly condemn the acts and their perpetrators, when they minimize their importance, reassure the public, and repeat their commitment to peace goals, then the chances are high that the peacemaking process will survive and gain momentum and reach the stage of conflict settlement. Cases of negotiators in South Africa and Northern Ireland illustrate the determination of the leaders to reach an agreement. In South Africa, the murder of ANC leader Chris Hani in 1993 and in Northern Ireland the terror attack by Real Irish Republican Army in Omagh in 1998 (29 people were killed) did not prevent successful conclusion of the peacemaking process.

Nelson Mandela provides an example of a leader's determination. After the murder of Chris Hani he said that "tonight I am reaching out to every single South African, black and white, from the very depths of my being. A white man, full of prejudice and hate, came to our country and committed a deed so foul that our whole nation now teeters on the brink of disaster. A white woman, of Afrikaner origin, risked her life so that we may know, and bring to justice, this assassin. The cold-blooded murder of Chris Hani has sent shock waves throughout the country and the world. . . . Now is the time for all South Africans to stand together against those who, from any quarter, wish to destroy what Chris Hani gave his life for – the freedom of all of us" (http://www.anc.org.za/show.php?doc=ancdocs/history/mandela/1993/pr930410.htm).

However, the process of peacemaking does not always succeed. Cases of conflict in Sri Lanka and the Middle East testify that it may fail, and the conflict may reescalate. Many reasons determine the success of this process. It is a test of the political culture of the society and of its leaders. The standing test is whether the society can bear the polarization and accept the process of changing the ethos of conflict. The political culture that is tolerant and pluralistic can accommodate the societal change with new challenges of serious polarization. But societies with a weak democratic culture can use a call to patriotism to delegitimize the supporters of the peace process and present them as traitors. It is easier to present the arguments for continuing the conflict as patriotic and benefiting the society than to support arguments for peacemaking. The former have only particularistic flavor and appeal to known and habituated practices, whereas the latter concern needed compromises and legitimization of the enemy, practices that are unknown or uncertain.

The success of the peacemaking process depends on various factors, such as the availability and free flow of new alternative information about the conflict, peacemaking, and the rival; the confidence and centrality with which the society holds its ethos of conflict; the responsiveness of the enemy to the changes, with corresponding lines of behaviors that signal peacemaking; determination of the leaders to pursue the new goals of peacemaking; the standing of the leaders who direct the peace process (their charisma, well-constructed rationale); the active support of the peace process by the involved societies (entrepreneurs, members, media); the low strength of the spoilers; significant reduction or elimination of violence; and the satisfaction of the basic needs of the societies involved.

Eventually, conflicts may deescalate and move toward their peaceful resolution when society members are demobilized from supporting the goals of the conflict and are mobilized for its peaceful resolution (Gidron, Katz, & Hasenfeld, 2002). But without determination and persistence of active peace forces, peace cannot be achieved, because it is not enough just to want peace. Almost everyone cherishes the value of peace. But real progress toward peacemaking requires parting from far-fetched and ideal dreams, adopting pragmatic steps, and transforming the socio-psychological repertoire that served for many years as a compass for continuing the conflict. Even goals that are underlined by justice and moral values eventually have to be compromised with practical considerations, if the peacemaking process is to succeed. In reality the formal process of peacemaking sometimes comprises a series of agreements on the way to the final settlement of the conflict. This was the case of the peacemaking process in Northern Ireland (see MacGinty, Muldoon, Ferguson, 2007) and in the Middle East between Israelis and Palestinians, where the rival parties did not reach the final settlement of the conflict but agreed only on principles that ended the violence and set the conditions for the mutual coexistence. In the latter case, these agreements did not lead to the settlement of the conflict, and eventually it reescalated with violence (see Bar-Siman-Tov, 2007).

Successful peacemaking processes in South Africa, Guatemala, and El Salvador testify that a peaceful settlement of the intractable conflict can be achieved, in spite of its durability, investments in its continuation, entrenchment of the socio-psychological infrastructure with the culture of conflict, and the operation of the spoilers who try actively to prevent its achievement. In all these and other cases, there were many conditions that facilitated reaching a peaceful settlement, but foremost were the society members, leaders and followers, who were determined to change the course of history and to overcome the barriers that would prevent peaceful resolution of the conflict. Those are human beings who eventually had to change their views, abandon the way of violence, and give their support to the peace-building process.

Conflict Settlement

Ending the conflict resolution process is a turning point in the relations between the rival parties engaged in intractable conflict. This point in most of the cases is reached after a long process of persuading society members to support it, and mostly after leaders decide to take the determinative decision to settle the conflict peacefully. It refers to a political process through which the parties in conflict eliminate the perceived incompatibility between their goals and interests and establish a new situation of perceived compatibility (Burton, 1990; Deutsch, 1973; Fisher, 1990; Kriesberg, 1992). It usually ends with an agreement, negotiated by the representatives of the two opposing groups, that outlines the details of the settlement such that the goals are viewed as not being contradictory. Harbom, Hogbladh, and Wallensteen (2006) report that out of 352 conflicts that erupted after World War II, 144 of them concluded with peace agreements.

Conflict resolution can be seen also as a psychological process, because it requires that the negotiators change their beliefs regarding their own goals, the other group's goals, the extent of contradiction between these two sets of goals, the conditions of the political environment, the situation of their own group, and the situation of the adversary group (see, e.g., Bar-Tal, Kruglanski, & Klar, 1989; Bercovitch, 1995; Burton, 1987, 1990; Fisher, 1990, 1997; Kelman, 1997; Kriesberg, 192; Pruitt, 2011; Ross, 1993; Worchel, 1999).

An agreement of conflict settlement is an important phase in the course of the confrontational relations between the rivals. It formally indicates an end to the conflict and specifies the terms of its settlement, which are based on uncertain and ambiguous future benefits. In most cases, they require putting aside dreams and aspirations in order to accept the possible and the practical present.

Rouhana (2004a, 2004b, 2011) differentiated between two types of conflict settlements. The first one, called *conflict settlement*, seeks a formal termination of open, violent conflict based on mutual interests that do not necessarily satisfy the needs of both parties. This settlement may especially hurt the needs of a weak society because it reflects the power relations that exist on the ground at the time of the settlement. In contrast, according to Rouhana, *conflict resolution* tries to satisfy the basic needs of the parties regardless of their power relations and then to address the underlying causes of conflict. These two types of settlements indicate that rival parties have a long way to go even after successfully ending the process of conflict resolution. Peaceful settlement of the conflict is only a phase in the long process of peace building, which requires also a phase of reconciliation in order to construct a lasting peace. Indeed, Ronald Fisher (2005, p. 189) provides a similar view of conflict settlement, defining it as "a transformation of the relationship and situation such that solutions developed by parties are sustainable and self-correcting in the long term. It also requires that an adequate degree of reconciliation occurs between the parties, in that harmony has been restored through processes such as acknowledgment of transgressions, forgiveness by the victims, and assurance of future peace."

But a movement toward the phase of reconciliation requires basic conditions that have to be fulfilled: it has to address satisfactorily the issues that stood at the core of the conflict; it has to satisfy the basic needs and goals of both parties; it has to address the justice within practical limitations; it has to provide observed changes in the conditions that benefit the ex-rivals; it has to create a basis for the emergence of the new psychological repertoire that supports peacemaking; it has to signal a strategic decision that changes the nature of the relations between the rival parties; and it has to provide a foundation for new policies and new courses of action that strengthen the peaceful settlement of the conflict and move the involved societies on the road of peace building. In short, the peaceful settlement has to be seen by at least a significant segment of the society as being fair in addressing the issues that stood at the heart of the conflict and as satisfying basic needs, especially those related to identity. Only when these conditions are fulfilled can new relations that aim at cementing the peace agreement later be built.

Nevertheless, peaceful settlement of the conflict does not have a unitary meaning, as peace can take many different forms once it is achieved. It can range from a cold peace that indicates a lack of violent acts and minimal relations to a warm peace that is geared toward a major transformation of building completely new peaceful relations (see the difference between negative and positive peace by Galtung, 1969). In any event, reaching a peaceful and satisfactory settlement of an intractable conflict with the support of the rival societies is probably one of the most impressive and significant achievements that human beings can attain.

It becomes apparent, though, that successfully reaching conflict settlement is only the first formal step in the peace-building process, which does not end necessarily with peacemaking (Cohr & Boehnke, 2008). Reykowski and Cisłak (2011, pp. 241–242) propose that "conflict resolution should not be looked upon as an achievement of a final state of equilibrium of a social system. Such equilibrium can never last for an extended period of time.... Thus, conflict resolution is rather an ongoing task that comprises prevention of the conflict escalation, elimination of its violent and destructive components, and facilitation of constructive change in people and in their social relations."

Of special importance is the societal process of peace building with the reconciliation that requires change of the socio-psychological repertoire of the culture of conflict among society members that fed the conflict and served as a barrier to the peace process. It has become evident that even when the formal peaceful settlement of the conflict is reached, it may fall far short of establishing genuine peaceful relations between the former adversaries. The repertoire that fed the conflict does not change overnight even when the groups' leaders resolve the conflict peacefully and sign a peace agreement. What is needed is a long process of peace building, which does not take place unintentionally but requires reciprocal planning and active efforts to overcome many obstacles and to reach its solidification. The next two chapters discuss the issues of building a stable and lasting peace embedded in culture of peace.

10

Peace Building

Concepts and Their Nature

The process of building stable and lasting peaceful relations between two parties that carried on a prolonged violent conflict (Christie, 2006; Cohrs & Boehnke, 2008; Vollhardt & Bilali, 2008) is probably among the most demanding challenges to achieve. It consists of a major societal change that often requires the restructuring of the society.

Such a major socio-psychological and cultural change is not simple but is possible, as various cases testify. Because the parties need to overcome strong emotions, attitudes, and beliefs included within the socio-psychological infrastructure, the challenge is immense. Prolonged adherence to ingroup conflict goals together with hatred, anger, fear, delegitimization of the rival, mistrust, self-perception as a victim, and animosity cannot be erased overnight and can be changed only through a long process of societal change.

The peace-building process was defined in Chapter 9 as continuous exerted efforts by society members, society's institutions, agents, channels of communications, and the international community to realize lasting peaceful relations with the past rival within the framework of the culture of peace. This process does not stop with the achievement of the peaceful settlement of the conflict but goes well beyond the historic event into a period with new qualitative meaning. In fact, in the past decades it has become evident that formal peace agreements fall far short of establishing genuine peaceful relations between the former adversaries (e.g., Knox & Quirk, 2000; Lederach, 1997; Lipschutz, 1998; Simpson, 1997; Wilmer, 1998). As the result, formal resolutions of conflicts may be unstable and may collapse, as was the case in Chechnya following the first war, or they may result in a cold peace, as is the case in Israeli-Egyptian relations. In these and similar cases, hopes of turning the conflictive relations of the past into peaceful societal relations have not materialized because the peace-building process with reconciliation either never actually began, was stalled, or has progressed very slowly. Formal conflict resolution sometimes abides mostly with the leaders who negotiated the agreement or with the narrow strata around them, a small part of the society. In these cases, the majority of society members may not accept the negotiated compromises or, even if they do, they may still hold a worldview that has fueled the conflict, not allowing the development of a stable peace but supporting maintenance of a cold peace only.

Before discussing peace building at length, I would first like to introduce two major factors that have determinative influence on this process: the nature of peaceful settlement of the conflict, with a focus on cold peace; and societal differences in peace building.

DETERMINATIVE FACTORS

Cold Peace

Cold peace takes place when states adhere to the signed agreements of peaceful resolution of their vicious conflict but do not continue to build stable peaceful and lasting peaceful relations between society members. Usually, cessation of the peace-building process following the formal agreement that ends the violent conflict signals that some problems dividing the rival sides remain unsettled, as in the case of the peace agreement between Israel and Egypt in 1978. In this specific case, the Palestinian issue remained unresolved, and therefore significant segments of the rival Egyptian society remained hostile and did not wish to move to the next phase of completely transforming the nature of Israeli-Egyptian relations. In this case and other similar cases, a cold peace prevails that focuses on the absence of violence (Barash & Webel, 2002; Christie & Louis, 2012; Galtung, 1969). Cold peace is often instrumental, serving the interests of the parties in a limited but predictive way, with calculus-based trust. This trust indicates that two parties might well come to cooperate without constructing deep and psychological trust, because their interests lie in developing safeguards such as commitments, interests, contracts, or monitoring agencies (Hoffman, 2002; Lewicki, 2006; Sztompka, 1999). The trust is based on a simple cost-benefit analysis between the parties and is maintained as long as the benefits of maintaining the peaceful relationship outweigh the costs of violating the agreement between the parties. These relations are often supported by leaders, economic elites, and certain segments of the society, who see maintaining peaceful relations as being in their interests, and it may last even for a long time. But such agreements preclude often the development of amiable and cordial relations between the two societies. As the result, formal resolution of the conflict can be unstable; it may collapse, as in the case of Sudan, or be maintained with much uncertainty and limitations. In these cases, hopes of turning the conflictive relations of the past into peaceful societal relations do not materialize because the societies do not transform their relationships in the process of building peace.

These restricted relations do not reflect warm peace, where there is complete restructuring of relations by building stable and lasting peace with complete transformation of the socio-psychological repertoire of the societies involved (see Clements, 2012; Lederach, 2005). Stable and lasting peace is based on fully nonviolent, normalized, and cooperative political, economic, and cultural relations in which both societies have a vested interest and goals in developing new peaceful relations and a secure coexistence. This type of relation can be successful only when it is constructed within the framework of a culture of peace that both societies construct.

Societal Differences

Discussions of the effort to build lasting peace benefit from two important classifications of conflicts. The first concerns the outcome of the conflict and the status of the groups involved after conflict resolution. Whereas in some conflicts, the two groups will live in two separate political entities (i.e., states) following the conflict resolution, as in the case of the German-French and the Israeli-Egyptian conflicts, in other instances, despite the vicious conflict, the two rival groups will have to continue to live together in one entity (a state), as in the case of South Africa, Guatemala, El Salvador, or Spain. This classification is important in deciding on the type of peace-building process chosen and the form of the final outcome. In general, rival groups that will be living together as an integrated peaceful society will need to restructure the society and construct mechanisms that foster integration with all that it signifies. In contrast, in the other cases the rival societies will need to construct mechanisms of intergroup relations in two different systems, which will involve different processes and outcomes. In both categories, however, the opposing parties must eventually undergo a similar psychological change to form a new socio-psychological repertoire.

The second classification is more complicated. It refers to the causes of the conflict with the performed injustices, attributed responsibility for the outbreak of the conflict, and blame for the harmful and immoral acts committed during the conflict (see Asmal et al., 1997; Kriesberg, 1998b). While some conflicts are more or less symmetrical with regard to these acts, other conflicts are not, and then the peace-building process requires that they be seriously addressed. First, some intractable conflicts erupt in order to correct unjust deprivation as a result of discrimination or oppression, as in the case of South Africa, Algeria, or Guatemala. Second, some intractable conflicts erupt as a result of an aggression by one side that is more responsible for the conflict's outbreak, as in the case of Chechnya. Third, in some intractable conflicts extreme immoral acts are performed, sometimes mainly by one group, as in the example of the Rwandan conflict. In all these conflicts, there are special requirements to achieve lasting peace between both societies. There is a need to address the injustice, maltreatment, and immoral behavior. This is a difficult challenge because in most of the intractable conflicts each involved party perceives itself as the victim and the other side as being responsible for the outbreak of the conflict and the negative acts committed (Bar-Tal, Chernyak-Chai, Schori, & Gundar, 2009). Also, societies tend to deny and repress wrongdoing and do not take responsibility for their own immoral behavior (Bandura, 1999; Cohen, 2001).

STABLE AND LASTING PEACE

The desired end point of intractable conflict is a stable and lasting peace, which can be defined as consisting of *mutual recognition and acceptance after the reconciliation process, whose supreme goal is the maintenance of peaceful relations characterized by full normalization with cooperation in all possible domains of collective life that provide secure and trustful coexistence.* This view may look unrealistic and somewhat utopian, but in all the cases it provides a compass to the desired nature of peaceful relations (Bar-Siman-Tov & Kacowicz, 2000).

Development of these characteristics requires both structural and psychological changes; in fact, building stable and lasting peaceful relations is a major societal change that includes all aspects of individual and collective life (Kacowicz, Bar-Siman-Tov, Elgstrom, & Jerneck, 2000). With regard to the socio-psychological repertoire of society members, a change is needed not only in their worldview, feelings, beliefs, attitudes, emotions, motivations, and behavioral intentions but also in societal, cultural, and educational products, such as new symbols and narratives, information in mass media, ceremonies, leaders' speeches, books, films, and school textbooks. The fundamental requirement is that the new socio-psychological basis will be shared by the majority of society members and penetrate deeply into societal institutions, organizations, and channels of communication (Asmal et al., 1997; Bar-Tal, 2000b; Kriesberg, 1998b; Lederach, 1997). Thus, the essence of the process of building peace is changing the socio-psychological repertoire of the majority of society members and the societal culture into a new one (De Soto, 1999; Kelman, 1999b; Lederach, 1997; Shonholtz, 1998; Wilmer, 1998). Construction of a new socio-psychological repertoire is a necessary condition for the establishment of lasting peaceful relations between former rival groups, because then stable foundations that are rooted in the psyche of the people are formed.

Nevertheless, this psychological basis has to be reflected in the people's subjective experience. As Lederach (1997, p. 21) notes, "To be at all germane to contemporary conflict, peacebuilding must be rooted in and responsive to the experiential and subjective realities shaping people's perspectives and needs." With this necessary requirement, it is clear that the major socio-psychological change cannot take place without real structural changes and observable acts that lead to satisfaction of the societies' needs. Thus, on the one hand, the criteria for successful establishment of lasting peace are within the realm of psychology as society members have to hold and express their views about the new relationship and the rival. But, on the other hand, it is clear that these views cannot be based on an imagined situation or formed images without a solid basis in reality. In order to establish stable and crystallized new views, they have to be based on real and experienced changes in the life conditions of the individuals and the collective, as well as in acts that directly rectify the immoral behavior carried out before the conflict and during its course.

Although some of the structural changes can be decided, ordered, and implemented relatively quickly, the socio-psychological changes do not occur in the same way. They take place through the slow socio-psychological processes of information processing, persuasion, learning, reframing, recategorization, and formation of the new socio-psychological repertoire. The changes are based on the unfreezing process that eventually leads to formation of the new repertoire. These processes are slow because the psychological repertoire formed during the conflict is central and held with high confidence. Therefore, its change, which must encompass the majority of society members, is a complex, arduous, prolonged, and multifaceted task that needs to overcome many inhibiting factors.

The formation of the new repertoire that facilitates and supports the peace-building process should not be carried out through indoctrination, manipulation, or instruction. The goal is not to substitute one closed-mindedness with another but to develop the new socio-psychological repertoire on the basis of critical thinking, skepticism, opened-mindedness, personal responsibility, and freedom of thought. (It is beyond the scope of the present book to develop this idea because it requires considerable diversion from the present lines of thought.) When the society eventually constructs this new repertoire, the process indicates solidification of the culture of peace, which testifies to the transformation of the nature of the relations between the former rivals.

It is important to stress again before moving to the discussion of culture of peace that stable and lasting peace with the culture of peace can be built only if the peaceful settlement of the conflict satisfies at least the great majority of the society members involved in the conflict. Specifically it means that they accept the agreement as finalizing the conflict, creating a new peaceful relations; they view the agreement as being just and equitable; and they perceive it as satisfying the needs and rights of their party.

THE NATURE OF THE CULTURE OF PEACE

The culture of peace has the same general generic features as the culture of conflict discussed in Chapter 7 when societies saliently integrate into their culture tangible and intangible symbols that create a particular meaning about living in the context of peace (Geertz, 1973). The development of culture requires building new symbols, narratives, and rituals that explain, maintain, justify, and even glorify peace. The symbols provide worldviews, values, norms, practices, and institutions that reflect the desire to live in stable and lasting peace (Boulding, 2000; de Rivera, 2010). A peace culture,[1] on a very basic level, is a culture in which individuals, groups, and nations have cooperative relations with one another and manage their inevitable conflicts constructively. The United Nations General Assembly proposed eight bases for the culture of peace (United Nations, 1998): education for the peaceful resolution of conflict and maintaining peace; sustainable development (viewed as involving the eradication of poverty, the reduction of inequalities, and environmental sustainability); human rights; gender equality; democratic participation; understanding, tolerance, and solidarity (among peoples, vulnerable groups, and migrants within the nation, and among nations); participatory communication and the free flow of information; international peace and security (including disarmament and various positive initiatives).

I would add mutual trust; values of justice; sensitivity and consideration of the other party's needs, interests, and goals; equality of relations; and acceptance and respect of cultural differences. Above all, it requires recognition of

---

[1] Peace culture is usually viewed in a wide form as extending beyond the specific relations between the former rivals to a general perspective on intergroup relations. It is "a set of values, attitudes, modes of behaviour and ways of life that reject violence and prevent conflicts by tackling their root causes to solve problems through dialogue and negotiation among individuals, groups and nations" (UN Resolutions A/RES/52/13-UNESCO, 1995). In the present chapter, I limit its nature to particular intergroup relations for the sake of the conception.

the superiority and importance of peace as a value, goal, and practice (see also Brenes & Weseels, 2001; de Rivera, 2004; Fernández-Dols, Hurtado-de-Mendoza, & Jiménez-de-Lucas, 2004). The development of all these bases after intractable conflict is not a simple societal task. It requires major socialization efforts with the following goals that solidify the culture of peace.

Valuing peace and creating a new common vision. It is essential for the peace culture that peace be a supreme value. Both sides should view peace as a desirable and important value and as a superordinate goal. Still, it should be viewed in concrete and relevant terms, that is, as a realistic and achievable goal. Thus, both parties have to accept the terms of the peace accord as ending the conflict, support it, and internalize it, with the recognition of its rewards and costs, seeing it as just and fair. They must establish a common moral as well as utilitarian epistemic basis that negates completely the use of violence and justifies the terms of peace. Beyond grounding the value of peace, the peace culture requires creation of a new shared vision by the parties that were involved in conflict about the nature of peace and peaceful relations. This vision outlines common aspirations and goals for maintaining peace and reinforcing it continuously. It provides the basis for peaceful coexistence that has new rules, means, and practices – all in the service of building a stable and lasting peace. This vision, together with the epistemic basis, needs to be imparted to society members.

Mutual knowledge. Past rivals acquire knowledge about each other. The scope of knowledge should cover various domains, such as cultural, religious, societal, political, geographic, and historical. Knowledge is essential for the development of the peace culture because ignorance and selective, biased, or distorted information are often the causes of hostility, prejudice, and hatred. Mutual knowledge facilitates the development of acquaintanceship, recognition, and respect.

Mutual acceptance. Both sides accept each other on personal and national levels. It means mutual inclusion, legitimization, and humanization. Mutual acceptance is a condition for developing cooperative and friendly relations. Building and maintaining trustful relations is the key aspect in mutual acceptance. It serves as a basis for establishing a secure existence for each group, which is a necessary condition for stabilizing peace. Mutual acceptance includes complete elimination of delegitimization and reduction of negative stereotyping, on the one hand, and imparting personalization and humanization, on the other hand; cultivation of positive attitudes and emotions toward the other; individuation of the other group members and differentiation among various groups; and legitimization of the other side's perspective with its narrative, identity, and culture.

Mutual understanding. Going beyond knowing and accepting, both sides understand each other by developing perspective taking, empathy, and sensitivity to each other's needs, goals, values, traditions, and experiences. The parties realize that the other side has legitimate needs, aspirations, and goals and that they have to be satisfied in order to maintain stable and lasting peace. Such an understanding goes beyond mere acceptance and thus prevents eruption of many of the conflicts, as the two sides realize that the relationship is governed by the principle of mixed motives, which indicates that in a conflict both sides may lose and in peaceful relations both sides can gain.

Equality of relations. The peace culture is based on equality between the societies involved in the peaceful relationship. This is an important requirement as many of the conflictive relations are characterized by clear asymmetry in which one party often treats the rival party with disrespect, discrimination, exploitation, and even oppression. The peace culture thus requires restructuring of the relations not only on the psychological level but also in reality. This requires concrete political, economic, and cultural acts that bring equality of relations.

Valuing human rights, freedom, and justice. The culture of peace is based not only on the value of peace but also on other values that maintain peaceful relations between societies. Values of human rights, with all their kinds, as well as freedom and justice, are foundations of peaceful relations, and they have to be respected and highly valued. They are the safeguards that neither of the societies will take steps that violate principles of peace, and they provide a moral basis for mutual understanding, as well as common norms and practices. Internalization of these values and adherence to them creates a societal-political-cultural climate conducive to harmony and peace.

Respect for differences and focus on commonalities. The peace culture, on the one hand, respects pluralism and differences and, on the other hand, stresses commonalties and constructs future common goals. Both parties look for the commonalities and identify the differences and respect both, as both are vitally important for peace. This respect provides assurance to secure the existence of their own particular socio-cultural foundation, which is a condition for peaceful coexistence. Each group has to be able to fulfill its own needs, aspirations, and goals, including the need to hold its own collective identity and culture to the condition that they do not harm the other group or groups.

Development of cooperative relations. The development of cooperative relations between the two sides is necessary, as such relations are concrete expressions of the peace culture. They apply especially to the structural and concrete side of the peace culture and are an essential part of the evolved common vision. The cooperation has unlimited scope as it can be part of economic, political, cultural, military, educational, and environmental relations. Significant within cooperative relations are military and security mechanisms that guard the peaceful relations and prevent misperceptions and misunderstandings.

Secure existence and mechanisms for maintaining peace. The fundamental basis of the culture of peace is secure existence. Members of both societies feel secure and are without fear and anxieties about their collective existence, which always impinges on their individual being. The culture of peace projects safety and security on their different levels, including physical, political, cultural, and economic levels in the context of relations with the past rival. Therefore, the culture of peace places great emphasis on mechanisms that allow the maintenance of peace. Thus, various kinds of institutions, organizations, cooperatives, and exchanges, which all serve to solidify and crystallize peaceful relations, should be developed.

These goals for solidification of the peace culture have to be developed and then implemented in order to build foundations for peace. A real peace is not only a political process; it is also a way of life reflected in the perceptions, thoughts, feelings, and behaviors of individuals and nations alike. Like any other culture, the peace culture includes abstract and concrete expressions and products such as symbols, myths, language, collective memories, values, and goals. The symbols consist of such tangible and intangible elements as artifacts, constructions, artworks, scripts, habits, rules, concepts, narratives, myths, and knowledge related to a group and to other categories. These symbols have to be constructed and then imparted to society members.

The culture of peace evolves slowly through time in view of lasting and meaningful experiences. Its development requires not only the construction and opening of channels of communication that provide messages of the peace culture but also the establishment of new institutions, procedures, and practices that maintain the peace culture. Continuous peace education courses can socialize the young generation into the culture of peace as well as develop a civil society to promote and carry out people-to-people and dialogue projects. In addition, mass media have a role and a mission in maintaining peace, as do various cultural channels such as literature, films, or theatrical plays.

Construction of the peace culture as a major societal political-cultural change is a long process that is gradual, moving step by step, and based on careful planning, implementation, and evaluation. Its success depends on its continuity and reciprocal nature. Actions should be part of an ongoing process that is coordinated by both parties in each society, with consideration to its conditions. Construction of the peace culture needs to involve all sectors of the societies but has to be tailored to their particular abilities and needs.

Eventually, when the process is successful, the culture of peace is shared by society members who were involved in conflict, and it provides meaning about the reality of the society and the world in general. It supplies the rules and norms for practice, and this is a crucial element that serves as a safeguard of peace. When society members, at least the great majority, internalize the values, beliefs, attitudes, norms, and practices of the culture of peace, it is possible to characterize the society as being peaceful, and then its collective identity is imprinted by this characteristic. Construction of the culture of peace is the ultimate achievement of societies that engaged in intractable conflict through many years. Societies have difficulty fully achieving a culture of peace, and in some respect it remains a desired culture by those who cherish its values and nature. Various conditions facilitate the achievement of the culture of peace, and probably one of the most important conditions is successful reconciliation between two past rivals.

RECONCILIATION

Most of the students of peace building agree that at the heart of the formation or restoration of genuine peaceful relationships between societies that have been involved in intractable conflict, after its formal resolution, lies reconciliation (Ackermann, 1994; Arthur, 1999; Asmal et al., 1997; Bar-Tal, 2000b; Brouneus, 2008a; Chadha, 1995; De Soto, 1999; Gardner Feldman, 1999; Kelman, 1999b; Kopstein, 1997; Kriesberg, 1998b; Lederach, 1997; Lipschutz, 1998; Murray & Greer, 1999; Nadler, 2002; Norval, 1999; Shonholtz, 1998; Wilmer, 1998). Reconciliation constitutes the psychological societal process that is a necessary condition for building stable and lasting peace. It involves changes of motivations, goals, beliefs, attitudes, and emotions by the majority of society members (De Soto, 1999; Kelman, 1999b; Lederach, 1997; Nadler, 2002; Shonholtz, 1998; Wilmer, 1998). In fact, it is necessary that these changes will begin in a preagreement phase in order to facilitate the peaceful resolution of the conflict and its support by the society members. It is by its nature gradual, reciprocal, and voluntary. The fundamental requirement is that the psychological basis will penetrate deep into societal fabric so as to be shared by the majority of both rival groups of society members (Asmal et al., 1997; Bar-Tal, 2000b; Kriesberg, 1998b; Lederach, 1997; Staub, 2006). Only such change guarantees first the successful conflict resolution and later solidification of the peaceful relations between rival groups, because then stable foundations that are rooted in the psyche of the people are formed.

Although the concept of reconciliation has been known and used in social sciences for a long time, only in the past two decades has the study of reconciliation emerged as a defined area of interest (e.g., Arnson, 1999a; Asmal, Asmal, & Roberts, 1997; Bar-Siman-Tov, 2004; Krepon & Sevak, 1995; Lederach, 1997; Long & Brecke, 2003; Nadler, Malloy, & Fisher, 2008; Rothstein, 1999a). It evolved out of the recognition that there is a need to go beyond the traditional focus on conflict resolution, to expand the study of peacemaking and peace building to a macrosocietal perspective, which concerns transformation of relations between societies that were engaged in bloody conflict into completely different peaceful and cooperative relations.

In addition, it became clear that violent conflict that involved extensive harm and especially atrocities cannot be easily resolved. Societies that experienced severe harm have difficulty forgetting it and moving forward to build new relations with the rival. These cases require various processes that go beyond the peaceful settlement of the conflict to achieve forgiveness or healing, on the one side, and recognition, compensation, apology, or even punishment, on the other side. Finally, and not the least, some of the peace agreements, in order to achieve meaningful change of intergroup relations, also require restructuring of the society in order to address the needs of society members. Thus, the new major challenge refers not only to the necessity of resolving the conflict peacefully but also to the goal of changing completely the nature of the relationship between the formal rivals in order to construct lasting satisfactory peace for both parties.

This main societal change via the reconciliation process supports the peace as a new form of positive intergroup relations. In this process is established a completely new worldview functional to these new relations that serves as a stable foundation for the cooperative and friendly acts that symbolize them. It provides new socio-psychological foundations that eventually serve as a prism for interpreting new experiences and information. This long and complex process goes beyond the agenda of formal conflict resolution and even peacemaking to profound societal change of culture and identity. The process of reconciliation is the precondition for the construction of the culture of peace.

Reconciliation, though, is not an automatic process, but one that begins and proceeds under conditions that allow its development. It begins when the parties in conflict start to change their beliefs, attitudes, goals, motivations, and emotions about the conflict, about each other, and about future relations – all in the direction of reconciliation. Such changes usually begin before the conflict is resolved peacefully and in fact can lead to its peaceful resolution because, without changes in the socio-psychological infrastructure that support continuation of the conflict, its peaceful settlement is impossible to achieve in most of the cases. Chapter 9 elaborated on the social changes that are required for peaceful conflict resolution. In turn, the peaceful resolution of the conflict with the initiation of various measures to establish formal relations serves as a crucial catalyst for further socio-psychological changes, including reconciliation.

Reconciliation is an informal process that lasts for a long time and does not have a formal beginning or ending. It begins often at the societal periphery and them moves to the mainstream. Nevertheless, it does require participation of the formal institutions with planning, policies, and actions to be legitimate and institutionalized (see, e.g., Brouneus, 2008a). It is not a linear process of continuous change in the direction of peaceful relations but one of regressions and progression; it even may stop at a certain level without its full completion. The initiation of reconciliation and its successful continuation depend on such factors as level of intractability of the conflict and especially level of violence; realization that continuation of the conflict will cause great costs, while there are gains in the peace process; satisfactory peaceful resolution of the conflict; emergence of some level of trust between the rivals; support for the peace process in both societies, especially among leaders; reciprocal and synchronized conciliatory, cooperative, and peaceful acts between the former rivals; weakness of the opposition to reconciliation and its course of action; satisfaction of needs through the process; and support from the international community.

The socio-psychological changes may not encompass all society members, because a small section of a society may continue to harbor the wish to maintain the conflict, despite its resolution and the new existing peaceful climate. An example of such a situation is the German irredentist groups, which do not accept even today the peace agreement and reconciliation between Germany and Poland or between Germany and the Czech Republic (Gardner Feldman, 1999; Handl, 1997). However, reconciliation is not affected if these groups are small and marginal (as in the case of Germany), whereas most of the society, including its dominant groups, has internalized the socio-psychological basis of reconciliation.

Nature of Reconciliation

While most of the researchers agree on the importance of the socio-psychological basis in reconciliation, they are vague or disagree about its specific components and the needed conditions for its success. On a general level, most thinkers on reconciliation have recognized the importance of creating a common socio-psychological framework in order to promote the process of reconciliation (Asmal et al., 1997; Hayes, 1998; Hayner, 1999; Kopstein, 1997; Kriesberg, 1998b, Lederach, 1997; Volkan, 1998; Whittaker, 1999). They realize that during the conflict the rival parties had different views about the nature of their relations, about each other, and about themselves. To ensure reconciliation, these different views have to adjust and synchronize dramatically. The major question that should be posed is, What, then is the nature of the common socio-psychological framework?

The first condition for reconciliation is a complete change of view with regard to the rival group as described in Chapter 9. The rival, as was noted, has to be legitimized, differentiated, equalized, and personalized (Bar-Tal & Teichman, 2005). This change allows viewing the rival as a partner to peace and as a human entity that deserves humane, equal, and just treatment, as well as a partner for building new peaceful and lasting relations. In addition, reconciliation goes beyond the peaceful conflict resolution to the desire to transform the relations into new ones that place cooperation and peace at the center, together with sensitivity and care about the needs of the other group. This transformation is based on the recognition that both sides have legitimate contentions, goals, and needs, and there is a need to satisfy them in order to solve the conflict and then establish peaceful relations. This recognition, though, does not have to be completely symmetrical. In some conflicts, the contentions of one side may be more morally based and justified, as in the case of the conflict between whites and blacks in South Africa. These basic changes open the way for the process of reconciliation to progress.

Various definitional specifications have been proposed by different researchers, and some of them included behaviors that are required to achieve it. Thus, for example, Marrow (1999, p. 132) points out that reconciliation "is reestablishment of friendship that can inspire sufficient trust across the traditional split." In emphasizing trust, he asserts that the basic thrust of reconciliation is to be sensitive to others' needs, the principal question being not what they have to do, but what we have to do to promote the reconciliation process. According to Asmal et al. (1997, p. 46), reconciliation focuses on dealing with contradicting narratives as well as performed injustices: "the facing of unwelcome truths in order to harmonize incommensurable world views so that inevitable and continuing conflicts and differences stand at least within a single universe of comprehensibility."

Lederach (1997) concentrates mainly on intrasocietal reconciliation and posits four elements that can be extended also to intersocietal conflicts: *truth*, which requires open revelation of the past, including admission, acknowledgment, and transparency; *mercy*, which requires acceptance, forgiveness, compassion, and healing for building new relations; *justice*, which requires rectification, restitution, compensation, and social restructuring; and *peace*, which underscores a common future, cooperation, coordination, well-being, harmony, respect, institutionalized mechanisms for conflict resolution, and security for all the parties. This view is similar to Long and Brecke's (2003) model, which suggests that reconciliation is based on truth telling about the harm done by both parties, forgiveness that requires a new view of both parties, giving up retribution, construction justice, and building a new positive relationship. Kriesberg (2004) added to the list *regard*, which includes mutual recognition of humanity and identity of the societies.

Kelman (1999b) presented elaborated components of reconciliation in what he calls a "positive peace." In his view, reconciliation consists of the following components: solution of the conflict, which satisfies the fundamental needs of the parties and fulfills their national aspiration; mutual acceptance and respect of the other group's life and welfare; development of a sense of security and dignity for each group; establishment of patterns of cooperative interactions in different spheres; and institutionalization of conflict resolution mechanisms (see also Bar-Siman-Tov, 2004). In a later paper, he defined reconciliation as "the development of working trust, the transformation of the relationship toward a partnership based on reciprocity and mutual responsiveness, and an agreement that addresses both parties' basic needs" (Kelman, 2004, p. 119). In his view, reconciliation requires change of identity via a process of internalization.

Nadler (2002) regards reconciliation as consisting of two processes: of instrumental and socio-emotional reconciliation. Instrumental reconciliation, which has restructuring characteristics, consists of different types of cooperation between former adversaries with the goal of achieving conflict-free coexistence (e.g., to improve economic conditions, to increase reciprocal trade, or to build tourism). Socio-emotional reconciliation, focusing on specific psychological elements, concerns the "deeper" identity-related process of removing conflict-related identity threats through interactions in which parties confront the pain and humiliation that they had inflicted on each other. This reconciliation is based on the psychological premise suggesting that adversaries in protracted intergroup conflict experience threats to basic human needs (e.g., need for security, esteem, control) and that addressing these threats is a prerequisite to ending conflict (Burton, 1969; Kelman, 1997a).

Nadler's model, called the need-based model of reconciliation, which applies to asymmetrical conflicts, suggests that the nature of these threats is different for victims and perpetrators (Nadler & Shnabel, 2008). Victims experience a threat to the basic human need for gaining power, self-esteem, and self-control. In contrast, perpetrators experience a threat to the basic human needs for belongingness and acceptance by others. They fear that others will view them as morally deficient and therefore will exclude them from the moral community to which they aspire to belong (Tavuchis, 1991). Thus, Nadler and his colleagues proposed that readiness for reconciliation is expected to increase if the needs of both parties are satisfied in a process of social exchange between the group that was victimized and the group that was the perpetrator. The perpetrating group empowers the victimized group by apologizing and seeking the victim's forgiveness. These acts give the formerly powerless victim the power to grant forgiveness, withhold it, or grant it only when certain conditions have been met (e.g., payment of reparations). This is an empowering and equalizing experience for the victim. On the other hand, if the victimized group grants forgiveness, it removes the perpetrator's moral debt and provides a moral permit to this group to enter into the relevant moral community.

Studies to confirm hypotheses derived from the model show that when Israeli Jews were made to feel as perpetrators, they showed greater willingness to reconcile after having received a message of acceptance from an Israeli Arab who represented the victimized group in that context. In turn, Israeli Arabs, the victimized group, were more ready to reconcile after having received a message of empowerment from a representative of the Israeli Jews (Shnabel, Nadler, Ullrich, Dovidio, & Carmi, 2009). Importantly, readiness to reconcile was mediated by an increase in victims' feelings of empowerment and perpetrators' feelings of acceptance, respectively.

Dealing with the Past

As the process of reconciliation proceeds, there is agreement that the successful outcome requires the formation of a new common outlook of the past (Asmal et al., 1997; Chirwa, 1997; Gardner Feldman, 1999; Hayes, 1998; Hayner, 1999; Kriesberg, 1998b; Lederach, 1998; Norval, 1998, 1999). This requirement is based on the demand to reach truth. During the conflict, both parties accumulated many grievances toward the other side. Years of violence leave deep scars of anger, grief, a sense of victimhood, and a desire for revenge. Also, parties in conflict propagated and internalized opposing collective memories that focused on the evilness and the wrongdoing of the rival. Indeed, there is a substantial body of research suggesting that truth telling about past human rights violations can contribute to the process of reconciliation (Gibson, 2006; Hayner, 2001; Minow, 1999). The revelations concern discrimination, oppression, massive atrocities, and acts of moral transgressions – whether one side was mostly responsible for the massive violations or both sides performed these acts (Crocker, 1999; Little, 1999; Minow, 1999). Truth telling may lead to the formation of a new shared narrative about the past. Once there is a shared knowledge of the past, both parties can take a significant step toward achieving reconciliation. As Hayner (1999, p. 373) notes, "Where fundamentally different versions or continued denials about such important and painful events still exist, reconciliation may be only superficial."

Reconciliation implies that each party not just get to know what did happen to the other party during the conflict but truly acknowledge what happened in the past (Asmal et al., 1997; Gardner Feldman, 1999; Hayes, 1998; Hayner, 1999; Lederach, 1998; Norval, 1999). Acknowledgment of the past implies at least going beyond knowledge of the two narratives of the conflict to the recognition in the performed misdeeds (Hayner, 1999; Kopstein, 1997; Norval, 1999; Salomon, 2004). This is an important factor in reconciliation, because the collective memories of each party about its own past underpin the continuation of the conflict and obstruct peacemaking (Bar-Tal, 2007a). Reconciliation thus necessitates changing these societal beliefs (i.e., collective memories) about the past by learning about the rival group's collective memory and recognizing one's own past misdeeds and responsibility for the outbreak and maintenance of the conflict. Through the process of negotiation about the collective memories, in which one's own past is critically revised and synchronized with that of the other group, a new narrative emerges (Asmal et al., 1997; Hayes, 1998; Norval, 1998). With time, this new historical account of events should substitute the reigning past collective memory.

Auerbach (2009) proposes a gradual dealing with the contrasting narratives of the rival group on the way to reconciliation. The starting point of the process is becoming *acquainted* with the clashing narratives. Familiarity with the narratives paves the way to full acknowledgment of them and may prepare the ground for the expressions of empathy. Empathizing with the enemy can lead to the assumption of at least partial responsibility for wrongdoing, which may be followed by material restitution (a legally based formal step) and requests for forgiveness. The process reaches its end when the two sides seriously and genuinely consider replacing their ethnocentric narratives with new, integrated narratives, based on the mutual acknowledgment of past miseries and a joint vision of the future.

Dealing with the narrative of the rival is one of the key issues in any intractable conflict and its peace building. During the conflict, the struggle to uphold one's own narrative and to delegitimize the narrative of the rival is one of the major goals (Bar-Tal, Oren, & Nets-Zehngut, 2012). During the peace-building process, one of the major goals is not only to cease this struggle but also to eventually reconcile between the two contracting narratives and construct a new integrative and united narrative that both groups adopt. This process is necessary if the past rival groups aspire to engage in constructing the ethos of peace and go through the reconciliation process, which requires assuming responsibility for past misdeeds and for making a radical change to the view of the rival group. Achievement of this goal requires a long process that has a number of phases. On the general level, it requires inclusion of events that were omitted from the ingroup narrative, balancing the narrative in various parts, and providing a balanced interpretation of various events and processes. Formal steps involve the authorities of each group in the process of constructing the new narrative. Informal steps refer to the changes on the individual level and through various informal societal institutions and channels of communication that are not controlled by the authorities such as mass media.

Describing this process in its general framework I would like to note the following phases. First members of each group need *to agree to be exposed to the narrative of the rival group*. Then it is necessary *to reflect on it and to understand it*. As the next step there is need *to acknowledge the legitimacy of the rival perspective* to the events of the conflict. In the next phase group members need *to recognize* that the narrative of the ingroup, not unlike that of the rival, is selective, biased, and distortive to some degree. On the basis of this phase may come *an acceptance* of at least some parts of the rival's narrative – those that were validated as reflecting facts and truthful accounts of certain events. This acceptance may lead further to *incorporation* of parts of the other's narrative into own narrative. The final phase is the attempt *to construct one integrative narrative for both groups* as it happens when formal committees are set to achieve this goal (see Chapter 11, which also provides examples of writing common history). This process takes years and does not necessarily have to end with the final phase. It may stop in any phase.

Indeed, preoccupation with the past requires more than just knowing and acknowledging the rival's past and constructing a new shared history. First, conflicts can be based on long-term injustices carried out by at least one party to the conflict. Often either one or both parties performed serious misdeeds that violated moral codes. In these cases, one party or both parties need to go through a process of finding factual truth and apologizing in order to establish a new relationship. These processes involve forgiveness by the harmed party and then healing (Arthur, 1999; Hayner, 1999; Lederach, 1998; Shriver, 1995; Staub, 2000). They create a space where forgiveness can be offered and accepted.

Forgiveness

Forgiveness is usually defined as an emotional process that involves letting go of past anger and resentment following experienced unjust and intentional misdeeds performed by the other and readiness to build new relations (Baumeister, Exline, & Sommers, 1998). Roe (2007, p. 4) proposes that in the forgiving process "those who forgive must look beyond the violent acts to the humanity they share with their victimizers and recognize the inherent equality between them." Intergroup forgiveness (collective forgiveness) has been found to be a meaningful concept in several cultures and can be transposed to the political realm and embodied in processes such as truth commissions (Kadima Kadiangandu, Gauche, Vinsonneau, & Mullet, 2007; Kadima Kadiangandu & Mullet, 2007; Neto, Pinto, & Mullet, 2007). The element of intergroup forgiveness as a condition for reconciliation is important in cases of unequal responsibility, when one party is responsible for the outbreak of, maintenance of, or misdeeds done during the conflict (see Auerbach, 2004; Hamber, 2007; Helmick & Petersen, 2001). In some cases, of course, it applies to both groups. Forgiveness symbolizes psychological departing from the past and progressing to new peaceful relations (Lederach, 1998; Norval, 1999), and it greatly facilitates reconciliation (Staub, 2000, 2006). It requires a decision to learn new aspects about one's own group, to open a new perspective on the rival group, and to develop a vision of the future that allows new positive relations with the perpetrator (see Noor, Brown, & Prentice, 2008).

Eventually, forgiveness is found to be associated with a release of negative feelings toward the adversarial group (Gobodo-Madikizela, 2008; Tutu, 1999), greater intention for reconciliation (Noor, Brown, & Prentice, 2008), and increased prosocial behavior and willingness to have contact with members of the adversarial group (Wohl & Branscombe, 2005). As an example, an empirical study by Čehajić, Brown, and Castano (2008) among Bosnian Serbs investigated their readiness to forgive the misdeeds committed by Serbs during the 1992–1995 war in Bosnia and Herzegovina. The results show that good-quality contact mediated by empathy and trust toward the perpetrator group with its perception as being heterogeneous predicted forgiveness (see also Moeschberger, Dixon, Niens, & Cairns, 2005). Also, minimal social distance and common-ingroup identification were good predictors of the readiness to forgive. According to two studies of Protestants and Catholics in Northern Ireland, willingness to forgive lessened negative emotions such as fear and anger toward the opponent group (Tam et al., 2007, 2008). But, at a minimum, an apology or public recognition of wrongdoing is needed for forgiveness to even be contemplated and to have an intergroup impact (Kadima

Kadiangandu et al., 2007; Kadima Kadiangandu & Mullet, 2007; Mellor, Bretherton, & Firth, 2007; Shriver, 2001). In multimethodological studies in Northern Ireland about forgiveness, McLernon, Cairns, Lewis, and Hewstone (2003) report that memories about past victimization are alive, especially within the Catholic community. They point to the need to deal with this feeling through forgiveness on a collective level, if the two past rival communities try to advance their reconciliation process. Indeed, Auerbach (2004) suggests that forgiveness is a necessary reconciliation step but is not always possible, and it is not a sufficient condition for a successful reconciliation between former rivals. In her view, the success of forgiveness depends on the compatibility of the religious-cultural context, importance of the interests promoted through this move, the power of the perpetrator, the status of leaders who are supposed to ask for forgiveness, the authenticity of the request, and the time that has passed since the harmful acts.

Long and Brecke (2003) distinguish between "forgiveness" and "signaling" models of reconciliation. A forgiveness model is an emotionally guided process that includes truth telling and redefinition of identities. Its aim is to promote social harmony between former opponents, usually in intrastate conflicts. In contrast, goals of a signaling model are more limited. It intends to signal to the adversary that interaction with him is safe and coexistence is possible. The signaling model is common in international conflicts in which the end of conflict means coexistence between two separate national identities. The forgiveness model is required in intrasocietal conflicts where the end of conflict means that the former opponents need to live harmoniously within the boundaries of the same collective identity (Long & Brecke, 2003).

Healing

Some of the students of reconciliation emphasize the importance of healing that often follows forgiveness. Staub (2011) proposes that healing from psychological wounds in the context of a postviolence era is an important requirement for forgiveness and reconciliation. Healing refers to the restoration of healthy conditions, including the spheres of psychological well-being, free of negative feelings and thoughts (Boraine & Levy, 1995; Staub, 1998). It is healing in this view that allows emergence of a common frame of reference and permits and encourages societies to acknowledge the past, confess former wrongs, relive the experiences under safe conditions, mourn the losses, validate the experienced pain and grief, receive empathy and support, and restore broken relationship (Lederach, 1998; Long & Brecke, 2003; Minow, 1998; Montville, 1993; Staub, 1998, 2000, 2006). It creates a space where forgiveness can be offered and accepted. Montville (1993, p. 112) notes that "healing and reconciliation in violent ethnic and religious conflicts depend on a process of transactional contrition and forgiveness between aggressors and victims which is indispensable to the establishment of a new relationship based on mutual acceptance and reasonable trust."

Not all the thinkers on the subject of reconciliation, however, agree with this view. Some seriously question whether forgiveness and healing are possible, or even necessary (Gardner Feldman, 1999; Hayes, 1998; Horowitz, 1993; Minow, 1999). They agree that a collective reconstruction of the past is a necessary element in any reconciliation process, but they wonder if this can lead to healing and forgiveness. Especially in severely divided societies, like South Africa and Northern Ireland, this will be a very hard, if not impossible, objective to obtain. Hayes (1998, p. 33), for example, argues, "Reconciliation is not about the (individualism of) forgiveness of the dreadful and vile acts committed in the name of apartheid, but how all of us are going to act to build a new society."

Nets-Zehngut (2012) proposes an existence of a collective self-healing process, in which parties to intractable conflicts treat their conflicts' wounds independently of their opponents. This can be applied to asymmetrical conflicts as well. This process can be easily observed in the strong groups involved in direct and intentional acts of rehabilitation and restoration to help the harmed ingroup members. But the weaker party may also through the collective self-healing process take control of its own destiny, determining if, when, and how it will overcome the injuries incurred during the conflict. The weaker group may elevate the perceived self-efficacy – its own beliefs regarding its capacity to bring about certain outcomes and influence the future – and ameliorate its self-esteem (Bandura, 1997). It may even provide support of a different kind to the victims, trying to rehabilitate them on the psychological and physical levels. Nets-Zehngut shows that Palestinians, citizens of Israel, since the late 1960s embarked on a self-collective healing process because the Israeli authorities were not helpful in dealing with their major national trauma of the 1948 war.

Nets-Zehngut (2009) also proposes the existence of a passive healing process. The passive part of the definition denotes that healing – that is, the improvement of the psychological repertoire and the mutual relations – is advanced in the absence of deliberate activities aimed at achieving this goal stems rather from instrumental activities that are taken for utilitarian reasons. The essence of passive healing is cooperation, which is motivated by the interests of the parties. For example, parties may engage in economic cooperation in the interest of earning profits or visit one another as tourists for pleasure.

Members of parties to the conflict who take part in such cooperation may thus come to know each other and slowly change their mutual psychological repertoire to be more positive. This process in the long run contributes to the healing and eventually to the reconciliation process. Examples of this process from the Japan–South Korean relationship, Polish-German relations, and Greek-Turkish relations testify to the utility of this process.

Reconciliation between two rival societies can be greatly aided by a third party or parties who provide the framework, moral support, and even economic aid that facilitates and guides this difficult process. For example, various European states and world organizations are involved in the attempts at reconciliation in Bosnia following the violent war in the 1990s (see, e.g., Haider, 2009).

In summarizing that preceding discussion about the nature of reconciliation I would like to propose that it pertains to *restoration of psychological well-being, free of negative thoughts and feelings toward the rival – from the psychological wounds of the conflict – that leads to socio-psychological restructuring of relations between past rivals*. This can be achieved through mutual recognition and acceptance, open and free deliberation about past conflict, and by taking responsibility and correcting past injustices and wrongdoing. Thus, reconciliation refers to building new relations that allow moving beyond the experiences accumulated before the conflict and during the conflict. Reconciliation allows forming a new socio-psychological repertoire that can accommodate the past grievances and contentions and construct new views about the rival and the conflict and collective self. It is this new socio-psychological repertoire as a result of the reconciliation process that enables building new relations in line with the culture of peace.

Ethos of Peace

Certain types of socio-psychological changes in my view are necessary for reconciliation (Bar-Tal, 2000b, 2009; Bar-Tal & Bennink, 2004). On this basis, and focusing on cognitive foundations, I suggest that achievement of reconciliation requires changes in five themes of societal beliefs that were formed during the conflict: societal beliefs about the group's goals, about the rival group, about relations with the past opponent, about one's own group, and about peace. These new clusters of societal beliefs constitute the ethos of peace when they become central, provide dominant characterization to the society, and give particular direction for future aspirations (Bar-Tal, 2000a). The ethos of peace can develop in a postconflict context in which two groups build peaceful relations in two separate political entities – in their separate states, as well as in a context in which the two rival groups continue to live in one political entity.

Societal Beliefs about the Group's Goals. An important challenge for the reconciliation process is changing the societal beliefs regarding the justness of the goals that underlie the outbreak and maintenance of the conflict (Bloomfield, Barnes, & Huyse, 2003; Lederach, 1997). The new beliefs must present new goals for the society that have been shaped by the conflict-resolution agreement. They center on maintaining peaceful relations with the former enemy; are based on the broader vision and aspiration for the future that can be fulfilled only in the context of maintaining peace; and provide rationalization and justification for the new goals, including new symbols and myths.

Societal Beliefs about the Past Rival Group. An additional crucial objective of reconciliation is a change of the images of the adversary group (Kaufman, 2006; Kelman, 1999b; Theidon, 2006). It is important to legitimize, equalize, differentiate, and personalize its members (Bar-Tal & Teichman, 2005). In addition, trusting the rival is a central belief in the set of beliefs about the past rival. Janoff-Bulman and Werther (2008) introduce the concept of respect as a necessary condition for reconciliation, defining it as recognition and acknowledgment that the rival group has the equal right to shape its own destiny. It allows viewing the opponent as belonging to the category of acceptable groups, with which it is desired to maintain peaceful relations.

Societal Beliefs about the Relationship with the Past Opponent. During the conflict, the societal beliefs support confrontation and animosity (Bar-Tal, 1998a, 2007b). They focus on the grievances, contentions, harm done, and perpetrations of the other side that lead to feelings of frustrations, hatred, humiliation, and anger. Reconciliation requires formation of new societal beliefs about the relations between the two groups that were engaged in conflict (Gardner Feldman, 1999; Krepon & Sevak, 1995). These beliefs stress fairness, justice, and equality of relations, and they in turn serve as a basis for new friendly and cooperative relations. Both sides to past conflicts have to feel that the new relations have a completely new foundation based on fulfilled needs and goals of the society as a whole and of the society members as individuals. This feeling has to be shared by at least the majority of society members.

Societal Beliefs about the History of the Conflict. Reconciliation requires also a change of collective memories that were dominating the engaged societies during the conflict. There is a need to revise these narratives that fueled the conflict into an outlook on the past that is synchronized with that of the former rival (Barkan, 2000; Borer, 2006; Borneman, 2002; Conway, 2003; Rotberg, 2006; Salomon, 2004). These new beliefs about the relationship should also present the past conflictive relations within a new framework that revises the collective memory and forms a new narrative.

Societal Beliefs about One's Own Group. Reconciliation requires changing societal beliefs about one's own group. During the conflict, groups tend to view themselves in a one-sided way with self-glorification and self-praise, ignoring and censoring any information that may shed negative light on the group. But in the reconciliation process, the group must take responsibility for its involvement in the outbreak of the conflict, if that was the case, as well as its contribution to the violence, including immoral acts, and refusal to engage in peaceful resolution of the conflict. Thus, the new societal beliefs present one's own group in a more "objective" light, more critically, especially regarding its past behavior.

Societal Beliefs about Peace. Reconciliation requires forming new societal beliefs about peace. During the intractable conflict, the parties yearn for peace but view it in general, amorphic, and utopist terms, without specifying its concrete nature and realistic ways to achieve it. Reconciliation requires forming new societal beliefs that describe the multidimensional nature of peace, realistically outline the costs and benefits of achieving it, connote the meaning of living in peace, and specify the conditions and mechanisms for its achievement and its maintenance. For lasting peace, the well-being of the two sides is in the interest of both parties, and hence peace also requires ongoing sensitivity, perspective taking, attention, and care for the needs and goals of the other group.

These themes of societal beliefs constitute the foundations of the *ethos of peace*, which is an opposing societal infrastructure to the ethos of conflict. It evolves when societies embark on the road to peace. But it takes a long time until these societal beliefs penetrate into the societal fabric and become an ethos, which underlies the peace culture.

Positive Emotional Orientation

Reconciliation also requires construction of general new collective emotional orientation that focuses on positive affect and specific emotions about the peaceful relations with the past opponent. Positive affects need to accompany the described beliefs and indicate good feelings that the parties have toward each other and toward the new relations. With regard to emotions, reconciliation requires a change in the collective emotional orientations of fear, anger, and hatred, which often dominate societies in intractable conflict. Instead, there is a need to develop at least an emotional orientation of hope as presented in Chapter 9, which reflects the desire for positive goals of maintaining peaceful and cooperative relations with the other party. This emotional orientation indicates a positive outlook for the future, expectations of pleasant events, and an absence of violence and hostilities (Averill, Catlin, & Chon, 1990; Bar-Tal, Halperin, & de Rivera, 2007; Jarymowicz & Bar-Tal, 2006; Kaufman, 2006; Snyder, 2000; Staub, Pearlman, Gubin, & Hagengimana, 2005).

Finally, a pillar of the new repertoire that is of crucial importance for reconciliation is a sense of security that society members have to experience. Maslow (1970) views security as one of the basic needs that has to be satisfied. A sense of security with feelings of satisfaction, tranquillity, contentment, and peace is important. Lack of security is accompanied with frustration, fear, and dissatisfaction and may lead to extreme behaviors, including violent conflicts, wars, and even genocide (Staub & Bar-Tal, 2003). Sense of security is similar to hope, as it also is based mainly on the cognitive foundations, accompanied by general good feelings (Bar-Tal & Jacobson, 1998; Smith & Lazarus, 1993). Lack of security is based on appraisal of an event, condition, or situation (all are parts of a context) as an indicator of possible threat or danger (primary appraisal) and on an evaluation of available defenses and the ability to cope with the perceived threat or danger (secondary appraisal). Accordingly, people form beliefs about being secure when they do not perceive threats or dangers, or even when they perceive threats or dangers, which they believe they are able to overcome. But it should be recognized that this is a multidimensional concept, as individuals and collectives differentiate among domains in which they can appraise security. Security may refer independently to such domains as physical survival, economic welfare, or cultural well-being. It can also refer to individual and collective security separately (Bar-Tal, Jacobson, & Freund, 1995). Reconciliation demands a sense of security in the relationship with the past rival. No threat and danger should be detected as coming from either side.

Reconciliation and Societal Changes

Lasting peace cannot develop without acts that directly deal with the foundations of the socio-psychological repertoire that evolved through the many years of conflict. In other words, it cannot be achieved without structural processes that are interwoven with the psychological processes. Rouhana (2011, p. 295) proposes that "reconciliation is a process that seeks a genuine, just, and enduring end to the conflict between the parties and transformation of the nature of the relationship between the societies through a course of action involving intertwined political and social changes and which addresses both politically tangible issues such as distribution of power and constitutional arrangements as well as intangible issues such as historical truth and historical responsibility; as such, this process has psychological correlates that emerge concurrently with the course of action." Reconciliation thus requires societal, legal, political, and psychological processes of restructuring of the power distribution, democratic arrangements, and constitutional guarantees for equality and human rights within a framework of restorative justice, and "reaching inter-subjective agreements on historical truths and addressing the issue of historical responsibilities for the mass violations of human rights that have occurred in whatever forms." This reconciliation process must address justice, truth, historical responsibility, and restructuring of the social and political relationship (Rouhana, 2004a, 2008). Similarly, Stephan (2008, p. 370) believes that reconciliation requires "repairing the fundamental institutions of a functioning society," with greater emphasis on inclusiveness and equality, enactment of new laws to prevent discrimination and exclusionary policies, establishment of "truth and reconciliation commissions," and prosecution of crimes against humanity.

In these approaches, the socio-psychological changes are concomitant to socio-political changes. This is a difficult, demanding, and complex process that is especially important in asymmetrical conflicts, if the strong party is interested in building completely new relations with the former rival by transforming the nature of the relationship and the structure of the institutions, power structure, and even wealth distribution. Such processes have taken place in South Africa, when eventually the majority of black people began to govern the state with the transformation of power with constitutional and institutional changes, after decades of apartheid. It is a unique case where the majority eventually assumed power. But it is hard to think about other examples of transformation processes of the same scope and depth. In other cases, the strong party does not willingly yield the power and resources, even if it agrees to a peaceful conflict settlement and a process of reconciliation. The processes of reconciliation in Guatemala and El Salvador are examples of these latter cases. Often the desired outcomes fall far behind the changes in reality.

In the next part I would like to elaborate on the lines of actions and structural changes that are needed in order to establish the socio-psychological repertoire that solidifies stable and lasting peaceful relations.

LINES OF ACTIONS AND STRUCTURAL CHANGES

The literature on the process of reconciliation specifies certain policies and practices that are considered necessary for constructing stable and lasting peaceful relations (e.g., Ackermann, 1994; Canas & Dada, 1999; Corm, 1994; Elhance & Ahmar, 1995; Gardner Feldman, 1999; Lederach, 1997; Weiwen & Deshingkar, 1995). In all the cases, however, the essential part in the structural acts is to treat the other side with respect, justice, equality, and sensitivity to its needs and goals. But an important prerequisite for building even cold peace is the cessation of violent acts. Continuation of violence is the most serious obstacle to the peace-building process. It serves as a signal and instigator to the evocation of emotions, attitudes, and beliefs of the culture of conflict that fuel continuation of the conflict. Therefore, one of the most important challenges for the parties in the peace-building process is to invest effort, persuasion, and resources to stop the violence of the members of one's own group and adhere to the principle of peaceful conflict resolution. This requires the establishment of mutually accepted structural mechanisms that can resolve any possible conflict and disagreement that can erupt after signing the documents of peaceful conflict resolution. But because it is almost impossible to control every member and group, there is a need to frame and act in view of the violence of the other society in a way that will calm down one's own society members and allow continuation of the peace-building process.

In the postconflict era, when both parties still lack trust and are insensitive to the other side's needs, establishing structural mechanisms to prevent violence represents a major challenge in their peace efforts. These may include not only the mechanisms to resolve conflicts but also many measures to reduce the perception of threat and feelings of fear that often underlie the eruptions of violence. Such measures may include establishment of military cooperation, building a system of warning, sharing information, demobilization of military forces, disarmament, and demilitarization of territories. All these steps facilitate the development of trust and positive perceptions (Ball, 1996; Canas & Dada, 1999; Spalding, 1999). An example of such acts can be seen in the reconciliation process in Nicaragua, which involved disarmament and demobilization of the Contras forces supervised successfully by the International Commission for Support and Verification (CIAV) set up by the Organization of American States (Sereseres, 1996). Another example is the confidence-building measures taken to improve the Israeli-Egyptian relations, which consisted of restricting military movements close to the borders and creating international forces (MFO) to supervise the disengaged parties.

In more advanced steps of peace building, there must be equalized interactions between the parties, together with political and economic restructurings that lead to new and cooperative links that stabilize peaceful relationships (Ackermann, 1994; Elhance & Ahmar, 1995; Gardner Feldman, 1999; Weiwen & Deshingkar, 1995). The literature focused on such structural elements as exchanging representatives in various political, economic, and cultural spheres; maintaining formal and regular channels of communication and consultation between the leaders of the states; developing joint institutions and organizations; developing reciprocal trade; developing cooperative economic ventures; exchanging information and developing cooperation in different areas; developing free and open tourism; developing educational coordination; and exchanging cultural products. These structural elements of stable and lasting peace described in the last chapter pertain mainly to cases in which the rivals live in two states, or in which they separate and begin to live in two states (see Charif, 1994; Corm, 1994; Lederach, 1997; Lipschutz, 1998; Murray & Greer, 1999; Saidi, 1994; Wilmer, 1998).

In cases where the rival parties will have to live under the same political system (as, e.g., in South Africa, El Salvador, Guatemala, Nicaragua, or Northern Ireland), the focus is on long-term processes of reconstruction, redistribution, restructure, restabilization, and rehabilitation of the society. They aim at internal institutional reforms, mostly in the political, legal, and economic systems. Stable and lasting peace requires political integration: the inclusion of all groups in the power system, the establishment of structural equality and justice, and the observance of human and civil rights, as well as democratic rules of political governance (Arnson, 1999b; Corm, 1994; Corr, 1995; Kriesberg, 1998b; Lederach, 1998; Murray & Greer, 1999; Zalaquett, 1999).

As a specific example, Fitzduff (2002) notes structural changes that took place in Northern Ireland on the way of peace building. Already in the early phase of peacemaking, there were programs to reduce and eliminate discrimination of Catholics in housing. Also, in order to correct political discrimination, new local council boundaries were drawn and a proportional representation system of voting was introduced. The government began to change policies in social and economic spheres to increase Catholics' employment and divide resources and funding in order to end their economic and social discrimination. Finally, special efforts were made to stop violence by delegitimizing use of the paramilitary forces and to change security policies by diversifying security forces and changing their way of operation.

In addition, the emphasis on the development of new rules of law and addressing questions of justice for human rights violations have became critical components of the attempts to deal with pervasive violence and ultimately a key part of ensuring reconciliation and lasting peace. Past experiences demonstrated clearly that the consolidation of peace in the immediate postconflict period, as well as the maintenance of peace in the long term, cannot be achieved unless the population is confident that redress for grievances can be obtained through legitimate structures for the peaceful settlement of disputes and the fair administration of justice. Thus, achievement of justice, peace, and democracy should be seen as complementary activities to socio-psychological change in these societies rather than as mutually exclusive objectives (UN Security Council, 2004). *Transitional justice*, which involves legal, political, and cultural restructuring, is useful here (Teitel, 2000).

Transitional Justice

Transitional justice is associated with political change, characterized by different legal responses to confront the wrongdoings of repressive predecessor regimes and generally mass violations of human rights during the conflict that may include ethnic cleansing and genocide (Deutsch, 2000; Freeman, 2006; Kritz, 1997; O'Donnell & Schmitter, 1986; Teitel, 2000, 2003a, 2003b). In some conflicts, one side is clearly responsible for unjust acts, but in others both sides share the blame. The restoration of justice depends much on the nature of the particular conflict and the nature of transgressions performed during its duration. The transitional justice process thus has directed its focus on the legitimized and institutionalized exploitation, discrimination, wrongdoing, and oppression of a group or groups. It concerns correction of the inequalities, punishing those responsible for the unjust system, prosecution of perpetrators, establishing inquiries into specific atrocities, undertaking truth commissions to investigate patterns of abuse, vetting major actors from a previous regime or dismissing them, and development of reparations and compensation programs to assist victims.

The fundamental assumption underlining these processes is that trials and prosecutions of human rights offenders are aimed at preventing perpetrators from reoffending, deterring others from committing similar crimes in the future, ensuring accountability for past crimes, and altering how individuals and groups might operate and relate to one another in a restructured society. Also, trials have the purpose of removing harmful elites, spoilers, or agents of conflict and entrepreneurs of violence from political life in order to reduce intergroup tension (Arthur, 2009). In essence, all these objectives come to strengthen greatly the process of reconciliation and solidify it by establishment of policies, practices, institutions, and mechanisms that construct more democratic, peaceful, and just societies.

The international community, according to defined international criteria of justice, sometimes blames one side more than the other (Asmal et al., 1997). Such international judgment can affect the reconciliation process. When one side is attributed more responsibility than the other for injustice performed in the course of the conflict (as in the cases of interstate conflict between Japan and Korea or between Germany and Poland and in the cases of intrastate conflict in South Africa or Chile), then this side is often required to take special steps in the reconciliation process (e.g., paying reparations, stating apology). In the Balkans, for example, the Dayton agreement gave each Bosnian family the right to return to its prewar home, if it so desires, or alternatively to receive compensation for the lost property (Woodward, 1999).

Through the years, concrete steps were taken to address the legal issues of justice following violent conflicts, some by the international community. As an illustration, the ad hoc International Criminal Tribunal for the former Yugoslavia (ICTY) was established in 1993, and the International Criminal Tribunal for Rwanda (ICTR) was established in 1994. In 1995 the International Committee of the Red Cross produced an explanatory interpretation of the amnesty provision of Article 6(5) of Protocol II to the 1949 Geneva Conventions, interpreting its broad wording as implicitly limited to the release of those detained for having participated in hostilities rather than those who violated international humanitarian law. In 1998 the Rome Statute established the International Criminal Court (ICC), which, although originally conceived as a response to interstate conflict, was eventually established against the backdrop of widespread intrastate conflict and associated transitional justice developments.

Of special note is the establishment of the International Center for Transitional Justice in 2001, which has become a major peace-promoting organization, working in dozens of countries and playing key roles promoting reconciliation and peace throughout the world. The importance of transitional justice is manifested also in a series of papers published in 2010 by the secretary-general to the United Nations on the role of law, some of which deal specifically with transitional justice. Also, the United Nations Human Rights Council has announced it will establish a mandate for a special rapporteur on the promotion of truth, justice, reparation, and guarantees of nonrecurrence of serious crimes and gross violations of human rights.

The landmark of transitional justice mechanisms that served as a paradigmatic example to many societies in building their stable and lasting peace is the establishment of the South African Truth and Reconciliation Commission (TRC) in 1995.

Political and Economic Restructuring

Many analysts suggest that democratization is the first condition for reconciliation in situations of intrastate conflict (Arnson, 1999b; Charif, 1994; Corr, 1995; Zalaquett, 1999). Democratization consists of establishing democratic rules and realizing formal democratic procedures that include freedoms of expression and the right to political organization and political activity (Arnson, 1999b; Azburu, 1999; Charif, 1994; Corr, 1995; El-Hoss, 1994; Lipschutz, 1998). The electoral system should be perceived by all parties as free and fair and should create incentives that reward moderation (Canas & Dada, 1999; Horowitz, 1993). Moreover, it should be possible to replace the political and military leaders who were associated with the abuses performed during the conflict. Democratization should lead to a new distribution of political power, restoration of civil and human rights, emergence of new democratic political institutions and organizations, enforcement of democratic principles and rules of governance, and wide political participation. Developing a political culture that centers around democratic values of freedom, equality, and justice is also one of the fundamental principal values for democratization. Reliance only on structural democracy without developing democratic culture hinders the functioning of democracy.

In this regard, it is also of importance to establish a legal system that is independent of the political, economic, and military bases of power. This system should be managed with the principles of justice, equality, and fairness (Azburu, 1999). In essence, the reconciliation process requires the evolvement of civil society, whose values, laws, and norms support peaceful and democratic life (Azburu, 1999; Clements, in press; Spalding, 1999).

Political restructuring may require the creation of new structures of governance. An example is participatory governance, which means a reduction in state activity and increased responsibility at the local level. Participatory governance is a way of involving the civil society in the process of reconciliation. This type of governance is promoted in some regions in Northern Ireland in the form of partnerships, which consist of local interest groups of elected community representatives and representatives from business, trade unions, and statutory agencies. The goal of these partnerships is to reinforce a peaceful and stable society and to promote reconciliation by increasing economic development and employment, promoting urban and rural regeneration, developing cross-border cooperation, and extending social inclusion (Murray & Greer, 1999).

In addition to political processes, economic processes are also an important condition for reconciliation. Whether the rival groups will live in one state or in two, the improvement of the economic situation of all members of the groups is always important (Rothstein, 1999b). Individuals in all the groups have to feel that peaceful relations are worthwhile, that is, are responsible for the reconstruction of the economy after the conflict, for facilitation of economic growth and employment, and for increased standards of living. These economic benefits constitute powerful tools of investment in peace because they mobilize group members to support the peace process and turn them into interest groups with the goal of maintaining peace. Therefore, special efforts are often made to provide financial support, investments, and economic planning in the postconflict period by various national and international organizations and institutions. An example of such efforts can be seen in Bosnia, where the World Bank, European Bank for Reconstruction and Development, and United Nations Development Program provided the money, plans, and personnel to reconstruct the country for all the groups that accepted and cooperated with the Dayton Agreement (Woodward, 1999).

Economic processes are necessary to foster economic interdependence, to include all groups in economic development, and to erase past discrimination and inequalities (Charif, 1994; Corm, 1994; Elhance & Ahmar, 1995; El-Hoss, 1994; Weiwen & Deshingkar, 1995). They can include redistributing land, wealth, and economic power; allowing equal opportunity for economic participation; and providing compensation to groups that have suffered systematic discrimination. This can be achieved by setting superordinate goals that are agreed on by all the parties, constructing inclusive identities, and abolishing all forms of discrimination (Charif, 1994; Corr, 1995; Horowitz, 1993; Kriesberg, 1998b; Lipschutz, 1998; Murray & Greer, 1999; Saidi, 1994; Wilmer, 1998; Zalaquett, 1999).

If the rival groups are going to live in different political systems, the focus should be on creating economic and political linkages that foster cooperation (Ackerman, 1994; Barua, 1995; Elhance & Ahmar, 1995; Ganguly, 1995; Gardner Feldman, 1999; Weiwen & Deshingkar, 1995). This can be achieved by stimulating political and economic interdependence. There are numerous structural measures that both groups can take in order to foster the reconciliation process. These include developing diplomatic relations, visits of leaders, trade, exchanges of delegations, developing joint economic projects, and developing cooperation in different areas of common interest. All the structural measures must be realized on the basis of equality and sensitivity to the parties' needs and goals. A successful example of structural process was the development of peaceful relations between France and Germany after War World II. In 1951 the two countries established an economic union for coal and steel production as

```
                    ┌─────────────────────────────┐
                    │ Context of Intractable Conflict │
                    └─────────────────────────────┘
                                 │  Change of conflict supporting
                                 │  repertoire
                                 ▼
                    ┌─────────────────────────────┐
                    │    Peace-Making Process      │
                    └─────────────────────────────┘
                                 │
                                 ▼
                    ┌─────────────────────────────┐
                    │  Peaceful Settlement of the  │
                    │          Conflict            │
                    └─────────────────────────────┘
                          ╱              ╲
                  Construction of
                  Ethos of Peace
                       ╱                      ╲
        ┌──────────────────────┐      ┌──────────────────────┐
        │ Socio-psychological  │      │  Acts of Peace Building │
        │Process of Reconciliation│   │                      │
        └──────────────────────┘      └──────────────────────┘
                       ╲     Construction of      ╱
                             Culture of Peace
                         ╲                    ╱
                         ┌──────────────────┐
                         │    Stable and    │
                         │  Lasting Peace   │
                         └──────────────────┘
```

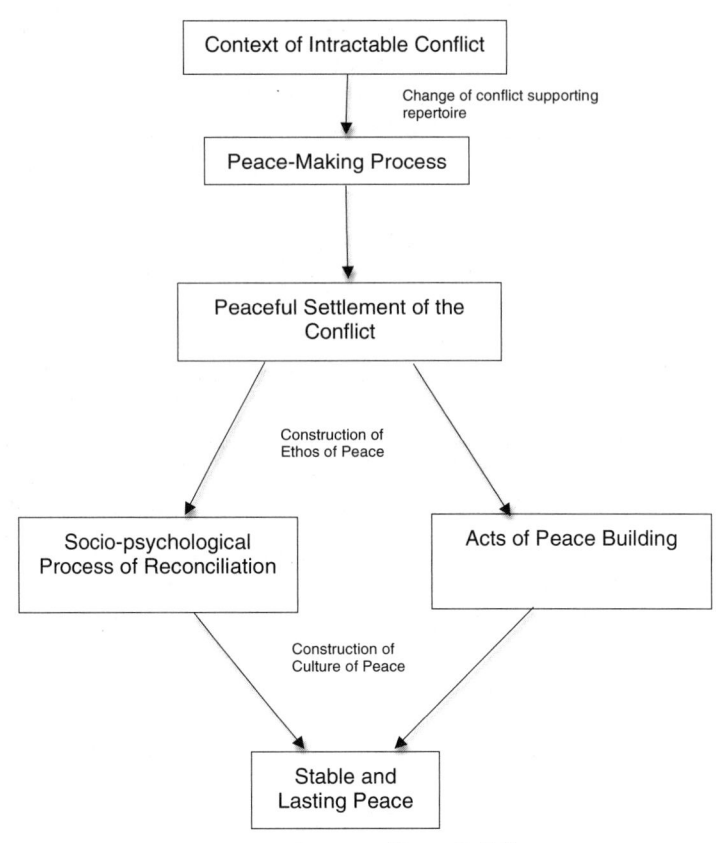

FIGURE 6. Process of Peace Building

one of the first steps in the reconciliation process. Later, in 1963 the Franco-German treaty was signed, which institutionalized many of the structural acts to speed the process of reconciliation (e.g., regular meetings between foreign, defense, and education ministers). In 1988 the Franco-German Cultural Council was established, and in 1995 even joint military units were formed (Ackermann, 1994). Another example of structural process is the creation of the extensive economic and political linkages between Germany and Poland. Building on the 1991 treaty, the two states established various cooperative ventures to promote reconciliation processes such as the Fund for German-Polish Cooperation, the German-Polish Economic Promotion Agency, the Committee for Cross-Border Collaboration, and the Committee for Interregional Collaboration (Gardner Feldman, 1999). On another continent, India and Pakistan have been trying to reconcile their differences for decades. In 1983 the two countries signed an agreement to establish a joint commission to strengthen their relations and to promote cooperation in economics, health, science and technology, sports, travel, tourism, and consular matters (Elhance & Ahmar, 1995).

The conception of a stable and lasting peace, the culture of peace, reconciliation, and the ethos of peace indicate the difficult, long, and complex way that societies have if they are interested in the transformation of their relations after being engaged in intractable conflict. Although these conceptions provide a general direction, reality often collides with the desired goals. Still, it is important to illuminate these goals in the same way that social scientists discuss concepts such as democracy, justice, freedom, or human rights as a desired reality. The present chapter tries to make this type of contribution. It elaborates on the nature of the stable and lasting peace with the culture of peace that is achieved through reconciliation as well as acts of political, societal, economic, and cultural restructuring. This part of the peace-building process is based on peacemaking process described in Chapter 9 (see Figure 6). In its totality, the peace-building process changes dramatically the nature of relations between the former rivals. The next chapter elaborates on a number of methods that facilitate and even enable this process.

11

Peace Building

Processes and Methods

On the general level it is important to recognize that while the process of building stable and lasting peace with reconciliation may begin with the leaders or the grass roots, to be effective it must always proceed from the top down and the bottom up simultaneously. Leaders with the elite and the grass roots have to make an active effort to transform the relations between the former rivals. While the socio-psychological change of leaders, especially from the mainstream, greatly influences the society members, the evolution of the mass movement that embraces the socio-psychological change has an effect on the position of the leaders. Still there are differences; for example, in Rwanda the attempt to promote the reconciliation is mostly characterized by a top-down process, where the postgenocide Tutsi-led government has tried to lead the peace-building process. In contrast, the movement in peace building in Northern Ireland, especially during the 1990s, can be characterized as being a bottom-up process with the help of the leaders. The grass-roots organizations embedded in the civil society have been the energizing forces in the peace-building process.

Eventually, however, leaders are of crucial importance, because they negotiate the peaceful resolution of the conflict and are in the position to direct the peace-building process with reconciliation (e.g., Mandela and de Klerk in South Africa; see Bargal & Sivan, 2004; Lieberfeld, 2009). For example, Lieberfeld (2009) points out that Mandela's capacities for emotional control, empathy, cognitive complexity, optimism about change, and his intellectual abilities influenced his way in leading blacks in South Africa toward peacemaking and reconciliation. But in many cases there was significant support for peace-building efforts. The success of the process depends on the dissemination of its ideas among the grass roots. An essential and necessary element is to convince the masses to change their socio-psychological repertoire, from supporting the conflict to favoring the emergence of stable and lasting peaceful relations with reconciliation. Nevertheless, there are cases in which peaceful settlement of a conflict takes place without the support of the society members (e.g., in the case of the Israeli-Egyptian peace agreement, there was lack of support in the Egyptian society). However, this type of settlement, termed a cold peace, does not allow progress in peace building beyond this phase.

In general, then, the process of peace building beyond the peaceful settlement of a conflict requires support of the grass roots. But it also requires policies set by leaders that aim at changing the socio-psychological repertoire of society members (Ackerman, 1994; Gardner Feldman, 1999; Kelman, 1999; Shonholtz, 1998; Volpe, 1998). These policies cannot merely be relayed in statements and speeches but must be reflected in formal acts that symbolically communicate to society the change in the relationship with the past rival. The formal acts, as already noted in Chapter 10, should occur in various spheres, beginning with formal meetings between the representatives of the rival groups, later between the leaders, then the establishment of formal relations, followed by political, economic, and cultural acts. These acts must be institutionalized and must encompass many society members, institutions, and organizations (Chadha, 1995; Kelman, 1999; Kriesberg, 1998b; Lederach, 1998; Norval, 1999).

The mobilization of the masses for the transformation of the relations is also performed by middle-level leaders – that is, prominent figures in ethnic, religious, economic academic, intellectual, and humanitarian circles (Khalaf, 1994; Lederach, 1997; Lipschutz, 1998; Thompson, 1997). In this process, elites play an important role. The elites include also those individuals who hold high-level positions in powerful public and private organizations and influential movements (Kotzé & Du Toit, 1996). These individuals can take an important part in initiating and implementing policies of peace building, including reconciliation and reconstruction (Ackermann, 1994; Chadha, 1995; Lederach, 1998). At the grass-roots level, local leaders, businessmen, community developers, local mental health experts, and educators can play an important role in initiating and implementing policies of peace building (Chetkow-Yanoov, 1986; Lederach, 1998; Thompson, 1997).

In essence, the evolvement and the solidification of stable and lasting peace are dependent on the development of the culture of peace. The culture of peace goes beyond acts and processes of reconciliation that focus on the repertoire of society members. It is the ultimate safeguard that the peace process is routinized deeply into the institutions and channels of communication of the society. Because the intractable conflict precedes it, facilitating the peace-building process requires different methods that entail two major goals: to change the socio-psychological repertoire of the societies involved and to transform the nature of the relations between former rivals. Both goals are interrelated. The change of the repertoire facilitates greatly the transformation of the relations, and then the transformation of the relations with real acts of reconstruction leads to change of the socio-psychological repertoire. This is the constructive circle that builds the stable peace.

METHODS OF PEACE BUILDING

Methods to facilitate peace building, and specifically reconciliation, have been proposed in the literature. Some are applied generally to the process of peace building, others only to the reconciliation process. They can be part of the formal policies or carried out voluntarily and informally. Some can be applied in an early stage of peace building, others only in later stages when the foundation of mutual trust is built and the relations are going through transformation. All, however, serve as mechanisms to change society members' motivations, goals, beliefs, attitudes, and emotions in the direction of building peace cultures and establishing a stable and lasting peace. These methods can be used for the interstate as well as the intrastate peace-building process. The process of peace building depends on the will and abilities of the society members. It does not happen by itself but requires resources, leadership, planning, organization, implementation, and persistence. This last part of the book will begin with the description of the methods that are important especially for the early phases of peace building, even without peaceful settlement of the conflict, and then move to methods that can be used in the advanced phases of the peace-building process.

Contact between People

Contact between members of the rival groups may take place in any phase of peace building and is the most general method to facilitate it. In fact, contact between members of the rival groups to change beliefs, attitudes, and emotions and improve the relations between them is one of the most commonly researched methods. This method was used by Sherif and his colleagues in their ingenious field experiments that investigated ways of resolving a conflict peacefully (Sherif, Harvey, White, Hood, & Sherif, 1961). After creating a conflict between two groups of campers, the researchers began to move the two groups toward conflict resolution, and contact between them was one of the used methods. Eventually the idea of bringing together members of two hostile groups to change their negative intergroup repertoire was conceptualized in the framework of a *contact theory* that was originally proposed by

Allport (1954) and then advanced by many social psychologists (e.g., Amir, 1969; Brown & Hewstone, 2005; Pettigrew, 1998). It suggests that when members of two groups, who initially have mutually negative repertoires involving each other, come in contact, they may change their repertoires in a more positive direction after they get to know each other in a personalized and humanized manner. This change is facilitated greatly when the encounter between the two groups takes place under the particularly favorable conditions that were specified by the researchers. They include equal status of the group members in contact, pursuit of common goals, intergroup cooperation, and institutional support. Pettigrew and Tropp (2006) summarize this line of research in a large-scale meta-analysis based on 713 independent empirical studies conducted over 60 years. This analysis supports the hypothesis that contact results in reduced prejudice and that the conditions specified by Allport for an ameliorative intergroup contact of positive, equal, cooperative cross-group contact within a supportive social context have salutary effects on intergroup relations.

In cases of peace building, contact between members of the rival societies may serve as a method of changing the negative view that each side has about the other. In the case of violent and prolonged conflict, contact is important because groups in conflict often live in separate places. Contact between members of rival societies can take place in any phase of peace building and even during the conflict, but encounters that are designed to improve intergroup relations can be critical in changing the negative sociopsychological repertoire. In many cases, the encounters take place during the conflict, but usually they are increasingly planned during the attempt to reconcile the two societies. In general, studies show that once the violence ends, contact contributes positively to reconciliation in the form of reducing prejudice and increasing forgiveness and trust (see Pettigrew & Tropp, 2006, 2008; Tropp & Pettigrew, 2005; Turner, Hewstone, Voci, Paolini, & Christ, 2007). Nevertheless, in cases of organized encounters between members of the rival groups, the effectiveness of the contact also depends on such factors as its duration, the underlying conception that guides the facilitators, characteristics of the participants, and their level of adherence to conflict-supporting societal beliefs (Bar-On, 2002, 2006; Maoz, 2011).

The line of research about the effects of contact on intergroup relations in situations of conflict is probably one of the most extensive ones in social sciences. The large-scale interventions in Northern Ireland sought to facilitate cross-community contact and thereby to promote values of tolerance and acceptance of cultural and political differences among local communities (Cairns, Dunn, & Giles, 1992). Later, research on reconciliation in Northern Ireland reported that cross-group contact between Catholics and Protestants was the key to trust building and empathy emergence and reduction of anger toward the outgroup (Tam, Hewstone, Kenworthy, & Cairns, 2009). Also in the same context of Northern Ireland, using a large-scale survey, Tausch et al. (2010) show positive effects of extended contact not only via ingroup friends and family members (i.e., more-intimate ties) but also via neighbors and work colleagues (i.e., less-intimate ties), especially if the relationship was judged to be close (see also Tausch, Kenworthy, & Hewstone, 2006). In a study on postapartheid reconciliation in South Africa, Gibson (2004a) reports that interracial contact was the most powerful predictor of reduced interracial prejudice. This finding was replicated in a study by Gibson and Claassen (2010). Malhotra and Liyange (2005) analyze the effect of a four-day peace camp in Sri Lanka on young Tamil and Sinhalese adults and report that, even one year after the intervention, workshop participants showed greater empathy for the outgroup and spent a higher amount of money for the support of outgroup children in need than did nonparticipants.

In the context of the Israeli-Palestinian conflict, dozens of planned contact programs between Israeli Jews and Palestinians have been conducted each year since the mid-1980s. They ranged from one-time meetings to long-term, continuous series of meetings, typically including 8 to 12 participants from each nationality and being handled by a Jewish and an Arab facilitator. They have been undertaken within a diverse range of demographic groups, including youths, university students, university professors, and other professionals (Adwan & Bar-On, 2000; Maoz, 2004, 2011). A series of public opinion surveys of representative samples of the Jewish Israeli population in the years 2002, 2003, and 2005 (Maoz, 2010) indicate that planned encounters have reached a remarkable number of Israeli Jews; about one in six Israeli Jews (about 16%) has participated in his or her lifetime in at least one program of planned encounters with Palestinian citizens of Israel. In general, participants in those meetings reported an increase in trust, empathy, better understanding of the complexity of the conflict situation, and in some cases even higher agreement with integrative compromise solutions than did nonparticipants (Maoz, 2011).

The idea of extended contact can be stretched to contact in aired programs of mass media. It was demonstrated that positive media portrayals of interactions and relations between ingroup and outgroup members (prosocial contact) can potentially change the intergroup orientations of millions of viewers, including, and perhaps especially, those whose opportunities for intergroup contact are rare (Schiappa, Gregg, & Hewes, 2005). This idea was even applied to radio programs in Rwanda, where a type of soap opera program focused on positive intergroup contact between Hutus and Tutsis (Paluck, 2009).

Peace Movement

The peace movement, which comprises various peace organizations, is an essential part of the peace-building process. Its objective is to advance peacemaking so as to reach a settlement of the conflict through mutually negotiated and agreed-upon compromises (De Vries & de Paor, 2005; Gidron, Katz, & Hasenfeld, 2002; Guelke, 2003; Meyer, 2004) and later to engage in the peace-building process toward solidification of a stable and lasting peace with the hegemonic peace culture. Usually, most of the activities of peace organizations are based on the involvement and actions of the civil society. While in general peace organizations act in a nonviolent way, they differ in the scope of their activities. The scope depends on the particular goal that peace organizations set, the context of the relations between the rival societies, the nature of the society, and the international climate. The peace movement can develop in very early phases of peacemaking and may continue its activities continuously into the period of building the peace culture. Its emergence is one of the signs that the peace-building process has begun. Gidron, Katz, and Hasenfeld (2002, p. 15) view peace organizations as "peace and conflict-resolution organizations," defining them as "citizens voluntary/nongovernmental organizations advocating peace/reconciliation/coexistence between the major contenders to the conflict..., on the basis of mutual recognition and/or use of dispute resolution strategies as means of addressing conflict."

In the early periods of peace building, even during the active conflict, the peace movement is a pioneer social force that tries to present an alternative socio-psychological repertoire that supports peacemaking in general. This repertoire advances the idea that the society needs to embark on the road to peace or can concern specific plans to resolve the conflict peacefully. Different peace organizations take different approaches with regard to the proposed goal, but almost all of them also present the rival as a trusted partner to the peace process and suggest peaceful relations with the rival.

Although peace organizations of the peace movement have a common general goal, they differ by focusing on specific objectives. Consequently, peace organizations differ with regard to the constituency they appeal to. While some are inclusive and try to mobilize the grass roots from every segment of the society, other are more exclusive and appeal to specific segments of the society – for example, women, or religious members or particular professions (Magal, 2012). Some organizations hope to change the policy of continuing the conflict by changing societal beliefs and attitudes in their own society (Gidron et al., 1999). While some try to include broad segments of the society and thus do not depart much from the consensual beliefs of the society, other peace organizations focus on alternative beliefs and care much less about the ideological gap between the beliefs they promote and those held by the mainstream of the society. Being at the vanguard of the peace movement, they try to advance the ideas they believe in without considering the scope of their mobilization efforts and are usually smaller than the previously described peace organizations.

On the basis of previous contributions to the study of social organizations, Magal (2013) proposes four dominant strategies that characterize peace organizations that try to change the policy of continuing the conflict. *Protest strategy* entails mobilizing grass-roots participation in a clear challenge to the dominant conflict-supporting view, which is maintained by the formal authorities. The protest repertoire may be further divided between legitimate protest activities (e.g., vigils, rallies, or marches), and unlawful or disruptive tactics (e.g., road blocks, sit-ins, or public disturbance). This strategy represents a direct challenge to the established practices of political participation and is intended to affect both political and public discourse and policies. *Litigation strategy* refers to legal action designed to challenge government policy on the issue of conflict. The litigation repertoire includes appealing to the courts to inhibit or roll back government activity; to force government officials to take action; or to enable new action venues, when these venues are blocked by government policy. Litigation activity creates new opportunities for action and legitimizes organizational ideology and discourse through court ruling. *Lobbying strategy* concerns persuasion attempts at the individual level, directed at political activists, political representatives (e.g., members of parliament), and public officials. Lobbying repertoire includes writing letters, informal conversations and small-group meetings with officials and political representatives, and participation in parliamentary proceedings. *Educational or cultural activity* refers to attempts at persuasion of the general public, at the individual and group levels. The educational repertoire includes lectures and conferences, information stands and petitions, press articles and ads, and position papers. These activities emphasize individual change through verbal and emotional persuasion and represent conformity to established political norms and practice.

At the same time, other peace organizations concentrate on collecting and disseminating information with the objective of shedding new light on the conflict reality: to change the view of society members about the conflict, about the rival, and often about one's own society (Gidron, Katz, & Hasenfeld, 2002). Specifically, they try to distribute information that pertains to the violation of human rights that the society performs, limitations of expression about the conflict, costs of the conflict, and specific proposals for a peaceful settlement of the conflict and new visions of the peace context. Some other organizations facilitate contact between people from both societies by bringing into contact members of the rival societies to change their views about each other and the conflict and promote informal dialogue between representatives of the rival parties (Maoz, 2011). Other organizations provide professional services and humanitarian assistance to the rival, usually the weaker side (Meyer, 2004).

Probably most of the societies involved in the peace-building process operate at least a few peace organizations to advance this process. Examples of activities of peace organizations can be found in Sri Lanka (e.g., Orjuela, 2003), Northern Ireland (e.g., Bosi, 2007; Gidron et al., 1999; Guelke, 2003; Maney, 2007; Racioppi & O'Sullivan, 2007), South Africa (e.g., Gidron et al., 2002; Meyer, 2004), and Israel (e.g., Chazan, 2006; Feige, 1998; Gidron et al., 2002; Helman, 1999; Hermann, 2009).

One of the salient examples is Northern Ireland's Women for Peace, organized by Protestant Betty Williams and Catholic Mairead Corrigan Maguire after witnessing the death of three children of Mairead's sister in August 1976. Eventually this organization became known as the Community for Peace People, organizing petitions and marches for supporting peace. Its first declaration stated:

We have a simple message to the world from this movement for Peace. We want to live and love and build a just and peaceful society. We want for our children, as we want for ourselves, our lives at home, at work, and at play to be lives of joy and Peace. We recognize that to build such a society demands dedication, hard work, and courage. We recognize that there are many problems in our society which are a source of conflict and violence. We recognize that every bullet fired and every exploding bomb make that work more difficult. We reject the use of the bomb and the bullet and all the techniques of violence. We dedicate ourselves to working with our neighbours, near and far, day in and day out, to build that peaceful society in which the tragedies we have known are a bad memory and a continuing warning. (http://www.peacepeople.com/PPDeclaration.htm)

Both women were awarded the Noble Peace Prize for their contribution to peacemaking (Beeman & Mahony, 1993).

Nevertheless, the role of peace organizations does not end with the achievement of peaceful settlement of the conflict. They continue to fulfill major functions in the next phase of peace building. Peace organizations can lay the foundations for healing, especially in societies that had vicious and violent conflict with severe violations of moral codes (Staub, 2011). They provide not only the framework for peace supporters but also the new ideas and visions, persuasive campaigns for peace building, behavioral expressions of these campaigns, and information about the peace-building process.

Mass Media

Mass media are among the most powerful agents that provide information and shape public opinion. The media not only reflect opinions of the society members but also play a role in creating and amplifying them by providing information and knowledge (Gitlin, 1980; McQuail, 1994). The role of the mass media becomes even more pivotal in times of war or peace negotiations (Norris, Kern, & Just, 2003; Wolfsfeld, 2004), especially when changes take place in the political environment. Then, according to Wolfsfeld (2004), mass media tend to provide temporal and narrative structure by constructing a frame and later validating it. It is this frame that provides meaning to the provided information (Gitlin, 1980). By framing the information in a specific way, the presentation suggests a particular organizing story line, which points out its scope and essence, the underlying causes, and possible consequences and thus provides a particular enlightenment for its understanding. Consequently, frames shape the view of the mass media's consumers about specific issues (Iyengar, 1991; Mutz, 1998). The public often relies on the media when they provide information about security issues, intergroup violent conflicts, wars, terror, conflict resolution, peacemaking, and peace building. This reliance serves as a basis for a formation of relatively uniform public opinion, which holds an essential role in a society by mediating and accommodating social change (Shamir & Shamir, 2000). Leaders use media to provide significant information to members of the society (Carmines & Stimson, 1989; Shamir & Shamir, 2000; Zaller, 1992). Zaller (1992) suggests that in most cases the public does not have alternative salient information, in a world in which events are ambiguous and in which the public must regularly have opinions about matters that are of importance to a society.

Thus, mass media have powerful tools for promoting peacemaking, reconciliation, and building the culture of peace (Barnes, 1997; Bruck & Roach, 1993; Calleja, 1994; Chadha, 1995; Elhance & Ahmar, 1995; Kopstein, 1997; Kriesberg, 1998b; Norval, 1999). They can be a crucially supportive agent through all the phases of peace building beginning with the emergence of the idea about the need to make pace with the rival. They can be used to transmit information to the public about the new peaceful goals, the past rival group, one's own group, and developing relations (Ross, 2011; Wolfsfeld, 2004). However, first and foremost the media provide a channel to communicate leaders' messages about peacemaking, reconciliation, and peace building. In democratic states, however, the media cannot be mobilized by means of decrees and orders but must likewise be persuaded in the importance of peace building.

Because in many cases mass media are mobilized and also mobilize themselves during violent intergroup conflict to support leaders' views to start or continue the conflict and thus frame the information in this light (e.g., Hunt, 1997), the beginning of the peace process provides an opportunity to change this practice. An example of such change is peace journalism, which has been developed on the basis of research that indicates that often news about conflict is biased toward reporting and encouragement of violence. In contrast, peace journalism comes not only to avoid this bias but also to report news in a way that promotes peace. It tries to frame news and stories in a broader, fairer, and more accurate way, drawing on the accumulated knowledge about conflict and peace-building analyses. Specifically, it presents a complex picture of the societies involved in conflict but differentiates among groups and points out groups that support peacemaking; it avoids widening the gap between one's own group and the rival group; it provides a background for understanding the causes for various specific acts related to conflict; it presents the suffering and victimhood of both sides; it avoids delegitimization of the rivals; and it points out the opportunities for peacemaking (Keeble, Tulloch, & Zollmann, 2010; Lynch, 2008; Lynch & Galtung, 2010; Shinhar & Kempf, 2007).

But mass media are not limited to supply news and commentaries only. They provide a range of programs about every subject matter and serve as major tools of mass entertainment. The variety of these themes and programs also provides an opportunity to support the peace-building process. Mass media can introduce humanized and personalized faces of the rival; can supply major information about the other group and its culture through films, theatrical plays, or entertainment programs; can enlighten in a balanced way the eruption of the conflict, its major events, costs that were paid for continuing the conflict, the immoral acts carried out by the ingroup, or rewards of peace building; can encourage contact between members of both societies; can provide new visions about the developing peaceful relations between the parties; and can be used as a tool to promote reconciliation.

In one example, the work of Staub (2011) and his colleagues on reconciliation in Rwanda has been based on the idea that understanding the roots of violence and avenues to reconciliation has many benefits. Victims need to become aware of the multicausal nature of violence and understand the pressure of social conditions that facilitate violence, their psychological effects and the social processes they create, and how these can turn groups and their individual members against others. In Staub's perspective, enlightenment follows, in the course of the learning and understanding process in which individuals and groups change (Staub, 1989).

One of the benefits of understanding these processes is to help victims realize that their victimizers are not evil. Another is that it can help people – victims as well as perpetrators and bystanders – begin to heal from the effects of violence. A third benefit is that they can become "active bystanders," resisting influences leading to violence and working to prevent violence (Staub, 2006, 2008, 2011). Both groups can become more open to each other, making it possible to engage in reconciliation processes.

These theoretical ideas, and an approach based on them to both prevention and reconciliation developed in the course of seminars and workshops conducted in Rwanda (Staub, 2006, 2011; Staub et al., 2005; Staub & Pearlman, 2006), served as the basis for the creation of a radio program that transmitted messages in a radio drama using a "soap opera" format. A field experiment that assessed the effectiveness of these messages after one year of broadcasting found that listening to the "reconciliation radio" did not lead to greater readiness for reconciliation as measured by some dimensions (beliefs that intermarriage brings peace, or that perpetrators can be traumatized), but it had an effect on a variety of other dimensions and behaviors (Paluck, 2009; see also Staub, 2011; Staub & Pearlman, 2009). These included greater empathy with varied groups (survivors, poor people, leaders, etc.), the belief that one should speak about painful experiences, and the belief that one should express one's disagreements. Listening to the radio drama also resulted in people actually expressing their views more and in being more independent of the authorities in their actions. While Paluck (2009) sees some of these changes as a result of changes in group norms, Staub and Pearlman (2009) see them as beliefs at the start, spreading in part as the result of active discussion in ongoing radio programs with fellow listeners, already highly popular in their first year. Over time, as beliefs or psychological orientations are shared, they are likely to become group beliefs and norms (Staub, 2011). Such radio dramas and other informational programs were also introduced in Burundi and Congo, and they lend themselves for use in any conflict setting.

Education

Education constitutes one of the most important methods for promoting the peace culture (Asmal et al., 1997; Calleja, 1994; Chadha, 1995; de Rivera, 2010; Gordon, 1994; Kriesberg, 1998b; Vargas-Barón & Alarcón, 2005). This method involves the school system, which is often the only institution that the society can use to change the socio-psychological repertoire of society members. Peace education *aims to construct students' worldview (i.e., their values, beliefs, attitudes, emotions, motivations, skills, and patterns of behavior) in a way that facilitates the peace-building process and prepares them to live in an era of reconciliation and peace* (see also Abu-Nimer, 2004; Bar-Tal, 2002; Fountain, 1999; Iram, 2006; Salomon, 2004; Salomon & Cairns, 2010). Harris (2010, p. 4) claims that "peace education is the process of teaching people about the threats of violence and strategies for peace. Peace educators strive to provide insights into how to transform a culture of violence into a peaceful culture." This is usually a process of societal change because peace education may be launched when society members still hold ideas that fuel the conflict and contradict the principles of peacemaking.

In using this method, it is assumed that the school system, as a major agent of socialization (Dreeben, 1968; Himmelweit & Swift, 1969), has significant power to influence. This assumption is based on a few reasons. First, education in schools reaches a whole segment of a society (i.e., the young generation) because schools are compulsory and all children and adolescents are required to attend them. Second, schools are often the only social institution that can formally, intentionally, and extensively achieve the mission of peace education as they have the authority, the legitimacy, the resources, the methods, and the conditions to carry it out. Third, schooling takes place during children's formative years, and the young generation, which still is in the process of acquiring a socio-psychological repertoire, is more open to new ideas and information. Finally, the young generation, which is required to learn the messages and information transmitted in schools, often treats them as truthful, and therefore students at least will be exposed to them.

In order to achieve the objectives of peace education, the educational system must go through major changes. It has to be institutionalized by the formal authorities as a mandatory curriculum that is used in various subject matters across all the grades. It has to be well prepared with plans, resources, curricula, textbooks, ceremonies, and other pedagogical means. It needs a systematic and continuous preparation of teachers through in-training. Furthermore, according to Salomon (2011), peace education in regions of intractable conflicts has at least four major challenges: to spread the messages to nonparticipants, to endure over time, to be tailored to the needs of the different groups in the society, and to be applicable to specific situations.

In terms of contents, peace education should include a number of themes (see also Bar-Tal, Rosen, & Nets-Zehngut 2010).

Conflicts and peace. This theme covers general knowledge about conflicts and peace building. It comes to demonstrate in a concrete and detailed manner the essence of conflicts, the reasons for their occurrence, the different categories of conflict (especially the violent ones), their results (including genocide), the meaning of wars and their cost, conflict resolution methods, the nature of peace and reconciliation processes, the meaning of peace, the different kinds of peace, methods of and obstacles to achieving it, ways of sustaining it, the roles of international institutions and agencies in promoting peace, international treaties regarding principles of conduct at wartime, and international courts and human rights (e.g., Avery, Johnson, Johnson, & Mitchell, 1999).

Specific conflict and its peace process. This theme refers directly to the conflict with which the society was engaged, beginning with a description of the violent conflict and the heavy price the society paid. It moves on to the peace-building process that is underway with its difficulties and achievements and refers to the differential but dynamic relations between one's own society and (different segments of) the past rival society. It is especially important to discuss the meaning of peace, closely consider the agreements that have been signed, describe obstacles to the peace process, and analyze the reconciliation process, which is crucial to sustaining peace (e.g., Fountain, 1999; Galtung, 1996).

Conflict resolution. The goal of learning about conflict resolution is to develop the main abilities and skills to negotiate, mediate, and collaboratively solve problems in the context of conflict situations (e.g., Bodine & Crawford, 1998; Deutsch, 1993; Jones, 2004; Raider, Coleman, & Gerson, 2000). Skills include (a) understanding that conflict is a natural and necessary part of life; (b) becoming a better conflict manager (knowing which type of peaceful conflict resolution method is best suited for a particular conflict problem); (c) becoming aware of how critical it is to understand the perspective of the other side in a constructive conflict resolution process; (d) effectively distinguishing positions from needs or interests; (e) expressing emotions in nonaggressive, noninflammatory ways; (f) reframing a conflict as a mutual problem that needs to be resolved collaboratively with compromises via negotiation or with the help of a third party, or both; and (g) brainstorming to create, elaborate, and enhance a variety of peaceful solutions.

Conflict resolution skills can be seen as one of the central components of peace education (e.g., Johnson & Johnson, 2005). The main concept of conflict resolution education is to promote an understanding of conflict and to assist individuals in developing a nonviolent constructive approach to conflict resolution (Raider, 1995). According to Deutsch (2005, p. 18), the key concept of conflict resolution education is "to instill the attitudes, knowledge, and skills that are conducive to effective, cooperative problem solving and to discourage the attitudes and habitual responses which give rise to win–lose struggles." Changing the students' perspective on different types of conflicts from a win-lose struggle to a mutual problem that can only be resolved collaboratively is an important component of peace education. It is assumed that this acquired perspective regarding conflict resolution will be transferred to the particular intractable conflict in which the society is involved (Van Slyck, Stern, & Elbedour, 1999). It will alert students to the need to resolve the conflict peacefully via negotiation.

In addition to the three previously noted themes directly related to conflicts and peace building, peace education also needs to impart themes that provide skills for maintaining stable peace.

Reflective thinking. This theme denotes questioning held beliefs, including dominant assumptions, and raising doubts and skepticism about the presently dominant understanding of an issue (Dewey, 1933, 1938). It requires open-mindedness defined as "freedom from prejudice, partisanship, and other such habits as close the mind and make it unwilling to consider new problems and entertain new ideas" (Dewey, 1933, p. 30). This view has prevailed through the years, and reflective thinking refers to the ability of not taking any knowledge for granted but of considering and reconsidering various alternatives in order to reach valid inferences, decisions, or evaluations (Rodgers, 2002). It increases awareness of the complexity of situations and enhances the ability to judge challenges in their complexity (Marsick, Sauquet, & Yorks, 2006; Marsick & Watkins, 1990). In addition, reflection leads to the exploration of alternative information that might otherwise be ignored (Coleman, 2006). This type of thinking allows openness, sophistication, and complexity, which are necessary foundations for elaborative information processing. Reflective thinking is needed during the intractable conflict and especially during the peace-building process. It allows resisting mobilized thinking and selective, biased, and distortive information processing that is so prevalent during the conflict. It is this thinking that may lead to the examination and possibly even the adoption of ideas that facilitate peacemaking.

Tolerance. Tolerance refers to the recognition and acceptance of the right of all individuals as well as groups to have their own thoughts, opinions, attitudes, will, and behavior (Agius & Ambrosewicz, 2003). Tolerance is related to a person's – or group's – readiness to bear, to allow, and even to hear opinions (thoughts or attitudes) that contradict their own. To become more tolerant means to reject negative stereotypes and prejudice, to learn about others' contributions to the world, to actively challenge bias, and to engage in thoughtful dialogue about controversial issues (Bullard, 1996; Vogt, 1997). Thus, education for tolerance may engender and facilitate public debate about peace building in societies that were involved in intractable conflict. It promotes opportunities to consider various views, develop openness, and engender high-level debates related to peace building.

Ethnoperspective taking. This theme refers to the ability to put oneself in the other's place and see the world through his or her eyes, feeling his or her emotions, and behaving as he or she would behave in a particular situation (e.g., Deutsch, 2000; Hoffman, 2000; Selman, 1980). But the core of the concept refers to the ability to take the perspective of the member of the other group and especially of the rival group. This is an important learned skill that, on the one hand, allows looking at the other, the rival, as a humane person and collective that has legitimate needs, goals, and aspirations and, on the other hand, enables seeing his suffering and victimhood. This view often underlies personalization and trust of the rival with whom one would want to maintain peaceful relations (Halpern & Weinstein, 2004). Thus, perspective taking is a pillar for peace building.

Human rights. The United Nations (2003, p. 3) defines human rights as "those rights which are inherent in our nature and without which we cannot live as human beings." Human rights, generally, concern the dignity of the person – this includes civil, political, social, economic, cultural, environmental, and developmental rights (e.g., United Nations, 1966a, 1966b). The main goal of education for human rights is strengthening the young generation's respect for human rights and fundamental freedoms (see, e.g., Andreopoulus & Claude, 1997; Davis, 2000; Flowers, Bernbaum, Rudelius-Palmer, & Tolman, 2000; Intercultural Education, 2005; Print, Ugarte, Naval, & Mihr, 2008; United Nations, 2003, for review). Human rights education presents the different types of human rights (e.g., cultural rights); explains their importance and relevance, including conflict situations; and attempts to persuade the students to behave according to them (Flowers et al., 2000).

Human rights education can promote more humane attitudes and a general awareness of the necessity to observe and respect the basic human rights. In addition, the perceived images of the other may change as a result of promoting a better understanding of human rights and their importance (Mertus & Helsing, 2006). Increasing the ability of analyzing situations in terms of human rights can also deepen awareness of abuses of those rights, of the costs for the societies caught up in the conflict, and of their respective contribution to the continuation of the conflict. Furthermore, becoming informed about human rights is supposed to develop a sense of responsibility for defending the rights of other groups.

The preceding description indicates that peace education is a large-scale endeavor that requires setting educational objectives, preparing curricula, specifying school textbook contents, developing instructional material, training teachers, and constructing a climate in the schools that is conducive to peace education (Bjerstedt, 1988, 1993; Burns & Aspeslagh, 1996; Harris, 1988; Hicks, 1988; Reardon, 1988; Salomon & Cairns, 2010). Peace education socializes new generations to a climate in which a culture of peace can emerge as a result of the process of reconciliation.

Examples of peace education that have advanced reconciliation can be found in different states. In Northern Ireland in the late 1990s, an entirely new subject was developed, education for mutual understanding (EMU), aimed at promoting values associated with better community relations. The main goal of EMU was to highlight the common cultural heritage of people in Northern Ireland and their interdependence, while also recognizing the diverse and distinctive aspects of those cultures. Also, this program tried to help young people to learn to respect themselves and others, to help them learn to appreciate other groups, and to show them nonviolent ways to deal with conflict (Duffy, 2000; Gallagher, 2010). Subsequently in the 2000s on the basis of EMU a new subject matter called local and global citizenship (LGC) was developed for ages 14–16. It centered around four main themes: democracy and participation, diversity and inclusion, justice and equality, and rights and responsibilities. The intention of LGC is to encourage the young generation to imagine how new intergroup relations might be in Northern Ireland. It provides the pupils with the concepts and language that allow them to become architects of a new future in Northern Ireland (Gallagher, 2010).

Another example of peace education is the project Education for Peace (EFP) in Bosnia and Herzegovina, which attempted to transform the lives of the students, teachers, and the whole community by directly confronting participants with the issues that were at the heart of the conflict (Clarke-Habibi, 2005; Danesh, 2010). The overall objective of the EFP pilot project is to assist the younger generations and their teachers and parents or guardians to become peacemakers through the processes of creating a culture of peace within and among the participating school communities. These objectives are pursued through an integrated combination of concepts, attitudes, skills, and activities all aimed at creating ever-greater levels of unity in intrapersonal, interpersonal, and intergroup life processes of all participants. The main emphasis in the EFP program is the study of unity in diversity, interethnic harmony, shared community beliefs, conflict prevention and peaceful conflict resolution, and dealing with trauma. All these themes are woven into the fabric of the school environment, and they become a framework for the study of every subject in every classroom throughout the year.

In the case of El Salvador, Guzmán (2005) argues that planning educational reform began even during the conflict. Educators in El Salvador initiated a reform process in the last phase of the domestic war before the peace accord was signed. This plan located five basic objectives: "better quality schooling at all levels; greater efficiency, effectiveness, and equity in the educational system; democratization of education; the creation of new service delivery models; and reinforced instruction for human, ethical, and civic values" (Guzmán, 2005, p. 47). Indeed, the implementation of the plan began in 1993 after the peace accord was signed with the establishment of the National Forum on Education and a Culture of Peace, which was organized by the government in April 1993, with the support of the United Nations Educational, Scientific and Cultural Organization (UNESCO).

Educating society members does not have to involve only the young generation in school. Educating society members involved in intractable conflict is an important part of the attempt to move them toward reconciliation and the establishment of lasting and stable peace. Society members have to acquire a new perspective about numerous themes including conflicts, peace, and peace building. They need to not only reframe their knowledge but also acquire new concepts, narratives, and symbols, as well as norms and practices. Staub and Pearlman report such an attempt in Rwanda. They conducted training workshops with members of local organizations who work with groups in the community. The contents of the workshops were about the influences that lead to mass killings, including genocide: the societal conditions, culture, the psychology of individuals and groups, and the evolution of increasing hostility and violence with its impact (see Pearlman, 2001; Staub, 1998, 2011). The information was elucidated by examples from other countries. The combination of these examples, and then participants applying the information to their own experience in Rwanda, led to what appeared to be a deep "experiential understanding" and meaningful change in the way they looked at the conflict and in particular at the humanization of the members of the rival group – either Tutsi or Hutu (Staub, 2006; Staub & Pearlman, 2006; Staub, Pearlman, Gubin, & Hagengimana, 2005). Later Staub applied these principles in workshops in which members of the media, national leaders, and members of the National Unity and Reconciliation Commission participated. In these workshops, he also included approaches to the prevention of group violence and to reconciliation (Staub, 2011; Staub & Pearlman, 2006). The same approach created for these trainings was used to develop the radio programs described earlier.

Joint Projects

Joint projects of different types offer an additional method of facilitating peace building by fostering links between members of the two groups at different levels of society, such as elites, professionals, and grass roots. This method provides opportunities for encounters in which past opponents can form personal relations (Brown, 1988; Chadha, 1995; Chetkow-Yanoov, 1986; Kriesberg, 1998b; Volpe, 1998), which, in turn, can help legitimize and personalize members of both groups. Joint projects may also create interdependence and common goals and provide benefits for society members. In this way, members of both groups learn about each other and about the importance of peaceful relations. They may begin in the presettlement phase of the conflict, often sponsored by nongovernmental organizations.

The Peres Center of Peace founded in 1996 has sponsored joint projects with Palestinians in areas of agriculture and water, business and economics, medicine and health care, and information technology. All these projects aim to bring both rival societies closer and to develop peaceful relations through cooperation. In later phases of peace building, the French-German reconciliation process provides an example in which a project of town twinning during 1950–1962 created 125 partnerships between French and German towns. By 1989, this project had expanded to include over 1,300 towns and went beyond towns to the establishment of twin relations between secondary schools and universities (Ackermann, 1994). In the case of the Czech-German reconciliation process, joint projects were initiated that included meetings between young people of the two nations and care for monuments and graves (Handl, 1997).

PUBLICIZED MEETINGS BETWEEN REPRESENTATIVES OF BOTH GROUPS

Much has been written about various types of meetings between members of the rival groups (e.g., Burton, 1969; Kelman, 1996). These encounters, which are sometimes secret, are aimed at gaining more understanding of the psychological dynamics of the conflict and may even contribute to conflict resolution, if the participants have influence over decision making or are leaders themselves. To promote peace building with reconciliation, however, these meetings must be well publicized because then they transmit a positive message to society members and influence the public opinion. Their influence is especially noted when the publicized meetings are between formal representatives of both groups. When these meetings are between leaders who also function as epistemic authorities and exhibit genuine respect, they can play an important role in transforming the relations between the groups. These meetings legitimize the rival groups and indicate that members of the other group are human beings with whom talk is possible, who can be treated as partners to agreements, and who can be trusted. They provide powerful symbols of humane, positive, and constructive interactions that stand in contradiction to the violent actions that take place during the conflict. These meetings have an effect even in the stage of peacemaking before the formal agreement. Montville (1993) offers two examples of the positive influence of such meetings on public opinion; one in Northern Ireland included representatives of different rival political parties who met publicly; the other, in the Middle East, included publicized meetings of highly respected theologians and scholars representing Christians, Muslims, and Jews of the region. In another example, the public meeting between de Klerk and Mandela in 1992 had an effect on the views that white and black constituencies held on the peace process. Also, publicized meetings and symbolic handshakes between the Israeli prime minister Benjamin Netanyahu and chairman of the PLO Yasser Arafat in 1997 and 1998 had significant positive influence on the Israeli supporters of the hawkish parties.

Tourism

Interstate and intrastate tourism is another important method for facilitating psychological peace building in cases of interstate conflict. It also may begin before the formal ending of the conflict. It must begin with the appearance of trust, because people do not visit places where they encounter inconvenience, danger, or rejection. If members of the past rival groups visit each other, it indicates that some psychological barriers to social relations have successfully been removed. Second, tourism provides an opportunity to learn about the past rival's readiness to form peaceful relations. Finally, tourism allows learning about the other group – its culture, history, economy, and so on. Social psychologists have long recognized the importance of tourism for improving intergroup relations (e.g., Allport, 1954; Amir, 1969; Hewstone, 1996). Ben-Ari and Amir (1988) demonstrate the positive influence of Israeli tourism in Egypt on changing the Israeli tourists' attitudes and beliefs.

Truth and Reconciliation Commissions

A truth commission is a temporary ad hoc inquiry mostly into systematic policies and practices over time that violated human rights or moral codes of behavior and took place with formal authorization (Hayner, 2001). It is a popular transitional justice method and, as a mechanism, is more readily associated with social goals than prosecution of perpetrators, such as alleviating intergroup conflict. It can begin its action after resolution of the conflict and usually indicates readiness to embark on a reconciliation process.

A truth commission is different from congressional hearings or parliamentary inquiries (e.g., the Bloody Sunday Inquiry in Northern Ireland), which generally focus on specific events. Establishment of a truth and reconciliation commission is a way of dealing extensively with the past. Its purpose is to reveal the truth about the past to the people and to serve as a mechanism of perpetuating justice (Gutmann & Thompson, 2000). Hayner (2001) proposed that a truth commission has five basic aims: to discover, clarify, and formally acknowledge past abuses; to respond to specific needs of victims; to contribute to justice and accountability; to outline institutional responsibility and recommend reforms; and to promote reconciliation and reduce conflict over the past. It tries to reduce biases at different stages of memory construction: fact creation, fact assembly, and fact retrieval (see Trouillot, 1995). Andrews (2003, p. 46) argues that "truth commissions act as conduits for collective memory; as individual stories are selected as being somehow representative, these stories come to frame the national experience. Truth commissions are not, however, mere conduits for stories; rather they wield an important influence on which stories are told and how they are to be interpreted. Thus they both produce and are produced by grand national narratives, and must be understood in the particular context(s) in which they emerge and the particular goals, either implicit or explicit, which guide their work."

A truth commission generally lasts from one to five years and is led by high-profile international or local figures with a human rights standing. Usually, through a team of investigators and support staff, it collects testimonies from victims and sometimes (but not always) from perpetrators and other documentation (Freeman & Hayner, 2003). This work is disseminated through public hearings and reports. This process attempts to uncover the causes and patterns of violence, including the role of individuals and institutions in the violence (Dimitrijevic, 2006). In most cases, though, individual compensation is not possible. It exposes acts of violence, violation of human and civil rights, discrimination, and other misdeeds perpetrated by the formal institutions of the state or by groups and individuals (Asmal et al., 1997; Barnes, 1997; Kaye, 1997; Kriesberg, 1998b; Liebenberg & Zegeye, 1998). In this process, the revelation of the past allows the groups to construct their new collective memory and thereby facilitates the recovery and healing (Asmal et al., 1997; Chirwa, 1997; Hayner, 1999; Norval, 1999; Zalaquett, 1999).

It is not typical for truth commissions to prosecute perpetrators of violence, but some have had the power to recommend prosecutions after their investigations conclude. Others, such as the South African Truth and Reconciliation Commission (SATRC), could grant individual amnesty to perpetrators of violence only if they fully disclosed the truth about their political crimes, if they have done so in a particular time frame, and if their crime was political in nature. Truth commissions normally conclude with a report and a set of recommendations outlining reforms to prevent political violence and violations of human rights from reoccurring. It is also commonplace for commissions to make recommendations for reparations to victims. These can include, among others, material compensation or payments, apologies, establishment of memorials, and administrative measures such as expunging criminal records. There have been more than 50 truth commissions until late in the first decade of 2000, including those in South Africa, Chile, Argentina, El Salvador, Honduras, Uruguay, and Rwanda (Backer, 2009). About half the countries undergoing transitions over the past 35 years have employed this approach (Backer, 2009).

The best-known truth and reconciliation commission (TRC) was established in South Africa in 1995, following termination of the conflict, when blacks under the leadership of Nelson Mandela assumed power and formed the government (Asmal et al., 1997; Chirwa, 1997; De la Rey & Owens, 1998; Gibson, 2004b; Hamber, 1998; Hayes, 1998; Liebenberg & Zegeye, 1998; Norval, 1998). Its principal objective was to promote "national unity and reconciliation in a spirit of understanding which transcends the conflict and divisions of the past." But it was also established to understand that apartheid was a crime against humanity, both sides committed gross offenses and human rights abuses, and apartheid was criminal because of the actions of both individuals and institutions. To this end, the TRC was supposed to (a) establish a comprehensive record of the nature, causes, and extent of gross human rights violations that occurred between March 1, 1960, and May 10, 1994; (b) decide on granting amnesty to individuals who made full disclosure about transgressions they had committed with a political motive; (c) restore the dignity of the victims by giving them the opportunity to recount their experiences; and (d) recommend measures for reparation and rehabilitation, as well as for preventing future human rights violations. More than 21,000 victims of apartheid have given testimony before the TRC in South Africa.

Gibson tried to evaluate the success of the South African Truth and Reconciliation Commission by focusing on the effects of interracial understanding, political tolerance, respect for human rights, and support for political institutions by individuals in a society (Gibson, 2004a, 2004b, 2006). In the first study, he examined the links between acceptances of the truths revealed during the TRC hearings and attitudes that reflect readiness for reconciliation with the outgroup (Gibson, 2004b). The findings indicate that among white and colored South Africans, truth acceptance was associated with better attitudes toward black South Africans and readiness for closer interaction with them. But such a relationship was not observed among black South Africans. Explaining these results, Gibson suggested that black South Africans, the victims of apartheid, had a thorough knowledge of its grim realities before the TRC had begun its hearings and therefore the testimonies and the report had no effects on their willingness for reconciliation.

In a second study, Gibson (2006) reports a positive relationship between truth acceptance and a structural-political index of reconciliation that included measures of support for the rule of law in South Africa, political tolerance, and beliefs in the legitimacy of South African political institutions. Although this relationship was more pronounced for white than black participants (.51 and .23, respectively), it existed in all the groups that make up postapartheid society. Importantly, the truth acceptance scale included items that reflected white South Africans' agreement with statements that horrible actions were committed in the name of defending apartheid, and nonwhites' agreement with statements that horrible things were done in the effort to defeat it. Thus, the more people believed in the relatively complex truth that came out of the TRC hearings, that both sides had committed cruelties against their adversary, the more they expressed pro-reconciliation attitudes. This indicates that "it is hard to reconcile with infinite evil" and that the acknowledgment that both sides to the conflict were "bad but not entirely evil" was essential for reconciliation (Gibson, 2006, p. 101).

Chapman (2007) evaluates the experiences of the South African TRC on promoting forgiveness and reconciliation by analyzing the transcripts of the TRC hearings and later contacting focus groups. She reports that on the one hand the victims were reluctant to forgive perpetrators and that on the other hand the perpetrators were not inclined to acknowledge their wrongdoing or to offer a meaningful apology. She explained these results by suggesting that the TRC in South Africa did not provide opportunities for meaningful interactions between the victims and the perpetrators, which are necessary for the moral reconstruction of the relationship after serious trauma.

Besides establishment of truth and reconciliation commissions, there are other methods to investigate the past. In Rwanda in order to speed the trials of about 120,000 imprisoned suspects participating in the genocide in 1994, the government initiated in March 2001 a nationwide program of Gacaca courts, which has evolved from traditional cultural communal law enforcement procedures (Clark, 2010; Fierens, 2005). This is a method of transitional justice of truth telling, designed to promote healing and moving on from the crisis. About 8,000 Gacaca courts were established with three main goals: reconstruction of what happened during the genocide, speeding up of the legal proceedings by using as many courts as possible, and reconciliation of all Rwandans and building their unity. Each court consists of weekly village meetings with an audience of at least 100 people in which victims tell their story in the presence of the perpetrators, their family and friends, and a locally elected group of judges. Staub (2011) points out that while this justice process was necessary and had benefits, the Gacaca had a mixed contribution to reconciliation. Telling painful stories of victimization is highly challenging, even in front of a supporting audience. Doing so in front of a predominantly Hutu group, which could be hostile to witnesses before, during, or after their testimony, made healing by all the parties difficult. In assessing the impact of the Gacaca process on the victims' well-being, Brouneus (2008b) notes that this process was replete with personal risks for the testifying victims, some of whom were women who had been raped by fellow villagers. Victims report that after they had given their testimony they were threatened by their perpetrator's friends and family. Some of them report having been ostracized by other villagers for having told the truth (Backer, 2007; Byrne, 2004). These experiences resulted in retraumatization and, compared to victims who had not testified, more symptoms of post-traumatic stress disorder. Not surprisingly perhaps, testifying also had negative emotional effects on "neighbors" of victim witnesses, presumably Hutus who testified against other Hutus (Bourneus, 2010; see also Staub, 2011).

More positive results of Gacaca were reported by Rimé, Kanyangara, Yzerbyt, and Paez (2011). Their study found that both victims and perpetrators who participated in the Gacaca manifested a considerable increase in negative emotions, in fear, sadness, and anxiety, in the period that followed their participation. In addition, enhancement of shame was found among perpetrators, which indicated internalization of social control as well as a decrease of shame among victims, which indicted empowerment – restoration of self-esteem and dignity. Participation also enhanced social integration by reducing perceived outgroup homogeneity, decreasing ingroup self-categorization, and increasing positive stereotypes among both victims and perpetrators.

Public Trials

Public trials of particular individuals, charged with violations of human rights and crimes against humanity, constitute another method that is regarded as facilitating the reconciliation process (Kritz, 1996). First, such trials provide an opportunity to reveal the misdeeds and so acknowledge the victims' suffering. Second, when the criminals are found guilty and are punished, the trials fulfill the deep-seated desire for retribution and give the victims the sense that justice has been carried out. In addition, the trials place the responsibility for crimes on particular individuals, thereby reducing the responsibility of the group to which they belong. Finally, these trials serve as warnings against recurrence of such crimes by showing that those who commit such crimes can be found, tried, and punished (Kriesberg, 1998b; Lederach, 1998; Liebenberg & Zegeye, 1998). In essence, they enable catharsis, foster a sense that grievances have been addressed, and thus allow progress toward reconciliation by satisfying the basic needs of the victims. An example of such trials is found in the War Crimes Tribunal in The Hague, where perpetrators from the Balkan conflict are being judged. Also, the International Criminal Tribunal for Rwanda (ICTR) was established in November 1994 by the United Nations Security Council. The tribunal targets genocide, crimes against humanity, and war crimes, defined as violations of the Geneva Conventions, and it convened in Rwanda between January 1 and December 31, 1994. Abuse of mass media and involvement with sexual crimes are also brought to justice. The tribunal is currently located in Arusha, Tanzania. So far, the tribunal has accomplished 50 trials and convicted 29 accused persons – all leaders of Hutu, who were responsible for the genocide.

Apology

As most analysts of reconciliation have pointed out, it requires confrontation with the past, especially in those cases in which transgressions were performed by one or both parties in the conflict (Bronkhorst, 1995). In these cases, the victims of the transgressions harbor strong negative feelings toward their perpetrators, which stand as major obstacles to reconciliation. Such negative feelings must be reduced to enable the socio-psychological change required for peace building including reconciliation. One of the methods to advance this process is a formal apology offered by the side or sides that committed the misdeeds (Blatz & Philpot, 2010; Scheff, 1994). Apology includes admitting the wrongdoing during the conflict, accepting responsibility, and expressing remorse (Barkan, 2000). It implies a commitment to pursuing justice and truth (Asmal et al., 1997; Gardner Feldman, 1999; Kriesberg, 1998b; Norval, 1999). It also allows for a symbolic redress of the historical transgression by acknowledging the harbored grievances, and thus it appeals to the victim for forgiveness. It restores power and dignity to the victim, affirms that the perpetrator group believes in norms of moral treatment and justice, and shows that the perpetrator group has suffered (Lazare, 2004; Thompson, 2008). It also reinstates the victim's belief that societal institutions are trustworthy (De Grief, 2008). Tavuchis (1991) argues that apology is a painful, self-punishing, symbolic gesture that can serve several purposes, especially to restore legitimacy to a claim of membership within the moral community.

Apology allows the victims to forgive and be healed so that eventually their negative feelings toward the past enemy will change. This reciprocal exchange is necessary to move toward complete reconciliation. If the apology is not accepted by the victim group, it does not advance the reconciliation process meaningfully. Questions thus arise when an apology is issued and when an apology is accepted by the victim. Blatz, Schumann, and Ross (2009) report that governments are more likely to acknowledge and apologize for historical injustices when victimized groups or their allies have political clout, the majority of voters do not strongly oppose an apology, some but not too much time has passed, and there appear to be ongoing negative effects of the original injustice. Their study also found that apologies are well accepted when they address the specific demands and psychological needs of those receiving the apology, when they express remorse, and when they refer to the major demands and concerns of the victimized group. But when the victim group demands compensation, a mere apology does not contribute toward reconciliation.

Acceptance of apology and forgiveness are affected by a number of factors. Among them are perceptions of sincerity by the victim, the time that passed after the wrongdoing, the nature of the relationship between the two groups, expectations of the victimized group, and acts that accompany apology. The more sincere the apology is perceived to be by the victimized group and the less time that has passed after the wrongdoing, the better the relations between the two groups are in the new postconflict era; and the more the apology is in line with the expectations and the accompanying acts reinforce the apology, then the more forgiving the victimized group will be toward the group that carried out the perpetrating acts. Blatz and Philpot (2010) note additional factors that influence the acceptance of the apology: effects of the nature of the harm (whether it was done intentionally, how severe it was, how long the suffering lasts), how costly the apology is for the perpetrator, and how trustworthy and powerful is the perpetrator.

In a specific study, analyzing a set of government apologies, Schumann and Ross (2010) found that the median interval between the end of the injustice and official apologies was 59 years. This finding indicates that societies have great difficulty in apologizing even after peaceful settlement of the conflict was achieved. Because societies involved in intractable conflict always view themselves as victims, only in rare cases does this perception change easily. It takes probably many years, which also enables the appearance of evidence that may shed a new light on the conflict and persuade a society that committed extensive violations of moral codes. But even if such evidence appears, societies still try to escape this act following an intractable conflict. Thus, for example, French president Nicolas Sarkozy refused to apologize for abuses, discrimination, oppression, and killings during 132 years of French colonial rule during his visit in 2007 in Algeria.

In contrast is the case of South Africa's former president, F. W. de Klerk, who in August 1996, after Nelson Mandela was elected president, publicly apologized for the pain and suffering caused by the former policies of the National Party. This apology, uncharacteristically, was offered relatively soon after termination of the conflict. It was issued in a short time because of the consensual view of the international community of who the perpetrator was and who the victim was in this conflict. He said:

I apologize... to the millions of South Africans who suffered the wrenching disruption of forced removals in respect of their homes, businesses and land. Who over the years suffered the shame of being arrested for past law offences. Who over the decades and indeed centuries suffered the indignities and humiliation of racial discrimination. Who for a long time were prevented from exercising their full democratic rights in the land of their birth. Who were unable to achieve their full potential because of job reservation. And who in any other way suffered as a result of discriminatory legislation and policies. (Brooks, 1999, p. 505)

In another case, the IRA in Northern Ireland issued in 2002 an apology to the families of civilians killed during the 30-year conflict between the Catholics and Protestants (Ferguson et al., 2007). It acknowledged the grief and pain caused to the families and even recognized its own past mistakes. In this statement it also expressed unequivocal commitment to the peace process as well as the search for freedom and justice. Of interest is the finding that while the Catholics tended to view the apology positively, the Protestants were inclined to see it more negatively. In fact, victims of the IRA violence were among the most vocal in rejecting the apology, seeing it as too little, too late.

Wohl, Hornsey, and Philpot (2011) propose a "staircase" model that suggests that apologies are well viewed, accepted, and contribute toward reconciliation if they follow five steps. As the first condition, the perpetrating group has to recognize that its harmful behavior deviated from moral codes and then it has to accept responsibly for this behavior. In the next step, formal discussions between representatives of the perpetrator and victimized groups are needed in order to reconstruct an accurate record of the past events. On this basis comes the next step in which reparations are discussed, which signals the sincerity of the remorse. With this progress, apology can be offered as the next step. Finally, a necessary step for reconciliation is the development of feelings of safety and trust with the goals of restoring human dignity. These humanizing acts allow establishment of new relations.

Payment of Reparations

Reparations are used when one or both sides accept responsibility for the misdeeds performed during the conflict and are willing to compensate the victims. It is often much more controversial than an apology because the perpetrator group is reluctant to surrender resources and because reparations are next to impossible to quantify. Reparations attempt to compensate for costs that cannot be compensated, such as lost lives, identity threats, and prevention of cultural development (Brooks, 1999). Still, it goes beyond apology and facilitates changes of the socio-psychological repertoire (see Iyer & Leach, 2010; Khatchadourian, 2007; Minow, 1998; Shriver, 1995). On the one hand, the offered reparation indicates an admission of guilt and regret by the perpetrator, while on the other hand, the victims' acceptance of the reparations signals readiness to forgive. These processes allow both victim and perpetrator groups to come to terms with the past and to move beyond it (Edwards, 2005). An example of the use of this method is the compensation paid to the Czech victims by the German government for their sufferings during German occupation in 1939–1945 (Handl, 1997; Kopstein, 1997).

Writing a Common History

This method involves re-creating a past that can be agreed on by groups that were involved in conflict. It usually takes place long after peaceful resolution of the conflict when both sides advance cooperatively to further stages of the peace-building process. The method usually involves a joint committee of historians, who work together to collect and select materials, and finally negotiate to establish an agreed account of the past events (Pingel, 2008). Such work requires exposure to the untold past of one's own group, which often includes the group's misdeeds, and to the unheard past of the other group. This method requires adhering to agreed facts and rejecting myths and unfounded stories. It puts new light on the conflict, its development, causes, involved societies and results, the price paid by the involved societies, failed mediation attempts, violence, and atrocities performed. The product of this joint work allows the construction of a well-founded and agreed-upon narrative, which sheds new light on the past of the two groups. It provides a basis for the eventual evolvement of new collective memory that is compatible with reconciliation and building a culture of peace.

The jointly published document not only has a symbolic value but should also have practical applications. It should serve as a basis for rewriting history textbooks, especially those used in schools, which can affect the beliefs and attitudes of new generations. In addition, the new rewritten narratives may infuse many cultural and educational products such as books, films, and television programs, all of which can influence society members.

An example of this method is the Franco-German commission of historians, which by the 1950s had already critically scrutinized the myths of hereditary enmity between the French and German peoples and revised the existing history textbooks. As a final product, the commission provided new accounts of the history of both nations, based on agreed-upon facts by the historians of the two groups (Willis, 1965). Another example is the committee of historians from both Germany and the Czech Republic, which produced a document providing an agreed-upon account of their common history (Kopstein, 1997). In the case of the Israeli-Palestinian conflict, two academics, a Palestinian and an Israeli Jew, initiated a project before peaceful resolution of this conflict to at least present to the Palestinian and the Israeli school students the two differing narratives side by side (Adwan & Bar-On, 2004; Bar-On & Adwan, 2006). Eventually, the Israeli Ministry of Education forbade the use of this unique history textbook.

It is not always necessary, however, to revise the entire history between nations. Sometimes reconciliation may require rewriting only the history of a significant and symbolic event. Thus, in the case of the Polish-Russian reconciliation a joint commission of historians investigated the murder of about 20,000 Polish officers by Soviets in Katyn in 1940. Through many years the Soviets had claimed that the Germans had performed the atrocity, while many Poles blamed the Russians. This event was one of the major obstacles to reconstructing Polish-Russian relations. The commission, which investigated the Soviet state archives, provided unequivocal evidence for Soviet responsibility. The work of the commission led to a formal Russian acknowledgment of responsibility and an apology to the Polish people.

In sum, the preceding discussion suggests that there are different methods to promote the process of peace building and that they can involve different sectors and layers of the society. The list is not exhaustive, and no single method is best; what is required is a combination of methods. In any event, the process of peace building requires the establishment of well-defined and unequivocal policies that are supported by the institutions and leadership of the states. These policies must be executed in a well-planned manner with the objective of involving as many society members as possible in the peace-building process. Fitzduff (2002) provides a comprehensive and enlightening analysis of the various methods used in Northern Ireland to advance the peace-building process in its various phases. By providing just a glimpse to these continuous efforts, it is possible to note the establishment of peace organizations and groups with the goal of increasing contact between Protestant and Catholic communities. While in 1985 there were about 47 groups with this objective, in 2001 there were 130 of them. Also within this goal of meeting the other side, Fitzduff notes that formal representatives of both communities met publicly at different phases of peace building to discuss issues that stand at the core of the conflict. Also, interface projects were developed to solve social and economic problems that were common to the two communities. Mediation networks had the goal of resolving local conflicts and disagreements between the two communities. Organizations and groups were established with the explicit goal of preventing violence as, for example, the Peace and Reconciliation Group (PRG) in Derry/Londonderry. Also of importance was a major effort to develop and then implement educational curricula and programs with the objective to promote peace education. These curricula and programs have introduced the ideas of living in peaceful relations, provided knowledge about the communities, and tried to construct new social common identity. Finally, the two communities have tried to develop a cultural tradition group (CTG), with the objective of constructing cultural commonality.

The use of the particular methods depends on many different factors, such as the nature of the conflict, the type of misdeeds perpetrated, the extent to which one side or both sides were responsible for its outbreak and the misdeeds committed, the history of relations between the groups, the culture of the groups involved, the availability of economic resources, and the involvement of the international community (see also discussions by Bar-Tal, 2000b; Gardner Feldman, 1999; Kriesberg, 1998b). In the last section we will briefly outline additional several major factors that in my opinion have a determinative influence on the success of the peace building process, which in essence refers to major societal change.

FACTORS AFFECTING THE PEACE-BUILDING PROCESS

First, the peace-building process depends on the peaceful resolution of the conflict. The resolution has to be satisfactory to both parties in the conflict, which must perceive that it has fulfilled their basic needs and addressed their fundamental aspirations (Kelman, 1999). These are decisive requirements for any progress in peace building; if they are not upheld, the process is doomed to fail. This does not mean that groups have to abandon their visions completely, alter their goals, or reframe their concerns. Every group, however, has existential needs and a raison d'être, and if these are compromised under pressure or weakness, the result will not only hamper the peace-building process but also plant the seeds for future conflict. Within this factor it is of great importance to add that societies involved in peace building have to recognize that pragmatic justice is made in this process. That is, within the peace-building process concrete steps are taken to address the immoral behaviors and violations of human rights that took place before and during the violent conflict.

Second, the peace-building process depends on real acts that symbolize peace building, both formal and informal, by both parties (Hayner, 1999; Zalaquett, 1999). After years of mistrust, hatred, and hostility, both parties must exhibit much goodwill in order to change these feelings. The peace-building process depends on overcoming deep suspicion, and this requires performing many different, often small symbolic acts that signal good intentions, the wish to build peaceful relations, adherence to aspirations of peace, and sensitivity to other group's needs and goals. These acts create and disseminate a new climate of relations among the masses. They set the tone for reciprocity, positive spirals of behavior, or even for the initiation of unilateral positive gestures. Peace building cannot rely on rhetoric only; societies involved in the peace-building process have to experience real change in their living conditions that signal to them that peace building is rewarding and benefiting them individually and collectively.

Third, the peace-building process requires a measure of complementary goals, policies, and practices between the former rivals (Asmal et al., 1997; Kriesberg, 1998b; Lederach, 1997). That is, both parties must undergo a similar socio-psychological change, and a majority of both parties has to support the peaceful relations. The complementary processes may progress in different ways and with different methods – but both societies have to perceive concrete and real moves that reflect the process. A considerable imbalance in these changes will impair the peace-building process, as one of the parties could feel betrayed and cheated.

Fourth, the peace-building process depends on the determination of the leaders involved in the peacemaking and also on the good and trusting relations that they build with each other. They have to become agents of change, entrepreneurs of peace, who, once joined, lead the parties toward peaceful settlement of the conflict and later toward lasting and stable peace. Their moves are often met with opposition within their own group in the form of pressure, public mobilization, and sometimes even smear campaigns or violence, all aimed at obstructing the peace process. Leaders must overcome these obstacles and show great resolve and devotion to the peace process. They must signal to group members that they are determined to advance the reconciliation process successfully despite the opposition. Nelson Mandela and F. W. de Klerk in South Africa or Helmut Kohl and Vaclav Havel in the case of Czech–German reconciliation were crucial players whose resolute stances provided the necessary catalyst for the progress of the reconciliation (Handl, 1997; Rothstein, 1999b).

Fifth, the peace-building process depends on the activism and strength of those who support it (Bar-Tal 2000b; Elhance & Ahmar, 1995; Gardner Feldman, 1999; Kriesberg, 1998b). It requires the involvement of individuals, groups, and organizations in persuading hesitating and opposing group members in the importance of the peace-building process. It requires formation of a mass movement to carry out dramatic societal change. The peace-building process also requires an active approach to cementing peaceful relations between past enemies. Therefore, activism on the part of the supporters may facilitate this process. That is, it is important to convey both to one's own group and to the other group that reconciliation is to be supported and cherished.

Sixth, the success of the peace-building process depends on mobilizing the support of society's institutions (Bar-Tal, 2000b; Gardner Feldman, 1999). This mobilization pertains to political, military, social, cultural, and educational institutions such as security forces, political parties, the school system, mass media, and the intellectual and cultural community (Asmal et al., 1997; Thompson, 1997; Zalaquett, 1999). The mission socializes the new generations in light of new goals and aspiration. Peace education has to be part of this mobilization.

Seventh, the peace-building process depends on the international context. That is, the extent to which the international community shows interest in the particular reconciliation, facilitates it, presses the parties to carry it out, and provides concrete assistance for pursuing it with involvement and economic aid (Bar-Tal, 2000b; Elhance & Ahmar, 1995; Gardner Feldman, 1999; Hume, 1993; Kriesberg, 1998b; Lederach, 1997, 1998). The international community has played a crucial role in facilitating conflict resolution and reconciliation in most cases of intractable conflict over the past decade (e.g., Northern Ireland, El Salvador, Nicaragua, Bosnia). In recent years, with the end of the Cold War, the international community through such organizations as the United Nations, the European Union, and the Organization of American States has had a great interest in promoting the peaceful resolution of conflicts followed by reconciliation.

CONCLUSION

Over the past decade, the discussion about the peace process has focused mostly on the issue of reconciliation. Years of study of conflict resolution have shown that peaceful resolution of a conflict does not guarantee stable and lasting peaceful relations. Parties to the conflict may negotiate an agreement of conflict resolution, but often it concerns mostly the negotiating leaders and is not relevant to the group members. In such cases, conflict can erupt again. To cement peaceful relations between the rival sides to an intractable conflict often requires a reconciliation process. The peace-building process requires major change in the socio-psychological repertoire. Peace building with the construction of a culture of peace can establish stable and lasting peaceful relations between former rivals on the basis of genuine support by the majority of the group members. Peace building then requires the formations of new beliefs, attitudes, emotions, motivations, and goals that support peaceful relations. This new socio-psychological repertoire includes evolvement of mutual respect, trust, positive attitudes, and sensitivity to other group's needs, fostering friendly and cooperative relations marked by equality and justice. The preceding conception suggests that peace building is in essence a socio-psychological endeavor achieved through a socio-psychological process of societal change. But this collective state of mind can come not as a result of persuasion, indoctrination, and propaganda but only from deep tangible and observable changes that touch on individual and collective lives. A mere psychological basis cannot hold for a long time. Society members have to experience the concrete changes before they can change their socio-psychological repertoire. The required changes – in lines of actions, practices, and restructurings, as well as in the political, legal, societal, cultural, and economic domains – range from acts that provide transitional justice to redistribution of wealth accumulated unjustly by one side.

On the basis of the concrete changes, socio-psychological change takes place that is the basis for establishing stable and lasting peaceful relations. It signals satisfaction and contentment with the new context of peace. This socio-psychological change is an arduous process. It requires a change of the socio-psychological infrastructure embedded in the culture of conflict that has been an essential part of individual and collective life for many years, sometimes many decades and even centuries. This culture was functional during the intractable conflict, in light of the ongoing experiences of individual society members and of the collective. In addition, this repertoire was propagated by all the groups' channels of communication and institutions, transmitted to new generations via the educational system, and grounded in the group's collective memory.

Establishment of new stable and lasting peaceful relations requires changing this repertoire, abolishing old fears, mistrust, hatred, animosity, delegitimization of the enemy, and often also adjusting the group's long-standing dreams and aspirations. Such change is long and complex, marked by progress and setbacks. It requires new experiences that can induce the change of the socio-psychological repertoire, transmitting a new message of peace and new image of the former enemy. However, these experiences do not come about by themselves. People have to create them, act upon them, and disseminate their meaning. That is, people have to perform acts that provide the new experiences, such as peaceful gestures, meetings, joint projects, exchanges, apologies, promoting justice, changing inequalities, and introducing peace education into the system. These acts supply in the best way the validating information that enables group members to look at their social world differently.

But changing group members' worldview requires accumulating new experiences that support peacemaking. A new culture of peace must indicate to all society members that a new reality evolves, free of threats, dangers, and fears. Such a reality is not always easy to form, because in societies engaged in a peace process and reconciliation, there is always a potent opposition to the process and small groups may even resort to violence to put a halt to it.

The evolvement of the new reality is an active process requiring the involvement of leaders, elites, professionals, and grass-roots organization and institutions. This is a major undertaking for the society. Just as in times of conflict the society was mobilized for waging the violent struggle with much resolve and sacrifice, building a peaceful society also requires determination and efforts to persuade the opposition of the genuine importance of the peace and its benefits.

The peace-building process requires not only persuading the members of one's own group but also convincing the rival side of one's sincere intentions and goals to build genuine peaceful relations. To do this, groups need to focus on their own efforts, shortcomings, misdeeds, and inhibitions and ask what they can do to facilitate reconciliation. This is a challenging requirement, because groups are conditioned to focus on the other group's shortcomings, obligations, and misdeeds and demand that it demonstrate its good intentions, while overlooking their own failings and malintentions. Groups usually tend to blame others for failures in the reconciliation process.

The peace-building process demands forming a new ethos embedded in a culture of peace. This entails a major societal transformation. New norms, values, opinions, symbols, and collective memory have to emerge. Groups have been able to undergo such transformation successfully, as the Franco-German case of reconciliation demonstrates. This process, however, took almost four decades to establish. Individuals and groups always rally sooner and easier to the banner of fear and hate than to the banner of trust and respect. But it is only trust and respect that provide hope for a better life, and it is the duty of humanity to enable groups to follow the path of the reconciliation process. As social scientists, we can contribute to a better understanding of this process and the factors that influence it. That is our mission to the well-being of human society, to preventing future bloodshed and suffering.

Epilogue

This Epilogue provides me with the unique opportunity to share with the readers in informal way, beyond the scholarly analysis presented in the chapters of this book, my thoughts about number of issues, as a kind of book summary. This summary touches on issues that are in my opinion of special importance for the understanding of the socio-psychological dynamics of intractable conflicts. The presented thoughts are grounded in my understanding of the situations of intractable conflict, which is based on observations of conflict situations in the world, reading professional literature, personal experiences in the Israeli-Arab conflict, and my own reflections. They can serve as bases for further scientific development. Finally, I want to note that I am aware that living in Israel and experiencing the Israeli-Arab conflict in general and specifically the Israeli-Palestinian conflict have had a major influence on my thinking about intractable conflict. Also, I recognize that my thoughts concern more the half-empty glass of the conflict's dynamics than the half-full glass. This is not only because intractable conflicts are extremely costly to humankind but also because we social scientists know more on a practical level how to ignite and escalate them than how to prevent and terminate them. Here, then, are "a few thoughts" about a number of issues.

CONFLICTS

Describing the roots of intractable conflicts sheds light on the difficulty of resolving them and explains their long durability and resistance to peaceful resolution.

Intergroup conflicts are an inseparable part of human life, and they cannot be avoided. Groups always have contradictory aspirations, interests, and goals and therefore can identify situations of intergroup conflicts. Once groups identify conflicts, they often act in line with this identification, and then conflicts move beyond the cognitive-emotional realm into courses of actions that are often violent. Nevertheless, it is important to remember that not all the conflicts are undesirable. Some of the conflicts serve as important processes to stop and correct deplorable practices such as oppression, occupation, discrimination, or exploitation that are part of the human world – the unbearable immorality of the world. The world was and is still plagued with injustices, inequalities, restrictions of freedom, and immoral acts that should be at least reduced, if not eliminated. Thus, unfortunately, in many cases conflicts are needed in order to change these situations because groups do not yield territories, power, wealth, or resources easily, even if it is clear that the territory that they occupy, the advantage that they have, the dominance that they hold, and the commodities that they possess were acquired in ways that contradict the contemporary moral standards.

To make this observation more complicated, it is possible to note that many of the intractable conflicts are not simple and unequivocal because they have foundations in completely different periods where the intergroup norms and moral codes were dissimilar to the contemporary ones. They have roots in times when discrimination, oppression, colonialism, occupation, and exploitation were a well-accepted and a normative part of intergroup relations in the civilized world. In addition, many of the contemporary intractable conflicts in different states were created by third powers, which through many years practiced immoral behaviors that disregarded needs and aspirations of various groups although these practices were in line with well-accepted codes in these periods. However, with time norms change and, with them, norms of intergroup moral conduct. But although the practices that were normative decades ago are not accepted any more, the serious deprivations created in the past are still present and underlie many of the conflicts. In fact, the emergence of new ideas, values, norms, and codes of behavior sheds new light on old intergroup relations. They brought new contentions, grievances, goals, and aspirations to deprived societies and fueled numerous conflicts.

Finding solutions to these conflicts is an extremely difficult challenge because they require redivision of territories, serious societal restructures, and redistribution of power, wealth, and resources – all major changes that are very difficult today to implement. In many cases, the needed changes are naturally viewed by the advantaged groups as an unacceptable change of the well-established conditions that causes harm to them, and therefore they strongly object to their implementation. Thus, there are still whole societies and layers in certain societies that profit and enjoy unjust gains and benefits in the present context in various political, economic, social, cultural, or religious domains. They do not like to lose these advantages and stand against those who try to change the status quo. Moreover, they develop elaborate justifications that are sometimes even accepted by significant parts of the society. The challenge thus for the other group is to find a way to change the situation within the developed context of conflict. In many serious and harsh conflicts, a party resorts to violence in order to change its unequal and unjust positions. It is unfortunate that, in spite of the progress in defining what are just intergroup relations, for these cases the civilization has not yet developed accepted mechanisms to rectify the situations that cause unjust deprivation among various groups. As a result, it is difficult or almost impossible to resolve many of the present conflicts, even with pragmatic justice. Thus, some of these conflicts continue, and some societies, at least for the time being, are doomed to live with immorality, injustice, and inequalities.

Contemporary intergroup violent conflicts do not erupt only about past grievances. Some also erupt because of present collective greediness to acquire more territory, wealth, power, and resources. Leaders and elites emerge who, in violation of moral codes, desire to dominate other groups, conquer territories, seize resources, increase wealth, and thus open new conflicts with the goal to benefit their group. The basic motives to enhance and extend what a group has is still a powerful cause of intergroup conflicts.

The nations and states of the world have differential power; some are considered superpowers, as reflected in their military might, political dominance, control of resources, and economic strength. This differential power also has a tremendous effect on the eruption of the intergroup conflicts, as different groups compete over various tangible and intangible resources and exercise influence to gain them. Stronger groups use their superiority to extend at least the influence and dominance of their group but often go beyond this objective to achieve control over resources or even territories that they believe they need. The stronger groups often achieve their desired dominance or resources by inflaming or supporting one side in a conflict, even without direct violent involvement. In these cases they play a role in the eruption and maintenance of intractable conflict. These exercises of power necessarily lead to intergroup conflicts, some of them violent. It is important to note that, although social scientists often prefer to analyze the described situations on macro-international relations that concern national interests and power, we need to realize and take into account that human beings decide on the national goals and policies. They then persuade the masses that these goals are essential for national survival and therefore have to be achieved.

There is something very basic in human nature that drives human beings to engage in conflicts. The first basic drive motivates human beings to change situations that violate newly established moral norms of intergroup relations and which are perceived by them as unjust. Then this drive operates against two other basic human drives: a drive that prevents human beings from yielding commodities that were achieved unjustly, and a drive that motivates them to have more than they have at present, even if the new aspirations are beyond their legitimate and moral goals and their achievement necessitates use of violent means.

Few conflicts are all black-and-white, whose raison d'être provides such direct contradiction to moral values as in the case of the Nazis, where there was a need to gain a complete victory in order to prevent massive crimes against humanity. Most of the conflicts have a gray color, even when they are asymmetrical in their moral evaluation. That is, each party has at least a few contentions that rest on grounded moral arguments, and today it is easier to judge conflicts from the perspectives of their justness and morality. The judgment of the conflicts rests on at least two major dimensional considerations that are often independent. The first consideration pertains to the causes that are accepted by the international community as justification to start a conflict. The other issue refers to the violence used during the conflict. The first consideration focuses on the extent of the injustice and immorality that a group suffered, formulated as contentions (i.e., contentions with a basis in experienced discrimination, oppression, inequality, and greediness) that eventually lead to the eruption of the conflict. The second consideration refers to the extent of violation of human rights, killings of civilians, and in general to crimes against humanity that a group performs during the course of the conflict. Groups differ with regard to their responsibility regarding the conditions that created a state of relative deprivation of another group. Some groups are fully responsible for the creation of these conditions, while other groups have only minor responsibility or even no responsibility. Also, groups differ with regard to the extent of violation of human rights and crimes against humanity during the conflict. Some groups perform more systematic atrocities than their rival group. However, all the societies involved in intractable conflict perform atrocities; perhaps there are justified violent conflicts, but none are without immoral misdeeds.

I note these two dimensions because in my mind both considerations not only affect judgment of conflicts but also have to be addressed in conflict resolution, if groups strive to build stable and lasting peace. One more important difference that contributes to the differential evaluation of parties in conflict is that groups differ with regard to their power to end an intractable conflict. While some groups, especially the powerful ones, have the keys to the solution because of their control over the disputed commodities, other groups can only struggle nonviolently and violently to achieve their goals. Also, in many cases the powerful groups have or achieved control over the disputed commodities in an unjust way, but because they have the military, political, and economic might, they refuse to give them up or even to compromise.

Although some social scientists may redirect these observations about conflicts to the domain of international relations or political sciences, I see in them a clear reflection of psycho-political dynamics because they all refer to perceptions, cognitions, emotions, motivations, and behaviors of individuals, groups, and societies. They relate strongly to three major foundations of intractable conflicts that have imprinting effects on their course: narratives, violence, and their long persistence because of the great difficulty to resolve them peacefully. The narrative provides the indispensable socio-psychological tool that enables participation in the conflict. Without this tool, it would be impossible to mobilize society members to take an active part in it. Moreover, the narrative not only provides the socio-psychological rationalization to sacrifice one's own life but also supplies a psychological permit to carry out violent acts against the rival group. Violence, as another distinguishing feature of an intractable conflict, is its extension. The use of violence throws it into a completely unique dynamic that has a determinative effect on its nature. Finally, an intractable conflict resists its peaceful ending and can last for many years. This prominent feature, together with violence, makes this human societal phenomenon so dangerous, causing suffering and misery to the participants.

Next, I discuss three features, beginning with narratives. First, I would like to make a point. Narratives are not baseless. Societies (or at least segments of the society) do experience conditions of deprivation that lead them into conflicts, and then they have harsh experiences during the violent conflict. Thus, the constructed narratives have their real basis. But the narratives also differ in their relations to reality, because the contentions and the course of the conflict differ in their moral ground. Some societies need more camouflage to hide their immoral contentions and misdeeds during the conflict. Thus, I do recognize asymmetry in moral responsibility in intractable conflicts and believe that they have a determinative effect on how conflicts are managed and then resolved.

NARRATIVES

Intergroup intractable conflicts always involve systems of societal beliefs constructed in narratives that are used by the involved parties. The major reason for the construction of the narratives is that human beings in general need a reasoned, coherent, and meaningful story that provides illumination, justification, and explanation of the reality in which they live. This need is especially essential in situations of violent and lasting conflicts because they all involve human losses, injuries, destruction, suffering, misery, and hardship that lead unavoidably to uncertainty, helplessness, unpredictability, chronic stress, and distress. It is in these, as well as in less severe intergroup conflicts, that the narrative provides the needed enlightenment about the confrontational context. In every intractable conflict the involved parties construct a conflict-supporting *collective master narrative* that focuses on its entirety and often becomes dominant. It explains the causes of the conflict, describes its nature, presents the image of the rival, portrays one's own presentation, elaborates on the conditions needed to win the conflict, and so on. In addition to this general master narrative about the conflict, there are also more specific narratives that concern major events in the conflict (e.g., wars) and mini-narratives that refer to a specific incident (e.g., a battle, a specific event in a battle, or a personality in the conflict). The master narrative appeals to the collective identity of the group, uses all available group symbols and myths, and arouses emotions. Together with the specific narratives it is constructed in a persuasive way and eventually they all serve as convincing epistemic frameworks that energize, mobilize, and activate group members to participate in conflicts. It is hard to imagine a serious and violent conflict without a master identity-related narrative that appeals to at least part of the group. As long as it is well accepted by society members, it maintains and fuels the continuation of the conflict. Only when society members begin to question its basic assumptions and start to create an alternative narrative is there a possibility that the conflict may be resolved peacefully.

The major contents of the conflict-supporting narratives outline the goals that lead to the conflict, justify its eruption and continuation, delegitimize the rival, present the ingroup in glorifying terms and as the sole victim of the conflict, and call for patriotic mobilization to participate in the conflict and even sacrifice one's life for the group's struggle. The narratives of sociopsychological infrastructure are collective memory of conflict and the ethos of conflict. It is important to note that these narratives are accompanied by emotions that play a crucial role in the conflict. They strengthen the contents of the narratives by being evoked with the major themes, and when they appear in various situations, they are appraised in line with the narratives. Thus, they also provide the fueling and maintain the ingredients for the continuation of the conflict.

Of importance is the fact that the described narratives are constructed in a selective way. First, knowledge and information that are inconsistent with the themes of the narrative of conflict are omitted. Second, the narrative is constructed in a biased way, as themes of the narrative are constructed on the basis of interpretations of evidence that support the themes of the narrative and disregard the contradictory implications. Third, the narrative is constructed through distortion because it contains contents that do not have any support in evidence but form support to match the themes of the narrative. The fourth principle, simplification, suggests that the narrative contains black-and-white arguments that support the major themes. In fact, this narrative constitutes *experienced and imagined reality* for the society members participating in intractable conflict. The experienced basis indicates that society members are greatly affected by the conditions of intractable conflict, while the imagined basis implies that the narrative is also based on misinformation, distortions, lies, and myths. It should be no surprise that most of the participants in intractable conflicts suffer from a blurred vision, which causes them to be selective, biased, distortive, and simplistic in their perception.

In the construction of their narrative, many of the groups practice manipulation and impose a double standard. Manipulation is practiced because all the groups, including those that try to achieve unjust goals, wrap the conflict-supporting narrative in line with acceptable moral justifications, such as defending democracy, ensuring security, or achieving justice. Use of double standards is apparent when groups judge and present in a narrative their own goals and behaviors according to moral standards but delegitimize similar goals and behaviors of the rival group. They insist on deploring evil acts carried out against them and judging them according to moral standards but tend to ignore their own similar evil acts and at best rationalize them. Groups tend to be self-righteous and have great difficulty looking at themselves.

From a socio-psychological perspective, all the conflict-supporting narratives play a major role in the eruption of violent conflicts, in their long continuation, in the difficulties of solving them peacefully, and in the use of violent means that often violate moral codes of accepted behaviors. They penetrate into the fabrics of the societal socio-psychological infrastructure and serve as pillars of the developed culture of conflict. These narratives, being constructed to appeal to the collective, maintain the conflict. They provide all the themes that are needed both to illuminate the conflict in a meaningful way to satisfy the individual and collective needs and to maintain the conflict.

They often serve as a dogma to socialize society members into closed-minded societies. These narratives are imparted, or more accurately indoctrinated, to young society members as well to older members and then serve as crucial mechanisms that fuel the continuation of the conflict. Society members who eventually acquire the conflict-supporting narratives and especially the master identity-related narrative adhere to it as it serves them as an ideology that guides their behaviors, including the performance of the most immoral acts. Together with the accompanied emotions it leads to psychological closure that prevents exposure and examination of information that may undermine its basic assumption. This repertoire becomes hegemonic and is maintained by societal institutions and channels of communication. Authorities of societies engaged in intractable conflicts attempt to close the societies to alternative information that may discredit the dominant narratives supporting the conflict. They are ready to sacrifice all the principles of freedom of expression and flow of information to preserve patriotic information. They frequently employ to different degrees a variety of methods, including control of channels of communication, use of censorship, or delegitimization of sources and messages that provide the alternative information. In this context society members have great difficulty identifying manipulations, indoctrinations, and propaganda that underlie acquisition of conflict-supporting narratives. In this climate individuals and groups that have objections to part of the narrative or to its whole often have difficulty expressing these reservations because of the societal formal and informal pressure. Some may become passive bystanders, contributing to the dominance of the conflict-supporting narratives, while other may pay a social and sometimes even a tangible price for their courage to express their alternative views.

Those are the conflict-supporting narratives that provide the permit to carry out violence, including deplorable atrocities and acts of genocide.

VIOLENCE

The second major feature of intractable conflicts is violence. There is no intractable conflict that does not involve the civilian population in vicious, violent, bloody, and severe harm and wide-scale violations of human rights. This is done in personal and impersonal ways. In the former the victims are harmed in face-to-face encounters, whereas in the latter the performer of the harm is distanced from the victims (e.g., being in a plane, in a command office, or on a ship). Human beings have not learned to carry on their violent conflicts without harming the civilian population. This is an inseparable part of every intractable conflict. Therefore, violence makes every group engaged in intractable conflict to feel as if it were a victim, independently of power or even responsibility for the eruption of the conflict. Once civilians and even military personnel fall, societies experience threat, sense of victimhood, wish to revenge, and desire to deter the rival.

This is the violence of various kinds that turns the conflicts into a nightmare for humankind. It is "incomprehensible" how and why individuals in violent intergroup conflict lose every shred of humanity and moral compass and perform the most brutal, cruel, and immoral acts. I assume that the society members who perform them often in other circumstances cannot hurt a neighbor who acts arrogantly toward them, behaving politely in interpersonal interactions in their society. The fundamental question that should preoccupy every *Homo sapiens* is how it happens that individuals who avoid raising a hand in an angry interpersonal encounter with a stranger hurt with great ease a rival human being in an intractable conflict. Many of them are good and warm fathers, husbands, sons, and friends, as well as good citizens of their country. But once the violent conflicts erupt and they become involved in them actively, some of them are turned into creatures capable of doing every evil act. They lose every moral restraint that guides their normal civil life, and this type of behavior encompasses individuals and collectives of every society, including those which consider themselves to be the carriers of civilized culture. In conflicts, human beings harm, maltreat, humiliate, rape, torture, and murder.

On a general scale, in the Rwandan conflict during the genocide that took place over a few months in 1994, an estimated 800,000 people were killed in their own villages or towns, often by their neighbors and fellow villagers, mostly by hand machetes. The Hutu gangs searched out victims hiding in churches and school buildings, massacred them, and even murdered those who refused to kill.

In a more specific case in Guatemala, where about 200,000 people lost their lives in the violent conflict and about 40,000 disappeared, in 1982 on December 6 about 200 civilians were massacred by government soldiers in the village of Las Dos Erres. Some were buried alive in the village well, infants were killed by slamming their heads against walls, fetuses ripped out of pregnant women, and young women kept alive to be raped over the course of three days.

In the Algerian conflict, the French army systematically used the most cruel ways of torture against many thousands, including innocent civilians, with such techniques as illegal executions and forced disappearances through what would later become known as "death flights" in which human beings were thrown from planes to the sea.

In the Sri Lankan conflict in the early morning of September 18, 1999, the Tamil military entered Gonagala village and hacked to death with knives or machetes more than 50 Sinhalese civilians, including women and children, most of them in their sleep.

A company of the United States Army on March 16, 1968, massacred at least 350 unarmed civilians in the Vietnamese village of My Lai, including women and children, who were not only murdered but also raped, beaten, and tortured.

These examples show the incredible cruelty that participants in intractable conflicts perform, and it takes place in all the intractable conflicts by both involved parties. Often it is carried out formally and authorized and legitimized by leaders through chains of command, and sometimes it is unauthorized by the local military personnel.

I stand before these atrocities speechless, not being able to grasp their scope, depth, methods, and especially roots. I cannot understand how people can take part in them and how other people can ignore them – these acts testify in my view to the imperfect programming of at least some human beings. Some human beings are able to perform unacceptable crimes against not only other groups but also members of their own group, acts that are justified by a well-established narrative. I believe that this ability is probably one of the most serious deficiencies of the human species. Use of violence reflects a chronic illness in some human beings for which at present a cure has not been found. The question why people commit evil acts that they try to prevent with all their might from occurring to themselves is essential for understanding human violence. Indeed, social scientists have spent years trying to understand the psychological mechanisms that give freedom to evil instincts that even animals do not commit against their own species with such an extensive and brutal scope. Studies of obedience, conformity, deindividuation, moral disengagement, deprivation of basic psychological needs, appeal of destructive ideologies, passivity of bystanders, mechanization, functioning of threats and fear, and routinization provide a glimpse into the dynamics of these behaviors. Human beings do all the possible acrobatic psychological exercises to be able to kill others in violent conflict. In my journey to understand these horrible human phenomena, I concentrated on the study of delegitimization that categorizes societies into some that are denied humanity and thus provides the psychological permit to carry out any act of cruel violence that one can imagine. Delegitimization represents an extreme form of moral exclusion, moral disengagement, and moral entitlement. It is probably one of the most destructive mind-sets that human beings construct to carry out evil acts. Delegitimization does not appear in every intergroup conflict, but it tends to emerge especially in every violent conflict when the contested goals are perceived as far-reaching, unjustified, and endangering the fundamental goals of the group.

The use of delegitimization in intractable conflict is not surprising because the rivals are viewed as an enemy. A group defined as an "enemy" is seen as a group that threatens unjust harm and therefore arouses feelings of hostility. Enemies are expected to be eliminated and destroyed. The word enemy is enough to condemn a human being to death. When trauma and insecurity support the delegitimizing discourse, this narrative has profound psychological appeal to the members of a society. Of special importance in evoking delegitimization and violence is the perception of threat that, on the one hand, freezes human reflective and moral thoughts with moral emotions that prevent unacceptable behaviors and, on the other hand, leads to the performance of the most unthinkable acts. I assume that at least some of those who carried out these acts look at themselves after some time with shame and guilt, realizing what they have done.

It is important to realize that delegitimization does not come just in an unexpected and surprising way. Delegitimization in intractable conflicts is part of the perpetuated narrative that is planned to be used, spelled out by the leaders who serve as epistemic authorities, repeated constantly, reflected in acts and products, institutionalized in the culture of conflict, and taught to the younger generations. It is thus sad but not unforeseen that eventually group members accepting or internalizing the delegitimizing terms of the rival are capable of losing all moral censors to perform the lowest evil human behaviors.

In reference to violence as an essential part of intractable conflict, a few comments are in order.

First, it is important to be aware that almost all nations glorify violence of their own group, and this glorification is well embedded in their culture. Nations see violence as an important part of their collective memory, which they worship. This violence is in most cases initiated and carried out by the ingroup, sometimes as a defense against the initiated violence of another group. Many of the nations glorify violence that was used to achieve self-determination and independence, lionize wars initiated or imposed, and idolize violent expansions of their states. Looking only on the initiated violence, I can note just a few examples: Americans glorify their war of independence and conquest of the West, Russians glorify their expansion toward the Asian East, the French glorify the Napoleonic Wars, and Israelis glorify their violent resistance to the British Mandate. We can go through nation after nation and find the same trend. Obviously, every ingroup violence is well justified in the national ethos, but I would like to claim that violence provides a fundamental ethos of the human being. Children learn about violence from their early years in every group, and this concept with all its implications is carried out with positive meaning as an inseparable part of every culture. Human beings learn to differentiate well between violence of their group, which is almost always justified, and violence carried out by other groups, which is presented almost always as unjustified. In many cases, a double standard is practiced where the same violence that is carried out by one's own group is glorified and the one carried out by the outgroup is viewed as being evil. In fact, part of the way that nations deal with their violence is related to persuasion regarding legitimization of its performance. Every nation involved in violent conflict tries to legitimize its own violence and delegitimize the violence of the rival. My observation is that the way ethnic groups, nations, states, and the international community deal with violence is in many cases plagued by political considerations, narrow interests, imposition of power, collective self-righteousness, double standards, persuasive ability, and credibility of the constructed narrative. For example, often because of political considerations and economic interests, third parties judge and evaluate by double standards the narratives and violent behaviors of various groups involved in violent conflict. They may support goals and violence of one group and reject justified goals and violent behavior of another group. In addition, a third party may use well-accepted moral arguments in one case but lead antimoral policies in another case.

Second, both parties in intractable conflicts commit severe violations of human rights. It is possible to find them among Russians and Chechens, among Catholics and Protestants in Northern Ireland, among Hutu and Tutsi in Rwanda, among Israeli Jews and Palestinians, Greek Cypriots and Turkish Cypriots, whites and blacks in South Africa, French and Algerians. They may differ in scope, in methods of brutality, or in chain of command, but all the groups practice atrocities that are defined as crimes against humanity.

Third, groups in intractable conflict make active efforts to bring to light the immoral behaviors of the opponent and hide their own acts of immorality with all possible tactics and methods. In fact, this is part of the active conflict that takes place in the psychological arena. In the first part, the involved parties exaggerate, magnify, and even fabricate the evil acts of the rival. They present them as reflecting an evil disposition, malintended, random, illogical, and unfounded. In the second part, the groups try minimize, present as exceptional, and omit and hide their own immoral acts. This is done through control of information but also by delegitimization of the sources, sometimes even by eliminating them. Groups try to bury very deeply their acts of immorality for as many years as possible. These attempts not only reflect the desire to keep up the dominant group narrative and to uphold the support of the international community but also to maintain the dominant group's self-image, though this may present great psychological difficulty. Such a self-assessment impinges not only on their collective self-esteem but also on their social identity, which plays a central role in the collective life. Thus, it is not surprising that groups suffer amnesia with regard to their own violent immoral acts and often ostracize ingroup members who bring these acts into light. Even some of the most moral preachers become mute when it comes to condemning the immorality of their own group.

Fourth, in asymmetrical intractable conflicts, states carry out vicious acts of violence that violate human rights sometimes no less than groups without a state. But the state violence is often better hidden because the state has control over the access to information and has more means to suppress the information. In contrast, groups without a state often lack institutionalized channels of communication to bring their version to light. States and stronger parties with resources dominate channels of communication and have the opportunities to bring their narrative to the international community. They also often have the power to define what is a legitimate violence or violent group and what is not. In addition, often violence by solders in uniform and by civilized nations is judged less severely than similar violence performed by fighters without uniforms, especially when they reside in the Third World.

Fifth, in violent conflicts it is often lost along the chain of events who was the instigator and who was the reactor in a particular violent conflict. They become one continuum of actions and reactions in which the logic vanishes but the propaganda remains, as each side tries to present the other side as innately and unpredictably intransigent. In reality, at any point in time an act of violence by one group can be seen as a retribution, prevention, or instigation at the same time, depending on the observer of the act.

Sixth, violence in its most immoral form is not only a result of degenerated individuals and groups who carry it out without a formal command. Violence in intractable conflict, with its most horrible atrocities including mass killings or ethnic cleansing, is often carried out with planned schemes by the highest military or civilian authorities. The military and paramilitary units who realize these plans perform these immoral acts not only as a result of conformity and obedience but also because of ideological convictions that contain the ethos of conflict with themes of justness of goals, delegitimization of the rivals, patriotism, and sense of self-collective victimhood. All these themes rationalize violent behavior. Eventually, all the intractable conflicts routinize violence. It becomes naturalized and normalized behavior that society members carry out as part of their role as participants in intractable conflict.

Seventh, it is remarkable how relatively few voices in many of the parties involved in intractable conflicts criticize and protest acts of atrocities performed by their own group and how many go out of the way to spread the information about the immoral behaviors of the rival. Group members practice self-censorship, take active part in silencing voices who try to stop the wrongdoing of their own group, and are ready to make all the efforts to deny, repress, and suppress this information.

Finally, it is deplorable that individuals (including leaders), groups, organizations, and nations often stand as passive bystanders, observing the most horrible acts of violence, without intervention to prevent them. Some individuals and groups are even direct observers of the misdeeds, being on the scene to witness the performance. Sometimes the same individuals and groups that make this complaint about the passivity of the bystanders later carry this practice too. This phenomenon is one of the reasons that wide-scale violence still continues in the world.

These phenomena have profound effects on how the intractable conflicts are managed and play a major role in the difficulty to resolve them. Group members collect information about the atrocities of the rival, memorize them, maintain them in the collective memory, and then evoke them often to justify policies and practices. Eventually violence serves as the major determinant of hostility, hatred, and delegitimization that all contribute to the continuation of the conflict.

I observe that human beings still have not learned how to manage their serious disagreements and contradiction of goals perceived as existential without using violent means. In spite of the fact that nonviolent ideology in conflicts is well established, it is rarely used in interethnic conflicts. Even in the prototypical conflicts where nonviolent struggle was used, violent confrontations were prevalent. The use of violence or nonviolence has become a political issue because often parties that condemn use of violence by another party use violence themselves when they believe it is needed.

I realize that I overstated my case, disregarding a portion of group members in many of the societies involved in intractable conflicts who object to the use of violence, sometimes being ostracized by their fellow group members and in some cases also literally endangering their lives in trying to stop bloodshed or save their victims. It is possible to find in almost every intractable conflict individuals and groups who make a real effort to stop the violence and lead the involved society to peaceful resolution of the conflict. Sometimes they even dare to report the violation of human rights performed by their own group and therefore are viewed as traitors. In some societies these forces are stronger, and in others they are weaker. In some societies they appear at the early stage of the conflict, and in others they evolve slowly. In some cases they even successfully manage the peace-building process and direct the conflict to peaceful resolution and even reconciliation. They are the real heroes in the conflict, whose persistence, adherence, and sacrifices save lives and suffering.

PERSISTENCE OF CONFLICTS

Intractable conflicts last for a long time and are extremely difficult to resolve peacefully. In fact, observation of these conflicts in the past few decades shows that, after the massive solution of the conflicts related to colonialism between colonialized and colonializing societies in the second half of the century, still considerable numbers of intractable conflicts continue to plague the world. Relatively few of the intractable conflicts are resolved formally; some of them are won by one side for the time being, and others continue to exist with fluctuating intensity. It is my premise that wining a military battle or even a war during an intractable conflict does not terminate it, except if the winning party satisfies the basic needs of the rival subjected society. But this process rarely happens as the wining party is confident that the victory determines the outcome of the conflict and therefore does not try to satisfy the needs of the defeated group. Thus, in most of the cases the needs and aspirations continue to exist and may even intensify. In these cases, members of the defeated group wait for another opportunity to renew their violent struggle to achieve their goals.

Many of the intractable conflicts do not end because the demands of both parties are difficult to reconcile. In the first part of this epilogue, I delineated some of the reasons for their resistance to peaceful resolution. The goals are often related to sacred values that cannot be traded off; they often require major distribution of wealth, power, and resources that parties have difficulty carrying out; they often refer to a correction of an injustice that after years of conflict is almost impossible to achieve. In many of the intractable conflicts, the culture of conflict is a special inhibitive force, with its narrative and accompanying emotions that are imparted through decades; it plays a major adaptive function during the conflict and is maintained by channels of communication and institutions. The repertoire of the culture of conflict provides a well-articulated rationale as to why the group should strive to achieve the goals and why it should carry out the conflict without compromises. In this process, agents of conflict, especially in leading positions, also play a major role in maintaining the dominant repertoire. They make an entire career of fueling the conflict. When this repertoire is central, shared by a majority of society members, and held by elites and leaders, then only miracles can terminate the conflict in a peaceful way. Peacemaking requires at least some changes of the repertoire. It is necessary to change at least some views about the rival and the goals in order to enable meaningful negotiation.

Indeed, conflicts cannot develop and be maintained for decades without active support by agents of conflict who have invested interest in their continuation because of various reasons, such as ideological conviction, personal interest, or even tangible profits. They include political, religious, military, and other leaders, together with media persons, NGO organizers, teachers, and other society members who in their position to influence the public make efforts to maintain the conflict by providing explanations, justifications, rationales, and illuminations, using narratives, symbols, myths, and every possible content and its representation in every possible channel of communication. This is a powerful machine that often successfully indoctrinates society members, closes their minds with propaganda, and prevents unbiased reflective and critical thinking. In this analysis, I do not imply that societies involved in intractable conflict do not have justified contentions in some cases. Some societies indeed do. In these cases, the driving forces are based on the accepted moral codes by the international community. But in this part I want to stress the massive organized effort to impart the ideological basis of conflict, which often blinds society members.

Focusing on leaders, I believe that they make a difference. They are often powerful agents or entrepreneurs of conflict. They are the ones who have the determinative weight in evaluating the nature of the conflict with its goals, the contradiction of the goals, the intentions of the rival, the means that are needed to continue the conflict, and the violence used. They could be dogmatic, close-minded ideologues or pragmatic, moral, and open-minded. In crucial points they can move the conflict into moderation, peacemaking, or escalation. They may even cause atrocities and massive violations of human rights. In many cases, they should be blamed for ordering their people to kill, even when they do not do it explicitly. They have often a determinative influence on shaping the views of their constituency, adherence to goals, and portrayal of the rival side. Because society members do not have access to the information that leaders have, they view leaders as epistemic authorities on issues of conflict and assume that leaders make rational decisions on the basis of valid information. In many cases they do not realize that leaders as normal human beings are affected by ideologies, may be closed-minded, promote biased policies, and encourage violence.

I also believe that there is ongoing interaction between the leaders and the society members. That is, leaders influence public opinion not only with their rhetoric but also with their line of action, which may either fuel the conflict or lead to peacemaking; however, they strive to get legitimization by reflecting in their policies and actions the views of society members. In democratic countries, leaders are elected, and they represent the views of the public. Leaders, in their attempt to be reelected, often follow the views of society members. Thus, leaders may escalate the conflict and create a sense of threat, which intensifies support for conflict continuation, and then in turn leaders may comply with the wishes of the public to further escalate the conflict. In any event, the influence of leaders depends on the societal closure, charisma of the leaders and their epistemic authority, freedom of expression, and tolerance toward alternative information. It is important, though, to note that leaders also direct processes of peacemaking. Some may even bravely change their mind from supporting and fueling the conflict to initiating and implementing its peaceful resolution.

I am sure that many different reasons can be added to the explanations that were already noted as to why intractable conflicts last a long time and why many are not resolved peacefully. Among them are the strength of the parties in conflict, lack of internalization of the moral codes, the self-righteousness of the societies involved in conflict, closure of the societies, lack of determination of the international community, indifference of the bystander parties, lack of power of the third parties, and lack of means to bring an end to the conflicts. Different conflicts have different combinations of reasons.

In addition, various powerful third parties, although not directly involved in conflicts, have an invested interest in the eruption and maintenance of one or more conflicts because they serve their interest of dominance, control of resources, and influence. Also, powerful parties that could terminate conflicts do not do so because of various considerations, including considerations of internal politics. I suspect that at least in some cases a powerful third party does not have an interest in ending intractable bloody conflicts. This observation is evident when one sees that in some cases a superpower intervenes and presses either one party or both parties to reach an agreement or takes an active role as mediator, but in other cases it avoids intervention and disrupts attempts of other third parties to carry out peacemaking missions. In fact, I am well aware that realistic politics plays an important role in the way intractable conflicts are managed and sometimes are terminated. While in some conflicts the international community does not reveal much interest and allows the parties to shed blood, in other conflicts a powerful party or third parties have an interest in its continuation because it serves their interests. Also, there are cases in which a powerful party supports unequivocally one side in the conflict and thus plays a detrimental role in its peaceful resolution. Although these factors are considered to be in the domain of international relations, as I already noted socio-psychological factors are also evident in these cases, because those are human beings who are leaders and make decisions. They form policies and lines of actions on the basis of their values, ideology, and system of beliefs. These decisions eventually determine the fate of people involved in conflicts, who pay the price for the taken direction.

In drawing this relatively pessimistic perspective about peaceful resolution of intractable conflict, I already recognized that there are conflicts that successfully achieved peaceful resolution, after years of violent struggle. In addition, in almost every intractable conflict there are segments of the involved society that actively press for the peacemaking process. They vary in size, influence, persistence, legitimization, and institutionalization. But in every society these attempts are viewed with rejection and hostility by those segments of the society striving to continue the conflict. In a few cases, the peace forces eventually succeed to lead their societies to peaceful settlement of the conflict and even to begin a process of reconciliation. In all these cases, it was a long, nonlinear, and complex process, which should seen as a great achievement.

THE EFFECTS OF INTRACTABLE CONFLICT ON THE SOCIETIES INVOLVED

The fundamental assumption is that intractable conflicts have a profound effect on the military-political-societal-economic-cultural system. Conflicts cannot operate separately from the normal cycles of individual and collective life, and the involved societies cannot seal themselves off from the intractable conflict, especially when it takes place within a state of the involved groups. In these cases, usually between a dominant society and a minority, there are continuous processes of interaction between the two societies. These processes touch upon every aspect of the collective life of the involved societies, including security, political, societal, economic, and cultural domains.

Groups are not passive entities. They take up lines of action in response to the situation of conflict. Some of these lines of action may be explicit, while others are not always easily detectable. These lines of action always must leave their marks on collective life. These marks may not appear overnight, but they will gradually penetrate the societies involved in intractable conflict and change their nature. If we focus here on only one example related to cycles of violence, it is possible to observe the following: acts of violence by one group lead to acts of violence by the other group. This influences such processes as redirecting military forces and resources to the new mission, mobilizing society members to participate in the conflict on different levels, constructing narratives by which society members can understand the new situation and act accordingly, developing a new diplomacy that will justify the violent conflict, and redirecting resources for the violent confrontation. These taken steps slowly lead to changes in a society, changes that are not always initially and externally observable.

Prolonged conflicts require many different activities by both societies in many different domains. Each society initiates well-planned and unplanned series of acts, beginning with the military sphere, but also in the legal, political, economic, and other arenas – and they in turn trigger new processes that lead to intended or unintended effects. New goals, interests, needs, trends, and developments appear at all levels of the society. New dogmas arise to justify the continuing conflict; new interest groups emerge, new norms, language, and moral standards develop to support the conflict; conflict-supporting economic investments are made; a new political culture evolves to maintain the conflict; new security needs and new military strategies are developed; new trade markets appear; new laws have to be legalized; the legal system always has to be involved, adapting new codes to the conflict situation; and sometimes groups emerge that object to the conflict and carry out a political struggle against it, reflecting the evolving socio-political polarization.

In general, the themes of the culture of conflict are central in the public debates and agendas, policy making, and courses of actions. They are hegemonic in the public repertoire and have great influence on individual and collective decision making, as, for example, in selecting leaders or voting in elections. In addition, they have influence over the functioning of various institutions of the society in different realms. They have an effect over set policies, legislations, decision making, and courses of actions; for example, they influence division of the national budget, approval of educational curricula, and even rulings in the courts.

An analysis of the influences, however, does not depend only on the formal and informal policies and the derived acts of both societies. It should be remembered that the individual participants in the conflict act and think when they actively participate in the conflict. They accumulate information, experiences, and political views, as well as aspirations and needs. Also, at least some of them leave the arena of the conflict with injuries and psychological wounds. Later they return to their original milieu with a new repertoire that necessarily affects their lives. This new repertoire becomes a new motivating force in their thoughts, feelings, and actions. In this respect, the norms, codes of behavior, morals, and practices that develop in the spheres of conflict do not stop at the conflict areas. They permeate, even unwittingly, into the society and leave their mark on its system of beliefs, attitudes, values, and patterns of behavior.

Conflicts require ideological justification, defense, resources, a legal system, and so on. The society has to adapt to the conflict conditions, to accommodate, to contain, to deal with, to live with the evolving context of prolonged conflict. But not all the effects are intended; many of them are unintended and even undesirable. Nevertheless, they become part of the dynamic processes of societal change in the society. Of importance for an understanding of these effects, we need to remember that societies carry out violent immoral acts that lead to reactions and counterreactions. These acts of violence, including terror, often have a profound effect on the societies engaged in conflict in many areas of personal and collective life. They cause losses and all kinds of injuries on a physical and psychological level that leave open wounds in the society that need to be addressed. Also, use of violence requires numerous steps that are taken to provide security to the involved societies. These steps in turn also have an impact on the life of individuals and the whole collective.

In addition, when a society violates the fundamental principles of justice, morality, and human rights during the intractable conflict, it is condemned to deterioration and decline, at least in regard to its democratic, humane, and moral qualities, which also lead to a corresponding political performance. Societies engaged in violent and vicious conflict become accustomed to mistreating the rival population. This process penetrates into the norms, values, beliefs, and attitudes of the societies and the culture. For example, the massive delegitimization of the rival leads frequently to atrocities and other immoral behaviors, including genocide, without feelings of guilt or shame. It becomes a major justification for violations of the moral standards. In addition, the prolonged conflict diminishes the sensitivity to breaches of moral values, and desensitizes the moral constraints of the societies. Eventually the immoral behavior is not only performed against the rival but also reaches into the intrasocietal system because society members generalize their behaviors and go beyond the boundaries to carry out the immoral acts also toward their co-patriots and their own institutions. All this leads to the weakening of the democratic principles. Societies that engage for a long time in intractable conflict have greater difficulty maintaining democratic values and principles because the essence of the conflict demands their transgression. For example, maintenance of security often requires violation of human rights principles. As a result, protracted violent conflicts frequently lead to penetration of illegality into the society. Societies involved in intractable conflicts minimize the universal values and emphasize the particularistic ones. They have to ignore moral standards and human rights because the actions violate these principles. They use them only in order to discredit the other side.

A few additional salient effects on societies involved in intractable conflicts are worth noting.

First, all the societies in intractable conflicts try to impose one view of the conflict that is in line with the conflict-supporting narrative: they manipulate the public, are intolerant to other views, close the flow of information, control information, and use various societal mechanisms to prevent reaching alterative information. These practices, if they last for many years, have an impact on the political culture of the society – on its openness, freedom of expression, level of tolerance, reflective thinking, and critical thinking. Societies that engage for a long period of violent conflict develop, to a different extent, dogmatic closure, blind patriotism, and monopolization of patriotism with all their implications. This development has to have an effect on the practices of the mass media and the educational system, which has the goal of preparing the young generation to participate in the conflict. Mass media in times of intractable conflict are often mobilized by the authorities and also mobilize themselves voluntarily for the group goals of providing information that is line with the themes of the conflict-supporting narrative. The educational system often not only provides a one-sided narrative but also indoctrinates students, prevents openness, and inhibits critical thinking. These practices often have an impact beyond the themes related to conflict, affecting the overall way of thinking, deliberation, and information processing.

Second, societies involved in conflict lose their grip over moral issues and human rights because they perform serious violations of moral codes continuously and constantly. The attempts to ignore their own violations cannot stop at the door of the society but enter into their own areas. Violations not only obscure the view of reality, judgment, harm, education, and socialization but also lead to their penetration into the psychological and physical space of the societies involved. They weaken the moral norms because once they are violated it is impossible to practice a double standard, carrying out the norms in one place and violating them in another.

Third, intractable conflicts, because of their nature, benefit the military echelon with all its sectors. This means that the military issues get super priority, the military personnel get special status in the society, the military leaders become extremely influential, the society directs much of the resources to the military struggle, and it eventually develops a military-industrial complex that not only becomes influential but also skews the economic development. These processes take place in every society that is involved in intractable conflict, whether it has a state or not. But they become very salient in states that are engaged in intractable conflicts because of the formal and institutionalized processes that are easily observable. On a general level, these societies absorb characteristics of militarism because of the developed values and norms that are needed to carry out violence and to withstand the rival militarily.

Fourth, lasting intractable conflict crystallizes the traditional gender roles and the gap between them. Because males take a major role in the conflict constituting most of the fighters, they are also rewarded for this participation and for their sacrifices by gaining rewards, glory, and stature. This effect causes discrimination and other effects that stabilize the gender differences.

Fifth, intractable conflicts that last for a long time and require mobilization of the society members and resources overshadow other problems and issues that a society confronts. The challenges of the conflict receive ultimate priority. Thus, in these times, societal, economic, or political problems that may plague a society because of societal inequality, discrimination, injustice, or other reasons are set aside. Conflicts lead to diversion of investments into the military struggle from other spheres such as education, health, and welfare. Societies involved in intractable conflicts pass over societal challenges because they want to avoid redirection of major goals; prevent loss of energies, psychological investments, and material resources; and are afraid of disagreements and polarization over issues unrelated to the conflict. Nevertheless, the unresolved problems exist and often grow, being a source of dissatisfaction, alienation, and deprivation. This process leaves an accumulating mark on societal life and causes chronic problems.

Sixth, intractable conflicts weaken democracy. Because of their nature and durability and because of the need to mobilize society members, concentration on the goals of the conflict and the military struggle leads to limitation of free expression, violation of norms of human rights, disproportional influence of the military sector, and the necessary effects on the legal system, which often supports the struggle.

Seventh, emergence of the culture of conflict has a profound effect on the societies involved in intractable conflict. It not only is developed and crystallized on the basis of a selective, biased, and distorting narrative but also carries symbols that idolize death, military power, and victimhood, while developing self-righteousness and insensitivity to the other. These symbols leave an imprint on the societies and serve as a prism to view reality.

Finally, societies involved in a long, violent, intractable conflict adapt to its conditions and become habituated to live with threats, stress, distress, and hardship without even knowing that life can be different; they pay a heavy psychological and social price when they live under these conditions. These conditions necessarily lead to various mental health problems, to development of various anomic societal symptoms, and to considerably reduced quality of life.

To this analysis it is essential to add – and, in fact, to begin – with the tremendous costs that societies in intractable conflict pay in terms of losses, injuries, destruction, suffering, and misery. It is estimated that at least about 50,000 Chechens and 10,000 Russians were killed in the two Chechen wars, at least 40,000 people were killed in Kashmir, and at least 70,000 people were killed in the violent conflict in El Salvador.

I realize that these effects are not unitary. They differ in extent and scope, but it is possible to find them in every society involved in intractable conflict. These differences are dependent on the nature of the intractable conflict, on the structure of the political system, on the grounded political culture and the culture in general, and on the carried collective memory.

In ending this part, I want to reiterate the points I made at the beginning of epilogue. Some of the societies involved in intractable conflict have clearly justified goals, as they come to change unacceptable situations of discrimination, occupation, oppression, or exploitation. These goals need to be achieved to stop injustice and immorality. These goals do not have to be camouflaged but should be stated openly and directly. The international community has the knowledge and codes to identify them. But the major point advanced in this book is that all the intractable conflicts cause harm to society members involved irrespectively of the justness of the goals. All the intractable conflicts involve immoral violence and use the narrative to justify it. Therefore, it is imperative to find ways to resolve these conflicts with a peaceful settlement.

HOW TO PREVENT VIOLENT CONFLICTS

In ending my long journey I deeply believe that one of the most serious challenges for the civilized international community is to find ways to terminate and prevent intractable conflicts.

With regard to solving intractable conflicts peacefully, much has been written about peacemaking processes that focus on the ingroup forces, processes, and dynamics that lead to peacemaking – among them pressures of the civil society and the education of peace. Therefore, I would like to focus here on the responsibility of the international community. This responsibility has to develop, in my view, because I came to believe that in many cases the involved societies do not have the ability or the will to save themselves from the losses, misery, and suffering of the conflict. In these cases, it is the responsibility of the international community and the superpowers to take active steps to help the rival parties to resolve the conflict peacefully. Much has been written concerning the international community about the steps that are needed in the involved societies in order to move them to the path of peacemaking. In addition, almost all the recent successful and unsuccessful attempts to resolve peacefully intractable conflicts included considerable active involvement of a third party – either particular states, international organizations, or even at least part of the international community.

In my view, the international community does not succeed in many cases in imposing what are now well-known moral codes. International mechanisms of mediation or arbitration must be established that in some cases even apply pressure for the parties to accept a solution. This is one of the most important challenges for the future generations. Only when such a practice is institutionalized will societies internalize this approach and accept it. In this way, we can overcome the closure, dogmatism, vicious cycles of violence, self-righteousness, blind patriotism, and adherence to the conflict goals typical of rival parties. Nobody imagined that the international community would be able to establish the International Court of Justice (ICJ) as the primary judicial organ of the United Nations based in The Hague. Its main functions are to settle legal disputes submitted to it by states and to provide advisory opinions on legal questions submitted to it by duly authorized international organs, agencies, and the UN General Assembly. Also, it would have been hard to imagine that states would establish the International Criminal Court (ICC) as a permanent tribunal to prosecute individuals for genocide, crimes against humanity, and war crimes. On the basis of these and other examples of progress, it is possible to imagine establishment of international organizations with enforcement mechanisms that can responsibly and peacefully end the intractable conflicts that cause so much damage to the involved societies and to the world in general.

It is important to curb the interests and greediness of the superpowers that disregard often the moral norms to advance their interests. Some of these powers practice double standards in which in certain cases they support conflicts and in other cases decide to terminate them. They compromise the moral norms and subject them to narrow interests that not only cause misery to the involved societies in intractable conflicts but also damage the moral order of the international community and credibility of justice. The major efforts for change depend to a large extent on the members of the international community. At present, few of the societies hold moral values as major principles of practice. Many like to talk about them and express support for them, but in reality most societies see them as being utopic and unpractical at best and often as negating their narrow interests, particularistic values, and collective identity.

In my view, the challenge that is posed before all of us is to establish a system of beliefs, attitudes, values, and norms that cherish peace, justice, and morality.

I know that to many it may look like an unrealistic goal and to others like a long-term goal. I prefer the latter view because it still gives hope. To achieve this goal, human beings wherever they live and especially in societies ridden by intractable conflict have to struggle to establish institutions, socialization patterns, and educational systems that encourage functioning of openness, tolerance, freedom of expression, critical and reflective thinking, personal and collective accountability, and responsibility. Then, with these skills societies should engage in ongoing deliberations on every societal level about human rights, the consequences of violence, the nature and outcomes of delegitimization, obedience, crimes against humanity, freedom of expression, the meaning of closed-mindedness, justice, equality, discrimination, and oppression – not only to elaborate the meaning and consequences in general but with a special focus on the ingroup context, with the central objective to establish new beliefs, attitudes, values, and norms of morality, peace, justice, and human rights. This is a tremendous challenge for civilization, if it desires to stop the continuous bloodshed, which seems so hard to eliminate.

I end my book with the vision:

> *And they shall beat their swords into plowshares,*
> *and their spears into pruning hooks;*
> *nation shall not lift up sword against nation,*
> *neither shall they learn war any more.*
>
> Isaiah 2:4

References

Abbott, H. P. (2002). *The Cambridge introduction to narrative.* Cambridge: Cambridge University Press.
Abelson, R. P., Aronson, E., McGuire, W. J., Newcomb, T. M., Rosenberg, M. J., & Tannenbaum, R. H. (Eds.), (1968). *Theories of cognitive consistency: A sourcebook.* Chicago: Rand McNally.
Abrams, D., & Hogg, M. (1990). Social identification, self-categorization and social influence. *European Review of Social Psychology, 1,* 195–228.
Abu-Lughod, L., & Sa'di, A. (2007). Introduction: The claims of memory. In A. Sa'di & L. Abu-Lughod (Eds.), *Nakba: Palestine, 1948, and the claims of memory* (pp. 1–24). New York: Columbia University Press.
Abu-Nimer, M. (2004). Education for coexistence and Arab-Jewish encounters in Israel: Potential and challenges. *Journal of Social Issues, 60*(2), 405–422.
Ackermann, A. (1994). Reconciliation as a peace-building process in post-war Europe: The Franco-German case. *Peace & Change, 19,* 229–250.
Adorno, T. W., Frenkel-Brunswik, E., Levinson, D. J., & Sanford, R. N. (1950). *The authoritarian personality.* New York: Harper.
Adwan, S., & Bar-On, D. (2000). *The role of non-governmental organizations in peace building between Palestinians and Israelis.* Jerusalem: Peace Research Institute in the Middle East.
   (2004). Shared history project: A PRIME example of peace building under fire. *International Journal of Politics, Culture and Society, 17,* 513–522.
Adwan, S., Bar-On, D., & Naveh, E. (Eds.), (2012). *Side by side: Parallel histories of Israel-Palestine.* New York: New Press.
Agence France Press (2008). Sudan: Darfur conflict timeline. July 11. Retrieved August 3, 2008, from http://www.reliefweb.int/rw/rwb.nsf/db900SID/YSAR-7GFMY6?OpenDocument.
Agius, E., & Ambrosewicz, J. (2003). *Towards a culture of tolerance and peace.* Montreal: International Bureau for Children's Rights (IBCR).
Agnew, J. (1989). Beyond reason: Spatial and temporal sources of ethnic conflicts. In L. Kriesberg, T. A. Northup, & S. J. Thorson (Eds.), *Intractable conflicts and their transformation* (pp. 41–52). Syracuse: Syracuse University Press.

Aguilar, P. (2002). *Memory and amnesia: The role of the Spanish civil war in the transition to democracy*. London: Berghahn Books.

Alexander, J. C. (2004). Toward a theory of cultural trauma. In J. C., Alexander, R. Eyerman, B. Giesen, N. J. Smelser, & P. Sztompka (Eds.), *Cultural trauma and collective identity* (pp. 1–30). Berkeley: University of California Press.

Alexander, M. G., Brewer, M. B., & Herrmann, R. K. (1999). Images and affect: A functional analysis of out-group stereotypes. *Journal of Personality and Social Psychology, 77*, 78–93.

Allen, V. I. (1965). Situational factors in conformity. In L. Berkowitz (Ed.), *Advances in experimental social psychology* (Vol. 2, pp. 133–175). San Diego: Academic Press.

Allport, G. W. (1954). *The nature of prejudice*. Cambridge, MA: Addison-Wesley.

Almagor (2011). Almagor Terror Victims Association's website. Retrieved March 27, 2011, from http://www.al-magor.com/index.htm.

Almog, O. (1992). *Israeli war memorials: A semiological analysis*. Master's thesis, Tel-Aviv University. (in Hebrew)

Almond, G. A., & Verba, S. (1989). *The civic culture: Political attitudes and democracy in five nations*. London: Sage.

Alonso, A. M. (1988). The effects of truth: Re-presentations of the past and the imagining of community. *Journal of Historical Sociology, 1*(1), 33–57.

Altemeyer, B. (1981). *Right-wing authoritarianism*. Winnipeg, Canada: University of Manitoba Press.

Amir, Y. (1969). Contact hypothesis in ethnic relations. *Psychological Bulletin, 71*, 319–341.

Amirav, M. (2009). *Jerusalem syndrome: The Palestinian-Israeli battle for the holy city*. Eastbourne: Sussex Academic Press.

Amstutz, M. R. (2005). *International ethics: Concepts, theories, and cases in global politics* (2nd ed.). Lanham, MD: Rowman & Littlefield.

Anderson, B. (1983). *Imagined communities: Reflections on the origins and spread of nationalism*. London: Verso.

Andreopoulus, G. J., & Claude, R. P. (Eds.), (1997). *Human rights education for the twenty-first century*. Philadelphia: University of Pennsylvania Press.

Andrews, M. (2002). Introduction: Counter-narratives and the power to oppose. *Narrative Inquiry, 12*, 1–6.

(2003). Grand national narratives and the project of truth commissions: A comparative analysis. *Media, Culture & Society, 25*, 45–65.

(2007). *Shaping history: Narratives of political change*. Cambridge: Cambridge University Press.

Antonovsky, A. (1987). *Unraveling the mystery of health: How people manage stress and stay well*. San Francisco: Jossey-Bass.

Antonovsky, A., & Arian, A. (1972). *Hopes and fears of Israelis: Consensus in a new society*. Jerusalem: Jerusalem Academic Press.

Anzulovic, B. (1999). *Heavenly Serbia: From myth to genocide*. New York: New York University Press.

Apter, D. E. (Ed.), (1997). *Legitimization of violence*. New York: New York University Press.

Archer, D., & Gartner, R. (1987). *Violence and crime in cross-national perspective*. New Haven, CT: Yale University Press.

Arian, A. (1989). A people apart: Coping with national security problems in Israel. *Journal of Conflict Resolution, 33,* 605–631.

(1995). *Security threatened: Surveying Israeli opinion on peace and war.* Cambridge: Cambridge University Press.

Armon-Jones, C. (1986). The social functions of emotions. In R. Harré (Ed.), *The social construction of emotions* (pp. 57–97). Oxford: Blackwell.

Armstrong, J. A. (1982). *Nations before nationalism.* Chapel Hill: University of North Carolina Press.

Arnold, M. B. (1960). *Emotion and personality* (Vols. 1 and 2). New York: Columbia University Press.

Arnson, C. J. (Ed.), (1999a). *Comparative peace processes in Latin America.* Stanford, CA: Stanford University Press.

(1999b). Conclusion: Lessons learned in comparative perspective. In C. J. Arnson (Ed.), *Comparative peace processes in Latin America* (pp. 447–463). Stanford, CA: Stanford University Press.

Arthur, P. (1999). The Anglo-Irish peace process: Obstacles to reconciliation. In R. L. Rothstein (Ed.), *After the peace: Resistance and reconciliation* (pp. 85–109). Boulder, CO: Lynne Rienner.

(2009). *Identities in transition: Developing better transitional justice initiatives in divided societies.* New York: International Center for Transitional Justice.

Arunatilake, N., Jayasuriya, S., & Kelegama, S. (2001). The economic cost of the war in Sri Lanka. *World Development, 29*(9), 1483–1500.

Arutiunov, S. (1995). Ethnicity and conflict in the Caucasus. In F. Wehling (Ed.), *Ethnic conflict and Russian intervention in the Caucasus* (pp. 15–18). San Diego: University of California.

Arviv-Abromovich, R. (2011). *Societal beliefs about the Israeli–Arab Palestinian conflict transmitted in national ceremonies – 1948–2006.* Ph.D. dissertation, Tel Aviv University. (in Hebrew)

Ashmore, D. R., Bird, D., Del-Boca, F. K., & Vanderet, R. C. (1979). An experimental investigation of the double standard in the perception of international affairs. *Political Behavior, 1,* 123–135.

Ashmore, R. D., Deaux, K., & McLaughlin-Volpe, T. (2004). An organizing framework for collective identity: Articulation and significance of multidimensionality. *Psychological Bulletin, 130,* 80–114.

Asmal, K., Asmal, L., & Roberts, R. S. (1997). *Reconciliation through truth: A reckoning of apartheid's criminal governance.* Cape Town: David Phillips Publishers.

Assmann, J. (1995). Collective memory and cultural identity. *New German Critique, 65,* 125–133.

Atran, S., & Axelrod, R. (2008). Reframing sacred values. *Negotiation Journal, 24,* 221–246.

Auerbach, Y. (1980). *Foreign policy decisions and attitude changes: Israel-Germany, 1950–1965.* Ph.D. dissertation, Hebrew University of Jerusalem. (in Hebrew)

(2004). The role of forgiveness in reconciliation. In Y. Bar-Siman-Tov (Ed.), *From conflict resolution to reconciliation* (pp. 149–175). New York: Oxford University Press.

(2009). The reconciliation pyramid: A narrative-based framework for analyzing identity conflicts. *Political Psychology, 30,* 292–318.

(2010). National narratives in a conflict of identity. In J. Bar-Siman-Tov (Ed.), *Barriers to peace in the Israeli-Palestinian conflict* (pp. 99–134). Jerusalem: The Jerusalem Institute for Israel Studies.

Averill, J. R. (1980). A constructivist view of emotion. In R. Plutchik & H. Kellerman (Eds.), *Theories of emotion* (pp. 305–340). New York: Academic Press.

(1982). *Anger and aggression: An essay on emotion*. New York: Springer-Verlag.

Averill, J. R., Catlin, G., & Chon, K. K. (1990). *Rules of hope*. New York: Springer-Verlag.

Avery, P. G., Johnson, D. W., Johnson, R. T., & Mitchell, J. M. (1999). Teaching and understanding of war and peace through structured academic controversies. In A. Raviv, L. Oppenheimer, & D. Bar-Tal (Eds.), *How children understand war and peace: A call for international peace education* (pp. 260–280). San Francisco: Jossey-Bass.

Avruch, K. (1998). *Culture & conflict resolution*. Washington, DC: United States Institute of Peace.

Avtgis, T. A., & Rancer, A. S. (Eds.), (2010). *Argument, aggression and conflict: New direction in theory and research*. New York: Routledge.

Axelrod, R. (1967). Conflict of interest: An axiomatic approach. *Journal of Conflict Resolution*, 11, 87–99.

Azar, E. E. (1986). Protracted international conflicts: Ten propositions. In E. E. Azar & J. W. Burton (Eds.), *International conflict resolution* (pp. 28–39). Sussex: Wheatsheaf Books.

(1990). *The management of protracted social conflict*. Hampshire: Dartmouth Publishing.

Azar, E. E., & Farah, N. (1981). The structure of inequalities and protracted social conflict: A theoretical framework. *International Interactions*, 7, 317–335.

Azaryahu, M. (1995). *State cults: Celebrating independence and commemorating the fallen in Israel, 1948–1956*. Beer Sheva: Ben-Gurion University of the Negev Press. (in Hebrew)

Azburu, D. (1999). Peace and democratization in Guatemala: Two parallel processes. In C. J. Arnson (Ed.), *Comparative peace processes in Latin America* (pp. 97–127). Stanford, CA: Stanford University Press.

Baas, D., Aleman, A., & Kahn, R. S. (2004). Lateralization of amygdale activation: A systematic review of functional neuroimaging studies. *Brain Research Reviews*, 45, 96–103.

Backer, D. (2007). Victims' responses to truth commissions: Evidence from South Africa. In M. Ndulo (Ed.), *Security, reconstruction and reconciliation: When the war ends* (pp. 165–196). London: University College London.

(2009). Cross-national comparative analysis. In H. van der Merwe, V. Baxter, & A. R. Chapman (Eds.), *Assessing the impact of transitional justice: Challenges for empirical research* (pp. 23–91). Washington, DC: United States Institute for Peace.

Baker, M. (2006). *Translation and conflict: A narrative account*. New York: Routledge.

Ball, N. (1996). The challenges of rebuilding war-torn societies. In C. A. Crocker, F. O. Hampson, & P. Aall (Eds.), *Managing global chaos: Sources of conflict and responses to international conflict* (pp. 607–622). Washington, DC: United States Institute of Peace Press.

Ball, P. D., Kobrak, P., & Spirer, H. F. (1999). *State violence in Guatemala, 1969–1966: A quantitative reflection*. Washington, DC: American Association for Advancement of Science.

Bamberg, M. G. W., & Andrews, M. (2004). *Considering counter narratives: Narrating, resisting, making sense.* Amsterdam: J. Benjamins.
Bandura, A. (1986). *Social foundations of thought and action: A social cognitive theory.* Englewood Cliffs, NJ: Prentice-Hall.
   (1990). Selective activation and disengagement of moral control. *Journal of Social Issues, 46*(1), 27–46.
   (1997). *Self-efficacy: The exercise of control.* New York: Freeman.
   (1999). Moral disengagement in the perpetration of inhumanities. *Personality and Social Psychology Review, 3*(3), 193–209.
   (2000). Exercise of human agency through collective efficacy. *Current Direction in Psychological Science,* 75–78.
Bandura, A., Caprara, G. V., Barbaranelli, C., Pastorelli, C., & Regalia, C. (2001). Sociocognitive self-regulatory mechanisms governing transgressive behavior. *Journal of Personality and Social Psychology, 80,* 125–135.
Bandura, A., Underwood, B., & Fromson, M. E. (1975). Disinhibition of aggression through diffusion of responsibility and dehumanization of victims. *Journal of Research in Personality, 9,* 253–269.
Bandura, A., & Walters, R. H. (1963). *Social learning and personality development.* New York: Holt, Rinehart & Winston.
Barash, D. P., & Webel, C. (2002). *Peace and conflict studies.* London: Sage.
Barbalet, J. M. (1998). *Emotion, social theory, and social structure: A macrosociological approach.* Cambridge: Cambridge University Press.
Barber, B. (1983). *The logic and limits of trust.* New Brunswick, NJ: Rutgers University Press.
Barber, J. (1999). *South Africa in the twentieth century.* Oxford: Blackwell.
Bar-Gal, Y. (1993). *Homeland and geography in a hundred years of Zionist education.* Tel Aviv: Am Oved (Hebrew).
Bargal, D., & Sivan, E. (2004). Leadership and reconciliation. In Y. Bar-Siman- Tov (Ed.), *From conflict resolution to reconciliation* (pp. 125–147). Oxford: Oxford University Press.
Bar-Gal, Y. (1993). *Homeland and geography in a hundred years of Zionist education.* Tel Aviv: Am Oved (Hebrew).
Bargh, J. A. (1997). Automaticity of everyday life. *Advances in Social Cognition, 10,* 1–61.
   (2001). Caution: automatic social cognition may not be habit forming. In R. K. Ohme (Ed.), *Polish Psychological Bulletin – special issue* 32(1), 1–8.
   (2007). *Social psychology and the unconsciousness: The automaticity of higher mental processes.* New York: Psychology Press.
Bargh, J. A., Chen, M., & Burrows, L. (1996). Automaticity of social behavior: Direct effects of trait construct and stereotype activation on action. *Journal of Personality and Social Psychology, 71*(2), 230–244.
Barkan, E. (2000). *The guilt of nations: Restitution and negotiating historical injustices.* New York: W. W. Norton.
Barnard, C. (2001). Isolating knowledge of the unpleasant: The rape of Nanking in Japanese high-school textbooks. *British Journal of Sociology of Education, 22*(4), 519–530.
Barnes, H. E. (1997). Theatre for reconciliation: Desire and South African students. *Theatre Journal, 49,* 41–52.

Bar-On, D. (2000). Cultural identity and demonization of the relevant other: Lessons from the Palestinian-Israeli conflict. In A. Y. Shalev, R. Yehuda, & A. C. McFarlane (Eds.), *International handbook of human response to trauma* (pp. 115–125). New York: Plenum.

(2002). Conciliation through storytelling: Beyond victimhood. In G. Salomon & B. Nevo (Eds.), *Peace education: The concept, principles and practices around the world* (pp. 109–116). Mahwah, NJ: Erlbaum.

(2006). *Tell your life story: Creating dialogue among Jews and Germans, Israelis and Palestinians.* New York: Central European University Press.

Bar-On, D., & Adwan, S. (2006). *The PRIME shared history project: Peacebuilding project under fire; Educating toward a culture of peace* (pp. 309–323). Charlotte, NC: Information Age Publishing.

Bar-On, M. (1996). *In pursuit of peace: A history of the Israeli Peace Movement.* Washington, DC: United States Institute of Peace Press.

(2006). Conflicting narratives of narratives of conflict: Can the Zionist and the Palestinian narratives of the 1948 War be bridged? In R. Rotberg (Ed.), *Israeli and Palestinian narratives of conflict – History's double helix* (pp. 142–173). Bloomington: Indiana University Press.

Baron, J., & Spranca, M. (1997). Protected values. *Organizational Behavior and Human Decision Processes, 70*(1), 1–16.

Baron, R. A., & Richardson, D. (1994). *Human aggression.* New York: Plenum.

Bar-Siman-Tov, Y. (1994). *Israel and the peace process, 1977–1982: In search of legitimacy for peace.* Albany: State University of New York Press.

(1995). Value-complexity in shifting form war to peace: The Israeli peace-making experience with Egypt. *Political Psychology, 16,* 545–565.

(1996). *The transition from war to peace: The complexity of decision making – The Israeli case.* Tel Aviv: Tel Aviv University, The Tami Steinmetz Center for Peace Research.

(Ed.), (2004). *From conflict resolution to reconciliation.* New York: Oxford University Press.

Bar-Siman-Tov, Y., & Kacowicz, A. M. (2000). Stable peace: A conceptual framework. In A. M. Kacowicz, Y. Bar-Siman-Tov, O. Elgstrom, & M. Jerneck (Eds.), *Stable peace among nations* (pp. 11–35). Lanham, MD: Rowman & Littlefield.

Bar-Siman-Tov, Y., Lavie, E., Michael, K., & Bar-Tal, D. (2007). The Israeli-Palestinian violent confrontation: An Israeli perspective. In Y. Bar-Siman-Tov (Ed.), *The Israeli-Palestinian conflict: From conflict resolution to conflict management* (pp. 69–100). Houndmills: Palgrave Macmillan.

Bar-Tal, D. (1988). Delegitimizing relations between Israeli Jews and Palestinians: A social psychological analysis. In J. Hofman (Ed.), *Arab-Jewish relations in Israel: A quest in human understanding* (pp. 217–248). Bristol, IN: Wyndham Hall Press.

(1989). Delegitimization: The extreme case of stereotyping and prejudice. In D. Bar-Tal, C. F. Graumann, A. W. Kruglanski, & W. Stroebe (Eds.), *Stereotyping and prejudice: Changing conceptions* (pp. 169–182). New York: Springer Verlag.

(1990a). Causes and consequences of delegitimization: Models of conflict and ethnocentrism. *Journal of Social Issues, 46,* 65–81.

(1990b). Israeli-Palestinian conflict: A cognitive analysis. *International Journal of Intercultural Relations, 14,* 7–29.

(1990c). *Group beliefs: A conception for analyzing group structure, processes and behavior.* New York: Springer-Verlag.
(1993). Patriotism as fundamental beliefs of group members. *Politics and Individual,* 3, 45–62.
(1997). The monopolization of patriotism. In D. Bar-Tal & E. Staub (Eds.), *Patriotism in the life of individuals and nations* (pp. 246–270). Chicago: Nelson Hall.
(1998a). Societal beliefs in times of intractable conflict: The Israeli case. *International Journal of Conflict Management,* 9, 22–50.
(1998b). The rocky road towards peace: Societal beliefs functional to intractable conflict in Israeli school textbooks. *Journal of Peace Research,* 35, 723–742.
(1998c). Group beliefs as an expression of social identity. In S. Worchel, J. F. Morales, D. Paez, & J. C. Deschamps (Eds.), *Social identity: International perspectives* (pp. 93–113). Thousand Oaks, CA: Sage.
(2000a). *Shared beliefs in a society: Social psychological analysis.* Thousand Oaks, CA: Sage.
(2000b). From intractable conflict through conflict resolution to reconciliation: Psychological analysis. *Political Psychology,* 21, 351–365.
(2001). Why does fear override hope in societies engulfed by intractable conflict, as it does in the Israeli society? *Political Psychology,* 22, 601–627.
(2002). The elusive nature of peace education. In G. Salomon & B. Nevo (Eds.), *Peace education: The concept, principles and practice around the world* (pp. 27–36). Mahwah, NJ: Erlbaum.
(2003). Collective memory of physical violence: Its contribution to the culture of violence. In E. Cairns & M. D. Roe (Eds.), *The role of memory in ethnic conflict* (pp. 77–93). Houndmills: Palgrave Macmillan.
(2007a). *Living with the conflict: Socio-psychological analysis of the Israeli-Jewish society.* Jerusalem: Carmel. (in Hebrew)
(2007b). Sociopsychological foundations of intractable conflicts. *American Behavioral Scientist,* 50, 1430–1453.
(2009). Reconciliation as a foundation of culture of peace. In J. de Rivera (Ed.), *Handbook on building cultures for peace* (pp. 363–377). New York: Springer.
(2010). Culture of conflict: Evolvement, institutionalization, and consequences. In R. Schwarzer & P. A. Frensch (Eds.), *Personality, human development, and culture: International perspectives on psychological science* (Vol. 2, pp. 183–198). New York: Psychology Press.
(Ed.), (2011a). *Intergroup conflicts and their resolution: Social psychological perspective.* New York: Psychology Press.
(2011b). Introduction: Conflicts and social psychology. In D. Bar-Tal (Ed.), *Intergroup conflicts and their resolution: Social psychological perspective* (pp. 1–38). New York: Psychology Press.
Bar-Tal, D., Abutbul, G., & Raviv, A. (in press). Routinization of the intractable conflict. In T. Capelos, H. Dekker, C. Kinvall, & P. Nesbitt-Larkin (Eds.), *The Palgrave handbook of global political psychology.* Houndmills: Palgrave Macmillan.
Bar-Tal, D., & Antebi, D. (1992a). Siege mentality in Israel. *International Journal of Intercultural Relations,* 16, 251–275.
(1992b). Beliefs about negative intentions of the world: A study of the Israeli siege mentality. *Political Psychology,* 13, 633–645.

Bar-Tal, D., & Bennink, G. H. (2004). The nature of reconciliation as an outcome and as a process. In Y. Bar-Siman-Tov (Ed.), *From conflict resolution to reconciliation* (pp. 11–38). Oxford: Oxford University Press.

Bar-Tal, D., & Čehajić-Clancy, S. (in press). From collective victimhood to social reconciliation: Outlining a conceptual framework. In D. Spini, D. Čorkalo Biruški, & G. Elcheroth (Eds.), *War and community: Collective experiences in the former Yugoslavia*. New York: Springer.

Bar-Tal, D., Chernyak-Hai, L., Schori, N., & Gundar, A. (2009). A sense of self-perceived collective victimhood in intractable conflicts. *International Red Cross Review*, 91, 229–277.

Bar-Tal, D., & Geva, N. (1986). A cognitive basis of international conflicts. In S. Worchel & W. B. Austin (Eds.), *Psychology of intergroup relations* (2nd ed., pp. 118–133). Chicago: Nelson-Hall.

Bar-Tal, D., & Halperin, E. (2009). Overcoming psychological barriers to peace process: The influence of beliefs about losses. In M. Mikulincer & P. R. Shaver (Eds.), *Prosocial motives, emotions and behaviors: The better angels of our nature* (pp. 431–448). Washington, DC: American Psychological Association Press.

(2011). Socio-psychological barriers to conflict resolution. In D. Bar-Tal (Ed.), *Intergroup conflicts and their resolution: Social psychological perspective* (pp. 217–240). New York: Psychology Press.

(in press). Intractable conflict: Eruption, escalation and peacemaking. In L. Huddy, D. Sears, & J. Levy (Eds.), *Oxford handbook of political psychology*. New York: Oxford University Press.

Bar-Tal, D., Halperin, E., & de Rivera, J. (2007). Collective emotions in conflict: Societal implications. *Journal of Social Issues*, 63, 441–460.

Bar-Tal, D., Halperin, E., & Oren, N. (2010). Socio-psychological barriers to peace making: The case of the Israeli Jewish society. *Social Issues and Policy Review*, 4, 63–109.

Bar-Tal, D., & Hammack, P. L. (2012). Conflict, delegitimization and violence In L. R. Tropp (Ed.), *Oxford handbook of intergroup conflict* (pp. 29–52). New York: Oxford University Press.

Bar-Tal, D., & Jacobson, D. (1998). Psychological perspective on security. *Applied Psychology: An International Review*, 47, 59–71.

Bar-Tal, D., Jacobson, D., & Freund, T. (1995). Security feelings among Jewish settlers in the occupied territories: A study of communal and personal antecedents. *Journal of Conflict Resolution*, 39, 353–377.

Bar-Tal, D., Jacobson, D., & Klieman, A. (Eds.), (1998). *Security concerns: Insights from the Israeli experience*. Stamford, CT: JAI Press.

Bar-Tal, D., Kahn, D., Raviv, A., & Halperin, E. (2010). *Trust and distrust in intergroup conflicts*. Unpublished manuscript, Tel Aviv University.

Bar-Tal, D., Kruglanski, A. W., & Klar, Y. (1989). Conflict termination: An epistemological analysis of international cases. *Political Psychology*, 10, 233–255.

Bar-Tal, D., Landman, S., Magal, T., & Rosler, N. (2009). *Societal-psychological dynamics of peace-making process – A conceptual framework*. Paper presented at the small meeting of the European Association of Social Psychology about "Resolving societal conflicts and building peace: Socio-psychological dynamics." Jerusalem, September 7–10.

Bar-Tal, D., Magal, T., & Halperin, E. (2009). The paradox of security views in Israel: Socio-psychological explanation. In G. Sheffer & O. Barak (Eds.), *Existential threats and civil security relations* (pp. 219–247). Lanham, MD: Lexington Books.

Bar-Tal, D., Ofek, R., & Shachar, R. (2002). *Expressions of peace societal beliefs in popular songs in Israel – 1948–2000*. Unpublished manuscript, Tel Aviv University.

Bar-Tal, D., & Oren, N. (2000). *Ethos as an expression of identity: Its changes in transition from conflict to peace in the Israeli case* (discussion paper No. 83). Jerusalem: The Leonard Davis Institute for International Relations, The Hebrew University of Jerusalem.

Bar-Tal, D., Oren, N., & Nets-Zehngut, R. (2012). *Socio-psychological analysis of conflict-supporting narratives*. Unpublished manuscript.

Bar-Tal, D., Raviv, A., & Freund, T. (1994). An anatomy of political beliefs: A study of their centrality, confidence, contents, and epistemic authority. *Journal of Applied Social Psychology, 24*, 849–872.

Bar-Tal, D., Raviv, A., Raviv, A., & Dgani-Hirsch, A. (2009). The influence of the ethos of conflict on the Israeli Jews' interpretation of Jewish-Palestinian encounters. *Journal of Conflict Resolution, 53*, 94–118.

Bar-Tal, D., Rosen, Y., & Nets-Zehngut, Z. R. (2010). Peace education in societies involved in intractable conflicts: Goals, conditions, and directions. In G. Salomon & E. Cairns (Eds.), *Handbook of peace education* (pp. 21–43). New York: Psychology Press.

Bar-Tal, D., & Salomon, G. (2006). Israeli-Jewish narratives of the Israeli-Palestinian conflict: Evolution, contents, functions and consequences. In R. Rotberg (Ed.), *Israeli and Palestinian narratives of conflict: History's double helix* (pp. 19–46). Bloomington: Indiana University Press.

Bar-Tal, D., & Saxe, L. (1990). Acquisition of political knowledge: A social psychological analysis. In O. Ichilov (Ed.), *Political socialization, citizenship education and democracy* (pp. 116–133). New York: Teachers College Press.

Bar-Tal, D., & Schnell, I. (Eds.), (2013a). *The impacts of lasting occupation: Lessons from Israel society*. New York: Oxford University Press.

(2013b). Introduction: Occupied and occupier –The Israeli case. In D. Bar-Tal & I. Schnell (Eds.), *The impacts of lasting occupation: Lessons from Israel society*. New York: Oxford University Press.

Bar-Tal, D., & Sharvit, K. (2008). The influence of the threatening transitional context on Israeli Jews' reactions to Al Aqsa Intifada. In V. M. Esses & R. A. Vernon (Eds.), *Explaining the breakdown of ethnic relations: Why neighbors kill* (pp. 147–170). Oxford: Blackwell.

Bar-Tal, D., Sharvit, K., Halperin, E., & Zafran, A. (2012). Ethos of conflict: The concept and its measurement. *Peace & Conflict. Journal of Peace Psychology, 18*, 4061.

Bar-Tal, D., & Staub, E. (Eds.), (1997). *Patriotism in the lives of individuals and nations*. New York: Nelson-Hall.

Bar-Tal, D., & Teichman Y. (2005). *Stereotypes and prejudice in conflict: Representations of Arabs in Israeli Jewish society*. Cambridge: Cambridge University Press.

Bar-Tal, Y. (1994). The effect of need and ability to achieve cognitive structure on mundane decision making. *European Journal of Personality, 8*, 45–58.

(2010). When the need for cognitive structure does not cause heuristic thinking: The moderating effect of perceived ability to achieve cognitive structure. *Psychology, 1*, 96–105.

Bar-Tal, Y., Bar-Tal, D., & Cohen-Hendeles, E. (2006). The influence of context and political identification on Israeli Jews' views of Palestinians. *Peace and Conflict: Journal of Peace Psychology, 12,* 229–250.

Bar-Tal, Y., Kishon-Rabin, L., & Tabak, N. (1997). The effect of need and ability to achieve cognitive structure on cognitive structuring. *Journal of Personality and Social Psychology, 73,* 1158–1176.

Bar-Tal, Y., Raviv, A., & Spitzer, A. (1999). Individual differences that moderate the effect of stress on information processing. *Journal of Personality and Social Psychology, 77,* 33–51.

Bar-Tal, Y., Shrira, A., & Keinan, G. (in press). The effect of stress on cognitive structuring: A cognitive motivational model. *Personality and Social Psychology Review.*

Bartels, L. M. (2002). Beyond the running tally: Partisan bias in political perceptions. *Political Behavior, 24,* 117–150.

Barth, F. (1969). *Ethnic groups and boundaries: The social organization of cultural difference.* Boston: Little, Brown.

Barthel D. (1996). *Historic preservation: Collective memory and historical identity.* New Brunswick, NJ: Rutgers University Press.

Barton, K. C., & McCully, A. W. (2005). History, identity, and the school curriculum in Northern Ireland: An empirical study of secondary students' ideas and perspectives. *Journal of Curriculum Studies, 37,* 85–116.

Bartunek, J. M. (1993). The multiple cognitions and conflict associated with second order organizational change. In J. K. Murnighan (Ed.), *Social psychology in organizations: Advances in theory and research* (pp. 322–349). Englewood Cliffs, NJ: Prentice Hall.

Barua, P. (1995). Economic CBMs between India and Pakistan. In M. Krepon & A. Sevak (Eds.), *Crisis prevention, confidence building and reconciliation in South Asia* (pp. 153–169). New York: St. Martin's Press.

Barzilai, G. (1992). *A democracy in wartime: Conflict and consensus in Israel.* Tel Aviv: Sifriat Poalim. (in Hebrew)

——— (1996). State, society, and national security: Mass communications and wars. In M. Lisak & B. Knei-Paz (Eds.), *Israel toward the third millennium: Society, politics and culture* (pp. 176–194). Jerusalem: Magnes Press. (in Hebrew)

Batson, C. D. (1991). *The altruism question: Toward a social-psychological answer.* Hillsdale, NJ: Erlbaum.

——— (2009). Two forms of perspective taking: Imagining how another feels and imagining how you would feel. In K. D. Markman, W. M. Klein, & J. A. Suhr (Eds.), *The handbook of imagination and mental simulation* (pp. 267–279). New York: Psychology Press.

Batson, C. D., & Ahmad, N. Y. (2009). Using empathy to improve intergroup attitudes and relations. *Social Issues and Policy Review, 3,* 141–177.

Batson, C. D., Ahmad, N., Lishner, D. A., & Tsang, J. (2005). Empathy and altruism. In C. R. Snyder & S. J. Lopez (Eds.), *Handbook of positive psychology* (pp. 485–498). New York: Oxford University Press.

Batson, C. D., Eklund, J. H., Chermok, V. L., Hoyt, J. L., & Ortiz, B. G. (2007). An additional antecedent of empathic concern: Valuing the welfare of the person in need. *Journal of Personality and Social Psychology, 93,* 65–74.

Batson, C. D., Polycarpou, M. P., Harmon-Jones, E., Imhoff, H. J., Mitchener, E. C., Bednar, L. L., Klein, T. R., & Highberger, L. (1997). Empathy and attitudes: Can feeling for a member of a stigmatized group improve feelings toward the group? *Journal of Personality and Social Psychology, 72*, 105–118.

Bauer, Y. (1982). *A history of the Holocaust*. New York: F. Watts.

Baumeister, R. F. (1991). *Meaning of life*. New York: Guilford.

(1997). *Evil: Inside human violence and cruelty*. New York: Freeman.

Baumeister, R. F., Bratslavsky, E., Finkenauer, C., & Vohs, K. (2001). Bad is stronger than good. *Review of General Psychology, 5*, 323–370.

Baumeister, R. F., & Butz, J. (2005). Roots of hate, violence and evil. In R. J. Sternberg (Ed.),(2005). *The psychology of hate* (pp. 87–102). Washington, DC: American Psychological Association.

Baumeister, R. F., Exline, J. J., & Sommer, K. L. (1998). The victim role, grudge theory, and two dimensions of forgiveness. In E. L. Worthington (Ed.), *Dimensions of forgiveness: Psychology research and theoretical perspectives* (pp. 79–104). Philadelphia: Templeton Foundation Press.

Baumeister, R. F., & Hastings, S. (1997). Distortions of collective memory: How groups flatter and deceive themselves. In J. W. Pennebaker, D. Paez, & B. Rimé (Eds.), *Collective memory of political events: Social psychological perspective* (pp. 277–293). Mahwah, NJ: Erlbaum.

BBC (2008). Timeline: Sri Lanka. July 17. Retrieved August 3 from http://news.bbc.co.uk/2/hi/south_asia/1166237.stm.

Beeman, J. H., & Mahony, R. (1993). The institutional churches and the process of reconciliation in Northern Ireland: Recent progress in Presbyterian-Roman Catholic relations. In D. Keogh & M. H. Haltzel (Eds.), *Northern Ireland and the politics of reconciliation* (pp. 150–159). Washington, DC: Woodrow Wilson Center Press.

Beeri, E. (1985). *The beginning of the Israeli-Arab conflict*. Tel Aviv: Sifriyat Poalim. (in Hebrew)

Beit-Hallahmi, B., & Argyle, M. (1997). *The psychology of religious behaviour, belief, and experience*. London: Routledge.

Beinart, W. (2001). *Twentieth-century South Africa*. Oxford: Oxford University Press.

Bem, D. J. (1970). *Beliefs, attitudes and human affairs*. Belmont, CA: Brooks/Cole.

Ben-Amos, A., & Bar-Tal, D., (Eds.), (2004). *Patriotism: Homeland love*. Tel Aviv: Hakibbutz Hameuhad. (in Hebrew)

Ben-Ari, R., & Amir, Y. (1988). Cultural information, intergroup contact and change in ethnic attitudes and relations. In W. Stroebe, A. W. Kruglanski, D. Bar-Tal, & M. Hewstone (Eds.), *The social psychology of intergroup relations: Theory, research and applications* (pp. 151–166). New York: Springer-Verlag.

Ben-Dor, G., Canetti-Nisim, D., & Halperin, E. (2007). *The social aspect of national security: Israeli public opinion and the second Lebanon war*. Haifa: National Security Studies Center. www.nssc.haifa.ac.il.

Ben-Ezer, E. (1977). War and siege in Israeli literature (1948–1967). *Jerusalem Quarterly*, 2(Winter), 94–112.

(1978). War and siege in Hebrew literature after 1967. *Jerusalem Quarterly, 9*, 20–37.

Ben-Ezer, E. (1992). *The Arab in Israeli fiction – An anthology*. Tel-Aviv: Zmora-Bitan. (in Hebrew)

Benjamin, L. T., Jr., & Simpson, J. A. (2009). The power of the situation: The impact of Milgram's obedience studies on personality and social psychology. *American Psychologist, 64*, 12–19.

Ben Meir, Y., & Bagno-Moldavsky, O. (2010). *Vox populi: Trends in Israeli public opinion on national security 2004–2009* (Memorandum 106). Tel Aviv: The Institute for National Security Studies.

Ben Shabat, C. (2010). *Collective memory and ethos of conflict acquisition during childhood: Comparing children attending state-secular and state-religious schools in Israel.* Master's thesis, School of Education, Tel Aviv University. (in Hebrew).

Ben-Yehuda, N. (1995). *The Masada myth: Collective memory and mythmaking in Israel.* Madison: University of Wisconsin Press.

Ben-Ze'ev, E. (2010). Imposed silences and self-censorship: *Palmach* soldiers remember 1948. In E. Ben-Ze'ev, R. Ginio, & J. Winter (Eds.), *Shadows of war – A social history of silence in the twentieth century* (pp. 173–180). Cambridge: Cambridge University Press.

(2011). *Remembering Palestine in 1948: Beyond national narratives.* Cambridge: Cambridge University Press.

Benziger, K. P. (2010). *Imre Nagy, martyr of the nation: Contested history, legitimacy, and popular memory in Hungary.* Lanham, MD: Rowman & Littlefield.

Bercovitch, J. (Ed.), (1995). *Resolving international conflicts.* Boulder, CO: Lynne Rienner.

(2005). Mediation in the most resistant cases. In C. A. Crocker, F. O. Hampson, & P. R. Aall (Eds.), *Grasping the nettle: Analyzing cases of intractable conflict* (pp. 99–121). Washington, DC: United States Institute of Peace Press.

Beristain, C. M., Pérez-Armiñan, M. L. C., & Lykes, M. B. (2007). Political violence, impunity, and emotional climate in Maya communities. *Journal of Social Issues, 63*, 369–385.

Berkowitz, L. (1968). Social motivation. In G. Lindzey & E. Aronson (Eds.), *The Handbook of social psychology* (2nd ed., Vol. 3, pp. 50–135). Reading, MA: Addison-Wesley.

(1990). On the formation and regulation of anger and aggression. *American Psychologist, 45*, 494–503.

(1993). *Aggression: Its causes, consequences and control.* Philadelphia: Temple University Press.

(2005). On hate and its determinants. In R. J. Sternberg (Ed.), (2005), *The psychology of hate* (pp. 155–184). Washington, DC: American Psychological Association.

Bernard, V. W., Ottenberg, P., & Redl, F. (2003). Dehumanization: A composite psychological defense in relation to modern war. In M. Schwebel (Ed.), *Behavioral science and human survival* (pp. 64–82). Lincoln, NE: iUniverse.

Berridge, K. C., & Winkielman, P. (2003). What is unconscious emotion: The case of unconscious "liking." *Cognition and Emotion, 17*, 181–211.

Bettencourt, B. A., Dorr, N., Charlton, K., & Hume, D. L. (2001). Status differences and ingroup bias: A meta analytic examination of the effects of status stability, status legitimacy and group permeability. *Psychological Bulletin, 127*, 520–542.

Bew, P., Gibbon, P., & Patterson, H. (1985). *The state and Northern Ireland.* Manchester: University of Manchester Press.

Bezalel, Y. (1989). *Changes in Zionist values as reflected in elementary school literature and language readers from the late fifties to the mid eighties.* Master's thesis, Ben Gurion University of the Negev.

Bialer, S. (1985). The psychology of U.S.-Soviet relations. *Political Psychology, 6*, 263–273.

Bilali, R. (2010). *Differential effect of ingroup glorification and identity centrality on historical memories.* Unpublished manuscript.
Billig, M. (1995). *Banal nationalism.* London: Sage.
Birnbaum, S. (2009). Historical discourse in the media of the Palestinian National Authority. In M. Litvak (Ed.), *Palestinian collective memory and national identity* (pp. 135–168). New York: Palgrave Macmillan.
Bjerstedt, A. (1988). *Peace education in different countries.* Malmo: Educational Information and Debate. No. 81.
 (Ed.), (1993). *Peace education: Global perspective.* Malmo: Almqvist & Wiksell.
Blanchard, R. J., & Blanchard, D. C. (1984). Affect and aggression: An animal model applied to human behavior. In R. J. Blanchard & D. C. Blanchard (Eds.), *Advances in the study of aggression* (Vol. 1, pp. 1–62). New York: Academic Press.
Blaney, P. H. (1986). Affect and memory: A review. *Psychological Bulletin, 99,* 229–246.
Blatz, C. W., & Philpot, C. (2010). On the outcomes of intergroup apologies: Review. *Social and Personality Psychology Compass, 4,* 995–1007.
Blatz, C. W., Schumann, K., & Ross, M. (2009). Government apologies for historical injustices. *Political Psychology, 30,* 219–241.
Bleich, A., Gelkopf, M., & Solomon, Z. (2003). Exposure to terrorism, stress-related mental health symptoms, and coping behaviors among a nationally representative sample in Israel. *JAMA: Journal of the American Medical Association, 290,* 612–620.
Bloomfield, D., Barnes, T., & Huyse, L. (Eds.), (2003). *Reconciliation after violent conflict: A handbook.* Stockholm: International IDEA.
Boccato, G., Capozza, D., Falvo, R., & Durante, F. (2008). The missing link: Ingroup, outgroup and the human species. *Social Cognition, 26*(2), 224–234.
Bodine, R. J., & Crawford, D. K. (1998). *The handbook of conflict resolution education: A guide to building quality programs in schools.* National Institute for Dispute Resolution. San Francisco: Jossey-Bass.
Boettcher, W. A. (2004). The prospects for prospect theory: An empirical evaluation of international relations applications of framing and loss aversion. *Political Psychology, 25,* 331–362.
Bond, M. H. (2004). Culture and aggression-from context to coercion. *Personality and Social Psychology Review, 8,* 62–78.
 (2007). Culture and collective violence: How good people, usually men, do bad things. In B. Drozdek & J. P. Wilson (Eds.), *Voices of trauma: Treating survivors across cultures* (pp. 27–57). New York: Springer.
Boraine, A., & Levy, J. (1995). *The healing of a nation.* Cape Town: Justice in Transition.
Borer, T. A. (Ed.), (2006). *Telling the truths: Truth telling and peace building in post-conflict societies.* Notre Dame, IN: University of Notre Dame Press.
Borman, W. (1986). *Gandhi and non-violence.* Albany: State University of New York Press.
Borneman, J. (2002). Reconciliation after ethnic cleansing: Listening, retribution, affiliation, *Public Culture, 14,* 283–304.
Bornstein, A. (2008). Military occupation as carceral society: Prisons, checkpoints, and walls in the Israeli-Palestinian struggle. *Social Analysis, 52,* 106–130.
Borovski-Sapir, L. (2004). *The process of socialization to the ethos of conflict at the paratrooper training base.* Master's thesis, Tel Aviv University. (in Hebrew)

Bose, S. (2007). *Contested lands: Israel-Palestine, Kashmir, Bosnia, Cyprus, and Sri Lanka.* Cambridge, MA: Harvard University Press.

Bosi, L. (2007). Social movement participation and the "timing" of involvement: The case of Northern Ireland civil rights movement. *Research in Social Movements, Conflicts and Change, 27,* 36–62.

(2008). Explaining the emergence process of the civil rights protest in Northern Ireland (1945–1968): Insights from a relational social movement approach. *Journal of Historical Sociology, 21,* 242–271.

Botcharova, O. (2001). Implementation of track two diplomacy: Developing a model for forgiveness. In G. Raymond, S. J. Helmick, & R. L. Peterson (Eds.), *Forgiveness and reconciliation: Religion, public policy, and conflict transformation* (pp. 304–279). Philadelphia: Temple Foundation Press.

Boulding, E. (2000). *Cultures of peace: The hidden side of human history.* Syracuse, NY: Syracuse University Press.

Bower, G. H. (1992). How might emotions affect learning? In S. A. Christianson (Ed.), *The handbook of emotion and memory: Research and theory* (pp. 3–31). Hillsdale, NJ: Erlbaum.

Boyd, C. (2008). The politics of history and memory in democratic Spain. *The ANNALS of the American Academy of Political and Social Science, 617,* 133–148.

Bozic-Roberson, A. (2004). Words before war: Milosevic's use of mass media and rhetoric to provoke ethnopolitical conflict in former Yugoslavia. *East European Quarterly, 38*(4), 395–408.

Branche, R., & House, J. (2010). Silences on state violence during the Algerian War of Independence: France and Algeria, 1962–2007. In E. Ben-Ze'ev, R. Ginio, & J. Winter (Eds.), *Shadows of war – A social history of silence in the twentieth century* (pp. 115–137). Cambridge: Cambridge University Press.

Brandenberger, D. (2009). A new short course? A. V. Filippov and the Russian State's search for a "Usable Past." *Kritika: Explorations in Russian and Eurasian History, 10*(4), 825–833.

Branscombe, N. R. (2004). A social psychological process perspective on collective guilt. In N. R. Branscombe & B. Doosje (Eds.), *Collective guilt: International perspectives* (pp. 320–334). Cambridge: Cambridge University Press.

Branscombe N. R., & Doosje, B. (Eds.), (2004). *Collective guilt: International perspectives.* Cambridge: Cambridge University Press.

Branscombe, N. R., Doosje, B., & McGarty, C. (2002). Antecedents and consequences of collective guilt. In D. M. Mackie & E. R. Smith (Eds.), *From prejudice to intergroup emotions: Differentiated reactions to social groups* (pp. 49–66). Philadelphia: Psychology Press.

Branscombe, N. R., Ellemers, N., Spears, R., & Doosje, B. (1999). The context and content of social identity threat. In N. Ellemers, R. Spears, & B. Doosje (Eds.), *Social identity: Context, commitment, content* (pp. 35–58). Oxford: Blackwell.

Branscombe, N. R., Schmitt, M. T., & Schiffhauer, K. (2007). Racial attitudes in response to thoughts of White privilege. *European Journal of Social Psychology, 37,* 203–215.

Branscombe, N. R., Slugoski, B., & Kappen, D. M. (2004). The measurement of collective guilt: What it is and what it is not. In N. R. Branscombe & B. Doosje (Eds.), *Collective guilt: International perspectives* (pp. 16–34). Cambridge: Cambridge University Press.

Bransford, J. D. (1979). *Human cognition: Learning, understanding and remembering.* Belmont, CA: Wadsworth.
Brecher, M., & Wilkenfeld, J. (1988). Protracted conflicts and crises. In M. Brecher & J. Wilkenfeld (Eds.), *Crisis, conflict and instability* (pp. 127–140). Oxford: Pergamon.
Brehm, J. (1956). Post-decision changes in desirability of alternatives. *Journal of Abnormal and Social Psychology,* 52, 384–389.
Brenes, A., & Weseels, M. (2001). Psychological contributions to building cultures of peace. *Peace and Conflict: Journal of Peace Psychology,* 7, 99–107.
Breuilly, J. (1982). *Nationalism and the state.* New York: St. Martin's Press.
Brewer, M. B. (1991). The social self: On being the same and different at the same time. *Personality and Social Psychology Bulletin,* 17, 475–482.
   (2001). Ingroup identification and intergroup conflict: When does ingroup love become outgroup hate? In R. D. Ashmore, L. Jussim, & D. Wilder (Eds.), *Social identity, intergroup conflict and conflict reduction* (pp. 17–41). Oxford: Oxford University Press.
   (2011). Identity and conflict. In D. Bar-Tal (Ed.), *Intergroup conflicts and their resolution: Social psychological perspectives* (pp. 125–143). New York: Psychology Press.
Brewer, M. B., & Campbell, D. T. (1976). *Ethnocentrism: East African evidence.* New York: Wiley.
Brewer, M. B., & Silver, M. D. (2000). Group distinctiveness, social identification and collective mobilization. In S. Stryker, T. J. Owens, & R. W. White (Eds.), *Self, identity, and social movement – Social movements, protest, and contention* (Vol. 13, pp. 153–171). Minneapolis: University of Minnesota Press.
Breznitz, S. (Ed.), (1983). *Stress in Israel.* New York: Van Nostrand Reinhold.
   (1986). The effect of hope on coping with stress. In M. H. Appley & R. Trumbull (Eds.), *Dynamics of stress: Physiological, psychological and social perspectives* (pp. 295–306). New York: Plenum.
Brockner, J., & Rubin, J. Z. (1985). *Entrapment in escalating conflicts: A social psychological analysis.* New York: Springer.
Bronfenbrenner, U. (1961). The mirror-image in Soviet-American relations: A social psychologist's report. *Journal of Social Issues,* 16, 45–56.
   (1977). Toward an experimental ecology of human development. *American Psychologist,* 32, 513–531.
Bronkhorst, D. (1995). *Truth and reconciliation: Obstacles and opportunities for human rights.* Amsterdam: Amnesty International.
Brooks, R. L. (Ed.), (1999). *When sorry isn't enough: The controversy over apologies and reparations for human injustice.* New York: New York University Press.
Brouneus, K. (2008a). Analyzing reconciliation: A structured methods for measuring national reconciliation initiatives. *Peace and Conflict: Journal Peace Psychology,* 14, 291–313.
   (2008b). Truth telling as talking cure? Insecurity and retraumatization in the Rwandan Gacaca courts. *Security Dialogue,* 39, 55–76.
   (2010). The trauma of truth-telling: Effects of witnessing in the Rwanda Gacaca courts on psychological health, *Journal of Conflict Resolution,* 54, 408–437.
Brown, D. (1966). *Against the world.* Garden City, NJ: Doubleday.
Brown, H. (1983). *Thinking about national security: Defense and foreign policy in a dangerous world.* Boulder, CO: Westview.

Brown, R. (1988). *Group processes: Dynamics within and between groups*. Oxford: Blackwell.

Brown, R., & Čehajić, S. (2008). Dealing with the past and facing the future: Mediators of the effects of collective guilt and shame in Bosnia and Herzegovina. *European Journal of Social Psychology, 38*, 669–684.

Brown, R., González, R., Zagefka, H., & Čehajić, S. (2008). Nuestra Culpa: Collective guilt and shame as predictors of reparation for historical wrongdoing. *Journal of Personality and Social Psychology, 94*, 75–90.

Brown, R., & Hewstone, M. (2005). An integrative theory of intergroup contact. *Advances in Experimental Social Psychology, 17*, 255–343.

Brown, R., Maras, P., Masser, B., Vivian, V., & Hewstone, M. (2001). Life on the ocean wave: Testing some intergroup hypotheses in a naturalistic setting. *Group Processes & Intergroup Relations, 4*, 81–97.

Brubaker, R. (2004). *Ethnicity without groups*. Cambridge, MA: Harvard University Press.

Brubaker, R., & Laitin, D. D. (1998). Ethnic and nationalist violence. *Annual Review of Sociology, 24*, 423–452.

Bruck, P., & Roach, C. (1993). Dealing with reality: The news media and the promotion of peace. In C. Roach (Ed.), *Communication and culture in war and peace* (pp. 71–95). Newbury Park, CA: Sage.

Bruner, J. (1990). *Acts of meaning*. Cambridge, MA: Harvard University Press.

Buck, R. (1999). The biological affect: A typology. *Psychological Review, 106*, 301–336.

Bullard, S. (1996). *Teaching tolerance: Raising open-minded, empathetic children*. New York: Doubleday.

Burgess, H., & Burgess, G. (1996). Constructive confrontation: A transformative approach to intractable conflicts. *Mediation Quarterly, 13*, 305–322.

Burke, B. L., Kosloff, S., & Landau, M. J. (in press). Death goes to the polls: A meta-analysis of mortality salience effects on political attitudes. *Political Psychology*.

Burke, B. L., Martens, A., & Faucher, E. H. (2010). Two decades of Terror Management Theory: A meta-analysis of mortality salience research. *Personality and Social psychology Review, 14*, 155–195.

Burn, S. M., & Oskamp, S. (1989). Ingroup biases and the US-Soviet conflict. *Journal of Social Issues, 45*(2), 73–990.

Burns, R. J., & Aspeslagh, R. (Eds.), (1996). *Three decades of peace education around the world*. New York: Garland.

Burns-Bisogno, L. (1997). *Censoring Irish Nationalism: The British, Irish and American Suppression of Republican Images in Film and Television, 1909–1995*. Jefferson, NC: McFarland.

Burton, J. W. (1969). *Conflict and communication: The use of controlled communication in international relations*. London: Macmillan.

(1987). *Resolving deep-rooted conflict: A handbook*. Lanham, MD: University Press of America.

(Ed.), (1990). *Conflict: Human needs theory*. New York: St. Martin's Press.

Buzan, B. (1991). *People states and fear: An agenda for international security studies in the post-Cold War era* (2nd ed.). Boulder, CO: Lynne Rienner.

(1997). Rethinking security after the Cold War. *Cooperation and Conflict, 32*(1), 5–28.

Byrne, C. (2004). Benefit of burden: Victims' reflections on TRC participation. *Peace and Conflict: Journal of Peace Psychology, 10*(3), 237–256.
Cacioppo, J. T., & Berntson, G. G. (1994). Relationship between attitudes and evaluative space: A critical review, with emphasis on the separability of positive and negative substrates. *Psychological Bulletin, 115*, 401–423.
Cacioppo, J. T., & Gardner, W. L. (1999). Emotion. *Annual Review of Psychology, 50*, 191–214.
Cacioppo, J. T., Gardner, W. L., & Berntson, G. G. (1997). Beyond bipolar conceptualizations and measures: The case of attitudes and evaluative space. *Personality and Social Psychology Review, 1*, 3–25.
  (1999). The affect system has parallel and integrative processing components: Form follows function. *Journal of Personality and Social Psychology, 76*, 839–855.
Cacioppo, J. T., Larsen, J. T., Smith, N. K., & Berntson, G. G. (2004). The affect system: What lurks below the surface of feelings? In A. S. R. Manstead, N. Frijda, & A. Fischer (Eds.), *Feelings and emotions: The Amsterdam symposium* (pp. 223–242). Cambridge: Cambridge University Press.
Cairns, E., Dunn, S., & Giles, M. (1992). *Surveys of integrated education in Northern Ireland.* Coleraine: Centre for the Study of Conflict.
Cairns, E., Lewis, C. A., Mumcu, O., & Waddell, N. (1998). Memories of recent ethnic conflict and their relationship to social identity. *Peace and Conflict: Journal of Peace Psychology, 4*, 13–22.
Cairns, E., Mallet, J., Lewis, C., & Wilson, R. (2003). *Who are the victims? Self-assessed victimhood and the Northern Irish conflict* (NIO Research & Statistical Series: Report No. 7). Belfast: Northern Ireland Office, Northern Ireland Statistics and Research Agency.
Cairns, E., & Roe, M. D. (Eds.), (2003). *The role of memory in ethnic conflict.* New York: Palgrave Macmillan.
Calhoun, C. (Ed.), (1994). *Social theory and the politics of identity.* Oxford: Blackwell.
Calleja, J. (1994). Educating for peace in the Mediterranean: A strategy for peace building. In E. Boulding (Ed.), *Building peace in the Middle East: Challenges for states and civil society* (pp. 279–285). Boulder, CO: Lynne Rienner.
Canas, A., & Dada, H. (1999). Political transition and institutionalization in El Salvador. In C. J. Arnson (Ed.), *Comparative peace processes in Latin America* (pp. 69–95). Stanford, CA: Stanford University Press.
Canetti, D., Galea, S., Hall, B. J., Johnson, R. J., Palmier, P. A., & Hobfoll, S. E. (2010). Exposure to prolonged socio-political conflict and the risk of PTSD and depression among Palestinians. *Psychiatry-Interpersonal and Biological Processes, 73*, 219–231.
Canetti, D., Guy, D., Lavi, I., Bar-Tal, D., & Hobfoll, E. S. (2012). *Exposure to conflict, ethos of conflict: Why Israelis and Palestinians say NO to peace?* Unpublished manuscript, Haifa University.
Canetti, D., Halperin, E., Sharvit, K., Hobfoll, E. S. (2009). A new stress-based model of political extremism: Personal exposure to terrorism, psychological distress and exclusionist political attitudes. *Journal of Conflict Resolution, 53*, 363–389.
Canetti, D., Rapaport, C., Wayne, C., Hall, B., & Hobfoll, S. (in press). An exposure effect? Evidence from a rigorous study on the psycho-political outcomes of terrorism. In S. J. Sinclair & D. Antonius (Eds.), *The political psychology of terrorism.* New York: Oxford University Press.

Canetti-Nisim, D., Halperin, E., Sharvit, K., Hobfoll, S. (2009). A new stress-based model of political extremism: Personal exposure to terrorism, psychological distress and exclusionist political attitudes. *Journal of Conflict Resolution*, 53, 363–389.

Caplan, N. (2009). *The Israeli-Palestine conflict: Contested history.* Malden, MA: Wiley-Blackwell.

Carmines, E., & Stimson, J. (1989). *Issue evolution: Race and the transformation of American politics.* Princeton, NJ: Princeton University Press.

Carrilo, J., Corning, A. F., Dennehy, T. C., & Crosby, F. J. (2011). Relative deprivation: Understanding the dynamics of discontent. In D. Chadee (Ed.), *Theories in social psychology* (pp. 140–160). Malden, MA: Wiley-Blackwell.

Carver, C. S., & Scheier, M. F. (1990). Origins and functions of positive and negative affect: A control-process view. *Psychological Review*, 97, 19–35.

Caryl, C. (2000). Objectivity to order: Access is the key problem for journalists reporting on the second Chechen war, and is under tight military control. *Index on Censorship*, 29, 17–20.

Cash, J. D. (1996). *Identity, ideology and conflict.* Cambridge: Cambridge University Press.

Caspi, D., & Limor. Y. (1992). *The mediators: The mass media in Israel, 1948–1990.* Tel Aviv: Am Oved. (in Hebrew)

Castano, E. (2008). On the perils of glorifying the in-group: Intergroup violence, in-group glorification, and moral disengagement. *Social and Personality Psychology Compass*, 2(1), 154–170.

Castano, E., & Giner-Sorolla, R. (2006). Not quite human: Infra-humanization as a response to collective responsibility for intergroup killing. *Journal of Personality and Social Psychology*, 90, 804–818.

Cecil, R. (1993). The marching season in Northern Ireland: An expression of politico-religious identity. In S. MacDonald (Ed.), *Inside European identities* (pp. 146–166). Providence, RI: Berg.

Čehajić, S., & Brown, R. (2008). Not in my name: A social psychological study of antecedents and consequences of acknowledgment of ingroup atrocities. *Genocide Studies and Prevention*, 3, 195–211.

Čehajić, S., Brown, R., & Castano, E. (2008). Forgive and forget? Antecedents and consequences of intergroup forgiveness in Bosnia and Herzegovina. *Political Psychology*, 29(3), 351–367.

Čehajić, S., Brown, R., & Gonzalez, R. (2009). What do I care? Perceived ingroup responsibility and dehumanization as predictors of empathy felt for the victim group. *Group Processes & Intergroup Relations*, 12, 715–729.

Čehajić. S., Effron, D., Halperin, E., Liberman, V., & Ross, L., (2011). Affirmation, acknowledgment of ingroup responsibility, group-based guilt, and support for reparative measures. *Journal of Personality and Social Psychology*, 101(2), 256–270.

Chadha, N. (1995). Enemy images: The media and Indo-Pakistani tensions. In M. Krepon & A. Sevak (Eds.), *Crisis prevention, confidence building and reconciliation in South Asia* (pp. 171–198). New York: St. Martin's Press.

Chaitin, J., & Steinberg, S. (2008). "You should know better": Expressions of empathy and disregard among victims of massive social trauma. *Journal of Aggression, Maltreatment and Trauma*, 17(2), 197–226.

Chambers, J. R., Baron, R. S., & Inman, M. L. (2006). Misperception in intergroup conflict: Disagreeing about what we disagree about. *Psychological Science, 17*, 38–45.

Chapman, A. R. (2007). Truth commissions and intergroup forgiveness: The case of the South Africa Truth and Reconciliation Commission. *Peace and Conflict: Journal Peace Psychology, 13*, 51–69.

Charif, H. (1994). Regional development and integration. In D. Collings (Ed.), *Peace for Lebanon? From war to reconstruction* (pp. 151–161). Boulder, CO: Lynne Rienner.

Chazan, N. (2006). Peace action and conflict resolution: An Israeli-Palestinian exploration. In E. Podeh, A. Kaufman, & M. Maoz (Eds.), *Arab-Jewish relations: From conflict to resolution?* (pp. 283–317). Brighton: Sussex Academic Press.

Chelvanayakam, S. J. V. (1975). Statement. February 7. Retrieved August 3, 2008, from http://www.tamilnation.org/selfdetermination/tamileelam/7504sjvstatement.htm.

Chetkow-Yanoov, B. (1986). Improving Arab-Jewish relations in Israel: The role of voluntary organizations. *Social Development Issues, 10*, 58–70.

Cheung-Blunden V., & Blunden, B. (2008). The emotional construal of war: Anger, fear and other negative emotions. *Peace and Conflict – Journal of Peace Psychology, 14*, 123–150.

Chigas, D. V. (1997). Unofficial interventions with official actors: Parallel negotiation training in violent intrastate conflicts. *International Negotiation, 2*, 409–436.

Chirot, D., & Seligman, M. E. P. (Eds.), (2001). *Ethnopolitical warfare: Causes, consequences and possible solutions.* Washington, DC: American Psychological Association.

Chirwa, W. (1997). Collective memory and the process of reconciliation and reconstruction. *Development in Practice, 7*, 479–482.

Christianson, S. A. (1992). Remembering emotional events: Potential mechanisms. In S. A. Christianson, *The handbook of emotion and memory* (pp. 307–340). Hillsdale, NJ: Erlbaum.

Christie, D. J. (2006). What is peace psychology the psychology of? *Journal of Social Issues, 62*, 1–17.

Christie, D. J., & Louis, W. R. (2012). Intervention and implementation. In L. R. Tropp (Ed.), *Oxford handbook of intergroup conflict (pp. 252–269).* New York: Oxford University Press.

Christie, D., Wagner, R., & Winter, D. D. (2001). *Peace, conflict, and violence: Peace psychology for the 21st century.* Upper Saddle River, NJ: Prentice Hall.

Cialdini, R. B., & Trost, M. (1998). Social influence: Social norms, conformity, and compliance. In D. T. Gilbert, S. T. Fiske, G. Lindzey (Eds.), *The handbook of social psychology* (4th ed., Vol. 2, pp. 151–192). Boston: McGraw Hill.

Cigar, N. (1995). *Genocide in Bosnia: The policy of "ethnic cleansing."* College Station: Texas A&M University Press.

Clark, P. (2010). *The Gacaca courts, post-genocide justice and reconciliation in Rwanda: Justice without lawyers.* Cambridge: Cambridge University Press.

Clarke-Habibi, S. (2005). Transforming world views: The case of education for peace in Bosnia and Herzegovina. *Journal of Transformative Education, 3*, 33–56.

Clayton, S., & Opotow, S. (2003). Justice and identity: Changing perspectives on what is fair. *Personality and Social Psychology Review, 7*, 298–310.

Clements K. P. (2012). Building sustainable peace. In L. R. Tropp (Ed.), *Oxford handbook of intergroup conflict* (pp. 344–357). New York: Oxford University Press.

Clore, G. L., Schwarz, N., & Conway, M. (1994). Affective causes and consequences of social information processing. In R. S. Wyer & T. K. Strull, *Handbook of social cognition* (Vol. 1, pp. 323–417). Hillsdale, NJ: Erlbaum.
Coats, S., Smith, E. R., Claypool, H. M., & Banner, M. J. (2000). Overlapping mental representations of self and in-group: Reaction time evidence and its relationship with explicit measures of group identification. *Journal of Experimental Social Psychology, 36*, 304–315.
Cohen, A. (1985). *An ugly face in the mirror: National stereotypes in Hebrew children's literature.* Tel Aviv: Reshafim. (in Hebrew)
Cohen, C. E. (1981). Person categories and social perception: Testing some boundaries of the processing effects of prior knowledge. *Journal of Personality and Social Psychology, 40*, 441–452.
Cohen, R. (1979). *Threat perception in international crisis.* Madison: University of Wisconsin Press.
Cohen, S. (2001). *States of denial: Knowing about atrocities and suffering.* Cambridge: Polity.
Cohen, S. F. (1986). *Sovieticus: American perceptions and Soviet realities.* New York: Norton.
Cohen, S. P. (2004). *The idea of Pakistan.* Washington, DC: Brookings Institution Press.
Cohen-Chen, S. (2012). *Inducing hope in intergroup conflict by increasing general beliefs in a dynamic reality.* Manuscript in preparation, University of Sheffield.
Cohen-Chen, S., Crisp, R. J., Lehman, T., & Halperin, E. (2012). *Inducing a conflict malleability belief increases hope.* Manuscript in preparation, University of Sheffield.
Cohrs, J. C., & Boehnke, K. (2008). Social psychology and peace: An introductory overview. *Social Psychology, 39*, 4–11.0
Coleman, P. T. (2000). Intractable conflict. In D. Deutsch & P. T. Coleman (Eds.), *The handbook of conflict reosolution: Theory and practice* (pp. 428–450). San Francisco: Jossey-Bass.
  (2003). Characteristics of protracted, intractable conflict: Towards the development of a metaframework - I. *Peace and Conflict: Journal of Peace Psychology, 9*(1), 1–37.
  (2006). Intractable conflict. In M. Deutsch, P. T. Coleman, & E. C. Marcus (Eds.), *The handbook of conflict resolution: Theory and practice* (2nd ed., pp. 533–559). San Francisco: Jossey-Bass.
Collier, P. (1999). On the economic consequences of civil war. *Oxford Economic Papers, 50*(4), 168–183.
Collins, R. (1975). *Conflict sociology: Toward an explanatory science.* New York: Academic Press.
Comisión de Esclarecimiento Histórico (CEH) [Commission for Historical Clarification]. (1999). *Memoria del silencio* [Memory of silence]. Guatemala: CEH.
Connerton, P. (1989). *How societies remember.* Cambridge: Cambridge University Press.
  (2009). *How modernity forgets.* Cambridge: Cambridge University Press.
Connor, W. (1993). Beyond reason: The nature of the ethnonational bond. *Ethnic and Racial Studies, 16*, 373–389.
  (1994). *Ethnonationalism: The quest for understanding.* Princeton, NJ: Princeton University Press.

Constantine, J. R. (1966). The ignoble savage, an eighteenth century literary stereotype. *Phylon, 27*, 171–179.

Conway, B. (2003). Active remembering, selective forgetting and collective identity: The case of Bloody Sunday. *Identity, 3*(4), 305–323.

Corkalo, D., Ajdukovic, D., Weinstein, H., Stover, E., Djipa, D. and Biro, M. (2004). Neighbors again? Inter-Community relations after ethnic violence. In E. Stover & H. Weinstein (Eds.), *My neighbor, my enemy: Justice and community in the aftermath of mass atrocity* (pp. 143–161). Cambridge: Cambridge University Press.

Corm, G. (1994). The war system: Militia hegemony and reestablishment of the state. In D. Collings (Ed.), *Peace for Lebanon? From war to reconstruction* (pp. 215–230). Boulder, CO: Lynn Rienner.

Corneille, O., Yzerbyt, V., Rogier, A., & Buidin, G. (2001). Threat and the group attribution error: When threat elicits judgments of extremity and homogeneity. *Personality and Social Psychology Bulletin, 27*, 437–496.

Corr, E. G. (1995). Societal transformation for peace in El Salvador. *Annals of the American Academy of Political and Social Science, 541*, 144–156.

Corradi, J. E., Fagen, P. W., & Garreton, M. A. (Eds.), (1992). *Fear at the edge: State terror and resistance in Latin America.* Berkeley: University of California Press.

Coser, L. A. (1956). *The functions of social conflict.* New York: Free Press.

Crane, S. A. (1997). Memory, distortion and history in the museum. *History and Theory, 36*, 44–63.

Crano, W. D., & Prislin, R. (2006). Attitudes and persuasion. *Annual Review of Psychology, 57*, 345–374.

Crighton, E., & Mac Iver, M. A. (1990). The evolution of protracted ethnic conflict: Group dominance and political underdevelopment in Northern Ireland and Lebanon. *Comparative Politics, 23*, 127–142.

Crocker, C. A., Hampson, F. O., & Aall, P. R. (Eds.), (2005a). *Grasping the nettle: Analyzing cases of intractable conflict.* Washington, DC: United States Institute of Peace Press.

(2005b). Introduction: Mapping the nettle field. In C. A., Crocker, F. O. Hampson, & P. R. Aall (Eds.), *Grasping the nettle: Analyzing cases of intractable conflict* (pp. 3–30). Washington, DC: United States Institute of Peace Press.

Crocker, D. A. (1999). Reckoning with past wrongs: A normative framework. *Ethics & International Affairs, 13*, 43–64.

Crosby, F. J. (1976). A model of egoistical relative deprivation. *Psychological Review, 83*, 85–113.

Czapinski, J. (1985). *Positive inclination: On the nature of optimism.* Wroclaw: Ossolineum. (in Polish)

(1988). *Negativity effect: on the nature of realism.* Wroclaw: Ossolineum. (in Polish)

Damasio, A. R. (1994). *Descartes' error: Emotion, reason, and the human brain.* New York: Putnam.

(2001). *A neurobiology for emotion and feeling.* Paper presented at the Amsterdam Conference on Feelings and Emotions (June 13–16).

(2003). *Looking for Spinoza: Joy, sorrow and the feeling brain.* New York: Harcourt.

(2004). Emotions and feelings: a neurobiological perspective. In A. S. R. Manstead, N. Frijda, & A. Fischer (Eds.), *Feelings and emotions. The Amsterdam Symposium* (pp. 49–57). Cambridge: Cambridge University Press.

Danesh, H. B. (2010). Unity-based education – Education for peace program in Bosnia and Herzegovina: A chronological case study. In G. Salomon & E. Cairns (Eds.), *Handbook of peace education* (pp. 253–268). New York: Psychology Press.

Darby, J. (2003). *Northern Ireland: The background to the peace process.* Retrieved April 16, 2006, from CAIN: http://cain.ulst.ac.uk/events/peace/darby03.htm.

Darley, J. M., & Gross, P. H. (1983). A hypothesis-confirming bias in labeling effects. *Journal of Personality and Social Psychology, 44*, 20–33.

David, O. (2007). *The crystallization and transformations of Jewish-Israeli identity: A study of identity reflection in Hebrew readers of the 20th century.* Ph.D. dissertation, Tel Aviv University. (in Hebrew)

David, O., & Bar-Tal, D. (2009). A socio-psychological conception of collective identity: The case of national identity. *Personality and Social Psychology Review, 13*, 354–379.

Davidson, R. J., & Fox, N. A. (1982). Asymmetrical brain activity discriminates between positive versus negative affective stimuli in human infants. *Science, 218*, 1235–1237.

Davidson, R. J., Jackson, D. C., & Kalin, N. H. (2000). Emotion, plasticity, context, and regulation: Perspectives from affective neuroscience. *Psychological Bulletin, 126*, 890–909.

Davis, C. G., Nolen-Hoeksema, S., & Larson, J. (1998). Making sense of loss and benefiting from the experience: Two construals of meaning. *Journal of Personality and Social Psychology, 75*, 561–574.

Davis, L. (2000). *Citizenship education and human rights education: An international overview.* London: The British Council.

Dawidowicz, L. S. (1975). *The war against the Jews: 1933–1945.* New York: Holt, Rinehart and Winston.

Deane, S. (1996). *The protection racket state: Elite politics, military extortion, and civil war in El Salvador.* Philadelphia: Temple University Press.

Deaux, K., Reid, A., Mizrahi, K., & Cotting, D. (1999). Connecting the person to the social: The functions of social identification. In T. Tyler, R. Kramer, & O. John (Eds.), *The psychology of the social self* (pp. 91–113). Mahwah, NJ: Erlbaum.

De Baets, A. (2002). *Censorship of historical thought: A world guide, 1945–2000.* Westport, CT: Greenwood Press.

Deci, E. L., & Ryan, R. M. (2000). The "what" and "why" of goal pursuits: Human needs and self-determination of behavior. *Psychological Inquiry, 11*(4), 227–268.

De Dreu, C. K. W. (2010). Social conflict: The emergence and consequence of struggle and negotiation. In S. T. Fiske, D. T. Gilbert, & G. Lindzey (Eds.), *Handbook of social psychology* (5th ed., Vol. 2. pp. 983–1023). Hoboken, NJ: John Wiley & Sons.

De Dreu, C. K. W., & Carnevale, P. J. (2003). Motivational bases of information processing and strategy in conflict and negotiation. *Advances in Experimental Social Psychology, 35*, 235–291.

De Dreu, C. K. W., & De Vries, N. K. (Eds.), (2001). *Group consensus and minority influence: Implications for innovation* (pp. 229–257). Oxford: Blackwell.

De Figueiredo, R. J. P., Jr., & Elkins, Z. (2003). Are patriots bigots? An inquiry into the vices of in-group pride. *American Journal of Political Science, 47*, 171–188.

De Grieff, P. (2008). The role of apologies in national reconciliation processes: On making trustworthy institutions trusted. In M. Gibney, R. E. Howard-Hasmann, J.-M. Coicaud, & N. Steiner (Eds.), *The age of apology: Facing up to the past* (pp. 120–134). Philadelphia: University of Pennsylvania Press.

de Jong, J. (Ed.), (2002). *Trauma, war, and violence: Public mental health in socio-cultural context*. New York: Kluwer Academic Publishers.

De la Rey, C., & Owens, I. (1998). Perceptions of psychological healing and the Truth and Reconciliation Commission in South Africa. *Peace and Conflict: Journal of Peace Psychology, 4*, 257–270.

De Mel, N. (2007). *Militarizing Sri Lanka: Popular culture, memory and narratives in the armed conflict*. Los Angles: Sage.

Denitch, B. (1994). Dismembering Yugoslavia: National ideologies and the symbolic revival of genocide. *American Ethnologist, 21*, 367–390.

de Rivera, J. (1992). Emotional climate: Social structure and emotional dynamics. In K. T. Strongman (Ed.), *International review of studies on emotion* (Vol. 2, pp. 199–218). New-York: John Wiley.

(2004). Assessing the basis for a culture of peace in contemporary societies. *Journal of Peace Research, 41*, 531–548.

(Ed.), (2009). *Handbook on building cultures for peace*. New York: Springer.

(2010). Teaching about the culture of peace as an approach to peace education. In G. Salomon & E. Cairns (Eds.), (*Handbook of peace education* (pp. 187–197). New York: Psychology Press.

de Rivera, J., & Paez, D. (Eds.), (2007). Emotional climate, human security, and culture of peace. *Journal of Social Issues, 63*, no. 2, whole issue.

Des Forges, A. (1999). *"Leave none to tell the story": Genocide in Rwanda*. New York: Human Rights Watch and International Federation of Human Rights.

De Soto, A. (1999). Reflections. In C. J. Arnson (Ed.), *Comparative peace processes in Latin America* (pp. 385–387). Stanford, CA: Stanford University Press.

Deutsch, M. (1973). *The resolution of conflict*. New Haven, CT: Yale University Press.

(1985). *The distributive justice: The social psychological perspective*. New Haven, CT: Yale University Press.

(1993). Educating for a peaceful world. *American Psychologist, 48*(5), 510–517.

(2000). Justice and conflict. In M. Deutsch & P. T. Coleman (Eds.), *The handbook of conflict resolution: Theory and practice* (pp. 41–64). San Francisco: Jossey-Bass.

(2005). Cooperation and conflict: A personal perspective on the history of the social psychological study of conflict resolution. In M. A. West, D. Tjosvold, & K. G. Smith (Eds.), *The essentials of teamworking: International perspectives* (pp. 1–35). New York: John Wiley & Sons.

Deutsch, M., & Gerard, H. B. (1955). A study of normative and informational influences upon individual judgment. *Journal of Abnormal and Social Psychology, 51*, 629–636.

Deutsch, K. W., & Merritt, R. C. (1965). Effect of events on national and international images. In H. C. Kelman (Ed.), *International behavior: a social-psychological analysis* (pp. 132–181). New York: Holt.

Devine, P. G. (1989). Stereotypes and prejudice: Their automatic and controlled components. *Journal of Personality and Social Psychology, 56*, 5–18.

Devine-Wright, P. (2001). History and identity in Northern Ireland: An explanatory investigation of the role of historical commemorations in the context intergroup conflict. *Peace and Conflict: Journal or Peace, 7*, 297–315.

(2003). A theoretical overview of memory and conflict. In E. Cairns & M. D. Roe (Eds.), *The role of memory in ethnic conflict* (pp. 9–33). Houndmills: Palgrave Macmillan.

Devos, T., Silver, L. A., Mackie, D. M., & Smith, E. R. (2002). Experiencing intergroup emotions. In D. M. Mackie & E. R. Smith (Eds.), *From prejudice to intergroup emotions: Differentiated reactions to social groups* (pp. 111–133). Philadelphia: Psychological Press.

De Vries, J. M. A., & de Paor, J. (2005). Healing and reconciliation in the L.I.V.E. program in Ireland. *Peace & Change, 30*, 329–358.

De Weerd, M., & Klandermans, B. (1999). Group identification and political protest: farmers' protest in the Netherlands. *European Journal of Social Psychology, 29*, 1073–1095.

Dewey, J. (1933). *How we think: A restatement of the relation of reflective thinking to the educative process.* New York: D. C. Heath.

——— (1938). *Experience and education.* New York: Collier Books.

Diani, M. (2004). Networks and participation. In D. A. Snow, A. Soule, & H. Kriesi (Eds.), *The Blackwell companion to social movements* (pp. 339–359). Malden, MA: Blackwell.

Dillard, J. P. (1994). Rethinking the study of fear appeals: An emotional perspective. *Communication Theory, 4*(4), 295–323.

Dimitrijevic, N. (2006). Justice beyond blame: Moral justification of (the idea of) a Truth Commission. *Journal of Conflict Resolution, 50*, 368–382.

Ditto, P. H., & Lopez, D. F. (1992). Motivated skepticism: Use of differential criteria for preferred and nonpreferred conclusions. *Journal of Personality and Social Psychology, 63*, 568–684.

Dixon, J. M. (2010a). Defending the nation? Maintaining Turkey's narrative of the Armenian genocide. *South European Society and Politics, 15*, 467–485.

——— (2010b). Education and national narratives: Changing representations of the Armenian genocide in history textbooks in Turkey. *The International Journal for Education Law and Policy*, special issue, 103–126.

Dohrenwend, B. S., & Dohrenwend, B. P. (Eds.), (1981). *Stressful life events and their contexts.* New York: Prodist.

Dollard, J., Doob, L., Miller, N. E., Mowrer, O. H., & Sears, R. R. (1939). *Frustration and aggression.* New Haven, CT: Yale University Press.

Domb, R. (1982). *The Arab in Hebrew prose.* London: Vallentine, Mitchell.

Donagan, A. (1979). *The theory of morality.* Chicago: University of Chicago Press.

Doosje, B., Branscombe, N. R., Spears, R., & Manstead, A. S. R. (1998). Guilty by association: When one's group has a negative history. *Journal of Personality and Social Psychology, 25*, 872–886.

Doosje, B., Ellemers, N., & Spears, R. (1999). Commitment and intergroup behaviour. In N. Ellemers, R. Spears, & B. Doosje (Eds.), *Social identity: Context, commitment, content* (pp. 84–106). Boston: Blackwell.

Dougherty, J. W. D. (Ed.), (1985). *Directions in cognitive anthropology.* Urbana: University of Illinois Press.

Dovidio, J. F., & Gaertner, S. (2010). Intergroup bias. In S. T. Fiske, D. T. Gilbert, & G. Lindzey (Eds.), *Handbook of social psychology* (5th ed., Vol. 2, pp. 1084–1121). Hoboken, NJ: John Wiley & Sons.

Dovidio, J. F., ten Vergert, M., Stewart, T. L., Gaertner, S. L., Johnson, J. D., Esses, V. M., Riek, B. M., & Pearson, A. R. (2004). Perspective and prejudice: Antecedents and mediating mechanisms. *Personality and Social Psychology Bulletin, 30*, 1537–1549.

Dowty, A. (2005). *Israel/Palestine*. Cambridge: Polity Press.
Dreeben, R. (1968). *On what is learned in school*. Reading, MA: Addison-Wesley.
Driskell, J. E., & Salas, E. M. (Eds.), (1996). *Stress and human performance*. Hillsdale, NJ: Erlbaum.
Drucker, R. (2002). *Hrakiri*. Tel Aviv: Miscal. (in Hebrew)
Drury, J., & Reicher, S. D. (1999). The intergroup dynamics of collective empowerment: Substantiating the social identity model of crowd behavior. *Group Processes and Intergroup Relations, 4*, 381–402.
Duffy, T. (2000). Peace education in divided society: Creating a culture of peace in Northern Ireland. *Prospects, 30*, 15–29.
Dunlop, J. B. (1998). *Russia confronts Chechnya: Roots of a separatist conflict*. Cambridge: Cambridge University Press.
Dunn, J. (1988). *The beginnings of social understanding*. Cambridge, MA: Harvard University Press.
Dweck, C. S. (1999). *Self-Theories: Their role in motivation, personality and development*. Philadelphia: Taylor and Francis/Psychology Press.
Dweck, C. S., & Ehrlinger, J. (2006). Implicit theories and conflict resolution. In M. Deutsch, P. T. Coleman, & E. C. Marcus (Eds.), *The handbook of conflict resolution: Theory and practice* (2nd ed., pp. 317–330). San Francisco: Jossey-Bass Publishers.
Eagleton, T. (1991). *Ideology: An introduction*. London: Verso.
Eagly, A. H., & Chaiken, S. (1993). *The psychology of attitudes*. Fort Worth: Harcourt Brace Jovanovich.
   (1998). Attitude structure and function. *In The handbook of social psychology* (4th ed., Vol. 1, pp. 269–322). New York: McGraw Hill.
Easterbrook, J. A. (1959). The effect of emotion on cue utilization and the organization of behavior. *Psychological Review, 66*, 183–201.
Ecker, U., Lewandowsky S., & Tang D. (2010). Explicit warnings reduce but do not eliminate the continued influence of misinformation. *Memory & Cognition, 38*(8), 1087–1100.
Edwards, J. A. (2005). Community-focused apologia in international affairs: Japanese Prime Minister Tomiichi Murayama's apology. *The Howard Journal of Communications, 16*, 317–336.
Edwards, K., & Smith, E. E. (1996). A disconfirmation bias in the evaluation of arguments. *Journal of Personality and Social Psychology, 71*, 5–24.
Eibl-Eibesfeldt, I. (1979). *The biology of peace and war*. New York: Viking.
Eibl-Eibesfeldt, I., & Sütterlin, C. (1990). Fear, defense and aggression in animals and man: Some ethological perspectives. In P. F. Brain, S. Parmigiani, R. J. Blanchard, & D. Mainardi (Eds.), *Fear and defense* (pp. 381–408). London: Harwood.
Eidelson, R. J., & Eidelson, J. I. (2003). Dangerous ideas: Five beliefs that propel groups toward conflict. *American Psychologist, 58*(3), 183–192.
Eisenberg, N. (2000). Emotion, regulation, and moral development. *Annual Review of Psychology, 51*, 665–697.
Ekman, P. (1992). An argument for basic emotions. *Cognition and Emotion, 6*, 169–200.
Ekman, P., & Davidson, R. J. (Eds.), (1994). *The nature of emotion: Fundamental question*. New York: Oxford University Press.
El Asmar, F. (1986). *Through the Hebrew looking-glass: Arab stereotypes in children's literature*. London: Zed Books.

Elcheroth, G., & Spini, D. (2011). Political violence, intergroup conflict, and ethnic categories. In D. Bar-Tal (Ed.), *Intergroup conflicts and their resolution: A social psychological perspective* (pp. 175–194). New York: Psychology Press.

Eldan, M. (2006). *Imparting collective memory by secular and religious kindergarten teachers.* Master's thesis, Tel Aviv University. (in Hebrew).

Elhance, A. P., & Ahmar, M. (1995). Nonmilitary CBMs. In M. Krepon & A. Sevak (Eds.), *Crisis prevention, confidence building and reconciliation in South Asia* (pp. 131–151). New York: St. Martin's Press.

El-Hoss, S. (1994). Prospective change in Lebanon. In D. Collings (Ed.), *Peace for Lebanon? From war to reconstruction* (pp. 249–258). Boulder, CO: Lynne Rienner.

Elizur, Y., & Yishay-Krien, N. (2009). Participation in atrocities among Israeli soldiers during the first intifada: A qualitative analysis. *Journal of Peace Research, 46,* 251–267.

Ellemers, N. (2002). Social identity and relative deprivation. In I. Walker & H. J. Smith (Eds.), *Relative deprivation: Specification, development and integration* (pp. 239–264). Cambridge: Cambridge University Press.

Ellemers, N., Spears, R., & Doosje, B. (2002). Self and social identity. *Annual Review of Psychology, 53,* 161–186.

Eller, J. D. (1999). *From culture to ethnicity to conflict: An anthropological perspective on international ethnic conflict.* Ann Arbor: University of Michigan Press.

Elon, A. (1971). *The Israelis: Founders and sons.* London: Weidenfeld and Nicolson.

Elster, J. (1999). *Alchemies of the mind: Rationality and the emotions.* Cambridge: Cambridge University Press.

Enderlin, C. (2003). *The shattered dreams: The failure of the peace process in the Middle East, 1995–2002.* New York: Other Press.

English, R., & Halperin, J. J. (1987). *The other side: How Soviet and Americans perceive each other.* New Brunswick, NJ: Transaction Books.

Entelis, J. P. (1981). The politics of partition: Christian perspectives on the Lebanese national identity. *International Insight,* May–June, 11–15.

Entessar, N. (2010). *Kurdish politics in the Middle East.* Lanham, MD: Lexington.

Eriksen, T. H. (2001). Ethic identity, national identity, and intergroup conflict. In R. D. Ashmore, L. Jussim, & D. Wilder (Eds.), *Social identity, intergroup conflict, and conflict resolution* (pp. 42–68). Oxford: Oxford University Press.

Eysenck, M. W. (1982). *Attention and arousal: Cognition and performance.* Berlin: Springer.

Farrell, M. (1976). *Northern Ireland: The Orange State.* London: Pluto.

Fay, M. T., Morrissey, M., & Smyth, M. (1998). *Mapping Troubles-Related Deaths in Northern Ireland, 1969–1998.* Londonderry: INCORE.

Fazio, R. H. (1995). Attitudes as object-evaluation associations. Determinants, consequences, and correlates of attitude accessibility. In R. E. Petty & J. A. Krosnick (Eds.), *Attitude strength: Antecedents and consequences* (pp. 247–283). Mahwah, NJ: Erlbaum.

Feige, M. (1998). Peace Now and the legitimization crisis of "Civil Militarism." *Israel Studies, 3,* 85–111.

Feldman, F. (1992). *Confrontations with the reaper: A philosophical study of the nature and value of death.* New York: Oxford University Press.

Feldman, S. (1982). *Israeli nuclear deterrence.* New York: Columbia University Press.

Feldman, S., & Stenner, K. (1997). Perceived threat and authoritarianism. *Psychological Psychology, 18*, 741–770.
Fenton, S. (1999). *Ethnicity: Racism, class and culture.* London: Macmillan.
Ferguson, N., Binks, E., Rose, M. D., Brown, J. N., Adams, T., Cruise, S. M., & Lewis, C. A. (2007). The IRA apology of 2002 and forgiveness in Northern Ireland's troubles: A cross-national study of printed media. *Peace and Conflict: Journal of Peace Psychology, 13*, 93–113.
Ferguson, N., Burgess, M., & Hollywood, I. (2010). Who are the victims? Victimhood experiences in postagreement Northern Ireland. *Political Psychology, 31*, 857–886.
Fernandez, R. M., & McAdam, D. (1988). Social networks and social movements: Multi-organizational fields and recruitment to Mississippi freedom summer." *Sociological Forum, 3*(3), 357–382.
Fernández-Dols, J., Hurtado-de-Mendoza, A., & Jiménez-de-Lucas, I. (2004). Culture of Peace: An Alternative Definition and Its Measurement. *Peace and Conflict: Journal of Peace Psychology, 10*, 117–124.
Festinger, L. (1954). A theory of social comparison process. *Human Relations, 7*, 117–140.
Fierens, J. (2005). Gacaca courts: Between fantasy and reality. *Journal of International Criminal Justice, 3*, 896–919.
Finlay, D. J., Holsti, O. R., & Fagen, R. R. (1967). *Enemies in politics.* Chicago: Rand McNally.
Firer, R. (1985). *The agents of Zionist education.* Tel Aviv: Hakibutz Hameuhad. (in Hebrew)
Fischer, A. H., & Roseman, I. J. (2007). Beat them or ban them: The characteristics and social functions of anger and contempt. *Journal of Personality and Social Psychology, 93*, 103–115.
Fischhoff, B., Gonzalez, R. M., Lerner, J. S., & Small, D. A. (2005). Evolving judgments of terror risks: Foresight, hindsight, and emotion. *Journal of Experimental Psychology: Applied, 11*, 124–139.
Fishbein, M., & Ajzen, I. (1975). *Belief, attitude, intention and behavior: An introduction to theory and research.* Reading, MA: Addison-Wesley.
Fisher, R. J. (1990). *The social psychology of intergroup and international conflict resolution.* New York: Springer-Verlag.
   (1997). Training as interactive conflict resolution: Characteristics and challenges. *International Negotiation, 2*, 331–351.
   (2000). Intergroup conflict. In M. Deutsch & P. T. Coleman (Eds.), *The handbook of conflict resolution: Theory and practice* (pp. 166–184). San Francisco: Jossey-Bass.
   (2001). Cyprus: The failure of mediation and the escalation of an identity-based conflict to an adversarial impasse. *Journal of Peace Research, 38*(3), 307–326.
   (2005). *Paving the way: Contributions of interactive conflict resolution to peacemaking.* Lanham, MD: Lexington Books.
Fisher, R. J., & Kelman, H. C. (2011). Perceptions in conflicts. In D. Bar-Tal (Ed.), *Intergroup conflicts and their resolution: A social psychological perspective* (pp. 61–81). New York: Psychology Press.
Fishman, J., & Marvin, C. (2003). Portrayals of violence and group difference in newspaper photographs: Nationalism and media. *Journal of Communication, 53*, 32–44.
Fiske, A. P. (1991). *Structures of social life.* New York: Free Press.

Fiske, A. P., & Tetlock, P. E. (1997). Taboo trade-offs: Reactions to transactions that transgress the spheres of justice. *Political Psychology, 18*(2), 255–297.
Fiske, S. S., & Taylor, S. E. (1991). *Social cognition* (2nd ed.). New York: McGraw-Hill.
Fiske, S. T. (1998). Stereotyping, prejudice, and discrimination. In D. T. Gilbert, S. T. Fiske, & G. Lindzey (Eds.), *The handbook of social psychology* (4th ed., Vol. 2, pp. 357–411). Boston: McGraw-Hill.
Fiske, S. T., & Taylor, S. E. (2007). *Social cognition: From brains to culture.* New York: McGraw-Hill.
Fitzduff, M. (2002). *Beyond violence: Conflict resolution process in Northern Ireland.* New York: United Nations University Press.
  (2006). Ending wars: Developments, theories, and practices. In M. Fitzduff & C. E. Stout (Eds.), *The psychology of resolving global conflicts: From war to peace* (Vol. 1, pp. ix–xl). Westport, CT: Praeger Security International.
Fitzduff, M., & Stout, C. E. (Eds.), (2006). *The psychology of resolving global conflicts: From war to peace* (Vols. 1–3). Westport CT: Praeger Security International.
Flood, G. (1996). *An introduction to Hinduism.* Cambridge: Cambridge University Press.
Flowers, N., Bernbaum, M., Rudelius-Palmer, K., & Tolman, J. (2000). *The human rights education handbook: Effective practices for learning, action and change.* Minneapolis: University of Minnesota Human Rights Resource Center.
Foster, K. (1999). *Fighting fictions: War, narrative and national identity.* London: Pluto Press.
Foster, M. D., & Matheson, K. (1995). Double relative deprivation: Combining the personal and political. *Personality and Social Psychology Bulletin, 21,* 1167–1177.
Fountain, S. (1999). *Peace education in UNICEF.* Working Paper Series, Programme Division, Education Section. New York: UNICEF.
Fox, R. (1992). Prejudice and the unfinished mind: A new look at an old failing. *Psychological Inquiry, 2,* 137–152.
  (1994). Nationalism: Hymns ancient and modern. *National Interest, 35,* 51–57.
Frank, J. D. (1967). *Sanity and survival: Psychological aspects of war and peace.* New York: Random House.
Frankl, V. E. (1963). *Man's search for meaning.* New York: Washington Square Press.
  (1978). *The unheard cry for meaning: Psychotherapy and humanism.* New York: Simon & Schuster.
Frazer, H., & Fitzduff, M. (1986). *Improving community relations.* Belfast: Standing Advisory Commission on Human Rights.
Freeman, M. (2006). *Truth Commissions and procedural fairness.* Cambridge: Cambridge University Press.
Freeman, M., & Hayner, P. B. (2003). Truth-telling. In D. Bloomfield, T. Barnes, & T. Huyse (Eds.), *Reconciliation after violent conflict: A handbook* (pp. 122–139). Stockholm: International Idea for Democracy and Electoral Assistance.
Frijda, N. H. (1986). *The emotions:* Cambridge: Cambridge University Press.
  (1997). Commemorating. In J. W. Pennebaker, D. Paez, & B. Rimé (Eds.), *Collective memory of political events: Social psychological perspective* (pp. 103–127). Mahwah, NJ: Erlbaum.
Fritsche, I., Jonas, E., & Kessler, T. (2011). Collective reactions to threat: Implications for intergroup conflict and for solving societal crises. *Social Issues and Policy Review, 5,* 101–136.
Fromm, E. (1968). *The revolution of hope.* New York: Bantam.

Funkeson, U., Schroder, E., Nzabonimpa, J., & Holmqvist, R. (2011). Witnesses to genocide: Experiences of witnessing in the Rwandan Gacaca courts. *Peace and Conflict: Journal Peace Psychology, 17*, 367–388.
Fuxman, S. (2012). *Learning the past, understanding the present, shaping the future: Israeli adolescents' narratives of the conflict.* Ph.D. dissertation, Harvard University.
Gagnon, V. P., Jr. (2004). *The myth of ethnic war: Serbia and Croatia in the 1990s.* Ithaca, NY: Cornell University Press.
Galinsky, A. D., & Moskowitz, G. B. (2000). Perspective-taking: Decreasing stereotype expression, stereotype accessibility, and in-group favoritism. *Journal of Personality and Social Psychology, 78*, 708–724.
Gallagher, A. M. (1989). Social identity and the Northern Ireland conflict. *Human Relations, 42*(10), 917–935.
Gallagher, T. (2010). Building a shared future from a divided past: Promoting peace through education in Northern Ireland. In G. Salomon & E. Cairns (Eds.), *Handbook of peace education* (pp. 241–251). New York: Psychology Press.
Galtung, J. (1969). Violence, peace, and peace research. *Journal of Peace Research, 6*, 167–191.
   (1975). Three approaches to peace: Peacekeeping, peacemaking and peace-building. In J. Galtung (Ed.), *Peace, war and defence: Essays in peace research* (pp. 282–304). Copenhagen: Christian Ejlers.
   (1990). Cultural violence. *Journal of Peace Research, 27*(3), 291–305.
   (1996). *Peace by peaceful means: Peace and conflict, development and civilization.* London: Sage.
Gamage, S., & Watson, I. B. (1999). *Conflict and community in contemporary Sri Lanka.* New Delhi: Sage.
Gamson, W. A. (1981). The political culture of Arab-Israeli conflict. *Conflict Management and Peace Sciences, 5*, 79–93.
   (1988). Political discourse and collective action. In B. Klandermans, H. Kriesi, & S. Tarrow (Eds.), *From structure to action: Comparing social movement research across cultures* (Vol. 1, pp. 219–244). Greenwich, CT: JAI Press.
   (1992). *Talking politics.* Cambridge: Cambridge University Press.
Ganguly, S. (1995). Mending fences. In M. Krepon & A. Sevak (Eds.), *Crisis prevention, confidence building and reconciliation in South Asia* (pp. 11–24). New York: St. Martin's Press.
   (1996). Explaining the Kashmir insurgency: Political mobilization and institutional decay. *International Security, 21*(2), 76–107.
Gardner Feldman, L. (1999). The principle and practice of "reconciliation" in German foreign policy: Relations with France, Israel, Poland and the Czech Republic. *International Affairs, 75*, 333–356.
Gavriely-Nuri, D. (2008). The "Metaphorical Annihilation" of the Second Lebanon War (2006). From the Israeli political discourse. *Discourse and Society, 19*(1), 5–20.
   (2009). Friendly fire: War-Normalizing metaphors in the Israeli political discourse. *Journal of Peace Education, 6*(2), 153–169.
   (2010). Rainbow, snow, and the Poplar's Song: The "Annihilative Naming" of Israeli military practices. *Armed Forces and Society, 36*, 825–842.
   (in press). War normalizing dialogue (WND): The Israeli case. In A. Fetzer & L. Berlin (Eds.), *Dialogue and politics.* Amsterdam: John Benjamins.

Gawerc, M. I. (2006). Peace-building: Theoretical and concrete perspectives. *Peace & Change, 31*, 435–478.
Gawronski, B. (2004). Theory-based bias correction in dispositional inference: The fundamental attribution error is dead, long live the correspondence bias. *European Review of Social Psychology, 15*, 183–217.
Gayer, C. (2012). *Gender intractability: National identity construction and gender in the Israeli-Palestinian conflict.* Ph.D. dissertation, Free University of Berlin.
Gayer, C., Landman, S., Halperin, E., & Bar-Tal, D. (2009). Overcoming psychological barriers to peaceful conflict resolution: The role of arguments about losses. *Journal of Conflict Resolution, 53*, 951–975.
Gazimestan speech. (2008, May 5). In *Wikisource, The Free Library*. Retrieved August 4, 2008, from http://en.wikisource.org/w/index.php?title=Gazimestan_speech&oldid=637618.
    (2008, June 30). In *Wikipedia, The Free Encyclopedia*. Retrieved August 4, 2008, from http://en.wikipedia.org/w/index.php?title=Gazimestan_speech&oldid=222610953.
Geertz, C. (1973). *The interpretation of cultures*: New York: Basic Books.
Geis, R. (2006). Asymmetric conflict structures. *International Review of the Red Cross, 88*, 757–777.
Gellner, E. (1983). *Nations and nationalism.* Ithaca, NY: Cornell University Press.
Gerhart, G. M. (1978). *Black power in South Africa: The evolution of an ideology.* Berkeley: University of California Press.
Gerolymatos, A. (2002). *The Balkan war: Conquest, revolution, and retribution from the Ottoman era to twentieth century and beyond.* New York: Basic books.
Geva, N., & Mintz, A. (Eds.), (1997). *Decision-making on war and peace: The cognitive-rational debate.* Boulder, CO: Lynne Rienner.
Gibson, J. L. (2004a). *Overcoming apartheid: Can truth reconcile a divided nation?* New York: Russell Sage Foundation.
    (2004b). Does truth lead to reconciliation? Testing the causal assumptions of the South African Truth and Reconciliation process. *American Journal of Political Science, 48*, 201–217.
    (2006). The contributions of truth to reconciliation: lessons from South Africa. *Journal of Conflict Resolution, 50*(3), 409–432.
Gibson, J. L., & Claassen, C. (2010). Racial reconciliation in South Africa: Interracial contact and changes over time, *Journal of Social Issues, 66*, 255–272.
Gidron, B., Katz, S. N., & Hasenfeld, Y. (Eds.), (2002). *Mobilizing for peace: Conflict resolution in Northern Ireland, Israel/Palestine, and South Africa.* Oxford: Oxford University Press.
Gidron, B., Katz, S. N., Meyer, M., Hasenfeld, Y., Schwartz, R., & Crane, J. K. (1999). Peace and conflict resolution organizations in three protracted conflicts: Structures, resources and ideology. *Voluntas: International Journal of Voluntary and Nonprofit Organizations, 10*, 275–298.
Giligan, E. (2010). *Terror in Chechnya: Russia and the tragedy of civilians in war.* Princeton, NJ: Princeton University Press.
Gillis, J. R. (Ed.), (1994). *Commemorations: The politics of national identity.* Princeton, NJ: Princeton University Press.
Gil-White, F. J. (2001). Are ethnic group biological "species" to the human brain? Essentialism in our cognition of some critical categories. *Current Anthropology, 42*, 515–554.

Ginges, J., & Atran, S. (2008). Humiliation and the inertia effect: Implications for understanding violence and compromise in intractable intergroup conflicts. *Journal of Cognition and Culture, 8*(3–4), 281–294.

(2009). What motivates participation in violent political action: Selective incentives or parochial altruism? *Annals of the New York Academy of Sciences, 1167*, 115–123.

(2011). War as a moral imperative (Not just practical policy by other means). *Proceedings of the Royal Society: Biological Sciences.* Online first publication, February 16.

Ginges, J., Atran, S., Medin, D., Shikaki, K. (2007). Sacred bounds on rational resolution of violent political conflict. *Proceedings of the National Academy of Science, 104*, 7357–7360.

Gitlin, T. (1980). *The whole world is watching.* Berkeley: University of California Press.

Glenny, M. (1993). *The fall of Yugoslavia: The third Balkan War.* Penguin Books.

Gobodo-Madikizela, P. (2008). Transforming trauma in the aftermath of gross human rights abuses: Making public spaces intimate through the South African Truth and Reconciliation Commission. In A. Nadler, E. M. Thomas, & J. D. Fisher (Eds.), *The social psychology of intergroup reconciliation* (pp. 57–75). New York: Oxford University Press.

Goertz, G., & Diehl, P. F. (1992). The empirical importance of enduring rivalries. *International Interactions, 18*, 151–163.

(1993). Enduring rivalries: Theoretical constructs and empirical patterns. *International Studies Quarterly, 37*, 147–171.

Goff, P. A., Eberhardt, J. L., Williams, M., & Jackson, M. C. (2008). Not yet human: Implicit knowledge, historical dehumanization, and contemporary consequences. *Journal of Personality and Social Psychology, 94*, 292–306.

Golan, G. (2006). *Youth journalism during Israeli wars: A comparative examination on the basis of the theory of ethos of conflict.* Master's thesis, Tel Aviv University. (in Hebrew)

Goldman, J. S., & Coleman, P. T. (2011). *A theoretical understanding of how emotions fuel intractable conflict: The case of humiliation.* Unpublished manuscript.

Golec, A., & Federico, C. M. (2004). Understanding responses to political conflict: Interactive effects of the need for closure and salient conflict schema. *Journal of Personality and Social Psychology, 87*, 750–762.

Goleman, D. (1995). *Emotional intelligence.* New York: Bantam Books.

Gómez, Á., Brooks, M. L., Buhrmester, M. D., Vázquez, A., Jetten, J., & Swann, W. B., Jr. (2011). On the nature of identity fusion: Insights into the construct and a new measure. *Journal of Personality and Social Psychology, 100*, 918–933.

Gonzalez-Allende, I. (2010). Masculinities in conflict: Representations of the other in narrative during the Spanish War. *Hispanic Research Journal, 11*, 193–209.

Goodwin, J. (2001). *No other way out: States and revolutionary movements, 1945–1991.* Cambridge: Cambridge University Press.

Goodwin, J., Jasper, J. M., & Polletta, F. (2004). Emotional dimension of social movements. In D. A. Snow, A. Soule, & H. Kriesi (Eds.), *The Blackwell companion to social movements* (pp. 413–432). Malden, MA: Blackwell.

Gopher, U. (2006). *Antecedents to the ethos of conflict in Israeli-Jewish society.* Master's thesis, Tel Aviv University. (in Hebrew)

Gordon, C., & Arian, A. (2001). Threat and decision making. *Journal of Conflict Resolution, 45*, 196–215.

Gordon, H. (1994). Working for peace in the Middle East: The educational task. In E. Boulding (Ed.), *Building peace in the Middle East: Challenges for states and civil society* (pp. 311–317). Boulder, CO: Lynne Rienner.

Gordon, S. T. (1990). Social structural effects on emotions. In T. D. Kemper, *Research agendas in the sociology of emotions* (pp. 145–179). Albany: State University of New York Press.

Goren, N. (2009). *The role of external incentives in promoting peace: The cases of Israel and Turkey*. Ph.D. dissertation, Hebrew University of Jerusalem.

(2010). *The role of external incentives in promoting peace: The cases of Israel and Turkey*. Ph.D. dissertation, Hebrew University of Jerusalem.

Govrin, N. (1989). Enemies or cousins?... Somewhere in between. The Arab problem and its reflection in Hebrew literature: Developments, trends, and examples. *Shofar*, 7, 13–23.

Gow, J. (2003). *The Serbian project and its adversaries: A Strategy of War Crimes*. London: Hurst.

Grabowska, A. (1999). Lateralisation of emotions in the brain – experimental and clinical data. In A. Herzyk & A. Borkowska (Eds.), *Neuropsychology of emotions* (pp. 59–79). Lublin: Wydawnictwo UMCS. (in Polish)

Grant, P. R., & Brown, R. (1995). From ethnocentrism, to collective protest: Responses to relative deprivation and threats to social identity. *Social Psychology Quarterly, 58*, 195–211.

Gray, B., Coleman, P., & Putnam, L. L. (2007). Introduction: Intractable conflict – New perspectives on the causes and conditions for change. *American Behavioral Scientist*, 50, 1415–1429.

Gray, J. A. (1987). *The psychology of fear and stress* (2nd ed.). Cambridge: Cambridge University Press.

Greenbaum, C. W., & Elizur, Y. (2013). The psychological and moral consequences for Israeli society of the occupation of Palestinian land. In D. Bar-Tal & I. Schnell (Eds.), *The impacts of lasting occupation: Lessons from Israeli society* (pp. 380–407). New York: Oxford University Press.

Greenberg, J., Pyszczynski, T., &. Solomon, S. (1997). Terror management theory of self-esteem and social behavior: Empirical assessments and conceptual refinements. In M. P. Zanna (Ed.), *Advances in experimental social psychology* (Vol. 29, pp. 61–139). New York: Academic Press.

Greenberg, J., Solomon, S., & Arndt, J. (2008). A basic but uniquely human motivation: Terror management. In J. Y. Shah & W. L. Gardner (Eds.), *Handbook of motivation science* (pp. 114–134). New York: Guilford Press.

Greenberg, J., Solomon, S., & Pyszczynski, T. (1997). Terror management theory of self-esteem and cultural worldviews: Empirical assessments and conceptual refinements. *Advances in Experimental Social Psychology*, 29, 61–139.

Greenstein, R. (2009). Class, nation, and political organization: The anti-Zionist left in Israel/Palestine. *International Labor and Working-Class History*, 75, 85–108.

Greitemeyer, T., Fischer, P., Frey, D., & Schulz-Hardt, S. (2009). Biased assimilation: The role of source position. *European Journal of Social Psychology*, 39, 22–39.

Grings, W. W., & Dawson, M. E. (1978). *Emotions and bodily responses: A psycho-physiological approach*. New York: Academic Press.

Gross, N., & Gross, Y. (1991). *The Hebrew film*. Jerusalem: Meor ve Lecha. (in Hebrew)

Grosser, P. E., & Halperin, E. G. (1979). *Semitism: The causes and effects of a prejudice.* Secaucus, NY: Citadel.
Grossman, D. (1995). *On killing: The psychological cost of learning to kill in war and society.* New York: Little, Brown.
Grundy, K. W., & Weinstein, M. A. (1974). *The ideologies of violence.* Columbus, Ohio: Charles E. Merrill.
Guelke, A. (2003). Civil society and the Northern Irish peace process. *Voluntas: International Journal of Voluntary and Nonprofit Organizations, 14,* 61–78.
Gurr, T. R. (1970). *Why men rebel.* Princeton, NJ: Princeton University Press.
 (1993). *Minorities at risk.* Washington, DC: U.S. Institute of Peace.
 (2010). *Why men rebel: Fortieth anniversary edition.* Boulder, CO: Paradigm Publishers.
Gurr, T. R., & Harff, B. (1994). *Ethnic conflict in world politics.* Boulder, CO: Westview.
Gutmann, A., & Thompson, D. (2000). The moral foundations of Truth Commissions. In R. I. Rotberg & D. Thompson (Eds.), *Truth vs justice: The morality of Truth Commissions* (pp. 22–44). Princeton, NJ: Princeton University Press.
Guzmán, J. L. (2005). Educational reform in post-war El Salvador. In E. Vargas-Barón & H. B. Alarcón (Eds.), *From bullets to blackboard: Education for peace in Latin America and Asia* (pp. 43–61). Washington, DC: Inter-American Development Bank.
Haaretz (2003). Special report: The cost of the settlements. September 26, pp. 44–46. (In Hebrew)
Hackett, C., & Rolston, B. (2009). The burden of memory: Victims, storytelling and resistance in Northern Ireland. *Memory Studies, 2*(3), 355–376.
Hadawi, S. (1968). *Palestine occupied* (Rev. ed.). New York: The Arab Information Center.
Hadjipavlou, M. (2004). The contribution of bicommunal contacts in building a civil society in Cyprus. In A. H. Eagly, R. M. Baron, & V. L. Hamilton (Eds.), *The social psychology of group identity and social conflict: Theory, application and practice* (pp. 193–211). Washington, DC: American Psychological Association.
 (2007). The Cyprus conflict: Root causes and implications for peacebuilding, *Journal of Peace Research, 44,* 349–365.
Hadjipavlou-Trigeorgis, M. (1987). *Identity Conflict in Divided Societies: The Case of Cyprus.* Ph.D. dissertation, Boston University.
Hafez, M. M. (2006). *Manufacturing human bombs: The making of Palestinian suicide bombers.* Washington, DC: United States Institute for Peace Press.
Haider, H. (2009). (Re)Imaging coexistence: Striving in sustainable return, reintegration and reconciliation in Bosnia and Herzegovina. *International Journal of Transitional Justice, 3,* 91–113.
Haidt, J., & Algoe, S. (2004). Moral amplification and the emotions that attach us to saints and demons. In J. Greenberg, S. L. Koole, & T. Pyszczynski (Eds.), *Handbook of experimental existential psychology* (pp. 322–335). New York: Guilford Press.
Hainsworth, P. (1996). Law and order. In A. Aughey & D. Morrow (Eds.), *Northern Ireland politics* (pp. 103–110). London: Longman.
Halbwachs, M. (1992). *On collective memory.* Chicago: University of Chicago Press.
Hall, M. (1999). *Conflict resolution: The missing element in the Northern Ireland peace process.* Belfast: Island Pamphlets.
Hall-Cathala, D. (1990). *The peace movement in Israel, 1967–1987.* London: Macmillan Press.

Halliday, W. (Eds.), (1915). *Propatria: A book of patriotic verse.* London: J. M. Dent and Sons.

Halperin, E. (2007). *On the group psychology of group-based hatred in political systems.* Ph.D. dissertation, Haifa University. (in Hebrew)

(2008). Group-based hatred in intractable conflict in Israel. *Journal of Conflict Resolution, 52,* 713–736.

(2010). The emotional roots of intergroup violence – The distinct role of anger and hatred. In M. Mikulincer & P. R. Shaver (Eds.), *Human aggression and violence: Causes, manifestations, and consequences* (pp. 315–332). Washington, DC: American Psychological Association Press.

(2011). Emotional barriers to peace: Negative emotions and public opinion about the peace process in the Middle East. *Peace and Conflict: Journal of Peace Psychology, 17,* 22–45.

(in press). Emotion, emotion regulation, and conflict resolution. *Emotion Review.*

Halperin, E., &. Bar-Tal, D. (2007). The fall of the peace camp in Israel: The influence of Prime Minister Ehud Barak on Israeli public opinion, July 2000–February 2001. *Conflict & Communication Online, 6*(2), 1–18.

(2011). Socio-psychological barriers to peace making: An empirical examination within the Israeli Jewish society. *Journal of Peace Research, 48,* 637–657.

Halperin, E., Bar-Tal, D., Nets-Zehngut, R., & Almog, E. (2008). Fear and hope in conflict: Some determinants in the Israeli-Jewish society. *Peace and Conflict: Journal of Peace Psychology, 14,* 1–26.

Halperin, E., Bar-Tal, D., Nets-Zehngut, R., & Drori, E. (2008). Emotions in conflict: Correlates of fear and hope in the Israeli-Jewish society. *Peace and Conflict: Journal of Peace Psychology, 14,* 1–26.

Halperin, E., Bar-Tal, D., Sharvit, K., Rosler, N., & Raviv, A. (2010). Social psychological implications for an occupying society: The case of Israel. *Journal of Peace Research, 47,* 59–70.

Halperin, E., Canetti-Nisim, D., & Hirsch-Hoefler, S. (2009). The central role of group based hatred as an emotional antecedent of political intolerance: Evidence from Israel. *Political Psychology, 30,* 93–123.

Halperin, E., & Gross, J. (2011a). Emotion regulation in violent conflict: Reappraisal, hope, and support for humanitarian aid to the opponent in wartime. *Cognition & Emotion, 25*(7), 1228–1236.

(2011b). Intergroup anger in intractable conflict: Long-term sentiments predict anger responses during the Gaza war. *Group Processes and Intergroup Relations, 14*(4), 477–488.

Halperin, E., Russell, A., Dweck, C., & Gross, J. J. (2011). Anger, hatred, and the quest for peace. Anger can be constructive in the absence of hatred. *Journal of Conflict Resolution, 55,* 274–291.

Halperin, E., Russell, A. G., Trzesniewski, K. H., Gross, J. J., & Dweck, C. S. (2011). Promoting the peace process by changing beliefs about group malleability. *Science, 333,* 1767–1769.

Halperin, E., Sharvit, K., & Gross, J. J. (2011). Emotions and emotion regulation in conflicts. In D. Bar-Tal (Ed.), *Intergroup conflicts and their resolution: A social psychological perspective* (pp. 83–103). New York: Psychology Press.

Halperin, E., Wohl, M. J. A., & Porat, R. (2011). *Coping with extinction threat: Collective angst predicts willingness to compromise in intractable intergroup conflicts.* Manuscript submitted for publication.

Halpern, J., & Weinstein, H. M. (2004). Rehumanizing the other: Empathy and reconciliation. *Human Rights Quarterly, 26*(3), 561–583.

Hamber, B. (1998). The burdens of truth: An evaluation of the psychological support services and initiatives undertaken by the South African Truth and Reconciliation Commission. *American Imago, 55,* 9–28.

(2007). Forgiveness and reconciliation: Paradise lost or pragmatism. *Peace and Conflict: Journal Peace Psychology, 13,* 115–125.

Hamburg, D. A., George, A., & Ballentine, K. (1999). Preventing deadly conflict: The critical role of leadership. *Archives of General Psychiatry, 56,* 971–976.

Hamilton, D. L., Sherman, S. J., & Ruvolo, C. M. (1990). Stereotype-based expectancies: Effects on information processing and social behavior. *Journal of Social Issues, 46*(2), 35–60.

Hamilton, V. (1982). Cognition and stress: An information processing model. In L. L. Goldberg & S. Breznitz (Eds.), *Handbook of stress: Theoretical and clinical aspects* (pp. 105–120). New York: Free Press.

Hammack, P. L. (2008). Narrative and the cultural psychology of identity. *Personality and Social Psychology Review, 12*(3), 222–247.

(2009). Exploring the reproduction of conflict through narrative: Israeli youth motivated to participate in a coexistence program. *Peace and Conflict: Journal of Peace Psychology., 15,* 49–74.

(2011). *Narrative and the politics of identity: The cultural psychology of Israeli and Palestinian youth.* New York: Oxford University Press.

Handelman, D. (1990). *Models and mirrors: Towards an anthropology of public events.* Cambridge: Cambridge University Press.

Handelman, S. (2011). *Conflict and peacemaking in Israel-Palestine.* New York: Routledge.

Handl, V. (1997). Czech-German declaration on reconciliation. *German Politics, 6,* 150–167.

Handy, J. (1994). *Revolution in the countryside: Rural conflict and agrarian reform in Guatemala, 1944–1954.* Chapel Hill: University of North Carolina Press.

Harbom, L., Hogbladh, S., & Wallensteen, P. (2006). Armed conflict and peace agreement. *Journal of Peace Research, 43,* 617–631.

Harbom, L., & Wallensteen, P. (2009). Armed conflicts, 1946–2008. *Journal of Peace Research, 46,* 577–587.

Harding, S. A. (2011). Translation and the circulation of competing narratives from the wars in Chechnya: A case study from the 2004 Beslan hostage disaster. *Meta, 56*(1), 42–62.

Harff, B., & Gurr, T. B. (2004). *Ethnic conflict in world politics* (2nd ed.). Boulder, CO: Westview.

Harkabi, Y. (1977). *Arab strategies and Israel's response.* New York: Free Press.

(1983). *The Bar Kokhba syndrome: Risk and realism in international politics.* Chappaqua, NY: Rossel Books.

Harmon-Jones, E., & Sigelman, J. (2001). State anger and prefrontal brain activity: Evidence that insult-related relative left prefrontal activity is associated with experienced anger and aggression. *Journal of Personality and Social Psychology, 80*, 797–803.
Harré, R. (Ed.), (1986). *The social construction of emotions*. Oxford: Blackwell.
Harris, I. (1988). *Peace education*. Jefferson, NC: McFarland.
  (2010). History of peace education. In G. Salomon & E. Cairns (Eds.), (*Handbook of peace education* (pp. 11–20). New York: Psychology Press.
Harris, R. (1972). *Prejudice and tolerance in Ulster: A study of neighbors and strangers in a border community*. Manchester: Manchester University Press.
Harrison, M. (1964). Government and press in France during the Algerian war. *American Political Science Review, 58*, 273–285.
Hartling, L. M., & Luchetta, T. (1999). Humiliation: Assessing the impact of derision, degradation, and debasement. *Journal of Primary Prevention, 19*, 259–278.
Haslam, N. (2006). Dehumanization: An integrative review. *Personality and Social Psychology Review, 10*, 252–264.
Haslam, S. A., Reicher, S. D., & Platow, M. J. (2010). *The new psychology of leadership: Identity, influence and power*. New York: Psychology Press.
Havel, B. (2005). In search of a theory of public memory: The State, the individual, and Marcel Proust. *Indiana Law Journal, 80*(3), 605–726.
Hayes, G. (1998). We suffer our memories: Thinking about the past, healing, and reconciliation. *American Imago, 55*, 29–50.
Hayner, P. B. (1999). In pursuit of justice and reconciliation: Contributions of truth telling. In C. J. Arnson (Ed.), *Comparative peace processes in Latin America* (pp. 363–383). Stanford, CA: Stanford University Press.
  (2001). *Unspeakable truths: Confronting state terror and atrocity*. New York: Routledge.
Heath, C., Larrick, R. P., & Wu, G. (1999). Goals as reference points. *Cognitive Psychology, 38*, 79–109.
Hein, L., & Selden, M. (Eds.), (2000). *Censoring history: Citizenship and memory in Japan, Germany, and the United States*. Armonk, NY: An East Gate Book.
Heine, S. J., Proulx, T., & Vohs, K. D. (2006). The meaning maintenance model: On the coherence of social motivations. *Personality and Social Psychology Review, 10*(2), 88–110.
Heisler, M. (2008). Challenged histories and collective self-concepts: Politics in history, memory, and time. *The ANNALS of the American Academy of Political and Social Science, 617*, 199–211.
Heller, W., Nitschke, J. B., & Miller, G. A. (1998). Lateralization in emotion and emotional disorders. *Current Directions in Psychological Science, 7*, 26–37.
Helman, S. (1999). From soldiering and motherhood to citizenship: A study of four Israeli peace protest movements. *Social Politics, 6*, 292–313.
Helmick, R. G., & Petersen R. L. (Eds.), (2001). *Forgiveness and reconciliation: Religion, public policy, and conflict transformation*. Radnor, PA: Templeton Foundation Press.
Heradstveit, D. (1981). *The Arab-Israeli conflict: Psychological obstacles to peace*. Oslo: Universitetsforlaget.
Hermann, T. (2009). *The Israeli peace movement: A shattered dream*. Cambridge, Cambridge University Press.
Herrmann, R. K. (1985). *Perceptions and behavior in Soviet foreign policy*. Pittsburgh: University of Pittsburgh Press.

Hever, S. (2013). Economic cost of the occupation to Israel. In D. Bar-Tal and I. Schnell (Eds.), *The impacts of lasting occupation: Lessons from Israeli society* (pp. 326–358). New York: Oxford University Press.

Hewstone, M. (1996). Contact and categorization: Social interventions to change intergroup relations. In C. N. Macrae, C. Stangor, & M. Hewston (Eds.), *Stereotype and stereotyping* (pp. 323–368). New York: Guilford.

Hicks, D., & Weisberg, W. (2004). Extending the interactive problem-solving method: Addressing multiple levels of conflict, unacknowledged trauma, and responsibility. In A. H. Eagly, R. M. Baron, & L. V. Hamilton (Eds.), *The social psychology of group identity and social conflict: Theory, application, and practice* (pp. 151–172). Washington, DC: American Psychological Association.

Hicks, D. W. (Ed.)., (1988). *Education for peace: Issues, principles and practices in the classroom.* London: Routledge.

Hilton, D. J., & Liu, J. H. (2008). Culture and inter-group relations: The role of social representations of history. In R. Sorrentino & S. Yamaguchi (Eds.), *The handbook of motivation and cognition: The cultural context* (pp. 343–368). New York: Guilford.

Himmelweit, H. T., & Swift, B. (1969). A model for the understanding of school as a socializing agent. In P. H. Mussen, J. Langer, & M. Covington (Eds.), *Trends and issues in developmental psychology* (pp. 154–180). New York: Holt, Rinehart, and Winston.

Hinkle, S., Fox-Cardamone, L., Haseleu, J., Brown, R., & Irwin, L. (1996). Grassroots political action as an intergroup phenomenon. *Journal of Social Issues*, 52(1), 39–51.

Hirshberg, M. S. (1993). The self-perpetuating national self-image: Cognitive biases in perceptions of international interventions. *Political Psychology*, 14(1), 77–98.

Hirschberger, G., & Pyszczynski, T. (2010). An existential perspective on ethnopolitical violence. In P. R. Shaver & M. Mikulincer (Eds.), *Understanding and reducing aggression, violence, and their consequences* (pp. 297–314). Washington, DC: American Psychological Association.

  (in press). Killing with a clean conscience: Existential angst and the paradox of morality. In M. Mikulincer & P. R. Shaver (Eds.), *Social psychology of morality: Exploring the causes of good and evil.* Washington, DC: APA.

Hobfoll, S. E. (1988). *The ecology of stress.* New York: Hemisphere.

  (1989). Conservation of resources: A new attempt at conceptualizing stress. *American Psychologist*, 44(3), 513–524.

  (1998). *Stress, culture and community: The psychology and philosophy of stress.* New York: Plenum.

Hobfoll, S. E., & deVries, M. W. (Eds.), (1995). *Extreme stress and communities: Impact and intervention.* New York: Kluwer Academic/Plenum Publishers.

Hobfoll, E. S., Hall, B., & Canetti, D. (in press). Political violence, psychological distress, and perceived health in a representative sample of Palestinians. *Trauma Psychology*.

Hobfoll, S. E., Lomranz, J., Bridges, A., Eyal, N., & Tzemach, M. (1989). Pulse of a nation: Depressive mood reactions of Israelis to the Israel-Lebanon War. *Journal of Personality and Social Psychology*, 56, 1002–1112.

Hobsbawm, E. (1990). *Nations and nationalism since 1780: Programme, myth, reality.* Cambridge: Cambridge University Press.

  (1992). Introduction: Inventing traditions. In E. Hobsbawm & T. Ranger (Eds.), *The invention of tradition* (pp. 1–15). Cambridge: Cambridge University Press.

Hobsbawm, E., & Ranger, T. (Eds.), (1983). *The invention of tradition*. Cambridge: Cambridge University Press.

Hochschild, A. R. (1983). *A managed beast*. Berkeley: University of California Press.

Hoffman, A. M. (2002). A conceptualization of trust in international relations. *European Journal of International Relations, 8*(3), 375–401.

Hoffman, M. L. (2000). *Empathy and moral development: Implications for caring and justice*. Cambridge: Cambridge University Press.

Hogg, M. A. (2004). Uncertainty and extremism: Identification with high entitativity groups under conditions of uncertainty. In V. Y. Yzerbyt, C. M. Judd, & O. Corneille (Eds.), *The psychology of group perception: Perceived variability, entitativity, and essentialism* (pp. 401–418). New York: Psychology Press.

Hogg, M. A., & Abrams, D. (1993). Towards a single-process uncertainty-reduction model of social motivation in groups. In M. Hogg & D. Abrams (Eds.), *Group motivation: Social psychological perspectives* (pp. 173–190). Hemel Hempstead: Harvester Wheatsheaf.

Hogg, M. A., & Mullin, B. A. (1999). Joining groups to reduce uncertainty: Subjective uncertainty reduction and group identification. In D. Abrams & M. A. Hogg (Eds.), *Social identity and social cognition* (pp. 249–279). Oxford: Blackwell.

Holbrooke, R. (1999). *To end a war*. New York: Modern Library.

Holmes, R., & Evans, M. M. (2006). *Battlefield: Decisive conflicts in history*. Oxford: Oxford University Press.

Holmes, T. H., & Rahe, R. H. (1967). The social readjustment rating scale. *Journal of Psychosomatic Research, 11*, 213–218.

Holt, R. R., & Silverstein, B. (1989). On the psychology of enemy images: Introduction and overview. *Journal of Social Issues, 45*(2), 1–11.

Horne, A. (2006). *A savage war of peace: Algeria, 1954–1962*. New York: New York Reviews Books.

Horowitz, D. (1984). Israeli perception of national security (1948–1972). In B. Neuberger (Ed.), *Diplomacy and confrontation: Selected issues in Israel's foreign relations, 1948–1978* (pp. 104–148). Tel Aviv: Everyman's University. (in Hebrew)

Horowitz, D. L. (1985). *Ethnic groups in conflict*. Berkeley: California University Press.

   (1993). Conflict and the incentives to political accommodation. In D. Keogh & M. H. Haltzel (Eds.), *Northern Ireland and the politics of reconciliation* (pp. 173–188). Washington, DC: Woodrow Wilson Center Press.

   (2000). *Ethnic groups in conflict*. Berkeley: University of California Press.

   (2001). *The deadly ethnic riot*. Berkeley: University of California Press.

Horowitz, M. J. (1986). *Stress response syndromes*. Northvale, NJ: Jason Aronson Inc.

Hrvatin, S., & Trampuz, M. (2000). Enjoy your enemy or how the Kosovo (media) war broke out. *The Public, 7*(3), 77–86.

Huddy, L. (2001). From social to political identity: Implication for political psychology. *Political Psychology, 22*, 127–156.

Huddy, L., Feldman, S., & Cassese, E. (2007). On the distinct political effects of anxiety and anger. In A. Crigler, M. MacKuen, G. Marcus, & W. R. Neuman (Eds.), *The dynamics of emotion in political thinking and behavior* (pp. 202–230). Chicago: Chicago University Press.

Huddy, L., & Khatib, N. (2007). American patriotism, national identity and political involvement. *American Journal of Political Science, 51*, 63–77.

Huge, B. (1996). *El Salvador's civil war: A study of revolution*. Boulder, CO: Lynne Rienner.
Hume, J. (1993). A new Ireland in new Europe. In D. Keogh & M. H. Haltzel (Eds.), *Northern Ireland and the politics of reconciliation* (pp. 226–233). Washington, DC: Woodrow Wilson Center Press.
Hunt, S. A., & Benford, R. D. (2004). Collective identity, solidarity and commitment. In D. A. Snow, A. Soule, & H. Kriesi (Eds.), *The Blackwell companion to social movements* (pp. 171–196). Malden, MA: Blackwell.
Hunt, W. P. (1997). *Getting to war: Predicting international conflict with mass media indicators*. Ann Arbor: University of Michigan Press.
Hunter, J. A., Stringer, M., & Watson, R. P. (1991). Intergroup violence and intergroup attributions. *British Journal of Social Psychology, 30*, 261–266.
Huth, P., & Russett, B. (1993). General deterrence between enduring rivals: Testing three competing models. *American Political Science Review, 87*, 61–72.
Hutt, M. (2006). Things that should not be said: Censorship and self-censorship in the Nepali press 2001–2002. *Journal of Asian Studies, 65*(2), 361–392.
Inbar, E. (1991). *War and peace in Israeli politics: Labor party positions in national security*. Boulder, CO: Lynne Rienner.
Ingelaere, B. (2009). "Does the truth pass across fire without burning?" Locating the short circuit in Rwanda's Gacaca courts. *Journal of African Studies, 47*, 507–528.
Intercultural Education (2005). Special issue on Human Rights Education and Transformational Learning, *16*(2).
Iram, Y. (2006). Culture of peace: Definition, scope, and application. In Y. Iram (Ed.), *Educating towards a culture of peace* (pp. 3–12). Greenwich, CT: Information Age Publishing.
Irwin-Zarecka, I. (1994). *Frames of remembrance: The dynamics of collective memory*. New Brunswick, NJ: Transaction.
Isen, A. M. (1984). Toward understanding the role of affect in cognition. In R. S. Wyer Jr. & T. K. Srull (Eds.), *Handbook of social cognition* (Vol. 3, pp. 179–236). Hillsdale, NJ: Erlbaum.
  (1990). The influence of positive and negative affect on cognitive organization: Some implications for development. In N. L. Stein, B. Leventhal, & T. Trabasso (Eds.), *Psychological and biological approaches to emotion* (pp. 75–94). Hillsdale, NJ: Erlbaum.
  (1999). Positive affect. In T. Dalgleish & M. Power, *Handbook of cognition and emotion* (pp. 521–539). New York: Wiley.
Ito, T. A., Larsen, J. T., Smith, N. K., & Cacioppo, J. T. (1998). Negative information weighs more heavily on the brain: The negativity bias in evaluative categorizations. *Journal of Personality and Social Psychology, 75*, 887–900.
Iyengar, S. (1991). *Is anyone responsible?* Chicago: Chicago University Press.
Iyengar, S., & Ottai, V. (1994). Cognitive perspective in political psychology. In R. S. Wyer Jr. & T. K. Srull (Eds.), *Handbook of social cognition* (2nd ed., Vol. 2, pp. 143–188). Hillsdale, NJ: Erlbaum.
Iyer, A., & Leach, C. W. (2010). Helping disadvantaged out-groups challenge unjust inequality: The role of group-based emotions. In S. Stürmer & M. Snyder (Eds.), *The psychology of prosocial behavior: Group processes, intergroup relations, and helping* (pp. 337–353). Malden, MA: Wiley-Blackwell.

Iyer, A., Leach, C. W., & Crosby, F. J. (2003). White guilt and racial compensation: The benefits and limits of self-focus. *Personality and Social Psychology Bulletin*, 29, 117–129.

Iyer, A., & van Zomeren, M. (Eds.), (2009). Social and psychological dynamics of collective action: From theory and research to practice and policy. *Journal of Social Issues*, 65, no. 4, whole issue.

Jabri, V. (1996). *Discourses on violence: Conflict analysis reconsidered*. Manchester: Manchester University Press.

Jacobson, D. (1991). The conceptual approach to job insecurity. In J. Hartley, D. Jacobson, and B. Klandermans (Eds.), *Job insecurity: Coping with jobs at risk* (pp. 23–29). London: Sage.

Jahoda, G. (1999). *The images of savages: Ancient roots of modern prejudice*. New York: Routledge.

Jaimoukha, A. (2005). *The Chechens: A handbook*. New York: Routledge.

Janis, I., Defares, P., & Grossman, P. (1983). Hypervigilant reactions to threat. In H. Selye (Ed.), *Selye's guide to stress research* (Vol. 3, pp. 1–42). New York: Van Nostrand Reinhold.

Janis, I. L., & Mann, L. (1977). *Decision making: A psychological analysis of conflict, choice, and commitment*. New York: Free Press.

Janoff-Bulman, R. (1992). *Shattered assumptions: Towards a new psychology of trauma*. New York: Free Press.

Janoff-Bulman, R., & Werther, A. (2008). The social psychology of respect: Implications for delegitimization and reconciliation. In A. Nadler, T. Malloy, & J. D. Fisher, *Social psychology of inter-group reconciliation: From violent conflict to peaceful co-existence* (pp. 145–171). Cambridge: Cambridge University Press.

Jarman, N. (1997). *Material conflicts: Parades and visual displays in Northern Ireland*. New York: Berg.

Jarymowicz, M. (1997). Questions about the nature of emotions: On unconscious and not spontaneous emotions. *Czasopismo Psychologiczne*, 3(3), 153–170 (in Polish).

(2001a). Affective reactions and evaluative judgments. *Polish Psychological Bulletin*, 2, 39–43.

(Ed.), (2001b). *Between affect and intellect: Empirical studies*. Warszawa: Wydawnictwo Instytutu Psychologii PAN. (in Polish)

(2002). Human aggressiveness in the light of knowledge about human emotions. In S. Amsterdamski (Ed.), *Human beings and aggression* (pp. 173–189). Warszawa: Wydawnictwo SIC! (in Polish).

(2006). *On the in-group favoritism and its alleged inescapability*. Warszawa: Wydawnictwo IP PAN. (in Polish)

(2009a). Emotions as evaluative processes: from primary affects to appraisals based on deliberative thinking. In A. Błachnio & A. Przepiórka (Eds.), *Closer to emotions* (pp. 55–72). Lublin: Wydawnictwo KUL. (in Polish)

(2009b). The heart-mind dichotomy: Toward understanding a very old idea. In J. Kozielecki (Ed.), *New ideas in psychology* (pp. 183–215), Gdańsk: GWP. (in Polish)

Jarymowicz, M., & Bar-Tal, D. (2006). The dominance of fear over hope in the life of individuals and collectives. *European Journal of Social Psychology*, 36, 367–392.

Jarymowicz, M., & Imbir, K. (2010). Toward a taxonomy of human emotions. *Przegląd Psychologiczny*, 53(4), 439–461. (in Polish)

Jenkins, R. (1996). *Social identity*. London: Routledge.

Jentleson, B. (1996). *Preventive diplomacy and ethnic conflict: Possible, difficult, necessary.* Berkeley: University of California, Institute on Global Conflict and Cooperation.

Jervis, R. (1976). *Perception and misperception in international politics.* Princeton, NJ: Princeton University Press.

Johnson, C., Ratwik, S. H., & Sawyer, T. J. (1987). The evocative significance of kin terms in patriotic speech. In V. Reynolds, V. Falger, & I. Vine (Eds.), *The sociobiology of ethnocentrism: Evolutionary dimensions of xenophobia, discrimination, racism and nationalism* (pp. 157–174). London: Croom Helm.

Johnson, D. W., & Johnson, R. (2005). Essential components of peace education. *Theory into Practice, 44*(4), 280–292.

Johnson, G. R. (1997). The evolutionary roots of patriotism. In D. Bar-Tal & E. Staub (Eds.), *Patriotism in the lives of individuals and nations* (pp. 45–90). Chicago: Nelson-Hall.

Johnson-Laird, P. N., & Oatley, K. (1989). The language of emotions: An analysis of semantic field. *Cognition and Emotion, 3,* 81–123.

(1992). Basic emotions, rationality and folk theory. *Cognition and Emotion, 6,* 201–223.

Jones, L. (2006). *Then they started shooting.* Harvard: Harvard University Press.

Jones, T. S. (2004). Conflict resolution education: The field, the findings, and the future. *Conflict Resolution Quarterly, 22*(1–2), 233–267.

Jordan, N. (1965). The asymmetry of liking and disliking: A phenomenon meriting further reflection and research. *Public Opinion Quarterly, 29,* 315–322.

Jost, J. T. (2006). The end of the end of ideology. *American Psychologist, 61,* 651–670.

Jost, J. T., & Banaji, M. R. (1994). The role of stereotyping in system-justification and the production of false consciousness. *British Journal of Social Psychology, 33,* 1–27.

Jost, J. T., Banaji, M. R., & Nosek, B. A. (2004). A decade of system justification theory: Accumulative evidence of conscious and unconscious bolstering of the status quo. *Political Psychology, 25,* 881–919.

Jost, J. T., Federico, C. M., & Napier, J. L. (2009). Political ideology: Its structure, functions and elective affinities. *Annual Review of Psychology, 60,* 307–337.

Jost, J. T., Glaser, J., Kruglanski, A. W., & Sulloway, F. J. (2003). Political conservatism as motivated social cognition. *Psychological Bulletin, 129,* 339–375.

Jost, J. T., & Hunyady, O. (2003). The psychology of system justification and the palliative function of ideology. *European Review of Social Psychology, 13,* 111–153.

Jost, J. T., Nosek, B. A., & Gosling, S. D. (2008). Ideology: its resurgence in social, personality, and political psychology. *Perspective on Psychological Science, 3,* 126–136.

Jowett, G., & O'Donnell, V. (2006). *Propaganda and persuasion* (4th ed.). Thousand Oaks, CA: Sage.

Judah, T. (2000). *The Serbs: History, Myth, and the Destruction of Yugoslavia.* New Haven, CT: Yale University Press.

Jussim, L., & Fleming, C. (1996). Self-fulfilling prophecies and the maintenance of social stereotypes: The role of dyadic interactions and social forces. In C. N. Macrae, C. Stangor, & M. Hewstone (Eds.), *Stereotypes and stereotyping* (pp. 161–192). New York: Guilford Press.

Kacowicz, A. M., Bar-Siman-Tov, Y., Elgstrom, O., & Jerneck M., (Eds.), (2000). *Stable peace among nations.* Lanham, MD: Rowman & Littlefield.

Kadima Kadiangandu, J., Gauche, M., Vinsonneau, G., & Mullet, E. (2007). Conceptualizations of forgiveness: Collectivist-Congolese versus individualist-French viewpoints. *Journal of Cross-Cultural Psychology, 38*(4), 432–437.

Kadima Kadiangandu, J., & Mullet, E. (2007). Intergroup forgiveness: A Congolese perspective. *Peace and Conflict: Journal of Peace Psychology, 13*, 35–47.

Kahneman, D. (1973). *Attention and effort.* Englewood Cliffs, NJ: Prentice Hall.

(2003). A perspective on judgment and choice: Mapping bounded rationality. *American Psychologist, 58*, 697–720.

Kahneman, D., & Tversky, A. (1979). Prospect theory: An analysis of decision under risk. *Econometrica, 47*, 263–291.

(1984). Choices, values, and frames. *American Psychologist, 39*, 341–350.

(1995). Conflict resolution: A cognitive perspective. In K. Arrow, R. Mnookin, L. Ross, A. Tversky, & R. Wilson (Eds.), *Barriers to conflict resolution* (pp. 44–61). New York: Norton.

Kalyvas, S. (2006). *The logic of violence in civil war.* Cambridge: Cambridge University Press.

Kaminer, R. (1996). *The politics of protest: The Israeli peace movement and the Palestinian Intifada.* Brighton: Sussex Academic Press.

Kammen, M. (1991). *Mystic chords of memory: The transformation of tradition in American culture.* New York: Knopf.

Kanouse, D. E., & Hanson, L. R. (1971). *Negativity in evaluation.* Morristown, NJ: General Learning Press.

(1972). Negativity in evaluations. In E. Jones et al., *Attribution: Perceiving the causes of behavior.* Morristown, NJ: General Learning Press.

Kansteiner, W. (2002). Finding meaning in memory: A methodological critique of collective memory studies. *History and Theory, 41*, 179–197.

Kaplowitz, N. (1990). National self-images, perception of enemies, and conflict strategies: Psychopolitical dimensions of international relations. *Political Psychology, 11*, 39–82.

Karpin, M., & Friedman, I. (1998). *Murder in the name of God: The plot to kill Yitzhak Rabin.* New York: Metropolitan Books.

Kashti, Y. (1997). Patriotism as identity and action. In D. Bar-Tal & E. Staub (Eds.), *Patriotism in the lives of individuals and nations* (pp. 213–228). Chicago: Nelson-Hall.

Kasabova, A. (2008). Memory, memorials, and commemoration. *History and Theory, 47*, 331–350.

Katz, D. (1960). The functional approach to the study of attitudes. *Public Opinion Quarterly, 24*, 163–204.

Kaufman, S. (2006). Escaping the symbolic political trap: Reconciliation initiatives and conflict resolution in ethnic wars. *Journal of Peace Research, 43*(2), 201–218.

(2001). *Modern hatred: The symbolic politics of ethnic wars.* Ithaca, NY: Cornell University Press.

Kaye, M. (1997). The role of the Truth Commissions in the search for justice, reconciliation and democratization: The Salvadorean and Honduran cases. *Journal of Latin American Studies, 29*, 693–716.

Keeble, R. L., Tulloch, J., & Zollmann, F. (Eds.), (2010). *Peace journalism, war and conflict resolution.* New York: Peter Lang.

Keen, S. (1986). *Faces of the enemy: Reflections of the hostile imagination.* San Francisco: Harper & Row.

Keinan, G. (1987). Decision making under stress: Scanning of alternatives under controllable and uncontrollable threats. *Journal of Personality and Social Psychology, 52*, 629–644.
Keinan, G., Friedland, N., & Arad, L. (1991). Chunking and integration: Effects of stress on the structuring of information. *Cognition and Emotion, 5*, 133–145.
Keinan, G., Friedland, N., & Even-Haim, G. (2000). The effects of stress and self esteem on social stereotyping. *Journal of Social and Clinical Psychology, 19*, 206–219.
Kelman, H. C. (1958). Compliance, identification and internalization: Three processes of attitude change. *Journal of Conflict Resolution, 2*, 51–60.
(1961). Processes of opinion change. *Public Opinion Queerly, 25*, 57–78.
(1995). Contributions of an unofficial conflict resolution effort to the Israeli-Palestinian breakthrough. *Negotiation Journal, 11*(1), 19–27.
(1996). The interactive problem-solving approach. In C. A. Crocker, F. O. Hampson, & P. Aall (Eds.), *Managing global chaos: Sources of conflict of and responses to international conflict* (pp. 501–519). Washington, DC: United States Institute of Peace Press.
(1997a). Group processes in the resolution of international conflicts: Experiences from the Israeli-Palestinian case. *American Psychologist, 52*, 212–220.
(1997b). Social-psychological dimensions of international conflict. In I. W. Zartman & J. L. Rasmussen (Ed.), *Peacemaking in international conflict: Methods and techniques* (pp. 191–237). Washington, DC: United States Institute of Peace Press.
(1999a). The interdependence of Israeli and Palestinian national identities: The role of the other in existential conflicts. *Journal of Social Issues, 55*, 581–600.
(1999b). Transforming the relationship between former enemies: A social-psychological analysis. In R. L. Rothstein (Ed.), *After the peace: Resistance and reconciliation* (pp. 193–205). Boulder, CO: Lynne Rienner.
(2001). The role of national identity in conflict resolution. In R. D. Ashmore, L. Jussim, & D. Wilder (Eds.), *Social identity, intergroup conflict, and conflict reduction* (pp. 187–212). New York: Oxford University Press.
(2004). Reconciliation as identity change: A social psychological perspective. In Y. Bar-Siman-Tov (Ed.), *From conflict resolution to reconciliation* (pp. 111–124). Oxford: Oxford University Press.
(2005). Building trust among enemies: The central challenge for international conflict resolution. *International Journal of Intercultural Relations, 29*, 639–650.
(2007). Social-psychological dimensions of international conflict. In I. W. Zartman (Ed.), *Peacemaking in international conflict: Methods and techniques* (Rev. ed., pp. 61–107). Washington, DC: United States Institute of Peace.
(2008). Evaluating the contributions of interactive problem solving to the resolution of ethnonational conflicts. *Peace and Conflict, 14*, 29–60.
Kelman, H. C., & Fisher, R. J. (2003). Conflict analysis and resolution. In D. O. Sears, L. Huddy, & R. Jervis (Eds.), *Oxford handbook of political psychology* (pp. 315–353). New York: Oxford University Press.
Keltner, D., & Robinson, R. J. (1993). Imagined ideological differences in conflict escalation and resolution. *International Journal of Conflict Management, 4*(3), 249–262.
Kemper, T. D (Ed.), (1990). *Research agendas in the sociology of emotions*. Albany: State University of New York Press.

Kennedy, K. A., & Pronin, E. (2008). When disagreement gets ugly: Perception of bias and the escalation of conflict. *Personality and Social Psychology Bulletin, 34*, 833–848.

Khalaf, S. (1994). Culture, collective memory, and the restoration of civility. In D. Collings (Ed.), *Peace for Lebanon? From war to reconstruction* (pp. 273–285). Boulder, CO: Lynne Rienner.

Khalidi, R. (2010). *Palestinian identity: The construction of modern national consciousness.* New York: Columbia University Press.

Khalili, L. (2007). *Heroes and martyrs of Palestine: The politics of national commemoration.* Cambridge: Cambridge University Press.

Khatchadourian, H. (2007). Compensation and reparation as forms of compensatory justice. In C. Card & A. T. Marsoobian (Eds.), *Genocide's aftermath: Responsibility and repair. Metaphilosophy series in philosophy* (pp. 147–165). Malden, MA: Blackwell.

Killgore, W. D. S., & Yurgelun-Todd, D. A. (2004). Activation of the amygdala and anterior cingulate during nonconscious processing of sad versus happy faces. *NeuroImage, 21*, 1215–1223.

Kim, S. H. (2005). The role of vengeance in conflict escalation. In I. W. Zartman & G. O. Faure (Eds.), *Escalation and negotiation in international conflicts* (pp. 141–162). Cambridge: Cambridge University Press.

Kimball, C. (2002). *When religion becomes evil.* San Francisco: Harper Collins Publishers.

Kimhi, S., Canetti-Nisim, D., & Hirschberger, G. (2009). Terrorism in the eyes of the beholders: The impact of causal attributions on perceptions of violence. *Peace and Conflict: Journal of Peace Psychology, 15*, 75–95.

Kimhi, S., & Sagy, S. (2008). *Moral justification and feelings of adjustment in military law-enforcement situations: The case of Israeli soldiers serving at army roadblocks.* Paper presented at International Society for Political Psychology conference, Paris.

Kirisci, K., & Winrow, G. M. (1997). *The Kurdish question and Turkey: An example of trans-state ethnic conflict.* London: Frank Cass.

Kitayama, S., & Markus, H. R. (Eds.), (1994). *Emotion and culture: Empirical studies of mutual influence.* Washington, DC: American Psychological Association.

Kızılyurek, N. (1999). National memory and Turkish Cypriot textbook. *International Textbook Research, 21*, 387–395.

Klandermans, B. (1984). Mobilization and participation: Social psychological expansions of resource mobilization theory. *American Sociological Review, 49*, 583–600.

(1988). The formation and mobilization of consensus. In B. Klandermans, H. Kriesi, & S. Tarrow (Eds.), *From structure to action: Comparing social movement research across cultures* (Vol. 1, pp. 173–196). Greenwich, CT: JAI Press.

(1997). *The social psychology of protest.* Oxford: Blackwell.

(2002). How group identification helps to overcome the dilemma of collective action. *American Behavioral Scientist, 45*, 887–900.

(2004). The demand and supply of participation: Social-psychological correlates of participation in social movement. In D. A. Snow, A. Soule, & H. Kriesi (Eds.), *The Blackwell companion to social movements* (pp. 360–379). Malden, MA: Blackwell.

Klandermans, B., & De Weerd, M. (2000). Group identification and political protest. In S. Stryker, T. J. Owens, & R. W. White (Eds.), *Self, identity, and social movements: Social movements, protest, and contentions* (Vol. 13, pp. 68–90). Minneapolis: University of Minnesota Press.

Klandermans, B., Kriesi, H., & Tarrow, S. (Eds.), (1988). *From structure to action: Comparing social movement research across cultures* (Vol. 1). Greenwich, CT: JAI Press.

Klandermans, B., Werner, M., & van Doorn, M. (2008). Redeeming Apartheid's legacy: Collective guilt, political ideology, and compensation. *Political Psychology, 29*, 331–349.

Klar, Y. (August 2011). *Barriers and prospects in Israel and Palestine: An experimental social psychology perspective.* Paper presented in the annual meeting of the American Psychological Association, Washington, DC, August.

Klar, Y., & Baram, H. (2011). *The taxing exposure to the other side's historical narrative and the attempts to "fence" the one's own narrative.* Paper presented in the Harvard-IDC Symposium in Political Psychology and Decision Making. Herzliya, Interdisciplinary Center of Herzliya, November 8–9.

Klar, Y., Schori, N., Pave. A., & Klar. Y. (in press). The "Never Again" State of Israel: The emergence of the Holocaust as a core feature of Israeli identity and its four incongruent voices. *Journal of Social Issues.*

Klare, M. T. (2005). *Blood and oil: The danger and consequences of America's growing dependency on imported petroleum.* New York: Henry Holt.

Klein, M. (2001). *Jerusalem: The contested city.* New York: New York University Press.

Kleinig, J. (1991). *Valuing life.* Princeton, NJ: Princeton University Press.

Knorr, K. (1976). Threat perception. In K. Knorr (Ed.), *Historical dimensions of national security problems* (pp. 78–119). Lawrence: University of Kansas Press.

Knox, C., & Quirk, P. (2000). *Peace building in Northern Ireland, Israel and South Africa: Transition, transformation and reconciliation.* London: Macmillan.

Kobasa, S. C. (1985). Stressful life events, personality, and health: An inquiry into hardiness. In A. Monat & R. S. Lazarus (Eds.), *Stress and coping: An anthology* (pp. 174–188). New York: Columbia University Press.

Kobylilska, D. (2003). *Implicit lateralized affective stimuli and explicit judgements.* Ph.D. dissertation, Uniwersytet Warszawski. (in Polish)

Kohl, P. L., & Fawcett, C. (Eds.), (1996). *Nationalism, politics, and the practice of archaeology.* Cambridge: Cambridge University Press.

Kohlberg, L. (1984). *The psychology of moral development: Essays on moral development* (Vol. 2). San Francisco: Harper & Row.

Koistinen, P. A. (1980). *The military-industrial complex: A historical perspective.* Westport, CT: Praeger.

Kolonimus, N., & Bar-Tal, D. (2011). Views of the ethos of conflict and the military service among soldiers of an elite unit in the Israeli army. *Public Space, 5*, 35–67. (in Hebrew).

(in press) Socialization to the ethos of conflict among soldiers of an elite unit in the Israeli army. *Public Space.* (in Hebrew)

Koltsova, E. (2000). Change in the coverage of the Chechen wars: Reasons and consequences. *The Public, 7*(3), 39–54.

Kopstein, J. S. (1997). The politics of national reconciliation: Memory and institutions in German-Czech relations since 1989. *Nationalism & Ethnic Politics, 3*, 57–78.

Korostelina, K. (2006). National identity formation and conflict intentions of ethnic minorities. In M. Fitzduff, & C. E. Stout (Eds.), *The psychology of resolving global conflicts: From war to peace* (Vol. 2, pp. 147–170). Westport, CT: Praeger Security International.

Kossowska, M., & Bar-Tal, Y. (in press). The interaction between the need for closer and efficacy at fulfilling the need for closer as a predictor of judgments and decisions. *British Journal of Psychology.*

Kössler, R. (2007). Facing a fragmented past: Memory, culture and politics in Namibia. *Journal of Southern African Studies, 33*(2), 361 - 382.

Kotzé, H., & Du Toit, P. (1996). Reconciliation, reconstruction and identity politics in South Africa: A 1994 survey of elite attitudes after apartheid. *Nationalism & Ethnic Politics, 2,* 1–17.

Kotzin, D. P. (2004). Transporting the American peace movement to British Palestine: Judah L. Magnes, American pacifist and Zionist. *Peace & Change 29,* 390–418.

Kouttab, A. (2007). Mapping the emotional terrain of peace: Palestinians and Israelis search for common ground. *Journal of Humanistic Psychology, 47,* 351–360.

Kramer, R. M. (2004). Collective paranoia: Distrust between social groups. In R. Hardin (Ed.), *Distrust: Russell Sage foundation series on trust* (pp. 136–166). New York: Russell Sage Foundation.

Kramer, R. M., & Brewer, M. (1986). Social group identity and the emergence of cooperation in resource conservation dilemmas. In H. Wilke, D. Messick, & C. Rutte (Eds.), *Psychology of decisions and conflict* (Vol. 3, pp. 205–230). Frankfurt: Verlag Peter Lang.

Kramer, R. M., Brewer, M. B., & Hanna, B. A. (1996). Collective trust and collective action: The decision to trust as a social decision. In R. M. Kramer & T. R. Tyler (Eds.), *Trust in organizations: Frontiers of theory and research* (pp. 357–389). Thousand Oaks, CA: Sage.

Kramer, R. M., & Carnevale, P. (2001). Trust in intergroup relations. In R. Brown and S. L. Gaertner (Eds.), *Blackwell handbook of social psychology: Intergroup processes* (pp. 431–450). Oxford: Blackwell.

Krause, K., & Williams, M. C. (1996). Broadening the agenda of security studies: Politics and methods. *Mershon International Studies Review, 40,* 229–254.

Krauss, R. M., & Fussell, S. R. (1991). Constructing shared communicative environments. In L. B. Resnick, J. M. Levine, & S. D. Teasly (Eds.), *Perspectives on socially shared cognition* (pp. 172–200). Washington, DC: American Psychological Association.

Krech, D., Crutchfield, R. S., & Ballachey, E. L. (1962). *Individual in society.* New York: McGraw-Hill.

Kreidie, L. H., & Monroe, K. R. (2002). Psychological boundaries and ethnic conflict: How identity constrained choices and worked to turn ordinary people into perpetrators of ethnic violence during the Lebanese civil war. *International Journal of Politics and Society, 16,* 5–36.

Krespon, M., & A. Sevak (Eds.), (1995). *Crisis prevention, confidence building and reconciliation in South Asia.* New York: St. Martin's Press.

Kressel, N. J. (1996). *Mass hate: The global rise of genocide and terror.* New York: Plenum.

Kreyenbroek, P. G., & Sperl, S. (Eds.), (1992). *The Kurds: A contemporary overview.* New York: Routledge.

Kriesberg, L. (1992). *International conflict resolution.* New Haven, CT: Yale University Press.

(1993). Intractable conflict. *Peace Review, 5,* 417–421.

(1998a). Intractable conflicts. In E. Weiner (Ed.), *The handbook of interethnic coexistence* (pp. 332–342). New York: Continuum.

(1998b). Coexistence and the reconciliation of communal conflicts. In E. Weiner (Ed.), *The handbook of interethnic coexistence* (pp. 182–198). New York: Continuum.

(2004). Comparing reconciliation actions within and between countries. In Y. Bar-Siman-Tov (Ed.), *From conflict resolution to reconciliation* (pp. 81–110). Oxford: Oxford University Press.

(2007). *Constructive conflicts: From escalation to resolution* (3rd ed.). Lanham, MD: Rowman & Littlefield.

(2009). Changing conflict asymmetries constructively. *Dynamics of Asymmetric Conflict, 2*(1), 4–22.

Kriesberg, L., Northrup, T. A., & Thorson, S. J. (Eds.), (1989). *Intractable conflicts and their transformation.* Syracuse: Syracuse University Press.

Kritz, N. J. (1996). The rule of law in the postconflict phase. In C. A. Crocker, F. O. Hampson, & P. Aall (Eds.), *Managing global chaos: Sources of conflict of and responses to international conflict* (pp. 587–606). Washington, DC: United States Institute of Peace Press.

(Ed.), (1997). *Transitional justice: How emerging democracies reckon with former regimes.* Washington, DC: U.S. Institute of Peace Press.

Krochik, M., & Jost, J. T. (2011). Ideological conflict and polarization: A social psychological perspective. In D. Bar-Tal (Ed.), *Intergroup conflicts and their resolution: Social psychological perspective* (pp. 145–174). New York: Psychology Press.

Krosnick, J. A. (1989). Attitude importance and attitude accessibility. *Personality and Social Psychology Bulletin, 15*, 297–308.

Kruglanski, A. W. (1989). *Lay epistemics and human knowledge.* New York: Plenum.

(1996). Goals as knowledge structures. In P. M. Gollwitzer & J. A. Bargh (Eds.), *The psychology of action: Linking cognition and motivation to behavior* (pp. 599–618). New York: Guilford.

(2004). *The psychology of closed mindedness.* New York: Psychology Press.

Kruglanski, A. W., & Kopetz, C. (2009). What is so special (and non-special) about goals? A view from the cognitive perspective. In G. Moscovitz & H. Grant (Eds.), *Goals* (pp. 27–55). New York: Guilford Press.

Kruglanski, A. W., Raviv, A., Bar-Tal, D., Raviv, A., Sharvit, K., Ellis, S., Bar, R., Pierro, A., & Mannetti, L. (2005). Says who? Epistemic authority effects in social judgment. In M. P. Zanna (Ed.), *Advances in experimental social psychology* (Vol. 37, pp. 346–392). San Diego: Elsevier Academic Press.

Kruglanski, A. W., Shah, Y. J., Fishbach, A., Friedman, R., Chun, W. Y., Sleeth-Keppler, D. (2002). A theory of goal-systems. In M. P. Zanna (Ed.), *Advances in Experimental Social Psychology* (pp. 331–376). San Diego: Academic Press.

Kruglanski, A. W., & Webster, D. M. (1996). Motivated closing of the mind: "Seizing" and "freezing." *Psychological Review, 103*(2), 263–283.

Kunda, Z. (1990). The case for motivated reasoning. *Psychological Bulletin, 108*, 480–498.

Lacey D. (2011). The role of humiliation in the Palestinian/Israeli conflict in Gaza. *Psychology & Society, 4*, 76–92.

Lactau, E. (Ed.), (1994). *The making of political identities.* London: Verso.

Lake, D. A., & Rothchild, D. (1996). Containing fear: The origins and management of ethnic conflict. *International Security, 21*, 41–75.

(Eds.), (1998). *The international spread of ethnic conflict: Fear, diffusion, and escalation.* Princeton, NJ: Princeton University Press.

Landau, M. J., Solomon, S., Greenberg, J., Cohen, F., Pyszczynski, T., Arndt, J., Miller, C. H., Ogilvie, D. M., & Cook, A. (2004). Deliver us from evil: The effects of mortality salience and reminders of 9/11 on support for President George W. Bush. *Personality and Social Psychology Bulletin, 30*, 1136–1150.

Landman, S. (2010). Barriers to peace: Protected values in the Israeli-Palestinian conflict. In Y. Bar-Siman-Tov, *Barriers to peace: The Israeli-Palestinian conflict* (pp. 135–177). Jerusalem: Jerusalem Institute for Israel Studies.

Lane, R. E. (1973). Patterns of political beliefs. In J. N. Knutson (Ed.), *Handbook of political psychology* (pp. 83–116). San Francisco: Jossey-Bass.

Langenbacher, E. (2010). Collective memory as a factor in political culture and international relations. In E. Langenbacher and Y. Shain (Eds.), *Power and the past – Collective memory and international relations* (pp. 13–49). Washington, DC: Georgetown University Press.

Larson, D. W. (1997). Trust and missed opportunities in international relations. *Political Psychology, 18*(3), 701–734.

László, J. (2003). History, identity and narratives. In J. László & W. Wagner (Eds.), *Theories and controversies in societal psychology* (pp. 180–182). Budapest: New Mandate Publishers.

László, J. C. (2008). *The science of stories: An introduction to narrative psychology*. New York: Routledge.

Lau, R. R. (1982). Negativity in political perception. *Political Behavior, 4*, 353–377.

Lau, R. R., & Sears, D. O. (1986). *Political cognition*. Hillsdale, NJ: Erlbaum.

Lauren, P. G. (2011). *The evolution of international human rights: Visions seen* (3rd ed.). Philadelphia: University of Pennsylvania Press.

Lavi, I., Canetti, D., Sharvit, K., Bar-Tal, D., & Hobfoll, S. (in press). A comparative study of the psycho-political consequences of conflict-related violence: The moderating influence of ethos of conflict among Israelis and Palestinians. *Journal of Conflict Resolution*.

Lavine, H., Borgida, E., & Sullivan, J. L. (2000). On the relationship between involvement and attitude accessibility: Toward a cognitive-motivational model of political information processing. *Political Psychology, 21*, 81–106.

Lazare, A. (2004). *On apology*. Oxford: Oxford University Press.

Lazarus, R. S. (1982). The psychology of stress and coping – with particular reference to Israel. *Series in Clinical and Community Psychology: Stress and Anxiety, 8*, 23–36.

(1991a). Cognition and motivation in emotion. *American Psychologist, 46*, 819–834.

(1991b). *Emotion and adaptation*. New York: Oxford University Press.

(1999). *Stress and emotion: A new synthesis*. London: Free Association Books.

Lazarus, R. S., & Folkman, S. (1984). *Stress, appraisal, and coping*. New York: Springer.

Leach, C. W., Ellemers, N., & Barreto, M. (2007). Group virtue: The importance of morality (vs. competence and sociability) in the positive evaluation of in-groups. *Journal of Personality and Social Psychology, 93*, 234–249.

Lebel, U. (2007). *The road to the pantheon*. Jerusalem: Carmel. (in Hebrew).

Lederach, J. P. (1997). *Building peace: Sustainable reconciliation in divided societies*. Washington, DC: United States Institute of Peace Press.

(1998). Beyond violence: Building sustainable peace. In E. Weiner (Ed.), *The handbook of interethnic coexistence* (pp. 236–245). New York: Continuum.

(2005). *The moral imagination: The art and soul of building peace.* New York: Oxford University Press.
Lederer, K. (Ed.), (1980). *Human needs.* Cambridge, MA: Oelgeshager, Gunn & Hain.
Ledgerwood, A., Liviatan, I., & Carnevale, P. (2007). Group-identity completion and the symbolic value of property. *Psychological Science, 18,* 873–878.
LeDoux, J. (1995). Emotion: Clues from the brain. *Annual Review of Psychology, 1,* 209–227.
(1996). *The emotional brain: The mysterious underpinnings of emotional life.* New York: Touchstone.
(2000). Emotion circuits in the brain. *Annual Review of Neuroscience, 23,* 155–184.
(2002). *Synaptic self: How our brains become who we are.* New York: Viking Penguin.
Legal Forum for Eretz Yisrael (2011, December 7). Retrieved from http://www.haforum.org.il/newsite/cat.asp?id=1146. (in Hebrew)
LeGoff, J. (1992). *History and memory.* New York: Columbia University Press.
Legum, C., & Legum, H. (1964). *South Africa: Crisis for the West.* London: Pall Mall Press.
Leidner, B., Castono, E., Zaiser, E., & Giner-Sorolla, R. (2010). Ingroup glorification, moral disengagement, and justice in the context of collective violence. *Personality and Social Psychology Bulletin, 36,* 115–1139.
Lemarchand, R. (1994). *Burundi: Ethnic conflict and genocide.* Cambridge: Woodrow Wilson Center Press and Cambridge University Press.
Lerner, M. (1980). *The belief in just world.* New York: Plenum.
Lerner, J. S., Gonzalez, R. M., Small, D. A., & Fischhoff, B. (2003). Effects of fear and anger on perceived risks of terrorism: A national field experiment. *Psychological Science, 14,* 144–150.
Lerner, J. S., & Keltner, D. (2000). Beyond valence: Toward a model of emotion-specific influences on judgment and choice. *Cognition and Emotion, 14,* 473–493.
(2001). Fear, anger and risk. *Journal of Personality and Social Psychology, 81,* 146–159.
Leung, K., & Bond, M. H. (2004): Social axioms: A model for social beliefs in a multi-cultural perspective. *Advances in Experimental Social Psychology, 36,* 119–197.
LeVine, R. A., & Campbell, D. T. (1972). *Ethnocentrism.* New York: Wiley.
Levinger, E. (1993). *War Memorials in Israel.* Tel Aviv: Hakibbutz Hameuchad. (in Hebrew)
Levy, J. S. (1996). Loss aversion, framing, and bargaining: The implications of prospect theory for international conflict. *International Political Science Review, 17,* 179–195.
Lewandowsky, S., Stritzke W., Oberauer K., & Morales M. (2009). Misinformation and the "War on Terror": When memory turns fiction into fact. In S. L. W. Stritzke, D. Denemark, J. Clare, & F. Morgan (Eds.), *Terrorism and torture: An interdisciplinary perspective* (pp. 179–203). Cambridge: Cambridge University Press.
Lewick, M., Czapinski, J., & Peeters, G. (1992). Positive-negative asymmetry or "when the heart needs a reason." *European Journal of Social Psychology, 22,* 425–434.
Lewicki, R. J. (2006). Trust, trust development, and trust repair. In M. Deutsch, P. T Coleman, & E. C. Marcus (Eds.), *Handbook of conflict resolution: Theory and Practice* (pp. 92–119). San Francisco: Jossey-Bass.
Lewicki, R. J., Gray, B., & Elliott, M. (Eds.), (2003). *Making sense of intractable environmental conflicts: Frames and cases.* Washington, DC: Island Press.

Lewicki, R. J., & McAllister, D. J. (1998). Trust and distrust: New relationships and realities. *Academy of Management Review, 23*(3), 438–458.

Lewin, K. (1942). Field theory and learning. *Year Book of the National Society for the Study of Education, 41*, 215–242.

(1947). Frontiers in group dynamics: I. *Human Relations, 1*, 5–41.

(1951). *Field theory in social science.* New York: Harper & Row.

Lewis, M. (1993). Self-conscious emotions: Embarrassment, pride, shame, and guilt. In M. Lewis & J. M. Haviland (Eds.), *Handbook of emotions* (pp. 623–636). New York: Guilford Press.

Lewis, M., & Haviland, J. M. (Eds.), (1993). *Handbook of emotions.* New York: Guilford.

Lewis, M., & Saarni, C. (Eds.), (1985). *The socialization of emotions.* New York: Plenum.

Lewis, M., Takai-Kawakami, K., Kawakami, K., & Sullivan, M. W. (2010). Cultural differences in emotional responses to success and failure. *International Journal of Behavioral Development, 34*(1), 53–61.

Lickel, B. (2012). Retribution and revenge. In L. R. Tropp (Ed.), *Oxford handbook of intergroup conflict* (pp. 89–105). New York: Oxford University Press.

Lickel, B., Miller, N., Stenstrom, D. M., Denson, T., & Schmader, T. (2006). Vicarious retribution: The role of collective blame in intergroup aggression. *Personality and Social Psychology Review, 10*, 372–390.

Liebenberg, I., & Zegeye, A. (1998). Pathway to democracy? The case of the South African Truth and Reconciliation process. *Social Identities, 4*, 541–558.

Lieberfeld, D. (2009). Media coverage and Israel's "Four Mothers" antiwar protest: Agendas, tactics and political context in movement success. *Media, War & Conflict, 2*(3), 317–338.

Lieberman, E. J. (1964). Threat and assurance in the conduct of conflict. In R. Fisher (Ed.), *International conflict and behavioral science* (pp. 110–122). New York: Basic Books.

Liebes, T., & Kampf, Z. (2007). Routinizing terror: Media coverage and public practices in Israel, 2000–2005. *Harvard International Journal of Press/Politics, 12*, 108–t116.

Liebman, C. (1978). Myth, tradition and values in Israeli society. *Midstream, 24*(1), 44–53.

Liebman, C. S., & Don-Yehiya, E. (1983). *Civil religion in Israel: Traditional Judaism and political culture in the Jewish state.* Berkeley: University of California Press.

Lifshitz, Y. (2000). *Defense economics: The general theory and the Israeli case.* Jerusalem: The Jerusalem Institute for Israeli Studies. (in Hebrew)

Lindemann, H. (2001). *Damaged identities, narrative repair.* Ithaca, NY: Cornell University Press.

Lindner, E. G. (2001). Humiliation and the human condition: Mapping a minefield, *Human Rights Review, 2*(2), 46–63.

(2002). Healing the cycles of humiliation: How to attend to the emotional aspects of "unsolvable" conflicts and the use of "humiliation entrepreneurship." *Peace and Conflict: Journal of Peace Psychology, 8*(2), 125–138.

(2006a). *Making enemies: Humiliation and international conflict.* Westport: CT: Praeger.

(2006b). Emotion and conflict: Why it is important to understand how emotions affect conflict and how conflict affects emotions. In M. Deutch, P. T. Coleman, & E. C. Marcus (Eds.), *The handbook of conflict resolution* (2nd ed., pp. 268–293). San Francisco: Jossey-Bass.

Linskold, S. (1978). Trust development, the GRIT proposal, and the effects of conciliatory acts on conflict and cooperation. *Psychological Bulletin, 85,* 772–793.

Linville, P., Fischer, G., & Salavoy, P. (1989). Perceived distribution of characteristics of in-group and out-group members: Empirical evidence and computer simulation. *Journal of Personality and Social Psychology, 57,* 167–188.

Lipschutz, R. D. (1998). Beyond the neoliberal peace: From conflict resolution to social reconciliation. *Social Justice: A Journal of Crime, Conflict and World Order, 25*(4), 5–19.

Little, A., & Silber, L. (1996). *The death of Yugoslavia* (Rev. ed.). London: Penguin Books.

Little, D. (1994). *Sri Lanka: The invention of enmity.* Washington, DC: United States Institute of Peace Press.

——— (1999). A different kind of justice: Dealing with human rights violations in transitional societies. *Ethics & International Affairs, 13,* 65–80.

Liu, J. H., & Atsumi, T. (2008). Historical conflict and resolution between Japan and China: Developing and applying a narrative theory of history and identity. In T. Sugiman, K. J. Gergen, W. Wagner, & Y. Yamada (Eds.), *Meaning in action: Constructions, narratives, and representations* (pp. 327–344). Tokyo: Springer-Verlag.

Liu, J. H., & Hilton, D. J. (2005). How the past weighs on the present: Social representations of history and their impact on identity politics. *British Journal of Social Psychology, 44,* 537–556.

Liu, J. H., Lawrence, B., Ward, C., & Abraham, S. (2002). Social representations of history in Malaysia and Singapore: On the relationship between national and ethnic identity. *Asian Journal of Social Psychology, 5*(1), 3–20.

Liu, J. H., & Liu, S. H. (2003). The role of the social psychologist in the Benevolent Authority and Plurality of Powers systems of historical affordance for authority. In K. S. Yang, K. K. Hwang, P. B. Pedersen, & I. Daibo (Eds.), *Progress in Asian social psychology: Conceptual and empirical contributions* (pp. 43–46). Westport, CT: Praeger.

Liu, J. H., Wilson, M. W., McClure, J., Higgins, T. R. (1999). Social identity and the perception of history: Cultural representations of Aotearoa/New Zealand. *European Journal of Social Psychology, 29,* 1021–1047.

Long, W. J., & Brecke, P. (2003). *War and reconciliation: Reason and emotion in conflict resolution.* Cambridge, MA: MIT Press.

Lundy, P., & McGovern, M. (2001). The politics of memory in post-conflict Northern Ireland. *Peace Review, 13*(1), 27–33.

Lynch, J. (2008). *Debates in peace journalism.* Sydney: Sydney University Press.

Lynch, J., & Galtung, J. (2010). *Reporting conflict: New directions in peace journalism.* St. Lucia: University of Queensland Press.

Maariv, May 9, 2011.

MacDonald, D. B. (2002). *Balkan holocausts? Serbian and Croatian victim-centred propaganda and the war in Yugoslavia.* Manchester: Manchester University Press.

MacGinty, R., & Darby, J. (2002). *Guns and government: The management of the Northern Ireland peace process.* Houndmills: Palgrave Macmillan.

Mac Iver, M. A. (1987). Ian Paisley and the reformed tradition. *Political Studies, 35,* 364–373.

Mack, J. E. (1990). The psychodynamics of victimization among national groups in conflict. In V. D. Volkan, D. A. Julius, & J. V. Montville (Eds.), *The psychodynamics of international relationships* (pp. 119–129). Lexington, MA: Lexington Books.

Mack, R. W., & Snyder, R. C. (1957). The analysis of social conflict: Toward an overview and synthesis. *Journal of Conflict Resolution, 1,* 212–248.

Mackie, D. M., Devos, T., & Smith, E. R. (2000). Intergroup emotions: Explaining offensive action tendencies in an intergroup context. *Journal of Personality and Social Psychology, 79,* 602–616.

Mackie, D. M., & Smith, E. R. (Eds.), (2002). *From prejudice to intergroup relations: Differentiated reactions to social groups.* Philadelphia: Psychology Press.

Macmaster, N. (2002). The torture controversy (1998–2002): Towards a "new history" of the Algerian War? *Modern & Contemporary France, 10,* 449–459.

Macrae, C. N., Milne, A. B., & Bodenhausen, G. V. (1994). Stereotypes as energy-saving devices: A peek inside the cognitive toolbox. *Journal of Personality and Social Psychology, 66,* 37–47.

Maddi, S. R. (1971). The search for meaning. In W. J. Arnold & M. M. Page (Eds.), *Nebraska Symposium on motivation, 1970* (pp. 137–186). Lincoln: University of Nebraska Press.

Magal, T. (2012). *Mobilization for peace making: The role of peace organizations.* Paper presented at the 28th annual conference of the Association of Israel Studies, Haifa, Israel.

(2013). *Mobilization for peace: The effects of organizational characteristics and political context on the mobilizing capacity of four Israeli peace organizations.* Ph.D. dissertation submitted to Haifa University.

Magal, T., Oren, N., Bar-Tal, D., & Halperin, E. (2013). Psychological legitimization – Views of the Israeli occupation by Jews in Israel: Data and implications. In D. Bar-Tal & I. Schnell (Eds.), *The impacts of lasting occupation: Lessons from Israeli society* (pp. 122–185). New York: Oxford University Press.

Maitner, A. T., Mackie, D. M., & Smith, E. R. (2007). Antecedents and consequences of satisfaction and guilt following ingroup aggression. *Group Processes & Intergroup Relations, 10,* 223–237.

Major, B. (1994). From social inequality to personal entitlement: The role of social comparisons, legitimacy appraisals, and group membership. *Advances in Experimental Social Psychology, 26,* 295–355.

Maksudyan N. (2009). Walls of silence: Translating the Armenian genocide into Turkish and self-censorship. *Critique, 37*(4), 635–649.

Malcolm, N. (1994). *Bosnia: A short history.* London: Macmillan.

Malhotra, D., & Liyanage, S. (2005). Long-term effects of peace workshops in protracted conflicts. *Journal of Education, 37,* 391–408.

Mallinson, W. (2005). *Cyprus: A modern history.* London: I. B. Tauris.

Mamdani, M. (2001). *When victims become killers: Colonialism, nativism, and the Genocide in Rwanda.* Princeton, NJ: Princeton University Press.

Mandel, N. J. (1976). *The Arabs and Zionism before World War I.* Berkeley: University of California Press.

Mandler, G. (1975). *Mind and emotion.* New York: Wiley.

(1993). Thought, memory, and learning: Effects of emotional stress. In L. Goldberger & S. Breznitz (Eds.), *Handbook of stress: Theoretical and clinical aspects* (pp. 40–55). New York: Free Press.

Maney, G. M. (2007). From civil war to civil rights and back again: The interrelation of rebellion and protest in Northern Ireland, 1955–1972. *Research in Social Movements, Conflicts and Change, 27*, 3–36.

Mannheim, K. (1952). *Ideology and utopia.* NY: Harcourt, Brace.

Manstead, A. S. R., Frijda, N. H., & Fischer, A. H. (Eds.), (2004). *Feelings and emotions. The Amsterdam Symposium.* Cambridge: Cambridge University Press.

Maoz, I. (2004a). Coexistence is in the eye of the beholder: Evaluating intergroup encounter interventions between Jews and Arabs in Israel. *Journal of Social Issues, 60*, 437–452.

(2004b). Peace building in violent conflict: Israeli-Palestinian post Oslo people to people activities. *International Journal of Politics, Culture and Society, 17*(3), 563–574.

(2006). The effect of news coverage concerning the opponents' reaction to a concession on its evaluation in the Israeli-Palestinian conflict. *International Journal of Press/Politics, 11*, 70–88.

(2010). Educating for peace through planned encounters between Arabs and Jews in Israel: A reappraisal of effectiveness. In G. Salomon & E. Cairns (Eds.), *Handbook of peace education* (pp. 303–314). New York: Psychology Press.

(2011). Does contact work in protracted asymmetrical conflict? Appraising 20 years of reconciliation-aimed encounters between Israeli Jews and Palestinians. *Journal of Peace Research, 48*(1), 115–125.

Maoz, I., & Eidelson, R. (2007). Psychological bases of extreme policy preferences: How the personal beliefs of Israeli-Jews predict their support for population transfer in the Israeli-Palestinian conflict. *American Behavioral Scientists, 50*, 1476–1497.

Maoz, I., & McCauley, R. (2005). Psychological correlates of support for compromise: A polling study of Jewish-Israeli attitudes towards solutions to the Israeli-Palestinian conflict. *Political Psychology, 26*, 791–807.

(2008). Threat, dehumanization, and support for retaliatory aggressive policies in asymmetric conflict. *Journal of Conflict Resolution, 52*, 93–116.

(2009). Threat perceptions and feelings as predictors of Jewish-Israeli support for compromise with Palestinians. *Journal of Peace Research, 46*, 525–539.

(2011). Explaining support for violating outgroup human rights in the Israeli-Palestinian conflict: The role of attitudes toward general principles of human rights, trust in the outgroup, religiosity and intergroup contact. *Journal of Applied Social Psychology, 41*(4), 889–905.

Maoz, I., Ward, A., Katz, M., & Ross L. (2002). Reactive devaluation of an Israeli and a Palestinian peace proposal. *Journal of Conflict Resolution, 46*, 515–546.

Maoz, Z. (2009). *Defending the Holy Land: A critical analysis of Israel's security & foreign policy.* Ann Arbor: University of Michigan Press.

Marcus, G. E., & MacKuen M. B. (1993). Anxiety, enthusiasm, and the vote: The emotional underpinnings of learning and involvement during presidential campaigns. *American Political Science Review, 87*, 672–685.

Marcus, G. E., Neuman, W. R., MacKuen, M., & Sullivan, J. L. (1996). Dynamic models of emotional response: The multiple roles of affect in politics. *Research in Micropolitics, 5*, 33–59.

Marcus, G. E., Sullivan, J. L., Theiss-Morse, E., & Wood, S. L. (1995). *With malice toward some: How people make civil liberties judgments.* Cambridge: Cambridge University Press.

Margalit, A. (2002). *The ethics of memory.* Cambridge, MA: Harvard University Press.

Markus, H. R., & Kitayama, S. (1994). The cultural shaping of emotion: A conceptual framework. In S. Kitayama & H. R. Markus (Eds.), *Emotion and culture: Empirical studies of mutual influence* (pp. 339–351). Washington, DC: American Psychological Association.

Markus, H., & Zajonc, R. B. (1985). The cognitive perspective in social psychology. In G. Lindzey & E. Aronson (Eds.), *Handbook of social psychology* (3rd ed., Vol. 1, pp. 137–230). New York: Random House.

Marrow, D. (1999). Seeking peace amid memories of war: Learning form the peace process in Northern Ireland. In R. L. Rothstein (Ed.), *After the peace: Resistance and reconciliation* (pp. 111–138). Boulder, CO: Lynne Rienner.

Marshall, M. G. (2002). Measuring the societal impact of war. *In* O. Hampson & D. M. Malone (Eds.), *From reaction to prevention.* Boulder, CO: Lynne Rienner.

Marsick, V. J., Sauquet, A., & Yorks, L. (2006). Learning through reflection. In M. Deutsch, P. T. Coleman, & E. C. Marcus (Eds.), *The handbook of conflict resolution: Theory and practice.* (2nd ed., pp. 486–506). San Francisco: Jossey-Bass.

Marsick, V. J., & Watkins, K. E. (1990). *Informal and incidental learning in the workplace.* New York: Routledge.

Maslow, A. H. (1963). The need to know and the fear of knowing. *Journal of General Psychology, 68*, 111–125.

  (1970). *Motivation and personality* (2nd ed.). New York: Harper & Row.

Matheson, C. (1986). War of words. *Index On Censorship, 15*, 31–36.

Mathias, Y. (2002). The crisis of the national paradigm history in Israel curriculum during the 1990s. *International Textbook Research, 24*, 427–443.

  (2005). Curriculum between politics and science: The case of history in Israel after the Six Day War. *Political Crossroads, 12*, 47–65.

Matsusaka, Y. T. (2003). *The making of Japanese Manchuria, 1904–1932.* Cambridge, MA: Harvard University Asia Center.

Mazur, J. (2012). *Zionism, post-Zionism & the Arab problem.* Bloomington, IN: WestBow Press.

McAdam, D. (1982). *Political process and the development of black insurgency.* Chicago: University of Chicago Press.

  (1986). Recruitment to high-risk activism: The case of freedom summer. *American Journal of Sociology, 92*, 64–90.

  (2003). Beyond structural analysis: Toward a more dynamic understanding of social movements. In M. Diani & D. McAdam (Eds.), *Social movements and networks: relational approaches to collective action* (pp. 281–298). Oxford: Oxford University Press.

McAdam, D., & Paulsen, R. (1993). Specifying the relationship between social ties and activism. *American Journal of Sociology, 99*, 640–667.

McAdams, D. P. (2006). *The redemptive self: Stories Americans live by.* Oxford: Oxford University Press.

McBride, I. (1997). *The siege of Derry in Ulster Protestant mythology.* Dublin: Four Courts Press.

McCarthy, J. D., & Zald, M. N. (1977). Resource mobilization and social movements: A partial theory. *American Journal of Sociology, 82*, 1212–1241.

McClosky, H., & Zaller, J. (1984). *The American ethos: Public attitudes toward capitalism and democracy*. Cambridge, MA: Harvard University Press.

McFarlane, G. (1986). Violence in rural Northern Ireland: Social scientific models, folk explanations and local variation. In D. Riches (Ed.), *The anthropology of violence* (pp. 184–203). Oxford: Blackwell.

McGarry, J., & O'Leary, B. (1995). *Explaining Northern Ireland*. Oxford: Blackwell.

McGarty, C., Bliuc, A-M., Thomas, E. E., & Bongiorno, R. (2009). Collective action as the material expression of opinion-based group membership. *Journal of Social Issues*, 65, 839–857.

McGraw, K. M. (2003). Political impressions: Formation and management. In D. O. Sears, L. Huddy, & R. Jervis (Eds.), *Oxford handbook of political psychology* (pp. 394–432). Oxford: Oxford University Press.

McLernon, F., Cairns, E., Lewis, C. A., & Hewstone, M. (2003). Memories of recent conflict and forgiveness in Northern Ireland. In E. Cairns & M. D. Roe (Eds.), *The role of memory in ethnic conflict* (pp. 125–143). London: Palgrave Macmillan.

McQuail, D. (1994). *Mass communication theory: An introduction* (3rd ed.). Thousand Oaks, CA: Sage.

Medjedovic, J., & Petrovic, B. (2011). *Personality traits, basic social attitudes and ethos of conflict as predictors of party affiliation in Serbia*. Unpublished Manuscript.

Mellor, D., Bretherton, D., & Firth, L. (2007). Aboriginal and non-Aboriginal Australia: The dilemma of apologies, forgiveness and reconciliation. *Peace and Conflict: Journal of Peace Psychology*, 13(1), 11–36.

Mellucci, A. (1989). *Nomads of the present: Social movements and individual needs in contemporary society*. London: Hutchinson Press.

Melvern, L. (2006). *Conspiracy to murder: The Rwandan genocide*. London: Verso.

Mennecke, M., & Markusen, E. (2004). Genocide in Bosnia and Herzegovina. In I. W. Charny, W. S. Parsons, & S. Totten (Eds.), *A century of genocide: Critical essays and eyewitness accounts* (pp. 415–447). New York: Routledge.

Merom, G. (1998). Outside history? Israel's security dilemma in a comparative perspective. In D. Bar-Tal, D. Jacobson, & A. Klieman (Eds.), *Security concerns: Insights from the Israeli experience* (pp. 37–52). Stamford, CT: JAI.

Mertus, J. A. (1999). *Kosovo: How myths and truths started a war*. Berkley: University of California Press.

Mertus, J., & Helsing, J. (2006). *Human rights and conflict: Exploring the links between rights, law, and peace building*. Washington, DC: USIP Press Books.

Mesquita, B., & Frijda, N. H. (1992). Cultural variations in emotion: A review. *Psychological Bulletin*, 112, 179–204.

Metsola, L. (2010). The struggle continues? The spectre of liberation, memory politics and 'war veterans' in Namibia. *Development and Change*, 41(4), 589–613.

Meyer, M. (2004). Organizational identity, political contexts, and SMO action: Explaining the tactical choices made by peace organizations in Israel, Northern Ireland, and South Africa. *Social Movement Studies*, 3, 167–197.

Michael, M. S. (2007). The Cyprus talks: A critical appraisal. *Journal of Peace Research*, 44, 587–604.

Middleton, D., & Edwards, D. (Eds.), (1990). *Collective remembering*. Thousand Oaks, CA: Sage.

Milgram, N. A. (Ed.), (1986). *Stress and coping in time of war: generalizations from the Israeli experience.* New York: Brunner/Mazel.

(1993). War-related trauma and victimization: Principles of traumatic stress prevention in Israel. In J. P. Wilson & B. Raphael (Eds.), *International handbook of traumatic stress syndromes* (pp. 811–820). New York: Plenum.

Milgram, S. (1974). *Obedience to authority: An experimental view.* New York: Harper and Row.

Miller, D. (1994). *Don't mention the war: Northern Ireland, propaganda, and the media.* London: Pluto.

Ministry of Culture and Sports, The (2011). Award for Creation in the Field of Zionism 2011. Retrieved from http://www.mcs.gov.il/Culture/Professional_Information/CallforScholarshipAward/Pages/PrasZionut2011.aspx. (in Hebrew).

Minow, M. (1999). *Between vengeance and forgiveness: Facing history after genocide and mass violence.* Boston: Beacon Press.

Mintz, A. (1983). The military-industrial complex: The Israeli case. *Journal of Strategic Studies, 6*(3), 103–127.

(2004). How do leaders make decisions: A poliheuristic perspective. *Journal of Conflict Resolution, 48,* 3–13.

Mintz, A., Geva, N., Redd, B. S., & Carnes, A. (1997). The effect of dynamic and static choice sets on political decision making: An analysis using the decision board platform. *American Political Science Review, 91*(3), 553–566.

Miron, A. M., & Branscombe, N. R. (2008). Social categorization, standard of justice, and collective guilt. In A. Nadler, T. Malloy, and J. Fisher (Ed.), *The social psychology of intergroup reconciliation* (pp. 77–96). Oxford, NY: Oxford University Press.

Mitchell, C. R. (1981). *The structure of international conflict.* London: Macmillan.

(1991). Classifying conflicts: Asymmetry and resolution. *Annals of the American Academy of Political and Social Sciences, 518,* 23–38.

Mitzen, J. (2006). Ontological security in world politics: State identity and the security dilemma. *European Journal of International Relations, 12,* 341–370.

Moeschberger, S. L., Dixon, D. N., Niens, U., & Cairns, E. (2005). Forgiveness in Northern Ireland: A model for peace in the midst of the "Troubles." *Peace and Conflict: Journal of Peace Psychology, 11,* 199–214.

Möllering, G. (2001). The nature of trust: From Georg Simmel to a theory of expectation, interpretation, and suspension. *Sociology, 35*(2), 403–420.

Montville, J. V. (1993). The healing function in political conflict resolution. In D. J. D. Sandole & H. van der Merve (Eds.), *Conflict resolution theory and practice: Integration and application* (pp. 112–127). Manchester: Manchester University Press.

Mor, B. D. (2007). The rhetoric of public diplomacy and propaganda wars: A view from self-presentation theory. *European Journal of Political Research, 46*(5), 661–683.

Mor, B. D., & Maoz, Z. (1999). Learning and the evolution of enduring rivalries: A strategic approach. *Conflict Management and Peace Science, 17,* 1–48.

Morris, B. (1993). *Israel's border wars: 1940–1956.* Oxford: Clarendon Press.

(2000). Israeli journalism in the "Kiviya" affair. In B. Morris (Ed.), *Jews and Arabs in Palestine/Israel, 1936–1956* (pp. 175–198). Tel-Aviv: Am-Oved. (in Hebrew).

(2001). *Righteous victims: A history of the Zionist-Arab conflict, 1881–2001.* New York: Vintage Books.

(2004). *The birth of the Palestinian refugee problem revisited.* Cambridge: Cambridge University Press.

Moscovici, S. (1972). Society and theory in social psychology. In J. Israel & H. Tajfel (Eds.), *The context of social psychology: A critical assessment* (pp. 17–68). London: Academic Press.

(1988). Notes towards a description of social representations. *European Journal of Social Psychology, 18,* 211–250.

Moscovici, S., & Doise, W. (1994). *Conflict & consensus: A general theory of collective decisions.* London: Sage.

Moscovici, S., & Faucheux, C. (1972). Social influence, conformity bias, and the study of active minorities. In L. Berkowitz (Ed.), *Advances in experimental social psychology* (Vol. 6, pp. 149–202). New York: Academic Press.

Moses, R. (1990). On dehumanizing enemy. In V. D. Volkan, D. A. Julius, & J. V. Montville (Eds.), *The psychodynamics of international relationships* (pp. 111–118). Lexington, MA: Lexington Books.

Moskalenko, S., & McCauley, C. (2009). Measuring political mobilization: The distinction between activism and radicalism. *Terrorism and Political Violence, 21,* 239–260.

Mosse, G. L. (1990). *Fallen soldiers: Reshaping the memory of the world wars.* New York: Oxford University Press.

Mowrer, O. H. (1960). *Learning theory and behavior.* New York: John Wiley.

Mufson, S. (1991). South Africa, 1990. *Foreign Affairs, 70,* 120–141.

Muldoon, O. T., & Downes, C. (2007). Social identification and post-traumatic stress symptoms in post-conflict Northern Ireland. *British Journal of Psychiatry, 191,* 146–149.

Mulholland, M. (2002). *The longest war: Northern Ireland's troubled history.* Oxford: Oxford University Press.

Mumendey, A., Klink, A., & Brown, R. (2001). Nationalism and patriotism: National identification and out-group rejection. *British Journal of Social Psychology, 40,* 159–172.

Murphy, S. T., & Zajonc, R. B. (1993). Affect, cognition, and awareness: Affective priming with optimal and suptimal stimulus exposures. *Journal of Personality and Social Psychology, 64,* 723–739.

Murray, M. R., and Greer, J. V. (1999). The changing governance of rural development: State-community interaction in Northern Ireland. *Policy Studies, 20,* 37–50.

Mutz, D. C. (1998). *Impersonal influence.* Cambridge: Cambridge University Press.

Nadler, A. (2002). Post resolution processes: An instrumental and socio-emotional routes to reconciliation. In G. Salomon & B. Nevo (Eds.), *Peace education worldwide: The concept, principles and practices around the world* (pp. 127–143). Mahwah, NJ: Erlbaum.

Nadler, A., & Liviatan, I. (2006). Intergroup reconciliation: Effects of adversary's expressions of empathy, responsibility, and recipients' trust. *Personality and Social Psychology Bulletin, 32,* 459–470.

Nadler, A., Malloy, T. E., & Fisher, J. D. (Eds.), (2008). *The social psychology of intergroup reconciliation.* Oxford: Oxford University Press.

Nadler, A., & Shnabel, N. (2008). Intergroup reconciliation: The instrumental and socio-emotional paths and the need-based model of socio-emotional reconciliation. In

A. Nadler, T. Malloy, & J. D. Fisher (Eds.), *Social psychology of intergroup reconciliation* (pp. 37–56). New York: Oxford University Press.

Nahhes, E. (2012). *Inter-generational transmission of collective memory of the 1948 War events among Palestinian citizens of Israel: Comparison between internally displaced and non-displaced.* Ph.D. dissertation, Harvard University.

Nasie, M., & Bar-Tal, D. (2012). Sociopsychological infrastructure of an intractable conflict through the eyes of Palestinian children and adolescents. *Peace and Conflict: Journal of Peace Psychology, 18*, 3–20.

Nasr, V. (2005). National identities and the India-Pakistan conflict. In T. V. Paul (Ed.), *The India-Pakistan conflict: An enduring rivalry* (pp. 178–201). Cambridge: Cambridge University Press.

Nasser, R., & Nasser, I. (2008). Textbooks as a vehicle for segregation and domination: state efforts to shape Palestinian Israelis' identities as citizens. *Journal of Curriculum Studies, 40*(5), 627–650.

National Technical Information Service of the Department of Commerce of the U.S., 2009.

Nave, E., & Yogev, E. (2002). *Histories – Towards a dialogue with the past.* Tel Aviv: Bavel. (in Hebrew).

Nemeth, C. J. (1986). Differential contributions of majority and minority influence. *Psychological Review, 93*, 23–32.

Neto, F., Pinto, C., & Mullet, E. (2007). Seeking forgiveness in an intergroup context: Angolan, Guinean, Mozambican, and East Timorese perspectives. *Regulation & Governance, 1*, 329–346.

Nets-Zehngut, R. (2008). The Israeli National Information Center and the collective memory of the Israeli-Arab conflict. *Middle East Journal, 62*(4), 653–670.

(2009). Passive healing of the aftermath of intractable conflicts. *International Journal of Peace Studies, 14*(1), 39–60.

(2011a). *Fixation and change of the Israeli official memory (1949–2004) regarding the causes of the Palestinians exodus during the 1948 war.* Ph.D. dissertation, Tel Aviv University. (in Hebrew)

(2011b). Origins of the Palestinian refugee problem: Changes in the historical memory of Israelis/Jews 1949–2004. *Journal of Peace Research, 48*(2), 235–248.

(2011c). Palestinian autobiographical memory regarding the 1948 Palestinian exodus. *Political Psychology, 32*(2), 271–295.

(2012a). *The collective self-healing process in the aftermath of intractable conflict.* Manuscript submitted for publication.

(2012b). The Israeli memory of the Palestinian refugee problem. *Peace Review, 24*(2), 187–194.

(2012c). *Israeli 1948 war veterans and the 1948 Palestinian exodus, 1949–2004.* Manuscript submitted for publication.

(in press). The Israeli Publications Agency and the 1948 Palestinian refugees – Official memory in times of conflict. In A. Sela & A. Kadish (Eds.), *Myth, memory, and historiography: Representations of the 1948 Palestine War.*

Nets-Zehngut, R., & Bar-Tal, D. (2009). *Popular collective memory of the Israeli-Arab/Palestinian conflict among Israeli Jews.* Unpublished manuscript.

(2012). *Transformation of the collective memory of conflicts: A conceptual framework and the Israeli case of 1948 Palestinian Exodus.* Manuscript submitted for publication.

Nets-Zehngut, R., Pliskin, R., & Bar-Tal, D. (2012). *Self-censorship of historical narratives of conflicts: Findings from Israel regarding the 1948 Palestinian exodus.* Manuscript submitted for publication.

Ney, J. S., & Lynn-Jones, S. M. (1988). International security studies: A report of a conference on the state of the field. *International Security, 12*(4), 5–27.

NGO Monitor. http://www.mgo_monitor.org?articles.php?type=about Nov 24, 2011.

Niedenthal, P. M., & Brauer, M. (2012). Social functionality of human emotion. *Annual Review of Psychology, 63*, 259–285.

Niedenthal, P. M., & Kitayama, S. (1994). *The heart's eye: Emotional influences in perception and attention.* San Diego: Academic.

Noor, M., Brown, R., & Prentice, G. (2008). Prospects for intergroup reconciliation: social-psychological predictors of intergroup forgiveness and reparation in Northern Ireland and Chile. In A. Nadler, T. Malloy, & J. Fisher (Ed.), *The social psychology of intergroup reconciliation* (pp. 97–116). Oxford: Oxford University Press.

Norris, P., Kern, M., & Just, M. (2003). *Framing terrorism: The news media, the government and the public.* New York: Routledge.

Northrup, T. A. (1989). The dynamic of identity in personal and social conflict. In L. Kriesberg, T. Northrup, & S. J. Thorson (Eds.), *Intractable conflicts and their transformation* (pp. 55–82). New York: Syracuse University Press.

Norval, A. J. (1998). Memory, identity and the (im)possibility of reconciliation: The work of the Truth and Reconciliation Commission in South Africa. *Constellations, 5*, 250–265.

——— (1999). Truth and reconciliation: The birth of the present and the reworking of history. *Journal of African Studies, 25*, 499–519.

Nosek, B. A., Graham, J., & Hawkins, B. C. (2010). Implicit political cognition. In B. Gawronski & B. K. Payne (Eds.), *Handbook of implicit social cognition: Measurement, theory and applications* (pp. 548–564). New York: Guilford Press.

Nosek, H., & Limor, Y. (1994). The military censorship in Israel: Prolonged temporary compromise between conflicting values. In D. Caspi & Y. Limor (Eds.), *The mass media in Israel* (pp. 362–390). Tel Aviv: Open University. (in Hebrew)

Oatley, K., & Jenkins, J. M. (1996). *Understanding emotions.* Cambridge, MA: Blackwell.

Oberschal, A. (2000). The manipulation of ethnicity: From ethnic cooperation to violence and war in Yugoslavia. *Ethnic and Racial Studies, 23*, 982–1000.

O'Boyle, G. (2002). Theories of justification and political violence: Examples from four groups. *Terrorism and Political Violence, 14*(2), 23–46.

ODHAG, Oficina de Derechos Humanos del Arzobispado de Guatemala: Informe Proyecto InterDiocesano de Recuperación de la Memoria Histórica (1998). *Guatemala: Nunca Más. Vol. I, II y III. Impactos de la Violencia.* Tibás, Costa Rica: LIL/Arzobispado de Guatemala. [Guatemalan Catholic Church Human Right's Department. Historical Memory Recovery Project Report, *Guatemala: Never Again*].

O'Donnell, G., & Schmitter, P., C. (Eds.), (1986). *Transitions from authoritarian rule: Tentative conclusions about uncertain democracies.* Baltimore: Johns Hopkins University Press.

Oegema, D., & Klandermans, B. (1994). Why social movement sympathizers don't participate: Erosion and non-conversion of support. *American Sociological Review, 59*(5), 703–722.

Ofrat, G. (1979). The Arab in Israeli drama. *Jerusalem Quarterly*, no. 11, pp. 70–92.

Öhman, A. (1993). Fear and anxiety as emotional phenomena: Clinical phenomenology evolutionary perspectives, and information-processing mechanisms. In M. Lewis & J. M. Haviland (Eds.), *Handbook of emotions* (pp. 511–536). New York: Guilford.

Öhman, A., & Wiens, S. (2001). *The concept of an evolved fear module as a challenge to cognitive theories of anxiety*. Keynote paper presented at the Amsterdam Conference on Feelings and Emotions, June 13–16.

Ohme, R. K., & Jarymowicz, M. (2001). *Implicit cues change explicit preferences, choice and behavior*. Poster presented at the Amsterdam Conference on Feelings and Emotions, June 13–16.

(Eds.), (1999). Influence of implicit affect on cognitive processes: Selected methods of research. *Studia Psychologiczne – special issue*, 37(1). (in Polish)

Olick, J. K. (2003). *States of memory: Continuities, conflicts, and transformations in national retrospection*. New York: Columbia University Press.

Olick, J. K., & Robbins, J. (1998). Social memory studies: From "collective memory" to the historical sociology of mnemonic practices. *Annual Review of Sociology*, 24, 105–140.

Olick, J. K., Vinitzky-Seroussi, V., & Levy, D. (2011). Introduction. In J. K. Olick, V. Vinitzky-Seroussi, & D. Levy (Eds.), *The collective memory reader* (pp. 3–61). Oxford: Oxford University Press.

Olmert, E. (2006). Active PM Ehud Olmert's speech at the Herzeliya conference. January 24. (in Hebrew).

Olson, J. M., Hermann, C. P., & Zanna, M. P. (Eds.), (1986). *Relative deprivation and social comparison: The Ontario symposium* (Vol. 4). Hillsdale, NJ: Erlbaum.

Olson, M. (1968). *The logic of collective action: Public goods and the theory of groups*. Cambridge, MA: Harvard University Press.

O'Malley – The Heart of Hope. (1992). F. W. de Klerk's speech at the opening of Parliament. February 2, 1990. Retrieved from http://www.nelsonmandela.org/omalley/index.php/site/q/03lv02039/04lv02103/05lv02104/06lv02105.htm.

Opotow, S. (1990). Moral exclusion and injustice: An introduction. *Journal of Social Issues*, 46, 1–20.

Opotow, S., & McClelland, S. I. (2007). The intensification of hating: A theory. *Social Justice Research*, 20, 68–97.

Ordeshook, P. C. (1986). *Game theory and political theory*. Cambridge: Cambridge University Press.

Oren, N. (2005). *The impact of major events in the Arab-Israel conflict on the ethos of conflict of the Israeli Jewish society (1967–2000)*. Ph.D. dissertation, Tel Aviv University. (in Hebrew)

(2009). *The Israeli ethos of conflict, 1967–2005*. Working Paper #27. Fairfax, VA: Institute for Conflict Analysis and Resolution, George Mason University. Retrieved from http://icar.gmu.edu/wp_27oren.pdf.

(2010). Israeli identity formation and the Arab–Israeli conflict in election platforms, 1969–2006. *Journal of Peace Research*, 47, 193–204.

Oren, N., & Bar-Tal, D. (2004). Monopolization of patriotism in the Israeli society. In A. Ben-Amos & D. Bar-Tal (Eds.), *Patriotism: Homeland love* (pp. 363–398). Tel Aviv: Hakibbutz Hameuhad. (in Hebrew)

(2006). Ethos and identity: Expressions and changes in the Israeli Jewish society. *Estudios de Psicología*, 27, 293–316.

(2007). The detrimental dynamics of delegitimization in intractable conflicts: The Israeli-Palestinian case. *International Journal of Intercultural Relations, 31*, 111–126.

(in press). Collective identity and intractable conflict. In G. M. Breakwell & R. Jaspal (Eds.), *Identity process theory: Identity, social action and social change*. Cambridge: Cambridge University Press.

Oren, N., Bar-Tal, D., & David, O. (2004). Conflict, identity and ethos: The Israeli-Palestinian case. In Y.-T. Lee, C. R. McCauley, F. M. Moghaddam, & S. Worchel (Eds.), *Psychology of ethnic and cultural conflict* (pp. 133–154). Westport, CT: Praeger.

Oren, N., Nets-Zehngut, R., & Bar-Tal, D. (2012). *Construction of the Israeli-Jewish conflict supportive narrative and the struggle over its dominance: A case study*. Manuscript submitted for publication.

Orjuela, C. (2003). Building peace in Sri Lanka: A role for civil society? *Journal of Peace Research, 40*, 195–212.

Ornstein, R. (1997). *The right mind: Making sense of the hemispheres*. New York: Harcourt Brace.

Orr, E. (1995). *Conflict as a cognitive schema*. Ph.D. dissertation, Bar-Ilan University, Israel. (in Hebrew)

Osgood, C. E. (1962). *An alternative to war or surrender*. Urbana: University of Illinois Press.

Osgood, R. E., & Tucker, R. W. (1967). *Force, order and justice*. Baltimore: John Hopkins Press.

Oskamp, S. (1965). Attitudes toward U.S. and Russian actions: A double standard. *Psychological Reports, 16*, 6–43.

Oskamp, S., & Levenson, H. (1968). *The double standard in international attitudes: Differences between doves and hawks*. Proceedings of the 76th annual convention of the American Psychological Association, pp. 379–380.

Ottati, V. C., & Wyer, R. S., Jr. (1993). Affect and political judgment. In S. Iyengar & W. McGuire (Eds.), *Explorations in political psychology* (pp. 296–315). Durham, NC: Duke University Press.

Paez, D., Basabe, N., & Gonzalez, J. L. (1997). Social processes and collective memory: A cross-cultural approach to remembering political events. In J. W. Pennebaker, D. Paez, & B. Riml (Eds.), *Collective memory of political events: Social psychological perspectives* (pp. 147–174). Mahwah, NJ: Erlbaum.

Paez, D., & Liu, J. H. (2011). Collective memory of conflicts. In D. Bar-Tal (Ed.), *Intergroup conflicts and their resolution: A social psychological perspective* (pp. 105–124). New York: Psychology Press.

Pally, S. (1955). Cognitive rigidity as a function of threat. *Journal of Personality, 23*, 346–355.

Paluck, E. L. (2009). Reducing intergroup prejudice and conflict using the media: A field experiment in Rwanda. *Journal of Personality and Social Psychology, 96*, 574–587.

Papadakis, Y. (1998). Greek Cypriot narratives of history and collective identity: Nationalism as a contested process. *American Ethnologist, 25*(2), 149–165.

(2003). Nation, narrative and commemoration: Political ritual in divided Cyprus. *History and Anthropology, 14*, 253–270.

(2005). *Echoes from the dead zone*. London: I. B. Tauris.

(2008). *History education in divided Cyprus: A comparison of Greek Cypriot and Turkish Cypriot school books on the "history of Cyprus."* PRIO report 2/2008. Oslo: International Peace Research Institute.

Papadakis, Y., Peristianis, N., & Welz, G. (Eds.), (2006a). *Divided Cyprus: Modernity, history, and an island in conflict.* Bloomington: Indiana University Press.

(2006b). Modernity, history, and Cyprus in divided Cyprus. In Y. Papadakis, N. Peristianis, & G. Welz (Eds.), *Divided Cyprus: Modernity, history, and an island in conflict* (pp. 1–29). Bloomington: Indiana University Press.

Parsons, T. (1951). *The social system.* Glencoe, IL: Free Press.

Passy, F. (2001). Socialization, connection, and the structure/agency gap: A specification of the impact of networks on participation in social movements. *Mobilization: An International Quarterly* 6(2): 173–192.

Patchen, M., Hofman, G., & Davidson, J. D. (1976). Interracial perceptions among high school students. *Sociometry, 39,* 341–354.

Paul, T. V. (2005). Causes of the India-Pakistan enduring rivalry. In T. V. Paul (Ed.), *The India-Pakistan conflict: An enduring rivalry* (pp. 3–24). Cambridge: Cambridge University Press.

Pavlov, I. P. (1930). A brief outline of the higher nervous activity. In W. C. Murchison (Ed.), *Psychologies of 1930* (pp. 207–220). Worcester, MA: Clark University Press.

Payne, J. W., Laughhunn, D. J., & Crum, R. (1981). Further tests of aspiration level effects in risky choice. *Management Science, 27,* 953–958.

Peace Index, (August, 2006). Peace Index project is conducted by The Tami Steinmetz Center for Peace Research at Tel-Aviv University. The data appears in The Tami Steinmetz Center's web site at www.tau.ac.il/peace.

Pearlman, L. A. (2001). The treatment of persons with complex PTSD and other trauma-related disruptions of the self. In J. P. Wilson, M. J. Friedman, & J. D. Lindy (Eds.), *Treating psychological trauma & PTSD* (pp. 205–236). New York: Guilford Press.

Peeters, G. (1971). The positive-negative asymmetry: On cognitive consistency and positivity bias. *European Journal of Social Psychology, 1,* 455–474.

(1991). Evaluative influence in social cognition: the roles of direct versus indirect evaluation and positive-negative asymmetry. *European Journal of Social Psychology, 21,* 131–146.

Peeters, G., & Czapinski, J. (1990). Positive-negative asymmetry in evaluations: The distinction between affective and informational negativity effects. *European Review of Social Psychology, 1,* 33–60.

Pena-Martin, J., & Opotow, S. (2011). The legitimization of political violence: A case study of ETA in the Basque country. *Peace and Conflict: Journal of Peace Psychology, 17,* 132–150.

Pennebaker, J. W., Paez, D., & Rimé, B. (1997). *Collective memory of political events: Social psychological perspective.* Mahwah, NJ: Erlbaum.

Peri, Y. (1998). The changed security discourse in the Israeli media. In D. Bar-Tal, D. Jacobson, & A. Klieman (Eds.), *Security concerns: Insights from the Israeli experience* (pp. 113–137). Stamford, CT: JAI Press.

(Ed.), (2000). *The assassination of Yitzhak Rabin.* Stanford, CA: Stanford University Press.

Petersen, R. D. (2002). *Understanding ethnic violence: Fear, hatred, and resentment in twentieth-century Eastern Europe.* Cambridge: Cambridge University Press.

Petrocelli, J. V., Tormala, Z. L., & Rucker, D. D. (2007). Unpacking attitude certainty: Attitude clarity and attitude correctness. *Journal of Personality and Social Psychology, 92*, 30–41.
Pettigrew, T. F. (1998). Intergroup contact theory. *Annual Review of Psychology, 19*, 185–209.
Pettigrew, T. F., & Tropp, L. R. (2006). Meta-analytic test of intergroup contact theory. *Journal of Personality and Social Psychology, 90*, 751–783.
  (2008). How does intergroup contact reduce prejudice? Meta-analytic tests of three mediators. *European Journal of Social Psychology, 38*, 922–934.
Pfeifer, J. E., & Ogloff, J. R. P. (1991). Ambiguity and guilt determinations: A modern racism perspective. *Journal of Applied Social Psychology, 21*, 1713–1725.
Pfetsch, F. R., & Rohloff, C. (2000). *International conflicts, 1945–1995: New empirical and theoretical approaches.* London: Routledge.
Piaget, J. (1970). Piaget's theory. In P. H. Mussen (Ed.), *Carmichael's handbook of child psychology* (Vol. 1, pp. 703–732). New York: Wiley.
Pingel, F. (Ed.), (2003). *Contested past, disputed present: Curricula and teaching in Israeli and Palestinian schools.* Hannover: Verlag Hahnsche Buchhandlung.
  (2008). Can truth be negotiated? History textbook revision as a means to reconciliation. *Annals of the American Academy of Political and Social Sciences, 617*, 181–198.
Plutchik, R. (1980). *Emotion: A psychoevolutionary synthesis.* New York: Harper & Row.
  (1990). Fear and aggression in suicide and violence: A psychoevolutionary perspective. In P. F. Brain, S. Parmigiani, R. J. Blanchard, & D. Mainarcli (Eds.), *Fear and defense* (pp. 359–379). London: Harwood.
Podeh, E. (2002). *The Arab-Israeli conflict in Israeli history textbooks, 1948–2000.* Westport, CT: Bergin & Garvey.
Poliakov, L. (1974). *The history of anti-Semitism* (Vols. 1 and 2). London: Routledge & Kegan Paul.
Police Service of Northern Ireland (PSNI). (2003). *Persons injured as a result of the Security Situation in Northern Ireland, 1969–2003 (by calendar year).* Retrieved August 3, 2008, from http://www.psni.police.uk/index/departments/statistics_branch.htm.
  (2008). *Parade Statistics, 2005–2007.* Retrieved August 4, 2008, from http://www.psni.police.uk/index/departments/statistics_branch.htm.
Polletta, F. (2002). Plotting protest: mobilizing stories in the 1960 student sit-ins. In J. E. Davis (Ed.), *Stories of change: Narrative and social movements* (pp. 270–299). Albany: State University of New York Press.
Polletta, F., & Jasper, J. M. (2001). Collective identity and social movements *Annual Review of Sociology, 27*, 283–305.
Poole, M. A. (1995). The spatial distribution of political violence in Northern Ireland. An update to 1993. In A. O'Day (Ed.), *Terrorism's laboratory: The case of Northern Ireland* (pp. 27–45). Aldershot: Dartmouth.
Porat, D. (2001). A contemporary past: History textbooks as sites of national memory. In A. Dickinson, P. Gordon, & P. Lee (Eds.), *International review of history education* (Vol. 3, pp. 36–55). London: Woburn Press.
Porat, R., Halperin, E., & Bar-Tal, D. (2012). *The effect of socio-psychological barriers on the processing of new information about peace opportunities.* Manuscript submitted for publication.
Pratto, F., & Glasford, D. (2008). How needs can motivate intergroup reconciliation in the face of intergroup conflict. In A. Nadler, T. E. Malloy, & J. D. Fisher (Eds.),

The social psychology of intergroup reconciliation (pp. 117–144). New York: Oxford University Press.

Pressman, J. (2003). Vision in collision: What happened at Camp David and Taba? *International Security, 28*, 5–43.

Preston, P. (1978). *The coming of the Spanish war.* London: Macmillan.

Print, M., Ugarte, C., Naval, C., & Mihr, A. (2008). Moral and human rights education: The contribution of the United Nations. *Journal of Moral Education, 37*, 115–132.

Prislin, R., & Christensen, P. N. (2005). Social change in the aftermath of successful minority influence. *European Review of Social Psychology, 16*, 43–73.

Prislin, R., & Wood, W. (2005). Social influence: The role of social consensus in attitude and attitude change. In D. Albarracín, B. T. Johnson, & M. P. Zanna (Eds.), *Handbook on attitudes and attitude change* (pp. 671–706). New York: Sage.

Pronin, E., Gilovich, T., & Ross, L. (2004). Objectivity in the eye of the beholder: Divergent perceptions of bias in self versus others. *Psychological Review, 111*, 781–799.

Prost, A. (1999). The Algerian war in French collective memory. In J. Winter & E. Sivan (Eds.), *War and remembrance in the twentieth century* (pp. 161–176). Cambridge: Cambridge University Press.

Pruitt, D. G. (2007). Readiness theory and the Northern Ireland peace process. *American Behavioral Scientist, 50*, 1520–1541.

(2011). Negotiation and mediation in intergroup conflict. In D., Bar-Tal (Ed.), *Intergroup conflicts and their resolution: A social psychological perspective* (pp. 267–289). New York: Psychology Press.

Pruitt, D. G., & Kim, S. H. (2004). *Social conflict: Escalation, stalemate, and settlement* (3rd ed.). New York: McGraw-Hill.

Pruitt, D. G., & Rubin, J. Z. (1986). *Social Conflict: Escalation, stalemate and settlement.* New York: Random House.

Prunier, G. (1998). *The Rwanda crisis: History of a genocide.* London: C. Hurst.

Putnam, L. L., & Wondolleck, J. M. (2003). Intractability: Definitions, dimensions and distinctions. In R. J. Lewicki, B. Gray, & M. Elliott, (Eds.). *Making sense of intractable environmental conflicts: Frames and cases* (pp. 35–62). Washington, DC: Island Press.

Pyszczynski, T., Greenberg, J., & Solomon, S. (1997). Why do we need what we need? A terror management perspective on the roots of human motivation. *Psychological Inquiry, 8*, 1–20.

Quattrone, G., & Jones, E. (1980). The perception of variability with in-group and outgroup: implications for the law of small number. *Journal of Personality and Social Psychology, 38*, 141–152.

Quillian, L. (1995). Prejudice as a response to perceived group threat: Population composition and anti-immigrant and racial prejudice in Europe. *American Sociological Review, 60*, 586–611.

Rachman, S. J. (1978). *Fear and courage.* San Francisco: W. H. Freeman.

Raider, E. (1995). Conflict resolution training in schools: Translation theory into applied skills. In B. B. Bunker & J. Z. Rubin (Eds.), *Conflict, cooperation and justice.* San Francisco: Jossey-Bass.

Raider, E., Coleman, S., & Gerson, J. (2000). Teaching conflict resolution skills in a workshop. In M. Deutsch & P. T. Coleman (Eds.), *The handbook of conflict resolution: Theory and practice* (pp. 499–521). San Francisco: Jossey-Bass.

Ramanathapillai, R. (2006). The politicizing of trauma: A case study of Sri Lanka. *Peace and Conflict: Journal of Peace Psychology, 12,* 1–18.

Ramet, S. P. (1996). *Balkan Babel: The disintegration of Yugoslav from the death of Tito to ethnic war* (2nd ed.). Boulder, CO: Westview.

Ratzabi, S. (2002). Between Zionism and Judaism: The radical circle in Brith Shalom, 1925–1933. Leiden: Brill.

Raviv, A., Bar-Tal, D., & Arviv-Abromovich, R. (in preparation). *In the eyes of the beholder: Views of the Israeli-Arab conflict by Jewish veteran residents in Israel.* Manuscript in preparation, Tel Aviv University.

Reardon, B. A. (1988). *Comprehensive peace education: Educating for global responsibility.* New York: Teachers College Press.

Reicher, S. (2004). The context of social identity: Domination, resistance, and change. *Political Psychology, 25,* 921–945.

Reicher, S., & Hopkins, N. (2001). *Self and nation.* London: Sage.

Reicher, S., Hopkins, N., Levine, M., & Rath, R. (2005). Entrepreneurs of hate and entrepreneurs of solidarity: Social identity as a basis for mass communication. *International Review of the Red Cross, 87*(860), 621–637.

Reicher, S. D. (1996a). Social identity and social change: Rethinking the context of social psychology. In W. P. Robinson (Ed.), *Social groups and identities: Developing the legacy of Henri Tajfel* (pp. 317–336). Oxford: Butterworth-Heinemann.

 (1996b). The battle of Westminster: Developing the social identity model of crowd behavior in order to explain the initiation and development of collective conflict. *European Journal of Social Psychology, 26,* 115–134.

Reifen, M., Halperin, E., & Federico, C. (2011). The positive effect of negative emotions in protracted conflict: The case of anger. *Journal of Experimental Social Psychology, 47,* 157–163.>

Reis, H. T. (2008). Reinvigorating the concept of situation in social psychology. *Personality and Social Psychology Review, 12,* 311–329.

Rettig, M. (2008). Gacaca: Truth, justice, and reconciliation in postconflict Rwanda? *Journal of African Studies, 51,* 25–50.

Rex, J. (1996). *Ethnic minorities in the modern nation state.* London: Macmillan.

Reykowski, J. (1968). *Experimental psychology of emotion.* Warszawa: Książka i Wiedza. (in Polish)

 (1982). Social motivation. *Annual Review of Psychology, 33,* 123–154.

 (1985). Evaluative standards: Genesis, functioning rules, and development. In A. Gołąb & J. Reykowski (Eds.), *Studies on the development of evaluative standards* (pp. 12–49). Wrocław: Ossolineum. (in Polish)

 (1989). Dimension of the development of moral values. In N. Eisenberg, J. Reykowski, & E. Staub (Ed.), *Social and moral values: Individual and societal perspectives* (pp. 23–44). Hillsdale, NJ: Erlbaum Associates.

 (1997). Patriotism and the collective system of meaning. In D. Bar-Tal & E. Staub (Eds.), *Patriotism in the lives of individuals and nations* (pp. 108–128). Chicago: NelsonHall.

Reykowski, J., & Cisłak, A. (2011). Socio-psychological approaches to conflict resolution. In D. Bar-Tal (Ed.), *Intergroup conflicts and their resolution: A social psychological perspective* (pp. 241–266). New York: Psychology Press.

Rice, J. S. (2002). Getting our histories straight: Culture, narrative, and identity in the self-help movement. In J. E. Davis (Ed.), *Stories of change: Narrative and social movements* (pp. 79–99). Albany: State University of New York Press.

Rieber, R. W. (Ed.), (1991). *The psychology of war and peace: The image of the enemy*. New York: Plenum Press.

Riek, B. M., Mania, E. W. M., & Gaertner, S. L. (2006). Intergroup threat and outcome attitudes: A meta-analytic review. *Personality and Social Psychology Review, 10*, 336–353.

Rime, B., & Christophe, V. (1997). How individual emotional episodes feed collective memory. In J. P. Pennebaker, D. Paez, & B. Rime (Eds.), *Collective memory of political events: Social psychological perspectives* (pp. 131–146). Mahwah, NJ: Erlbaum.

Rimé, B., Kanyangara, P., Yzerbyt, V., & Paez, D. (2011). The impact of Gacaca tribunals in Rwanda: Psychosocial effects of participation in a truth and reconciliation process after a genocide. *European Journal of Social Psychology, 41*, 695–706.

Riskedahl, D. (2007). A sign of war: The strategic use of violent imagery in contemporary Lebanese political rhetoric. *Language & Communication, 27*(3), 307–319.

Roccas, S., & Elster, A. (2012). Group identities. In L. R. Tropp (Ed.), *Oxford handbook of intergroup conflict* (pp. 106–122). New York: Oxford University Press.

Roccas, S., Klar, Y., & Liviatan, I. (2006). The paradox of group-based guilt: modes of conflict identification, conflict vehemence, and reactions to the in-group's moral violations. *Journal of Personality and Social Psychology, 91*, 698–711.

Roccas, S., Sagiv, L., Schwartz, S., Halevy, N., & Eidelson, R. (2008). Towards a unifying model of identification with groups: Integrating theoretical perspectives. *Personality and Social Psychology Review, 12*, 280–306.

Rodgers, C. (2002). Defining reflection: Another look at John Dewey and reflective thinking. *Teachers College Record, 104*(4), 842–866.

Roe, M. D. (2007). Intergroup forgiveness in settings of political violence: Complexities, ambiguities, and potentialities. *Peace and Conflict: Journal Peace Psychology, 13*, 3–9.

Roe, M. D., & Cairns, E. (2003). Memories in conflict: Review and a look to the future. In E. Cairns & M. D. Roe (Eds.), *The role of memory in ethnic conflict* (pp. 171–180). Houndmills: Palgrave Macmillan.

Rogers, R. F. (1975). A protection motivation theory of fear appeals and attitude change. *Journal of Psychology, 91*, 93–114.

Rojahn, K., & Pettigrew, P. F. (1992). Memory for schemata-relevant information: A meta-analytic resolution. *British Journal of Social Psychology, 31*, 81–109.

Rokeach, M. (1960). *The open and closed mind*. New York: Basic Books.

Rose, R. (1985). National pride in cross-national perspective. *International Social Science Journal, 37*, 85–96.

Roseman, I. J. (1984). Cognitive determinants of emotions: A structural theory. In P. Shaver (Ed.), *Review of Personality and Social Psychology* (Vol. 5, pp. 11–36). Beverly Hills, CA: Sage.

Roseman, I. J., Wiest, C., & Swartz, T. S. (1994). Phenomenology, behaviors, and goals differentiate discrete emotions. *Journal of Personality and Social Psychology, 67*, 206–221.

Rosenberg, S. W., & Wolfsfeld, G. (1977). International conflict and the problem of attribution. *Journal of Conflict Resolution, 21*, 75–103.

Rosler, N. (2012). *Political context, social challenges, and leadership: Rhetorical expressions of psycho-social roles of leaders in intractable conflict and its resolution process – the Israeli-Palestinian case*. Ph.D. dissertation, Hebrew University of Jerusalem. (in Hebrew)

Rosler, N., Gross, J. J., & Halperin, E. (2009, July). *The role of transitional psycho-social repertoire in ending intractable conflict: The case of intergroup emotions*. Paper presented at the annual meeting of the International Society of Political Psychology, Dublin, Ireland.

Rosoux, V. B. (2001). National identity in France and Germany: From mutual exclusion to negotiation. *International Negotiation, 6*, 175–198.

Ross, L., & Nisbett, R. E. (1991). *The person and the situation: Perspectives of social psychology*. New York: McGraw.

Ross, L., & Ward, A. (1995). Psychological barriers to dispute resolution. In M. Zanna (Ed.), *Advances in Experimental Social Psychology* (Vol. 27, pp. 255–304). San Diego: Academic Press.

Ross, M. H. (1993). *The culture of conflict: Interpretations and interests in comparative perspective*. New Haven, CT: Yale University Press.

(1995a). *The management of conflict: Interpretations and interests in comparative perspective*. New Haven, CT: Yale University Press.

(1995b). Psychocultural interpretation theory and peacemaking in ethnic conflicts. *Political Psychology, 16*, 523–544.

(1998). The cultural dynamics of ethnic conflict. In D. Jacquin, A. Oros, & M. Verweij (Eds.), *Culture in world politics* (pp. 156–186). Houndmills: Macmillan.

(2001). Psychocultural interpretations and dramas: Identity dynamics in ethnic conflict. *Political Psychology, 22*, 157–198.

(2007). *Cultural contestation in ethnic conflict*. Cambridge: Cambridge University Press.

Ross, S. D. (2011). Media discourses of peace: An imperfect but important tool of peace, security and Kyosei. In N. Kawamura, Y. Murakami, & S. Chip (Eds.), *Building new pathways to peace* (pp. 126–140). Seattle: University of Washington Press.

Rotberg, R. (Ed.), (2006). *Israeli and Palestinian narratives of conflict – History's double helix*. Bloomington and Indianapolis: Indiana University Press.

Rothbart, D., & Korostelina, K. V. (2006). *Identity, morality, and threat: Studies in violent conflict*. Lanham, MD: Lexington Books.

Rothbart, M., Evans, M., & Fulero, S. (1979). Recall for confirming events: Memory processes and the maintenance of social stereotypes. *Journal of Experimental Social Psychology, 15*, 343–355.

Rothgerber, H. (1997). External intergroup threat as an antecedent to perceptions of in-group and out-group homogeneity. *Journal of Personality and Social Psychology, 73*, 1206–1211.

Rothman, J. (1997). *Resolving identity-based conflict in nations, organizations, and communities*. San Francisco: Jossey-Bass.

Rothstein, R. L. (Ed.), (1999a). *After the peace: Resistance and reconciliation*. Boulder, CO: Lynne Rienner.

(1999b). In fear of peace: Getting past maybe. In R. L. Rothstein (Ed.), *After the peace: Resistance and reconciliation* (pp. 1–25). Boulder, CO: Lynne Rienner.

Rouhana N. N. (2004a) Identity and power in the reconciliation of national conflict. In A. Eagly, R. Baron, & V. Hamilton (Eds.), *The social psychology of group identity and social conflict: Theory, application, and practice* (pp. 173–187). Washington, DC: American Psychological Association.

(2004b). Group identity and power asymmetry in reconciliation processes: The Israeli-Palestinian case. *Peace and Conflict: Journal of Peace Psychology*, 10, 33–52.

(2008). Reconciling history and equal citizenship in Israel: democracy and the politics of historical denial. In B. Bashir & W. Kymlicka (Ed.), *The politics of reconciliation in multicultural societies* (pp. 70–93). Oxford: Oxford University Press.

(2011). Key issues in reconciliation: Challenging traditional assumptions on conflict resolution and power dynamics. In D. Bar-Tal (Ed.), *Intergroup conflicts and their resolution: A social psychological perspective* (pp. 291–314). New York: Psychology Press.

Rouhana, N. N., & Bar-Tal, D. (1998). Psychological dynamics of intractable conflicts: The Israeli-Palestinian case. *American Psychologist*, 53, 761–770.

Rouhana, N. N., & Fiske, S. T. (1995). Perception of power, threat and conflict interest in asymmetric intergroup conflict. *Journal of Conflict Resolution*, 39, 49–81.

Rouhana, N. N., & Kelman, H. C. (1994). Promoting joint thinking in international conflicts: An Israeli-Palestinian continuing workshop. *Journal of Social Issues*, 50, 157–178.

Rouhana, N. N., O'Dwyer, A., & Morrison Vaso, S. K. (1997). Cognitive biases and political party affiliation in intergroup conflict. *Journal of Applied Social Psychology*, 27, 37–57.

Royzman, E. B., McCauley, C., & Rosin, P. (2005). From Plato to Putnam: Four ways to think about hate. In R. J. Sternberg (Ed.), *The psychology of hate* (pp. 3–36). Washington, DC: American Psychological Association.

Rozin, P., & Royzman, E. B. (2001). Negativity bias, negativity dominance, and contagion. *Personality and Social Psychology Review*, 5(4), 296–320.

Ruane, J., & Todd, J. (1996). *The dynamics of conflict in Northern Ireland: Power, conflict and emancipation*. Cambridge: Cambridge University Press.

Runciman, W. G. (1966). *Relative deprivation and social justice: A study of attitudes to social inequality in twentieth century*. London: Routledge & Kegan Paul.

Rupesinghe, K., & Rubio, M. C. (1994). *The culture of violence*. New York: United Nations University Press.

Russell, J. (2002). Mujahedeen, mafia, madmen: Russian perspectives of Chechens during the wars in Chechnya, 1994–96 and 1999–2001. In R. Fawn & S. White (Ed.), *Russia in retrospect: Ten years since the end of the USSR* (pp. 73–96). London: Frank Cass.

(2005). Terrorists, bandits, spooks and thieves: Russian demonisation of the Chechens prior to and since 9/11. *Third World Quarterly*, 26(1), 101–116.

(2007). *Chechnya-Russia's war on terror*. New York: Routledge.

Rutkoff, P. M. (1981). *Revenge and revision*. Athens: Ohio University Press.

Rydell, R. J., Mackie, D. M., Maitner, A. T., Claypool, H. M., Ryan, M. J., & Smith, E. R. (2008). Arousal, processing, and risk-taking: The consequences of intergroup anger. *Personality and Social Psychology Bulletin*, 34, 1141–1152.

Saarni, C. I., & Harris, P. (Eds.), (1989). *Children's understanding of emotions*. Cambridge: Cambridge University Press.

Sabucedo, J. M., Blanco, A., & De la Corte, L. (2003). Beliefs which legitimize political violence against the innocent. *Psicothema, 15*, 550–555.

Sack, R. D. (1986). *Human territoriality: Its theory and history.* Cambridge: Cambridge University Press.

Sa'di, A. H. (2002). Catastrophe, memory and identity: Al-Nakbah as a component of Palestinian identity, *Israel Studies, 7*, 175–198.

Sarafian, A. (1999). The Ottoman archives debate and the Armenian genocide. *Armenian Forum, 2*(1), 35–44.

Sagy, S., Adwan, S., & Kaplan, A. (2002). Interpretations of the past and expectations for the future of Israeli and Palestinian youth. *American Journal of Orthopsychiatry, 72,* 26–38.

Saideman, S. M. (2005). At the heart of the conflict: Irredentism and Kashmir. In T. V. Paul (Ed.), *The India-Pakistan conflict: An enduring rivalry* (pp. 202–224). Cambridge: Cambridge University Press.

Saidi, N. H. (1994). The economic construction of Lebanon: War, peace, and modernization. In D. Collings (Ed.), *Peace for Lebanon? From war to reconstruction* (pp. 195–212). Boulder, CO: Lynne Rienner.

Salomon, G. (2004). A narrative-based view of coexistence education. *Journal of Social Issues, 60*(2), 273–287.

(2011). Four major challenges facing peace education in regions of intractable conflict. *Peace and Conflict: Journal Peace Psychology, 17*, 46–59.

Salomon, G., & Cairns, E. (Eds.), (2010). *Handbook of peace education.* New York: Psychology Press.

Sande, G. N., Goethals, G. R., Ferrari, L., & Worth, L. T. (1989). Value-guided attributions: Maintaining the moral self-image and the diabolical enemy-image. *Journal of Social Issues, 45*(2), 91–118.

Sandole. D. (1999). *Capturing the complexity of conflict: Dealing with violent ethnic conflicts of the Post-Cold War era.* London: Pinter/Continuum.

(2002). Virulent ethnocentrism: A major challenge for transformational conflict resolution and peacebuilding in the post-cold war era. *Global Review of Ethnopolitics, 1*(4), 4–27.

Sani, F., Bowe, M., Herrera, M., Manna, C., Cossa, T., Miao, X., & Znou, Y. (2007). Perceived collective continuity: Seeing groups as entities that move through time. *European Journal of Social Psychology, 37,* 1118–1134.

Sani, F., Herrera, M., & Bowe, M. (2009). Perceived collective continuity and ingroup identification as defence against death awareness. *Journal of Experimental Social Psychology, 45,* 242–245.

Savage, R. (2006). "Vermin to be cleared off the face of the Earth": Perpetrator representations of genocide victims as animals. In C. Tatz, P. Arnold, & S. Tatz (Eds.), *Genocide perspectives III: Essays on the Holocaust and other genocides* (pp. 1–32). Sydney: Brandl & Schlesinger.

(2007). "Disease incarnate": Biopolitical discourse and genocidal dehumanisation in the age of modernity. *Journal of Historical Sociology, 20,* 404–440.

Schaffer, H. B., & Schaffer, T. C. (2005). Kashmir: Fifty years of running in place. In C. A. Crocker, F. O. Hampson, & P. Aall (Eds.), *Grasping the Nettle: Analyzing cases of intractable conflict* (pp. 295–318). Washington, DC: United States Institute of Peace Press.

Schatz, R. T., Staub, E., & Lavine, H. (1999). On the varieties of national attachment: Blind versus constructive patriotism. *Political Psychology, 20,* 151–174.

Scheff, T. J. (1994). *Bloody revenge: Emotions, nationalism, and war.* Boulder, CO: Westview.

Schiappa, E., Gregg, P. B., & Hewes, D. E. (2005). The parasocial contact hypothesis. *Communication Monographs, 72,* 92–115.

Schleifer, R. (2009). Psyoping Hezbollah: The Israeli psychological warfare campaign during the 2006 Lebanon War. *Terrorism and Political Violence, 21*(2), 221–238.

Schofield, V. (2000). *India, Pakistan and the unfinished war.* London: I. B. Tauris.

Schori-Eyal, N., Halperin, E., & Bar-Tal, D. (2011). *The three levels of collective victimhood: Effects of multilayered victimhood on intergroup conflicts.* Manuscript submitted for publication.

Schori-Eyal, N., Klar, Y., & Roccas, S. (2011). *The Shadows of the past: Effects of historical group trauma on current intergroup conflicts.* Manuscript submitted for publication.

Schramm, K. (2011). Introduction: Landscapes of violence: Memory and sacred space. *History and Memory, 23*(1), 5–22.

Schultz-Hardt, S., Frey, D., Luthgens, C., & Moscovici, S. (2000). Biases information search in group decision making. *Journal of Personality and Social Psychology, 78,* 655–669.

Schuman, H., & Scott, J. (1989). Generations and collective memory. *American Sociological Review, 54,* 359–381.

Schumann, K., & Ross, M. (2010). The antecedents, nature and effectiveness of political apologies for historical injustices. In D. R. Bobocel, A. C. Kay, M. P. Zanna, & J. M. Olson (Eds.), *The Ontario Symposium: The psychology of justice and legitimacy* (Vol. 11, pp. 299–324). New York: Psychology Press.

Schwartz, B. (1996). Memory as a cultural system: Abraham Lincoln in World War II. *American Sociological Review, 61,* 908–927.

Schwartz, N. (1990). Feelings as information: Informational and motivational functions of affective states. In E. T. Higgins & R. M. Sorrentino (Eds.), *Handbook of motivation and cognition: Foundations of social behavior* (Vol. 2, pp. 527–561). New York: Guilford.

Schwartz, S. H. (1992). Universals in the content and structure of values: Theoretical advances and empirical tests in 20 countries. In M. P. Zanna (Ed.), *Advances in experimental social psychology* (Vol. 25, pp. 1–65). New York: Academic Press.

Sears, D. O. (2002). Long-term psychological consequences of political events. In K. R. Monroe (Ed.), *Political psychology* (pp. 249–269). Mahwah, NJ: Erlbaum.

Seger, C. R., Smith, E. R., & Mackie, D. M. (2009). Subtle activation of a social categorization triggers group-level emotions. *Journal of Experimental Social Psychology, 45,* 460–467.

Segev, T. (2000). *The seventh million: The Israelis and the Holocaust.* New York: Henry Holt.

Sekulic, D. (in press). Ethnic intolerance as a product rather than a cause of war: Revisiting the state of the art. In D. Spini, D. Čorkalo Biruški, & G. Elcheroth (Eds.), *War and community: Collective experiences in the former Yugoslavia.* New York: Springer.

Selman, R. L. (1980). *The growth of interpersonal understanding.* New York: Academic Press.

Sen, R., & Wagner, W. (2005). History, emotions and hetero-referential representations in inter-group conflict: The example of Hindu-Muslim relations in India. *Papers on Social Representations, 14*, 2.1–2.23.

Sereseres, C. (1996). The regional peacekeeping role of the organization of American States: Nicaragua, 1990–1993. In C. A. Crocker, F. O. Hampson, & P. Aall (Eds.), *Managing global chaos: Sources of conflict of and responses to international conflict* (pp. 531–562). Washington, DC: United States Institute of Peace Press.

Seton-Watson. H. (1977). *Nations and states: An enquiry into the origins of nations and the politics of nationalism.* Boulder, CO: Westview.

Shaked, G. (1989). The Arab in Israeli fiction. *Modern Hebrew Literature*, no. 3, pp. 17–20.

Shalev, A. Y., Yehuda, R., & McFarlane,-A. C. (Eds.), (2000). *International handbook of human response to trauma.* Dordrecht, Netherlands: Kluwer Academic Publishers.

Shamir, B., Arthur, M. B., & House, R. J. (1994). The rhetoric of charismatic leadership: A theoretical extension, a case study, and implications for research. *Leadership Quarterly, 5*(1), 25–42.

Shamir, I. (Ed.), (1976). *The perpetuation of the memory of the fallen and its meaning.* Tel Aviv: Ministry of Defence Press. (in Hebrew)

Shamir, J., & Shamir, M. (2000). *The anatomy of public opinion.* Ann Arbor: University of Michigan Press.

Shamir, J., & Shikaki, K. (2002). Self serving perceptions of terrorism among Israelis and Palestinians. *Political Psychology, 23*, 537–557.

Sharp, G. (2005). *Waging nonviolent struggle: 20th century practice and 21st century potential.* Boston: Extending Horizons Books.

Sharvit, K. (2008). *Activation of the ethos of conflict while coping with stress resulting from intractable conflict.* Ph.D. dissertation, Tel Aviv University.

Sharvit, K., & Bar-Tal, D. (2007). Ethos of conflict in the Israeli media during the period of the violent confrontation. In Y. Bar-Siman-Tov (Ed.), *The Israeli-Palestinian conflict: From conflict resolution to conflict management* (pp. 203–232). Houndmills: Palgrave Macmillan.

Sharvit, K., Bar-Tal, D., Raviv, A., Raviv, A., & Gurevich, R. (2010). Ideological orientation and social context as moderators of the effect of terrorism: The case of Israeli-Jewish public opinion regarding peace. *European Journal of Social Psychology, 40*, 105–121.

Sharvit, K., Halperin, E., & Rosler, N. (2011). *Forces of stability and change in prolonged domination: Empathy, justifying beliefs and moral emotions.* Manuscript submitted for publication.

Sharvit, K., Kruglanski, A. W., Wang, M., Sheveland, A., Ganor, B., & Azani, E. (2010). *Palestinian public opinion and terrorism: A two-way street?* Manuscript submitted for publication.

Shechtman, Z., & Basheer, O. (2005). Normative beliefs supporting aggression of Arab children in an intergroup conflict. *Aggressive Behavior, 31*, 324–335.

Sheffer, G., & Barak, O. (Eds.), (2009). *Existential threats and civil security relations.* Lanham, MD: Lexington Books.

(Eds.), (2010). *Militarism and Israeli society.* Bloomington: Indiana University Press.

Shepard, T. (2006). *The invention of the decolonization: The Algerian war and the remaking of France.* Ithaca, NY: Cornell University Press.

Sher, G. (2001). *Within reach: The peace negotiations: 1999–2001.* Tel Aviv: Yedioth Aharonot. (in Hebrew)

Sherif, M., Harvey, O. J., White, B. J., Hood, W. R., & Sherif, C. W. (1961). *Intergroup cooperation and competition: The Robbers Cave experiment.* Norman, OK: University Book Exchange.

Shils, E. (1968). Ideology: The concept and function of ideology. In D. E. Sills (Ed.), *International Encyclopedia of the Social Sciences* (Vol. 7, pp. 66–75). New York: Macmillan & Free Press.

Shinhar, D., & Kempf, W. F. (2007). *Peace journalism: The state of the art.* Berlin: Verlag Irena Regener.

Shnabel, N., Nadler, A., Ullrich, J., Dovidio, J. F., & Carmi, D. (2009). Promoting reconciliation through the satisfaction of the emotional needs of victimized and perpetrating group members: The needs-based model of reconciliation. *Personality and Social Psychology Bulletin, 35,* 1021–1030.

Shohat, E. (1989). *Israeli cinema: East/west and the politics of representation.* Austin: University of Texas Press.

Shonholtz, R. (1998). Conflict resolution moves East: How the emerging democracies of Central and Eastern Europe are facing interethnic conflict. In E. Weiner (Ed.), *The handbook of interethnic coexistence* (pp. 359–368). New York: Continuum.

Shriver, D. W., Jr. (1995). *An ethic for enemies: Forgiveness in politics.* New York: Oxford University Press.

(2001). Forgiveness: A bridge across abysses of revenge. In R. G. Helmick & R. L. Petersen (Eds.), *Forgiveness and reconciliation: Religion, public policy, and conflict transformation* (pp. 151–167). Radnor, PA: Templeton Foundation Press.

Sibley, C. G., & Duckitt, J. (2008). Personality and prejudice: A meta-analysis and theoretical review. *Personality and Social Psychology Review, 12,* 248–279.

Sibley, C. S., Liu, J. H., Duckitt, J., & Khan, S. S. (2008). Social representations of history and the legitimation of social inequality: The form and function of historical negation. *European Journal of Psychology, 38,* 542–565.

Sidanius, J., & Pratto, F. (1999). *Social dominance.* Cambridge: Cambridge University Press.

Silke, A. (2006). The role of suicide in politics, conflict, and terrorism. *Terrorism and Political Violence, 18,* 35–46.

Silove, D. (1999). The psychosocial effects of torture, mass human rights violations, and refugee trauma: Toward an integrated conceptual framework. *Journal of Nervous and Mental Disease, 187,* 200–207.

Silverstein, B., & Flamenbaum, C. (1989). Biases in the perception and cognition of the actions of enemies. *Journal of Social Issues, 45*(2), 51–72.

Simon, B., & Klandermans, B. (2001). Politicized collective identity: A social psychological analysis. *American Psychologist, 56,* 319–331.

Simpson, G. (1997). Reconstruction and reconciliation: Emerging from transition. *Development in Practice, 7,* 475–478.

Sivan, E. (1991). *The 1948 generation: Myth, profile and memory.* Tel Aviv: Maarchot. (in Hebrew)

(1999). Private pain and public remembrance in Israel. In J. Winter & E. Sivan (Eds.), *War and remembrance in the twentieth century* (pp. 177–204). Cambridge: Cambridge University Press.

Skitka, L. J. (2002). Do the means justify the ends, or do the ends justify the means? A test of the value protection model of justice. *Personality and Social Psychology Bulletin, 28,* 588–597.

(2003). Of different minds: An accessible identity model of justice reasoning. *Personality and Social Psychology Review, 7,* 286–297.

Skitka, L. J., & Bauman, C. W. (2008). Moral conviction and political engagement. *Political Psychology, 29,* 29–54.

Skitka, L. J., Bauman, C. W., Aramovich, N. P., & Morgan, G. C. (2006). Confrontational and preventative policy responses to terrorism: Anger wants a fight and fear wants "them" to go away. *Basic and Applied Social Psychology, 28,* 375 – 384.

Skitka, L. J., Bauman, C. W., & Sargis, E. G. (2005). Moral conviction: Another contributor to attitude strength or something more? *Journal of Personality and Social Psychology, 88,* 895–917.

Skitka, L. J., Mullen, E., Griffin, T., Hutchinson, S., & Chamberlin, B. (2002). Dispositions, ideological scripts, or motivated correction? Understanding ideological differences in attributions for social problems. *Journal of Personality and Social Psychology, 83,* 470–487.

Slocum-Bradley, N. R. (2008). Discursive production of conflict in Rwanda. In F. M. Moghaddam, R. Harré, & N. Lee (Eds.), *Global conflict resolution through positioning analysis* (pp. 207–226). New York: Springer.

Slone, M., & Hallis, D. (1999). The impact of political life events on children's psychological adjustment. *Anxiety, Stress, and Coping, 12,* 1–21.

Small, D. A., Lerner, J. S., & Fischhoff, B. (2006). Emotion priming and attributions for terrorism: Americans' reactions in a national field experiment. *Political Psychology, 27,* 289–298.

Smith, A. D. (1986). *The ethnic origin of nations.* Oxford: Blackwell.

(1991). *National identity.* London: Penguin.

(2000). *The nation in history: Historiographical debates about ethnicity and nationalism.* Cambridge: Polity Press.

(2008). *The cultural foundations of nations: Hierarchy, covenant, and republic.* Malden, MA: Blackwell.

Smith, C. A., & Lazarus, R. S. (1993). Appraisal components, relational themes, and the emotion. *Cognition and Emotion, 7,* 233–269.

Smith, E. R. (1993). Social identity and social emotions: Toward new conceptualization of prejudice. In D. M. Mackie & D. L. Hamilton (Eds.), *Affect, cognition and stereotyping: Interactive processes in group perception* (pp. 297–315). San Diego: Academic Press.

(1998). Mental representation and memory. In D. T. Gilbert, S. T. Fiske, & G. Lindzey (Eds.), *The handbook of social psychology* (4th ed., Vol. 1, pp. 391–445). Boston: McGraw Hill.

(1999). Affective and cognitive implications of a group becoming part of the self: New models of prejudice and of the self concept. In D. Abrams & M. A. Hogg (Eds.), *Social identity and social cognition* (pp. 183–196). Oxford: Blackwell.

Smith, E. R., & Mackie, D. M. (2008). Intergroup emotions. In M. Lewis, J. M. Haviland-Jones, & L. F. Barrett (Eds.), *Handbook of emotions* (3rd ed., pp. 428–439). New York: Guilford.

Smith, E. R., Seger, C. R., & Mackie, D. M. (2007). Can emotions be truly group level? Evidence regarding four conceptual criteria. *Journal of Personality and Social Psychology*, 93, 431–446.

Smith, H. J., & Ortiz, D. J. (2002). Is it just me? The different consequences of personal and group relative deprivation. In I. Walker & H. J. Smith (Eds.), *Relative deprivation: Specification, development, and integration* (pp. 91–115). Cambridge: Cambridge University Press.

Smith, M. B. (1968). Personality in politics: A conceptual map with application to the problem of political rationality. In O. Gareau (Ed.), *Political research and political theory* (pp. 77–101). Cambridge, MA: Harvard University Press.

Smith, S. (2001). *Allah's mountains: The battle for Chechnya* (Rev. ed.). London: I. B. Tauris.

Smith, T. W., & Kim, S. (2006). National pride in comparative perspective: 1995/96 and 2003/04. *International Journal of Public Opinion Research*, 18, 127–136.

Smith-Lovin, L. (1990). Emotion as the confirmation and disconfirmation of identity: An affect control model. In T. D. Kemper, *Research agendas in the sociology of emotions* (pp. 238–270). Albany: State University of New York Press.

Smyth, M. (2001). Putting the past in its place: Issues of victimhood and reconciliation in Northern Ireland's peace process. In N. Biggar (Ed.), *Burying the past: Making peace and doing justice after civil conflict* (pp. 107–130). Washington, DC: Georgetown University Press.

Sniderman, P. M. (1975). *Personality and democratic politics*. Berkeley: University of California Press.

Snow, D. A., & Benford, R. D. (1988). Ideology, frame resonance, and participant mobilization. In B. Klandermans, H., Kriesi, & S. Tarrow (Eds.), *From structure to action: Comparing social movement research across cultures* (Vol. 1, pp. 197–217). Greenwich, CT: JAI Press.

Snow, D. A., Soule, A., & Kriesi, H. (Eds.), (2004). *The Blackwell companion to social movements*. Malden, MA: Blackwell.

Snyder, C. R. (1994). *The psychology of hope*. New York: Free Press.

(Ed.), (2000). *Handbook of hope: Theory, measures, & applications*. San Diego: Academic Press.

Snyder, S. (2005). "Intractable" confrontation on the Korean Peninsula: A contribution to regional stability? In C. A. Crocker, F. O. Hampson, & P. Aall (Eds.), *Grasping the Nettle: Analyzing cases of intractable conflict* (pp. 319–341). Washington: United States Institute of Peace Press.

Solomon, S., Greenberg, J., & Pyszczynski, T. (1991). A terror management theory of social behavior: The psychological functions of self esteem and cultural worldviews. In M. P. Zanna (Ed.), *Advances of experimental social psychology* (Vol. 24, pp. 91–159). San Diego: Academic Press.

Solomon, Z. (1995). *Coping with war-induced stress: The Gulf War and the Israeli response*. New York: Plenum Press.

Solzhenitsyn, I. A. (1979). *The gulag archipelago* (3 Volumes). New York: Harper/ Collins.

Somerville, J. (1981). Patriotism and war. *Ethics*, 91, 568–578.

Sommers, S. R., & Ellsworth, P. C. (2000). Race in the courtroom: Perceptions of guilt and dispositional attributions. *Personality and Social Psychology Bulletin*, 26, 1367–1379.

Southgate, B. (2005). *What is history for?* New York: Routledge.
Spalding, R. J. (1999). From low-intensity war to low-intensity peace: The Nicaraguan peace process. In C. J. Arnson (Ed.), *Comparative peace processes in Latin America* (pp. 31–64). Stanford, CA: Stanford University Press.
Spanovic, M., Lickel, B., Denson, T. F., & Petrovic, N. (2010). Fear and anger as predictors of motivation for intergroup aggression: Evidence from Serbia and Republika Srpska. *Group Processes & Intergroup Relations, 13,* 725–739.
Spencer, J. (Ed.), (1990). *Sri Lanka: History and the roots of conflict.* New York: Routledge.
Sperber, D. (1996). *Explaining culture: A naturalistic approach.* Oxford: Blackwell.
Spiro, M. (1984). Some reflections on cultural determinism and relativism with special reference to emotion and reason. In R. A. Shweder & R. A. LeVine (Eds.), *Culture theory: Essays on mind, self, and emotion* (pp. 323–346). Cambridge: Cambridge University Press.
Springer, S. P., & Deutsch, G. (1998). *Left brain – right brain: Perspectives from cognitive neuroscience* (5th ed.). New York: W. H. Freeman.
Spyrou, S. (2002). Images of 'the other': The Turk in Greek Cypriot children's imaginations. *Race, Ethnicity & Education, 5*(3), 255–272.
Staal, M. A. (2004). *Stress, cognition and human performance: A literature review and conceptual framework.* Hanover MD: NASA, Center for Aerospace Information.
Staats, S. R., & Stassen, M. A. (1985). Hope: An affective cognition. *Social Indicators Research, 17,* 235–242.
Stagner, R. (1967). *Psychological aspects of international conflict.* Belmont, CA: Brooks/Cole.
Stangor, C., & McMillan, D. (1992). Memory for expectancy-congruent and expectancy-incongruent information: A review of the social and developmental literatures. *Psychological Bulletin, 111,* 42–61.
Statman, D. (2002). Humiliation, dignity and self-respect. In D. Kretzmer & E. Klein (Eds.), *The concept of human dignity in human rights law* (pp. 209–229). Amsterdam: Kluwer Press.
Staub, E. (1989). *The roots of evil: The origins of genocide and other group violence.* Cambridge: Cambridge University Press.
   (1996). Cultural-societal roots of violence: The examples of genocidal violence and of contemporary youth violence in the United States. *American Psychologist, 51,* 117–132.
   (1997). Blind versus constructive patriotism: Moving from embeddedness in the group to critical loyalty and action. In D. Bar-Tal & E. Staub (Eds.), *Patriotism in the lives of individuals and nations* (pp. 213–228). New York: Nelson-Hall.
   (1998). Breaking the cycle of genocidal violence: Healing and reconciliation. In J. H. Harvey (Ed.), *Perspectives on loss: A sourcebook* (pp. 231–238). Philadelphia: Brunner/Mazel.
   (1999). The roots of evil: personality, social conditions, culture and basic human needs. *Personality and Social Psychology Review, 3,* 179–192.
   (2000). Genocide and mass killing: Origins, prevention, healing, and reconciliation. *Political Psychology, 21,* 367–382.
   (2003). *The psychology of good and evil: the roots of benefiting and harming other.* Cambridge: Cambridge University Press.

(2005). The origins and evolution of hate, with notes on prevention. In R. J. Sternberg (Ed.), *The psychology of hate* (pp. 51–66). Washington, DC: American Psychological Association.

(2006). Reconciliation after genocide, mass killing and intractable conflict: Understanding the roots of violence, psychological recovery, and steps toward a general theory. *Political Psychology, 27*(6), 867–894.

(2011). *Overcoming evil: Genocide, violent conflict, and terrorism.* Oxford: Oxford University Press.

Staub, E., & Bar-Tal, D. (2003). Genocide, mass killing and intractable conflict: Roots, evolution, prevention and reconciliation. In D. O. Sears, L. Huddy, R. Jervis (Eds.), *Oxford handbook of political psychology* (pp. 710–751). New York: Oxford University Press.

Staub, E., & Pearlman, L. (2006). Advancing healing and reconciliation. In L. Barbanel & R. Sternberg (Eds.), *Psychological interventions in times of crisis* (pp. 213–243). New York: Springer.

(2009). Reducing intergroup prejudice and conflict: A commentary. *Journal of Personality and Social psychology, 96*, 588–594.

(in press). Healing and forgiveness and reconciliation after genocide and other collective violence. In R. G. Helmick & R. L. Peterson (Eds.), *Forgiveness and reconciliation: Religion, public policy and conflict transformation.* Radnor, PA: Templeton Foundation Press.

Staub, E., Pearlman, L. A., Gubin, A., & Hagengimana, A. (2005). Healing, reconciliation, forgiving and the prevention of violence after genocide or mass killing: An intervention and its experimental evaluation in Rwanda. *Journal of Social and Clinical Psychology, 24*(3), 297–334.

Staw, R. M., Sandelands, L. E., & Dutton, J. E. (1981). Threat-rigidity effects in organizational behavior: A multi-level analysis. *Administrative Science Quarterly, 26*, 501–524.

Stein, H. F. (1978). Judaism and the group-fantasy of martyrdom: The psycho-dynamic paradox of survival through persecution. *Journal of Psychohistory, 6*, 151–210.

Stenstrom, D. M., Lickel, B., Denson, T. F., & Miller, N. (2008). The roles of ingroup identification and outgroup entitativity in intergroup retribution. *Personality and Social Psychology Bulletin, 34*, 1570–1582.

Stephan, W. G. (1999). *Reducing prejudice and stereotyping in schools.* New York: Teachers College Press.

(2008). The road to reconciliation. In A. Nadler, T. Malloy, and J. Fisher (Ed.), *The social psychology of intergroup reconciliation* (pp. 369–394). Oxford: Oxford University Press.

Stephan, W. G., & Finlay, K. (1999). The role of empathy in improving intergroup relations. *Journal of Social Issues, 55*, 729–742.

Stephan, W. G., & Renfro, C. L. (2002). The role of threat in intergroup relations. In Mackie, D. M., & Smith, E. R. (Eds.), *From prejudice to inter-group emotions: Differential reactions to social groups* (pp. 191–207). New York: Psychology Press.

Stephan, W. G., Renfro, C. L., & Davis, M. D. (2008). The role of threat in intergroup relations. In U. Wagner, L. R. Tropp, G., Finchilescu, & C. Tredoux (Eds.), *Improving intergroup relations* (pp. 55–72). Oxford: Blackwell.

Stephan, W. G., & Stephan, C. W. (2000). An integrated threat theory of prejudice. In S. Oskamp (Ed.), *Reducing prejudice and discrimination* (pp. 225–246). Hillsdale, NJ: Erlbaum.
Sternberg, R., & Sternberg, K. (2008). *The nature of hatred.* Cambridge: Cambridge University Press.
Sternberg, R. J. (2003). A duplex theory of hate: Development and application to terrorism, massacres and genocide. *Review of General Psychology, 7,* 299–328.
  (Ed.), (2005). *The psychology of hate.* Washington, DC: American Psychological Association.
Stokke, K., & Ryntveit, A. K. (2000). The struggle of Tamil Ealam in Sri Lanka. *Growth and Change, 31,* 285–304.
Stone, M. (1997). *The agony of Algeria.* New York: Columbia University Press.
Stone, R. A. (1982). *Social change in Israel: Attitudes and events, 1967–79.* New York: Praeger.
Stotland, E. (1969). *The psychology of hope.* San Francisco: Jossey-Bass.
Strategic Foresight Group [Semu Bhatt, Devika Mistry] (2006). *Cost of conflict in Sri Lanka.* Mumbai, India: Strategic Foresight Group.
Struch, N., & Schwartz, S. H. (1989). Intergroup aggression: Its predictors and distinctness from in-group bias. *Journal of Personally and Social Psychology, 56,* 364–373.
Stryker, S., Owens, T. J., & White, R. W. (Eds.), (2000). *Self, identity, and social movement: Social movements, protest, and contention* (Vol. 13). Minneapolis: University of Minnesota Press.
Sturmer, S., & Simon, B. (2009). Pathways to collective protest: Calculation, identification, or emotion? A critical analysis of the role of group-based anger. *Journal of Social Issues, 65,* 681–706.
Suedfeld, P., & Jhangiani, R. (2009). Cognitive management in enduring international rivalry: The case of India and Pakistan. *Political Psychology, 30,* 937–951.
Suedfeld, P., Tetlock, P. E., & Ramirez, C. (1977). War, peace, and integrative complexity. *Journal of Conflict Resolution, 21,* 427–442.
Sullivan, D., Landau, M. J., Branscombe. N. R., & Rothschild, Z. K. (2012). Competitive victimhood as a response to accusations of ingroup harm doing. *Journal of Personality and Social Psychology, 102,* 778–795.
Sumner, W. G. (1906). *Folkways: A study of the sociological importance of usages, manners, customs, mores, and morals.* Boston: Ginn.
Svasek, M. (2005). *Mixed emotions: Anthropological studies of feeling.* New York: Berg.
Svenson, O., & Maule, J. A. (Eds.), (1993). *Time pressure and stress in human judgment and decision making.* New York: Plenum Press.
Swann, W. B., Jr., Gómez, Á., Huici, C., Morales, J. F., & Hixon, J. G. (2010). Identity fusion and self-sacrifice: Arousal as catalyst of extreme and altruistic group behaviour. *Journal of Personality and Social Psychology, 96,* 824–841.
Swann, W. B., Jr., Gómez, A., Seyle, C. D., Morales, J. F., & Huici, C. (2009). Identity fusion: The interplay of personal and social identities in extreme group behavior. *Journal of Personality and Social Psychology, 96,* 995–1011.
Sweeney, P. D., & Gruber, K. L. (1984). Subjective exposure: Voter information preferences and the Watergate affair. *Journal of Personality and Social Psychology, 46,* 1208–1221.

Swidler, A. (1986). Culture in action: Symbols and strategies. *American Sociological Review, 51*, 273–286.

Swirski, S. (2005). *The price of occupation*. Tel Aviv: ADVA Center & MAPA Publishers. (in Hebrew)

Swisher, C. E. (2004). *The truth about Camp David: The untold story about the collapse of the Middle East peace process*. New York: Nation Books.

Szalay, L. B., & Mir-Djalali, E. (1991). Image of the Enemy: Critical parameters, cultural variations. In R. W. Rieber (Ed.), *The psychology of war and peace: The image of the enemy* (pp. 213–250). New York: Plenum Press.

Sztompka, P. (1999). *Trust: A sociological theory*. Cambridge: Cambridge University Press.

Taber, C. S. (2003). Information processing and public opinion. In D. O. Sears, L. Huddy, & R. Jervis (Eds.), *Oxford handbook of political psychology* (pp. 433–476). Oxford: Oxford University Press.

Tajfel, H. (1972). Experiments in a vacuum. In J. Israel & H. Tajfel (Eds.), *The context of social psychology: A critical assessment*. London: Academic Press.

(1978). Social categorization, social identity and social comparison. In H. Tajfel (Ed.), *Differentiation between social groups* (pp. 61–76). London: Academic Press.

(1981). *Human groups and social categories*. Cambridge: Cambridge University Press.

(1982). *Social identity and intergroup relations*. Cambridge: Cambridge University Press; Paris: Maison des Sciences de l'Homme.

Tajfel, H., & Turner, J. C. (1986). The social identity theory of intergroup relations. In S. Worchel & W. G. Austin (Eds.), *Psychology of intergroup relations* (2nd ed., pp. 7–24). Chicago: Nelson-Hall.

Tam, T., Hewstone, M., Cairns, E., Tausch, N., Maio, G., & Kenworthy, J. (2007). The impact of intergroup emotions on forgiveness in Northern Ireland. *Group Processes and Intergroup Relations, 10*, 119–135.

Tam, T., Hewstone, M., Kenworthy, J. B., & Cairns, E. (2009). Intergroup trust in Northern Ireland. *Personality and Social Psychology Bulletin, 35*, 45–59.

Tam, T., Hewstone, M., Kenworthy, J. B., Cairns, E., Marinetti, C., Geddes, L., & Parkinson, B. (2008). Postconflict reconciliation: Intergroup forgiveness and implicit biases in Northern Ireland. *Journal of Social Issues, 64*, 303–320.

Tangney, J. P., & Fischer, K. W. (Eds.), (1995). *Self-conscious emotions: The psychology of shame, guilt, embarrassment, and pride*. New York: Guilford Press.

Tangney, J. P., Wagner, P., Fletcher, C., & Gramzow, R. (1992). Shamed into anger? The relation of shame and guilt to anger and self-reported aggression. *Journal of Personality and Social Psychology, 62*, 669–675.

Tarrow, S. (1998). *Power in movement: Social movements and contentious politics*. Cambridge: Cambridge University Press.

Tausch, N., Hewstone, M., Kenworthy, J. B., Psaltis, C., Schmid, K., Popan, J., Cairns, E., & Hughes, J. (2010). Secondary transfer effects of intergroup contact: Alternative accounts and underlying processes. *Journal of Personality and Social Psychology, 99*, 282–302.

Tausch, N., Kenworthy, J., & Hewstone, M. (2006). The contribution of intergroup contact to the reduction of intergroup conflict. In M. Fitzduff & C. E. Stout (Eds.), *The psychology of global conflicts: From war to peace* (Vol. 2, pp. 67–108). New York: Praeger.

Tavuchis, N. (1991). *Mea culpa: A sociology of apology and reconciliation.* Stanford, CA: Stanford University Press.
Taylor, D. M., & Jaggi, V. (1974). Ethnocentrism and causal attribution in a South Indian context. *Journal of Cross-Cultural Psychology, 5*, 162–171.
Taylor, D. M., Moghaddam, F. M., Gamble, I., & Zeller. E. (1987). Disadvantaged group responses to perceived inequity: From passive acceptance to collective action. *Journal of Social Psychology, 127*, 259–272.
Taylor, S. E. (1983). Adjustment to threatening events: A theory of cognitive adaptation. *American Psychologist, 38*, 1161–1173.
   (1991). Asymmetrical effects of positive and negative events: The mobilization-minimization hypothesis. *Psychological Bulletin, 110*, 67–85.
Teff-Seker, Y. (2012). *The representation of the Arab-Israeli conflict in Israeli children's literature.* Ph.D. dissertation, Hebrew University of Jerusalem. (in Hebrew)
Teitel, R. G. (2000). *Transitional justice.* Oxford: Oxford University Press,
   (2003a). Transitional justice genealogy. *Harvard Human Rights Journal, 16*(Spring), 69–94.
   (2003b). Transitional justice in a new era. *Fordham International Law Journal, 26*(4), 893–906.
Tessler, M. (2009). *A history of the Israeli-Palestinian conflict* (2nd ed.). Bloomington, IN: Indiana University Press.
Tetlock, P. E. (1989). Structure and function in political belief systems. In A. R. Pratkanis, S. J. Breckler, & A. G. Greenwald (Eds.), *Attitude structure and function* (pp. 129–152). Hillsdale, NJ: Erlbaum.
   (1999). Coping with tradeoffs: Psychological constraints and political implications. In L. A. McCubbins & S. L. Popkin (Eds.), *Elements of reason: Cognition, choice, and the bounds of rationality* (pp. 239–263). Cambridge: Cambridge University Press.
   (2002). Social functionalist frameworks for judgment and choice: Intuitive politicians, theologians, and prosecutors. *Psychological Review, 109*, 451–471.
   (2003). Thinking the unthinkable: Sacred values and taboo cognitions. *Trends in Cognitive Science, 7*, 320–324.
Tetlock, P. E., Kristel, O. V., Elson, S. B., Green, M. C., & Lerner, J. F. (2000). The psychology of the unthinkable: Taboo trade-offs, forbidden base-rates, and heretical counterfactuals. *Journal of Personality and Social Psychology, 78*(5), 853–870.
Thackrah, J. R. (2009). *The Routledge companion to military conflict since 1945.* New York: Routledge.
Theidon, K. (2006). Justice in transition. *Journal of Conflict Resolution, 50*(3), 433–457.
Thomas, R. (1999). *The Politics of Serbia in the 1990s.* New York: Columbia University Press.
Thompson, A. (Ed.), (2007). *The media and the Rwanda genocide.* London: Pluto Press.
Thompson, I., & Nadler, J. (2000). Judgmental biases in conflict resolution and how to overcome them. In M. Deutsch & P. T. Coleman (Eds.), *The handbook of conflict resolution: Theory and practice* (pp. 213–235). San Francisco: Jossey-Bass.
Thompson, M. (1997). Conflict, reconstruction and reconciliation: Reciprocal lessons for NGOs in Southern Africa and Central Africa. *Development in Practice, 7*, 505–509.
Thórisdóttir, H., & Jost, J. T. (2011). Motivated closed-mindedness mediates the effect of threat on political conservatism. *Political Psychology, 32*, 785–811.

Thorson, S. J. (1989). Introduction: Conceptual issues. In L. Kriesberg, T. A. Northup, & S. J. Thorson (Eds.), *Intractable conflicts and their transformation* (pp. 1–10). Syracuse: Syracuse University Press.

Tilly, C. (2002). *Stories, identities, and political change.* Oxford: Rowman & Littlefield Publishers.

Tindall, D. B. (2002). Social network, identification and participation in an environmental movement: Low-medium cost activism within the British Columbia wilderness preservation movement. *The Canadian Review of Sociology and Anthropology, 39,* 413–452.

Tint, B. (2010). History, memory, and intractable conflict. *Conflict Resolution Quarterly, 27*(3), 239–256.

Tonge, J. (2002). *Northern Ireland: Conflict and change* (2nd ed.). Harlow: Longman.

Tooby, J., & Cosmides, L. (1990). The past explains the present: Emotional adaptations and the structure of ancestral environments. *Ethology and Sociobiology, 11,* 375–424.

Torsti, P. (2007). How to deal with a difficult past? History textbooks supporting enemy images in post-war Bosnia and Herzegovina. *Journal of Curriculum Studies, 39*(1), 77–96.

Tracy, J. L., & Robins, R. W. (2004). Show your pride: Evidence for a discrete emotion expression. *Psychological Science, 15,* 194–197.

Tracy, J. L., Robins, R. W., & Schriber, R. A. (2009). Development of a FACS-verified set of basic and self-conscious emotion expressions. *Emotion, 9*(4), 554–559.

Tropp, L. R. (Ed.), (2012). *Oxford handbook of intergroup conflict.* New York: Oxford University Press.

Tropp, L. R., & Pettigrew, T. F. (2005). Relationships between intergroup contact and prejudice among minority and majority status groups. *Psychological Science, 16,* 651–653.

Tropp, L. R., & Wright, S. C. (2001). Ingroup identification as the inclusion of ingroup in the self. *Personality and Social Psychology Bulletin, 27,* 585–600.

Trouillot, M. (1995). *Silencing the past: Power and the production of history.* Boston: Beacon Press.

Tsur, N. (2013). Vocabulary and the discourse on the 1967 territories. In D. Bar-Tal & I. Schnell (Eds.), *The impacts of lasting occupation: Lessons from Israeli society* (pp. 471–506). New York: Oxford University Press.

Turner, J. C. (1991). *Social influence.* Milton Keynes: Open University.

(1999). Some current issues in research on social identity and self-categorization theories. In N. Ellemers, R. Spears, & B. Doosje (Eds.), *Social identity: Context, commitment, content* (pp. 6–34). Oxford: Blackwell.

Turner, J. C., Hogg, M. A., Oakes, P. J., Reicher, S. D., & Wetherell, M. S. (1987). *Rediscovering the social group: A self-categorization theory.* Cambridge, MA: Blackwell.

Turner, J. C., Oakes, P. J., Haslam, S. A., & McGarty, C. A. (1994). Self and collective: Cognition and social context. *Personality and Social Psychology Bulletin, 20,* 454–463.

Turner, R. N., Hewstone, M., Voci, A., Paolini, S., Christ, O. (2007). Reducing prejudice via direct and extended cross-group friendship. In W. Stroebe & M. Hewstone (Eds.), *European Review of Social Psychology* (Vol. 18, pp. 212–255). Hove, E. Sussex: Psychology Press.

Turney-High, H. H. (1949). *Primitive war.* Columbia: University of South Carolina Press.

Tutu, D. (1999). *No future without forgiveness.* New York: Doubleday.

Tversky, A., & Kahneman, D. (1986). Rational choice and the framing of decisions. *The Journal of Business*, 59(4), 251–278.
Tyerman. D. (1973). Crying for the moon Sri Lanka's new Press Council law. *Index on Censorship*, 2, 37–42.
Tyler, T. R., & Smith, H. J. (1998). Social justice and social movements. In D. T. Gilbert, S. T. Fiske, & G. Lindzey (Eds.), *The handbook of social psychology* (4th ed., Vol. 1, Chapter 1, pp. 595–632). New York: McGraw-Hill.
Ugolnik, A. (1983). The Godlessness within: Stereotyping the Russians. *The Christian Century*, 100, 1011–1014.
Ulug, O. M., & Cohrs, C. (2012). *Laypeople's representations of the Turkish-Kurdish conflict: A Q methodological exploration.* Manuscript submitted for publication.
UNESCO and a culture of peace: Promoting a global movement (1995). UN Resolutions A/RES/52/13-UNESCO. Paris: UNESCO Publishing.
United Nations. (1966a). *International covenant on civil and political rights.* The General Assembly Press.
  (1966b). *International covenant on economic, social and cultural rights.* The General Assembly Press.
  (1998). UN resolution (A/RES/52/13), culture of peace.
  (2003). *ABC: Teaching human rights: Practical activities for primary and secondary schools.* New York and Geneva: United Nations.
Urian, D. (1997). *The Arab in the Israeli drama and theatre.* Amsterdam: Harwood.
  (2013). The occupation as represented in the arts in Israel. In D. Bar-Tal & I. Schnell (Eds.), *The impacts of lasting occupation: Lessons from Israeli society* (pp. 438–470). New York: Oxford University Press.
Vallacher, R. R., Coleman, P. T., Nowak, A., & Bui-Wrzosinska, L. (2010). Rethinking intractable conflict: The perspective of dynamical systems. *American Psychologist*, 65, 262–278.
Vallone, R. P., Ross, L., & Lepper, M. R. (1985). The hostile media phenomenon: Biased perceptions of media bias in coverage of the Beirut massacre. *Journal of Personality and Social Psychology*, 49, 577–585.
Van den Berghe, P. L. (1981). *The ethnic phenomenon.* New York: Elsevier.
Van den Broek, H. (2004). BORROKA – The legitimation of street violence in the political discourse of radical Basque nationalists. *Terrorism and Political Violence*, 16, 714–736.
Van Dijk, T. A. (1998). *Ideology: A multidisciplinary study.* London: Sage.
Van Slyck, M. R., Stern, M., & Elbedour, S. (1999). Adolescents' beliefs about their conflict behavior. In A. Raviv, L. Oppenheimer, & D. Bar-Tal (Eds.), *How children understand war and peace: A call for international peace education* (pp. 208–230). San Francisco: Jossey-Bass.
Van Stekelenburg, J., & Klandermans, B. (2007). Individuals in movements: A social psychology of contention. In B. Klandermans & C. Roggeband (Eds.), *Social movements across disciplines* (pp. 157–204). New York: Springer.
van Zomeren, M., & Iyer, A. (2009). Introduction to the social and psychological dynamics of collective action. *Journal of Social Issues*, 65, 645–660.
van Zomeren, M., Postmes, T., & Spears, R. (2008). Toward an integrative Social Identity Model of Collective Action: A quantitative research synthesis of three socio-psychological perspectives. *Psychological Bulletin*, 134, 504–535.

(2012). On conviction's collective consequences: Integrating moral conviction with the social identity model of collective action. *British Journal of Social Psychology, 51*, 52–71.
van Zomeren, M., Spears, R., Fischer, A. H., Leach, C. W. (2004). Put your money where your mouth is! Explaining collective action tendencies through group-based anger and group efficacy. *Journal of Personality and Social Psychology, 87*, 649–664.
Vargas-Barón E., & Alarcón H. B. (2005). Educating children and youth in countries with conflicts. In E. Vargas-Barón & H. B. Alarcón (Eds.), *From Bullets to blackboard: Education for peace in Latin America and Asia* (pp. 3–39). Washington, DC: Inter-American Development Bank.
Vertzberger, Y. (1991). *The world in their minds*. Palo Alto, CA: Stanford University Press.
Vescio, T. K., Sechrist, G. B., & Paolucci, M. P. (2003). Perspective-taking and prejudice reduction: The mediational role of empathy arousal and situational attributions. *European Journal of Social Psychology, 33*, 455–472.
Vignoles, V. L., Chryssochoou, Z., & Breakwell, G. M. (2000). The distinctiveness principle: Identity, meaning, and the bounds of cultural relativity. *Personality and Social Psychology Review, 4*, 337–354.
Vogt, W. P. (1997). *Tolerance and education: Learning to live with diversity and difference*. Thousand Oaks, CA: Sage.
Volkan, V. D. (1988). *The need to have enemies & allies*. Northdale, NJ: Jason Aronson.
  (1997). *Bloodlines: From ethnic pride to ethnic terrorism*. New York: Farrar, Straus and Giroux.
  (1998). The three model: Psychopolitical dialogues and the promotion of coexistence. In E. Weiner (Ed.), *The handbook of interethnic coexistence* (pp. 343–358). New York: Continuum.
  (2001). Transgenerational transmissions and chosen traumas: An aspect of large-group identity. *Group Analysis, 34*(1), 79–97.
Vollhardt, J. R. (2012). Collective victimization. In L. R. Tropp (Ed.), *Oxford handbook of intergroup conflict* (pp. 136–157). New York: Oxford University Press.
Vollhardt, J. R., & Bilali, R. (2008). Social psychology's contribution to the psychological study of peace: A review. *Social Psychology, 39*, 12–25.
Volpe, M. R. (1998). Using town meetings to foster peaceful coexistence. In E. Weiner (Ed.), *The handbook of interethnic coexistence* (pp. 382–396). New York: Continuum.
Waganaar, W. A., & Groeneweg, J. (1990). The memory of concentration camp survivors. *Applied Cognitive Psychology, 4*, 77–88.
Walker, I., & Smith, H. J. (Eds.), (2002). *Relative deprivation: Specification, development and integration*. Cambridge: Cambridge University Press.
Walker, J. S. (1995). The origins of the Cold War in United States history textbooks. *The Journal of American History, 81*, 1652–1661.
Wallbott, H. G., & Scherer, K. S. (1986). The antecedents of emotional experiences. In K. S. Scherer, H. G. Wallbott, & A. B. Summerfeld (Eds.), *Experiencing emotion: A cross-cultural study* (pp. 69–83). Cambridge: Cambridge University Press.
Wallensteen, P. (2002). *Understanding conflict resolution: War, peace and the global system*. London: Sage.
Waller, J. (2002). *Becoming evil: How ordinary people commit genocide and mass killing*. New York: Oxford University Press.

Walsh, E. J. (1981). Resource mobilization and citizen protest in communities around Three Mile Island. *Social Problems, 29*, 1–21.
Walshe, P. (1970). *The rise of African nationalism in South Africa: The African national Congress, 1912–1952*. Berkeley: University of California Press.
Walzer, M. (1994). *Thick and thin: Moral argument at home and abroad*. Notre Dame, IN: University of Notre Dame Press.
　(2006). *Just and unjust wars: A moral argument with historical illustrations*. (4th edition). New York: Basic Books.
Wasserstein, B. (2003). *Israelis and Palestinians: Why do they fight? Can they stop?* New Haven, CT: Yale University Press.
Webb, W. M., & Worchel, P. (1986). Trust and distrust. In S. Worchel & W. G. Austin (Eds.), *Psychology of intergroup relations* (pp. 116–143). Chicago: Nelson-Hall.
Weiner, B. (1985). An attributional theory of achievement motivation and emotion. *Psychological Review, 92*, 548–573.
Weiner, E. (Ed.), (1998). *The handbook of interethnic coexistence*. New York: Continuum.
Weinstein, J. (2007). *Inside rebellion: The politics of insurgent violence*. Cambridge: Cambridge University Press.
Weiss, M. (1997). Bereavement, commemoration, and collective identity in contemporary Israeli society. *Anthropological Quarterly, 70*(2), 91–101.
Weiwen, Z., & Deshingkar, G. (1995). Improving Sino-Indo relations. In M. Krepon & A. Sevak (Eds.), *Crisis prevention, confidence building and reconciliation in South Asia* (pp. 227–238). New York: St. Martin's Press.
Wertsch, J. V. (2002). *Voices of collective remembering*. Cambridge: Cambridge University Press.
White, H. (1978). *Tropics of discourse: Essays in cultural criticism*. Baltimore, MD: John Hopkins University Press.
White, R. K. (1969). Three not-so-obvious contributions of psychology to peace. *Journal of Social Issues, 25*(4), 23–40.
　(1970). *Nobody wanted war: Misperception in Vietnam and other wars*. Garden City, NY: Anchor Books.
　(1984). *Fearful warriors: A psychological profile of U.S.-Soviet relations*. New York: Free Press.
　(1996). Why the Serbs fought: Motives and misperceptions. *Peace and Conflict: Journal of Peace Psychology, 2*(2), 109–128.
　(2004). Misperception and war. *Peace and Conflict: Journal of Peace Psychology, 10*(4), 399–409.
White, R. W., & Fraser, M. R. (2000). Personal and collective identity and long-term movement activism: Republican Sinn Fein. In S. Stryker, T. J. Owens, & R. W. White (Eds.), *Self, identity, and social movement: Social movements, protest, and contention* (Vol. 13, pp. 321–346). Minneapolis: University of Minnesota Press.
Whittaker, D. J. (1999). *Conflict and reconciliation in the contemporary world*. London: Routledge.
Wichert, S. (1994). *Northern Ireland in 1945*. London: Longman.
Wickham-Crowley, T. P. (1992). *Guerrillas and revolution in Latin America: A comparative study of insurgents and regimes since 1956*. Princeton, NJ: Princeton University Press.
Williams R. M. (1994). The sociology of ethnic conflicts: Comparative international perspectives, *Annual Review of Sociology, 20*, 49–79.

Willis, F. R. (1965). *France, Germany, and the New Europe, 1945–1963*. Palo Alto, CA: Stanford University Press.
Wilmer, F. (1998). The social construction of conflict and reconciliation in the former Yugoslavia. *Social Justice: A Journal of Crime, Conflict & World Order*, 25(4), 90–113.
Wilson, A. J. (2000). *Sri Lankan Tamil nationalism: Its origins and development in the nineties and twenties century*. Sydney: C. Hurst.
Wilson, J., & Stapleton, K. (2007). The discourse of resistance: Social change and policing in Northern Ireland. *Language in Society*, 36, 393–425.
Wiltfang, G. L., & McAdam, D. (1991). The costs and risks of social activism: A study of sanctuary movement activism. *Social Forces*, 69, 987–1010.
Winograd, T. (1972). Understanding natural language. *Cognitive Psychology*, 3, 1–191.
Winter, J. (1995). *Sites of memory, sites of mourning: The Great War in European cultural history*. Cambridge: Cambridge University Press.
  (2010). Thinking about silence. In E. Ben-Ze'ev, R. Ginio, & J. Winter (Eds.), *Shadows of war – A social history of silence in the twentieth century* (pp. 3–31). Cambridge: Cambridge University Press.
Winter, J., & Sivan E. (1999a). Setting the framework. In J. Winter & E. Sivan (Eds.), *War and remembrance in the twentieth century* (pp. 6–39). Cambridge: Cambridge University Press.
  (Eds.), (1999b). *War and remembrance in the twentieth century*. Cambridge: Cambridge University Press.
Wistrich, R. S. (Ed.), (1999). *Demonizing the other: Antisemitism, racism, and xenophobia*. Amsterdam: Harwood Academic Publishers.
Witztum, E., & Malkinson, R. (1993). Bereavement and perpetuation: The double face of the national myth. In R. Malkinson, S. S. Rubin, & E. Witztum (Eds.), *Loss and bereavement in Jewish society in Israel* (pp. 231–258). Jerusalem: Kana. (in Hebrew)
Wohl, M. J. A., & Branscombe, N. R. (2004). Importance of social categorization for forgiveness and collective guilt assignment for the Holocaust. In N. R. Branscombe & B. Doosje (Eds.), *Collective guilt: International perspectives* (pp. 284–305). Cambridge: Cambridge University Press.
Wohl, M. J. A., & Branscombe, N. R. (2005). Forgiveness and collective guilt assignment to historical perpetrator groups depend on level of social category inclusiveness. *Journal of Personality and Social Psychology*, 88, 288–303.
  (2008a). Collective angst: How threats to the future vitality of the ingroup shape intergroup emotion. In H. Wayment & J. Bauer (Eds.), *Transcending self-interest: Psychological explorations of the quiet ego* (pp. 171–181). Washington, DC: American Psychological Association.
  (2008b). Collective guilt for current ingroup transgressions. *Journal of Personality and Social Psychology*, 94(6), 988–1006.
  (2009). Group threat, collective angst, and ingroup forgiveness for the war in Iraq. *Political Psychology*, 30, 193–217.
Wohl, M. J. A., Branscombe, N. R., & Klar, Y. (2006). Collective guilt: Emotional reactions when one's group has done wrong or been wronged. *European Review of Social Psychology*, 17, 1–37.

Wohl M. J. A., Branscombe, N. R., & Reysen, S. (2010). Perceiving your group's future to be in jeopardy: Extinction threat induces collective angst and the desire to strengthen the ingroup. *Personality and Social Psychology Bulletin, 36,* 898–910.

Wohl, M. J. A., Hornsey, M. J., & Philpot, C. R. (2011). A critical review of official public apologies: Aims, pitfalls, and a staircase model of effectiveness. *Social Issues and Policy Review, 5,* 70–100.

Wohl, M. J. A., & Reeder, G. D. (2004). When bad deeds are forgiven: Judgments of morality and forgiveness for intergroup aggression. In J. P. Morgan (Ed.), *Focus on aggression research* (pp. 59–74). New York: Nova Science Publishers.

Wolfsfeld, G. (1997). *Media and political conflict: News from the Middle East.* Cambridge: Cambridge University Press.

(2004). *Media and path to peace.* Cambridge: Cambridge University Press.

Wolfsfeld, G., Frosh, P., & Awabdy, M. (2008). Covering death in conflicts: Coverage of the Second Intifada on Israeli and Palestinian television. *Journal of Peace Research, 45*(3), 401–417.

Wood, E. J. (2003). *Insurgent collective action and civil war in El Salvador.* Cambridge: Cambridge University Press.

Woodward, S. L. (1999). Bosnia after Dayton: Transforming a compromise into a state. In R. L. Rothstein (Ed.), *After the peace: Resistance and reconciliation* (pp. 139–166). Boulder, CO: Lynne Rienner.

Worchel, S. (1999). *Written in blood: Ethnic identity and the struggle for human harmony.* New York: Worth.

Worchel, S., Morales, J. F., Paez, D., & Deschamps J. C. (Eds.), (1998). *Social identity: International perspectives.* Thousand Oaks, CA: Sage.

World Development Report 2011: Conflict, security and development (2011). Washington, DC: The World Bank.

Wright, S. C. (2001). Strategic collective action: Social psychology and social change. In R. Brown & S. L. Gaertner (Eds.), *Intergroup processes: Blackwell handbook of social psychology* (Vol. 4, pp. 409–430). Oxford: Blackwell.

Wright, S. C., Taylor, D. M., & Moghaddam, F. M. (1990). Responding to membership in a disadvantaged group: From acceptance to collective protest. *Journal of Personality and Social Psychology, 58,* 994–1003.

Wright, S. C., & Tropp, L. R. (2002). Collective action in response to disadvantage: Intergroup perceptions, social identification and social change. In I. Walker & H. J. Smith (Eds.), *Relative deprivation: Specification, development and integration* (pp. 200–237). Cambridge: Cambridge University Press.

Wyer, R. S., Jr., & Srull, T. K. (1980). The processing of social stimulus information: A conceptual integration. In R. Hastie, T. M. Ostrom, E. B. Ebbesen, R. S. Wyer, R. S. Hamiton, & D. E. Carston (Eds.), *Person memory: The cognitive basis of social perception* (pp. 227–300). Hillsdale, NJ: Erlbaum.

(1989). *Memory and cognition in its social context.* Hillsdale, NJ: Erlbaum.

Yadgar, Y. (2004). *Out story: The national narratives in the Israeli press.* Haifa: Haifa University Press.

Yahya, A. (1999). *The Palestinian refugees.* Ramallah: PACE.

Yanay, N. (2002). Understanding collective hatred. *Analyses of Social Issues and Public Policy, 2,* 53–60.

Yaniv, A. (Ed.), (1993a). *National security and democracy in Israel*. Boulder, CO: Lynne Rienner.

(1993b). *A question of survival: The military and politics under siege*. In A. Yaniv (Ed.), National security and democracy in Israel (pp. 81–103). Boulder, CO: Lynne Rienner.

Yilmaz, M. (2005). The Cyprus conflict and the Annan plan: Why one more failure? *Edge Academic Review, 5*(1), 29–39.

Yogev, E. (2010). A crossroads: History textbooks and curricula in Israel. *Journal of Peace Education, 7*, 1–14.

Yzerbyt, V. Y., Dumont, M., Gordijn, E., & Wigboldus, D. (2002). Intergroup emotions and self-categorization: The impact of perspective-taking on reactions to victims of harmful behavior. In D. M. Mackie & E. R. Smith (Eds.), *From prejudice to intergroup emotions: Differentiated reactions to social groups* (pp. 67–87). Philadelphia: Psychological Press.

Yzerbyt, V., Dumont, M., Wigboldus, D., & Gordin, E. (2003). I feel for us: The impact of categorization and identification on emotions and action tendencies. *British Journal of Social Psychology, 42*, 533–549.

Zafran, A. (2002). *Measuring Israeli ethos of conflict: Antecedents and outcomes*. Master's thesis, Tel Aviv University.

Zafran, A., & Bar-Tal, D. (2002). *The dominance of fear over hope in situations of intractable conflict: The Israeli case*. Paper presented at the annual meeting of the International Society of Political Psychology, Berlin.

(2003). Holocaust memory and its implications for peace process: The influence of fear and self-image as a victim on the Israeli security beliefs. In M. Al-Haj & U. Ben-Eliezer (Eds.), *In the name of security: The sociology of peace and war in Israel in changing times* (pp. 329–367). Haifa: Haifa University Press. (in Hebrew).

Zajonc R. B. (1980). Feeling and thinking: Preferences need no inferences. *American Psychologist, 35*, 151–175.

(1998). Emotions. In D. Gilbert, S. T. Fiske, & G. Lindzey (Eds.), *The handbook of social psychology* (4th ed., Vol. 1, pp. 591–632). Boston: McGraw-Hill.

Zalaquett, J. (1999). Truth, justice, and reconciliation: Lessons for the international community. In C. J. Arnson (Ed.), *Comparative peace processes in Latin America* (pp. 341–361). Stanford, CA: Stanford University Press.

Zaller, J. (1992). *The nature and origins of mass opinion*. Cambridge: Cambridge University Press.

Zand, S. (2004). *The historian, the time and the imagination*. Tel Aviv: Am Oved. (in Hebrew).

Zanna, M. P., & Rempel, J. K. (1988). Attitudes: A new look at an old concept. In D. Bar-Tal & A. Kruglanski (Eds.), *The social psychology of knowledge* (pp. 315–334). Cambridge: Cambridge University Press.

Zartman, I. W. (2000). Ripeness: The hurting stalemate and beyond. In P. C. Stern & D. Druckman (Eds.), *International conflict resolution after the cold war* (pp. 225–250). Washington, DC: National Academy Press.

(2005). Analyzing intractability. In C. A., Crocker, F. O. Hampson, & P. R. Aall (Eds.), *Grasping the nettle: Analyzing cases of intractable conflict* (pp. 47–64). Washington, DC: United States Institute of Peace Press.

(Ed.), (2007). *Peacemaking in international conflict: Methods and techniques* (Rev. ed.). Washington, DC: United States Institute of Peace.

Zertal, I. (2005). *Israel's Holocaust and the politics of nationhood.* Cambridge: Cambridge University Press.

Zertal, I., & Eldar, A. (2007). *Lords of the land: the war over Israel's settlements in the occupied territories, 1967–2007.* New York: Nation Books.

Zerubavel, Y. (1995). *Recovered roots: Collective memory and the making of Israeli national tradition.* Chicago: University of Chicago Press.

Zheng, W. (2008). National humiliation, history education, and the politics of historical memory: Patriotic education campaign in China. *International Studies Quarterly, 52,* 783–806.

Zhou, Q., Valiente, C., & Eisenberg, N. (2003). Empathy and its measurement. In S. J. Lopez & C. R. Snyder (Eds.), *Positive psychological assessment: A handbook of models and measures* (pp. 269–284). Washington, DC: American Psychological Association.

Zohar, N. (1972). *Arab's image in a reader.* Master's thesis, Hebrew University of Jerusalem. (in Hebrew)

Zomer, E., & Bleich, A. (Eds.). (2005). *Mental health in the shadow of terror: The Israeli experience.* Tel Aviv: Ramot – Tel Aviv University. (in Hebrew)

Index

Abbass, Ferhart, 73, 82
ability of the rival, perceptions of, 115–116
Abromovich, Arviv, 265
Abu-Lughod, L., 147
academic research, monitoring and control of, 284–285, 286
acceptance between former rivals, 373
action
    action mobilization, 78
    decision to act, 11–12, 69
    escalation as response to, 116
    personal motivations to act, 84
active bystanders, 410
addition (information processing), 318
Adorno, T. W., 210
African National Congress (ANC), 71, 96, 102, 302–303
agents of conflict. *See also* leaders
    as barrier to peaceful resolution, 448–449
    blocking of alternative information, 284, 286, 315
    construction of narratives of conflict, 254
    as invested in the conflict, 301
    as mobilizers of society for conflict, 91–92, 198, 448–449
    transitional justice and, 394–395
agents of peace, 360, 408, 429–430
aggression and anger, 239
Agnew, J., 56–57
Al-Aqsa mosque, 177–178
Algeria-France conflict
    change in French policies, 303
    costs of continuation of, 332–333
    epistemic basis for, 73, 82
    escalation of, 114

French censorship, 285
French manipulation of collective memory of, 165–166
French refusal to apologize for, 425
French unity in, 199
justification of goals in, 180, 279
major events in, 114
relative deprivation and, 69
violence in, 442
violent efforts to stop peacemaking, 361–362
Allport, G., 236, 402–403
Altemeyer, B., 212
alternative culture and openness of society, 274
alternative information. *See also* information
    barriers to dissemination of, 315, 316–317, 441, 446–447
    omission and marginalization of, 255, 256
    openness to and peacemaking process, 329–331
    peace movement and dissemination of, 406–407
    reflective thinking and, 413
alternative narratives
    degree of adherence to, 305
    in institutionalization phase of peacemaking process, 356
    in legitimization phase of peacemaking process, 353–354
ambiguous information, 255–256, 303, 307–308, 318
ambiguous situations, 10–11, 95–96
Amir, Y., 418
amnesty for perpetrators of immoral acts, 395, 419–420
Andrews, M., 419

547

anger. *See also* negative emotions
  in collective emotional orientation, 222, 225, 236–237, 238–240
  forgiveness and reconciliation and, 384, 403–404
  in mobilizing messages, 93–94
  vengeance and, 109–110
Annapolis peace summit, 293
Antebi, Dikla, 235
Antonovsky, A., 127
apartheid. *See* South African conflict
apologies, 384, 423–426
appraisal tendency framework, 221
appraisal theory, 129
Arab Information Center, 167
Arab-Israeli conflict. *See* Israeli-Arab conflict
Arabs
  delegitimization in Hebrew literature, 231, 265–267
  fear of, 232–233
  portrayal in Israeli textbooks, 268–269
Arafat, Yasser, 191–192, 197, 361, 418
archives, closure of, 287
Arian, A., 233
Armenian genocide, 165–166, 287
art. *See* cultural products
Arunatilake, N., 50
Arutiunov, Sergei, 106
Arviv-Abramovich, R., 204
Ashmore, R. D., 275
Asmal, K., 379
Assmann, J., 139
associations, manipulation of, 164
asymmetrical conflicts
  dissemination of collective memory and, 168
  equalization of rivals in, 374
  escalation of conflict and, 114–115, 116
  failure of powerful side to win, 58
  humiliation of the weaker rival, 241
  immoral acts and peace building, 369–370, 380–381
  levels of societal censoring in, 288
  mobilization and, 79
  overview, 26–29
  socio-political change in aftermath of, 390–392
  violence and, 102–103
Atran, S., 177–178, 241–242
atrocities. *See* immoral acts; violence
Atsumi, T., 165
attainability of goals, 6

attitudes
  collective identity and, 83
  defined, 19
  regarding violation of Palestinian human rights, 186
Auerbach, T., 382, 385
authoritarian societies, peacemaking process in, 350
autobiographical memory, 159–160
automatic activation of societal beliefs, 306
automatic mental processes, 129, 215–217, 226
Averill, J. R., 239, 243
axiological rules of behavior, 216–217
Azar, Edward, 35

Balkan Wars. *See* Yugoslavia conflict
Ballachey, E. L., 17
Bandaranaike, S. W. R. D., 89
Bandura, A., 92, 109–110, 250, 312
Barak, Ehud, 11, 34–35, 114
Baram, H., 303, 305
Bar Kochva rebellion, 155, 271
Barreto, M., 191
barriers to conflict resolution. *See* conflict resolution, socio-psychological barriers to
Bar-Tal, Daniel, 83–84, 128–129, 169–170, 184, 187, 195, 201, 204, 207, 225, 232–233, 243, 277, 304, 308, 311, 317, 342
Barzani, Massoud, 199
Basque conflict, 111–112, 113
Batson, C. D., 343, 344
Battle of Kosovo, 18, 89–90, 147, 154–155
Bauman, C. W., 87
Baumeister, R. F., 164, 183–184
Becker, J. C., 67–68
Beeri, E., 103
Begin, Menachem, 169
behavior. *See also* functional beliefs, emotions, and behaviors; moral codes of behavior
  emotional arousal of, 214–215
  societal beliefs' influence over, 309
beliefs. *See also* functional beliefs, emotions, and behaviors; societal beliefs
  compromising beliefs, 337–338
  instigating and mediating beliefs, 327–329
  overview, 18–19
Ben-Ari, R., 418
Ben-Ezer, E., 231, 265
Benford, R. D., 62–63
Ben Shabat, C., 303–304
Ben-Yehuda, N., 155

Ben Ze'ev, E., 317
Bercovitch, J., 12
Berkowitz, L., 239
Bernard, V. W., 313
Berntson, G. G., 215
bias
   bias perception, 309–310
   in construction of conflict narratives, 254, 439–440
   in information processing, 306, 318
biased assimilation, 311
Bilali, R., 165–166
biographical memory, 159–160
blame, 157, 164, 239
Blatz, C. W., 424
Bleich, A., 122
blind patriotism, 196, 198
Bloody Sunday (Northern Ireland), 34, 98, 114
Boehnke, K., 111
Bond, H. M., 258
Borovski-Sapir, L., 201
Bosnia-Herzegovina conflict. *See also* Serbia; Yugoslavia conflict
   collective memory in, 147
   peace education in, 415
   reconciliation process, 384, 387, 397
   transitional justice in, 395
   violence in, 40
Botcharova, O., 109–110
Botha, P. W., 302–303, 329
brain, localization of emotions in, 217–218
Branscombe, N. R., 157, 347
Brazil, 11
Brecke, P., 380, 385
Brit Shalom (peace organization), 352
Brockner, J., 57
Brouneus, K., 422
Brown, R., 186, 251, 313, 345, 384
Brubaker, R., 11, 102
Bruner, J., 22
Bui-Wrzosinska, L., 36
Burgess, G., 64
Burgess, H., 64
Burn, S. M., 308
Burton, J. W., 354–355
Burundi conflict, 94–95, 167, 410
Bush, George W., 10–11

Cacioppo, J. T., 215
Cairns, E., 187, 341, 384–385

Campaign for Social Justice (Northern Ireland), 85–86
Campbell, D. T., 191
Camp David summit (2000), 11, 152–153, 262
Canetti, D., 123, 128–129
Castano, E., 191, 313, 384
category representation, 344
Catholic-Protestant conflict. *See* Northern Ireland conflict
Catlin, G., 243
Čehajić, S., 186, 251, 313, 345, 384
censorship, 164, 264–265, 285, 316–317
change
   of collective memory, 168–172
   in ethos of conflict, 201–204
   ethos of conflict and resistance to, 211–212
Chapman, A. R., 421
charismatic leaders, 91–92
Chechen-Russian conflict
   centrality of, 46
   Chechen collective experiences, 119–120
   collective emotional response to violence in, 106
   delegitimization of the rival in, 185
   humiliation of Russians in, 241
   identification of conflict, 62
   investment in, 50
   justness of goals in, 178
   longevity of, 16, 35
   manipulation of collective memory in, 165
   mobilizing messages in, 88–89
   perceived unsolvability of, 49
   political instability and, 71
   Russian control of information about, 284
   threat perception as barrier to resolution of, 296–297
   violence in, 41
   zero-sum approach to, 44
Chelvanayakam, S. J. F., 179
Chernyak-Hai, L., 187
children. *See also* educational institutions and materials
   children's literature, 231, 266–267
   peace education and, 411
Chon, K. K., 243
chosen traumas and chosen glories, 146–148, 182–183
Cisłak, A., 366
civilian deaths and casualties. *See also* genocide; mass killings/massacres
   as characteristic of intractable conflict, 441

civilian deaths and casualties (*cont.*)
  in Chechen-Russian conflict, 41
  in Israeli-Arab conflict, 103, 197
  as moral issue, 105
  in Northern Ireland conflict, 41
Claassen, C., 404
clarity of situations and mobilization, 95–96
closure of societies in conflicts, 281–282, 441, 454
coexistence, peaceful, 367–369, 374, 385
cognitive adaptive approach, 127
cognitive factors for freezing of societal beliefs, 290–291
Cohen, Adir, 231, 266
Cohrs, J. C., 111
cold peace, 325, 366, 367–369, 401
Cold War, 308, 310
Coleman, P. T., 36, 48, 71, 122
collective action theory, 69
collective deprivation, 68
collective efficacy, 69, 92–93
collective emotional orientation
  characteristics and development of, 223–226
  collective anger, 238–240
  collective angst, 234
  collective fear, 226–230
  collective fear in Israeli Jewish society, 230–234
  collective hatred, 236–238
  collective hope, 243–244
  collective humiliation, 240–242
  collective memory and, 141–142, 213–214, 222, 224, 231–232
  collective pride, 242–243
  as component of socio-psychological infrastructure, 130–131
  emotions as basis of actions, 214–215
  negative emotions as dominant over positive, 217–219
  overview, 23–24, 213–214, 244
  positive emotional orientation and reconciliation, 389–390
  primary and secondary emotions, 215–217
  shared emotions, 219–223
  siege mentality, 235
  violence and, 105–106
collective experience, 21, 118–124
collective goals, 6
collective guilt, 345–348
collective identity
  collective memory and, 157–158

culture of conflict and, 274–278
definition and theory of, 83–84
of ethnic groups, 12–14
reconciliation and, 380
violence and, 105–106
collective master narratives, 145, 439
collective memory. *See also* commemoration; ideology; narrative, generally
  changes in, 142, 161, 167–172
  characteristics of, 140–142
  collective emotional orientation and, 141–142, 213–214, 222, 224, 231–232
  common history vs., 426
  competing collective memories of rivals, 140, 166–168
  as component of socio-psychological infrastructure, 130
  contents not related to the conflict, 153–156
  contents related to the conflict, defined, 137–138
  emotions and, 156–157
  escalation of conflicts and, 118
  ethos of conflict and, 212
  ethos of peace and, 388–389
  functions of, 157–158, 172–173
  incorporation of rival's perspective, 356
  mobilization and, 88, 90
  nature of, 145–148
  protractedness of conflict and, 51–52
  reconciliation and, 382–383
  selectivity of, 163–166
  social identity and, 142–144
  transmission and dissemination of, 159–163
  truth commissions and, 419
  types of, 138–140
  victimization as encoded in, 187–188
  violence and, 43
collective needs, 65–66. *See also* needs
collective self-healing, 386–387. *See also* healing
collective self-image, 164, 169, 178, 190–192, 237–238, 250
colonialism, termination of, 356–357
commemoration
  as active remembering, 139–140
  ethos of conflict and, 175, 269
  of fallen comrades, 150–151, 299
  Israeli tradition of, 269
  as transmission of collective memory, 162
Commission for Historical Clarification (Guatemala), 110–111
commonality between former rivals, 374

commonality of beliefs and attitudes, 83
common fate, sense of, 83–84, 275–276
communicative memory, 139
comprehensibility of intractable conflicts, 126–127
comprehensibility of messages of mobilization, 86
compromise. *See also* conflict resolution; zero-sum nature of intractable conflicts
　compromising beliefs, 337–338
　emotions and, 229, 233, 238, 240, 293, 341–342
　ethos of conflict and resistance to, 211–212
　goals of conflict and, 72–73, 75–76, 158, 177–178, 327
　investment in conflict and resistance to, 300, 362
　Israeli peace movement and, 355
　losses of continuing conflict vs. losses of, 335
　nature of intractable conflicts and resistance to, 36, 42, 43–45, 59–60
　new socio-psychological repertoire and, 325
　as possible in tractable conflicts, 37
　symbolic compromises, 234, 238, 293
confirmation bias, 306–307
conflict
　decision to act, 11–12
　defined, 4–5
　eruption of, 14–17
　human nature and, 436–437
　identification of a situation as, 7–11
　positive aspects of, 7, 434–435
　socio-psychological framework of, 17–26, 29–30
conflict resolution. *See also* institutionalized mechanisms of conflict resolution
　conflict settlement vs., 365–366
　constructive use of anger and, 240
　defined, 325
　existential threats and, 37–39
　nonviolent means of, 42
　as peace education component, 412–413
　perceived impossibility of, 47–49, 57
　psychological change leading to, 59
conflict resolution, socio-psychological barriers to
　closure process, 281–282, 315–318
　cognitive and motivational factors, 290–291
　consequences of, 306
　contextual factors, 294–297
　emotional factors, 291–294
　at the individual level, 283–290, 319
　investments in conflict as factor, 299–303
　mistrust and habituation as factors, 297–299
　overview and summary, 283–290, 306, 450
　societal mechanisms, 315, 319
conflict settlement phase of peace building, 364–366
conformity, 198–199, 315–316
Congo conflict, 410
Connerton, P., 141
conscious emotions. *See* secondary appraisal/emotions
Conservation of Resources (COR) theory, 121
conservatism, 211–212, 229, 290, 348
construction of conflict-supporting narratives. *See also* narratives of conflict
　methods of, 255–256
　principles of, 254
constructive patriotism, 196
contact theory, 402–403
contact with the rival, 384, 402–404
context of intractable conflicts
　context as threat to social identity, 75
　context defined, 33–34
　context for evolvement of goals, 63–64
　context of conflict, 35–36
　contextual framing, 164
　facilitating conditions for peacemaking, 331–334
　overview, 118–119
　peace-building process and duality of, 359–364
　transitional context, 34–35
continuity with the past, 83, 158, 228, 292
contradictory information, 255, 303, 306–307, 318. *See also* alternative information
control over one's life, 124
cooperation between former rivals, 374–375, 398–399, 416–417
coordinated collective activity, 84
coping with conflict, 115, 118, 125, 126–130, 226–230, 239, 248–249, 292
core cultural ideas, 219–220
Corradi, 227
correspondence bias, 310–311
costs to society of continuing conflict, 332–334
Council for Peace and Security (Israeli organization), 352, 358
counternarratives, 22–23, 140, 160, 167–168, 169, 198
Crighton, E., 75, 234

Crimean conflict, 82–83
Crutchfield, R. S., 17
cues
   contextual cues, 98–99
   emotion and, 20, 23–24, 215, 217, 223–226, 228, 292, 306
   for identifying conflict situation, 9
cultural products
   collective emotional orientation and, 224, 231
   collective memory and, 139, 142, 160–161
   control of information in, 287–288
   dissemination of culture of conflict, 272
   enemy depictions in, 182
   societal beliefs in, 175, 200–204, 260, 265–267
culture
   cultural differences in interpretation of conflict situation, 10
   cultural heritage, 14
   cultural influence over shared emotions, 219–220
   cultural memory, 139
   cultural symbols, 258
   defined, 257–258
   terror management and, 128
culture of conflict
   as barrier to peaceful resolution, 448
   characteristics of, 270–274
   construction of conflict supporting narratives, 254–257
   degree of homogeneity of, 261–262
   education and perpetuation of, 52
   evolution of, 257–261, 269–270, 273–274, 278–280
   features of, 131–132
   functions of socio-psychological infrastructure, 247–253, 278–280, 431–432
   hegemony of, 452
   identity and, 274–278
   in Israeli Jewish society, 262–270
   violence and, 43, 149–150
culture of peace, 371, 401, 415
cycles of violence
   culture of conflict and, 133, 280, 318–319
   expectations and, 308–309
   humiliation and, 94–95
   instigation and reaction in, 446
   societal changes and, 451–452
   variations in level of violence, 103–113
   victimhood and, 109–110
Cyprus conflict
   collective memory in, 144, 161–162, 171–172
   culture of conflict in, 273
   delegitimization of alternative information sources, 286
   delegitimization of the rival in, 182–183, 185
   habituation to conflict as barrier to peacemaking, 299
   incentives for Turkey to resolve, 333
   justification of conflict goals, 178
   mobilization in, 96
   protractedness of, 52
Czech-German reconciliation, 417, 426, 427
Czechoslovakia, dissolution of, 69

Darby, 335–336
David, O., 83–84
Dawson, 226–227
Dayton Peace Agreement, 333, 395, 397
death. *See also* loss of life
   culture as buffer for fear of, 128
   salience of and freezing of societal beliefs, 296
Deaux, K., 275
Deci, E. L., 123
decision-making processes
   collective emotional orientation and, 224, 225–226
   decision to act, 11–12, 69
   escalation of conflict and, 113–114
   negativity bias and, 293
de Clerk, F. W., 302–303, 336–337, 357, 418, 425
deescalation of conflict, 3, 55, 114, 323–324, 340, 354. *See also* escalation of intractable conflicts; peacemaking
defeat and collective memory, 149–150
defense budgets, 51
Degani-Hirsch, 308
de Gaulle, Charles, 303, 332–333, 361–362
dehumanization of the rival
   of Chechens, 297
   fear and, 231
   moral disengagement and, 109–110
   of Palestinians, 231, 233
   rationalization of violence and, 109–110, 186, 191, 313
   as theme in ethos of conflict, 181
   zero-sum perceptions and, 44
delegitimization of alternative information sources, 285–286
delegitimization of the rival

in collective memory, 149
defined, 180–181
examples of, 184–186
form and function of, 181–184
glorification of the ingroup vs., 251–252, 263–264
hatred and, 236–238
Israeli delegitimization of Arabs, 265–267, 342
legitimization vs., 339
moral disengagement and, 313
obedience and, 316
violence and, 251, 443–444
democracy and democratization
as American societal belief, 23
as condition for reconciliation, 396
political restructuring, 396
as weakened by intractable conflicts, 453, 455
denial of wrong doing, 164, 165
Denson, T., 108
depersonalization, 80, 340
deprivation
escalation of conflict and, 114–115
in messages of mobilization, 87
overview, 66–69
of psychological needs, 123–125
recognition of and setting of goals, 70–72, 76
de Rivera, J., 220
desensitization to violence, 110
Deutsch, M., 43, 412
Devine-Wright, P., 242–243
Dgani-Hirsch, A., 207
diaspora of the Jews, 188, 268–269
Diehl, P. F., 53
differences, respect for, 374
differentiation between ingroup and rival, 251–252, 309
differentiation of the rival, 340
diplomatic relations, 397–399
direct violence, 112
disarmament, 392–393
discrimination
of Chechens, 119–120
epistemic basis for goals against, 288
gender discrimination, 455
in Kurdish conflict, 87–88
moral responsibility for, 369–370
in Northern Ireland, 85–86, 393
reconciliation and ending of, 374, 397
in Rwanda, 148

in South Africa, 71, 425
in Sri Lanka conflict, 151
dissent in peace-building process, 378
distortion in narratives of conflict, 254, 318, 440
distributive injustice, 67, 397
Dome of the Rock, 177–178
dominant narrative, 22–23
Doosje, B., 83–84
double standards, 310, 440, 445
doves. See hawks and doves
Downes, C., 123
drama and film, 267
Drori, E., 232–233, 342
duality of society over peacemaking process, 354, 356, 358
Dweck, C., 240
dynamic nature of intractable conflicts, 35

"early risers" in peacemaking process, 350–353
economic issues in intractable conflicts. See also political-economic structure
economic cooperation of formal rivals, 397–399
economic mobilization for conflict, 452
economic unpredictability, 252–253
hardship resulting from conflict, 119
reconciliation and reconstruction of the economy, 397
redirection of resources to military, 454–455
educational institutions and materials
collective emotional orientation and, 224
culture of conflict in, 260, 268–269
culture of peace in, 375–376
ethos of conflict in textbooks, 204, 268–269
major events in, 146
omissions in textbooks, 165
peace-building role of, 410–416
peace education, 406
as perpetuating conflicts, 52, 58
sense of fear in textbooks, 252
symbols of conflict in textbooks, 132
transformation of collective memory in textbooks, 170–172, 427
as transmitters of collective memory, 161–162
Education for Mutual Understanding (Northern Ireland), 415
Education for Peace (Bosnia and Herzegovina), 415
Eidelson, J. I., 190
Eidelson, R. J., 190

El Asmar, Fouzi
Elcheroth, G., 101
electoral system reform, 396
Elizur, Y., 314
Ellemers, N., 83–84, 191
Eller, J. D., 13
El Salvador conflict, 81, 92–93, 287, 301
emotions. *See also* collective emotional orientation; *specific emotions*
  as basis for action, 214–215
  emotional climate vs. emotional culture, 220
  freezing of societal beliefs and, 291–294
  negativity bias, 217–219, 292–294, 334
  overview, 19–20
  about participation in collective action, 67–68
  in response to collective threats, 82
  vengeance in response to, 107–108
empathy for the rival, 109, 163, 186, 188, 311–312, 318, 343–345, 382, 403–404
"enemy" as delegitimizing term, 182, 444
entrepreneurs. *See* agents of conflict; agents of peace
epistemic authorities, 34–35, 91–92, 260
epistemic basis
  collective memory and, 138, 158
  conflict goals, 72–74, 91, 176–177
  ethos as providing, 174
  international moral codes and, 288
  for peaceful resolution of conflict, 351
  for unequal relations, 70–71
epistemic psychological needs, 125, 248–249
equalization of the rival, 339–340, 374, 384
Eretz Israel, 268, 337
eruption of intractable conflicts
  agents of conflict, 91–92
  context for evolvement of goals of conflict, 63–64, 100
  context of mobilization process, 95–98
  epistemic basis for goals of conflict, 72–74
  goals in conflict, 64–66, 149
  mobilization and emotions, 93–95
  mobilization and identity, 79–84
  mobilization for the conflict, 76–79, 84–86
  mobilization messages, 86–90
  overview, 61–63, 98–99
  recognition of deprivation and setting goals, 70–72, 100
  relative deprivation and conflict, 66–69

socio-psychological repertoire and, 99
escalation of intractable conflicts. *See also* violence and escalation of intractable conflicts
  collective emotional involvement and, 105–106
  collective experience and, 118–124
  conditions leading to escalation, 114–118
  evolution of socio-psychological repertoire and, 126–130
  irreversibility of conflict situation, 107
  overview, 101, 113–114
  rationalization of violence, 108–111
  role of leaders in, 449–450
  salience of conflict and, 209
  sanctity of life and, 104–105
  socio-psychological framework and, 130–133
  vengeance and, 107–108
  violence in, 101–104
ETA (Basque Homeland and Freedom), 111–112
ethnic conflicts. *See also* genocide
  as asymmetrical, 113
  eruption of, 14–16
  longevity of, 72, 113
  overview, 12–14
  recognition of deprivation in, 70–71
ethno-perspective taking. *See* perspective taking
ethos of conflict. *See also* ideology; narratives of conflict; societal beliefs
  children's socialization to, 303–304
  collective emotional orientation and, 213–214
  collective memory and, 212
  as component of socio-psychological infrastructure, 130
  ethos defined, 23, 174–175
  as ideology, 210–212
  as illuminating the conflict, 249
  in Israeli Jewish society, 128–129, 201–207
  psychological needs satisfied by, 209–211
  themes of, 175–176
ethos of peace, 338
euphemization, 111
European Bank for Reconstruction and Development, 397
everyday life, culture of conflict in, 272–273
evil of the rival, 149, 182, 183–184, 237, 251–252, 310
exaggeration in collective memory, 164
existential threats

collective angst and, 234
collective memory and, 149
identity and, 75–76
impossibility of conflict resolution and, 57
justice of goals of conflict and, 176
totality of intractable conflicts and, 37–39
explanation of the conflict situation, 248–249, 438–439
external support. *See* international community

fabrication in conflict supporting narratives, 256
fabrication of false memories, 164
facilitating conditions, 331–334
Fagen, 227
fallen comrades in collective memory, 150–151
false polarization, 309
family and transmission of collective memory, 159–160
Farabundo Martí National Liberation Front (FMLN), 301. *See also* El Salvador conflict
fear
  collective fear, 226–230
  freezing of societal beliefs and, 292, 293
  in Israeli-Arab conflict, 157, 252, 263
  in mobilizing messages, 94
  in socio-psychological repertoire, 222
  vengeance and, 109–110
fedayin, 197
Federico, C. M., 9
Festinger, 328
fighters. *See also* the military
  commemoration of the fallen, 150–151
  in culture of conflict, 270–271
  glorification of, 194, 270, 455
  obedience of, 316
  psychological effects of perpetrating violence, 120–121
  recruitment of, 253
fight or flight instinct, 227
film, Israeli, 267
Finlay, K., 343–344
Firer, R., 268–269
Firmly Entrenched Narrative Closure (FENCE) scale, 305
Fisher, Ronald, 364
Fitzduff, M., 393, 427–428
FLN (Algerian National Liberation Front), 114, 303
forgiveness, 381, 384–385, 403
forgiveness model of reconciliation, 385

framing
  of anger, 240
  in construction of conflict supporting narratives, 256
  emotional appraisal and, 221–222
  of intractable conflicts, 62–63
  by mass media, 408
  of peace process, 362
France-Algeria conflict. *See* Algeria-France conflict
France-Germany conflict
  common history of, 427
  joint projects, 417
  peace building of, 324–325
  reconciliation and economic/political interdependence, 397–399
France-Vietnam conflict, 333–334
Franco-Prussian War, 108
Frankl, Victor, 126–127
Fraser, M. R., 81
freedom and culture of peace, 374
freezing of societal beliefs
  cognitive and motivational factors for, 290–291
  consequences of, 306
  contextual factors for, 294–297
  emotional factors for, 291–294
  at the individual level, 283–290
  investments in conflict as factor for, 299–303
  mistrust and habituation as factors for, 297–299
  overview, 283–290
  unfreezing process, 327–331
Friel, Brian, 46
Fritsche, I., 97
Fromm, 342
functional beliefs, emotions, and behaviors
  as adaptations to conditions of conflict, 278–280
  belief in self-victimization, 188–189
  beliefs about peace, 200
  beliefs about security, 193–194
  fear as, 228
Fuxman, S., 206–207

Gacaca courts (Rwanda), 421–422
Gamson, W. A., 176
Gandhi, Mohandas, 42
Garreton, 227
Gavriely-Nuri, D., 111
Gayer, C., 207

Gazimestan speech of Milošević, 192, 197, 199–200
Geertz, C., 257
Gelkopf, M., 122
gender roles in intractable conflicts, 455
Geneva Conventions, 395, 423
genocide. *See also* immoral acts
  Armenian genocide, 162, 165–166, 287
  of Chechens, 41
  as end of interethnic conflict, 113
  in Holocaust, 188, 232
  as major event, 34
  in Rwanda conflict, 27, 40, 110, 116, 186, 421–422, 442
geographic context of intractable conflicts, 33
geopolitical change as facilitating condition for peacemaking, 333
Germany. *See also* France-Germany conflict; Holocaust
  groups dissenting with peace agreements, 378
  reconciliation with European neighbors, 397–399, 417
Gibson, J. L., 420–421
Gidron, B., 405
Giner-Sorolla, R., 191, 313
Ginges, J., 177–178, 241–242
glorification of the ingroup, 149, 191, 251–252, 254, 268–269, 389
glorification of violence, 42–43, 79, 194, 197, 270–271, 444–445
glory, chosen, 146–148
goals in ethos of peace, 388
goals of intractable conflicts
  adherence to, 300
  context for evolvement of, 63–64
  contradictory nature of, 61–63
  justification and morality of, 60, 176–180, 279, 456
  overview, 5–7
  relative deprivation and, 66–69
  societal beliefs relating to, 193–194
  totality of, 37–39
  types of, 64–66
Goal System Theory, 5–6
Goertz, G., 53
Golec, A., 9
Gonzalez, R., 186
Goodwin, J., 81
Gopher, U., 201
Goren, N., 333

governance and political restructuring, 396
governments, apologies by, 424–425
Graduated and Reciprocated Initiatives in Tension Reduction (GRIT), 341
grass-roots organizing for peace, 400–401, 406, 430
greed, 436, 457
Greek Cypriots. *See* Cyprus conflict
Greenbaum, C. W., 314
Green Book, The, 65
Grings, W. W., 226–227
Gross, J., 220–222, 240
Gross, N., and Y. Gross, 267
Grossman, D., 109–110, 313
group-based emotions, 23, 220
group comparison, 181
group identification. *See also* collective identity; social identity
  clarity of context and, 96
  collective emotional orientation and, 213
  collective guilt and, 348
  of "early risers" in peacemaking process, 350–351
  overview, 81–83
Guatemalan conflict
  distributive injustice in, 67
  fear in Mayan society, 230
  overview of, 1–2
  violence in, 110–111, 442
guilt
  delegitimization of rival and, 183
  hatred of the rival and, 237–238
  moral disengagement and, 250–251, 312–314
  in peacemaking process, 339, 345–348
  rejection of, 157
  self-glorification and, 191
Gundar, A., 187

habituation to conflict conditions, 455
Hadawi, Sami, 167
Hadjipavlou, M., 52, 185, 273
Halbwachs, M., 137
Hallis, D., 122
Halperin, E., 157, 195, 201, 220–222, 233, 234, 236–237, 238, 240, 277, 293, 304, 342, 347
Harbom, L., 364
Harris, I., 411
Harrison, M., 285
Hasenfeld, Y., 405
Hastings, S., 164
hatred

anger and, 240
as barrier to conflict resolution, 293
collective hatred, 236–238
in mobilizing messages, 95
vengeance and, 108
hawks and doves
collective fear and, 232
ethos of conflict and, 206, 207
evaluation of peace proposals, 314
perception of conflict by, 9
societal beliefs and, 304, 309
Hayes, G., 386
Hayner, P. B., 382, 419
healing, 385–387
Hebrew literature, drama and film, 231, 265–267. *See also* cultural products
Hever, S., 50
Hewstone, M., 341, 384–385
hierarchy of needs, 65–66
Hindu caste system, 68
Hirschberger, G., 128
historical affordances, 188
history
as background of intractable conflicts, 29
portrayal in collective memory narrative, 138, 140–141, 268
social identity and, 143
societal beliefs about conflict history, 388–389
writing a common history with former rival, 426–428
Hobfoll, S., 128–129
Hogbladh, S., 364
Hogg, M. A., 211, 220
Holocaust
as chosen trauma for Israeli Jews, 148, 154
collective sense of victimization and, 188
fear of Arabs and, 156, 232
holy sites, 177–178
homogenizing of the rival, 255, 311, 340
honor, vengeance as a matter of, 108
hope
collective hope, 243–244
in Palestinian children's writing, 225
in peacemaking process, 341–342
reconciliation and, 390
Hopkins, N., 80
Horne, A., 199
Hornsey, M. J., 425–426
Horowitz, D. L., 38
human beings

capacity for immoral acts, 443
conflict and human nature, 436–437
peace as highest attainment of, 366
humanizing the rival, 269–270, 315, 340, 356, 373, 414, 416
human rights
in culture of peace, 374
dehumanization of the rival and, 186
in peace education, 414
violation of and judgment of conflict, 437
human rights violations
adjudication of, 394–396
as committed by both parties in conflict, 445
in Guatemalan conflict, 2, 230
reconciliation and, 381–382, 391, 418–422
transitional justice and, 394–395
humiliation
collective humiliation, 240–242
in mobilizing messages, 94–95
hunger strikes, 93
Hunter, J. A., 252, 310–311
Hutu society. *See* Burundi conflict; Rwandan conflict

identification, social. *See* social identity
identification of conflict, 62
identity. *See* collective identity; social identity
identity-based conflict, 74–76
identity fusion, 81
ideology
beliefs and attitudes as, 19
information processing and, 305
Ihud (peace organization), 352
illumination of conflict situation, 248–249, 438–439
"imagined community," 144
immoral acts. *See also* human rights violations; moral codes of behavior; violence
collective guilt for, 346
hatred as leading to, 237–238
human capacity for, 443–444
inclusion/omission from collective memory, 163–164, 445–446
justifications for, 249–251
moral entitlement and, 312
obedience and, 316
peace building and, 369–370
as planned by military, 446
positive collective self-image and, 190

immoral acts (*cont.*)
  reconciliation and, 380–381
  social effects of committing, 453
imposed grievances, 70
incentives for conflict resolution, 333
India
  Hindu caste system, 68
  involvement in Sri Lanka, 48–49
India-Pakistan conflict
  escalation of, 114, 115
  external support for Kashmir insurgency, 117–118
  recognition of deprivation in, 72
  reconciliation and economic cooperation, 398–399
  totality of, 38–39
  zero-sum approach to, 44
individual, the
  effects of intractable conflict upon, 452
  identification of conflict by, 9
  individual differences in interpretation of conflict, 10
  unfreezing at level of, 327–328
inequality
  as basis for conflicts, 66
  reconciliation and correction of, 397
inertia effect of humiliation, 241–242
information. *See also* alternative information; major information
  ambiguous information, 255–256, 303, 307–308, 318
  control over, 315, 316–317, 445–446
  evaluation of trustworthiness of, 206–207
  fear acquired from, 226–227
  gatekeepers to, 317
  information searching behavior, 307
  major information, 34–35
  use of in conflict narratives, 255–256
information processing
  biases in, 292–294, 306, 318
  of competing narratives, 303
  effects of freezing of societal beliefs on, 289, 291, 304, 306
  overview, 318
  threat and, 294–297
  unconscious vs. conscious, 19–20
ingroup, the
  change in societal beliefs about, 389
  differentiation between rival and, 251–252
  glorification of, 149, 191, 251–252, 254, 268–269, 389

justification of actions by, 249–251
  transformation by violence into confrontational society, 101
injustice. *See also* justice
  recognition of, 68–69
  types of, 67
insecurity. *See* security
instigating beliefs, 328
institutionalization phase of peacemaking, 355–359
institutionalized mechanisms of conflict resolution
  in culture of peace, 375
  international institutions, 457
  lack of, 60, 66, 436
  reconciliation and creation of, 392–394
  tractable conflicts and, 36–37
institutions. *See* societal institutions
instrumental reconciliation, 380–381
intentions of the rival, perception of, 115–116
Interactive Problem Solving method, 354–355
interethnic conflicts. *See* ethnic conflicts
internal disagreements, 311
International Center for Transitional Justice, 395
International Committee of the Red Cross, 395
international community
  attitude toward colonialism, 356–357
  epistemic basis of conflicts and persuasion of, 73–74
  forms of support from, 117–118
  justification of violence and, 111–112, 178
  rival as member of, 339
  role in prevention of intractable conflicts, 456–457
  selectivity of collective memory and, 163, 168
  siege mentality and, 235
  support for peace movements, 354, 430
  support for victims, 189–190
  transformative justice role, 395
  zero-sum competition for support from, 43
International Court of Justice (The Hague), 457
International Criminal Court (ICC), 395, 457
International Criminal Trial for Rwanda (ICTR), 423
International Criminal Tribunal for the former Yugoslavia (ICTY), 395
interpretations of information, 255–256, 307–308, 310
In the Desert Plains of the Negev (drama), 267

Intifada, first and second, 115, 122–123, 152, 169–170
intractable conflicts
    centrality of, 45–47
    characteristics of, 59–60, 438
    emergence of characteristics of, 53–55
    historical dimension of, 29
    interrelation between, 334
    intractability defined, 35–36
    justice of goals in, 60
    moral basis for, 99–100
    nature of intractability, 56–59
    perceived uniqueness of, 28–29
    psychological basis for characteristics of, 55–56
    psychological challenges of living in, 124–126, 210–211
    spatial and temporal dimensions of, 56–57
    tractable conflicts vs., 36
    types of, 26–29
    vested interests and, 58, 435
    zero-sum nature of, 43–45
intractable syndrome, 56
intrasocietal conflicts, 26, 276
investments in intractable conflicts, 49–51, 299–303
Iran as threat to Israel, 234
Iraqi-American conflict, 6, 10–11
Iraqi-Kurd conflict, 199
Iraqi Sunni-Shiite conflict, 65–66
Irish Catholics and Protestants. *See* Northern Ireland conflict
Irish Republican Army (IRA), 65, 425
irreversibility of loss of live, 107
Islam, sacred sites of, 177–178
Israel Academia Monitor (organization), 286
Israeli-Arab conflict
    Arab readiness to reconcile, 381
    contradictory nature of goals in, 62
    deescalation and reescalation of, 262
    extremity of, 54
    fear of the other in, 232–233
    Israeli Jewish attitudes about, 204–207
    Israeli peace movement and, 355
    major events and major information in, 34–35
    major events in, 34
    security of Israel as issue in, 195
    violence in, 103, 113
Israeli Council for Israeli-Palestinian Peace (ICIPP), 352–353

Israeli-Egyptian conflict, 262, 325, 332, 368, 401
Israeli Jewish society
    collective emotional orientation of, 222
    collective fear in, 230–234
    collective guilt in, 348
    control of information about Palestinian exodus, 284–285
    correspondence bias in, 311
    culture of conflict in, 262–270, 272
    empathy for Palestinians, 345
    ethos of conflict in, 207
    goals of Jewish homeland, 38
    hatred of Palestinians in, 238
    Holocaust as chosen trauma, 154
    hope for peace, 342
    literature, drama and film in, 231, 265–267
    monopolization of patriotism in, 198
    moral disengagement of, 250–251, 313–314
    moral entitlement of, 312
    openness to alternate narratives, 269–270
    peacemaking process, 352–353, 355, 358
    self-censorship in, 317
    settlers' investment in conflict continuation, 301, 362
    societal beliefs about security, 194–195
    societal beliefs and interpretation of information, 308
    societal beliefs as barrier to conflict resolution, 304
    state control over academia, 284–285, 427
    themes of peace in popular songs, 200–201
    willingness to reconcile, 381
Israeli-Jordanian peace treaty, 262
Israeli National Information Center, 165, 166
Israeli-Palestinian conflict, 50–51. *See also* Israeli Jewish society; Palestinian society
    centrality of, 46
    civilian losses in, 105
    collective emotional response to violence, 106
    collective memory in, 118, 140, 152–153, 155–156, 165, 166, 169–171
    delegitimization of the rival in, 184–185, 186
    escalation of, 104, 114
    geopolitical events affecting, 333
    humiliation in, 241–242
    interests vested in continuation of, 58
    Jewish ethos of conflict, 129
    losses as facilitating condition for unfreezing, 337
    loss of life and investment in, 300

Israeli-Palestinian conflict (*cont.*)
  overview, 2–3
  peace process, 152–153
  planned contact between Jews and Palestinians, 404
  pride and, 242–243
  psychological stress, 122–123
  sacred values in, 177–178
  threat perception and violence in, 295
  trust in the rival, 341
  victimhood in, 188, 190, 313–314
  violence in, 40, 42
  zero-sum nature of, 276–277
Iyer, A., 220

Jabri, V., 148
Jammu/Yammu (region of India/Pakistan), 38–39
Janoff-Bulman, R., 388
Japan
  conquest of Manchuria, 71, 87, 102
  healing in South Korea relationship, 387
  management of collective memory in, 165
Jarymowicz, M., 216–217
Jayasuriya, S., 50
Jerusalem, 177–178
Jervis, R., 315
Jews. *See* Israeli Jewish society; Israeli-Palestinian conflict
joint projects of former rivals, 416–417
Jonas, E., 97, 210
Jordan-Israel peace treaty, 262
Jost, J. T., 210, 211
journalists and journalism, 284, 409
justice
  culture of peace, 374
  of goals of intractable conflicts, 60, 175, 176–180, 256, 356–357, 437, 456
  reconciliation and administration of, 394, 396

Kahneman, D., 334
Kansteiner, W., 137
Kanyangara, P., 422
Karadžić, Radovan, 185–186
Kashmir conflict. *See also* India-Pakistan conflict
  external support for, 117–118
  perceived insolvability of, 48
  totality of India-Pakistan conflict and, 38–39
Katz, S. N., 314, 405

Keen, S., 182
Kelegama, S., 50
Kelman, H. C., 276–277, 354–355, 380
Kennedy, K. A., 309–310
Kennedy, John F., 11
Kenworthy, J. B., 341
Kessler, T., 97
killing and the sanctity of life, 104–105, 249, 299–300, 313
Kim, S. H., 101
kinship terms and collective identity, 105–106
Kirisci, K., 87–88
Kitayama, S., 219–220
Klandermans, B., 77–78, 83, 85
Klar, Y., 188, 191, 303, 305, 312, 347
knowledge about former rival, 373
knowledge perspective theory, 21
Korean conflict, 65–66, 76
Korostelina, K., 82–83
Kosovo. *See* Battle of Kosovo; Serbia; Yugoslavia conflict
Krech, D., 17
Kreidie, L. H., 277–278
Kriesberg, L., 35–36
Kruglanski, A. W., 5–6, 64
Kumaratunga (president of Sri Lanka), 200
Kurdish conflict
  discrimination in, 67
  identity and territory issues, 14, 74–75, 87–88, 180
  incentives for Turkey to resolve, 333
  in Iraq, 74–75, 199
  moral convictions in messages of mobilization, 87–88
  procedural injustice in, 67

labels, delegitimizing, 181, 183, 184, 185
Laitin, D. D., 11, 102
Landau, M. J., 128
language
  culture of conflict in everyday language, 272
  identity and, 75, 89
Larsen, J. T., 215
Lavi, I., 128–129
Lazarus, R. S., 121, 238–239
Leach, C. W., 191, 220
leaders. *See also* agents of conflict
  agents of conflict and, 91–92, 449–450
  difficulty accepting alternative information, 301–303
  as epistemic authorities, 34–35, 417

public meetings of rival leaders, 417–418
reconciliation and replacement of, 396
role in constructing master narrative of conflict, 254
role in peace building, 400–401, 429–430
support for peacemaking, 356, 357, 362–363
Lebanon, 75, 277–278, 355
Lederach, J. P., 371, 379–380
legal systems, 396
legitimization of the rival, 339, 417–419, 423–424
legitimization of violence, 111, 148
legitimization stage of peacemaking process, 353–355
Legum, C., 235
Legum, H., 235
Leidner, B., 191
Levine, M., 80
Levy-Paluck, E., 410
Lewin, K., 327
Lewis, C., 187, 384–385
Lickel, B., 108
Lieberfeld, D., 400
life, loss of. *See* loss of life
Lindner, E. G., 94–95, 241
literature, Hebrew, 231, 265–267
litigation strategy of peace movement, 406
Liu, J. H., 146, 165, 188
Liviatan, I., 191, 345, 348
Liyange, S., 404
lobbying strategy of peace movement, 406
Long, W. J., 380, 385
longevity of conflict, 35, 51–52, 448–451
loss aversion, 314
losses as facilitating condition for peacemaking, 334–338, 339
loss of life. *See also* death
  collective emotional experience of, 105–106
  in collective memory, 150–151
  investment in continuation of conflict and, 299–300
  irreversibility of, 107
  mobilization and, 93, 98
  as societal cost, 456
lost causes, 92
LTTE (Tamil rebel group), 41, 48–49, 151

MacGinty, R., 335–336
Mac Iver, M. A., 75, 234
Mack, J. E., 311–312
Magal, T., 195, 406

magnification of themes in conflict narratives, 255
Maguire, Mairead Corrigan, 407
Mai Lai massacre, 443
major events
  collective memory and, 142, 145–146, 155–156
  eruption of conflict and, 100
  escalation of conflict and, 114
  overview, 34
major information. *See also* information
  change of collective memory and, 169
  defined, 34–35
  escalation of conflict and, 114
  ethos of conflict and reception of, 201
  about own immoral actions, 334
Malhotra, D., 404
malintentions of the rival, 95, 104, 116, 227–228, 297
Mallet, J., 187
Mamdani, M., 110
manageability of intractable conflicts, 126–127
Manchuria, 71, 87, 102
Mandela, Nelson, 92, 357, 362–363, 400–401, 418
manipulation of associations, 164
Maoz, I., 186, 233, 295, 314, 341
marches/parades in Northern Ireland conflict, 47, 86
Markus, H. R., 219–220
Maronite Christians, 75
Marrow, D., 379
Marshall, M. G., 12
martyrs, 197
Masada siege, 155–156, 271
Maslow, A. H., 65–66, 228, 390
mass killings/massacres. *See also* genocide
  in Bosnia-Herzegovina, 40
  in Guatemala, 110–111
mass media
  alternative information and, 284
  contact with rival via, 404, 409–410
  control over, 284, 287
  in culture of peace, 375–376
  framing done by, 408
  in Israeli Jewish society, 264–265
  role in peacemaking and peace building, 326–327, 408–410
  as transmitter of collective memory, 162
mastery as psychological need, 124, 125, 127, 252
material investments in intractable conflicts, 49, 117, 300–301
Maya people. *See* Guatemalan conflict

Mazen, Abu, 337
Mazur, J., 62
McAdam, D., 85
McCauley, R., 186, 233, 295, 341
McClelland, S. I., 236
McClosky, H., 23
McFarlane, G., 109
McLaughlin-Volpe, T., 275
McLernon, F., 384–385
meaning
    in coping process, 126–127
    emotions as decoders of, 214–215
    ideology and, 210–211
    socio-psychological infrastructure as illuminating, 248
mechanisms of conflict resolution
    in culture of peace, 375
    international mechanisms, 457
    lack of, 60, 66, 436
    reconciliation and creation of, 392–394
    tractable conflicts and, 36–37
media. *See* mass media
mediating beliefs, 328–329
Medin, D., 177–178
Medjedovic, J., 207
meetings between rival groups, 417–418
Meir, Golda, 312
memoirs and transmission of collective memory, 160
memory and cognition, 307. *See also* collective memory
mercy, 379–380
Merom, G., 314
Mertus, J. A., 162
messages of mobilization
    contents of, 88–90
    principles of, 86–88
messages of peace, legitimization of, 353–354
Milgram, N. A., 121, 249
Milgram, Stanley, 316
military, the. *See also* fighters
    demobilization of, 392–393
    militarization of society, 454–455
    planning of immoral acts, 446
    transmission of ethos of conflict by, 201, 206–207
    as transmitter of collective memory, 162
military budgets, 51
military cooperation, 392–393
military personnel. *See* fighters
military victory, 49, 57–58, 113, 448

Miller, N., 108
Milošević, Slobodan, 45, 89–90, 154–155, 192, 199–200
minority influence and persuasion, 351–352
Minow, M., 108
mirror image of rivals, 133, 184, 185, 207, 318–319, 429
mistrust, 297–298. *See also* trust
Mitzen, J., 298
mobilization for conflict
    acts facilitating mobilization, 93
    agents of conflict, 91–92
    collective efficacy and, 92–93
    collective memory and, 158
    contextual factors, 95–98, 99
    delegitimizing beliefs and, 184
    emotions and, 93–95
    as escalating the conflict, 117
    evolvement of conflicts and, 53
    as function of socio-psychological infrastructure, 253
    identity and, 79–84
    justness of conflict goals and, 178
    messages of mobilization, 86–90
    methods of, 84–86
    overview, 76–79
mobilization for peace, 325, 352, 357, 360, 401, 430, 432
monitoring of alternative information sources, 286–287
monopolization of patriotism, 198
Monroe, K. R., 277–278
Montville, J. V., 386, 418
moral amplification, 310
moral basis for intractable conflicts, 99–100, 178, 279
moral codes of behavior. *See also* immoral acts
    as changing over time, 435
    international mechanisms for enforcing, 456–457
    killing and the sanctity of life, 104–105, 249, 299–300, 313
    reflective thinking about, 216–217
    as weakened by intractable conflict, 454
moral convictions
    of early risers in peacemaking process, 351
moral disengagement, 250, 312–314
moral entitlement, 312
moral evaluation of conflicts, 28, 437
moral mandates, sacred values and, 177

moral support, 118
Morris, B., 103
mortality. *See* death; loss of life
Mosse, G. L., 151
Mossinsohn, Yigal, 267
motivated reasoning, 291
Mufson, S., 336–337
Muldoon, O. T., 123
multiethnic states. *See* ethnic conflicts
murals in Northern Ireland conflict, 47, 273
mutual acceptance, 373
mutual knowledge, 373

Nadler, A., 190, 345, 380–381
Nahhes, E., 139–140, 159–160
naive realism, 309–310
Nakba (Palestinian catastrophe), 147, 159–160
Nanking Massacre, 165
narrative. *See also* alternative narratives; collective memory
  collective memory as, 137–138
  counternarratives, 140, 152
  defined, 22–23, 130
  ethos of conflict as, 175
  ethos of peace and, 388–389
  master vs. specific narratives, 145, 439
  overview, 22–23
narratives of conflict. *See also* ethos of conflict
  construction of, 254–257, 439–440
  development over time, 52
  epistemic basis as, 72
  as maintaining the conflict, 440, 454
  in mobilizing messages, 89–90
  reconciliation and, 379, 382–383
Nasie, M., 209, 225, 243
nation, defined, 14
national information centers, 162, 165, 166, 167, 284, 314
nationhood and collective identity, 143
NATO (North Atlantic Treaty Alliance), 333
naturalization of violence, 111
Nazis
  accusation of Chechens of collaboration with, 41, 88–89, 119, 185
  attack on Soviet Union, 10–11
  delegitimizing comparisons to, 181, 183, 190
Need Based Model of Reconciliation, 380–381
needs
  collective memory and satisfaction of, 158
  conflict settlement/resolution and, 364, 388

ethos of conflict as satisfying, 209–211
hierarchy of, 65–66
psychological response to deprivation of, 123–125
reconciliation and, 380, 428
for security, 192–196
societal beliefs as satisfying, 290
negative emotions. *See also* anger; fear; hatred
  arising from Gacaca court, 422
  collective memory and, 156–157, 227–228
  negativity bias, 217–219, 292–294, 334
negotiating partner, rival as, 339–340, 351, 354, 357, 417–419
negotiation. *See* peace-building process; peacemaking
Netanyahu, Benjamin, 262, 362, 418
Nets-Zehngut, R., 161, 165, 169–170, 232–233, 284–285, 317, 342, 386–387
NGO Monitor (Israeli organization), 286–287
Nicaragua, disarmament and demobilization in, 392–393
"Nomad and the Viper" (Oz), 265
nongovernment organizations (NGOs)
  in Israeli-Palestinian conflict, 286–287
  in Northern Ireland conflict, 85–86
  in peace movement, 405
nontangible goals of intractable conflicts, 65
nonviolent struggle, 42, 447
Noor, M., 190
normalization of conflict, 46, 111
Northern Ireland Civil Rights Association, 85–86, 98, 114
Northern Ireland conflict
  alternative information in, 282
  Catholic goals in, 65
  centrality of, 46–47
  collective memory in, 143–144, 148, 153–154
  collective self-image in, 192
  delegitimization of the rival in, 184, 252
  external support for the IRA, 117–118
  forgiveness in, 384–385
  hope of peace in, 342
  identity issues in, 75, 81
  investment in, 50, 300
  IRA apology for civilian deaths in, 425
  losses as facilitating condition for ending of, 335–336
  major events in, 34, 98
  mobilization methods in, 85–86, 93
  murals and parades, 46–47, 86, 242–243, 273
  peace education, 415

Northern Ireland conflict (*cont.*)
  peacemaking/building process in, 362, 400, 427–428
  peace movement in, 407
  pride and, 242–243
  psychological stress and, 123
  rationalization of violence, 109
  recognition of deprivation in, 71–72
  reconciliation in, 393, 396, 403–404
  security in, 195
  trust in the rival, 341
  victimization and, 187, 190
  violence in, 41, 112–113, 310–311
  zero-sum approach to, 44–45
Nowak, A., 36

Oakes, P. J., 220
obedience, 316
Oberschal, A., 90
occupied territories (Israel), 50–51, 206, 233, 263, 299, 358
official memory, 138–139
Ofrat, G., 267
Olmert, Ehud, 337
one-state conflict resolutions, 369, 385, 393
Opotow, S., 236
optimistic overconfidence, 314
Orange marches (Northern Ireland), 47, 86
Oren, N., 184, 201–204, 304, 332
Orr, E., 9
Osgood, C. E., 341
Oskamp, S., 308
Oslo agreements (Israel and PLO), 185, 262, 358, 361
Ottenberg, P., 313
outcasting, 181
Oz, Amos, 265

Paez, D., 146, 422
Paisley, Ian, 44–45, 153–154
Pakistan. *See also* India-Pakistan conflict
  collective identity and culture of conflict, 277
Palestine as place-name, 268
Palestine Liberation Organization (PLO), 184–185, 198, 333, 352–353, 358
Palestinian society. *See also* Israeli-Palestinian conflict
  collective memory of, 139, 147, 167
  collective self-healing, 386–387
  collective self-image, 191–192
  cultural symbols of, 271
  emotional expression in, 225
  ethos of conflict in, 207–209
  exodus in 1948, 284–285, 317
  first Intifada, 152
  goals of homeland, 38
  humiliation in, 241–242
  Palestinian nationalism, 2, 171–172, 263, 268
  patriotism in, 197
  pride in, 242–243
  second Intifada, 115
Paluck, E. L., 410
Pan Africanist Congress (PAC), 102
Papadakis, Y., 144, 171–172
parades in Northern Ireland conflict, 47, 86, 242–243, 273
parallel empathy, 343
Parsons, T., 21
participation in intractable conflicts, 76–79, 253
participatory governance, 396
partnerships (participatory governance), 396
passive healing process, 386–387
past, the
  continuity of present with, 83, 158, 228, 292
  experience as factor in conflict escalation, 118
  reconciliation and dealing with the past, 381–383
patriotism
  blind patriotism, 196, 198
  as collective emotional involvement, 105–106
  monopolization of, 363, 454
  in narratives of conflict, 89
  pride and, 242
  societal beliefs about, 196–198, 206–207, 209, 264
peace. *See also* culture of peace
  in Israeli Jewish children's literature, 266–267
  mechanisms for maintaining, 375
  societal beliefs about, 200–201, 264, 389
  as a value, 372–373
Peace and Reconciliation Group (Northern Ireland), 427–428
peace-building methods
  apology, 423–426
  contact between rival groups, 402–404
  education, 410–416
  joint projects, 416–417
  of mass media, 408–410

overview, 400–402
payment of reparations, 426
peace movement strategies, 405–408
publicized meetings between rival groups, 417–418
public trials, 422–423
tourism, 418
truth and reconciliation commissions, 418–422
writing a common history, 426–428
peace-building process. *See also* reconciliation
in asymmetrical conflicts, 369–370
as continuation of peacemaking, 366
culture of peace, 372–376
defined, 324–325, 367
factors affecting, 428–430
goal of stable and lasting peace, 370–372, 431–433
one- vs. two-state conflict resolutions, 369
peace education, 411–415, 430
peaceful coexistence, 367–369, 374, 385
peaceful settlement of conflict, 324
peace journalism, 409
peacemaking. *See also* conflict resolution
challenges of, 323–326
collective guilt and shame, 345–348
conditions for change, 331–334
conflict settlement phase of, 325, 364–366
deescalation of conflict, 3, 55, 114, 323–324, 340, 354
dual contexts in peace-building process, 359–364
emergence of peacemaking ideas, 350–353
ethos of conflict and, 201
failure of, 363
fear as hindering, 228
hope for conflict resolution, 341–342
institutionalization stage of, 355–359
legitimization stage of, 353–355
losses as a facilitating condition, 334–339
new views of the rival, 339–340
overview, 323–326, 348–350
peace building as continuation of, 366
perspective taking and empathy, 343–345
reconciliation phase of peace building, 366
shared negative emotions and, 213
trust in rival, 340–341
unfreezing process, 327–331
peace movement
emergence of, 350–353
in Israeli-Palestinian conflict, 355, 358

role in peacemaking process, 354, 405–408, 430, 451
violence and, 447–448
Peace Now (Israeli peace organization), 355
peace proposals, reactive devaluation of, 314
Pearlman, L. A., 410, 416
perception
of contradictory goals, 5
differences in how two sides perceive a conflict, 42
ethos of conflict effects on, 207
perceived threat, 96–98
of rival's ability and intentions, 115–116
of situation as a conflict, 7–8, 55–56
of uniqueness of the society, 83, 275–276, 314
of unsolvability of conflicts, 47–49
Peres Center of Peace, 417
personalization of the rival, 340, 344, 402–403
perspective taking, 311–312, 343–345, 414
persuasion
by agents of peace, 331
epistemic basis for conflict as, 73–74
evolvement of conflicts and, 53
negativity bias and, 293
Petrovic, B., 207
Pettigrew, T. F., 403
Philpot, C. R., 424, 425–426
Pliskin, R., 317
Podeh, E., 170–171, 252, 268
Poland
cultural memory in, 142
passive healing in, 387
reconciliation with Germany, 398
reconciliation with Russia, 427
polarization of rivals, 309
polarization of society over peacemaking, 354, 356, 358
political-economic structure. *See also* economic issues in intractable conflicts
alternative information emergence and, 288–317
one- vs. two-state conflict resolutions, 369
peacemaking process and, 350, 363
reconciliation and changes in, 392–394, 396–399
social identity and, 75
political labeling, 181, 183, 184, 185
political parties
in Israeli Jewish society, 265
in Northern Ireland conflict, 85–86
Polycarpou, M. P., 344

popular collective memory, 138, 145, 149–150, 152–153, 159–160
Porat, R., 234, 304
positive collective self-image. *See* collective self-image
positive emotional orientation. *See* collective emotional orientation
positive experiences in intractable conflicts, 124
"positive peace," 380
positive vs. negative events, memory of, 147
post traumatic stress disorders (PTSD), 122–123
power differential between rivals, 27, 436
predictability, 122, 125, 127, 174, 252, 253, 360
preparedness for conflict, 252–253
prevention of violent conflicts, 456–458
pride, 242–243
primary appraisal/emotions, 129, 215–217, 226
primitive societies, vengeance in, 107
privately held beliefs, 315–316
problem-solving workshops, 354–355
procedural injustice, 67
progress and conflict, 7
projection of wrong doing, 164
Pronin, E., 309–310
propositions, defined, 18–19
prosecution of perpetrators of immoral acts, 419–420, 457
prospect theory, 294, 334–335
"protected value," 43
protest strategy of peace movement, 406
protracted nature of intractable conflicts, 35, 51–52, 448–451
Pruitt, D. G., 101, 331
psychological investments in intractable conflicts, 49
psychological needs of society members. *See* needs
psychological warfare, 179–180
public discourse
  collective emotional orientation and, 223–224
  collective memory in, 159
  culture of conflict in, 260
  ethos of conflict in, 264–265
public opinion polls
  ethos of conflict and, 201–204, 263–264
  in Israeli Jewish society, 230–234, 263–264, 332, 404
public trials, 422–423
Putin, Vladimir, 34–35, 185

Putnam, L. L., 36
Pyszczynski, T., 128

Rabin, Itzhak, 198, 358, 362
Ramanathapillai, R., 110, 253
Rath, R., 80
Raviv, A., 204, 207, 308
reactive devaluation, 314
reactive empathy, 343–344
realistic threats, 96–97, 120
recognition of relative deprivation, 68, 70–72
reconciliation. *See also* peace-building process
  conflict settlement without, 325, 365–366
  dealing with the past, 381–383
  ethos of peace, 387–389
  forgiveness, 384–385
  healing, 385–387
  overview, 376–381, 399
  political/economic changes, 396–399
  positive emotional orientation, 389–390
  socio-political changes, 390–392
  structural changes, 392–394
  transitional justice, 394–396
redistribution of land, wealth, and power, 397
Redl, F., 313
reescalation
  of Israeli-Palestinian conflict, 3, 51, 262, 363
  military victory and, 113
  peacemaking process and, 323–324, 363
  protracted nature of conflict and, 51
reflective thinking, 413
refugees
  in Bosnia-Herzegovina conflict, 40
  in Guatemalan conflict, 110–111
  in Israeli-Palestinian conflict, 3, 40, 41, 169–171
Reicher, S., 80, 86, 91, 220
relative deprivation. *See* deprivation
relevance of messages of mobilization, 87
religious conflicts, 65–66
remembering. *See also* collective memory
  mental vs. active, 139–140
reparations
  guilt and, 346, 347
  payment of, 426
  truth commission recommendations for, 420
resources required by intractable conflicts, 78–79, 103, 117, 454–455
respect as condition for reconciliation, 388
restructuring of society, 377

retaliation, 109, 116, 233, 295–296, 342. *See also* cycles of violence
revenge. *See* cycles of violence; vengeance
Reykowski, J., 366
right-wing authoritarianism (RWA), 212
Rimé, B., 422
ripeness of conflict for resolution, 331
risk taking
   anger and, 239
   decisions about, 294
   fear and, 233
   trust in rival and risks of negotiation, 341
rituals of memory. *See* commemoration
rival groups
   contact between, 384, 402–404
   contradictory collective memory between, 166–168
   correspondence bias and, 310–311
   differentiation from ingroup, 251–252
   empathy for the rival, 109, 163, 186, 188, 311–312, 318, 343–345, 382, 403–404
   homogenizing of, 255, 311
   as mirror images of each other, 133, 184, 185, 207, 318–319
   perceived ability and intentions of, 115–116
   as potential partner to peace, 339–340, 351, 354, 357, 417–419
   segregation from each other, 182
   trust-building actions by, 332, 429
rival groups, former
   change in societal beliefs about, 388
   complementary new goals of, 429
   culture of peace between, 372–376
   economic and political cooperation between, 397–399
   joint projects, 416–417
Roccas, S., 188, 191, 312, 348
Roe, M. D., 384
Rose, R., 196
Ross, Lee, 309–310
Ross, M., 424
Ross, M. H., 258, 273, 314
Rothman, J., 74–75
Rouhana, N. N., 309, 365–366, 391
Ruane, J., 50, 144, 192
Rubin, J. Z., 57
Russell, A., 240
Russell, J., 185
Russian-Chechen conflict. *See* Chechen-Russian conflict
Russian Information Center, 284

Russian-Polish relations, 427
Rutkoff, P. M., 108
Rwandan conflict
   asymmetry of, 27
   collective memory and, 140, 148
   contradictory goals in, 8
   delegitimization of the rival in, 186
   genocide in, 27, 40, 110, 116, 186, 421–422, 442
   humiliation in, 94–95
   major events in, 34
   peace-building process, 400, 404, 409–410
   peace education workshops, 416
   perceived intentions in, 116
   transitional justice, 395, 421–422
   unity in, 200
   violence in, 40, 110
Ryan, R. M., 123
Ryntveit, A. K., 86

sacred values, goals of conflict as, 177–178
sacrifice. *See also* loss of life
   collective identity and, 84
   goals of conflict and, 176, 178
   investments in conflict as, 78, 300
   mobilization and, 78, 117, 158
   patriotism and, 197–198, 253, 264
Sadat, Anwar, 34, 263, 332, 355
Sa'di, A. H., 147
safety needs, 65, 125, 192–193, 290
salience of mortality, 128
Salomon, G., 411
sanctity of life, 104–105, 109, 249
Sande, G. N., 310
Sarig, On, 266
Sarkozy, Nicolas, 425
Scheff, T. J., 107–108
Schmader, T., 108
schools. *See* educational institutions and materials
Schori, N., 187, 312
Schori-Eyal, N., 188
Schuman, H., 139
Schumann, K., 424
Schwartz, B., 153
Schwartz, S. H., 191
Scott, J., 139
secondary appraisal/emotions
   fear as, 226
   guilt as, 346
   hatred as, 236
   hope as, 243

secondary appraisal/emotions (*cont.*)
  humiliation as, 241
  ideology and, 129
  long-term emotional sentiments effects on, 220–222
  overview, 216–217
  pride as, 242
securatism, 195
security
  reconciliation and, 380, 390
  societal beliefs about, 192–196, 206–207, 229–230, 263
Sekulic, D., 90, 104
selective attention, 306–307
selectivity in construction of conflict narratives, 254, 383, 439
selectivity of collective memory, 163–166
self, the, 80, 81–83
self-categorization, 142–143, 220, 275, 344
self-censorship, 316–317, 446–447
self-defense in collective memory, 167
self-enhancement, 127
self-fulfilling prophecy phenomenon, 308–309
self-image, positive collective, 164, 169, 178, 190–192, 237–238, 250
separatist conflicts, 26
Serbia. *See also* Battle of Kosovo; Bosnia-Herzegovina conflict; Yugoslavia conflict
  chosen trauma of, 147, 154–155
  collective memory in, 162
  collective self-image, 192
  dehumanization of the rival, 186
  empathy for Bosnian Muslims in, 345
  ethos of conflict in, 207
  justification of conflict goals, 179
  moral disengagement and victimhood, 251, 313
  moral entitlement, 312
  patriotism of, 197
  unity among, 199–200
  zero-sum nature of conflict in, 43–45
Serbian Academy of Sciences and Arts, 179, 312
severity of conflicts, 35–36
shahids (martyrs), 197
shame
  delegitimizing the rival and, 183
  hatred of rival and, 237–238
  moral disengagement and, 250–251, 312–314
  in peace-building process, 348
  truth commissions and, 422

shared emotions, 23–24, 219–223. *See also* collective emotional orientation
shared fate, sense of, 83–84, 275–276
shared societal beliefs, 20–21, 130
Sharon, Ariel, 104
Sharpeville, South Africa, 98, 114
Sharvit, K., 128–129, 201, 220–222, 249, 277, 306–307
Sherif, M., 402
Shikaki, K., 177–178
Shnabel, N., 190
siege mentality, 235, 252
signaling model of reconciliation, 385
Simon, B., 83
simplification in narratives of conflict, 254, 440
Singh, Hari, 114
Sinhalese society. *See* Sri Lankan conflict
Sinn Fein (Northern Ireland), 81
situational factors, 310–311
Sivan, E., 138
sixth commandment ("thou shalt not kill"), 104–105
Skitka, L. J., 87
Slone, M., 122
Smith, M. B., 13, 87, 220
Smith, N. K., 215
Snow, D. A., 62–63
Snyder, C. R., 243
social categorization theory, 106
social contagion of fear, 228
Social Democratic and Labour Party (Northern Ireland), 85–86
social distance, 384
social identity. *See also* collective self-image; group identification; identity-based conflict
  collective memory and, 142–144, 148
  conflict goals and, 15
  ethnicity and, 13
  identity symbols in mobilizing messages, 88
  mobilization for participation in conflict, 81
  overview, 79–84
  of peace activists, 350–351
  shared emotion and, 220
  total participation in intractable conflicts and, 78
social identity theory, 76
socialization. *See also* educational institutions and materials
  collective memory and, 162–163
  conformity as a form of, 316

culture of conflict and, 272, 273
in Israeli Jewish society, 249
patriotism and, 197
for peaceful settlement of conflict, 411
shared beliefs and emotions, 20, 105–106, 132, 259, 260, 272
of soldiers, 201
social networks
dissemination of societal beliefs through, 260
in mobilization process, 85–86
societal beliefs. *See also* ethos of conflict; freezing of societal beliefs; narrative
collective identity and, 83
in collective memory, 141
as a conservative ideology, 290
as constituting an ethos, 174–175
defined, 275
degrees of consensus about, 259
about delegitimization of rival, 180–186
effects of freezing of, 306
in ethos of peace, 387–389
influence on collective emotion orientation, 225
about justness of ingroup goals, 176–180
overview, 20–21
about patriotism, 196–198
peace movement and, 405–406
about positive collective self-image, 190–192
rival narrative and changing of, 382–383
about security, 192–196
about unity, 198–200
about victimization, 186–190
societal institutions. *See also* educational institutions and materials; institutionalized mechanisms of conflict resolution
collective memory transmission and, 160
mobilization for conflict, 452
reconciliation and change to, 390–392
societies in intractable conflict
effects on conflict upon, 451–456
restructuring of, 377
socio-emotional reconciliation, 380–381
socio-political changes
as mobilization for conflict, 452
reconciliation and, 390
socio-psychological infrastructure. *See also* conflict resolution, socio-psychological barriers to
conceptual model of, 130–133

as detrimental to peace process, 280
functions of, 247–253, 278–280, 440
guilt in context of, 346–347
levels of adherence to, 305
overview, 24–25
sharing of, in culture of conflict, 259
socio-psychological process of closure
conformity, 315–316
obedience, 316
self-censorship, 316–317
socio-psychological repertoire. *See also* collective emotional orientation; collective memory; ethos of conflict
contact with rival and change in, 403
defined, 130
development/evolvement over time, 52, 58, 99, 126–130
of intractable conflicts, 55–56
levels of sharing of, 132
openness to alternative information and change in, 329–331
peace building as creation of new, 323–324, 325, 360, 370–372, 387, 431–433
peace movement and, 405
resistance to change, 16–17
of tractable conflicts, 37
transformation into socio-psychological infrastructure, 130
Solomon, Z., 122
Solzhenitsyn, Alexander, 139
Somalia conflict, 94–95
sources of information, 255, 328, 446–447
South African conflict
apology by de Klerk, 425
asymmetry of, 27
boycott of apartheid system, 118
collective guilt in, 348
contact and reconciliation, 404
forgiveness and healing in, 386
leaders' difficulty in changing policy, 302–303
mediating beliefs in, 329
morality of conflict goals, 279
peacemaking process in, 357, 362–363, 400–401
recognition of deprivation in, 70–71, 96
siege mentality in, 235
socio-political changes in, 391
totality of, 39
Truth and Reconciliation Commission, 395–396, 419–421

Soviet Union, 10–11, 55, 71, 119, 139. *See also* Chechen-Russian conflict
Spanish Civil War, 75, 140
Spears, R., 83–84
Spini, D., 101
Srebrenica massacre, 40
Sri Lankan conflict
  censorship in, 285
  collective memory in, 151
  contact between rivals, 404
  epistemic basis for, 73, 82
  escalation of, 115
  identity issues in, 75
  investment in, 50
  justification of conflict goals, 179
  mobilization for participation in, 86, 253
  mobilizing messages in, 89
  perceived unsolvability of, 48–49
  violence in, 41, 110, 442
  zero-sum approach to, 44
staircase model of apology acceptance, 425–426
stalemate/deadlock, 35–36
stateless societies. *See also* asymmetrical conflicts
  forms of violence of, 103
  infrastructure and resource issues, 79, 117
  as nations, 14
  security of, 193
state power
  control over resources, 78–79, 103, 117
  decision to act and, 69
  dissemination of collective memory and, 168
  human rights violation and, 446
  maintaining security and control of, 192–193
  mobilization to conflict participation, 78–79
Staub, E., 109–110, 187, 196, 385, 409–410, 416, 422
Stenstrom, D. M., 108
Stephan, W. G., 96–97, 120, 343–344, 391
Sternberg, R. J., 236
Stokke, K., 86
stress of living under intractable conflict, 121–123, 125, 128–129, 252
Stringer, M., 252, 310–311
Suedfeld, P., 302
superpowers, 64, 333, 450, 456–457
suppression of collective memory, 139, 159–160
suppression of evidence, 256
Swidler, A., 258
symbolic annihilation, 111
symbolic compromises, 234, 238, 293
symbolic immortality, 128

symbolic threats, 96–97, 120
symbols
  of conflict, 131–132, 271–272
  cultural, 258
  of social identity, 88
symmetry in conflicts. *See* asymmetrical conflicts
system justification theory, 176, 211

Tajfel, H., 190
Talabani, Jalal, 199
Tam, T., 341
Tamil society, 110, 253. *See also* Sri Lankan conflict
Tamil Tigers, 48–49
tangible goals of conflict, 64–65
Tarrow, S., 70
Tausch, N., 67–68, 403–404
Tavuchis, N., 423–424
Taylor, S. E., 127
Teff-Seker, Y., 266–267
Temple Mount, 177–178
temporal context of intractable conflicts, 33, 57–58
territorial issues
  as conflict goals, 64–65, 71, 177–178
  identity issues in, 74–75
  Israeli-occupied territories, 50–51, 206, 233, 263, 299, 358
  nationhood and, 14
terrorism
  definitions of, 42
  ETA justification of, 111–112
  LTTE use of, 151
  perception of threat and, 296
  use by weaker groups, 112
Terror Management Theory (TMT), 97, 128, 296
Tetlock, P. E., 177
textbooks. *See* educational institutions and materials
Thatcher, Margaret, 44–45
themes of ethos of conflict. *See* societal beliefs
third parties
  creation of intractable conflicts by, 435
  interests in continuation of conflict, 450
  intervention by, 333, 387, 403, 430, 456–457
Thórisdóttir, H., 211
threat
  conflict escalation and perceptions of, 116
  consensus and levels of threat perception, 261

fear as response to, 229, 233
Israeli Jewish perceptions of, 263
mobilization and perceptions of, 96–98
perception of, as barrier to conflict resolution, 294–297
realistic vs. symbolic, 120
societal beliefs about, 193
Todd, J., 50, 144, 192
tolerance, 413–414
totality as characteristic of intractable conflicts, 37–39
total participation in intractable conflicts, 78
tourism, 380, 386–387, 398–399, 418
tractable conflicts, 36–37
trait characterization, 181
transitional context, 34–35, 55, 114
transitional justice, 394–396, 418
transmission of collective memory, 159–163
trauma, chosen, 146–148
trials, public, 422–423
Tropp, L. R., 403
"The Troubles." *See* Northern Ireland conflict
Trumpeldor, Joseph, 271
trust
 calculated trust in cold peace, 368–369
 contact with rival and, 403
 delegitimization of the rival as obstacle to, 166
 development of trust in rival, 340–341
 mistrust as barrier to conflict resolution, 297–298
 reconciliation and, 379
 trust-building actions by the rival, 332, 429
truth
 reconciliation and acknowledgment of, 379–380, 381–382
 truth and reconciliation commissions, 384, 418–422
truth acceptance, 420–421
Truth and Reconciliation Commission (South Africa), 395–396, 419–421
Tsur, D., 265
Turkey. *See* Armenian genocide; Cyprus conflict; Kurdish conflict
Turkish Cypriots. *See* Cyprus conflict
Turner, J. C., 220
Turney-High, H. H., 107
Tutsi society. *See* Rwandan conflict
Tversky, A., 334
two-state conflict resolutions, 369, 385

Ulster Defence Association (UDA), 195
unconscious emotions, 129, 215–217, 226
underground groups, 169
understanding between former rivals, 374
unfreezing process, 327–331, 337–338, 371. *See also* freezing of societal beliefs; peacemaking
unilateral initiatives toward peacemaking, 341
unintentional escalation of conflicts, 114
uniqueness of the conflict, 28–29
uniqueness of the ingroup, 24, 75, 83, 143, 275–276, 314
United Nations Development Program, 397
United Nations Human Rights Council, 395
United Nations International Court of Justice, 457
United States
 activities in Guatemala, 1–2
 ethos of, 23
 intervention in Yugoslavia conflict, 333
 Iraq War, 6
 Vietnam War, 334, 356, 443
unity, societal beliefs about, 198–200, 264
unsolvability, perception of, 47–49
Urian, D., 267
USSR, 333
utilitarian arguments for peace, 338, 351

validity of messages of mobilization, 86–87
Vallacher, R. R., 36
vengeance
 continuation of conflict and, 299
 escalation of intractable conflicts and, 107–108
 human losses and, 42–43, 299
 negative emotions and, 95, 157, 225, 237, 239
 victimhood and, 109
 in Yugoslavia conflict, 200
victimization/victimhood
 collective memory and, 149, 168
 cycles of violence and, 109–110
 forgiveness and, 384–385
 hatred and, 238
 inability to take rival's perspective and, 311–312
 moral disengagement and, 250–251, 313–314
 moral entitlement and, 312
 societal beliefs about, 186–190, 209
 as theme in mobilizing messages, 88, 98
 truth telling and, 421–422
victims of immoral acts, 380–381, 409–410, 423

victory in collective memory, 149–150. *See also* military victory
Vietnamese-French conflict, 333–334
Vietnam War, 334, 356, 443
violence. *See also* immoral acts
  cessation of, 392–393
  as characteristic of intractable conflicts, 39–43, 53–54, 441–443
  collective emotions and, 216–217, 234
  in culture of conflict, 270–271
  definitions of, 103–104, 109
  delegitimization of rival and, 183–184
  fear as motivation for, 227, 229
  glorification of, 444–445
  group identification and participation in, 83
  humiliation and cycles of, 94–95
  mobilization toward, 91
  moral disengagement and, 250
  morality of violence by ingroup vs. rival, 104, 190–191, 249–251
  in peacemaking process, 361–362
  psychological effects on perpetrators of, 120–121
  psychological reactions to, 119, 122, 128–129
  reconciliation and, 377
  social effects of, 451–452
  threat perception and, 97–98, 295–296
violence and escalation of intractable conflicts
  in asymmetrical conflicts, 103
  collective emotional involvement arising from, 105–106
  eruption of violence, 41–42, 101–104
  in interethnic conflicts, 113
  irreversibility of loss of life, 107
  justification of, 111–112
  rationalization for, 108–111
  sanctity of life and, 104–105
  vengeance for, 107–108
Volkan, V. D., 146

Wagner, U., 67–68
Wallensteen, P., 364
Walsh, E. J., 70
War Crimes Tribunal (The Hague), 423
Ward, C., 314
War of 1948 (Israeli-Palestinian), 169–171
Warsaw Ghetto uprising, 92, 271
Watson, R. P., 252, 310–311
Weiner, B., 242
Werther, A., 388
West Bank and Gaza settlements, 152

Wetherell, M. S., 220
White, R. K., 182, 237
White, R. W., 81
Wickham-Crowley, T. P., 66, 91
Williams, Betty, 407
Wilson, R., 187
Winrow, G. M., 87–88
Winter, J., 138
Wohl, M. J. A., 157, 234, 235, 347, 425–426
Wolfsfeld, G., 408
Women for Peace (Northern Ireland), 407
Wondolleck, J. M., 36
Wood, E. J., 81, 92–93
World Bank, 397
worldviews
  culture of conflict as, 270, 455
  culture of peace as, 377
  in dominant narratives, 22–23
  effects on societal beliefs about conflict, 290–291
  role in terror management, 128
World Wars I and II, 54

Yadlin, Aaron, 268
Yom Kippur War (1973), 156
Yugoslavia conflict. *See also* Bosnia-Herzegovina conflict; Serbia
  collective memory in Balkan Wars, 154
  delegitimization of the rival in, 185–186
  failure to compromise in, 45
  justification of conflict goals, 179
  mobilizing messages in, 89–90
  Serbian chosen traumas, 147, 154–155
  third party intervention in, 333
  transitional justice, 395
  violence in, 104
  war crimes trials, 423
Yzerbyt, V., 422

Zafran, A., 201, 232, 277
Zaiser, E., 191
Zaller, J., 23, 408
Zartman, I. W., 58, 331
zero-sum nature of intractable conflicts, 43–45, 276–277, 344–345, 413
Zerubavel, Y., 156
Zionism
  in culture of conflict, 287–288
  as delegitimizing label, 185
  in Israeli version of collective memory, 166
  as national movement, 2